Mississippi Writers
Reflections of Childhood and Youth

MISSISSIPPI WRITERS

Reflections of Childhood and Youth

Volume I: FICTION

Edited by
DOROTHY ABBOTT

UNIVERSITY PRESS OF MISSISSIPPI
Jackson

Center for the Study of Southern Culture Series

Manufactured in the United States of America
Second Printing 1985
Library of Congress Cataloging in Publication Data
(Revised for volume 2)
Main entry under title:

Mississippi writers.

(Center for the Study of Southern Culture series)
Contents: v. 1. Fiction—v. 2. Non fiction.
1. American literature—Mississippi. 2. American literature—20th century. 3. Mississippi—Literary collections. 4. Children—Literary collections. 5. Youth—Literary collections. [1. Mississippi—Literary collections. 2. American literature—Collections] I. Abbott, Dorothy, 1944- . II. Series.
PS558.M7M55 1984 813'.008'09762 84-5131
ISBN 0-87805-231-3
ISBN 0-87805-232-1 (pbk.)

CONTENTS

ACKNOWLEDGMENTS

THE EDITOR wishes to thank the following authors and publishers or magazines for permission to reprint the designated selections. Rights in all cases are reserved by the owner of the copyright.

Excerpt from *Blood on the Forge* by William Attaway. Published by Doubleday & Company, Inc. Copyright © 1941 by Doubleday & Company, Inc. Reprinted by permission of the publisher.

"Gila Flambé" by Frederick Barthelme first appeared in *The New Yorker*. Copyright © 1983 by Frederick Barthelme. Reprinted by permission of Simon & Schuster, Inc., from *Moon Deluxe* by Frederick Barthelme.

Excerpt from *The Married Land* by Charles G. Bell. Published by Houghton Mifflin Company. Copyright © 1962 by Charles G. Bell. Reprinted by permission of the publisher.

"The Convert" by Lerone Bennett, Jr. Copyright © 1963 by Lerone Bennett, Jr. Reprinted by permission of the author.

"The Lottery Drawing" by besmilr brigham first appeared in *The Southern Review*. Copyright © 1982 by besmilr brigham. Reprinted by permission of the author.

"Without Any Ears" by Jack Butler first appeared in *The Black Warrior Review*. Copyright © 1982 by Jack Butler. Reprinted by permission of August House, Inc., from *Hawk Gumbo* by Jack Butler.

"A Sense of Place" by Price Caldwell first appeared in *The Georgia Review*. Copyright © 1971 by Price Caldwell. Reprinted by permission of the author.

"The Harp of the Winds" by Robert Canzoneri first appeared in *Barbed Wire and Other Stories*. Published by The Dial Press. Copyright © 1970 by Robert Canzoneri. Reprinted by permission of the author.

Excerpt from *The Chain in the Heart* by Hubert Creekmore. Published by Random House, Inc. Copyright © 1953 by Hubert Creekmore. Reprinted by permission of John Schaffner Associates, Inc.

"Antaeus" by Borden Deal first appeared in *Southwest Review*. Copyright © 1961 by The Borden Deal Family Trust. Reprinted by permission of the author.

"The Gift" by Louis Dollarhide first appeared in *The Georgia Review*. Copyright © 1969 by the University of Georgia. Reprinted by permission of the publisher.

"On the Lake" by Ellen Douglas first appeared in *The New Yorker*. Published by Houghton Mifflin Company in *Black Cloud, White Cloud* by Ellen Douglas. Copyright © 1961 by Houghton Mifflin Company. Reprinted by permission of the publisher and by permission of The New Yorker Magazine, Inc.

"A Tribute to The General" by Charles East. Copyright © 1965 by Charles East. Reprinted by permission of Harcourt Brace Jovanovich, Publishers, Inc., from *Where the Music Was* by Charles East.

"Barn Burning" by William Faulkner first appeared in *Harper's Magazine.* Copyright © 1939; renewed 1967 by Estelle Faulkner and Jill Faulkner Summers. Reprinted by permission of Random House, Inc., from *Collected Stories of William Faulkner* by William Faulkner.

"That Evening Sun" by William Faulkner. Copyright © 1931; renewed 1959 by William Faulkner. Reprinted by permission of Random House, Inc., from *Collected Stories of William Faulkner* by William Faulkner.

Excerpt from *Shiloh* by Shelby Foote. Published by Random House, Inc. Copyright © 1952 by Shelby Foote; renewed 1980. Reprinted by permission of the publisher.

Excerpt from *Jordan County* by Shelby Foote. Published by The Dial Press. Copyright © 1954 by Shelby Foote; renewed 1982. Reprinted by permission of the author.

Excerpt from *A Piece of My Heart* by Richard Ford. Published by Harper & Row, Publishers, Inc. Copyright © 1976 by Richard Ford. Reprinted by permission of the author.

"Revenge" by Ellen Gilchrist first appeared in *Prairie Schooner.* Published by The University of Arkansas Press in *In the Land of Dreamy Dreams.* Copyright © 1981 by Ellen Gilchrist. Reprinted by permission of the author.

"A Trip to Czardis" by Edwin Granberry first appeared in *The Forum.* Copyright © 1966 by Edwin Granberry. Reprinted by permission of Harold Matson Company, Inc.

"The Revolt of Brud Bascomb" by Loyle Hairston. Copyright © 1984 by Loyle Hairston. Printed by permission of the author.

"The Peaceful Eye" by Martha Lacy Hall first appeared in *The Southern Review.* Copyright © 1970 by Martha Lacy Hall. Reprinted by permission of the author.

"Testimony of Pilot" by Barry Hannah first appeared in *Esquire.* Copyright © 1978 by Barry Hannah. Reprinted by permission of Alfred A. Knopf, Inc., from *Airships* by Barry Hannah.

Excerpt from *The Prisoners* by Evans Harrington. Published by Harper & Row, Publishers, Inc. Copyright © 1956 by Evans Burnham Harrington. Reprinted by permission of the publisher.

Excerpt from *Hub* by Robert Herring. Published by Viking Penguin Inc. Copyright © 1981 by Robert Herring. Reprinted by permission of the publisher.

Excerpt from *Blue Rise* by Rebecca Hill. Published by William Morrow and Company, Inc. Copyright © 1983 by Rebecca Hill. Reprinted by permission of the publisher.

"One of These Mornings" by Kenneth Holditch first appeared in *Phylon.* Copyright © 1965 by Kenneth Holditch. Reprinted by permission of the author.

"An Open House" by James Hughes first appeared in *The New Yorker.* Copyright © 1980 by the New Yorker Magazine, Inc. Reprinted by permission of the publisher.

"When the Morning Comes" by Don Lee Keith first appeared in *Contempora.* Copyright © 1971 by Don Lee Keith. Reprinted by permission of the author.

"Wild Rabbits" by John Little first appeared in *North Dakota Quarterly.* Copyright © 1979 by John Little. Reprinted by permission of Bloodroot, Inc., from *Whistling Dixie* by John Little.

"The Great Speckled Bird" by P. H. Lowrey. Published by Henry Regnery Company in *The Great Speckled Bird and Other Stories* by P. H. Lowrey. Copyright © 1964 by P. H. Lowrey. Reprinted by permission of Janet Lowrey.

Excerpt from *Come Back, Lolly Ray* by Beverly Lowry. Published by Doubleday & Company, Inc. Copyright © 1976 by Beverly Lowry. Reprinted by permis-

sion of the author.
"The Habits of Guineas" by Tom McHaney first appeared in *The Georgia Review.* Copyright © 1971 by Tom McHaney. Reprinted by permission of the author.
"The Lonesomes Ain't No Spring Picnic" by Birthalene Miller first appeared in *Southern Exposure.* Copyright © 1977 by Southern Exposure. Reprinted by permission of the publisher.
"To Pass Him Out" by William Mills. Copyright © 1976 by William Mills. Reprinted by permission of the author.
"The Organ Piece" by Berry Morgan first appeared in *The New Yorker.* Copyright © 1974 by Berry Morgan. Reprinted by permission of Houghton Mifflin Company from *The Mystic Adventures of Roxie Stoner* by Berry Morgan.
Excerpt from *Good Old Boy* by Willie Morris. Published by Harper & Row, Publishers, Inc. Second edition published by Yoknapatawpha Press, Inc. Copyright © 1971 by Willie Morris; renewed 1980. Reprinted by permission of the author.
"The Sin Eater" by Lewis Nordan first appeared in *Redbook.* Copyright © 1983 by Lewis Nordan. Reprinted by permission of Louisiana State University Press from *Welcome to the Arrow-Catcher Fair* by Lewis Nordan.
"Revive Us Again" by Gloria Norris first appeared in *The Sewanee Review.* Copyright © 1983 by Gloria Norris. Reprinted by permission of the author.
Excerpt from *The Moviegoer* by Walker Percy. Published by Alfred A. Knopf, Inc. Copyright © 1961 by Walker Percy. Reprinted by permission of the publisher.
Excerpt from *The Last Gentleman* by Walker Percy. Published by Farrar, Straus & Giroux, Inc. Copyright © 1966 by Walker Percy. Reprinted by permission of the publisher.
Excerpt from *The Second Coming* by Walker Percy. Published by Farrar, Straus & Giroux, Inc. Copyright © 1980 by Walker Percy. Reprinted by permission of the publisher.
"The Shadow of an Arm" by Thomas Hal Phillips first appeared in *The Virginia Quarterly Review.* Copyright © 1950 by Thomas Hal Phillips. Reprinted by permission of the author.
"Mighty Long Time" by Sterling D. Plumpp first appeared in *The Black Scholar.* Copyright © 1981 by Sterling D. Plumpp. Reprinted by permission of the author.
"Alvira, Lettie, and Pip" by Jessie Schell first appeared in *The Greensboro Review.* Copyright © 1973 by The University of North Carolina at Greensboro. Reprinted by permission of the publisher.
Excerpt from *Forever Island* by Patrick D. Smith. Published by W. W. Norton & Company, Inc. Copyright © 1973 by Patrick D. Smith. Reprinted by permission of the publisher.
"The Day Before" by Elizabeth Spencer first appeared in *Ship Island and Other Stories.* Published by McGraw-Hill Book Company. Copyright © 1968 by Elizabeth Spencer. Reprinted by permission of Doubleday & Company, Inc., from *The Stories of Elizabeth Spencer* by Elizabeth Spencer.
"A Southern Landscape" by Elizabeth Spencer first appeared in *The New Yorker.* Copyright © 1960 by Elizabeth Spencer. Reprinted by permission of Doubleday & Company, Inc., from *The Stories of Elizabeth Spencer* by Elizabeth Spencer.
"Weep No More, My Lady" by James Street. Copyright © 1941 by Curtis Publishing Company; renewed 1969 by Lucy Nash Street. Reprinted by permission of the Harold Matson Company, Inc.
"The Horse in the Bedroom" by Chester Sullivan first appeared in *Southern*

World. Copyright © 1979 by Chester Sullivan. Reprinted by permission of the author.

Excerpt from *Roll of Thunder, Hear My Cry* by Mildred D. Taylor. Published by Dial Books for Young Readers, a division of E. P. Dutton, Inc. Copyright © 1976 by Mildred D. Taylor. Reprinted by permission of the publisher.

Excerpt from *Child Ellen* by Frank Trippett. Published by Prentice-Hall, Inc. Coypright © 1975 by Frank Trippett. Reprinted by permission of the author.

Excerpt from *Jubilee* by Margaret Walker. Published by Houghton Mifflin Company. Copyright © 1966 by Margaret Walker Alexander. Reprinted by permission of the publisher.

Excerpt from *The Redneck Poacher's Son* by Luke Wallin. Published by Bradbury Press, Inc. Copyright © 1981 by Luke Wallin. Reprinted by permission of the publisher.

"A Memory" by Eudora Welty first appeared in *The Southern Review.* Copyright © 1937; renewed 1980 by Eudora Welty. Reprinted by permission of Harcourt Brace Jovanovich, Publishers, Inc., from *The Collected Stories of Eudora Welty* by Eudora Welty.

"First Love" by Eudora Welty first appeared in *Harper's Bazaar.* Copyright © 1942; renewed 1980 by Eudora Welty. Reprinted by permission of Harcourt Brace Jovanovich, Publishers, Inc., from *The Collected Stories of Eudora Welty* by Eudora Welty.

"Why I Live at the P.O." by Eudora Welty first appeared in *The Atlantic Monthly.* Copyright © 1941; renewed 1980 by Eudora Welty. Reprinted by permission of Harcourt Brace Jovanovich, Publishers, Inc., from *The Collected Stories of Eudora Welty* by Eudora Welty.

Excerpt from *Joiner* by James Whitehead. Published by Alfred A. Knopf, Inc. Copyright © 1971 by James Whitehead. Reprinted by permission of the publisher.

Excerpt from *Captain Blackman* by John A. Williams. Published by Doubleday & Company, Inc. Copyright © 1972 by John A. Williams. Reprinted by permission of the publisher.

"The Field of Blue Children" by Tennessee Williams. Copyright © 1939 by Tennessee Williams. Reprinted by permission of New Directions Publishing Corp., from *One Arm and Other Stories* by Tennessee Williams.

"Portrait of a Girl in Glass" by Tennessee Williams. Copyright © 1948 by Tennessee Williams. Reprinted by permission of New Directions Publishing Corp., from *One Arm and Other Stories* by Tennessee Williams.

"Paul's Eyes" by Austin Wilson. Copyright © 1984 by Austin Wilson. Printed by permission of the author.

Excerpt from "Big Boy Leaves Home" by Richard Wright. Copyright © 1936 by Richard Wright; renewed 1964 by Ellen Wright. Reprinted by permission of Harper & Row, Publishers, Inc., from *Uncle Tom's Children* by Richard Wright.

"Almos' a Man" by Richard Wright first appeared in *Harper's Bazaar.* Published (with slight revision) in *Eight Men* by World Publishing Company. Copyright © 1940 by Richard Wright; renewed 1961 by Ellen Wright. Reprinted by permission of Paul R. Reynolds, Inc.

Excerpt from *Snakes* by Al Young. Published by Creative Arts Book Company. Copyright © 1970 by Al Young. Reprinted by permission of the publisher.

Excerpt from *River House* by Stark Young. Published by Charles Scribner's Sons. Copyright © 1929 by Stark Young. Reprinted by permission of the publisher.

PREFACE

I SUPPOSE THAT only retrospection adequately explains the intent of any project—especially when the project is an anthology in which each writer's nuances and variations of the initial notion of theme move that notion a little farther from the original idea. So, it seems that I need to say something to draw a line between the task of editing these volumes and the inevitably ensuing speculation about what my intent was and to what extent these pages hit, or miss, the mark.

My intentions at the beginning were simple. I wanted to present Mississippi as portrayed by its writers in this century. I believed that the presentation, its implications, scope, and depth would be of universal importance. The idea isn't new. In speaking of the beginnings of his own writing career, Faulkner said, "I discovered that my own little postage stamp of native soil was worth writing about and that I would never live long enough to exhaust it." While the statement is often quoted and, I feel sure, was never meant to become a credo, Mississippi writers are noted for doing just that—transforming their lives here in Mississippi into literature. As Sterling D. Plumpp said:

> It dawned on me that the greatest wealth I possessed was my rural upbringing in Mississippi. This is so because my Mississippi is peopled with wonderful characters and has a close affinity with nature and animals. I began writing as a black writer and came to write as a black writer whose legacy is both the violence and the beauty of Mississippi. You can say I found my voice in my Mississippi background. In Mississippi I found a place to house the uncertainty of chaos ushered in by fear and anxiety, and I found in the people I had known a language and a music to compliment my voice. The southern experience is invaluable because it gives one a sense of permanence, roots which are not easily dug up by any caprice.

Having defined my intention, and being faced with a staggering amount of material, I realized that what remained was my need of a theme that would both limit and direct my work. I found the theme I needed in reading the letters of Richard Wright. To David L. Cohn, he wrote: "Youth is the turning point in life, the most sensitive and volatile period, the state that registers most vividly the impressions and experiences of life; and an artist likes to work with sensitive material."

Having found a theme, the title suggested itself—*Mississippi Writers: Reflections of Childhood and Youth.* That was how I began. This anthology is the finished product, and each selection expresses the theme of Mississippi childhood and youth or its relevance to the life of the writer. Between that point and this, between the idea and the reality (Eliot wasn't a Mississippian, but I'll cite him here anyway) falls the shadow. And in the shadow, in the process of becoming, lay the editorial limitations and policies that formed these volumes and also determined what *did not* form them.

I chose to include only Mississippi writers of the twentieth century. My reasons were several. I felt that Mississippi writers of this century would be more accessible to the modern reader—in language, concerns, and just plain reading enjoyment. Mississippi writers of the twentieth century are also much more widely known—there are more of them to celebrate, and they offer much more material worth the effort of celebration. I wanted this book to be a tool for the young writers of our state, an aid to the craft of writing. In my conversations with writers, one of the recurring statements I heard was that in growing up in Mississippi they had little or no instruction in the craft of writing (the omniscient English teacher aside). I wanted an anthology that presented Mississippi authors writing about Mississippi and the South, an anthology that could be used by tomorrow's writers to learn not only how to write, but where their roots came from, and, perhaps more importantly, the standards of excellence that have been set.

Having established limitations as to time and topic, I began the long process of reading and searching archives, libraries, bookstores, and literary supplements to discover not only who was to be included, what materials were to be included, but the locations of the authors I sought to include.

Some of the authors came to me when word of the project

spread. One man appeared on my porch at 8:00 a.m. one Saturday to recite his poetry and spread his arrowhead collection across my lawn. Others I had to look for. Mississippi writers are scattered from Natchez to Nepal, from Yazoo City to New York, and the remainder are sprinkled liberally between these four points. Some of the people I searched for were dead; others I thought were dead, but, after searching, I found them to be very much alive and still writing. For example, I had been led to believe that William Attaway was dead, though no one could supply me with any proof. I searched to find him, with no success, until I learned that, in addition to novels, he had written calypso music lyrics for Harry Belafonte. I wrote Belafonte's office in New York and was sent Attaway's California number. I called him. The news that he was not dead was of great relief to us both.

The astonishingly large amount of Mississippi literature I discovered made me at times concede to the notion that virtually everyone in Mississippi must have written at least one book. The sheer volume of materials made me almost believe that when Faulkner's "last ding-dong of doom" *did* sound, the final voice on earth would be that of a Mississippian talking about a book his great aunt, his nephew, his cousin, or some marginally related, half-removed relative had written. One man couldn't understand why his aunt wasn't included in my collection when I would "take a heathen like William Faulkner."

Early on, it became apparent that there would be no shortage of materials or writers. But the term "Mississippi writer" bothered me. I wasn't sure what criteria to use in determining who was or who was not a Mississippi writer. The standards evolved, and when the dust settled, I had established a workable editorial stance. I would accept all writers born in Mississippi; I would accept writers who, while not native Mississippians, are at present living here and are translating their experiences into fiction; I would accept writers who spent a large part of their growing-up time residing in Mississippi. In short, I came to accept those writers whose work has become infused with what has popularly come to be called Mississippi's "sense of place." As Eudora Welty wrote:

> Rich in writers, Mississippi is rich in resources for the writer. Our primary resource is the place itself. Place is where the writer has his roots. In his experience, out of which he learns to write, and will always write, place provides the base of reference. In his work it

> frames his initial point of view. I think the sense of place is as essential to good and honest writing as a logical mind. Our critical powers spring up from the study of place and the growth of experience within it. Place never stops informing us, for it is forever astir, changing, reflecting, like the mind of man itself.

Even with a broad definition, there were borderline writers who either did not fit the classification thematically or whose geographic influences were more firmly rooted elsewhere. Among the writers I excluded were Alice Walker. I wanted to include her, especially after I discovered she wrote parts of *The Third Life of Grange Copeland, Meridian, Revolutionary Petunias and Other Poems,* and *In Love and Trouble* in Mississippi. Ms. Walker wrote me, "Mississippi is the only place in this country that I could have conceived of *Meridian.* Maybe." In the end, I decided it would be unfair to include this writer so closely associated with Georgia.

Another group of writers I had to exclude were those who visited relatives in Mississippi and were influenced accordingly, and those who went to colleges or universities here but grew up in other places. This first group included Joan Williams, who has written beautiful prose about Mississippi and who wrote me: "The Civil Rights movement of the sixties had a strong influence on my work—the changes it brought into peoples' lives." But Williams grew up in Memphis. I laughed uproariously at Candyce Barnes's "I Saw Rock City" and "Work for the Night Will Come," but in the end felt I had to exclude her for the same reason (even though David L. Cohn wrote in *Where I Was Born and Raised* that "the Mississippi Delta begins in the lobby of the Peabody Hotel in Memphis"), much to my regret and to the anthology's loss.

There are other writers not included for a variety of reasons. Some I simply did not find in time to make my deadline. Jean Davidson and her Pushcart Prize story, "Robo-wash," Charles Henley, who recently was awarded a National Endowment for the Arts grant, and Bonna Whitten-Stovall all fit into this category. There were writers I thoroughly enjoyed reading, but who did no discernable work that fit into my thematic category: Herschel Brickell, Ben Ames Williams, Blanche Colton Williams, and Wirt Williams among others. In short, there are many writers who, for one reason or another, are not included. Any oversight was not intentional; many omissions were made after serious deliberation and discussion with editorial assistants, friends, and the writers themselves.

The details of the gathering of material would be incomplete if I did not mention the tremendous amount of help I received, both in the way of suggestions of writers' names that I did not realize were Mississippians and the cooperation I received in trying to track down the writers I was looking for. Dr. Jim Ewing, Erin Clayton Pitner, Sterling D. Plumpp, Samuel Prestridge, and Professor Jerry W. Ward, Jr., are to be especially commended.

Many teachers from around the state—Karen Conwill of Tupelo, Harriet DeCell of Yazoo City, Patsy Pace of Aberdeen, Gwen Porter of McComb, and Nell Thomas of Greenville—gave guidance and evaluation. Members of the Mississippi Council of Teachers of English were an important sounding board for curriculum development.

I would like to thank all the writers with whom I corresponded—so many times that I'm sure they started watching the sky thinking I might swing down from a magnolia tree to ask about a comma or a semicolon. In all, they were gracious and responded to every question I had.

In *The Second Coming* Walker Percy wrote, "All you need to do anything is time to do it, being let alone long enough to do it and a center to do it from." I would especially like to express my heartfelt gratitude to the Center for the Study of Southern Culture. Without the support of its director William Ferris and associate director Ann J. Abadie this anthology would not have been completed. To the staff of the center—especially Sue Hart, Elizabeth Makowski, Sarah Dixon, Martha Doyel, Frank Childrey, Ann Holmes, and Charles R. Wilson—I am grateful for their aid in many ways. I am appreciative also to members of the center's state advisory committee—Lyle Cashion, Lee Dearman, Doyce Deas, Twick Morrison, Bruce Moses, Frances Patterson, John Squires, Pat Stevens, and Betsy Vick—for the special time they gave this project.

Director Barney McKee, executive editor Seetha Srinivasan, marketing manager Hunter Cole, and editor Joanne Prichard at the University Press of Mississippi have offered valuable assistance and advice. They know how to add beauty to the printed word.

Just as philanthropist Andrew Carnegie held the philosophy that "the man who dies . . . rich dies disgraced," so did Phil B. Hardin of Meridian. Before his death he established the Phil Hardin Foundation through which the bulk of his estate would be used to further education in Mississippi. This anthology moved from the stage of ideas and research to publication because the Phil Hardin Foundation awarded the project a challenge grant. I would like to thank C. Thompson Wacaster, vice president for educational programs and research, and the board of directors of the Phil Hardin Foundation—S. A. Rosenbaum, Mark M. Porter, Archie R. McDonnell, R. B. Deen, Jr., Joe S. Covington, M.D., William B. Crooks, Jr., Edwin E. Downer, Otho R. Smith, Walter Smith, and Robert F. Ward—for their important contribution.

CREATE, Inc., in Tupelo and many people from around the state came forward to meet the challenge by generously donating funds to match the grant. For this, I thank them all. Their names are appropriately listed in this collection.

My family members are the greatest blessings of my life, and this book is for them: for my parents Jack and Jeanette Renshaw, who gave me a love for books; for my children Rush and Erin, who are carrying on the tradition; and for my brother Bob, because when he's around it's always a celebration.

And now, as Beverly Lowry wrote in *Daddy's Girl*, "turn up the music, I plan to dance."

Dorothy Abbott
The University of Mississippi

INTRODUCTION
A Sense of Place and Time: Common Experience, Common Values

GORDON WEAVER

THERE IS A southern tradition in literature, a tradition that occupies a prominent place in the larger American tradition of this century. Critics have remarked its characteristics in both general and special, narrower studies of modern writing, and they, along with common readers, have praised its achievements. There is some consensus that, overall, viewing the total spectrum of American literature produced in this century, the work—especially the fiction—produced by Deep South writers constitutes a high-water mark of excellence.

Any literate undergraduate can recite a list of great American fiction writers who both called the Deep South home and who chose that "home" as the substance and focus of the fictional words they created. An inordinate number of these great fiction writers in the southern tradition are identified with the state of Mississippi, perhaps the most essentially "southern" state in this region of our nation.

Think of southern literature, of fiction, and one thinks at once of William Faulkner, of Walker Percy, of Eudora Welty, of Richard Wright. But scholars and serious readers know a tradition, a literary heritage, is neither created nor sustained by the efforts of its "superstars" alone, that the achievement and the celebrity that achievement earns with the literate national public for those great artists depends on a broad base of literary activity. The marvelous creations of a Faulkner, a Welty, or a Richard Wright cannot be considered in isolation from the whole of the literary culture that underlies them, and from which they rose to such eminence.

This anthology presents not only an excellent sampling of the work of those most widely known "classic" fiction writers who hail from Mississippi, it presents them in the larger context of their fellow writers, all fellow Mississippi natives or residents, and the totality of this collection provides the reader with a rich and varied casebook on just what southern fiction (Mississippi-style), is.

Herein the reader will find, in addition to authors who have, deservedly, become literary household names, the work of no less accomplished artists such as Robert Canzoneri, Borden Deal, Ellen Douglas, Shelby Foote, Berry Morgan, Willie Morris, Elizabeth Spencer, Margaret Walker, and Stark Young. These are writers who, although they have not attained the international renown of a Faulkner or a Welty, have won a national audience for their fiction.

This anthology aims at inclusiveness, and so the reader will also find the work of a younger generation that is even now succeeding in its reach for wider acceptance by the American public: Richard Ford, Ellen Gilchrist, Barry Hannah, Beverly Lowry, Chester Sullivan, James Whitehead (also a prominent American poet), John A. Williams, and Al Young, for instance.

And we have also gathered fiction by a number of new, as yet not widely known fiction writers, men and women of Mississippi whose creative accomplishments, nevertheless, make their inclusion here obligatory: Price Caldwell, Martha Lacy Hall, James Hughes, William Mills (like Whitehead, a well-known poet), and Gloria Norris are but a few of these.

The names cited above do not begin to exhaust the contents of this comprehensive anthology. Herein, the reader will find—to his delight and instruction—the broadest possible gallery of fictions, short stories and novel excerpts, a panorama of Mississippi fiction, which provides a clear definition of what the southern literary tradition is in this century.

Writers—like any collection of individuals—are unique, distinctive human beings. Consequently, each of their creations is a unique microcosm. It is this infinite variety of fictional characters and *milieu* that provides the reader's continually renewed delight in the literary experience. At the same time, writers native to a common place—in this instance the state of Mississippi—and a common era, our century over the past several generations, share not only a common heritage, they share a regional language and more important, a common way of responding to their varied particular experiences, a common way of seeing, of feeling, and of believing—what can be called a common faith against which they measure life.

These shared properties will emerge for the reader as he confronts the fictions that follow hereafter, whether he read through systematically from the first page to the last, or, should that be his wont, more eclectically, opening this book at random to begin, casually skipping over selections from the last read to one further on, attracted perhaps by a title or the familiarity of an author's name. Whatever the reader's method, and however unique the qualities that distinguish one writer's fiction from another's, there will, however gradually, emerge a set of characteristics that, in sum, define both southern (Mississippi) writing and the Mississippi experience, an experience easily recognized by a native or longtime resident of the state, one possible for the non-Mississippian to share equally in, because that is what fiction of genuine literary merit does permit. We read for at least two reasons: to know both the world we share with an author, and to know the world only that author knows and can create for us.

What are the terms of the world of Mississippi writers the reader will recognize (or discover) in these fictions?

Logically enough, the very presence of the environment of the region depicted in these fictions is a constant element. The reader will see, again and again, the evocation of the particular world of nature, flora and fauna, weather, the landscape, as the setting for the human experiences dramatized. Leaf and bird, wind and water, searing heat and biting cold are phenomena of nature the reader will find most Mississippi authors emphasizing to establish the milieu of a given story. And it is more than just perfunctory limning of enough of the natural world to erect a credible backdrop for dramatic narrative. Nature, in Mississippi fictional tradition, is not only a significant atmosphere establishing tone and mood, not only a subtle and pervasive ambience permeating the sensibilities of characters, it is often a primary agent of action, a dramatic catalyst in and of itself. And as it can be a source of beauty and satisfaction, it can also be a malevolent, destructive force in several of the fictions assembled here.

History is another constant presence in the work of the fiction writers collected in this book. It may take the form of a concern with oral tradition and unspoken social mores, or it may exist via explicit reference to the past; a family scandal may weigh equally with the Lost Cause of the Confederacy. Within this fixation on history, how things were and have been for generations, there lies the broad value of "tradition," the value placed on ways of being and doing, folkways that are valued *because* they are traditional. Much of the conflict portrayed in these fictions can be seen as arising from the confrontation between the traditional and the new, the "modern" versus the past, the encroachment of outside, alien cultural forces on a region whose cultural integrity is both cause and effect of that regional identity. This conflict is accompanied by emotions running the gamut from pain to a nostalgia that is sometimes sentimental.

Perhaps the most frequent focus of these forces of historical fact and traditional custom is the matter of race. The "peculiar institution" ended with Appomattox, but the present century's obsession, both within and without the South, with race continued. Again and again in these stories and novel excerpts, relations between white and black people come to the fore, sometimes only incidentally to the central narrative, but frequently as the focus of scrutiny. White and black writers anthologized here examine and reexamine the facts and implications of this racial agony, and this scrutiny or introspection is more than merely historical or sociological, it is an unending exercise, often excruciating, in moral evaluation. The depiction and analysis of race relations in these fictions is so central to their reason for being that the subject may safely be said to be the single most important moral concern of fiction writers from Mississippi.

Writers from Mississippi and other Deep South states have long been noted for the creation and presentation of memorable characters. A careful reading of the fictions that follow reveals a pantheon of, not "stock" characters—at least not in the pejorative sense of the term—but of "types." These writers have evolved a rich typology of character, almost always effectively individuated, but a typology nonetheless. And this is not surprising, given a common environment and a self-consciously shared history and set of cultural folkways. The reader will recognize individual facets of this typology of character as they step forth in the pages of story after story. They are not interchangeable—this is possible only in very bad writing—but they are recognizable as types. The respective visions of character these authors produce, if not a characteristic "southern" or Mississippi personality, do constitute at least a limited range of such personalities.

Nor is it surprising that a geographically stable—and relatively, until recent times, isolated culture—peopled by two distinct and homogenous strains, the Anglo-Saxon and the Afro-American, should produce a common and distinct language, a regional dialect. The reader will "hear" the language he already knows if he knows the Deep South, a vernacular that includes elegant refinement no less than earthy imagery, rhythmic and rough, oblique and euphemistic, blunt and crude, strewn with metaphors from an elevated, literary tradition as often as with those taken directly from vulgar experience. It is a language spoken nowhere else in the world, however much it has been diluted by its popular imitation. These authors have preserved it on the page in its pristine, oral texture, unsullied by the incursion of the electronic media that threatens, in our lifetime, to eradicate it.

A common ground, a shared history, shared traditions, a central moral question of cataclysmic significance, a gallery of character types, and a common dialect—all preserved and reinforced, chronicled, archived by a body of serious literature of which this collection is a vivid cross-section: it is reasonable that some common themes should begin to articulate themselves in the fictions the reader has before him.

What it comes to, seen in perspective over the whole of this book's contents, is that Mississippi fiction writers, recreating the Mississippi experience of this century, arrive at a fairly unified vision of the meaning of this experience. The thematic strain of these fictions is, generally, tragic, often elegiac, but is also one of celebration, the celebration of the human spirit, of human fortitude, courage, and endurance. If this is distinctly southern, it is also American.

The themes of these short stories and novel excerpts provide readers not only with a vision of how excruciatingly cruel and blindly chaotic the life of man can be, they counter this with repeated assertions of the infinite capacity of man to withstand and cope, even overcome (on occasion) these assaults on his being and his sensibility. It would be difficult to imagine, ultimately, a more positive response to being alive in Mississippi (and America) today than that which the reader will partake of in the contents of this book of fictions.

Particular illustrations abound. In Price Caldwell's touching "A Sense of Place," the very title indicates the centrality of milieu. Bo, Caldwell's forty-six-year-old viewpoint character, is a cripple, house-bound in the small town of Carny, Mississippi. Severely and pathetically limited by his physical handicap—he is a spastic who has great difficulty even with his speech when he is excited—he is fascinated by the limitless geography of the universe, depicted in a Map of the Heavens published in *National Geographic;* in particular, he watches the moon as it waxes and wanes in the night skies over Carny, his source of information on that planet a 1932 edition of the Rand McNally *World Atlas.*

But Caldwell's portrait of Bo's yearning for a larger world is an inverse metaphor for his character's exact knowledge of and feel for the excruciatingly limited world of his mother's house in Carny, to which his congenital affliction has restricted him. Lovingly, Bo sketches the minute dimensions of that world—his room, the kitchen, his mother, who cares for him, the porch they share in good weather, the side yard with its flowers and hedges, the bayou behind the house. What Caldwell gives the reader in Bo is a character who would be pathetic except that his enthusiastic attachment to place (as the story's title points out) gives him an integrity, a dignity, and an identity approaching the noble and the heroic.

In the selection by Hubert Creekmore, an excerpt from his *The Chain in the Heart,* we have an oppressive view of poverty as seen by George, a black boy who learns the hard lesson of his color and the system of segregation and prescribed social inferiority that comes with it. But George's ultimate triumph—he beats a white bully in a fight over a marble, and shares the joy of that victory with his father—is inextricably related to the strong sense of identity he draws from the world around him he knows so well.

> He could see no possibilities for fun—only the swing with broken slats, the lard cans of sword fern and purple cane, the grubby yard, the field across the road, the pasture at the foot of the hill, the seven porches below him—sun-drowned, deserted, dotted with pails of geranium and petunia. A hum of life seeped from the dingy windows behind which the families hid from the heat.

Creekmore's George *is* oppressed by the atmosphere of this environment—as he is oppressed by the racism of his society—but there is mitigating beauty in it, sword fern and purple cane, geraniums and petunias—and George's fight for his "rights" against a racist bully derives as much from the strength and security he draws from his environment as it does from his knowledge that "right" is on his side in the conflict.

Borden Deal's "Antaeus" applies the ancient Greek myth about a giant whose strength comes from contact with the earth to the situation of T.J., a boy from "somewhere down South" (Alabama) who has been wrenched from his roots on the land, transplanted to the alien, hostile North, an industrial city. T.J.'s family is one of thousands who migrated north to find work in wartime, and though they find work, they lose the life-giving contact with the soil that was their Deep South heritage. T.J.'s response is to lead a gang of city urchins in establishing a garden on the roof of a factory. The effort fails in the end, and T.J. runs away, back to the land, to the South. Deal's story is narrated by an anonymous city boy, one who cannot fully understand either the attraction or the power of life lived on and close to the land. "Antaeus" is an explicit statement of the supreme value of a life lived naturally, in concert with nature, a value that underlies so many of the stories collected here.

In Louis Dollarhide's "The Gift," nature threatens in the shape of a devastating flood. An old woman, marooned in her house, suddenly finds herself confronted with a panther that has sought refuge on her porch. She placates the beast—and thus survives the threat of nature—with the "gift" of a cured ham. It is as if, in this story, a necessary reciprocity between man and nature is posited; each owes the other something in a natural system of symbiosis.

In virtually every fiction collected here, the reader will come, again and again, to descriptions of nature, the environment, the shared "place" that Mississippi writers must include in any artistic effort to catch hold of the texture and ambience of life in this region. This shared physical world is more than just a common feature in the southern literary tradition, it is the ultimate basis for a culture that has so consistently expressed itself in the literary fiction in our century.

Mississippi fiction's preoccupation with history—the sense that Mississippi writers have that those who live now remain, always, connected in vital, essential ways with those who have gone before them—is demonstrated amply in a great many of these stories and novel excerpts. Unlike any other distinctive and distinguishable region of America, the South alone has the living memory of a Lost Cause always present in its contemporary consciousness. The historical experience of the Confederacy exists as an explicit point of reference in many of the works collected here, and is implicit in those where it is not tangibly articulated.

In Charles East's fine "A Tribute to The General," the title of which is ironic, the legacy of the Lost Cause is dramatized in his character, Miss Jenny, now aged ninety-one. The widow of a Confederate general she married when she was young—he was already past his prime, a widower, totally absorbed in vicarious refighting of a lost battle—she continually asks him, "What was it like?" She never gets an answer, and so she lives her married life with the tantalizing mystery of that historical experience. Widowed, she is often called upon to attend and speak at celebrations of that conflict, a prisoner into her dotage of a past she never knew, but which lives on in the present, affects her existence as fully as if she had been there, at her general's lost battle, herself. The message for the reader is perhaps psychologically overobvious: that who and what we are is a function of what we have been, and done, is no less valid for its being a commonplace.

In a chapter reprinted here from Shelby Foote's *Shiloh,* the reader is made intimate with the first-person narration of a Confederate infantryman who follows Beauregard into close combat on April 6, 1862, the Battle of Shiloh, one of the most bloody encounters between blue and gray in that bloody war. Foote's description of the infantry charge is as harrowingly real as any in our literature. The sheer facts of war, the hysteria it produces, produce in turn an almost surreal—horribly so—sense of what it was like to be there on that day, in that place, in American history. If there is a romantic aura often surrounding the Lost Cause, Foote's fiction effectively debunks it. The chapter concludes with the agonized death of General Johnston, and, aptly, Foote's infantryman says, "I didn't want to have any more to do with the war if this was the way it was going to be."

Eudora Welty's excellent "First Love" reaches back even further into Mississippi history—and the meaning of that history for the present. Set in January, 1807 the locale is the Natchez Trace. In the sensitive consciousness of Joel Mayes, a twelve-year-old deaf-mute, Welty registers the charismatic impact of the unsuccessful treason conspiracy of Aaron Burr and Harman Blennerhassett—an event that seems to have received strangely little attention in popular American histories. Welty's marvelous story creates the utterly mystical bewilderment of the "common" man confronted by the complexity, moral and otherwise, of history-making events and personalities, demonstrating the web that history casts for even the least sophisticated, that every man lives in and of history, despite how narrow and personal his preoccupations.

It is this web of history, southern history, the reader will find informing these fictions, and informing the reader with an awareness of the extent to which the past informs our present, in the South, and in Mississippi.

"Tradition," the complex of traditional ways of feeling, thinking, and doing, is the product of history, the palpable evidence that history lives, is a force in the day-to-day existence of people who may be only partially aware of the force of that history in their lives. In no regional art is it more clear that what we are is a function of what we have been than in the literary art of the South, and of the state of Mississippi; the reader will find the truth of this contention manifest in myriad forms in the fictions that follow. Any selection for the purpose of illustrating this point is at best arbitrary.

William Faulkner's great classic story, "Barn Burning," like the whole of his literary canon, is a vivid proof. In "Barn Burning" which also invokes the spectre of the Lost Cause—it is the spirit which most basically animates the story—the emotions of the boy, Colonel Sartoris Snopes, are tortured because he only dimly recognizes the forces of tradition that structure the world in which he must balance the conflict between love and loyalty to his poor-white renegade father—himself a creature driven by his rebellion against social and moral tradition—and the loyalty due the larger society, if only by virtue of the necessary membership in that society ascribed to all men who must live with their fellows. The dichotomy of formal law and justice and the powerful—because based on the blood tie of family—"law" of allegiance to father and family is starkly dramatized in the boy's agonized decision to warn Major de Spain against his father's act of arson.

In the end, the boy does choose allegiance to society, but at a terrible cost, for his father has told him, "You got to learn to stick to your own blood or you ain't going to have any blood to stick to you." Tradition, then, in the Mississippi ethos, is ambiguous, blood ties in conflict with prescribed formal allegiances to a larger and anonymous humanity in the abstract, and there is no resolution of this conflict without costly moral and emotional suffering.

In the brief excerpt from Robert Herring's *Hub* included here, a casual reading might impress the reader with the presentation of the phenomenon of nature and man's necessary relationship with it, but more careful analysis will reveal that the profound thrust of this piece is in the direction of rendering the wild pig hunt as an initiation ritual. The boy, Percy, is inducted into manhood by this experience, conducted by his father in a ritual as traditional in its context as the legal and ethical codes that are the framework of Faulkner's story. A ritual is, after all, only a rigidly structured, traditional way of doing things toward a commonly understood end. In Herring's fiction, while the ritual is frightening, it is successful, the resolution clear and definitive.

In the excerpt from Walker Percy's celebrated *The Second Coming*, we see another hunting experience rendered as ritual, the remembered moment having become archetypal, because it was so traumatic, for the author's hero. And his hero's obsession with that experience both shapes and illuminates the whole of his adult life. Percy's hero is what he is because of what happened to him when bird hunting with his father, and his recognition and understanding of this allow him to see his existence in a new and utterly different way for the remainder of his life. The dimension of "tradition" in this fiction is not one of legal or social codes, nor one of folk or family practice, but one that is private and personal. It is no less a matter of tradition's role in contemporary life for that narrower scope.

The title of Elizabeth Spencer's story, "A Southern Landscape," employs a physical metaphor, a reference to geography, as the vehicle for the exposition of the intangible, though no less real forces of tradition that govern the lives of people in her fictional town of Port Claiborne, Mississippi. The physical landscape *is* important to this story, but of far greater significance is the omnipresence of tradition, symbolized in the ruins of the Windsor mansion. Spencer's Marilee Summerall is kissed for the first time—a ritual of initiation—only after viewing the ruin of Windsor, and that ruin of a once magnificent structure, with its attendant way of life is reflected in the character of Foster Hamilton, a prematurely decadent and charming alcoholic; it is Foster who kisses Marilee, and the implication of doom that informs that kiss is evident in the atmosphere of decay that prevails over Port Claiborne and its citizens.

In the chapter of his *River House* reprinted herein, Stark Young explores decadence in the context of a son's chaffing at the bonds of a genteel culture. The specific context here is plantation life, but its implications are broader. The pathos—sometimes the tragedy—of the force of tradition in contemporary southern life as recreated in fiction by these Mississippi writers is that the traditions governing lives derive from a dead culture—the antebellum South, the Lost Cause—and though a sentimental nostalgia for that dead, romanticized culture may generate significant human feelings, traditions whose roots are dead—dying, in a state of decay, however gradually—cannot sustain or nurture dynamic life in the present society.

The most profoundly moral—and the morally darkest—aspect of the literary fiction written by Mississippi writers treats the racial "question." No aspect of southern history, not even the Lost Cause itself, has more consistently challenged the sensibilities of Mississippi authors. The Lost Cause was just that, *lost,* and as a force in contemporary southern culture its vitality diminishes with each passing decade. But the issue of race, stemming from the institution of chattel slavery that ended with the Lost Cause, remains as significant as ever in the fictions assembled here for the reader, and any such collection that scanted this issue could not pretend to a true representation of Mississippi literature in our century.

Ellen Douglas's "On The Lake" creates an exquisitely subtle, yet dramatic sense of the barrier that still remains between white and black people, despite the efforts of well meaning whites to transcend that obstacle to human interaction. This obstacle, so deeply and firmly rooted in historical experience and social tradition, is presented to the reader from the perspective of a white woman, Anna Glover. She takes her black former housekeeper, Estella Mosely, along with her and three children on a fishing outing on a reservoir. Douglas's narrative beautifully captures the strained and uncertain communication between the two women, and culminates in a boating accident—their rowboat is swamped.

Anna Glover, to save herself and the children, pushes the drowning, panic-stricken Estella away from her. The fishing party is rescued, and Estella is revived, but her instinctive act of survival leaves Anna with a feeling of guilt that she cannot assuage, a guilt that speaks to the total historical and social scope of the white oppression of blacks in the South. The sins of the past, in Ellen Douglas's excellent story, are visited upon the unsuspecting heirs of the present, however benevolent their intentions.

There is at least a momentary substantial optimism regarding the relations of black and white in Berry Morgan's "The Organ Piece," one of her Roxie Stoner stories. Roxie, a black woman, is invited by a young white boy—he is myopically indifferent to the dictates of segregation—to hear him play an organ recital in a white church. The boy, Laurance Ingles, is an isolated character who seeks Roxie's approval and understanding. Morgan's story, like those discussed above, argues that this fundamental understanding between the races is impossible, but their mutual response to the beauty of fine music, and the essentially religious nature of Roxie's character, bordering on the saintly, argue that such an understanding may yet be possible in generations to come.

Richard Wright's "Almos' a Man" directly addresses the yearning of Dave, a young black man, to own a gun, which he sees as the ultimate symbol of manhood (he is seventeen). Ownership of a gun will, he believes, confer manhood on him, earn him the same respect a white man is given by virtue of nothing more than the color of his skin. Dave accidently kills a white man's mule with his pistol, and, humiliated, an object of scorn to both black and white alike, he flees, hopping a train going north, ". . . where he could be a man."

These are only a few of the fictions herein that expose the reader to the central position in the consciousness of the southern literary artist that the fact of race has assumed. Stories and novel excerpts portray aspects of this southern reality from the point of view of both black and white (and black and white authors), and indicate the range of judgments from the darkest pessimism to the bright hope that, however clouded the present, the future must be better, if only because of the endurance and courage of noble blacks and whites working and living together.

One has to look to a source as rich as Shakespeare or the Russian novelists to find a cast of characters as varied and memorable as the ones created by the Mississippi writers whose fictions are arrayed here for the reader. An interest in *character,* the character of individual people, is a trait of personality in southern culture, so it is not surprising that this region's literature should exhibit that trait, highlighting the particulars and peculiarities that distinguish one man—or woman—or child—from another. At its worst, this focus has produced some popular stereotypes, but at its best, as in these stories and novel excerpts, the reader finds characters so deftly, exactly individuated as to linger in one's memory and sensibility long after reading. What makes the characters created by Mississippi writers memorable is, in the best sense of the word, their *eccentricity,* that amalgam of details that goes to make an individual character, fictional or real, inimitably unique.

In Ellen Gilchrist's "Revenge," the author captures the voice—the voice of her most inner consciousness—of ten-year-old Rhoda, a girl at an awkward age, her emotions focused on a desire to join her brothers in the unfeminine sport of pole-vaulting. She sneaks away from a wedding reception to try her skill, unwilling to accept the docile female role prescribed for her, determined to equal her brothers' feats, to know their experience before she goes on to grow into the young woman she will become.

> I knew exactly what to do first. I picked up the pole and hoisted it over my head. It felt solid and balanced and alive. I hoisted it up and down a few times . . . getting the feel of it.
>
> Then I laid it ceremoniously down on the ground, reached behind me, and unhooked the plaid formal. I left it lying in a heap on the ground. There I stood, in my cotton underpants, ready to take up pole-vaulting.

Rhoda's efforts end in comic disaster, but her voice lingers in the reader's ear, poignant and pathetic, saved from sentimentality by her fundamental human dignity.

In "Testimony of Pilot," Barry Hannah gives the reader the saxophone playing Quadberry. We see him leading a high school band in concert competition, having taken over for the beloved director, who has been killed in an automobile accident:

> All I know is that he looked grief-stricken and pale, and small. Sweat had popped out on his forehead. He bent over extremely. He was wearing the red brass-button jacket and black pants, black bow tie at the throat, just like the rest of us. In this outfit he bent over his horn almost out of sight. For a moment, before I caught the glint of his horn through the music stands, I thought he had pitched forward off the stage. He went down so far to do his deep oral thing, his con-

> ducting arm disappeared so quickly, I didn't know but what he was having a seizure. . . . When *Bolero* was over, the audience stood up and made meat out of their hands applauding.

So *present* at the scene of Quadberry's triumph are we that the reader is tempted to join the audience and the competition judges in applauding.

It is this, the felt presence of characters, the reader will perhaps enjoy most in these fictions. Rhoda, Quadberry, the Gospelers who change forever the life of Niewatha Cardwell in P. H. Lowrey's "The Great Speckled Bird":

> . . . she recognized the older one, though he looked now like a prophet. He had climbed into the pulpit—the bald womanish one with steel spectacles was off to the right in front of him; the heavy red-headed one who had the harmonica strapped into a contraption that fitted around his neck was on the other side. They were all waving their snakes and chanting, and somewhere on the other side of the church a man was yelling . . . for somebody for God's sake phone up the Marshall, and off in the grove a woman still screamed faintly but steadily. Niewatha was too busy watching to mind.

These characters *live* for the reader, whose consciousness is as taken with these bizarre revivalist hucksters as Niewatha is.

Old men, little girls, pubescent boys, the naive Niewatha and her flamboyant Gospelers, the gallery of striking characters who live in these fictions defies neat categorization. And these portraits are not all memorable simply because the authors have chosen the unusual or exotic to depict. Consider Tennessee Williams's Laura Wingfield, seen in his "Portrait of a Girl in Glass" (later brought to a world-wide audience in *The Glass Menagerie*); Laura is sketched in quiet tones, her tortured, stunted sensibility brought to a momentary bloom as she dances with the young man her brother has brought home to dinner:

> As far as I knew she had never danced in her life. But to my everlasting wonder she slipped quite naturally into those huge arms of Jim's, and they danced round and around the small steam-heated parlor, bumping against the sofa and chairs and laughing loudly and happily together. Something opened up in my sister's face.

With this economical description, Williams presents the reader with a brief moment of joy in the life of Laura, the more touching for its inevitable sad aftermath. Mississippi writers are always taken with the dimension of character in their fictions, and the reader's experience is the richer and greater for this propensity.

There is no such thing as a Mississippi "language," but there does exist a regional dialect that the whole of our nation has come to know from the literature created in and of this region; in its popular dissemination, this dialect has evolved into something of a parody. But in the fictions here, the reader's delight will be continually renewed as he encounters it in its purest, authentic form, the transcription of the speech of Mississippi characters created by Mississippi authors. This dialect does have its cliches, but when rendered by the literary artist comes off the page with refreshing originality and striking vividness. Any more or less random sampling from the work that follows makes the point.

Consider Edwin Granberry's "A Trip to Czardis," in which two young, rural poor-white boys, Daniel and Jim, are taken by their mother for a farewell visit with their father, a condemned criminal about to be executed in the penitentiary:

> "Hit's the day, Dan'l. This day that's right here now, we are goen. You'll recollect it all in a minute."
>
> "I recollect. We are goen in the wagon to see Papa—"
>
> "Then hush and don't whine."
>
> "I were dreamen, Jim."
>
> "What dreamen did you have?"
>
> "I can't tell. But it were fearful what I dreamt."
>
> "All the way we are goen this time. We won't stop at any places, but we will go all the way to Czardis to see Papa. I never see such a place as Czardis."
>
> "I recollect the water tower—"
>
> "Not in your own right, Dan'l. Hit's by my tellen it you see it in your mind."
>
> "And lemonade with ice in it I saw—"
>
> "That too I seen and told to you."
>
> "Then I never seen it at all?"
>
> "Hit's me were there, Dan'l. I let you play like, but hit's me who went to Czardis. Yet I never till this day told half how much I see. There's sights I never told."
>
> They stopped talking, listening for their mother's stir in the kitchen. But the night stillness was unlifted. Daniel began to shiver again.
>
> "Hit's dark," he said.

The powerful effect of Granberry's dialogue comes not only from the faithful rendition of the boys' speech—not only as a result of the accuracy of the author's ear for such speech—but from the oblique nature of their conversation, the unspoken spectre of what is to become of their father, who haunts the dialogue like a third, silent party to the exchange.

In Sterling D. Plumpp's "Mighty Long Time," a young black Sonny Boy, wants to learn to play the blues on a harmonica. This is how he expresses his fascinated frustration:

> "I can blow the harp—just can't blow blues out it. Not like eating, this blues-playing—you can't just use your own spoon to clean your plate—gotta dip from somebody else's too. Ebenezzer got them blues—had'em most his life. Took me in, they say when my momma died with pneumonia and I was three years old. Been with him and Miss Mae ever since; she the only momma I knowed and he my daddy. Miss Mae say ain't nobody never can blow the blues like Ebenezzer Smith; say he could stop folks from playing baseball at a picnic. Then one night in a honky-tonk in Vicksburg he blowed so low folks broke down and cried like they at a revival. He was the best til they took him away. Some no-good nigger said Ebenezzer Smith was in with him in stealing cotton; when all he'd done was help some fella load cotton one night up in Clarksdale—"

In addition to the authenticity of black dialect that the author gives us, he presents the intensity of Sonny Boy's ambition and the mini-tale of the tragedy of Ebenezzer Smith, a great folk blues musician.

The reader who knows the South, knows Mississippi, will hear that familiar, special quality of expression that is unknown, in its genuine texture, outside the region. In James Street's "Weep No More, My Lady," the bark of a basenji, lost in a swamp, is remarked thusly: "That ain't no animal. That's a thing." In a chapter from Luke Wallin's novel, *The Redneck Poacher's Son,* a moonshiner and his sons catch an enormous alligator snapping turtle in a seining net:

> . . . "I was thinking Aunt May could flat cook us some stews from that sucker."
>
> "Let's let him go," Jesse said. "We'll get some little ones for the pot."
>
> "Let him go?" Robert Elmer said. "Let him go and us have to wade in there again?"

"He could take off your foot, couldn't he?" Bean laughed.
"More than that," Paw said.

One of the reasons for the marvelous accomplishment of Mississippi fiction writers, one of the reasons the reader of that fiction *experiences* the substance, the palpable stuff of the life depicted in it, is that the reader cannot help but *hear* the characters talk. This regional dialect rings true—eccentric, ungrammatical, hard with metaphors taken directly from the reality of daily life.

Common ground, a common milieu, a shared history manifest in the living fabric of explicit and unspoken social traditions, the moral focus of race relations stemming from the awful institution of slavery, memorable characters, and a distinctive regional dialect, these are features readers will encounter over and over again in the fiction of Mississippi native and resident authors collected hereafter.

If these elements can be said to constitute the *stuff* of this fiction, is there any thematic focus, however broadly discerned, that can be said to characterize the work of Mississippi fiction writers? Is there perhaps an archetypal fictional situation common to this body of literary art?

It is a broad concept, but the reader will repeatedly confront the situation of youthful innocence thrust into or against a situation of complex—often corrupt or violent—adult "sophistication." The juxtaposition of these factors is always poignant, and sometimes traumatic, a fictional paradigm in which the intricacies of the world of adults are always seen afresh, via a perspective that is unclouded by the heritage of the past, unburdened by the weight of social mores, uncorrupted by the amoral or immoral streak that can run so deep in human nature. In these fictions, Mississippi authors repeatedly depict the first significant experience of an innocent consciousness as it registers the sheer fact and substance of the life that must be lived, must be accepted if it cannot be overcome.

Jack Butler's "Without Any Ears" is an instance of Southern Gothic, the juxtaposition of the grotesque and the sentimental, in which the horror of the human capacity for cruelty is tempered by the human instinct to reach out to suffering, to comfort it, expressed by a naive young man in an essay written for an English composition class.

The title of Martha Lacy Hall's "The Peaceful Eye" is deceptive, for what Mary, her central character, sees in the behavior of Miss Emma, a suicide, is another instance of human instinct and desire twisted toward the grotesque. Fundamental impulses are stymied, and the innocent witness, Mary, a sixth grader, must transcend the trauma of what she learns of the adult world, must come to accept the suffering that "life" in that adult world can mean.

The juvenile observer of adult behavior is very common in these fictions. William Mills's "To Pass Him Out" presents ten-year-old Tommy, an innocent outsider, as witness to Miz Fanny's "murder" of Mr. Emmett Tillman; the author's method is skillfully oblique, the reader able to know so much more of what is happening, and why, than the naive Tommy can—the reader knows Miz Fanny is, almost as a kind of horrible service, assisting the decrepit Mr. Tillman to his necessary demise, so that the reader shares equally in the boy's anxious bewilderment and the terrible necessities of the adult world.

In the portion of James Whitehead's excellent *Joiner* reprinted here, his Sonny Joiner recalls the early trauma of his sister Lucy's death by fire. The adult Sonny Joiner must "worry" the meaning of that awful childhood experience, the accident, his sister's death from shock, the funeral, in an unending effort to understand and accept it, though it is clear Sonny Joiner will never wholly "accept" the fact that life brings such deaths with it.

In an excerpt from Al Young's *Snakes,* a young black outsider is sent to live with relatives in Mississippi. Like Mills's Tommy, Young's viewpoint character is only ten. Living with an uncle who keeps a "blind pig," the boy is initiated into a world of adult corruption that is mitigated by its vitality, and he emerges from the experience with the prize of having been taught to play the piano.

So the thematic implications of this archetypal situation, the innocent facing adult reality, are not always unrelievedly bleak. One value almost always posited, almost as the sole haven from the frustration and pain of the world's "sophistication," is that of family. In no literature is family more important than in that produced by Mississippi artists.

In no fiction is this more true than in James Hughes's "An Open House," wherein, despite all the irony expressed at the expense of the contemporary middle class family, it is that family, with its solid bonds of love and tolerance, that salves the wounds incurred in the course of living. Fig Remberg, a musician, loses a finger in the garbage disposal. His mother suffers a nervous collapse as a result. His father seems ineffectual, unable to cope with the crisis, and Fig's brother—the innocent—must sort out at least an emotional solution to the dilemma if the family is to survive. He does, and it does.

Decadence, corruption, violence, the grotesque—these *are* embedded themes of many of the fictions gathered here for the reader, but these grim visions are more often than not tempered by fine emotions and insights, by nostalgia, love, courage, and endurance. In the end, the reader will see that no matter how pessimistic a literary artist's vision can seem to be, it is always countered by a fundamental optimism. The very act of literary endeavor—of all artistic endeavor—is an act of faith, faith in imagined possibilities, if not in easy practical solutions. And the themes of these fictions posit, ultimately, not only an unflinching picture of the way things are, or have been, but also assert, if only by implication sometimes, how they might be, or should be.

In the end, Mississippi literature is at one with all serious literary art. No comment on literature can speak for that art; art speaks for itself—it is its own message for its audience. The reader is invited to open these pages, to read . . . and listen.

Gordon Weaver
Oklahoma State University

THE PHIL HARDIN FOUNDATION AND THE MISSISSIPPI WRITERS SERIES

In 1964 Mr. Phil B. Hardin of Meridian, Mississippi, established an educational foundation. At the Foundation's organizational meeting, Mr. Hardin made the following statement:

> My material wealth has been principally acquired by the operation of my bakery business in the State of Mississippi and from the good people of that state. For a long time I have been considering how my estate could best be used after my death. I have finally conceived the idea of creating a charitable foundation through which the bulk of my estate can be used for furthering . . . the education of Mississippians.

Upon his death in 1972, Mr. Hardin willed a portfolio of stocks and bonds, as well as the bakeries, to the Phil Hardin Foundation. The directors of the Foundation use income from these sources to make grants intended to improve the education of Mississippians. Since the transfer of Mr. Hardin's estate to the Foundation in 1976, the Phil Hardin Foundation has distributed over 3.8 million dollars for this purpose.

In 1983 the Foundation directors authorized a challenge grant to support the publication of the series of anthologies entitled *Mississippi Writers: Reflections of Childhood and Youth.* This series recognizes the accomplishments of our state's authors. The series also introduces young Mississippians to their state's literary heritage, perhaps providing thereby a "shock of recognition" and the transmission of values revealed in that heritage: family, community, a sense of place and history, the meaning of justice and honor, the importance of enduring in the struggle for just causes, the significance as we live out our lives one with another of "courage . . . and hope and pride and compassion and pity and sacrifice." By so doing the series may help young Mississippians come to grips with the complexities of Mississippi culture and heritage and of the larger society that now more than ever impinges on this place. As importantly, the series may help forge a sense of common identity and interest.

The major values, themes, and situations found in these writings, however, have substantial significance beyond the borders of our state—as Mr. Faulkner demonstrated with his "postage stamp of native soil." This series, then, to the extent that its pieces touch the human heart and give expression and meaning to human experience, may encourage a love of good literature and develop interest in the craft of writing.

The Phil Hardin Foundation is honored to join with other Mississippians to make possible the publication of the *Mississippi Writers* series. Mississippians can accomplish more working together than working alone.

C. Thompson Wacaster
The Phil Hardin Foundation

The Following People, Organizations, and Businesses Generously Contributed Funds to Match the Challenge Grant Awarded by the Phil Hardin Foundation

Dr. and Mrs. Joe Bailey
Mrs. and Mrs. Charles G. Bell
Ms. Jane Rule Burdine
Mrs. Roberta J. Burns-Howard
Mrs. Betty W. Carter
Centennial Study Club (Oxford)
Mr. Henry Chambers
Coca-Cola Bottling Co. (Vicksburg)
Mr. and Mrs. Sam W. Crawford
CREATE, Inc.
Ms. Carole H. Currie
Mr. and Mrs. Glen H. Davidson
Mr. and Mrs. William Deas
Mr. and Mrs. Herman B. DeCell
Mrs. Keith Dockery
Mr. and Mrs. Robert B. Dodge
Fortnightly Matinee Club (Tupelo)
Dr. and Mrs. Jan Goff
Dr. and Mrs. William Hilbun
Mr. and Mrs. Howard Hinds
Mrs. Mary Hohenberg
Mr. Irwin T. Holtzman
Mr. Stuart C. Irby, Jr.
Stuart Irby Construction Company
Dr. and Mrs. David Irwin
The Honorable and Mrs. Trent Lott
Mr. and Mrs. T. M. McMillan, Jr.
Miss Marjorie Milam
Mrs. Blewett Mitchell
The Honorable G. V. Montgomery
Mrs. Gaines Moore
Mrs. L. K. Morgan
R. R. Morrison and Son, Inc.
Mr. Richard A. Moss
National Association of Treasury Agents
Mr. William M. Pace
Mrs. A. E. Patterson

Dr. Max Pegram
Mr. and Mrs. Jack R. Reed
Dr. and Mrs. Pete Rhymes
Dr. Stephen L. Silberman
Mr. and Mrs. Bill Spigner
Mr. and Mrs. Landman V. Teller
Dr. and Mrs. P. K. Thomas
United Southern Bank (Clarksdale)
University Press of Mississippi
Mr. and Mrs. Harold Wilson
Mr. Sam Woodward

Mississippi Writers
Reflections of Childhood and Youth

FROM

Blood on the Forge

William Attaway

He never had a craving in him that he couldn't slick away on his guitar. You have to be native to the red-clay hills of Kentucky to understand that. There the guitar players don't bother with any fingering; they do it by running a knife blade up and down the stops. Most of the good slickers down where he was born would say that a thin blade made the most music. But he liked the heft of a good, heavy hog sticker. It took a born player to handle one of those. And maybe that's why his mother changed his name to Melody when he got old enough for a name to mean something beside "Come get tit."

Nineteen-nineteen—early spring: the last time, there among the red-clay hills, he was to reach down his guitar. It was a hunger craving yanking at his vitals. That wasn't unusual; share-cropping and being hungry went together. He had never thought about white pork, molasses and salt water cornbread as food anyhow. They were just something to take the wrinkles out of his stomach. Maybe thinking like that had something to do with his not growing up tall and hefty like his half brothers, Big Mat and Chinatown—that and making music when he should have been fighting over the little balls of fat left in the kettle.

Chinatown was in the dust by the shack, playing mumblety-peg with the hog sticker. His back was flattened against a tin patent-medicine sign that covered the chinks in the cabin. Because the tin held the heat of the last sun he rubbed his back up and down and grinned. His gold tooth flashed. There had never been anything wrong with his teeth; he had just had a front one pulled to make space for the gold.

Melody plopped down on the lopsided stoop and arranged his guitar. Chinatown looked out of the corners of his little slant eyes.

"What blues you chordin'?"

"Hungry blues." And Melody plucked the thrown hog sticker out of the air.

"Won't be no more hungry blues come night."

Hattie came and stood in the doorway. She was Big Mat's wife. The marks on her told that much. But although she was hardly bigger than Melody's music box nobody could take the spunk out of her. She leaned against the doorjamb and rubbed one bare foot against the other.

"I hear what you say, China."

"What you hear I say?"

"That you goin' out stealin' come night."

"You hear wrong, woman. I say ain't gonna be no more hungry blues, come night. An' you know why?"

"'Cause we be doin' ninety days on the road gang for your thievin'?"

"Naw," squealed Chinatown, "'cause, come night, we all be sleepin'." He laughed, and his gold tooth shone as he laughed, only you couldn't call it laughter by his face. His slant eyes and the tight skin drawing the lips back off his teeth made laughing his natural look.

"Maybe Mat bring somethin' back." Hattie sighed. "He gone over Moaningreen way to kill them ailin' hogs for Mr Johnston."

"Maybe he git a whole hog," said Chinatown. "They gonna die anyways."

"Mr Johnston ain't givin' niggers no well hog an' he ain't givin' 'em no sick hog. He ain't givin' 'em no hog a-tall." And with that Melody struck up a chord, running his knife the full length of the guitar. It was mellow, like the sound of hound dogs baying across a river.

Done scratched at the hills,
But the 'taters refuse to grow. . . .
Done scratched at the hills,
But the 'taters refuse to grow. . . .
Mister Bossman, Mister Bossman,
Lemme mark in the book once mo'. . . .

There were more verses like that than any one man knew. And after each verse the refrain:

Hungry blues done got me listenin' to my
love one cry. . . .

Put some vittles in my belly, or yo' honey
gonna lay down and die. . . .

He quit singing to just slick a little while. There was no need to think; his hand wouldn't stop until it had found every minor chord in the box.

"It ain't no two ways about it," breathed Hattie. "Blues sure is a help."

"Hungry blues ain't nothin'," he told her, never stopping. "It ain't like you tryin' to blues away a love cravin' that git so mixed up with the music you can't know which is which."

"Lawd, now!" she breathed.

"Ain't never hear tell of a creeper singin' no love blues," said Chinatown through his golden grin.

"Ain't never seen no creeper without razor marks on him somewhere, you mean," said Hattie.

"There ain't no mark on me."

"Well, what you lay that to?"

"Reckon I jest too slick to git caught."

"You jest got more space to cook up devilment than anybody else. A body ought to be 'shamed to lay round in the dust all day, lettin' his two brothers go out in the fields and earn his somethin'-to-eat for him."

"I lazy, and they smart." He grinned. "I lazy and hungry—they smart and hungry." He helped his point with a bigger grin.

Hattie did not know what to say. She fussed around with her feet. Then, snorting, she went into the shack. Chinatown winked at Melody.

From the southwest came a flock of coots, flying high, straining forward like all water fowl. All day they had been passing overhead, curving north. It would not be long before the wild ducks and geese would make the same passage. Chinatown looked up.

"When coots come afore the duck tomorrow goin' to bring bad luck." Extending his hands, he sighted along an imaginary rifle. "Bop! Bop! Bop!" He settled back, satisfied with the number of coots he had killed in his mind.

Hattie popped into the doorway. She had thought of the right answer for Chinatown. "It ain't needin' for none of us to be hungry, an' you with a hunk of gold in your mouth."

Chinatown looked scared, and Hattie watched him with satisfaction. She knew he would rather die than part with that shiny tooth but she was out to plague him.

"Maybe it ain't worth nothin'," he mumbled.

"It worth a full belly."

He could not look at her eyes. His toes searched the dust.

"I know what," she said.

"What?" mumbled Chinatown.

"Tonight I talk to Big Mat, so he yank it outen your head and take it in to Madison."

Chinatown half rose. "No!" His voice went into falsetto and cracked. "I work in the bossman's fields all season for that tooth."

Hattie backed. "Onliest time you stir since is to look at that gold in the glass." She disappeared in the shack.

He sat back against the tin. After a time he mumbled, "Ain't no use in a man stirrin' round and gettin' all lathered up. He ain't gittin' no place."

He was talking to himself, but Hattie heard and called out, "Now what you tryin' to say?"

"Only seem like good sense to stay where you was in the first place and save yourself the trouble of comin' back."

She came to the door again. "How the crop goin' to git made?"

"We jest niggers, makin' the white man crop for him. Leave him make his own crop, then we don't end up owin' him money every season."

"Lawd, you never will be no good!" Hattie sighed. "Maybe you git straightened out if you gits a woman of your own to feed."

Melody entered the conversation in an old song:

Now the berry always sweeter
on the other man's bush. . . .
What you reckon make that?

Chinatown guffawed. "Now that there the truth."

"Your poor dead maw musta had a conjure, to set a bad egg like you without spoilin' the brook," she said.

"Better be careful not to say nothin' 'bout Maw when Big Mat around," Chinatown warned.

"Sure said he'd belt you," put in Melody.

"An' I ain't never knowed Mat to grin when he say somethin'," said Chinatown.

"Mat know he in the wrong," she scolded.

"Forgit about it," advised Melody.

"I got cause to talk as much as I please."

"Jest forgit about it."

"Mat jest afeared I goin' to talk about how come we ain't got no mule and what the reason we ain't got nothin' to cook up in the house."

To cut Hattie off Melody started up another spell of the blues. Maw hadn't been in the ground but about four weeks. Neither of them wanted to hear any talk about her or that mule. Talk brought back the homemade burial box, the light rain falling and the thud of falling clods still ringing in their ears as they went homeward across the pastures, before sunup Maw out pushing that one-mule plow, Chinatown sitting around in the dust, Melody dodging the fields for his guitar. They thought of it now. She had dropped dead between the gaping handles of the plow. The lines had been double looped under her arms, so she was dragged through the damp, rocky clay by a mule trained never to balk in the middle of a row. The mule dragged her in. The rocks in the red hills are sharp. She didn't look like their maw any more. Hattie went to work on the body with yellow hog-fat soap. Chinatown and Melody sat against the house and cried. Big Mat went away for a long time. He came back hog wild and he took a piece of flint rock and tore the life out of that mule, so that even the hide wasn't fit to sell.

Melody had fallen out on the ground and vomited and for three days afterward hc couldn't hold food on his stomach. The sight of blood always acted on him like that.

Four weeks had stopped them from wailing. It was better for her to be in heaven, was Hattie's word on their maw, than making a crop for Mr Johnston. . . . Still, you couldn't stop her from working. If that mule went to the same place she did she probably started in right away to plow for God.

Mr Johnston said that they could not have any more food credit. He claimed their share of the crop for the next two years in payment for his mule. He didn't say where the crop was coming from when there was no animal to plow with. He didn't say how they were going to eat without food credit. All they could do was to wait for him to change his mind.

Hattie had kept at Big Mat, driving him crazy with her talk, blaming him for everything. One day it had taken both Chinatown and Melody to keep him from lighting into her with the butt end of a hoe. But he swore he'd belt her if she even mentioned Maw again.

Melody sang softer and softer. Soon he was just singing for himself. Going onto verse fifty, or thereabout, he got weary and barely hit the strings. He looked away over the rolling country to the place where the sun had about given up fighting the dark hills. Most of the country beyond Vagermound Common was bunched with crab-apple trees, posing crookedly, like tired old Negroes against the sky. Big Mat was going to come walking out of those hills, over the Vagermound Common, down the red, packed road that wound past their door. He was going to have a greasy sack over his shoulders, Melody hoped. To keep from hoping too hard about that sack he made out to play the wish game with Chinatown.

"China," he half sang, "you know where I wish I was at now?"

Chinatown hunched forward in the dust. He liked the wishing game. They had played at it all their lives, most times wishing they were at the grand places pictured in the old newspapers that livened the walls of the shack.

"Where at?" He grinned eagerly.

"Me—me," pondered Melody, "me—I wish I was in town. That's it—smack in town—and it's a Saturday noontime."

"What you be doin'?"

"Jest standin'—all made out in a white-checkered vest and a ice-cream suit, and you can't hardly see the vest for a gold watch chain. I got on shoes, too—yeller shoes with dimes in the toes. Man, man!"

"The gals is passing by. . . . " Chinatown tried to help.

"Naw, that ain't till evenin'. Now I aimin' to shoot some pool."

"You can't shoot no pool."

"But I wish I can," said Melody.

"Ain't you aimin' to make no music?"

"Jest aimin' to shoot some pool," he told him. "Course, I got my guitar with me, jest in case. But I'm feelin' too good to make my guitar cry."

"Now ain't that awful you can't make no music, and you feelin' good?" sympathized Chinatown.

"It don't make no never mind, 'cause my box is shinin' with silver, and the stops all covered with mother-of-pearl. An' everybody see me say that must be Mr Melody. They say howdy to Mr Dressin'-man Melody."

Hattie was in the doorway again.

"Stuff!" she snorted, but she was listening hard.

"What you do, come night?" asked Chinatown.

Melody thought hard and struck a long chord to make his thoughts swell with the music.

"Come night—come night . . . Well, I guess I spark around the gals and drink a little corn. Maybe I'm on a church picnic. The gal and me has got our bellies full and slipped away in the bushes at the edge of the river. Had the corn in my pocket all the time."

Chinatown had a pucker around his slant eyes.

"Goin' to drink anythin' but corn?" he asked hopefully.

Chinatown wanted him to put a bottle of red pop into the story. Chinatown lived on red pop whenever they were in Masonville. He had loved it from the first bottle given him by a white man who thought it would be funny to see a little slant-eyed pickaninny drink red pop. When asked how he liked it Chinatown had told the man:

"Taste kinda like your foots is 'sleep."

He was right.

"I say you goin' to drink anythin' but corn?" repeated Chinatown.

"Jest corn." Then, seeing how Chinatown was caught in the story, he added: "Maybe I mix it with a little red pop though."

"That make it good." Chinatown grinned.

It was deep dusk.

"Wish night gone and real night come on." Hattie sighed. "Guess I light the rag for Big Mat." Melody looked up, caught by the rhythm of her words. She went in to light the scrap in a dish of black tallow. The kerosene had been gone a long time.

Chinatown took an old quid out of his pocket. He wrapped it in a dried corn husk and tied the cigar-shaped mass with Johnson grass.

"Smoke always spoil my feelin' for eatin'," he said. He called to Hattie: "Hand me out a lighted stick."

"What you want a fire stick for?" she called back.

"Gonna set the house on fire." He laughed.

Grumbling, she brought a glowing twig.

"Ain't but one place you coulda got any tobacco," she said. "You done found one of Mat's hunks o' chewin' tobacco and crumbled it up."

"That's right," he said.

"Mat take the hide off you."

"What for? He chewed this piece already about ten times."

"Well, can't say I hold no blame. . . . What I wouldn't give for a pinch of snuff under the lip!"

"Wish night gone and real night come on," Melody repeated. "That sound like the blues, Hattie."

"Too bad you didn't bring some wish snuff back with you from Wish Town," was her answer.

"Night creep up like a old woman," Melody said softly to himself. "Can't see her—can't hear her. She jest creep up when your back turned."

"Smoke makin' me light in the head. My stomach growlin'. Guess that mean I got fast business in some white man's smokehouse." Chinatown snuffed his smoke. He got to his feet, cleaning his hands by spitting on them and wiping them on his overalls.

"She got on a black skirt," Melody dreamed. "She black, too, so's you can't see her legs when she shackle her skirt to the floors o' the earth."

"Keep the kettle bilin', Hattie," said Chinatown. "Bilin' water for meat or for buckshots."

Melody began to sway.

"At night the hills ain't red no more. There ain't no crab-apple trees squat in the hills, no more land to hoe in the red-hot sun—white the same as black. . . . Where the mule gone at? He only a voice in the pasture land. . . ."

Of a sudden he became conscious of what he was doing. He grabbed for the guitar. "Listen, China; listen, Hattie—listen what I'm doin'." He went on lightly: "Now the chigger ain't nothin' but bite. All the crickets is is a big chirp in the grass. Night bird call out the deathwatch. . . . Night-flyers is glow buckles on the garters of old creepin' night. The mosquitoes is her swamp-fever sting. . . . But it don't last long, 'cause she say, 'Git along,' an' be nothin', 'cause black ain't nothin', an' I is black. . . ."

"Hallo, hallo . . ." It came like an echo lost in the hills beyond Vagermound.

Hattie was peering into the night, listening.

"Hallo, hallo . . ." the echo answered itself.

"It's Big Mat," she cried.

"Well, git the kettle bilin', woman," cried Chinatown. "He ain't holler lessen he got somethin' in a sack."

Nigger, nigger never die.
Black face and shiny eye,
Kinky hair and pigeon toe—
That the way the nigger go. . . .

Because he was blacker than his half brothers the white share croppers' kids had sung that little chant at him. They had said that Big Mat's father must have been a lump of charcoal. And Big Mat had learned to draw to a safe distance within himself everything that could be hurt. The years had given him a shell. But within that tight *casure* his emotions were under great pressure. Sometimes they broke through, and he filled with red madness—like a boar at mating—hog wild. Few folks had seen him like that. To almost everybody but his close kin he was a stupid, unfeeling giant, a good man to butcher hogs and veal cattle. Melody alone knew him completely. Melody, from his dream world, could read the wounds in Big Mat's eyes.

Now seven carcasses glistened on the sacks at Big Mat's feet. Flies struggled in the sticky blood that oozed from the box of entrails. He threw the chain around the hind leg of the last hog. Passing the free end of the chain over the low branch of a tree, he began to hoist the struggling, squealing animal off the ground. Out of the corners of his eyes he saw Mr Johnston and the riding boss. Mr Johnston had always been a landowner, but the riding boss had been a poor white share cropper. Big Mat remembered him as a little ragged boy singing the hated chant. The two men stood in the shade of the barn, mixing their talk and spit. That talk was about him. He could see it in their little gestures. So he bent closer to the chain, lifting the hog in easy jerks. When the hog was well off the ground Mat fastened the chain to a stake and reached down into the box of guts for his knife.

"Oh, Mat," called Mr Johnston.

"Yessuh?" Mat waited.

Mr Johnston came toward him.

"This here's the last hog, ain't it?"

"This the brood sow, suh."

"Well, I want to catch her blood."

Mat went and got a bucket and set it under the hanging animal.

"Figger to make some blood sausages," said Mr Johnston. "Damn good eatin' when they made right."

Mr Johnston stood watching while Big Mat wiped the knife across the hog's teats. The animal had grown quiet. Its little eyes sucked back out of sight. The snout dripped a rope of saliva halfway to the ground. Big Mat touched the hog's neck tentatively with the point of the knife. The animal quivered. The shining rope broke and made a bubble on the ground.

"Mr Johnston."

"What it is, Mat?"

"This here the last hog, and the sun almost down. I was jest wonderin'——"

"Say what's on your mind, boy," said Mr Johnston.

"My folks is waitin'——"

"For what?"

"For me, Mr Johnston. They hungry. . . ."

"Go on."

"If I could jest scald this one and leave the butcherin' until tomorrow—take somethin' home to my folks . . ."

Mr Johnston spat his quid into the box of entrails.

"Well, that there's a good idee, Mat. What you figger on takin' home?"

"Why, anythin' you gives me, suh." Mat played the knife over the sow's throat. The animal held its breath and then gagged. Saliva ran like unraveling silk.

"What makes you think I'm goin' to give you anythin', Mat?"

Big Mat did not answer.

Mr Johnston said, "It ain't my fault your folks ain't got nothin' to eat."

The knife point found a spot on the hog's neck.

"I figger this here labor can jest go on what you owe me for my mule."

The blade slid out of sight. The haft socked against the bristled neck. A quick wiggle of the knife found the great blood vessel. Big Mat drew the blade. Dark blood gushed in its wake. Mr Johnston looked admiringly.

"You know the needs of a knife, Mat," he said.

Big Mat stood watching the hog bleed. He shifted the bucket a trifle with his toe.

"Mr Johnston."

"Yes, Mat?"

"How we goin' to make a crop this year? We already late on plowin'."

Mr Johnston grinned. "Well, Mat, I figger on you all makin' a good crop with corn and molasses cane."

"We got to have a mule, suh."

Mr Johnston's eyes grew small and sharp. "Looka here, I contract with you for a crop. It ain't my business how you make it. Them hills has always growed a crop and they'll grow one this season if you folks have to scratch it outen the bare rocks."

So Big Mat told him what he already knew about the land: "It ain't jest the mule, suh. It's everythin'. Wind and rain comin' outen the heavens ever' season, takin' the good dirt down to the bottoms. Last season over the big hill the plow don't go six inches in the dirt afore it strike hard rock. Stuff jest don't come up like it use to. Us'll have a hard time makin' it on our share, mule or no—a hard time. . . ."

Mr Johnston caught Big Mat with his eyes. He came forward. Big Mat looked doggedly into the hard eyes. For a long second they hung on the edge of violence.

Mr Johnston said, "You ain't kickin', are you, Mat?"

Big Mat's eyes dropped to the bloody entrails. He presented a dull, stupid exterior.

"Nosuh, I ain't kickin'."

Mr Johnston smiled and drew out a plug. He bit a chaw and settled it in his cheek to soften.

"Mat," he said, "you know I don't have nothin' but niggers work my land. You know why?"

"Nosuh."

"Well, they's three reasons: niggers ain't bothered with the itch; they knows how to make it the best way they kin and they don't kick none."

The hog suddenly started its final death struggles. It threshed about on the chain, throwing blood in a wide circle. Mr Johnston jumped back. Big Mat grabbed hold of the animal's ears and held the big body steady.

"They don't jump till they 'most dead," said Big Mat.

Mr Johnston laughed. "What I say jest past your understandin', Mat—slips off your head like water offen a duck's back."

"Yessuh."

"You a good boy though. What I really come over here for is to tell you I'm goin' to let you have a mule tomorrow."

"Yessuh." Big Mat's outward self did not change, but his heart jumped. A mule was life.

"An' about what's on the book against you—you send them brothers of yourn over here. They can work some of it off. Give them fifty cents a week to boot. That'll keep you goin'."

"Yessuh."

"You kin take along a bag of them guts when you go. Throw the rest of them back to the other hogs."

Mr Johnston started toward the house. He turned. "Oh, Mat, my ridin' boss tells me there some jacklegs around, lyin' to the niggers about how much work they is up North. Jest you remember how I treat you and don't be took in by no lies."

It was dark when Big Mat picked up his greasy sack and started for home. The moon would not be up yet, but he knew the rolling hills by night. His feet would find the road. Deep inside him was his familiar hatred of the white boss, but the thought of a mule was hot, like elderberry wine. Against the dark sky the darker crab-apple trees kept pace with him as he walked. When he reached the edge of Vagermound Common he threw back his head and gave a long "Hallo . . . hallo . . ."

Gila Flambé

FREDERICK BARTHELME

THE WOMAN WITH the menus stops me by the cash register because the restaurant is crowded and she doesn't think she has a table for one. I'm soaked after running across the jammed parking lot in the hot rain, so I'm not sympathetic when the woman, whose lips are a juicy red, shakes her head and gazes forlornly around the room. "Nobody ever comes in alone," she says.

I point to a small man sitting by himself in a corner.

"Oh," she says, straightening the menus on her arm. "That's Mr. Pelham. I forgot about him."

"Well, maybe he'd like company?" I don't want to sit there, but it's better than nothing.

"No. He always eats alone."

Mr. Pelham occupies a small table near the kitchen doors—not a good table at all, but it has two chairs, one of them empty, and there isn't another unoccupied chair in the room. The restaurant used to be a hardware store; now it's all done up in cheesy L.A. late-thirties gear, the hard-boiled version—palms, ratty paintings, neon, ersatz columns, colored lights, pale-salmon walls in bad plaster, black tile floor. The waitresses slink around in period evening dress; the blondes make an effort at Veronica Lake. There's a lot of smoke-colored taffeta and lamé in evidence. This is my first trip.

"Why don't you ask him," I say. "He looks like he could use a friend."

The woman with the menus doesn't want to do this, but after another look around she agrees, and slides across the room toward his table, narrowly missing a waitress in a shiny dress who's carrying a tray of squat cocktails.

There's a commotion in the corner; abruptly Mr. Pelham gets up and pushes the menu woman aside. He's short. He stands awkwardly, bent forward, his fists planted on the table, his black raincoat still tight around him, and he stares across the room at me. I point at him, then at myself, then back at him; he says something to the woman, then sits down. She flaps her hand at me, telling me it's all right, I should come over.

Pelham looks fifty. At the neck of his raincoat—only the topmost button is undone—the bright, starched, tightly buttoned collar of a white dress shirt is visible. He isn't wearing a tie. On the table, half covering the chrome wire rack of sugar packets, there's a black hat with a ribbed band. I remove my raincoat and drop it onto the floor next to the second chair. "Thanks," I say. "I didn't want to bother you, but"—I turn and look quickly around the room—"there's no place left to sit. My name's Harold. Sometimes I'm called Zoot." I stick out my hand, but Pelham doesn't look up from his soup. He's bent over the shallow dish, blowing on the soup, pulling away occasionally to whisk his spoon around the rim. "I'll move if something opens up, O.K.?"

Pelham's hair is thin and sticking to his scalp. "I'm waiting for somebody," he says. "You'll have to move when she comes."

A woman who can't be twenty hands me a glassy scarlet menu. She's wearing a black dress with thin straps and a feather motif in sequins up under the bodice. She looks good. I ask her to keep an eye out for a vacant table, but she doesn't seem to understand.

"Mr. Pelham has been kind enough to let me join him until another table becomes available."

"Oh," the waitress says, reaching for the menu she's just given me.

"I'll keep it." We have a little tug-of-war over the menu, very quick, which she gracefully allows me to win. She's not sure about the water glass she's holding, but finally decides to leave it.

Pelham says, "Don't stain the table," so I open the menu and slide the glass onto one corner of it. There's an eight-foot-high potted palm behind him, and every time the kitchen doors swing open, one of the largest fronds sways, brushing the back of his head, and he jerks out of the way.

"I'm not alone all the time," he says. "I've got people come to see me night and day." He's looking very carefully through his soup, picking up spoonfuls, twisting them to catch the light, then dripping the soup back into the dish. "Don't get the idea that I'm bad off."

"O.K.," I say, and drink my water. There's a dark, irregular stain on the corner of the menu; I try to put the glass back exactly where it was. "You come often? Here, I mean?"

"What're you, an accountant? You run a small store or something? You're not from the Board of Health, are you?"

"No." I wish I'd waited at the door. "No, I just came to try the food."

He laughs and drops the spoon into the saucer. "Yeah, and I love yams," he says. "Slinky's food is nothing. She goes off to Vassar or someplace and suddenly everybody's stiff for her."

"The desserts—somebody said they were good."

"Her aunt. Slinky's idea of dessert is a weekend with wet hair in a station wagon." He presses a hand to his forehead, then slides the fingers back over his scalp, gluing new points of dark hair to the skin. He rolls his eyes. "Look at these people—why the hell don't they go home? Go to Bonanza, for Christ's sake."

Looking around the room, I wonder the same thing. Bonanza's not so bad, and you can usually get a table.

Pelham looks at me for the first time since I sat down. "What're you doing here, Mac? You're out of town and it's raining and you're here alone—don't that beat all. Where's your beautiful wife? Where's your beautiful house?"

I grin and shrug stupidly, aiming for camaraderie. "No wife, no house. My beautiful car's in the lot outside, only it's a Chevrolet."

Pelham shreds four crackers into his soup, which must be room temperature by now. "Zoot? What kind of name is that? That's a stupid name."

I nod and study the menu, trying to decide whether I want to stay. I've been called Zoot since I was a kid—my father played lousy saxophone and loved Zoot Sims. "It's all tongue, boy," he used to say while we listened together to a Sims record so loud it rattled the figurines in my mother's china cabinet. "Tongue and breath." And we sat, listening, my father's open saxophone case on the sofa, the horn a light, glistening gold, until late into the weekend nights. As nicknames go, Zoot isn't so bad. "My dad was a musician. He gave me the name."

"I know a guy named Stick," Pelham says. "And I used to know a guy named Nipple, but he got his throat cut on a rig in the Gulf. Stick's a bowling champion somewhere—Little Rock, maybe. He's got himself set up with a bar called the 7–10 Club, something like that." Pelham flakes more crackers into the dish. His soup is beginning to look like day-old cereal.

"Stick," I repeat.

Two couples come in together and are seated at a table against the far wall. I catch the eye of the woman with the menus, and she tosses her head a little to indicate that she gets the message.

"Yeah. Stick. And you're Zoot. And I'm Blink, because I never do. Ain't that wonderful."

I eat a small steak while Pelham watches, still nursing his soup. The steak isn't bad. The waitress with the sequins says she's sorry ten or fifteen times, talking, it seems, more to Pelham than to me. She suggests a dessert that turns out to be a circle of fresh pineapple embedded in a square of white chocolate and topped with curled almond shavings.

"I need a ride," Pelham says while I add the tip on the Visa slip. "Hot young thing like you can afford to give me a ride, can't you?"

"Sure. Where're you headed?" It's a reflex; I don't know why I'm agreeing. Maybe it's the way Pelham looks—the eyebrows and the sallow skin and the disdain. Maybe I want to prove I'm not such a rotten felow.

"It ain't far," he says. "I'll buy gas if you want to be pissy about it. I've got to meet somebody, and my Lamborghini's in the shop."

"Fine. O.K."

"Course if you're too busy I'll just crawl." He pushes his chair back from the table, deposits the hat on his head, then falls to his knees and crawls toward the entrance. For a minute I think he's crippled, but at the door he gets up and gives the menu woman a hug, then brushes his knees. He signals for me to hurry up. I'm still seated at the table, trying to figure out what's going on, when he shouts, "Let's move it, kid," as if we were Marines in a movie.

The first thing I do when I get the car started is look at the gas gauge: half a tank, plenty. Then I turn on the windshield wipers and turn off the radio. Pelham jams his hands in his raincoat pockets and says, "That way," jerking his head to the right. "How old are you, thirty? Thirty-five?"

"Two," I say, wheeling out of the parking lot. "Where're we going?"

"I'll tell you where to turn." He stares straight out the windshield. "I'm fifty today. When you're fifty, it goes very fast. You people don't know that."

We drive through town, which is eight blocks of two- and three-story buildings, then go out a winding road past the industrial section, past some kind of all-lit-up oil refinery, and out onto an old highway that used to be a truck route; it's raining heavily, so I can't see much except the occasional brights of a passing tanker truck.

"I'm going to help you out, kid," Pelham says after we've been driving a few minutes in silence. "I'm going to introduce you to Melba."

Oncoming lights make the rain on the windshield look alive, the way the water pops off the glass and flies into midair. I wait for Pelham to tell me about Melba. Suddenly he says, "Here. Turn here."

I spin the Chevrolet onto a red clay road full of potholes and brown standing water. We buck and heave in the front seat of the car, and there's nothing to see but the hood, the rain, the almost pumpkin-colored road. We go a little way, and I start to say something but Pelham pulls his hand out of his raincoat pocket and grabs my arm. "O.K.," he says. "Here. Stop. Cut the lights and sit tight." Then he yanks the hat down over his forehead, opens the door, and pushes out into the rain.

I do what he says. With the lights off I can't see anything at all; at first I can't even see the steering wheel in my lap. I know where we are, how far we are from town, but when lightning cracks somewhere in the distance to the left, I'm too slow to catch it, and see only empty space, a field—no trees or buildings—before the blackness closes in again. Pelham's only been gone a minute or two, but it seems longer. I pull the knob that turns on the instrument lights so I can read the clock: nine-eighteen. It's ridiculous—I can't leave the poor bastard in the rain in the middle of nowhere. There's no place to turn the car around anyway; I'd have to back up the three-quarters of a mile to the highway. I feel stupid for getting into this. I start the car, snap on the lights, and punch the horn button a couple of times; he doesn't show, so I lock all four doors, then turn the engine and lights off and listen to the chatter of the rain.

Pelham knocks on my window, and I roll it down. "Come on out, kid. It's O.K." He's got an umbrella—one of those oversize golf umbrellas with alternating wedges of color, red and white. "Got to get you inside, get you into some dry clothes."

"Inside what?" I say. "There isn't a place for miles. I'm leaving."

I begin to close my window, starting the car at the same time. He shouts, "Wait a minute, kid. Hold on."

"You want a ride back to town, Pelham?" He's got on different clothes—a red checked shirt under the raincoat. "I'm going."

"Sure, kid. Sure. Hold on a minute. Let me get Melba." He goes off again, and I sit there with the motor running. It's nine-thirty-seven.

Melba's a dog—coal black and the size of a small pony. When we get her into the back seat, she shakes herself off, throwing water all over the inside of the car. Pelham hammers on the passenger window; that door's still locked. "Fifty yards up, there's a drive," he says, getting into the car. "You can turn there."

I go out a lot faster than I came in, the car bouncing and sliding through the holes and the slop; when I make the highway, we head for town, driving fast. Pelham is talking to the dog, which has vanished from the rearview mirror. "I knew right where you'd be, Melba," Pelham says. "Came for you just like I said I would, didn't I?" He talks all the way. When I take the turn into the parking lot outside the restaurant too fast and slide the rear end into the back fender of somebody's white Mercedes, Pelham says, "Attaboy."

"O.K." I say, pushing the shift lever into park and turning off the engine. "Get the dog out." I go around to the back of the car to see how bad the damage is. Pelham eases the dog out of the rear seat, holds her on a tight chain, and heads for the restaurant, twirling the bright umbrella. People are lining up at the windows of the building, rubbing the glass and peering out. It looks as if my bumper is caught in the Mercedes' rear wheel well, and the tire there is flattening fast. I jump on the trunk of my car, trying to free the bumper, but the jumping doesn't do any good; the cars are hooked tight.

At the cash register inside I tell the woman what's happened and give her the Mercedes' license number.

"That's Miss Landson's car," the woman says. "You sure know how to pick 'em. Wait here and I'll get her."

I look around the restaurant. There are lots of empty tables now. Back toward the corner where I ate dinner, Pelham comes out of the kitchen carrying what must be a new bowl of soup, the huge dog right behind him.

Miss Landson looks twenty-five and calm, like a hippie girl who suddenly got rich. Her hair is long, straight, thin, and brown. She comes out through the swinging doors of the kitchen talking to the cashier; she's wearing Levi's and lime-yellow running shoes—Nikes, from the look of the decoration—and a denim jacket. As she passes Pelham, who's sitting at the same table playing with the soup, she taps him on the back. She extends her hand when she's still ten feet away from me. "Ericka Landson," she says. "We had a wreck?"

"Only a small wreck, but you lost a tire. I'm sure there's no problem—I mean, Allstate will take care of it."

"Maybe we ought to have a look." She smiles at me and walks toward the door. "It's still raining, I guess." The tail of the jacket is curled at the bottom in back; she doesn't seem to have a shirt on underneath. "Betsy," she says, turning to the cashier, "bring a couple of umbrellas, will you?"

"I'm sorry about this. I was going too fast coming in. It got away from me."

Ericka stands with the door slightly open, looking out into the parking lot. "I heard that. My husband tells me you were mad at him for making you go get Melba."

"Excuse me?" I heard what she said; I just need a minute to get used to the idea. "Oh, yes. Pretty dog. Big."

She laughs. "Dumb. She's afraid of the rain. That's why Warren wanted to go get her, although I don't know why he didn't drive himself." She lets the door close, then looks at her watch, which is black and digital, like an underwater watch. The cuffs of her jacket are rolled twice; she has small, masculine hands, long fingers, clear nails, no wedding ring.

"I sat with him at dinner. You husband, I mean. Only I didn't know he was your husband."

Ericka looks across the room at Pelham. "He likes soup," she says. "Today's his birthday."

Betsy comes out of the kitchen with Pelham's red-and-white umbrella and a second, tan one. Pelham looks up as she passes him, then looks at the two of us standing inside the front door. He seems to chuckle to himself, a vague grin creeping up on one side of his face. "This is all I could find, Miss Landson. This brown one is busted. Carlos has a good umbrella, but he couldn't find it."

"Take one," Ericka says, pointing to the umbrellas. I take the tan and follow her out into the rain. Her shoulders are broad; she's a big woman but not heavy—like an athlete, a runner.

Our cars are awkwardly banged together at the edge of the now almost empty lot. A street light hanging off a telephone pole just beyond the entrance to the lot throws a ghoulish green-white light on the wet cars, and they glisten. The Mercedes is covered with thousands of mirrorlike bubbles. Ericka squats between the cars to assess the damage; the tire on her Mercedes is spread out like a pool of tar under the chromed wheel. She fingers the lug nuts as she surveys the situation.

"I tried jumping on mine, but it didn't help."

"No. It wouldn't," she says, standing. "It'll come out when we jack this one up to replace the tire. The fender's torn a little." She comes out from between the cars, fishing in a breast pocket, from which she pulls a ring of keys. "Let me check the spare. I don't want to get somebody out here if the spare's no good."

She opens the trunk of the Mercedes, then bends under the lid and flips up the carpet to get at the spare. When she closes the trunk, she looks at my car and says, "You didn't do so badly, outside of the taillight. It's Warren's fault, really—he likes intrigue."

We go back inside. She suggests I sit down at the round table near the cash register while she takes care of the cars. "I'll bring coffee in a minute," she says, heading for the kitchen. Pelham watches me strip off the raincoat, shake it lightly, and drape it over the back of a chair. When I sit down to inspect my shoes, Betsy arrives with two cups of coffee. "Miss Landson'll be out in a minute," she says. "Did you want something else? A nice dessert?"

"I don't know." I look past her at Pelham; he's working on the soup. "No. I guess I'm fine."

Betsy turns to look at Pelham too, then whispers to me, "It's his birthday today. He's a nice man—he really is. I don't think it makes any difference that he's so much older than she is."

"No," I say, nodding. "I agree with you. Thanks, Betsy."

The last diners are leaving, pushing arms into raincoats, picking up purses, straightening clothes. A small fellow in a navy chalk-stripe suit, coral shirt, and regimental tie stops alongside my table and hands Betsy a ten-dollar bill. She says, "Thank you," and folds the bill twice, then slips it under her wide patent-leather belt.

The guy turns to me. "What, you staying all night?"

I look at Betsy; she raises her eyebrows and rolls her eyes in a quick half circle. The guy looks at me as if he expects an answer.

"What's that mean? Who're you?"

Ericka slips up behind him before he has a chance to answer. "Hello, Bill," she says. "Did you enjoy dinner?"

Bill grins uncomfortably and catches up with a weak-faced woman who is waiting for him in the aisle.

Three Chicano busboys are noisily stacking dishes in spattered gray rubber trays. Betsy and two waitresses cluster around the cash register, smoking and counting the evening's receipts. Pelham has put his soup on the floor for the dog, which laps hungrily at the dish while Pelham watches, expressionless.

"You dance?" Ericka says, holding her coffee to her lips with both hands. Her eyes seem very bright.

"Not much. You?"

"Sometimes I go to this cowboy bar out on the bypass—Boots, it's called—and dance all night. I love it. It's going to take a while for the Triple A people to get here—maybe we should go out?"

"I don't think so, thanks," I say watching Pelham and the dog. "We've got no cars."

"Oh, I've got a truck in back. Warren can stay here and take care of the accident."

"He'll love that."

"It's O.K." She turns and looks over her shoulder, her elbows still planted on the table. "Hey, Warren. We're going out to Boots; you come out when the wreckers get finished, O.K.?"

Pelham looks up from the dog, then closes his eyes and drops his head maybe a quarter of an inch. He reaches into his coat pocket and pulls out two car keys on a thick yellow string.

"Toss it," Ericka says. He does, and she shoves her chair back, leaping off the floor to make a one-handed catch. "Come on, buzzard," she says, grabbing my arm. "I'll teach you every dance I know. Let me have your keys for Warren, so he can bring your car out."

I give her my keys, and she takes them across the room and hands them to Pelham, then squats down and cups the dog's ears. The dog stops eating long enough to look up and lick its lips, soup dropping off its black jaw. Ericka says something to Pelham, then pats his calf, and they both laugh.

I put on my raincoat. For a minute I leave the collar of the coat turned up, but then decide it looks too stupid that way, and fold it neatly down.

"Let's go, youngster," Ericka calls. "Don't be shy, now."

The truck is parked in a narrow alley in back of the restaurant; the passenger side is so close to the brick wall that I can't even squeeze between the fender and the wall, much less get into the truck. The rain has let up.

"I'm already having a good time," Ericka says. "You want to drive?"

"I don't want to go."

"Listen to the man, will you? The man's got 'Born to Bop' tattooed on his neck and he's talking about retirement. Try this side over here, Slick." She does a little two-step, opening the door for me.

Ericka Landson did a year at Sarah Lawrence, hated it, and went to Georgia Tech, where she took bachelor's and master's degrees in chemical engineering. She delivered the diplomas to her father on a Thursday and bought the building for her restaurant the next day. That was almost a year ago; since then her father died and left her half a million dollars in cash and three times that in land.

"So I married Warren," she says while we're sitting in the cab of the Ford Ranchero waiting for the attendant at the Sinclair station to return with her credit card. "I'd been in love with him since I was a kid. He had a lot more money than I did, so I figured I was safe."

The attendant, a boy with wet blond shoulder-length hair and giant lips, stops in back of the car to write the license number on a charge slip, then pushes the green plastic clipboard in Ericka's window. "I like this weather," he says. "Brings out the bugs. Get me plenty of food for my Gila monsters."

"I want those lizards," Ericka says. "I need them for my menu. The palates of the customers demand monster."

The boy grins messily; the grin distorts his face, drawing the lips tight over a row of brown teeth. "I believe you'd try it, too, Mrs. Landson," he says. "But they gonna come dear."

"And go dearer," Ericka says, passing the clipboard back out the

My fork is wrapped tight in a paper napkin. "That's funny. Is he going to kill you if you hurt me?"

"Eat your pie, why don't you?"

"Happily," I say, pulling the fork out of the end of the rolled napkin. One of the tines is missing. I show this to Ericka and then start on the pie. "We're not doing so well, are we?"

"We're not supposed to," she says. "How is it?"

"Pretty good. You want some?"

"Dessert is later." She grabs my free hand and yanks it across the table, then pins it to the red linoleum and bends over to inspect the fingernails. "These are a mess. I can clean them up if you want me to."

"Maybe later."

Her food arrives on a brown oval plate with portion dividers; the dirty-whitish gravy has been liberally applied so that it seeps from one section to the next in an uninterrupted flow. Ericka starts with the toast, plunging the corner of the first piece into the thick pool on top of the potatoes. I finish the pie and then watch her eat. She asks a couple of questions—what do I do, where was I born?—but then she loses interest and concentrates on the food. We go through the rest of the dinner in silence. I'm tired.

"Now," she says, when she's finished. "Now we dance." She tears a couple of napkins trying to get a whole one out of the chrome-faced dispenser screwed to the table just under the window.

"Please—no dancing tonight, O.K.? Tonight let's go home."

She unbuttons one of the pockets of her denim jacket and brings out a five-dollar bill. She puts the money on the table and gets up. "No dancing?" she says, affecting a hurt expression. "You seem like kind of a drip, Harold."

"Thanks."

In the car she says, "We'll have cake with Warren and then you can go, O.K.?"

The house is modern, white as ice and lit up like a circus. My car is parked in the U-shaped drive next to the Mercedes. Warren is inside watching a bank of three Sonys; he's wearing a black silk robe with scarlet piping, and under that he's got on green pajamas. Melba is asleep beside his chair. "You have fun?" he asks his wife.

"We decided to have cake," she says. "You need cake."

"What's on?" I ask, motioning toward the televisions.

"A movie, Tom Snyder, and 'Love Boat.'"

"I got the truck filled up," Ericka says. "Harold didn't have such a great time. We went out to the diner. I don't think he knows what's going on." She sits on the arm of Pelham's chair, facing the televisions. She rubs the back of the dog's neck.

"We don't have any problems," he says. "That's easy enough. Slinky's looking for a companion because I wear out fast."

"Me too," I say. "Sorry."

"I'll get the cake," Ericka says, heading for the kitchen. "I made it myself, Harold. It's really good."

"Her aunt made it. I've had it before," Pelham says when Ericka's out of the room. "It's pitiful looking."

I laugh sympathetically. "What about the cars? How're we going to work that out?"

"Don't worry about the cars."

"I won't if you'll send me something I can give the insurance guy."

"Yeah, well," Pelham says, waving at the sofa, "it just isn't necessary. What you're supposed to do is distract Slinky, but I don't guess you're going to."

I drop my raincoat over a ladder-back chair near the door, then take a seat at one end of the sofa. We sit there in silence watching the televisions. All three of them have the sound on, so that what we hear is a garbled, random mix of talk and music. Pelham pets the dog and looks from one screen to the next, his eyes shifting from left to right with habitual precision. Then all three stations start commercials at the same time—a Pepsi ad, a car ad, and an ad for perfume—and all three look the same: dramatic silvery colors, surreal spaces, glittering sexy women. "Look at that," I say pointing.

"I know," Pelham says, without turning around. "Good."

Ericka comes back into the room carrying a tray on which is a large flat cake stuck full of lighted candles. The icing is sherbety orange. She puts the tray on the coffee table and starts to sing "Happy Birthday," gesturing for me to join in. I'm embarrassed, but I sing along. Pelham hangs on to his composure for a minute, then grins and starts singing. When we finish the chorus, Ericka starts it again, and everybody sings loudly this time, complete with conductor's gestures, vibrato, and three-part home-made harmony. The singing wakes Melba, who yawns and shakes, then steps up to the coffee table waving her big tail and rips a four-inch hole in the cake's fruity icing.

FROM

The Married Land

Charles G. Bell

THE PLANE TOOK the runway south. It seemed with the body's beginning to travel, the mind had already arrived. The surprise might have been that his aunt's accident had waited until now, that her supreme gesture of independence, her driving, had not long ago become the pit into which she had fallen.

Was she a type of something—the South, decadence? What could eccentricity typify but itself? "You, with your historical trends and bridges between shores; it's poppycock; she's Betsy Byrne, or if anything else, she's old; age is ubiquitous." The skeptical voice, to which the other answered: "Yes, but there are trends: species, entelechy, *Zeitgeist*, styles. Madmen have represented history. There are drifts in the particular, symbolic riders, always doubtful, always *there* . . ."

There she was over the decades, from that time two generations ago, when she got her first bouncy little red Dodge and learned, more or less, to jerk it around town, swerving and stalling, but never stripping the gears, never, by some ludicrous chance, traffic being thin and slow, quite hitting anything; until she was cited in the newspaper among Delta wonders: "Miss Betsy Byrne has driven the same car fifteen years and never had an accident"—she ignoring the touch of malice, so confirmed in her self-esteem, she never saw the other cars slam on brakes when she strayed to the wrong side of the road, or heard the horns and cries as she stalled at intersections—fell out in fact with one of her friends for venturing to warn her at a cross street of an approaching car, turned on her furiously with: "You let me drive, will you? I'm perfectly capable." And never took her out again.

She bounced that Dodge over town, her little form puffy and pasty-fleshed, streaked with powder as if she'd thrown herself in the flour barrel, and wearing the black lace of what amounted to a perpetual mourning (the clothes, it seemed, along with the mother's opinions and everything else but her meticulous housekeeping, taken over from her and enlarged); they were together in the car, that arrogant Kentucky belle, blind now and fierce, a mere wasp of a woman, and beside her the daughter, pasty-fat, propped up with pillows beneath and behind, so that she seemed in her bosomy inflation to be blown up against the wheel, that wheel which always, in the nervously energetic manner of her walking and talking (tiny fretful steps and short exclamatory sentences full of so's and very's), she jiggled and wiggled from side to side, as if the only approved method of driving a car was to keep it swerving like a stalking cat, an unpredictable progress from which it might dart off at any moment in any direction.

Daniel remembered a ride the whole family took, soon after the reconciliation when they tried to be a family and went with both cars on a common outing, this time to the low dam and locks on the Sunflower River, the banks dense with oak forests and the water racing with fish. His father's car had gone in front with the grandmother, Daniel and little Gerald; Aunt Betsy came behind with her mother, Hilda, and her school friend—these consigned in an abortive effort at sociability to the risk of that driving. They were creeping along a narrow strip of concrete road with gravel shoulders, the pride of the country, over the wide flat land through the hot air. The fields of rowed cotton succeeded one another. The bordering masses of wood blended into an horizon on all sides that moved as the cars moved. Now they were bumping down from the concrete ribbon, one wheel on the gravel shoulder, to meet an approaching car, and again on the other side to pass a cotton wagon. Now a couple of cars were coming, and on their side of the road, blocking the shoulder, was a stalled Model T, a Negro peering into the engine. So they had to pull over and wait behind while the other cars got by. The grandmother leaned out in her self-righteous fury and scolded the man: "Why don't you get that wreck off the road?" (Though there was no place to move it to but the flooded ditch.) "As if you had any right to a car anyway, you Colored Man!"

The concrete road had played out. Also the gravel. Under a summer shower they were crossing a swamp on a built-up hard embankment of buckshot mud. Hilda had shifted to the larger car, pleading car-sickness. So Daniel was on the spot, with his mother. But he liked it. Aunt Betsy, following the Willys Knight, which was already skidding a bit, would slide clear across the road, almost into the ditch. "Whooee! Almost got me that time!" she would shriek, gambling as always against dangerous gods. Flinging the wheel over, she would skid toward the other slippery edge, and there: "Whooee! Almost had me again!" would fling it back as before.

Thus she graduated from the Dodge to her second car. The mother was dead now; the daughter lived on in the stingy solitude the old woman had spun her in. A black robed, graying form, propped up, her pinch-nose glasses on her head, she went swerving at somewhat faster clip in the green Buick. She was more forgetful of the gears, would put on the brakes without the clutch and jerk to a stall, or start from a stop without shifting out of high. The fenders too were showing signs of the increased hazards of the road. Her sight was worse, at night impossible, but she refused to surrender the wheel to anybody, nephew, brother, hired help or friend—assured, even as she scraped and dented the cars parked by the curb, of the matchless skill of her newspaper-cited handling.

Daniel remembered: on a summer's visit how she had driven him to tea with one of her friends, the Impeccable, and finding the house on the left, had crossed over the crowded street and parked in the wrong direction, and then starting up afterwards, had gone ahead on the left, the cars honking at her, until she reached the corner, where the sign forbade a U turn, but she made one anyway, beginning on the left of the road and swinging clockwise, to wind up still on the wrong side, going the other way, while traffic in all four branches stopped dead, honking.

Her reputation went on increasing, deepening the irony of that first citation, as police fines and revoking of licences failed to arrest the always more perilous trajectory. The law knuckled under, as it will in the deep South before the defiance of female eccentric age.

Her driveway backed onto Bolivar, one of those more and more trafficked ways, into which, without warning or a rearward glance, she would come tail-first any hour of the day or night, bumping over the sidewalk and roughly hacked-out curb, between concealing masses of crape myrtle bushes, backing into the road and cutting left or right, in either case occupying both lanes, stalling as a rule before she could shift gears and grind off to a jerky forward—why she had grown as famous in the town as the Sirens or Scylla in the legends of the Greeks, one of those father-to-child expounded dangers of the place.

He remembered about then, with the wartime influx of airmen

to the base, overhearing (it was at a summer party, and a native youth had come back in uniform, with his northern wife) the wife complaining—for they lived down Bolivar: "I don't know what to do when I go by that place. Half the time some old woman comes backing out of there. I honk and try to get by, but I don't think she hears me. I get so nervous coming there I start praying: 'Don't let that old woman back out, Lord, don't let her;' because when she backs out I don't know what to do."

"Honey," said the boy, "there's things you've got to learn about this town, and it might as well be now. That old woman you talk about is Miss Betsy Byrne, and when she backs out of that drive, I tell you what you do. You pull clear out of the road, clear out mind you, and cut off the engine. And if you want to go on praying, it can't do any harm."

Miss Betsy sold the Buick and came to the third car, the blue Studebaker with the automatic shift. That took care of the shifting and stalling—which was better and worse. For in her increasing feebleness and diabetic forgetfulness, she might have had to quit driving if she'd gone on struggling with a clutch and gears; but with this car all she had to do was give it the gun and it would go; and she gave it more gun than she should, and more often.

Though she did cut out the night business. "No," she would say, "I'm afraid I don't see very well at night." She wouldn't tell you how she learned that. It was one fall evening on her way home from visiting a country friend. The best she could do at night was to follow the red taillight of the car in front of her, but this turned out to be a cotton picker, working late. When it left the road and veered into the field, she lit out after it down the embankment, and mired in the furrow; so they had to get a tractor to haul her out. "I don't like to drive at night," she would say shaking her head. "My eyes are getting bad." But of course she was perfectly competent in the daytime.

It was no longer the pneumatically inflated form propped up and juggling the wheel with excess of energy. She was actually lean—the surplus that had fattened her gone to blood sugar. The hollow face, as the outward energy decayed, was assuming by sheer loss the secret fierce demonism of the mother. The pillows had long since disappeared. She was unbuoyed, shrinking down into the seat almost out of sight, the eyes too retiring into the sunken face. Yet still she drove around to her houses, collected rents, or sometimes, when they were threateningly overdue, paid the bills for water, light and gas.

By now her glasses were recurrently lost in the house which had become a quicksand of objects stored and misplaced, into which anything laid down sank without trace, so that though she bought a new pair every few months, she was mostly without, and couldn't see to read her mail or the newspaper, or to transact the simplest business or maintain the necessary checks on an environment that would otherwise, from carelessness if not design, cheat, bungle and overcharge at every turn of the road.

She came into the water office with a purse full of random bills paid and unpaid and asked the clerk to put them in order and tell her what she owed on all her houses. "I can't do it," she said; "I'm ashamed of myself; I've always done it; but now I can't see."

"Why, Miss Betsy," they said, "if you can't see, how'd you get down here?"

"Oh that's nothing," she said. "I drove my car."

And when one of the crew of bosom or bosom-fallen friends she had gossiped and quarreled with since childhood and written cards to on all her bus tours over the nation, asked her in the same connection: "But Betsy, if you can't see, how on earth do you drive?" she had countered (one could have thought a year and never have hit on the answer that flowed off her tongue with the bright unassailable defiance of her being): "Well, I only drive out on bright days . . ."

Daniel kept his eyes on the window as the power thrust bore him back into the seat. The ground whirred. The bumping and lurching went air-smooth. Descents and returns stretched in a series back into childhood, indistinguishable. It was here, settling towards the delineations of the city, that he had laid aside the Delta after the last return, here, where he shouldered it again, the buildings going gray in the mist below him.

And now, like one of those things called up in the mind where it had waited all along, unnoticed, as if you were sitting in a twilight room and a voice sounded, and you would turn, startled, and see by the window a form emerging, the puffy po-white form and pasty scar-cheeked face, one eye knocked asquint in some undivulged feat of heroism or folly, a look not unkind, but shifty—Daniel had said on the phone he did not know the Colesons, but he only needed the connection to bring it back: Bud Coleson, like something transported from Dickens down the Mississippi, over the gullied clay hills to the Depression Delta, and slowly in the war boom that followed, finding work, claiming to be a plumber, though he might as well have said electrician, or carpenter, or jack of all trades, earning enough at least for himself and his leathery, lean, officious wife and increasing family of kids, and then by the chance of renting one of Miss Betsy's houses, coming, out of fondness, and self interest too, that loyalty of the Southern poor to some heir of tradition and pride they serve, yet hope one way or another to get something out of, becoming her hanger-on, fixer of all breakages and shiftless maintainer of her property—Bud Coleson, the man, and now the voice, the drawling low voice: "Yes sir, Miss Byrne's a driver; she's quite a driver."

That had been when Daniel first found out anything about his aunt's property. She had been secret as the grave until a year ago when she broke down and said things were vacant and she couldn't get around the way she did, she wished he'd see what should be done. So he went to the insurance company for the list.

"Daniel," said Mr. Laurence in his doddering old voice that had been too soft years ago, and that got more secret as he got older, until you had to lean forward saying: "What's that, Mr. Laurence? I can't hear you."

"Daniel, I wish you'd think about the insurance your aunt's got on those houses. She won't listen to me, but something's got to be done."

They took the schedule and drove around. First they parked on Walnut Street. "You see that, Daniel? She's got that house insured for twenty thousand dollars, a four-apartment house, it says, furnished. I like the premiums, but my company won't let me keep that house insured that way. And the furniture for five thousand. There's not a stick of furniture in it. It's been vacant three years, every window is broke and the doors are off the hinges. And now the roof is falling in. That's not a house, that's a ruin.

"I tell you how it is, Daniel." He lowered his voice as if this one was too hot to bear repetition.

Daniel crowded up: "Louder, Mr. Laurence, I can't hear you."

"You know Miss Betsy's not as clear as she once was. She's been after me to sell some of her property. Well, I had a good offer on this lot—three thousand—because nobody's going to buy it except for the lot.

"'Mr. Laurence,' she said to me, 'don't talk nonsense. I want to sell that house, I don't want to give it away. I wouldn't take a bit less than twenty-five thousand dollars for it. That's a big house, with four apartments in it.'

"'Miss Betsy,' I told her, 'that house is in bad shape. It would take thousands to get it where it would rent, and the best thing would be to tear it down and start over again.'

"'Oh sha! Mr. Laurence,' she said, 'that house don't need a thing but a little paper and paint to spruce it up. That's a fine house. You tell your buyer twenty-five thousand.'"

They drove on. One place Daniel thought he had Mr. Laurence. Two little trailers had been run into the yard behind a duplex house and hitched to the light and plumbing and rented for a while, when you could rent anything. They were a wreck now, the roofs off and weeds inside, and there along the outer wall the boards were charred—My Lord, they were charred; those houses had burned, and they were insured each one for three thousand dollars with their furnishings. "We'll put in a claim right now," Daniel said.

Mr. Laurence shook his head. "Those trailers fell apart," he whispered. "They were empty for years and the boys tore 'em apart. They weren't insured against boys. Then the grass was burned and that smoked the walls. Burning weeds is what did it. You couldn't collect on 'em. They aren't worth insuring."

"Look here, Mr. Laurence, you can't have it both ways. If they can be insured they can be collected on, and if they can't be collected on, she shouldn't have been paying premiums all these years."

"I been telling her to drop those premiums, haven't I?" Mr. Laurence almost raised his voice. "You know she won't change a thing. That's why I had to talk with you. It's doing her no good to have insurance on that junk."

"You mean all the premiums she's paid are lost, and she couldn't collect if the houses had burned?"

"If she'll cancel the insurance, I'll get her back some of the premiums. I told her so, but she won't sign a thing."

In desperation Daniel went to the colored houses, which were at least rented. At the first house, he got on the trail of Coleson. The tenants all knew Daniel, even when he didn't remember them. This was Winnie Bloomer, as broad as she was tall, with a droll face, elfish, no doubt, in her youth, but spread now into the likeness of a great frog. She worked for Lawyer Hargreaves and was one of the best cooks in town.

"Misser Dan," she said, "you see those steps? I hate to fall down and break a leg on those steps. Can't you get me some new boards there? And I wish you look at my bathroom. Mr. Coleson pertend to be fixin me a bathroom. He a nice man, but he don't know nothin tall bout no bathroom. He done got it so low you have to go down squattin, like dis here."

She went backing off from him, bent over, bracing herself with one hand on the chair, her belly swagging between her knees, breasts like hams, the monstrous buttocks going lower and lower, as she heaved and grunted with the strain, looking up at him with grotesque, unvoiced question. "Yes suh," she said, "you have to go way down on that bathroom. It's a mess."

The word bathroom had thrown him at first, but the demonstration was enough. He walked around to the outhouse, a latrine once, fitted up now with water as the city required. (That was during the campaign of a few years back when Segeen Wright was engineer, and the local paper had written: "We believe this situation is going to get cleaned up, because Segeen Wright is in charge, and as everybody knows, he is not the kind of a man to let his end drag.") So Miss Betsy had dug up a secondhand toilet with a long pipe and pull-chain, and Mr. Coleson had set it in a chunk of cement before he thought about flooring the place. He built the floor in afterwards, running from the sill of the door, which was six inches off the ground, back around the toilet base, the boards cut out hit-or-miss to fit there, so what was left of the toilet was not a foot high, like a toadstool half out of the ground.

Winnie flung open the door, turned to Daniel and wrinkled her fat face: "Dah," she said, slapping her thigh. "You laughin, Misser Dan. Ain't dat sumpin? Mr. Coleson call that a bathroom. He the limit. You got to go way down . . ." And she backed off again, squatting. Daniel left her with promises.

Late in the afternoon, at the last shotgun house, he found Bud Coleson putting on a ripped-off screen door. He had rebuilt the door partly with the old wood that would go to pieces in no time, partly with patches of the lowest grade of splitting pine. Now he was screwing it on the jamb, but he had set it so low there was an inch above where flies and mosquitoes could make a freeway, and the thing was dragging at the bottom, so there was no way to open it over the rough floorboards without catching it again and ripping it off the hinges.

"Hadn't you better put it higher?" Daniel asked.

"Should be a mite higher, I reckon," said Mr. Coleson; "but 'tain't worth movin now."

"I'd move it though," said Daniel. "It'll get ripped up that way. Why don't you set a board under it while you screw it on, and then when you're done it'll be off the floor?"

"Sure," said Mr. Coleson, "ony I didn't find a board handy."

Daniel looked under the house. There were two bundles of termite-eaten flooring. He pulled out a board. "What's all that lumber doing under there, anyway?"

"Lumber?" said Coleson. "Oh, that. Gonna be used to fix the floorin. It should a been did before now, but I haven't got to it, ony workin nights and on weekends."

So they unscrewed the door and in three minutes reset it, while Mr. Laurence stood by and watched. He was one of those planter offshoots who had taken up insurance in the Depression, and you'd no more have expected him to screw on a door or drive a nail, even into his own house, than you'd have expected an angel to hoe cotton.

But he went on talking, in his dying tones, to be cranked up now and then by Daniel's proddings. And being agent also for Miss Betsy's automobile policy, he mentioned her driving:

"You know, Daniel, she oughtn't to be allowed in that car. They tell me the police have taken her license away, but she goes right on. If my company finds out about it, I'll have to snatch that policy out from under her."

It was Mr. Coleson's turn: "Sho nuff, Daniel" (they called him by the first name like a boy, because his aunt did, and in fact the whole town), "she ought to be kep off the road."

"Who's going to keep her off?" said Daniel. "I can't, and you can't, and I don't imagine the law can, either."

Mr. Coleson shook a gray face: "No, I reckon she'll keep on. But she ought to be stopped. She's liable to git killed.

"It was jest yestiddy I was comin from work and I see Miss Betsy limpin toward her driveway, the car grindin like a sawmill. She went out wide like she was going to turn in, but it wouldn't turn, so she angled across traffic slow and parked against her curb headin the wrong way, where you can't park anyway, even headin right. I said: 'Now, Miss Byrne, they're goin to give you another ticket parkin there. Why don't you go in the driveway?' And she said: 'I can't turn in. I don't know what's the matter with it, but it won't turn.' So I looked under it and the steerin rod was bent all out of shape. 'Who'd you hit, Miss Byrne?' I ast her. 'You've done hit somethin.' 'No,' she said, 'I never hit anything at all. I backed over some trash up there and a stick or somethin caught in it.' 'No stick goin to bend it like that,' I said. 'Where was that trash?' 'Oh back yonder a piece'; she waved her hand. I figgered it must be at them nigger houses of hern back up Bolivar. I got a hammer and straightened out the steerin rod. Then I put her car in the drive and turned my truck around and went up there. There was a nigger in front of the first house. 'Did Miss Betsy Byrne run over some trash up here?' 'Trash?' he said. 'She run over a plow.' She had backed plumb up over the curb and onto the yard and gone clean over the plow backard and forrard and drug it a considerable piece, trying to turn around, and not even knowed what she hit. Yes sir, Miss Byrne's quite a driver. If you don't look out, she'll git killed." They had all cautioned and warned, but she had gone on with her jaunty reply: "I only drive out on bright days." Except the Sunday she drove herself to church, her friends having phoned they would come for her, but she unwilling to depend on anybody but herself—that day seems not to have been quite bright enough. So she moved toward the intersection where blindness, eccentricity and defiance of age, limitation and law, baited their traps against her.

Which was it that prompted her to drive through the stop light at that busiest corner? Had the newfangled green arrow for the right turn, beckoning simultaneously with the flaring red, blurred on the merely physical organ? Or was she thinking of those houses vacant and falling to pieces, on which she was always waiting for some tomorrow when she would wake with the old energy and get them spruced up and rented again?

Or was it a temporary shock from the diabetes and too much or too little insulin? For she injected herself whenever she thought of it, or when she could find one of countless old needles mislaid, or get out to buy a new one; and if the insulin so taken was irregular and the doses at best guessed at and blindly groped for, the food which was to have balanced it was even more haphazardly administered, cooked up for herself—opened from any of the rusty cans that had accumulated through the years in the pantry, and mixed with old rice or corn meal or grits left in five-gallon glass screw-top jars by the mother, and now so mouldy that the malodorous unscrewing of the lid would have turned any stomach but hers—fried on the stove that had lost its oven door and had no broiler, so the only place to cook was on top, and the only utensil any way operant (the rest on the floor under the sink or stove rusted out and filled with dirt and spider webs) was a clumsy skillet with a convex base, which would have been rusty too if it hadn't been protected any time this last fifteen years with a deep layer of roach-traversed rancid grease, into which she had thrown her bacon, eggs, stale rice, grits, old canned tomatoes, whatever else she could locate, to fry on the back-burning leaky jet and call it a fit diet for one not only afflicted with diabetes, but guessing at the doses of insulin required—would it be any wonder if returning from the new church at the edge of town (if a body couldn't pray with any better success than that, Daniel thought, why bother?) she should miss a red light, or a dozen of them?

Or could it have been her determination to pay no attention to these novel devices and changing rules of the aftercomers to a town she had once been at the center of? She did not submit to any of their regulations. "Young man," she told the cop who whistled at her for jumping a red light, "don't you ever let me catch you blowing that whistle at me again!"—bawling him out while the traffic waited.

She would never put a coin in a parking meter, and the police, after leaving her summons after summons and revoking her license with no effect, had got to where they recognized her car, and left it alone, even the immigrant greenhorns on the force, admired her in fact, as officials with any of the unregenerate man in them always will those who ignore or defy their social rigmarole: "Hello, Miss Betsy. You know you should put a coin in that meter. That's what it's there for."

And she with a start: "Is there a meter? I didn't know. We never had meters in town before. So many changes. Well, I only parked for a minute."

"That's all right, Miss Betsy," he would say. "How you feelin?"

Worst was along the main avenue of the town. In the old days it was wider than the traffic needed, and cars parked diagonally to the curb. But as traffic increased one had to park alongside, as in most places, and the marks and meters were spaced that way. But she would never do anything but slant her nose in to the curb as she had done for twenty years. Maybe it was inability (power and will being hard to separate), since she could hardly have wormed into one of those marked-off lateral spaces if she had tried—backward or forward. But she never tried. So it was defiance as much as incapacity. And when the police took after her about it, it was the same story, call it intransigence or failure to understand what was being talked about: "No, officer, I never park that way. I've parked like this all my life, and I'm going to keep right on."

"Well, Miss Betsy, you know you're supposed to get up there inside those lines and put a coin in that meter."

She: "I can't see the lines. They change the lines all the time. So many changes. I'm too old to change now. But I won't blame you. You're new to the force, aren't you? How is Judge Harper? Give him my best."

Judge Harper had been dead for years.

So it might have been sheer intransigence, one could not tell. And of course she would remember nothing. She would not have seen the car coming fast from the left strike her amidships, stave in the door and the whole driver's side of the car, tear the seat assembly from its moorings, burst out the opposite door with the thrust, and hurl her, along with the seat, clear of the car, through the air and onto the pavement on the far side—except she would fall half on the seat, and so preserve herself for what the phone call had announced to Daniel a thousand miles away in the quiet of Woodruff Farm . . .

Announced: and initiated this voyage, through a window of which he peered, observing: the plane's reflected interior, lights, travelers. Also the self: mouth, nose, eyes, separate pools of vision. Approach. They merge: one cave of sight, one great cyclopean eye. That is what you see through. And what you see is a tundra of cloud, from which the Appalachians roll up in long folds and ridges.

The conjunction caught him. He remembered a pool, not one of those cloudy blue-holes of the Delta, but away from there, on a summer trip long ago, in the Ozarks perhaps, or these Appalachians—clear water between rocks, a surface of mirrored limestone and trees, a sky broken with leaf shapes.

From the branches something falls to the water, insect or seed pod, sending out luminous ripples, a diverging iris, into which rises a vortex of flesh, subliminal Grendel through a plane of reflected earth, defining the complementarity: facet and depth, pattern and *dynamis* . . .

What energy was stirring under that mottled surface of a world, cresting beneath him like a wave?

The Convert

Lerone Bennett, Jr.

A MAN DON'T KNOW what he'll do, a man don't know what he is till he gets his back pressed up against a wall. Now you take Aaron Lott: there ain't no other way to explain the crazy thing he did. He was going alone fine, preaching the gospel, saving souls, and getting along with the white folks; and then, all of a sudden, he felt wood pressing against his back. The funny thing was that nobody knew he was hurting till he preached that Red Sea sermon where he got mixed up and seemed to think Mississippi was Egypt. As chairman of the deacons' board, I felt it was my duty to reason with him. I appreciated his position and told him so, but I didn't think it was right for him to push us all in a hole. The old fool—he just laughed.

"Brother Booker," he said, "the Lord—He'll take care of me."

I knew then that that man was heading for trouble. And the very next thing he did confirmed it. The white folks called the old fool downtown to bear witness that the colored folks were happy. And you know what he did: he got down there amongst all them big white folks and he said: "Things ain't gonna change here overnight, but they gonna change. It's inevitable. The Lord wants it."

Well sir, you could have bought them white folks for a penny. Aaron Lott, pastor of the Rock of Zion Baptist Church, a man white folks had said was wise and sound and sensible, had come close—too close—to saying that the Supreme Court was coming to Melina, Mississippi. The surprising thing was that the white folks didn't do nothing. There was a lot of mumbling and whispering but nothing bad happened till the terrible morning when Aaron came a-knocking at the door of my funeral home. Now things had been tightening up—you could feel it in the air—and I didn't want no part of no crazy scheme and I told him so right off. He walked on past me and sat down on the couch. He had on his preaching clothes, a shiny blue suit, a fresh starched white shirt, a black tie, and his Sunday black shoes. I remember thinking at the time that Aaron was too black to be wearing all them dark clothes. The thought tickled me and I started to smile but then I noticed something about him that didn't seem quite right. I ran my eyes over him closely. He was kinda middle-sized and he had a big clean-shaven head, a big nose, and thin lips. I stood there looking at him for a long time but I couldn't figure out what it was till I looked at his eyes: they were burning bright, like light bulbs do just before they go out. And yet he looked contented, like his mind was resting somewheres else.

"I wanna talk with you, Booker," he said, glancing sideways at my wife. "If you don't mind, Sister Brown——"

Sarah got up and went into the living quarters. Aaron didn't say nothing for a long time; he just sat there looking out the window. Then he spoke so soft I had to strain my ears to hear.

"I'm leaving for the Baptist convention," he said. He pulled out his gold watch and looked at it. "Train leaves in 'bout two hours."

"I know *that,* Aaron."

"Yeah, but what I wanted to tell you was that I ain't going Jim Crow. I'm going first class, Booker, right through the white waiting room. That's the law."

A cold shiver ran through me.

"Aaron," I said, "don't you go talking crazy now."

The old fool laughed, a great big body-shaking laugh. He started talking 'bout God and Jesus and all that stuff. Now, I'm a God-fearing man myself, but I holds that God helps those who help themselves. I told him so.

"You can't mix God up with these white folks," I said. "When you start to messing around with segregation, they'll burn you up and the Bible, too."

He looked at me like I was Satan.

"I sweated over this thing," he said. "I prayed. I got down on my knees and I asked God not to give me this cup. But He said I was the one. I heard Him, Booker, right here—he tapped his chest—in my heart."

The old fool's been having visions, I thought. I sat down and tried to figure out a way to hold him, but he got up, without saying a word, and started for the door.

"Wait!" I shouted. "I'll get my coat."

"I don't need you," he said. "I just came by to tell you so you could tell the board in case something happened."

"You wait," I shouted, and ran out of the room to get my coat.

We got in his beat-up old Ford and went by the parsonage to get his suitcase. Rachel—that was his wife—and Jonah were sitting in the living room, wringing their hands. Aaron got his bag, shook Jonah's hand, and said, "Take care of your Mamma, boy." Jonah nodded. Aaron hugged Rachel and pecked at her cheek. Rachel broke down. She throwed her arms around his neck and carried on something awful. Aaron shoved her away.

"Don't go making no fuss over it, woman. I ain't gonna be gone forever. Can't a man go to a church meeting 'thout women screaming and crying."

He tried to make light of it, but you could see he was touched by the way his lips trembled. He held his hand out to me, but I wouldn't take it. I told him off good, told him it was a sin and a shame for a man of God to be carrying on like he was, worrying his wife and everything.

"I'm coming with you," I said. "Somebody's gotta see that you don't make a fool of yourself."

He shrugged, picked up his suitcase, and started for the door. Then he stopped and turned around and looked at his wife and his boy and from the way he looked I knew that there was still a chance. He looked at the one and then at the other. For a moment there, I thought he was going to cry, but he turned, quick-like, and walked out of the door.

I ran after him and tried to talk some sense in his head. But he shook me off, turned the corner, and went on up Adams Street. I caught up with him and we walked in silence, crossing the street in front of the First Baptist Church for whites, going on around the Confederate monument where, once, they hung a boy for fooling around with white women.

"Put it off, Aaron," I begged. "Sleep on it."

He didn't say nothing.

"What you need is a vacation. I'll get the board to approve, full pay and everything."

He smiled and shifted the suitcase over to his left hand. Big drops of sweat were running down his face and spotting up his shirt. His eyes were awful, all lit up and burning.

"Aaron, Aaron, can't you hear me?"

We passed the feed store, Bill Williams' grocery store, and the movie house.

"A man's gotta think about his family, Aaron. A man ain't free.

Didn't you say that once, didn't you?"

He shaded his eyes with his hand and looked into the sun. He put the suitcase on the ground and checked his watch.

"Why don't you think about Jonah?" I asked. "Answer that. Why don't you think about your own son?"

"I am," he said. "That's exactly what I'm doing, thinking about Jonah. Matter of fact, he started *me* to thinking. I ain't never mentioned it before, but the boy's been worrying me. One day we was downtown here and he asked me something that hurt. 'Daddy,' he said, 'how come you ain't a man?' I got mad, I did, and told him: 'I am a man.' He said that wasn't what he meant. 'I mean,' he said, 'how come you ain't a man where white folks concerned.' I couldn't answer him, Booker. I'll never forget it till the day I die. I couldn't answer my own son, and I been preaching forty years."

"He don't know nothing 'bout it," I said. "He's hot-headed, like my boy. He'll find out when he grows up."

"I hopes not," Aaron said, shaking his head. "I hopes not."

Some white folks passed and we shut up till they were out of hearing. Aaron, who was acting real strange, looked up in the sky and moved his lips. He came back to himself after a little bit, and he said: "This thing of being a man, Booker, is a big thing. The Supreme Court can't make you a man. The NAACP can't do it. God Almighty can do a lot, but even He can't do it. Ain't nobody can do it but you."

He said that like he was preaching and when he got through he was all filled up with emotion and he seemed kind of ashamed—he was a man who didn't like emotion outside the church. He looked at his watch, picked up his bag, and said, "Well, let's git it over with."

We turned into Elm and the first thing I saw at the end of the Street was the train station. It was an old red building, flat like a slab. A group of white men were fooling around in front of the door. I couldn't make them out from that distance, but I could tell they weren't the kind of white folks to be fooling around with.

We walked on, passing the dry goods store, the barber shop, and the new building that was going up. Across the street from that was the sheriff's office. I looked in the window and saw Bull Sampson sitting at his desk, his feet propped up on a chair, a fat brown cigar sticking out of his mouth. A ball about the size of a sweet potato started burning in my stomach.

"Please Aaron," I said. "Please. You can't get away with it. I know how you feel. Sometimes I feel the same way myself, but I wouldn't risk my neck to do nothing for these people. They won't appreciate it; they'll laugh at you."

We were almost to the station and I could make out the faces of the men sitting on the benches. One of them must have been telling a joke. He finished and the group broke out laughing.

I whispered to Aaron: "I'm through with it. I wash my hands of the whole mess."

I don't know whether he heard me or not. He turned to the right without saying a word and went on in the front door. The string-beany man who told the joke was so shocked that his cigarette fell out of his mouth.

"Y'all see that," he said. "Why, I'll——"

"Shut up," another man said. "Go git Bull."

I kept walking, fast, turned at the corner, and ran around to the colored waiting room. When I got in there, I looked through the ticket window and saw Aaron standing in front of the clerk. Aaron stood there for a minute or more, but the clerk didn't see him. And that took some not seeing. In that room Aaron Lott stood out like a pig in a chicken coop.

There were, I'd say, about ten or fifteen people in there, but didn't none of them move. They just sat there with their eyes glued on Aaron's back. Aaron cleared his throat. The clerk didn't look up; he got real busy with some papers. Aaron cleared his throat again and opened his mouth to speak. The screen door of the waiting room opened and clattered shut.

It got real quiet in that room, hospital quiet. It got so quiet I could hear my own heart beating. Now Aaron knew who opened that door, but he didn't bat an eyelid. He turned around real slow and faced High Sheriff Sampson, the baddest man in South Mississippi.

Mr. Sampson stood there with his legs wide open, like the men you see on television. His beefy face was blood-red and his gray eyes were rattlesnake hard. He was mad; no doubt about it. I had never seen him so mad.

"Preacher," he said, "you done gone crazy?" He was talking low-like and mean.

"Nosir," Aaron said. "Nosir, Mr. Sampson."

"What you think you doing?"

"Going to St. Louis, Mr. Sampson."

"You must done lost yo' mind, boy."

Mr. Sampson started walking toward Aaron with his hand on his gun. Twenty or thirty men pushed through the front door and fanned out over the room. Mr. Sampson stopped about two paces from Aaron and looked him up and down. That look had paralyzed hundreds of niggers; but it didn't faze Aaron none—he stood his ground.

"I'm gonna give you a chance, preacher. Git on over to the nigger side and git quick."

"I ain't bothering nobody, Mr. Sampson."

Somebody in the crowd yelled: "Don't reason wit' the nigger, Bull. Hit 'im."

Mr. Sampson walked up to Aaron and grabbed him in the collar and throwed him up against the ticket counter. He pulled out his gun.

"Did you hear me, deacon. I said, 'Git.'"

"I'm going to St. Louis, Mr. Sampson. That's cross state lines. The court done said——"

Aaron didn't have a chance. The blow came from nowhere. Laying there on the floor with blood spurting from his mouth, Aaron looked up at Mr. Sampson and he did another crazy thing: He grinned. Bull Sampson jumped up in the air and came down on Aaron with all his two hundred pounds. It made a crunchy sound. He jumped again and the mob, maddened by the blood and heat, moved in to help him. They fell on Aaron like mad dogs. They beat him with chairs; they beat him with sticks; they beat him with guns.

Till this day, I don't know what come over me. The first thing I know I was running and then I was standing in the middle of the white waiting room. Mr. Sampson was the first to see me. He backed off, cocked his pistol, and said: "Booker, boy, you come one mo' step and I'll kill you. What's a matter with you niggers today? All y'all gone crazy?"

"Please don't kill him," I begged. "You ain't got no call to treat him like that."

"So you saw it all, did you? Well, then, Booker you musta saw the nigger preacher reach for my gun?"

"He didn't do that, Mr. Sampson," I said. "He didn't——"

Mr. Sampson put a big hairy hand on my tie and pulled me to him.

"Booker," he said sweetly. "You saw the nigger preacher reach for my gun, didn't you?"

I didn't open my mouth—I couldn't I was so scared—but I guess my eyes answered for me. Whatever Mr. Sampson saw there musta convinced him 'cause he throwed me on the floor besides Aaron.

"Git this nigger out of here," he said, "and be quick about it."

Dropping to my knees, I put my hand on Aaron's chest; I didn't feel nothing. I felt his wrist; I didn't feel nothing. I got up and looked at them white folks with tears in my eyes. I looked at the women, sitting crying on the benches. I looked at the men. I looked at Mr. Sampson. I said, "He was a good man."

Mr. Sampson said, "Move the nigger."

A big sigh came out of me and I wrung my hands.

Mr. Sampson said, "Move the nigger."

He grabbed my tie and twisted it, but I didn't feel nothing. My eyes were glued to his hands; there was blood under the fingernails, and the fingers—they looked like fat little red sausages. I screamed and Mr. Sampson flung me down on the floor.

He said, "*Move the nigger.*"

I picked Aaron up and fixed his body over my shoulder and carried him outside. I sent for one of my boys and we dressed him up and put him away real nice-like and Rachael and the boy came and they cried and carried on and yet, somehow, they seemed prouder of Aaron than ever before. And the colored folks—they seemed proud, too. Crazy people. Didn't they know? Couldn't they see? It hadn't done no good. In fact, things got worse. The Northern newspapers started kicking up a stink and Mr. Rivers, the solicitor, announced they were going to hold a hearing. All of a sudden, Booker Taliaferro Brown became the biggest man in that town. My phone rang day and night: I got threats, I got promises, and I was offered bribes. Everywhere I turned somebody was waiting to ask me: "Whatcha gonna do? Whatcha gonna say?" To tell the truth, I didn't know myself. One day I would decide one thing and the next day I would decide another.

It was Mr. Rivers and Mr. Sampson who called my attention to that. They came to my office one day and called me a shifty, no-good nigger. They said they expected me to stand by "my statement" in the train station that I saw Aaron reach for the gun. I hadn't said no such thing, but Mr. Sampson said I said it and he said he had witnesses who heard me say it. "And if you say anything else," he said, "I can't be responsible for your health. Now you know"—he put that bloody hand on my shoulder and smiled his sweet death smile—"you *know* I wouldn't threaten you, but the boys"—he shook his head—"the boys are real worked up over this one."

It was long about then that I began to hate Aaron Lott. I'm ashamed to admit it now, but it's true: I hated him. He had lived his life; he had made his choice. Why should he live my life, too, and make me choose? It wasn't fair; it wasn't right; it wasn't Christian. What made me so mad was the fact that nothing I said would help Aaron. He was dead and it wouldn't help one whit for me to say that he didn't reach for that gun. I tried to explain that to Rachel when she came to my office, moaning and crying, the night before the hearing.

"Listen to me, woman," I said. "Listen. Aaron was a good man. He lived a good life. He did a lot of good things, but he's *dead, dead, dead!* Nothing I say will bring him back. Bull Sampson's got ten niggers who are going to swear on a stack of Bibles that they saw Aaron reach for that gun. It won't do me or you or Aaron no good for me to swear otherwise."

What did I say that for? That woman liked to had a fit. She got down on her knees and she begged me to go with Aaron.

"Go wit' him," she cried. "Booker. *Booker!* If you's a man, if you's a father, if you's a friend, go wit' Aaron."

That woman tore my heart up. I ain't never heard nobody beg like that.

"Tell the truth, Booker," she said. "That's all I'm asking. Tell the truth."

"Truth!" I said. "Hah! That's all you people talk about: truth. What do you know about truth? Truth is eating good and sleeping good. Truth is living, Rachel. Be loyal to the living."

Rachel backed off from me. You would have thought that I had cursed her or something. She didn't say nothing; she just stood there pressed against the door. She stood there saying nothing for so long that my nerves snapped.

"Say something," I shouted. "Say something—anything!"

She shook her head, slowly at first, and then her head started moving like it wasn't attached to her body. It went back and forth, back and forth, back and forth. I started toward her, but she jerked open the door and ran out into the night screaming.

That did it. I ran across the room to the filing cabinet, opened the bottom drawer, and took out a dusty bottle of Scotch. I started drinking, but the more I drank the soberer I got. I guess I fell asleep 'cause I dreamed I buried Rachel and that everything went along fine until she jumped out of the casket and started screaming. I came awake with a start and knocked over the bottle. I reached for a rag and my hand stopped in mid-air.

"O course," I said out loud and slammed my fist down on the Scotch-soaked papers.

I didn't see nothing.

Why didn't I think of it before?

I didn't see nothing.

Jumping up, I walked to and fro in the office. Would it work? I rehearsed it in my mind. All I could see was Aaron's back. I don't know whether he reached for the gun or not. All I know is that *for some reason* the men beat him to death.

Rehearsing the thing in my mind, I felt a great weight slip off my shoulders. I did a little jig in the middle of the floor and went upstairs to my bed, whistling. Sarah turned over and looked me up and down.

"What you happy about?"

"Can't a man be happy?" I asked.

She sniffed the air, said, "Oh," turned over, and mumbled something in her pillow. It came to me then for the first time that she was 'bout the only person in town who hadn't asked me what I was going to do. I thought about it for a little while, shrugged, and fell into bed with all my clothes on.

When I woke up the next morning, I had a terrible headache and my tongue was a piece of sandpaper. For a long while I couldn't figure out what I was doing laying there with all my clothes on. Then it came to me: this was the big day. I put on my black silk suit, the one I wore for big funerals, and went downstairs to breakfast. I walked into the dining room without looking and bumped into Russell, the last person in the world I wanted to see. He was my only child, but he didn't act like it. He was always finding fault. He didn't like the way I talked to Negroes; he didn't like the way I talked to white folks. He didn't like this; he didn't like that. And to top it off, the young whippersnapper wanted to be an artist. Undertaking wasn't good enough for him. He wanted to paint pictures.

I sat down and grunted.

"Good morning, Papa." He said it like he meant it. He wants something, I thought, looking him over closely, noticing that his right eye was swollen.

"You been fighting again, boy?"

"Yes, Papa."

"You younguns. Education—that's what it is. Education! It's ruining you."

He didn't say nothing. He just sat there, looking down when I looked up and looking up when I looked down. This went on through the grits and the eggs and the second cup of coffee.

"Whatcha looking at?" I asked.

"Nothing, Papa."

"Whatcha thinking?"

"Nothing, Papa."

"You lying, boy. It's written all over your face."

He didn't say nothing.

I dismissed him with a wave of my hand, picked up the paper, and turned to the sports page.

"What are you going to do, Papa?"

The question caught me unawares. I know now that I was expecting it, that I wanted him to ask it; but he put it so bluntly that I was flabbergasted. I pretended I didn't understand.

"Do 'bout what, boy? Speak up!"

"About the trial, Papa."

I didn't say nothing for a long time. There wasn't much, in fact, I could say; so I got mad.

"Questions, questions, questions," I shouted. "That's all I get in this house—questions. You never have a civil word for your pa. I go out of here and work my tail off and you keep yourself shut up in that room of yours looking at them fool books and now soon as your old man gets his back against the wall you join the pack. I expected better than that of you, boy. A son ought to back his pa."

That hurt him. He picked up the coffeepot and poured himself another cup of coffee and his hand trembled. He took a sip and watched me over the rim.

"They say you are going to chicken out, Papa."

"Chicken out? What that mean?"

"They're betting you'll 'Tom.'"

I leaned back in the chair and took a sip of coffee.

"So they're betting, huh?" The idea appealed to me. "Crazy people—they'd bet on a funeral."

I saw pain on his face. He sighed and said: "I bet, too, Papa."

The cup fell out of my hand and broke, spilling black water over the tablecloth.

"You did what?"

"I bet you wouldn't 'Tom.'"

"You little fool." I fell out laughing and then I stopped suddenly and looked at him closely. "How much you bet?"

"One hundred dollars."

I stood up.

"You're lying," I said. "Where'd you get that kind of money?"

"From Mamma."

"Sarah!" I shouted. "Sarah! You get in here. What kind of house you running, sneaking behind my back, giving this boy money to gamble with?"

Sarah leaned against the doorjamb. She was in her hot iron mood. There was no expression on her face. And her eyes were hard.

"I gave it to him, Booker," she said. "They called you an Uncle Tom. He got in a fight about it. He wanted to bet on you, Booker. *He* believes in you."

Suddenly I felt old and used up. I pulled a chair to me and sat down.

"Please," I said, waving my hand. "Please. Go away. Leave me alone. Please."

I sat there for maybe ten or fifteen minutes, thinking, praying. The phone rang. It was Mr. Withers, the president of the bank. I had put in for a loan and it had been turned down, but Mr. Withers said there'd been a mistake. "New fellow, you know," he said, clucking his tongue. He said he knew that it was my lifelong dream to build a modern funeral home and to buy a Cadillac hearse. He said he sympathized with that dream, supported it, thought the town needed it, and thought I deserved it. "The loan will go through," he said. "Drop by and see me this morning after the hearing."

When I put that phone down, it was wet with sweat. I couldn't turn that new funeral home down and Mr. Withers knew it. My father had raised me on that dream and before he died he made me swear on a Bible that I would make it good. And here it was on a platter, just for a word, a word that wouldn't hurt nobody.

I put on my hat and hurried to the courthouse. When they called my name, I walked in with my head held high. The courtroom was packed. The white folks had all the seats and the colored folks were standing in the rear. Whoever arranged the seating had set aside the first two rows for white men. They were sitting almost on top of each other, looking mean and uncomfortable in their best white shirts.

I walked up to the bench and swore on the Bible and took a seat. Mr. Rivers gave me a little smile and waited for me to get myself set.

"State your name," he said.

"Booker Taliaferro Brown." I took a quick look at the first two rows and recognized at least ten of the men who killed Aaron.

"And your age?"

"Fifty-seven."

"You're an undertaker?"

"Yessir."

"You been living in this town all your life?"

"Yessir."

"You like it here, don't you, Booker?"

Was this a threat? I looked Mr. Rivers in the face for the first time. He smiled.

I told the truth. I said, "Yessir."

"Now, calling your attention to the day of May 17th, did anything unusual happen on that day?"

The question threw me. I shook my head. Then it dawned on me. He was talking about——

"Yessir," I said. "That's the day Aaron got—" Something in Mr. River's face warned me and I pulled up— "that's the day of the trouble at the train station."

Mr. Rivers smiled. He looked like a trainer who'd just put a monkey through a new trick. You could feel the confidence and the contempt oozing out of him. I looked at his prissy little mustache and his smiling lips and I got mad. Lifting my head a little bit, I looked him full in the eyes; I held the eyes for a moment and I tried to tell the man behind the eyes that I was a man like him and that he didn't have no right to be using me and laughing about it. But he didn't get the message. The bastard—he chuckled softly, turned his back to me, and faced the audience.

"I believe you were with the preacher that day."

The water was getting deep. I scrooched down in my seat, closed the lids of my eyes, and looked dense.

"Yessir, Mr. Rivers," I drawled. "Ah was."

"Now, Booker—" he turned around—"I believe you tried to keep the nigger preacher from getting out of line."

I hesitated. It wasn't a fair question. Finally, I said: "Yessir."

"You begged him not to go in the white side?"

"Yessir."

"And when that failed, you went over to *your* side—the *colored* side—and looked through the window?"

"Yessir."

He put his hand in his coat pocket and studied my face.

"You saw *everything*, didn't you?"

"Just about." A muscle on the inside of my thigh started tingling.

Mr. Rivers shuffled some papers he had in his hand. He seemed to be thinking real hard. I pushed myself against the back of the chair. Mr. Rivers moved close, quick, and stabbed his finger into my chest.

"Booker, did you see the nigger preacher reach for Mr. Sampson's gun?"

He backed away, smiling. I looked away from him and I felt my heart trying to tear out of my skin. I looked out over the courtroom. It was still; wasn't even a fly moving. I looked at the white folks in front and the colored folks in back and I turned the question over in my mind. While I was doing that, waiting, taking my time, I noticed, out of the corner of my eye, that the smile on Mr. Rivers' face was dying away. Suddenly, I had a terrible itch to know what that smile would turn into.

I said, "Nosir."

Mr. Rivers stumbled backwards like he had been shot. Old Judge Sloan took off his glasses and pushed his head out over the bench. The whole courtroom seemed to be leaning in to me and I saw Aaron's widow leaning back with her eyes closed and it seemed to me at that distance that her lips were moving in prayer.

Mr. Rivers was the first to recover. He put his smile back on and he acted like my answer was in the script.

"You mean," he said, "that you didn't see it. It happened so quickly that you missed it?"

I looked at the bait and I ain't gonna lie: I was tempted. He knew as well as I did what I meant, but he was gambling on my weakness. I had thrown away my funeral home, my hearse, everything I owned, and he was standing there like a magician, pulling them out of a hat, one at a time, dangling them, saying: "Looka here, looka here, don't they look pretty?" I was on top of a house and he was betting that if he gave me a ladder I would come down. He was wrong, but you can't fault him for trying. He hadn't never met no black man who would go all the way. I looked him in the eye and went the last mile.

"Aaron didn't reach for that gun," I said "Them people, they just fell on——"

"Hold it," he shouted. "I want to remind you that there are laws in this state against perjury. You can go to jail for five years for what you just said. Now I know you've been conferring with those NAACP fellows, but I want to remind you of the statements you made to Sheriff Sampson and me. Judge—" he dismissed me with a wave of his hand—"Judge, this *man*—" he caught himself and it was my turn to smile—"this *boy* is lying. Ten niggers have testified that they saw the preacher reach for the gun. Twenty white people saw it. You've heard their testimony. I want to withdraw this witness and I want to reserve the right to file perjury charges against him."

Judge Sloan nodded. He pushed his bottom lip over his top one. "You can step down," he said. "I want to warn you that perjury is a very grave offense. You——"

"Judge, I didn't——"

"Nigger!" He banged his gavel. "Don't you interrupt me. Now git out of here."

Two guards pushed me outside and waved away the reporters. Billy Giles, Mr. Sampson's assistant, came out and told me Mr. Sampson wanted me out of town before sundown. "And he says you'd better get out before the Northern reporters leave. He won't be responsible for your safety after that."

I nodded and went on down the stairs and started out the door.

"Booker!"

Rachel and a whole line of Negroes were running down the stairs. I stepped outside and waited for them. Rachel ran up and throwed her arms around me. "It don't take but one, Booker," she said. "It don't take but one." Somebody else said: "They whitewashed it, they whitewashed it, but you spoiled it for'em."

Russell came out then and stood over to the side while the others crowded around to shake my hands. Then the others sensed that he was waiting and they made a little aisle. He walked up to me kind of slow-like and he said, "Thank you, sir." That was the first time in his whole seventeen years that that boy had said "sir" to me. I cleared my throat and when I opened my eyes Sarah was standing beside me. She didn't say nothing; she just put her hand in mine and stood there. It was long about then, I guess, when I realized that I wasn't seeing so good. They say I cried, but I don't believe a word of it. It was such a hot day and the sun was shining so bright that the sweat rolling down my face blinded me. I wiped the sweat out of my eyes and some more people came up and said a lot of foolish things about me showing the white folks and following in Aaron's footsteps. I wasn't doing no such fool thing. Ol' Man Rivers just put the thing to me in a way it hadn't been put before—man to man. It was simple, really. Any man would have done it.

The Lottery Drawing

besmilr brigham

SATURDAY MORNING—and when the old man got up, it was sleeting. A fresh spread of tiny solid crystals drifted, an icy mass on the door stoop, banked over the bare-earth mound where the septic tank had been dug. As he opened the screen, a splatter near to snow dislodged from the door frame and fell in his face; he stood clutching his son Elbert's old coat that was too small for him, tight against his lower belly, looking at the falling, dull settlement.

Hard and not melting . . . cold against cold, the sleet piled in corrugated ridges on the low flap shed he had put up over the cellar opening, and beyond the hackberry on the tin roof of the chicken barn, heaped laid out in drifts against the frost-dead grass. The stiff grass stalks raised, blown and struck up frozen to the ground, broke absorbed with weight and looked to him the way beard does when a man is old; the way his own sick stubble was, caught naked on the razor.

"I ought to pile out ashes—" he said. He could hear that the old woman Bett was up, dressing by the fire in the kitchen. "A dog couldn't make it down the steps."

And he remembered that he didn't use the fireplace anymore but burned butane, so that he kept no wood in the house. Sawed log cuts, back of a wood pile where the grown-up garden started, long ago had rotted . . . and the axe he'd lost, forgotten in the watermelon field that last year he planted; cut sprouts, laid the sprawling rows and placed glass fruit jars over to hold in warmth to the emerging vines. Later, he stretched barbed wire and dug post holes to put in a fence.

Sold his land back—couldn't work it, seventy-seven years old; and that was six years ago. With the money he built a lean-on section to the house, extending from the kitchen and the old woman's bedroom, made a porch sitting place for himself and installed a bath, put in a hot water tank and an electric lift pump. And when the piping was laid, "You might as well, right now—" the old woman said, "it's as easy to lay out lines for gas."

All of the whole world that was left to him, that same year he had marked off with wire—no farther than he could once throw. Straight beyond old Bett's clothes line and the chicken house, he had to look on another man's field.

Not waiting to put on his shoes, he went down the board steps in his heavy socks that he slept in. The ice stuck to the soles and wool, and he took a rock and broke in the thick hard-massed freeze on the wash tub under the hydrant, freeing the water for the chickens. From the corner of the house, the wind lifted in gusts of sleet that fell hurled against his face and onto the old woman's knitted head covering that he wore, warm and stretched like a cap down over his ears. It took a long time for him to get to the exposed tub and faucet and to make his way back—and his hands turned numb, burning from lifting the ice cakes out of the water.

The hands hung onto him like stubborn leaves that won't fall. His body felt cold as the pear tree that stayed with its limbs lifted up and not prepared for winter. Above the wrapped well pump, its trunk stretched bare and caked with transparent flakes; and the uneven little stones whirled fast from the sky now, full of light and obliterating the earth like a shower of snow. They looked stiff as frozen feathers to him, absorbing down brittle and hard against him and covering his face.

"If it don't clear," he said, coming back in and knocking the firm meltings that went liquid as frost from his coat, "we can't go to town today."

"But we have to," Bett said.

"Not if I can't get the car out."

"Oh my—" and the old woman pushed past his big oak rocker that took up the full space in front of the heater. He bent over pulling at the wet toes of the socks to get the soggy weave loose. Moisture, turning to vapor, steamed off the stove front from where the red flames flared high and spurted from the radiants, as he sat shaking the socks, until at last he put them to dry on a rack above the fire.

"The pipes are freezing . . . " Bett dipped a slush of ice from the sink, "the water won't go down." And the old man turned up the already high blaze that sent fire licking onto the upper stove frame. "Shut the faucets off," he said, "don't let the water run."

"Hettie Floyd before they moved to town let their water run. That's the way water won't freeze!" she objected. "She and Ira opened their taps all night."

"I don't care what Ira Floyd does. It'll freeze in the drain-off. The water trickles down that cold pipe, and—" to him the metal caked over inside and the run drew in narrow the way people's old arteries did. He wasn't worried about standing water. "It's like a hollow icicle. You have to keep the drain-off empty," he said. "Put on the tea kettle." He'd pour boiling water down till the ice already collected was unchoked.

"If we don't go to town, I don't know what we'll do—" and not to open the tap, she dipped with a cup to fill the coffeepot from water in one of the dish pans she'd run full the night before. "It's the last Saturday before Christmas."

"That don't matter," he said. "Christmas don't matter."

"But there'll be two drawings."

"Do we have any tickets—?"

"Of course we have tickets. I haven't put mine in yet," she said, "and you never did get yours from the gas station. You paid twenty dollars, didn't you?" And when he didn't answer, "That'd be twenty tickets. Why do you always wait for me to get your trade tickets?"

"If you want them, you can get them," he was warmer now. "We never win anything."

"Because it's crooked—" she said.

"I know it's crooked; so what's the use to put the numbers in?"

The old woman didn't know that and the old man didn't know. As long as the merchants gave chances, before three o'clock when Harvy Walker came out from the drugstore with the rotating lottery hamper on his shoulder—when the whole town drew in from its two directions, along one straight line of dull brick and wood two-story buildings and stores, to that point where the high platform was placed next to the post office—the red stubs stayed hot in the hand, if you didn't drop them in. And people did win! The old woman had drawn twenty-five dollars twice, but that was almost eight years ago. It seemed to her the winning had never happened, though she couldn't forget it.

The old man leaned back, watching his strips of toast set up straight against the heater radiants and burning to make ash—good for the blood, somebody said. "That Walker decides before he totes the hamper out. He knows . . . who's going to win," he complained. "Those that buy on and on, week in and week out the same, it don't matter how many counts they have. They don't get the money."

"It's Pauline decides," a point the old woman always came to, "and anyway, you don't know."

"It's a fraud," he sucked in his breath. He always hoped, and he knew that the old woman hoped. She put his tickets in. And it'd be a good day. Because Harvey Walker wouldn't carry the drawing money over, not this near Christmas. He'd keep on if it took an hour until a stub he pulled matched. You had to be right on the lot to holler if you got it, and with the weather so bad. . . .

"We need to get to town before eleven—" the old woman thought about meals, one after the other, straight. With breakfast on the stove, "What'll I fix for dinner?" she'd say.

"I'll go out and try the car," he said, "soon as I drink coffee." And the old man suddenly felt very light, as though a gust of warm air had gone blowing up into his head. "Maybe we'll fix dinner in town—" he laughed, moving quickly, "and stay all day."

"What if the roads are froze?"

But he kept the feeling. "Maybe it'll clear," he said.

Bending over in the bulky rocking chair, old Abe struggled to get his half-dry socks back on. The damp substance stuck to his feet and he jerked, holding his legs out, flung the socks whole again above the stove onto the tin guard that extended from behind and was turned to throw the heat out. "Can't I have a dry pair of these things?" he asked.

"Wait a minute," the old woman was busy and he sat back, watching with his old face as she stirred the thick oatmeal full with raisins and slowly let the gruel cook until gummy, the way he liked to eat it now.

"Aren't you going to have breakfast?"

"Not yet," he said.

So she went to the bedroom, where he didn't sleep or go anymore, and found the big socks. "Why did Elbert buy the damn things?" he quarreled, stretching a long foot up as he pushed the sleeves of his outing pajamas and thermal underwear back to bare his forearm. He held the loose extended toe in his fist. "The heel comes to my elbow."

The old woman brought out another pair. They were exactly the same, like the first and of a dirty, cream-colored wool composition. He took them and held them out, letting the long tops fall. "That fool Elbert," he said. "Must have thought he got more for his money."

"They're to go on over your socks," Bett explained.

"Can't you shrink them?"

"Wool will shrink—but these won't."

"Did you boil them?"

"They're ten percent cotton," she said, "and anyway, they're warm and you can wear them pulled on over others," as though he didn't understand.

"Makes my feet too big to go into the shoes," and he jerked, trying to tear the wadded threads. "I raised an idiot fool!" And he got up and went to his room. When the added-on section was built, he had lined his part on the sides and back with rows of windows, and that first year he moved his high three-quarter bedstead in with a huge stuffed chair. The old woman brought out a small dressing stand with drawers in it where he could keep the planting seeds he still collected and his tobacco. She continued to put her empty fruit canning jars she never used now in stacked cardboard boxes under his bed, and in the extra space behind the great chair she kept hidden the sack of throw-away cans. Directly off from the door they kept open to the kitchen stood the big trash hamper. Egg cartons cluttered an under support strip built onto the large table against the bathroom wall and where the old man culled eggs. Empty boxes and sacks of dog food, the smelly cans and trash, a dirty clothes basket, all had found their places on the porch that was his room—and he sat in the wide high-base stuffed chair with wooden arms that he liked and felt at ease among the discard, struggling with his hard old bones to get his feet into the socks.

When he forced his boots on, he couldn't catch-to the buckles, and he let the high flaps flare. And all the morning back and forth he went out into the cold bundled in his coat, or returned as he worked with the car, heating water, scraping and thawing the windshield, or sitting with the dog in the front seat. When the car did start, he roared the motor to excess to let the black exhaust smoke spread in defiance against the falling sleet.

And the old woman stayed dressed for town in front of the kitchen fire, huddled stiff and subdued as the hens were that squatted for protection under the house edge. Until as the hours passed, she put on a pot of rice. "We have to eat," she said—they couldn't get in by eleven! And they ate their hot rice, the old woman in a straight chair and the old man close to the open heater, the door closed to the back because of the cold, shut in, shut off, thinking of town. Until, "I think we can go," he decided.

"Is the sleet slacking up?"

"Turning to rain," he estimated. "It comes down not froze."

"We don't have to. We could kill a chicken." But her voice went high, "Remember the time we drove back from town in the snow and no place to see out except one small hole we kept scraped clear from the windshield?"

"That was a long time ago."

"Maybe ten years," and she looked at the clock. Twelve-thirty.

"Sun's come out," though he couldn't actually see the sun. But the sun was out, he knew. It threw a cast of light over the whole sky through the steady slow rain, and he went out and wiped the remaining frosted ice carefully from the windshield. "It freezes as soon as it hits," he said.

"Make the dog get out."

"If we go, the dog goes. You want him to get his feet froze off?"

"It's not that cold—" but she opened the door and the dog stayed. When Abe got in the dog raised up, quickly jumped to the back seat. And before the car had gone a half mile to the first creek bridge, the old man had to get out to scrape a thick slush off the glass again. At the main blacktop tediously he stopped. "It's freezing on the new road," he said. "Better stay with the gravel." And he raked his arm and heavy jacket sleeve inside to absorb the settled moisture their breaths had made. "Roll your window down, wife."

"It's cold."

"I can't see to cross over." So she rolled down the window, and as soon as the bend and crossing was cleared and the wheels hit the wider straight gravel, she ran it back up. All the way in, she sat with her body hunched over, her face close to the dull windshield glass as she watched, while the old man kept the car creeping up the longer road.

"Lord in Heaven," she cried once, when they slipped on a hill. In caution, old Abe jerked his arm, the tires whirled, and they missed the side ditch.

"Take me by the Floyd house," she said entering town, and he turned on a side residence street. "But you'll have to come after me in time."

"If you've got to stop," he said, "why can't you walk on?"

"Well I can't, not on a day like this. So you come after me," but she hesitated. Ira Floyd's truck wasn't home. Ira might have gone back out to his cattle pasture, but their daughter Effie's car wasn't home either. Effie lived next door and Lena Polk, Ira's sister, lived farther up on the other side of the Floyds' new house.

"Wait, I think nobody's home," the old woman became excited, but she got out and rang the house buzzer. "It's too bad a day. Something's happened. You knock at Effie's and I'll go to Lena's," she called, and the old man blew loud on the car horn. He kept blowing the repetitious horn though nobody from any of the houses came out, while the old woman went slipping on the dead grass across to each of the yards. He heard her, the voice raised distant and subdued from behind Lena Polk's back door; coming back, she rang the Floyd doorbell again, and knocked at Effie's.

"I just know Hettie's in the hospital," she said. "Maybe she had another heart attack. She looked awfully bad the last time I saw her."

"What are you going to do?" he asked. Then, "We might as well go on into town," she decided.

"All of them gone! You know Ira. In Hettie's condition, he wouldn't let her be out like this," the old woman was near crying.

"Maybe they all went to Houston, for the holidays," Abe said. And in town she'd ask, so she got out near Holden's hardware.

But Mrs. Holden was busy making wreaths and hadn't heard. Janice Holden sat on a high stool behind the shining glass show case, winding green and tinseled leaves and bright red berries to sell for pretty house-door arrangements, to be put up in windows and on graves at the cemetery. "They trade at Dunham's," Janice said. "I haven't heard any ambulance sirens," and she thought about it. "She wouldn't be up, out in this weather—not even with Effie."

Past the sparkling decorations, the old woman went back out with care to the slushy sidewalk, walking on by the desolate gaudy displays of Christmas, the vacant glass sections of what once had been the front lobby of the hotel, since turned into a grocery store—now closed; and crossed the windy side street with empty lot, where the drawing would be and beside it the post office, to the other end of the little town and Dunham's grocery.

"None of them's been in town all day," Oscar Dunham told her, cutting meat on a block behind the meat counter; and the old woman remembered that a relative of Ira's had a job at the garage across the street from the hardware, so that she went cautiously again through the rain and wet. "What if I broke a leg, who would take care of me," she thought. Ahead, she saw the old man walking toward her. He wasn't close enough for her to call, and from a distance he looked like any other old man, heavy and stocky and bundled into his birthday jacket their son Elbert had given him. He walked with his head bent against the wind, hard as a bull that stands in open pasture, driving himself before the gusts of light rain, and then he turned under a porch roof in front of Sally Vaughn's store and went in, and the old woman hurried not to miss him going out again. It seemed warm, knowing he was there, knowing where he was. Sally sent a boy to the Nix garage.

"You don't need to be in this weather, either of you," Sally Vaughn scolded.

So Hettie Floyd was sick. Hettie was in the hospital, lying there pale and her hair fixed, fine as if Effie had done it right in the beauty parlor that morning before she let her mother be carried out to the ambulance. The other Floyd daughter would come home from the coast! They'd be waiting also for married grandsons and Lena for her son who had studied to be a barber. All would arrive at the Floyd houses for Christmas, with cakes and pies and chicken, good things the old woman couldn't think about. For her and Abe, not even their son Elbert could be home this year. Their granddaughter, Barbara, had four babies—and Mary Jo had written she still had a job she had to hold down. She wished Mary Jo could be here to sit in a booth with her in the drugstore, to talk for awhile and drink a coke. She wished she could see Elbert.

"What kind of meat do you want?" the old man said.

"For next week," she said "—I don't know. But you can go on to the service station."

"Oh, Dad likes T-bone steak," she laughed to Sally Vaughn. "Everything is so high!" And she stood disturbed before the glass-enclosed meat counter. The cut-up sections of meat seemed to run together the way lights and icicles and fabulous presents melted on a Christmas tree . . . and you hung on trying to make a choice, to find your own name on a package. All she could see was the handwritten signs with enormous prices.

"I'll take a pound of hamburger and a pound of sausage," she said, remembering that for a meat loaf, sausage could be mixed with beef—she didn't know why. The rest of the shopping was easy, and she took out her list. Flour. Always a bad week when flour had to be bought or a three-pound can of shortening, though now because of the old man's blood vessels she tried to cook with less frying. And she walked about the few counters. You could get things cheaper at Dunham's. Every morning over the radio, Bett listened to Mr. Dunham's ads. But Oscar Dunham wouldn't buy Abe's eggs. Though Dunham gave credit—! And you had to stay with a person who already gave you credit, at least for as long as you still owed a bill; you couldn't leave in debt at one store while you made new charge accounts up the street.

Following a ritual through the aisles, she brought each separate purchase one at a time to the counter. Abe's forty dollars, his whole Veteran's compensation check for the death of their eldest son, had gone to Sally Vaughn on the first and that made the old woman feel better. "I shouldn't buy the buttermilk," she said, "but Dad likes it. I drink dried milk," and she became very excited telling about dried milk. "It's just as good. I can't tell the difference . . ." and through her disquiet she kept on talking. Though she wanted to stop, she couldn't. Not to have Sally notice, in defiance she hurried over to the shelves and came back with a thirty-five cent jar of pickles.

"Don't put this on Dad's bill," she cautioned. "Please—I'll pay cash for it." She'd buy a fruit cake too, a four-pound one you could get at Dunham's for a dollar. Anybody ought to have something special for Christmas! And onions. "Put the onions on the bill. Three's enough." If they killed a chicken, she'd need onions for dressing. Jello. Later, she'd get the jello.

"For the onions, ten cents." Sally counted, "That makes it with tax, eight dollars and a little over . . . sixty-four cents," she corrected.

"That much," and the old woman looked over the stack of what she'd bought. "I'll pay a dollar of it," she said. But she couldn't!

"Honest, he spends at least half this much every week for tobacco, cigarettes—" Sally cried. "When he goes to pay his bill, I tell him. For awhile I just kept the accounts separate. Tobacco and food. A third's not food, and I made him stand right there before me while I showed him. He fusses so about what you spend, I had to do it," Sally laughed. "He sure got mad. I was afraid he wouldn't come back."

"I bet he did—" and the old woman fumbled in her purse for her billfold. "For the pickles," she said. "There's no way I can change anything." She knew she would cry if she didn't get away.

"Thirty-six cents, a cent is for tax," Sally apologized, and the old woman hurried out of the store.

The lips had gone stiff. She wanted to smile, to think of something that would obliterate what she felt. And the old woman wanted to feel it was Christmas. From a record player in the drawing lot, also emerging out from speaker systems in some of the stores, she could hear music . . . songs and carols that sounded distinct and echoing in the moist atmosphere of the sordid little town, as though coming from a church choir of angels. After awhile Claude Haimes, the town marshal dressed as Santa Claus, would ride with his helpers up the street in the city council's decorated fire truck and throw out candy—when all the people, like a big family, gathered on the curb and children raced to catch the sweets, pick up the little wrapped gifts. And as she kept hearing the strange remembered tones with intonations that so affected a listener from his own childhood, a sense of continuity came and with a false exuberance in her voice, louder than she meant the tone to be, she joined in singing the words: "Joy to the world!" Oh Joy—joy to it, and to all simple creatures as herself. Beyond a side street cut that led to another that ran parallel to the town, she could see houses. On these, wreaths would be gaily hung against doors for the Christ child, and because of the low-cast weather and rain a few had their colored lights left burning. "The Lord is come—" she said, and the meaning filled her. But the Lord wasn't 'come.' He hadn't and he wasn't—not in her time, not soon enough. Her life had been rained on and washed over and rushed away and nothing was left. "Oh, come to the church in the Wildwood—come come come come . . ." she sang, and her steps moved with the rhythm of little lambs' feet emerging into the fold. She was back and young, a child, a young girl to become a woman, going with her brothers and sisters to a religious festival, a singing in Mississippi, driving to the church in a wagon. Long, long ago, so very long ago, and with her head erect and not observing where she stepped her foot slipped on the wet surface of the concrete walk space, past the wide closed doors to the post office. Her body jerked and her face went up, and into her face came the Lord's face, that she didn't know at first, because it took her a time before she recognized it was Jack Fuller's face. He held his hands on her . . . laughing.

"Why you almost fell," he said, his arms to her back as she righted herself, and the old hand clutched frantically. Reaching out to him, "I thought you were the Lord—" she said, and she began to cry, going on across the gravel side street where farther on down Mrs. Harper's house had been built, and passing the brick arches of the old abandoned hotel front. Marlene Harper had operated a dry goods business next door beyond the big building—the store closed now, show windows bare as the street. Bett wanted to stop, stand in the shelter that the broad hotel entrance made, under the jutting portion beneath what had been upper office floors, but Willard's pool hall for more than twenty years had taken over one bottom section as part of the big structure—and now, old men roomed above. Outside, the old men and stragglers stood lonely as a drove of solitary homeless dogs brought together, looking up into the diminishing sleet. They watched the thick air, the changing light and weather, protecting themselves—hot in August sun they stood in the cool there, or in the year's first fierce blizzards. The men congregated on the low steps and between the tall, square, inlaid brick posts, always close and intent as buzzards in flock, and they watched the women that passed. Even if you were old as they were the men looked at you. Their still faces held a desolate contentment, not bawdy in what was said or their movements the way young men would be; and in their eyes was a sadness, as when after Christmas is over and all accumulated passion of the season has been washed out—a body could go through paper snowflakes and gaudy elaborate cheap cards and not quite throw them away. The gathered old men looked on, remembering because of the women as they passed.

Walking again past the drugstore, the old woman turned and went back into Holden's. She stopped before the counter and display tables of bowls and plates and bright expensive dishes, but left quickly not to look at the objects, and went out again. She felt separated and lost in part because she wanted to sit in the drugstore, but she knew that she couldn't go in—though she did sometimes stop to talk with Pauline. Abe owed a bill for medicine and Harvey Joe Walker had asked for payment. If Mr. Walker was busy with prescriptions it wouldn't matter, though at any time he might come out to the cash register.

The old woman didn't know all of what happened. Mr. Walker spoke to the old man nicely as he could . . . he said no being had a right to talk to another the way Abe did. And the old man had kept cursing and saying he didn't owe the money and that Harvey Walker poisoned people. Harvey Walker sold dope! As Pauline said, "He made a shit-ass of himself." Everybody knew that Arnold Smith, who owned the store, let Walker sell medicines without prescriptions, but if you were sick you could go into that drugstore and get relief; you didn't have to pay a doctor every time to tell you what to buy. Though many could have reported him and had the store's license taken away, no one ever did.

And that same afternoon, Mr. Walker sent Pauline to Sally Vaughn's to hunt for the old woman. Fourteen dollars and eighty-five cents, and could she pay the two-year-old bill? "But don't you two old people go without medicine—" he said.

Abe had made a four hundred dollar mortgage on the place to buy chickens, and the old woman was settling that, clearing the loan at ten dollars a month for forty months, all to come out of her portion of the war compensation and security. She didn't know how much longer it would take, because each January one of two months' payment went for interest. And she was responsible for the butane: "If you want to have a false fire," Abe had said, "you sure as hell can pay for it." Of course, Abe bought his chicken feed. . . . "Some months the chickens eat more than you do," Sally Vaughn would complain. She also sold him the feed. And Bett now bought his clothes, though Elbert kept him supplied in shoes. Now Elbert sent a lot of things, secondhand out of Salvation Army, and such. But she had burial insurance, and her tithe to the church, and any over—for extras, she spent at Dunham's. Abe wouldn't pay for a bar of soap bought at Dunham's.

And the old woman sat in the corner booth at Doc Knight's cafe, drinking hot tea, where she hoped she could cry and nobody would see her.

"She's crying over there," Doc's wife said at the counter.

"She almost fell down in the street awhile ago," Jack Fuller said. "Would have, except that I caught her."

"Poor old thing."

And after awhile, the old woman got up and went out. She kept thinking about Hettie in the hospital with a hundred-and-four fever, but her first fright returned and . . . she decided the Floyd family was holding something back. "She's dying," the old woman said. And in her mind she saw herself dead in the room the interns put a body in—a form covered, the bed rolled out, down through the halls of desolate suffering—before a man, dressed in black, drew all the blood out. She saw her own blanched face in the casket, waiting for Jesus to come for her. But she couldn't feel the reality of actually being dead.

It was a day she had waited most of her life for, to see God . . . to see God at last. "Oh, that will be glory, be glory for me—" she sang off in herself somewhere. Though nothing consoled her.

"I always buy myself a present—for Christmas," she thought, passing the closed movie house, remembering the holiday wreaths, the whole front section of Holden's hardware where Janice Holden kept gifts, the spread rows of shiny glass, placed so you could look at everything and touch the rich china. And she walked back and forth through the aisles as though anything she wanted she could have gotten, all held within her choice, wandering there, until suddenly she found the salt shaker. The glittering clear shaker, very large, had deep blue rings that reflected from the cut-in shape against the glass, with a shiny screw-on top set with a small spindle knob that turned and opened the sprinkler holes. A token one selected from a treasure of great riches, and she held it.

It couldn't cost too much, she thought—no more than thirty cents, holding the jar-like container against the high counter where Mrs. Holden sat with her wreaths.

Janice Holden carelessly turned the bottom up.

"I couldn't see the price," the old woman said.

"Eighty-nine cents," Janice said. "Ninety-two with tax. Honey, the top is aluminum."

"That much?" the old woman asked. "And it's the only one . . . it's not a set," not daring to part with it. She remembered the platter with painted turkey on it that Mrs. Holden had sold her—was it four years ago? She mentioned that she still enjoyed the platter, and she told Janice about Hettie Floyd; and then Cherry Rhoton came in.

"Come on to the drugstore with me," Cherry said "—before the drawing. And I'll buy you a coke," so that the old woman felt comfortable again, all warm and not fluttering.

"I'll put the shaker back," Mrs. Holden offered.

"Oh no. I'll do it," Bett insisted, picking up the almost forgotten shaker. But she stopped. "Would you please gift wrap it for me?" and her voice stayed low. "Can I make a ticket," she said, as she put the small box, wrapped in gold with a tiny wreath upon it, into her purse.

"We've still got thirty minutes to wait," Cherry said. "No rush—" and the old woman wondered if Abe had picked up his drawing tickets! Her own lay secure in her purse, and the station tickets were his—so he could look after them, she decided, as she stopped to drop those she had been saving into the big wire hamper. There was someone to talk with now, and soon Pauline would bring the cokes. It was as though nothing had ever happened. Ruby Hines and Myrtle Bates were at one of the tables in the full booths, and the two crowded over to give room for her and Cherry. To the side on a high stand the TV kept going, but nobody watched or listened. From back of them people were just leaving . . . and a girl kept laughing.

"It's Mildred," Cherry said. "Mildred Sellers. Home for the holidays."

"I know Mildred," the old woman cried. "She used to go to our Sunday School."

". . . three babies now, expecting another."

"But she's only been married—"

"Seven years," Cherry Rhoton studied. "Come February."

Pauline stooped over, "I'd say it was time she told that husband of hers—" finishing in a whisper, "to put the tap on. Well, you know, there are things a woman can do," she said.

"I had twelve," Cherry laughed, "though three of my children died."

"But now things are different," Pauline went on. "We can't afford to have all the children a man can get on us. Can we? I should hope not! I told mine—!"

"We were very poor," Cherry Rhoton said.

"I had three and one died, and I thought I didn't want any more," the old woman confided. "Then I had another. That was Elbert. You know Elbert? He was the sweetest baby of the lot. Of course, my other boy—the one that lived to be grown, was killed in the war . . . ."

"That was a terrible thing," Pauline had been told many times.

"He was married you know, and we didn't get the insurance.

Now, the only ones I have left are Elbert and Mary Jo," the old woman said "—and Barbara. But Barbara's my granddaughter." And though the old woman and the others kept saying the things all had said for so many years, Saturdays and week days, to Pauline and to one another, telling the hurts, the joys that had shaped their lives and that each had repeated many, many times for pleasure or from grief, to the old woman the booths and counters seemed a familiar glistening place, open and belonging. She forgot about the drawing and old Abe's tickets and the cold. Until she saw him, lumbering against the tight aisle places between the center row of shelves that had been put up and the glass counters with perfumes and cosmetics. He might come too close and break any number of the delicate vials, and she called to him.

"Here, I got the tickets," he said, shoving the string of tabs toward her face.

"Then put them in—" the old woman looked up unconcerned. "They haven't taken the bin out yet, have they?" she asked Pauline. "Go back up front and put your stubs in," she directed, pointing toward the soda fountain on the opposite side of the store's entrance where the wheel was kept. But soon the old man returned. He couldn't find it. "It's no good, I can't see to read the numbers," he said, and the old woman took them, hurried with him to the hamper to tear the thick strips apart and get the shorter drawing ends into the hole. "Tell them to wait," she kept saying, "There are ten whole sheets—how'd you get so many? Oh, you must not have picked them up for months," and down the little red papers went, separated . . . each one floating in a sea of squares and numbers and chances.

"You will be out there?" the old man asked.

"Of course I'll go for the drawing. I've got tickets in, myself."

"You'd better go now," he said.

"I'll leave when everybody else does and the bin is taken," she said, but she stayed close to the big doors not to miss it.

All the people attached to one another through loneliness, knowing one another's names, slowly came together at the drawing lot . . . and an air of festivity went up, out over their heads and faces, from where knotted little groups stood in their coats, some with umbrellas, their feet held firm against the hard tramped grass and mud. At a height even with their shoulders, at the center spread the rough board platform where the rotating hopper soon would be whirled with a chance more certain than any of them in other ways knew. An hilarity about the brief gathering also, as in summers when election speeches were held and chairs rented to be put in place to cover the whole empty side block, back to the trees!

But Harvey Walker was standing now and there was plenty of time; first, the handle would be turned and the gala wheel set rolling with its wire barrel where all could see the heavy weights of paper surging upward, falling, and the red and green and yellow slips flying down separately . . . at last to settle, and a child would be lifted to touch into the opened place and draw out a number; a man also would come from the crowd and read the card.

And then Mr. Walker would call out the figures on the loud speaker; and hands rushed to lift the sections of colored trade receipts they held, torn from long, thick binding pads that had been kept up and down the street in either direction in the row of small stores and business places. Nobody expected to win, but as in a raffle, in a game of sharing in anticipation and illusion each kept his own secrets. Smiles and laughter, a communion of stark pleasure, when a man answered, "I think I've got it," and hurried to the bare edge of the platform planks to hold up a sheaf of tickets, or one single ticket, and receive back an envelope. But there was another drawing, and the game went on. The colored barrel moved again with its load and went dancing with little colored squares against the wire.

It had stopped raining now. Soon, with the ceremony over, all would go home . . . to houses their separate friends knew and ways that were for none of them very different from those of most of the people who stood below the platform. Nobody lived in a singular world, and pleasure came from their bodies being close and touching, touching in wonder, as though by some unperceived process in this repetitious act, bound in place, they belonged to one another. Their children grew up, emerging outward with other children, as slowly from house by house the same teachers taught the succeeding families of young ones. The same stores supplied their goods, sons and daughters courted one another and some married—and some went away, and some returned. Until at last, the reproducing generations of parents took their proper responsibilities in the cycle, opened their arms to another that was new, and found comfort in sharing . . . it didn't matter who won the money, and Bett's eyes grew moist and brilliant, thinking of it.

After the old woman had received the envelope, she went back to the drugstore. "Pauline," she whispered, as though someone not seen might take the bills from her, "mine was the second winner."

"You mean," Pauline leaned close, "you got one of the twenty-five dollars?"

"And for me Mr. Walker only drew once—" still talking low. "There's something I want to do with it. That old drug account, the one he—you know, Abe's . . . Mr. Walker talked to me about it. I don't want everybody to know. I want to pay five dollars on that. Tell Mr. Walker; he'll remember," she paused. "And can I take home the receipt?"

"We'll sure see to that," Pauline laughed. "We don't want it to come up again—do we?"

Even if she paid the bill, she'd still have to give Abe half, Bett thought, and that would leave . . . five dollars from twelve-fifty—but her tithe would be two-fifty! Lately, the tithe had disturbed the old woman, since before Thanksgiving when the church budget had been made public. Rev. Tyson Sellers drew forty-five hundred dollars in salary for a year and worked under a fifteen hundred dollar expense account. Six thousand dollars! Of course, if she kept only half, then her tithe should be half, but "—I am giving my money straight to Rev. Sellers," she reasoned. "And he has more than I do." The church organization had light bills to be paid, and they hired a man for cleaning, also literature and song books had to be bought, but nothing consoled her. She tried to imagine she helped pay for the song books, though she knew that most of the church expense went to pay Sellers.

"It's all fixed," Pauline said. "Nine dollars and eighty-five cents left owing, and here's your receipt—" and the old woman at that moment had to hold herself not to pay the whole amount. "I'm awfully glad," Pauline said. "That you won the money, I mean."

"Oh—yes!" the old woman felt giddy as a child, with a secret held only to herself, for nobody talked about it yet. Nobody seemed to know. But she wanted to find Abe. To her, it was time to go home, and she walked back along the strung-out store fronts, as though a circle of strange reality spread, suddenly surrounding her.

When she saw Jack Fuller she was about to ask him, "Have you seen Abe?" but waited, expecting Jack to say, "I hear you won!" And she'd answer, "Thank you," because she'd know he felt happy for her—by his voice. It would be like Pauline's voice and her Elbert's, truly glad.

"You'd better watch out," Jack Fuller said. "That old man of yours—he's looking for you. He says he's the one that should'a got that money."

"But how could he?" And a flutter of moths ran through her head.

"I don't know. I was over at the station, and Bud Thurman recognized the series. Soon as he heard it called. From a row Bud had just pulled off, and there was the book and on it the next run. And Thurman looked. He showed old Abe, and you ought to 'a heard him."

"Oh my Lord," and already she had spent the five dollars. She saw the car yet standing with the dog in it under the washrack shed at the station. "I'll go to the car and wait," she said, "if you see him—tell him." At once the closed car looked safe to her, and she wanted to be on across the street away from Jack . . . away from other faces and other voices. All seemed mocking to her now. Whatever the old man had to say, he could say it in the car, where nobody would hear.

Abe saw her and rushed out of the gas station. "Of course it was my ticket," he said. "You pulled it off a row, didn't you?"

"I don't know," she cried. "I was so excited. I went through all the tickets, I saw the drawing number. I thought it was right. I handed the stubs I had up to Mr. Walker on the stand, for him to check. They're not any good if it's not the right one. And he read the figures out, said I had it and held up mine. Mr. Walker said . . ." for a moment she couldn't remember. "'Yes, you have the right ticket,' that's what he said. 'You have the number, you've won the money.' He said I had the ticket, I know that. And I thought . . . I thought it was mine."

"The hell you did!" And the old man grabbed the money from her. "Where's the rest of it?"

"That's all—" Bett was crying now. "I didn't buy anything. I paid—" she struggled to get the words out, "I did pay five dollars on your drug bill," she remembered. "And I ought to have paid more. There's no need to look at me like that," she said. "I wish I'd paid the whole bill off."

He drew back his hand to hit her and his face swelled. "You paid Harvey Walker!"

"You won't strike me," she warned. "Not right here. I thought I had won the money and I meant to give you half, and the five dollars was to come out of my part," she explained. "Now that you won it, you ought to know it's right to divide with me. If for no other reason, because I held the tickets!"

He turned in a rush back for the gas station and came out waving two ten-dollar bills. He threw one on her lap.

Bett waited, knowing his anger wasn't passed and afraid to ride with him if he started cursing. She tried to hold herself at peace. "I don't want to cause him to damn his soul," she said, vowing to keep her mouth shut . . . but once in the yard, "If I do keep the ten dollars," she told him, "I'll pay the rest of that medicine account for you."

The old man didn't move from the wheel. A pain lay hard against him to understand how the old woman's mind worked. Harvey Walker had insulted him—insulted them . . . talked to him worse than he would to a Negro, and she sat declaring herself, the ten dollars he'd given her folded away in her bag. There was nothing he could do, and he knew it. To stop her from paying the bill, or to hurt Harvey Walker as he had been hurt. Not to pay Harvey Joe Walker had been the only way he knew to absolve himself, the only action he could take that made him look upon himself justifiably.

"I'll swear to God," he said, "if you pay one more cent on that account—I'll kill you." And she took the ten dollars out her purse and gave it back to him. "I wish I could think you'd keep the twenty dollars," she said, "to buy the car license with next month. It's going to be awfully hard then, to get up the money."

"Next month I'll pay half the car license," he was so angry his voice broke, "and you will pay the other half. I buy the food. I pay for all the gasoline! You ride in the car."

"And I'll go on riding in it," the old woman defied him. "I'll pray for you," she said, as she got out of the car.

"Damn your soul," he said. But her mind was still, she wouldn't hear him. "Don't pray for me," he cried. And in pain he said it again . . . "damn you. Damn you—" He had worked all his life. Damn ignorance. Damn poverty, he thought. Damn money and the lack of it.

Full with hurt, the old woman went into the house. The money appeared now a curse to her, and she wished that it never existed. She tried to feel that nothing had happened, that the twenty-five dollars had not been won—that she had not stood out in that squared-off lot, fumbling through the lengths of red rectangles, and that all those pieces stretched blank without anything on them.

And she thought of Hettie Floyd. She didn't feel sorry for Hettie any more. Hettie wouldn't die; she wanted to live too much. And she didn't want to leave Ira.

"I don't find anything wrong with Ira," Hettie had said once, "I don't criticize him, because there's no fault I find—" and the old woman thought of this. Hettie and Ira Floyd had lived for forty years right up the road from where she and Abe now lived—next house, and only one year ago moved to town, before Thanksgiving. The old woman remembered the rush to get into the new house before the holiday. "We have to sell out," Hettie had said, "though Ira is to keep one pasture—. We're too old. We have to move closer to the children . . . Effie can't come out here every time we're sick," and Ira just seventy! Abe would never leave the farm. He'd die on it and leave her to do "whatever you damn well please," sell the place that wasn't worth much, pay bills, rent a room. She couldn't even count on Elbert to help.

In the late spring a few years back when the tail of a tornado hit, blew the big hickory down that grew in the front yard and smashed in part of the front porch, the old woman had lain in the bedroom through all the storm and prayed. And when she heard the tree fall, she thought the whole asbestos roof must have blown off. Telling Hettie afterward, "Where were you?" she asked. And Hettie laughed.

"When the first blow started," Hettie said, "I ran and jumped in Ira's lap . . . and there I stayed with my arms around him." It was hard to believe, the old woman thought, and she sat in her straight chair in front of the stove and cried. She didn't have anywhere to turn. She felt in those moments that she'd never been able to look to Abe for anything, not even physical protection.

And the old man stayed on sitting in the car outside. He kept the door open, but he wouldn't get out. The dog wouldn't jump from the car either and leave him. Though anger would not stay long with him and he knew that he would go in where warmth was. His life had become old and worn as the house, the boards that went into the walls, and like the trees that he lived with—many that he had planted. He had become durable as earth. (And if women were durable, they also had great sentiment and love, that was different from a man's.

When he was truly old, her hands would comfort him.) But until then, he understood only a stubborn determination to live by his will and whatever chance until breath stopped him.

Old Abe sat on in the car until near dark, moist clouds settling again like sleet, and he remembered many things . . . in his mind he was in the hills and Mississippi, at his home there—the old place of his father's that was no more; and all the qualities of earth seemed gone that had held him together. He wasn't certain that his father's life had been any better than his. The old man had died on his own land, that stretched for as far as he could see; he took sick one night and he died in the night, and his children were about him—all his sons, except Abe. Abe didn't remember where he was.

South Texas, he supposed. He was in the Rio Grande valley . . . but that was long ago. It never snowed there and it never sleeted; the land lay rich and flat with no hills and no timber, palms and the gulf. You could drive on a straight road and see from sky to sky, like a dream to think of it, here and already a drizzle thickening, the hardest cold yet to come on them . . . after Christmas, after the holidays, early January and all the empty whiteness of illusion would bank this narrow field he lived in with burning ice—.

But now it was Christmas! One year on March 5 the pears were full of white blooms, the bright limbs covered, and even then snow came. He remembered the tiny flakes, petals being blown falling in the storm. How strange they had looked, not melting.

Without Any Ears

JACK BUTLER

PEOPLE WITHOUT EARS wont die. But an ear is a necessity for most of us, we wouldn't know what to do without them.

You will probably think this is a bad topic, but I think you are prejudice against me because I talk back, but I can't help it because you or so wrong.

I have known two people who didn't have an ear and please don't be prejudice; because you said use your imagination, "don't just write the same o stuff." You said you open your mouth and in the modern world of today floats out. So I said if he wants a theme about ears but with imagination, why not write about not an ear. But I just know you will give me an F because I argue with you about the Watergate. But I still say he is our president. I wrote a theme on it last year and Mrs. Hallikan she gave me an A! So I know you have just made up your mind to flunk me.

Now I don't have but forty-two minutes. Oh!

The first man I knew he didn't have ears was when I went with Daddy one time to visit Mr. Blasingame. He knocked on the door with a big brass knocker and after a while Mr. Blasingame came to the door he was *real big.*

He said hello Ed and Daddy said hello Mr. Blasingame. That's what I would call him but on the way over Daddy didn't call him that, he called him Charley, so I wondered.

"What a pretty little girl."

"She's a corker, alright." He was in the shadow kind of so I didn't make out about his ears till we went in the livingroom. Then I saw he didn't have hair on the sides of his face and the skin was all melted and purple. One was just a little hole and the other had stuff around it like a candle. Mr. Blasingame ask did he want some coffee, and Daddy said he better hear why he come first, and Mr. Blasingame said he kind of figured why he come, but what he wanted to know was if Daddy was on his side or the insurance company's.

"You know it wouldn't be like they could put me in jail, but everybody would still think I done it."

"Yeah, but I don't work for you, I work for the company—honey git away from that china cabinet!"

"Oh let her ramble, Ed, she won't hurt nothing."

"Honey! Git over here, why don't you run along and play outside, Daddy'll be along in a minute."

So I went down to the creek and played. It was just one of them o mud creeks it wasn't clear or nothing, but you could pretend it was a big river with cliffs. I counted a minute but Daddy wasn't over with and then I counted another but he still wasn't. I don't have but twenty-two minutes left and I'm writing as fast as I can and I still haven't got to Pauly. It was a long time till I heard them at the door and the light was all yellow and long and I was tired. Then when I had to cross the chicken-yard I was afraid of the rooster and Daddy come and swung me up. Mr. Blasingame followed us to the pick-up. "I can't tell you how much I appreciate it, Ed. This thing has been eaten on me, I know that's the way they all do but its still been eaten on me."

"I'm sorry I even had to ask, that's all," said Daddy. "But you got to see a man face to face on something like that. Well, we been missing you down to Little Hope." That's our church we go to down there, Brother Cotton is the preacher.

When we were driving home I ask Daddy what happened to Brother Blasingame's ears.

"He was caught in a fire, honey. Don't you remember No I guess that was a little far back for you. How old are you Five?" That was Daddy's game, He would say Three or Five like he didn't know.

I said no, I was Four. He said don't you remember the big fire about three years ago. Well Charley and his wife and son and o Mrs. Odeneill were in the upstair den when the furnace exploded. They tried to get down but they couldn't. Then Mrs. Odeneill caught on fire and Charley let her down the window onto the porch roof and she rolled onto the ground and he jumped out and flung her in the ditch and put her out. Then he ran back and climbed up the post when the floor fell in and Marie and Jerry were burned up. His ears got melted off when he tried to get back in but he just couldn't even when he heard her scream. And then he went unconscious. A lot of times he wanted to kill himself but he figures he'll just wait.

"You mean o Mrs. Odeneill was there? She's ugly as sin."

"Ain't that the truth. Goes to show. People got to talk, be there a thing to talk about or not."

"Well I'm mad. She never said word one. How come him to grab her first?"

"It was so bad she don't remember it honey," Daddy said. "Because she was company," he said.

You will probably flunk me because it is so gorey, but I can't help it, you said use your imagination. But this is all the truth, really. But I used my imagination to think up to even talk about it. Now I don't have but ten minutes left for Pauly.

His Daddy burn his ears off with a kerosene lantern, this was after they move to Rolling Fork. He didn't mean to he just swung around with a skillet and it knocked off and blowed up and run all over Pauly and melted off his ears and his face all over. Pauly's face is not ok like Brother Blasingame it has run down and melted all over and he cant even grin. He can laugh, though, I just mean his face won't move. He has a little topknot of hair in the back of his head that didn't get burn. He has to roll his eyes around alot to keep them wet; he can't blink all the way.

I knew him in school but he is a Methodist, and then they moved to Rolling Fork. His Daddy hugged him in some blankets. After that I only seen him twice, once was when we played them in baseball and he was pitching! We went to watch Troy, that is my oldest brother. He came behind the screen and told Daddy everybody feels sorry for Pauly, but I am going to try and knock him out of the box. Do you think that's ok? Daddy said, "It was the only way to be." Then Troy went back and hit it a long way, but their left outfield run his tail off and caught it and everybody hollered.

Oh, no! Well I am just going to have to be late for biology and finish and its all your fault, when you use your imagination it takes longer than it's suppose to. I didn't know there was so much to say about not having an ear but you'll probably give me an F anyhow you're so prejudice.

The other time I seen Pauly was when a bunch of us went up to Delta State in our Senior Year to see if we would want to go there next year. I wish I had of now. We were in the Student Union when somebody calls "Eileen! Eileen!" and Pauly come running up. I saw it was Pauly and his face didn't bother me none because I seen worse, but I heard some of them biddies catch their breaths. Then he took me over to a table for some coffee. I don't hardly drink coffee, but in college you do so I did. I had a lot of sugar and cream and Mrs. Mohon watched us right along.

He said was I going to school here and I said I didn't know yet but I might. I said how was he, and he said fine. I ask could he hear good, and he said yes. Brother Blasingame could to, so I guess the fire didn't get inside. Only I wonder what the outside of an ear is for now. He said you know it's nice of you not to look at me like a Frankenstein. I said anybody could get burnt. Anyway, I said, it's not what's on the outside that counts, but what's on the inside? But really it does count, but you have to fight against it.

"You're a smart girl," he says, "That's how it is. Besides it could be worse, I could've broke my neck like o Bobbie diving in shallow-water and just have to lay there the rest of my life." I thought that wouldn't be so bad, because then you're still pretty, but I didn't say it to be polite.

"I've got a girl friend," he said. "We're going to be married when I get out."

"Oh, Pauly, that's wonderful. I bet she's a big o fat girl won't anybody date but you can date each other and be happy."

"You're a smart girl," he said. He said that twice, but you will probably mark a F on me anyhow.

"But she's a great—" he said, and then he said a word that I wont say what it is but if you don't know what it is by now you ought not to be teaching in College. I know I might should of got mad, but then he went and laughed and tried to wink at me right after he said it and it was so funny to see him try to wink I like to died laughing. And it's not any use you getting onto me, because I already went to Daddy and told him and he said I done the right thing.

So that's my imagination and if you aren't prejudice you ought to give me an A or at least a C. I was real happy for Pauly because sometimes you see these people something terrible has happened to and they come in the grocery store, or maybe its a family with a idiot without any teeth, or maybe a idiot and a cripple and all grown up and being ashamed they leave it in the car in the parking lot with the windows all rolled up and it gets real hot, and it cries and slobbers just like a baby. But its ugly ugly ugly because it's not a baby it's a grown-up.

And they live way out in the country and only come in when they have to. And don't know how to act, all dirty and with overalls on, like they was afraid, like they could come out and arrest them for being so ugly.

A Sense of Place

PRICE CALDWELL

BO, HAVING PLACED a great deal of importance in place, thought a lot about the moon. It was a very marvelous place, he had decided many years ago, but it had no place. At the age of forty-six he understood that its location was predictable: the farmers always seemed to know when it was going to rise and when it was going to set, and when the eclipse was going to happen. But he had never quite understood how to account for it.

Not that it was any great bother. From his position on the porch swing he could see only a relatively small triangular patch of the southeastern sky anyway. Sometimes the moon was there and sometimes it wasn't. He studied the Map of the Heavens that came in the *National Geographic* magazine and figured out when Orion and Cassiopeia would swing through his part of the sky. But there was no accounting for the moon.

As a place, the moon had provoked great thought on his part in a year some time past. He had a Rand McNally *World Atlas*, the International Edition of 1932 that his great-aunt had given him on his twelfth birthday. It said, "The Moon is an opaque body like the Earth and has no light or heat other than that received from the sun." Bo knew that it was a smaller place than the world, and that it had no air. The *Atlas* told how big it was and how far away, and that because of the slight oddness of its path, you could sometimes see a little bit around the right side of the moon, and sometimes a bit around the left side. Other than that, not very much was said about it, as a place. Perhaps, Bo felt, there was just not very much to say.

Bo was sympathetic. There was not very much to say about his own place, either. His own place was the town of Carny, Mississippi, and Bo had thought a great deal about it. Once he had imagined that a man from Rand McNally came to see him, to ask him to write a description of Carny. His name was Mr. Ed Bridger, Bo remembered, a pleasant, round-bodied man with funny little eyes, who smiled all the time he was talking. Bo remembered how he had argued with Mr. Bridger. He told him that there were places in Carny that he hadn't even seen yet. Because of the affliction that he had from birth, he couldn't go anywhere except when his mother pushed him in his wheel chair. He tried to tell Mr. Bridger that he couldn't write, either, except very slowly on a typewriter, because when he tried to print, his hands wouldn't go straight long enough to make the letters. Everything twisted when he wanted it to go straight, and even when he talked it came out a kind of twisted roar that only his mother could understand. But Mr. Bridger said it didn't matter. He said that Bo knew as much as anybody about Carny, Mississippi. He didn't come right out and tell Bo that his description would be published in the next edition of the *World Atlas,* but Bo had the feeling after he had left that he would use whatever influence he had, and would get as much of it published as possible.

First Bo thought about the part he knew the most about. In his room, on the ceiling, there were three brown splotches that the rain had made one time when it came through the roof. Bo had always thought of them as dishes of ice cream, but now that he wanted to describe them for Mr. Bridger he could only think of two great wheels riding over a mountain that had fluted edges like a butter cookie. He thought about the wheels for a while, trying to figure out where they were going. When he had finished thinking about them, he thought about the bedspread that his mother had made, with tulips crocheted in red and green and brown, and then the oval-shaped hook rug, pink and green, that he had to be very careful about when he lifted himself into his wheel chair. It slipped very easily, and one edge turned up treacherously.

In the kitchen there was black and white linoleum, with a curiously intricate pattern. He wondered if he should speak of the blue and green flowers that intertwined on the edges of the white dishes, or of how he tried not to touch his plate when he ate because he might too easily knock if off onto the floor. On a little shelf in the living room there were more cups and plates, with whole pictures painted on them. His mother dusted them every day. He wondered if he should describe her. "She was always the same," he decided to say. "She was always there, moving around the house in her old cotton dress and white socks, old woman with white hands and white hair shooing dust away." He thought, suddenly: "shooing shadows and pains away too."

And he could talk about the porch. He and his mother spent

most of their time there, when the weather was good. The porch went all the way around the side of the house. He would describe the square strips of wood that the swing was made of, and the thick, strong links of the chains that held it up.

From the swing he could see the side yard. There were his mother's flowers and then the high hedge that surrounded the whole yard, even behind the house. At night a street light shone through the upper part, and where the sidewalk went through in front, he could see a narrow part of the street and some of the green house across the way. If he looked hard he could even see a bit of the cotton gin that was back behind it on another street. To the left of the green house, behind the hedge, was the church his mother took him to sometimes on Sundays. From out there on the street he could see a good part of the rest of town.

Behind the house, he knew, there was the bayou, full of cypress trees and blackbirds. Every year Dr. Thompson or one of his mother's friends took him in a car to Memphis to see a specialist. When they went over the bridge in the center of town, he could see the brown water lying slackly around the cypress knees, and the birds, and the curve in the bank that made the bayou go around behind his house. The other part of town, the part that he did not know very well, lay on the far side of the bayou. There was one long crowded street that more or less followed the bank of the bayou. Only colored people lived there, in houses smaller than his own house. The only place white people went to was at the very end of that street, where the little square cemetery lay, green under four great pecan trees. Anyone could tell who the oldest families in town were, because they had the most stones with their names on them.

When he had finished thinking about all the parts of town he knew, he made his mother draw him a map of all the streets. She had forgotten where some of them went, and he had to tell her. Still there were some streets he wasn't sure about. So he waited for the summer when his friend Gip, who was Dr. Thompson's grandson, would come to town for a visit and could help him finish the map. When it was finished Bo realized the town was just like he knew it was. Even the streets he had never been on went where he thought they would go. He realized the Rand McNally man was right. You didn't really have to go to a place to know about it.

Gip was fourteen years old that summer he came over to help

with the map, and Bo was thirty. That was when he started again to look at the maps in his *World Atlas*, and to look at the pictures of far places. When a letter came to his mother he cut out the postmark, and read about the place it came from, so he would know as much as he could about it. One summer when Gip came they made a scrapbook for the postmarks, and Gip told him as much as he could about the places he had been to. He had been to Chicago once, and Washington, D. C. Over the years Bo collected quite a number of postmarks, but there were many he couldn't find out much about because the *Atlas* didn't have very much to say about near places. It only told about big or famous or far-away places, even though there were maps of everywhere. So he was happy when his mother subscribed to a small magazine that was published in Memphis, and which told about places in his own state of Mississippi and about the other states between Nashville and New Orleans. That was how he learned about the story that his friend Gip had written.

When Bo read the story he shook all over with excitement. He had a strong feeling that he knew what was going to happen even before he finished. It was about a man who built his own special place to die in, a little mausoleum in his front yard. There he would be preserved intact so his friends could come to visit him after he passed away. In the story he asked his oldest Negro retainer to come into the monument and open the drawer where he would be lying and put him on a fresh shirt and tie every other day. Bo trembled because Mr. Charlie Connors, who lived only eight and a half miles up the highway north of Carny, had just last year built just such a little building for himself. And Bo cried out when he saw the author's name at the end of the story, because it was the same as Gip's name.

As quick as he could, Bo rolled his wheelchair into the kitchen where his mother was and waved the magazine in the air with his hand. He was so excited he had to say "is it Gip?" to her four times before she knew what he said.

She got the magazine away from him and looked. "Why, Bo, maybe it is," she said. "That is his name, all right."

She turned to the Table of Contents to see if his name was there, too. It was the same. "I'll tell you what we'll do, Bo," she said. "I'll just call up Dr. Thompson on the telephone and we'll just see."

And Bo held his hands as still as he could because Gip was his friend, who had helped him with the map. Gip had been born here in Carny, Mississippi, in Dr. Thompson's back bedroom, and Bo had called him Gip ever since he first saw him as a baby. Even though, Bo thought suddenly, that must have been almost thirty years ago now.

"Bo, it is Gip," his mother said when she came back.

"It is Gip," Bo roared happily. They sat still for a long time smiling at each other, trying to understand how Gip could have become a famous author who wrote stories about places they knew about, only eight and a half miles away. But then his mother said that just last week she had talked to Mrs. Wylie in the grocery store and she had said that Mr. Connors' monument was really one of the prettiest in this part of the country. They sat silently for a while thinking about that. Then Bo went to his typewriter, and, though it was very difficult to do, he wrote a letter to Gip. He told Gip how proud he was to see his story in the magazine, and when he finished the letter, he wrote at the end, "Your friend always." Then he made his mother call up Dr. Thompson again to find out where Gip lived. When he learned that his friend lived on Napoleon Avenue, in New Orleans, Louisiana, he went to his bedroom to read in his *World Atlas.*

The *World Atlas* did not have very much to say about New Orleans, as a place, and nothing about Napoleon Avenue. "French Town is the most marked feature of the place," it said, "with its varied attractions of ancient mold. Here may be seen the Cathedral of St. Louis, the second oldest built on American soil, and the Cabildo, in which the formal transfer of Louisiana to the United States was made. The city is the annual scene of the festival of Mardi Gras."

Bo wondered if Napoleon Avenue was in French Town, and if the festival of Mardi Gras was anything like the celebrations that he knew happened on the street across the bayou almost every night. On cold nights he could hear the laughter and the shouting from his porch swing.

It was almost Christmas when Bo read his friend's story, so he waited for Gip to come to Carny as he sometimes did at Christmas. But Gip didn't come. Bo's mother reminded him that Gip was married now and had a little girl, and maybe it wasn't as easy for him to visit his grandfather as it had been in the past. And Bo waited for an answer to the letter he had written, but that didn't come either. So he waited for the summer. The last time Gip had come to see him it had been in the summer.

In the summer Bo learned that the Astronauts had flown all the way to the moon. It happened on July 20, but Bo didn't know about it until the next day, when his mother heard it from somebody at the grocery store. Bo made his mother buy a newspaper every day then, until there was no more news about the moon to read. The more he read the more excited he got. And when the paper talked about what the moon was like, as a place, it was exactly as he thought it might be. The only thing that was different was that he had never imagined people actually standing there on the moon looking at it. Bo could imagine what it looked like up close perfectly well. But it worried him because up until now nobody had known about it any better than he. Now that wasn't so any more. When it got dark Bo went out on the porch to see if the moon still looked the same from his place on the swing.

But when he looked, the moon wasn't up. He watched for it until bedtime, but it did not appear. The next day he read everything there was in the paper about the Astronauts and looked for a long time at the Map of the Heavens. But the moon did not appear that night either.

The next day Bo tried to make his mother help him figure out when the moon came up, but she did not know how. He looked at the Map of the Heavens, but that didn't help. The *Almanac* would know, he thought, but he didn't have an *Almanac*. He thought about it for a week, and still the moon didn't come up. Finally he called his mother.

"I know what," Bo roared to her. "The moon goes around the world in twenty-eight days. And the world goes around itself in twenty-four hours."

"Oh," his mother said. "I knew you could do it, Bo. I knew you would get it if you just tried."

"No," Bo said. "Is it twenty-four hours divided by twenty-eight days? Or the other way? How do you do that?"

"I don't know, Bo," his mother said. "You know I could never figure out things like that. We'll just have to ask somebody."

"When Gip comes," Bo said. "He will know." But still the moon did not appear in his part of the sky.

Every night he watched the sky, and thought. One night he noticed that a part of the gutter was beginning to come loose from the edge of the roof. It had edged out a whole inch so that he could see a little slice of the sky between the gutter and the roof. The hedge had grown higher across the side yard, too. He couldn't see as much of the sky as he had before. One night he saw the shadow of a big wasp nest just outside the screen on the corner of the porch. It had grown there as big as his elbow before he had noticed it. Still the moon did not come out.

"I know what," Bo said at last. "Twenty-four is almost the same as twenty-eight. That means the moon comes up a little bit more or a little bit less than an hour from when it came up the day before."

"Oh," his mother said. "You can figure out anything when you put your mind to it, Bo."

"But earlier or later?" Bo said. "From when?"

"When?" his mother said. "Oh, Bo, I meant to tell you what Mrs. Wylie said in the grocery store yesterday. She said the reason the moon hasn't come out is because the Astronauts stole it. She said they packed it up in their space ship and brought it back with them and now the Government is hiding it from the Russians. Now isn't that just the silliest thing you ever heard?"

Bo roared with laughter at that. They both laughed for a long time. Then they sat still looking out at the street lamp which shone through the hedge and at their part of the sky in which the moon had still not appeared. Bo put his feet up on the swing and pulled them tightly under his body. He thought about two men standing by the space craft staring out at a deepening grey plain with huge shadows across it in the near distance.

The next morning Bo read in his *World Atlas* until twelve o'clock. He looked for a long time at the pencil drawing of the Capitol Building in Washington, D. C., by Carpenter, which was opposite the title page. Then he turned to his favorite picture in the whole book, at page 218, entitled "Footbridge at Mostar, Yugoslavia." The book said that Mostar had once been the capitol of all Hercegovina, yet it looked even smaller than Carny, Mississippi. It was one of the most beautiful places he had ever seen.

As best he could tell, it was a photograph that had been painted by hand. He thought no place in this world could have colors like that. Purplish brown buildings leaned against a yellow hill. The windows looked like eyes watching the people down below. The old footbridge was in the center, and underneath it lay the Narenta River, smiling happily. Its color was a whitish blue, bright as robin's eggs. Underneath the picture, it said, "The city derives its name from the unique bridge here built over the Narenta which dates from the 15th or 16th Century, *most* signifying bridge and *star* old. Mostar lies in a narrow valley of wild and rugged beauty.

Situated off the beaten track of tourist travel, the city and its ancient bridge are not visited by the countless throngs of tourists to whom Wien (Vienna), Budapest, and other famous places are familiar ground. Those who are so fortunate to visit Mostar to-day wonder what the picturesque town was like when the 'old bridge' was new, and they find themselves thinking, with Longfellow, 'how many thousands of care-encumbered men, each bearing his burden of sorrow, must have crossed the bridge since then.'"

While Bo was thinking about this the doorbell rang, and when he had lifted himself into his chair and wheeled into the living room there was Gip. He was standing in the doorway with a little girl in his arms, and his wife was there too with a baby boy in her arms. Bo roared with pleasure.

Gip and his family only stayed for a few minutes. They said they had to get back for lunch, and after they had gone Bo remembered that he had forgotten to ask Gip about the moon. There had been so much else to think of.

They had talked about the man who built the monument. Gip said he had heard about it from his grandfather, but that he had used his imagination to write the story. He didn't know who the man was and he had never seen the monument. So Bo told him about Mr. Charlie Connors, and how it was only eight and a half miles up the highway. He told him everything he could, except that he was so excited that even his mother had to ask him to slow down his talk before she could tell them what he said.

After that he wanted Gip to tell him about Napoleon Avenue, in New Orleans. But Gip's wife said they didn't live there any more. She said they lived in Chapel Hill, in North Carolina.

Bo stopped then. North Carolina! He would look it up. Then he thought of what he wanted to ask. "When you wrote the story, did you live on Napoleon Avenue in New Orleans?"

But Gip laughed and said no. "We were in Europe then," he said. "I wrote it while I sat for several afternoons in a café, in Vienna."

Vienna! Bo thought about that. Then he asked, "Where in Vienna?"

Gip thought for a minute. "At the end of a little street called Fasziehergasse." Gip found a piece of paper in his pocket and wrote it down. "Fasziehergasse Zwölf," the paper said, when Bo looked at it.

By suppertime Bo read everything he could find about Vienna, and discovered where Chapel Hill, North Carolina, was on the map. He could not find out about Fasziehergasse Zwölf. He would have to have more books, he thought, and more maps. And he would have to decide about the moon.

"Weren't those children just darling?" his mother said.

The children were too young to be frightened of him, Bo thought. They laughed and smiled at him. He thought about Gip's wife, too. "They were beautiful," he roared at his mother. "They were beautiful."

After supper they sat on the porch swing and looked for the moon. They waited for a long time, but it did not appear. When it was time to go to bed, Bo said, "I know what. If it goes like the sun goes, it must come up almost an hour later every day. At the equator at least."

"Maybe so," his mother said.

"But an hour later from when?" Bo said. Then he saw it. Suddenly it peeked up over the top of the hedge, near the corner of the porch. It was already mostly full.

"Well, there you are," Bo roared at the moon. "Where have you been all this time?" He looked at it more closely then, and it looked just the same as it did before. Just exactly.

The Harp of the Winds

ROBERT CANZONERI

"MAMA, YOU KNOW you can't work in the graveyard," his uncle said again. "It'll be a hundred in the shade, and you out in the sun."

His aunt was washing dishes. She did not turn; her elbows worked beside her thin back. "Let her go," she said. "She won't be satisfied, anyway, until she's buried."

"Pshaw," his grandmother said, as if that answered all argument.

"She's always cared more for the dead than for the living." His aunt's voice had in it the ridge of her nose, the knobs of her cheekbones.

"Come along," his grandmother told him. "Make haste!"

She said things the boy heard nowhere else. Pshaw and Make haste and Shake a leg. He carried the hoe and shovel. She carried two buckets of water; wherever they sloshed, the thick dust of the road rolled up like doodlebugs. He was sweating already, and he would have liked to stay in the shade of the wellhouse, where she had drawn the water hand over hand. His uncle had put in a motor and pump, but she would not use that water. "Pshaw," she would say. "After it goes through that thing?" She had her own way to do whatever came up. Last night when his aunt had been cooking supper, his grandmother suddenly cried, "Here! You don't know how to do that!" She pulled the sack of cornmeal to her, brushing aside the measuring cup and spoons. "Lord a mercy. You can taste those things in the bread." As if to be sure it was really meal, she felt it carefully before scooping up a handful and dumping it into the mixing bowl.

Dust was in the air, settling in the sweat on his arms, lining the creases where his elbows closed. He could feel the grit. His grandmother moved on ahead, stooped, a faded work dress under a wide straw hat. She might have been a chunk of the clay she would soon be hoeing. The whole countryside was clay. The roadside banks were eroded; though they would show blood red when it rained, now they were dry and pale. The barn and, farther along, the empty tenant house were weathered gray and powdered with hot dust. The fields of runty cotton were still, stifling, dusty.

It seemed to the boy that he was always seeing people from behind. His grandmother sloshed farther and farther ahead, ghostly in the blinding haze. "Here!" she cried. "Shake a leg! You'd think the dead lice was dropping off of you."

The boy tried to walk faster. Sweat ran into his eyes; the hoe and the shovel would drag if he did not keep lifting them, and his arms ached. He wondered if he could recognize people the way his grandmother did, by the back of the neck, but her neck was hidden by the brim of her hat.

"Now, Mama," his uncle had said, winking at him, "what do you think the Lord gave people faces for?"

"Hold on!" she said. She seemed always to be hauling people forward or backward to where she was. "Hold on, there! I know what I know."

The boy could see the tops of the pine trees beyond the graveyard. It wasn't much farther. There was no shade at all, but at least he could put down the shovel and the hoe. He heard immediately, clearly, the tinny voice on the Victrola:

So lay down the shovel and the ho-o-o-oe. . . .

His uncle had let him wind it and put the needle on and release the spring.

The pines rose higher and higher, all in a line in somebody's dry pasture, angled off away from the graveyard. Green tufts against the brazen sky, long slender trunks like palm trees. The boy had never seen palm trees, had never seen the ocean, but he knew about them; he had a hunger for them. He would go to the island on a sailing ship with the salt air blowing in his face, and there would be the graceful palm trees curving down a clean white beach with blue-green water nudging softly up the sand, and it would be his place, where he belonged.

"Come along," his grandmother said. A warped gray board was laid across the bottom of the raw ditch. Up the bank were a few green shrubs—boxwoods, she called them—and some wilted flowers. Tall grass and bitterweeds edged into the open graveyard. Faint mounds of weathered dirt or long sunken places stretched like shadows from small markers. His grandfather's grave was the only one covered with grass; it was as green as anything in sight except the high pine tops. Marigolds rimmed it, trying to keep blooming. The headstone was marble with letters chiseled in it:

HE IS NOT DEAD,
BUT SLEEPING.

His grandfather was under there. His grandmother, now hoeing around the flowers, would be put in beside him, right there. She was humming "Beulah Land" as she worked, bent over, her face only a few feet above the upturned face of the grandfather.

The boy walked as casually as he could toward the back of the graveyard, where the markers were mostly boards, and pretended to read the names. His grandfather had been tall and thin. A gentleman, he had heard him called. A Christian gentleman. He could see him coming out of the little bedroom—Granddaddy's room—into the front room where they all sat and talked by the yellow light of kerosene lamps. He could see him laid out for burial on the daybed in the front room, coins on his eyelids, skin drawn along his cheekbones, thin hands folded.

When the sun was halfway up the sky she fancied she could smell the pines, all in a row, straight trunks running cleanly to the high green tops, half a dozen of them, like the Harp of the Winds picture. She raised up, holding her stiff back with one hand, and looked at the pines. Wind through the high needles made the thin constant shhh her mother used to whisper to her when she stirred, just at the edge of sleep.

The Harp of the Winds. It had a good ring to it, like a phrase from the Bible. Her father used to tell about riding horseback, as a young man, all the way to the Mississippi, just to see it, and he had sat in the saddle and looked out over the mighty river and said, "The Father of Waters," and then he turned the horse around and rode back home. She could remember his exact tone, and she used it now aloud: "The Harp of the Winds." It stood there over the grave, over the plot where she would lie.

"You call me, Grandmama?"

She had forgotten about the boy. She bent back to the ground, hearing the shhh of the pines change as her head moved. The pine trunks would have lines of pungent resin binding the bits of rough bark. The Harp of the Winds. When her father was a young man, and the Choctaws were still wild, this had been a forest of pines.

That was why there were no branches until the very top. She could smell the copper, feel the dark, of the big kettle her mother had turned down over her and her brother once when there was an uprising. Now the Indians went to the whitewashed schoolhouse over toward Carthage; they wore old felt hats and cast-off britches and walked silently down the side of the road. Nothing was the way it used to be.

Her hoe scraped cleanly. She had loosened the soil around the marigolds before she watered them, and now she was cutting the few weeds out around the grave. Bare clay. People left and went to the city and watered green lawns with garden hoses, but it wasn't real. The earth is the Lord's. She pinched a bit of the pale dirt between her thumb and forefinger the way people used to take snuff, and then she straightened and touched her tongue to it. Clay soil, just as the Lord put it there.

Off beyond the tall pines, away over past the old Freeny place, she could see other pines. But those were second growth, where the land had been cut over in the first days of the sawmills. The smells came on her all in a rush: the smell of fresh-cut pine logs, ends moist to the touch with good strong sap; smoke from mountainous sawdust piles that glowed in great patches at night; steam from molasses cooking down in crisp air, and thin sweet cane juice right out of the mill, drunk with the foam still on it while the old mule walked his slow blindered round. That was where it all was, right in the soil. Everything grew from it and it took everything back.

When the sun was directly overhead, she rose with an effort from pulling bitterweeds. There was the boy—she had forgotten him again—fallen asleep across the grave of one of the Scott children. "Here, you . . ." She could not sort his name out from among those of her sons and grandsons. "Hsst!" she called, as though shooing a cat. "Hsst! Don't you know not to get on people's graves?"

He watched her put one water bucket into the other and pick up the shovel, leaving the hoe for him. His leg was asleep; he began to limp toward her, hot and dirty, his head full of heat waves. "Respect the dead," she said. He had not meant to lie on a grave. He had a horror that one would cave in with him. The bitter voice of his aunt and the impatient tones of his grandmother had soured his half-sleep like some dream of bees and hot yellowjackets.

A week hadn't seemed so long when he was planning to come here. He had tried picking cotton yesterday, but he had only thirteen pounds when finally his uncle came stepping over the rows to tell him he'd better go in. His grandmother had been out with the chickens, and his aunt had been the only one in the house. She gave him a piece of cold apple pie and a glass of cold milk. She was dark-haired and thin and nervous, and she said, "That's just like him!" about something his uncle had done wrong, and, "She couldn't be happy without some complaint," about his grandmother, but she said these things as if she didn't know any other way to talk. She even smiled at him, her eyes dark and intent, and he noticed before he looked away that her skin was like the clay, eroded and hard with the red drying out of it.

"Make haste," his grandmother told him. "Dinner'll be on the table." She stopped, suddenly, buckets in one hand and shovel in the other, looking past the grandfather's grave. "She won't be buried here," she said. "She wants to go back to her own."

The boy wanted to ask who, but he couldn't. Their voices began knocking together in his head, his aunt saying, "You won't have to put up with me much longer. Take comfort in that!" And his grandmother, "Pshaw! How you talk," as she swished her hands around in the dishpan and wiped them on her apron. "Here, now, dry that skillet good or give it to me." Once, wakened in the night to the thick half-words of his grandmother's snoring, he had heard his aunt's voice from another room, like a rope stretched so tight it was hard: "Out all hours of the night! I've sat here . . ." And his uncle, stung: "You didn't need to wait up." And she: "Me with no idea where on earth . . ." Something clunked, his uncle's watch on the bureau, maybe. "I was just playing a few games of pool." And his aunt: "I'll see to it Otis Shepherd gets that pool table out of his store if it's the last thing I do!" The town had only two stores and another one boarded up, the way his grandfather's office was. He walked there by himself every day; after the blinding sun he would stand a long time before he could see to pick out which candy he wanted. The showcase was grimy, too, and there was no light in the store. "Everything all right?" Mr. Shepherd would ask him every time, not getting up from his cane-bottom chair.

The boy realized that he was standing very still. There was no wind at all, and beyond his grandmother the tall pines were as still as he was. "I reckon it's her right," his grandmother said.

He had said almost nothing since he had been there, and now he heard himself say only one hesitant word: "She . . .?"

It was enough. His grandmother went on from there. "She won't last long. Pshaw, a body could tell that by looking, without the doctor."

What the boy wanted to say, he couldn't get into his head as words. He would try later to think what it was, but to ask weren't you supposed to be nice to dying people was not enough. He found himself talking, anyway, fast, as he did sometimes when it would seem he had to get it all out while somebody was there to hear. He told her he had a tree at home, only it was an oak, and he could just barely reach the bottom limb, but it was easy to climb the rest of the way, and he would sit in the very top and hold on tight when the wind was blowing, and he could see a long, long way. He stopped, overcome with a craving for the high leaves, the sway of the wind, the rough woody bark hugged hard against his shirtless ribs.

She was not looking at him, but he could not help seeing her face, wrinkled with age, mottled. And now suddenly it drew together, and behind the thin-rimmed glasses her eyes shut tight and tears squeezed out the sides. Her jaw trembled for a moment, and then she took a breath and she was in motion again. "Shake a leg!" she said. "Her beans taste greasy unless they're hot off the stove."

The boy could not turn away from the pines. He felt as if he were being baked into the ground.

"Come along," his grandmother said behind him. "Come along, now." And then she must have stopped and looked, too, because in a minute she said, "The Harp of the Winds." It was as if she had recognized him by the back of his neck. He heard in her voice what he himself was feeling, and the ache in his chest began to seem unbearable.

"I want to go home," he said. "I don't want to go back there."

"Hush!" his grandmother cried. "Be ashamed! You don't know what you're talking about!"

When he turned, she was crossing the weathered board back to the road, plodding steadily on, blending again with the dust, and there was nothing for him to do but follow.

FROM

The Chain in the Heart

HUBERT CREEKMORE

GEORGE SAT FRETFULLY on the shady back step. Miss Lucy's boy, Lincoln, had gone off somewhere without him and without telling him. Lincoln went to school five days a week, but afternoons and Saturdays and Sundays they spent their spare time inventing ways to amuse themselves. Sometimes, in the winter, they took the BB gun Lincoln's father had given him and went across the swamps and wet-brown woodlands to shoot at birds and squirrels. In summer, they played marbles, roamed the woods or the town, built dens of packing crates salvaged from behind stores and even put together a frail wagon in which they pulled the clean laundry to the Murchison home every Saturday. Sometimes Albert Rosson, the son of the white landlord who lived at the entrance of the Row, would join them, but never for very long.

Years ago, when they were really children and not entering their teens as now, he and Lincoln played in the road with a group from all along the Row—hopscotch, jump-rope and tag. Every month or so their games would suffer a hideous rout when a wagon driven by a red-faced balding man headed into the lane. "Here come the shit-wagon!" they'd scream and all tear down the hill to romp under the trees at the bottom until the impervious driver had cleaned out the privies and departed to another section of the town.

Today must be Monday, George thought, because a sheet full of dirty clothes from the Murchisons' bulged at the kitchen door where his father had dropped them. If he stayed home now his mother and Cora would have him hauling water from the faucet to the wash kettle, or bringing wood for the fire under it. He hurried around the house as they passed through it.

In front he jumped up on the warped, split boards of the porch, undecided what to do. The sound of water splashing into the pot came from the back yard. He wriggled his toes up and down on the boards warming in the high summer sun. He could see no possibilities for fun—only the swing with broken slats, the lard cans of sword fern and purple cane, the grubby yard, the field across the road, the pasture at the foot of the hill, the seven porches below him—sun-drowned, deserted, dotted with pails of geranium and petunia. A hum of life seeped from the dingy windows behind which the families hid from the heat.

He heard his mother singing as she rounded the house for another bucket of water, and skipped swiftly down the yard path, lined with zinnias and ruddy cockscombs, and down the sagging steps in the clay bank. He leaped from the wooden walk and crouched in the ditch below. Nothing moved along the powdery road but the wind shaking the trees and grass. Something pressed against the ball of his bare foot and he shifted backward and peeped down at the offending pebble.

Then he almost ignored the marble, for the fine dust had dulled its shine except for one bright arc that caught the sun. He picked it up, a brown and scarlet agate, leaving a tiny round cup in the firm bed, and rubbed off the dirt. He put it into his mouth and rolled his tongue over it to clean it more thoroughly. Having wiped the saliva on his pants, he curled his fingers around the smooth ball and with eyes squinted made an imaginary shot. He must have knocked two out of the ring. Then he let it lie, as if on display, in the palm of his left hand. His only aggie. Three other marbles he drew from his pocket and held in his right hand: two glassies and a steely.

The steely he had won from Albert Rosson two weeks ago. Albert had hated to give it up to a Negro, but he had been the one who wanted to play for keeps. He had a lot of marbles—all kinds and all pretty—but then his father could give him money. George had to win his, playing for keeps; or swap a lot of chalkies for one glassy; or, whenever he had a penny, buy one of those marshmallows that had a marble in the center.

For a long time he sat on the edge of the ditch waiting for Lincoln to appear. The sickly leaves of stinkweeds at the corner began to droop in the heat. Some ants crawled from a nest and bit his ankles. He rubbed his feet along the ground, the dust making a pleasant friction.

Miss Lucy came out, a puffy feathered hat set on her piled-up hair, her high-buttoned shoes darting from under the flaring bell skirt, and started down the walk. She never let her son have such fine clothes as she wore, because, she said, he'd mess them up.

Just the same, Lincoln had sort of fine ideas in his head. One day he had stuck his pale arm alongside George's and said, "Look what light skin I got. See? Mr. Theo gi' me that. It's a lot better'n yo ole black skin."

"Yo mama's got black skin, sort of," George had said heatedly, never having thought about skin color before.

As she passed him, Miss Lucy looked down at George and in a luxurious voice asked, "What you settin in the ditch fo?"

"When's Lincoln comin back?" he returned moodily.

"He be back soon," she called over her shoulder, and in a few moments her handsome figure had passed beyond the paling fence of Rosson's back yard and out of sight.

George could wait no longer; he must show the aggie to someone. He climbed the bank and went to the back yard where, from a big iron pot propped on stones over a wood fire, wisps of sudsy steam drifted upward in the smoke. Henry sat in a hickory chair leaning against the house in the thin line of shade that the mounting sun ate away. Annie was sorting the white clothes from the dyed before dropping them into the hot water. George held out his fist to his father and opened it to show the marble, as some gracious oyster might open on a pearl. "Look what I found," he said.

"Where'd you find that, George?" asked Henry, taking it between his thick fingers.

"Out in the ditch," he answered.

Hearing them, Annie dropped the clothes on a bench and came over to see what it was. "Oh, ain't it pretty!" she exclaimed.

"It's a aggie," said George proudly.

"Wouldn't a string of em look pretty roun my neck," said Annie, holding it to the light.

Henry let out a whoop of laughter. "Marbles roun yo neck! If you cain't do no better'n marbles, you better crawl off an die."

"They cost fifteen cents in town," George said defensively. "Ain't it any good?" He reached for it fearfully.

Annie gave it back and kicked at Henry as she went away giggling. "Shut yo mouth," she grumbled, "'F you'd get up an stir aroun, you might be able to buy me some beads sometime." She poked the clothes in the pot with a long stick and wiped her forearm across the sweat that crept down from the edge of her hair.

"Yeah, it's a good aggie, George," said Henry. "You take good care of it."

George left them, feeling his spiritual property restored, and walked the path through the weeds to the front yard. "Lincoln" he called to Miss Lucy's house next door. "Lincoln!" But there was no answer. He wandered down the steps, into the road, slapping the four marbles in his pocket, and listening to their pleasant chink. Walking slowly up the road, he built up a frail rhythm, striking the marbles between each hushed footfall. Opposite the dense odorous chinaberry trees of Mr. Rosson's yard, George hesitated.

Before he could decide whether or not he should show Albert the aggie and maybe lose it playing for keeps, even before Lincoln had seen it, a voice called, "Hey," through the fence. George answered guardedly. The white skin and tan hair raised a strange barrier without his knowing why. Albert seemed always to want to boss everything, and usually his mother yelled for him to come in before they finished their games. At first, an animal shyness overwhelmed him, as it did when white people came down the Row asking questions about where folks lived. He and his friends would stand fascinated, repelled and speechless. In earlier years, they had simply turned and run silently away, followed by the naked youngest tots. Now they could not show such indignity, but still they choked on words. So before Albert he waited timidly and silent.

"What you doin?" asked Albert, holding on to the fence palings.

"Nothin," said George.

"Le's play something," suggested Albert.

"What?"

"Marbles, huh?"

Suspicion and fear stirred in George. He couldn't answer.

"Wanna play marbles?" asked the white boy again.

"I don know."

"Aw, I bet you ain't got none," sneered Albert. "You never do have more than one or two."

"I got more'n that now," said George with assurance.

"How many? Aw, you ain't got none."

"Yes, I have, too. I got four."

"I got eighteen."

George's face relaxed wistfully, but he remembered he had never before had four marbles and one of them an aggie.

"Le's play for keeps," said Albert.

"Unh-unh. Not fo keeps."

"Scared you'll lose, ain't you?"

"I'm not either. I just got a new marble I want a show to Lincoln." He wished he hadn't said it now. He put his hand into the pocket and let the marbles drop from his fingers one by one.

"Where'd you get it?"

"Pa give it to me. It's a aggie."

"Where'd your pa get money to give you a aggie?"

"Well, he did. See?" George drew out the marbles and held up the aggie.

"Come on over here," said Albert. "I can't see that far."

George jumped the ditch and stood on the walk by the fence. Albert held out his hand.

"See?" said George, his confidence rising with his delight, as he continued to hold it up. He put the other marbles back in his pocket.

"Lemme hold it. I can't see it that way."

After a moment's hesitation, George laid it in the outstretched palm. He saw it drawn through the fence and held under Albert's freckled nose. Horror rose up in him almost simultaneously with Albert's cry.

"This is *my* aggie!"

George choked; his lips fell open and fluttered.

"Where'd you get it?" screamed Albert. "This is my aggie. I lost it a week ago."

"It's not yours," George managed to say. Hopefully he repeated the old magical incantation, "Finders keepers, losers weepers."

"Maybe I didn't lose it. Maybe you stole it," said Albert.

"I didn't. I found it in the ditch."

"Said yo pa give it to you."

"Well, I found it. It's mine. Give it back."

"Try an get it."

"I found it. That makes it mine." George advanced to the fence and put his hand through. "Gimme, now—please. It's mine."

"Here's all I'll give you," said Albert and spat a meager spray into George's hand.

George jerked his hand away and stood taut as if the earth were falling away and he trying to hold himself up by sheer volition. He blinked his black wide eyes. He must get his aggie back; Lincoln hadn't seen it and would never believe him. He wiped his hand on the back of his pants and swallowed the choke in his throat.

"Come on, Albert. Finders keepers."

"You're loser now," taunted Albert. "Don't you wish you had it?"

He stuck his hand out with the marble cupped in it. George grabbed for it, but the hand was snatched back.

Albert began chanting, "Don't you wish you had it? Don't you wish you had it?" and poking his hand between the palings at intervals as he walked toward the house. George rushed forward at each emergence of the hand and always missed it. Exasperation had smothered his voice, and he ran in silent spurts for the tantalizing arm.

Near the corner of the house, the fence was interrupted by a wide opening where Mr. Rosson's carriage went in to the stable. The gate across the opening was off one hinge and had been turned against the fence. When George saw Albert nearing this gateway, he realized the opportunity and darted through it, catching Albert before he could escape into the house.

He clung to Albert's arm and tried to unclench his fingers from the marble. Albert gripped it tightly and kept saying, "Turn loose. Turn loose." Then he leaned over and bit George's fingers. George howled and released him, but his eyes burned with fury.

"Gimme my aggie," he said in a low voice.

"I'll show you how to jump on me, you ole nigger," said Albert.

"What'll you do?" challenged George.

They stood glaring at each other.

"I'll show you."

"Gimme my aggie."

"I'm gonna knock yo brains out."

"I don want a fight, Albert. Now gimme my aggie an le's quit. You know it's mine."

"I'll fix you. Wait'll my dad comes home." The words seemed to give him courage, and he shouted suddenly, "Now get out of here. Get out." Then in a triumphant tone, "Get out, you ole blue-gum!"

He turned to go into the house, but George leaped on him. "I want my aggie," he cried, and began pounding Albert with his fists.

Albert struck out, not very forcibly, then backed away, flailing the air with one arm, while he put the marble into his pocket with the other. He let out two shouts for his mother, but did not dare turn to see if she appeared.

George felt insane with courage from the time he first struck out his fists and felt the impact on Albert. It meant regaining the treasure. He knew nothing of any punches he may have received and did not know that he was forcing his opponent backward. When Albert fell down, George straddled his stomach and beat his face and poured dirt into his eyes and mouth and rubbed it in. Albert screamed and spluttered, while George reached into his pocket and found the aggie. Then he jumped up and ran out of the yard, hearing the voice of Mrs. Rosson, who had just come out on the back porch, shouting and asking what was the matter.

George ran home, panting and trembling, the marble clutched in his hand, sweaty and dirty and bloody. He opened his hand to look, when he got to the weather-beaten porch, and satisfaction filled him at the sight. But in such a disheveled and agitated state, he could not meet his family. With a furtive glance toward the Rosson home, he went down the road as far as the sycamore tree at the bottom of the hill. Here he sat down and dug his toes into the sand and finally calmed his turmoil.

He was modeling a sand track to roll the marbles in, when Lincoln came up and had to be told about the fight. Though he admired the prize with proper enthusiasm, Lincoln only stared when he heard the story, and moaned, "Oh . . . oh . . ." George showed his bitten fingers, still hurting a little and caked with red sand about the wounds.

They decided to spend the afternoon together and skip their slim noon meal. As the sun sank, they emerged from the pastures and woods and sauntered toward their homes. At Aunt Martha's shack they lingered, to grow accustomed to the sense of family authority; but since Aunt Martha, knowing nothing of their actions, wouldn't think to scold them, they ventured on homeward more easily.

It was the pale time of a summer afternoon, before the long twilight, when the Negroes usually sat on their porches behind the ranked lard cans of fern and geranium. Today not one was outside taking his rest in the cool of the day. George and Lincoln, laughing and talking, did not notice. They parted unapprehensively before Miss Lucy's house, and Lincoln was on his own porch before George had climbed his steps.

Then the sound burst out fiercely and paralyzed them both. Neither could have said why they had not heard it sooner, for it was loud enough to have been heard at some distance in the stillness. Now it rooted them momentarily where they stood.

"Well, where is he? He stole it and I'm gonna get it back if I have to kill every nigger in this block!"

George's heart quaked. A dizziness came over him as he faltered on the steps. Lincoln gave one terrified look at his chum and popped inside the door. George heard his father's voice earnestly and quietly trying to explain that the marble had been found in the ditch.

He kept telling himself to run away. If he weren't there, they couldn't harm him. Why must Mr. Rosson demand the marble anyway? Run away, he said; but no action came from his urging. Something required him to stay and show he was right. He had found the marble. It was his; he knew that.

Then he heard his mother's voice saying "Here e is." She was in the doorway. "I was jus comin to look fo you. Come on in, George. Yo pa wants to see you."

He thought it was a long time before he could make his legs move. But his mother didn't speak again, and he was able to get inside the door.

Mr. Rosson, his face and bald head flushed and perspiring, was standing in the center of the room. He was nervous with anger, and almost charged at George when he entered. The boy shrank against Annie's hip and she put her arm about his shoulder.

"Well—gimme that marble, you little black bastard," Mr. Rosson shouted.

George recoiled fearfully. Mr. Rosson was a big man, with piggish eyes sunken into the bulging flesh of his cheeks, and a thick fold over the neck of his collarless shirt.

There was no answer in his father's eyes when George looked there. Mr. Rosson came closer and held out a fat hand.

"If you was old enough, they'd hang you for fightin a white boy. I ought to throw all of you out." His breath wheezed. He jerked at the belt that sagged under the weight of his belly. "Where's the marble?"

"It's mine. I found it—in the ditch," George gasped.

"You stole it from my boy. Albert told me so."

"I didn't."

Mr. Rosson whacked his palm against the boy's face. "Shut up," he cried. "Don't call me a liar!"

Annie was holding George by the shoulders, but he swung his feet and kicked the white man's trousers. She pulled her son aside and guarded him, and Henry stepped forward quickly.

"Please, Mr. Rosson," Henry was saying, "please. I'll get it. Please. 'Scuse him. He's jus a little boy."

Mr. Rosson cursed and shivered. But before he had brushed his trousers and decided what to do, he heard Henry say in a quiet and unnatural voice, "George—gimme that marble."

With a bewildered ache, George held it out and watched his father give it to Mr. Rosson. The big pinkish man examined the marble and grunted and looked angrily at each of them.

"You all better watch your step," Mr. Rosson growled. "You're a bad set of niggers and you're gonna get in trouble. I ought to throw you out now, but you owe me a month's rent, so I'll try to overlook it. An don't let me catch your boy stealin any more."

Henry followed him to the door. "Yessuh. Thank you, suh; thank you," he was saying automatically.

Mr. Rosson turned. "I ought to brought Albert down so he could apologize to im. Maybe he better apologize to me, and I'll tell Albert."

"Yessuh," said Henry. "Come 'ere, George. 'Pologize to Mr. Rosson fo fightin Albert."

George moved nearer but didn't say anything.

"Say you're sorry," said Henry.

George trusted his father. He had given him the marble, but his father had given it away. He wasn't sorry and didn't understand why his father let the man call him a thief and thanked him for it, and wanted him to say he was sorry. Henry spoke to him again, and he looked up. Maybe this would work it out all right, though; older men should know what was best.

"Say you're sorry bout Albert."

George wasn't sure he could do it. Then in the silence he heard his voice faintly. "I'm sorry."

"Well, that's better," said Mr. Rosson.

But George felt like crying. As soon as the words were out, he itched all over and his face puckered in shame. He went back to Annie and pressed his face against her side. But he could not feel any tears come. There was too much anger.

Mr. Rosson was still speaking. "But if I ever hear of that brat laying hands on a white child again, I'll whip im to death. It's better'n he deserves now. He ought to know a nigger can't never hit a white man."

The sickening, chaining words wrapped around his soul: Never. Never. Then that was what he had felt and hadn't realized about Albert. Albert knew it all the time. That was why Lincoln bragged so much about the light color of his skin.

"Yessir, thank you," Henry went on. "He's sho a bad boy. We got a tend to im."

George turned a suffering face toward his father. He was betrayed and forsaken.

Mr. Rosson walked away in the deepening twilight. George wrenched out of Annie's embrace and went to the kitchen door where he sat on the single step and stared at the gray clouds on the horizon. He heard the high voice of Columbus suddenly asking, "He gone now?" and Cora answering softly, "Yeh, it's all right, Columbus. Go on an play." They must have been crouching in a corner of the other room while Mr. Rosson's storming filled the house.

In a few moments, Henry came through the kitchen and stood in the doorway above George. The boy did not look up. He was afraid his father would touch him. But Henry sat on the floor inside the threshold, with his son's back by his shoulder. Darkness sank down over the land.

Then, miraculously, the bitter flower of understanding unfolded in George, and his anger went. There came something deeper than what had seemed broken trust and a lost aggie.

A scratch of matches and a stream of light came from the room.

Soon a voice rose in song far down the Row.

"Pa," said George, peacefully. "I whupped im."

"Yeah," said Henry.

In the black of night their lips spread into tranquil smiles.

Antaeus

Borden Deal

This was during the wartime, when lots of people were coming North for jobs in factories and war industries, when people moved around a lot more than they do now and sometimes kids were thrown into new groups and new lives that were completely different from anything they had ever known before. I remember this one kid, T. J. his name was, from somewhere down South, whose family moved into our building during that time. They'd come North with everything they owned piled into the back seat of an old-model sedan that you wouldn't expect could make the trip, with T. J. and his three younger sisters riding shakily atop the load of junk.

Our building was just like all the others there, with families crowded into a few rooms, and I guess there were twenty-five or thirty kids about my age in that one building. Of course, there were a few of us who formed a gang and ran together all the time after school, and I was the one who brought T. J. in and started the whole thing.

The building right next door to us was a factory where they made walking dolls. It was a low building with a flat, tarred roof that had a parapet all around it about head-high, and we'd found out a long time before that no one, not even the watchman, paid any attention to the roof because it was higher than any of the other buildings around. So my gang used the roof as a headquarters. We could get up there by crossing over to the fire escape from our own roof on a plank and then going on up. It was a secret place for us, where nobody else could go without our permission.

I remember the day I first took T. J. up there to meet the gang. He was a stocky, robust kid with a shock of white hair, nothing sissy about him except his voice—he talked different from any of us, and you noticed it right away. But I liked him anyway, so I told him to come on up.

We climbed up over the parapet and dropped down on the roof. The rest of the gang were already there.

"Hi," I said. I jerked my thumb at T. J. "He just moved into the building yesterday."

He just stood there, not scared or anything, just looking, like the first time you see somebody you're not sure you're going to like.

"Hi," Blackie said. "Where you from?"

"Marion County," T. J. said.

We laughed. "Marion County?" I said. "Where's that?"

He looked at me like I was a stranger, too. "It's in Alabama," he said, like I ought to know where it was.

"What's your name?" Charley said.

"T. J.," he said, looking back at him. He had pale blue eyes that looked washed-out, but he looked directly at Charley, waiting for his reaction. He'll be all right, I thought. No sissy in him . . . except that voice. Who ever talked like that?

"T. J.," Blackie said. "That's just initials. What's your real name? Nobody in the world has just initials."

"I do," he said. "And they're T. J. That's all the name I got."

His voice was resolute with the knowledge of his rightness, and for a moment no one had anything to say. T. J. looked around at the rooftop and down at the black tar under his feet. "Down yonder where I come from," he said, "we played out in the woods. Don't you-all have no woods around here?"

"Naw," Blackie said. "There's the park a few blocks over, but it's full of kids and cops and old women. You can't do a thing."

T. J. kept looking at the tar under his feet. "You mean you ain't got no fields to raise nothing in? No watermelons or nothing?"

"Naw," I said scornfully. "What do you want to grow something for? The folks can buy everything they need at the store."

He looked at me again with that strange, unknowing look. "In Marion County," he said, "I had my own acre of cotton and my own acre of corn. It was mine to plant ever' year."

He sounded like it was something to be proud of, and in some obscure way it made the rest of us angry. "Heck!" Blackie said. "Who'd want to have their own acre of cotton and corn? That's just work. What can you do with an acre of cotton and corn?"

T. J. looked at him. "Well, you get part of the bale offen your acre," he said seriously. "And I fed my acre of corn to my calf."

We didn't really know what he was talking about, so we were more puzzled than angry; otherwise, I guess, we'd have chased him off the roof and wouldn't let him be part of our gang. But he was strange and different, and we were all attracted by his stolid sense of rightness and belonging, maybe by the strange softness of his voice contrasting our own tones of speech into harshness.

He moved his foot against the black tar. "We could make our own field right here," he said softly, thoughtfully. "Come spring we could raise us what we want to . . . watermelons and garden truck and no telling what all."

"You'd have to be a good farmer to make these tar roofs grow any watermelons," I said. We all laughed.

But T. J. looked serious. "We could haul us some dirt up here," he said. "And spread it out even and water it, and before you know it, we'd have us a crop in here." He looked at us intently. "Wouldn't that be fun?"

"They wouldn't let us," Blackie said quickly.

"I thought you said this was you-all's roof," T. J. said to me. "That you-all could do anything you wanted up here."

"They've never bothered us," I said. I felt the idea beginning to catch fire in me. It was a big idea, and it took a while for it to sink in, but the more I thought about it, the better I liked it. "Say," I said to the gang, "he might have something there. Just make us a regular roof garden, with flowers and grass and trees and everything. And all ours, too," I said. "We wouldn't let anybody up here except the ones we wanted to."

"It'd take a while to grow trees," T. J. said quickly, but we weren't paying any attention to him. They were all talking about it suddenly, all excited with the idea after I'd put it in a way they could catch hold of it. Only rich people had roof gardens, we knew, and the idea of our own private domain excited them.

"We could bring it up in sacks and boxes," Blackie said. "We'd have to do it while the folks weren't paying any attention to us. We'd have to come up to the roof of our building and then cross over with it."

"Where could we get the dirt?" somebody said worriedly.

"Out of those vacant lots over close to school," Blackie said. "Nobody'd notice if we scraped it up."

I slapped T. J. on the shoulder. "Man, you had a wonderful idea,"

I said, and everybody grinned at him, remembering he had started it. "Our own private roof garden."

He grinned back. "It'll be ourn," he said. "All ourn." Then he looked thoughtful again. "Maybe I can lay my hands on some cotton seed, too. You think we could raise us some cotton?"

We'd started big projects before at one time or another, like any gang of kids, but they'd always petered out for lack of organization and direction. But this one didn't . . . somehow or other T. J. kept it going all through the winter months. He kept talking about the watermelons and the cotton we'd raise, come spring, and when even that wouldn't work, he'd switch around to my idea of flowers and grass and trees, though he was always honest enough to add that it'd take a while to get any trees started. He always had it on his mind, and he'd mention it in school, getting them lined up to carry dirt that afternoon, saying in a casual way that he reckoned a few more weeks ought to see the job through.

Our little area of private earth grew slowly. T. J. was smart enough to start in one corner of the building, heaping up the carried earth two or three feet thick, so that we had an immediate result to look at, to contemplate with awe. Some of the evenings T. J. alone was carrying earth up to the building, the rest of the gang distracted by other enterprises or interests, but T. J. kept plugging along on his own, and eventually we'd all come back to him again, and then our own little acre would grow more rapidly.

He was careful about the kind of dirt he'd let us carry up there, and more than once he dumped a sandy load over the parapet into the areaway below because it wasn't good enough. He found out the kinds of earth in all the vacant lots for blocks around. He'd pick it up and feel it and smell it, frozen though it was sometimes, and then he'd say it was good growing soil or it wasn't worth anything and we'd have to go on somewhere else.

Thinking about it now, I don't see how he kept us at it. It was hard work, lugging paper sacks and boxes of dirt all the way up the stairs of our own building, keeping out of the way of the grownups so they wouldn't catch on to what we were doing. They probably wouldn't have cared, for they didn't pay much attention to us, but we wanted to keep it secret anyway. Then we had to go through the trap door to our roof, teeter over a plank to the fire escape, then climb two or three stories to the parapet and drop down onto the roof. All that for a small pile of earth that sometimes didn't seem worth the effort. But T. J. kept the vision bright within us, his words shrewd and calculated toward the fulfillment of his dream; and he worked harder than any of us. He seemed driven toward a goal that we couldn't see, a particular point in time that would be definitely marked by signs and wonders that only he could see.

The laborious earth just lay there during the cold months, inert and lifeless, the clods lumpy and cold under our feet when we walked over it. But one day it rained, and afterward there was a softness in the air and the earth was alive and giving again with moisture and warmth. That evening T. J. smelled the air, his nostrils dilating with the odor of the earth under his feet.

"It's spring," he said, and there was a gladness rising in his voice that filled us all with the same feeling. "It's mighty late for it, but it's spring. I'd just about decided it wasn't never gonna get here at all."

We were all sniffing at the air, too, trying to smell it the way that T. J. did, and I can still remember the sweet odor of the earth under our feet. It was the first time in my life that spring and spring earth had meant anything to me. I looked at T. J. then, knowing in a faint way the hunger within him through the toilsome winter months, knowing the dream that lay behind his plan. He was a new Antaeus, preparing his own bed of strength.

"Planting time," he said. "We'll have to find us some seed."

"What do we do?" Blackie said. "How do we do it?"

"First we'll have to break up the clods," T. J. said. "That won't be hard to do. Then we plant the seed, and after a while they come up. Then you got you a crop." He frowned. "But you ain't got it raised yet. You got to tend it and hoe it and take care of it, and all the time it's growing and growing while you're awake and while you're asleep. Then you lay it by when it's growed and let it ripen, and then you got you a crop."

"There's those wholesale seed houses over on Sixth," I said. "We could probably swipe some grass seed over there."

T. J. looked at the earth. "You-all seem mighty set on raising some grass," he said. "I ain't never put no effort into that. I spent all my life trying not to raise grass."

"But it's pretty," Blackie said. "We could play on it and take sunbaths on it. Like having our own lawn. Lots of people got lawns."

"Well," T. J. said. He looked at the rest of us, hesitant for the first time. He kept on looking at us for a moment. "I did have it in mind to raise some corn and vegetables. But we'll plant grass."

He was smart. He knew where to give in. And I don't suppose it made any difference to him really. He just wanted to grow something, even if it was grass.

"Of course," he said, "I do think we ought to plant a row of watermelons. They'd be mighty nice to eat while we was a-laying on that grass."

We all laughed. "All right," I said. "We'll plant us a row of watermelons."

Things went very quickly then. Perhaps half the roof was covered with the earth, the half that wasn't broken by ventilators, and we swiped pocketfuls of grass seed from the open bins in the wholesale seed house, mingling among the buyers on Saturdays and during the school lunch hour. T. J. showed us how to prepare the earth, breaking up the clods and smoothing it and sowing the grass seed. It looked rich and black now with moisture, receiving of the seed, and it seemed that the grass sprang up overnight, pale green in the early spring.

We couldn't keep from looking at it, unable to believe that we had created this delicate growth. We looked at T. J. with understanding now, knowing the fulfillment of the plan he had carried alone within his mind. We had worked without full understanding of the task, but he had known all the time.

We found that we couldn't walk or play on the delicate blades, as we had expected to, but we didn't mind. It was enough just to look at it, to realize that it was the work of our own hands, and each evening the whole gang was there, trying to measure the growth that had been achieved that day.

One time a foot was placed on the plot of ground . . . one time only, Blackie stepping onto it with sudden bravado. Then he looked at the crushed blades, and there was shame in his face. He did not do it again. This was his grass, too, and not to be desecrated. No one said anything, for it was not necessary.

T. J. had reserved a small section for watermelons, and he was still trying to find some seed for it. The wholesale house didn't have any watermelon seed, and we didn't know where we could lay our hands on them. T. J. shaped the earth into mounds, ready to receive them, three mounds lying in a straight line along the edge of the grass plot.

We had just about decided that we'd have to buy the seed if we were to get them. It was a violation of our principles, but we were anxious to get the watermelons started. Somewhere or other, T. J. got his hands on a seed catalogue and brought it one evening to our roof garden.

"We can order them now," he said, showing us the catalogue. "Look!"

We all crowded around, looking at the fat, green watermelons pictured in full color on the pages. Some of them were split open, showing the red, tempting meat, making our mouths water.

"Now we got to scrape up some seed money," T. J. said, looking at us. "I got a quarter. How much you-all got?"

We made up a couple of dollars between us, and T. J. nodded his head. "That'll be more than enough. Now we got to decide what kind to get. I think them Kleckley Sweets. What do you-all think?"

He was going into esoteric matters beyond our reach. We hadn't even known there were different kinds of melons. So we just nodded our heads and agreed that yes, we thought the Kleckley Sweets too.

"I'll order them tonight," T. J. said. "We ought to have them in a few days."

Then an adult voice said behind us: "What are you boys doing up here?"

It startled us, for no one had ever come up here before, in all the time we had been using the roof of the factory. We jerked around and saw three men standing near the trap door at the other end of the roof. They weren't policemen, or night watchmen, but three men in plump business suits, looking at us. They walked toward us.

"What are you boys doing up here?" the one in the middle said again.

We stood still, guilt heavy among us, levied by the tone of voice, and looked at the three strangers.

The men stared at the grass flourishing behind us. "What's this?" the man said. "How did this get up here?"

"Sure is growing good, ain't it?" T. J. said conversationally. "We planted it."

The men kept looking at the grass as if they didn't believe it. It was a thick carpet over the earth now, a patch of deep greenness startling in the sterile industrial surroundings.

"Yes, sir," T. J. said proudly. "We toted that earth up here and planted that grass." He fluttered the seed catalogue. "And we're just fixing to plant us some watermelon."

The man looked at him then, his eyes strange and faraway. "What do you mean, putting this on the roof of my building?" he said. "Do you want to go to jail?"

T. J. looked shaken. The rest of us were silent, frightened by the authority of his voice. We had grown up aware of adult authority, of policemen and night watchmen and teachers, and this man sounded like all the others. But it was a new thing to T. J.

"Well, you wan't using the roof," T. J. said. He paused a moment and added shrewdly, "So we just thought to pretty it up a little bit."

"And sag it so I'd have to rebuild it," the man said sharply. He turned away, saying to a man beside him, "See that all that junk is shoveled off by tomorrow."

"Yes, sir," the man said.

T. J. started forward. "You can't do that," he said. "We toted it up here, and it's our earth. We planted it and raised it and toted it up here."

The man stared at him coldly. "But it's my building," he said. "It's to be shoveled off tomorrow."

"It's our earth," T. J. said desperately. "You ain't got no right!"

The men walked on without listening and descended clumsily through the trap door. T. J. stood looking after them, his body tense with anger, until they had disappeared. They wouldn't even argue with him, wouldn't let him defend his earth-rights.

He turned to us. "We won't let 'em do it," he said fiercely. "We'll stay up here all day tomorrow and the day after that, and we won't let 'em do it."

We just looked at him. We knew that there was no stopping it. He saw it in our faces, and his face wavered for a moment before he gripped it into determination.

"They ain't got no right," he said. "It's our earth. It's our land. Can't nobody touch a man's own land."

We kept on looking at him, listening to the words but knowing that it was no use. The adult world had descended on us even in our richest dream, and we knew there was no calculating the adult world, no fighting it, no winning against it.

We started moving slowly toward the parapet and the fire escape, avoiding a last look at the green beauty of the earth that T. J. had planted for us . . . had planted deeply in our minds as well as in our experience. We filed slowly over the edge and down the steps to the plank, T. J. coming last, and all of us could feel the weight of his grief behind us.

"Wait a minute," he said suddenly, his voice harsh with the effort of calling. We stopped and turned, held by the tone of his voice, and looked up at him standing above us on the fire escape.

"We can't stop them?" he said, looking down at us, his face strange in the dusky light. "There ain't no way to stop 'em?"

"No," Blackie said with finality. "They own the building."

We stood still for a moment, looking up at T. J., caught into inaction by the decision working in his face. He stared back at us, and his face was pale and mean in the poor light, with a bald nakedness in his skin like cripples have sometimes.

"They ain't gonna touch my earth," he said fiercely. "They ain't gonna lay a hand on it! Come on."

He turned around and started up the fire escape again, almost running against the effort of climbing. We followed more slowly, not knowing what he intended. By the time we reached him, he had seized a board and thrust it into the soil, scooping it up and flinging it over the parapet into the areaway below. He straightened and looked us squarely in the face.

"They can't touch it," he said. "I won't let 'em lay a dirty hand on it!"

We saw it then. He stooped to his labor again and we followed, the gusts of his anger moving in frenzied labor among us as we scattered along the edge of earth, scooping it and throwing it over the parapet, destroying with anger the growth we had nurtured with such tender care. The soil carried so laboriously upward to the light and the sun cascaded swiftly into the dark areaway, the green blades of grass crumpled and twisted in the falling.

It took less time than you would think . . . the task of destruction is infinitely easier than that of creation. We stopped at the end, leaving only a scattering of loose soil, and when it was finally over, a stillness stood among the group and over the factory building. We looked down at the bare sterility of black tar, felt the harsh texture of it under the soles of our shoes, and the anger had gone out of us, leaving only a sore aching in our minds like over-stretched muscles.

T. J. stood for a moment, his breathing slowing from anger and effort, caught into the same contemplation of destruction as all of us. He stooped slowly, finally, and picked up a lonely blade of grass left trampled under our feet and put it between his teeth, tasting it, sucking the greenness out of it into his mouth. Then he started walking toward the fire escape, moving before any of us were ready to move, and disappeared over the edge while we stared after him.

We followed him, but he was already halfway down to the ground, going on past the board where we crossed over, climbing down into the areaway. We saw the last section swing down with his weight, and then he stood on the concrete below us, looking at the small pile of anonymous earth scattered by our throwing. Then he walked across the place where we could see him and disappeared toward the street without glancing back, without looking up to see us watching him.

They did not find him for two weeks. Then the Nashville police caught him just outside the Nashville freight yards. He was walking along the railroad track; still heading south, still heading home.

As for us, who had no remembered home to call us . . . none of us ever again climbed the escape-way to the roof.

The Gift

Louis Dollarhide

HOW MANY DAYS, she wondered, had she sat like this, watching the cold brown water inch up the dissolving bluff. She could just faintly remember the beginning of the rain, driving in across the swamp from the south and beating against the shell of her house. Then the river itself started rising, slowly at first until at last it paused as if to turn back. From hour to hour it slithered up creeks and ditches and poured over low places. In the night, while she slept, it claimed the road and surrounded her so that she sat alone, her boat gone, the house like a piece of drift lodged on its bluff. Now even against the tarred planks of the supports the waters touched. And still they rose.

As far as she could see, to the treetops where the opposite banks had been, the swamp was an empty sea, awash with sheets of rain, the river lost somewhere in its vastness. Her house with its boat bottom had been built to ride just such a flood, if one ever came, but now it was old. Maybe the boards underneath were partly rotted away. Maybe the cable mooring the house to the great live oak would snap loose and let her go turning downstream, the way her boat had gone.

No one could come now. She could cry out but it would be no use, no one would hear. Down the length and breadth of the swamp others were fighting to save what little they could, maybe even their lives. She had seen a whole house go floating by, so quiet she was reminded of sitting at a funeral. She thought when she saw it she knew whose house it was. It had been bad seeing it drift by, but the owners must have escaped to higher ground. Later, with the rain and darkness pressing in, she had heard a panther scream upriver.

Now the house seemed to shudder around her like something alive. She reached out to catch a lamp as it tilted off the table by her bed and put it between her feet to hold it steady. Then creaking and groaning with effort the house struggled up from the clay, floated free, bobbing like a cork, and swung out slowly with the pull of the river. She gripped the edge of the bed. Swaying from side to side, the house moved to the length of its mooring. There was a jolt and a complaining of old timbers and then a pause. Slowly the current released it and let it swing back, rasping across its resting place. She caught her breath and sat for a long time feeling the slow pendulous sweeps. The dark sifted down through the incessant rain, and, head on arm, she slept holding on to the bed.

Sometime in the night the cry awoke her, a sound so anguished she was on her feet before she was awake. In the dark she stumbled against the bed. It came from out there, from the river. She could hear something moving, something large that made a dredging, sweeping sound. It could be another house. Then it hit, not head on but glancing and sliding down the length of her house. It was a tree. She listened as the branches and leaves cleared themselves and went on downstream, leaving only the rain and the lappings of the flood, sounds so constant now that they seemed a part of the silence. Huddled on the bed, she was almost asleep again when another cry sounded, this time so close it could have been in the room. Staring into the dark, she eased back on the bed until her hand caught the cold shape of the rifle. Then crouched on the pillow, she cradled the gun across her knees. "Who's there?" she called.

The answer was a repeated cry, but less shrill, tired sounding, then the empty silence closing in. She drew back against the bed. Whatever was there she could hear it moving about on the porch. Planks creaked and she could distinguish the sounds of objects being knocked over. There was a scratching on the wall as if it would tear its way in. She knew now what it was, a big cat, deposited by the uprooted tree that had passed her. It had come with the flood, a gift.

Unconsciously she pressed her hand against her face and along her tightened throat. The rifle rocked across her knees. She had never seen a panther in her life. She had heard about them from others and had heard their cries, like suffering, in the distance. The cat was scratching on the wall again, rattling the window by the door. As long as she guarded the window and kept the cat hemmed in by the wall and water, caged, she would be all right. Outside, the animal paused to rake his claws across the rusted outer screen. Now and then, it whined and growled.

When the light filtered down through the rain at last, coming like another kind of dark, she was still sitting on the bed, stiff and cold. Her arms, used to rowing on the river, ached from the stillness of holding the rifle. She had hardly allowed herself to move for fear any sound might give strength to the cat. Rigid, she swayed with the movement of the house. The rain still fell as if it would never stop. Through the gray light, finally, she could see the rain-pitted flood and far away the cloudy shape of drowned treetops. The cat was not moving now. Maybe he had gone away. Laying the gun aside she slipped off the bed and moved without a sound to the window. It was still there, crouched at the edge of the porch, staring up at the live oak, the mooring of her house, as if gauging its chances of leaping to an overhanging branch. It did not seem so frightening now that she could see it, its coarse fur napped into twigs, its sides pinched and ribs showing. It would be easy to shoot it where it sat, its long tail whipping back and forth. She was moving back to get the gun when it turned around. With no warning, no crouch or tensing of muscles, it sprang at the window, shattering a pane of glass. She fell back, stifling a scream, and taking up the rifle, she fired through the window. She could not see the panther now, but she had missed. It began to pace again. She could glimpse its head and the arch of its back as it passed the window.

Shivering, she pulled back on the bed and lay down. The lulling constant sound of the river and the rain, the penetrating chill, drained away her purpose. She watched the window and kept the gun ready. After waiting a long while she moved again to look. The panther had fallen asleep, its head on its paws, like a housecat. For the first time since the rains began she wanted to cry, for herself, for all the people, for everything in the flood. Sliding down on the bed, she pulled the quilt around her shoulders. She should have got out when she could, while the roads were still open or before her boat was washed away. As she rocked back and forth with the sway of the house a deep ache in her stomach reminded her she hadn't eaten. She couldn't remember for how long. Like the cat, she was starving. Easing into the kitchen, she made a fire with the few remaining sticks of wood. If the flood lasted she would have to burn the chair, maybe even the table itself. Taking down the remains of a smoked ham from the ceiling, she cut thick slices of the brownish red meat and placed them in a skillet. The smell of the frying meat made her dizzy. There were stale biscuits from the last time she had cooked and she could make some coffee. There was plenty of water.

While she was cooking her food, she almost forgot about the cat until it whined. It was hungry too. "Let me eat," she called to it, "and then I'll see to *you*." And she laughed under her breath. As she hung the rest of the ham back on its nail the cat growled a deep throaty rumble that made her hand shake.

After she had eaten, she went to the bed again and took up the rifle. The house had risen so high now it no longer scraped across the bluff when it swung back from the river. The food had warmed her. She could get rid of the cat while light still hung in the rain. She crept slowly to the window. It was still there, mewing, beginning again to move about the porch. She stared at it a long time, unafraid. Then without thinking what she was doing, she laid the gun aside and started around the edge of the bed to the kitchen. Behind her the cat was moving, fretting. She took down what was left of the ham and making her way back across the swaying floor to the window she shoved it through the broken pane. On the other side there was a hungry snarl and something like a shock passed from the animal to her. Stunned by what she had done, she drew back to the bed. She heard the sounds of the panther tearing at the meat. The house rocked around her.

The next time she awoke she knew at once that everything had changed. The rain had stopped. She felt for the movement of the house but it no longer swayed on the flood. Drawing her door open, she saw through the torn screen a different world. The house was resting on the bluff where it always had. A few feet down, the river still raced on in a torrent, but it no longer covered the few feet between the house and the live oak. And the cat was gone. Leading from the porch to the live oak and doubtless on into the swamp were tracks, indistinct and already disappearing in the soft mud. And there on the porch, gnawed to whiteness, was what was left of the ham.

On the Lake

Ellen Douglas

LATE SUMMER IN Philippi is a deadly time of year. Other parts of the United States are hot, it is true, but not like the lower Mississippi Valley. Here the shimmering heat—the thermometer standing day after day in the high nineties and the nights breathless and oppressive—is compounded, even in a drought, by the saturated air. Thunderheads, piling up miles high in the afternoon sky, dwarf the great jet planes that fly through them. The air is heavy with moisture, but for weeks in July and August there is no rain.

In July, Lake Okatukla begins to fall. The lake, named from a meandering bayou that flows into it on the Arkansas side, bounds the town of Philippi on the west. It was once a horseshoe-shaped bend of the Mississippi, but its northern arm is blocked off from the river now by the Nine-Mile Dike, built years ago when a cut-through was made to straighten the river's course. The southern arm of the lake is still a channel into the Mississippi, through which pass towboats pushing strings of barges loaded with gravel, sand, cotton, scrap iron, soybeans, fertilizer, or oil.

In August, the lake drops steadily lower, and at the foot of the levee mud flats begin to appear around the rusty barges that serve as Philippi's municipal terminal and around the old stern-wheeler moored just above them that has been converted into the Philippi Yacht Club. The surface of the mud, covered with discarded beer cans, broken bottles, and tangles of baling wire, cracks and scales like the skin of some scrofulous river beast, and a deathlike stench pervades the hot, still air. But the lake is deep and broad—more than a mile wide at the bend, close to the town—and fifty feet out from the lowest mud flat the steely surface water hides unplumbed black depths.

Late in August, if rain falls all along the course of the Mississippi, there will be a rise of the lake as the river backs into it. The mud flats are covered again. The trees put on pale spikes of new growth. The sandbars are washed clean. Mud runnels stream from the rain-heavy willow fronds, and the willows lift their heads. The fish begin to bite. For a week or two, from the crest of the rise, when the still water begins to clear, dropping the mud that the river has poured into the lake, until another drop has begun to expose the mud flats, Lake Okatukla is beautiful—a serene, broad wilderness of green trees and bright water, bounded at the horizon by the green range of levee sweeping in a slow curve against the sky. Looking down into the water, one can see through drifting forests of moss the quick flash of frightened bream, the shadowy threat of great saw-toothed gar. In the town, there has been little to do for weeks but wait out the heat. Only a few Negroes have braved the stench of the mud flats for the sake of a slimy catfish or a half-dead bream. After the rise, however, fishermen are out again in their skiffs, casting for bass around the trunks of the big willow trees or fishing with cane poles and minnows for white perch along the fringe willows. Family parties picnic here and there along the shore. The lake is big—twelve miles long, with dozens of curving inlets and white sandy islands. Hundreds of fishermen can spend their day trolling its shores and scarcely disturb one another.

One morning just after the August rise a few years ago, Anna Glover set out with two of her three sons, Ralph and Steve, and one of Ralph's friends, Murray McCrae, for a day on the lake. Her oldest son, who at fifteen considered himself too old for such family expeditions, and her husband, Richard, an architect, for whom summer was the busiest season of the year, had stayed behind. It was early, and the waterfront was deserted when Anna drove over the crest of the levee. She parked the car close to the Yacht Club mooring float, where the Glovers kept their fishing skiff tied up, and began to unload the gear—life jackets for the children, tackle box, bait, poles, gas can, and Skotch cooler full of beer, soft drinks, and sandwiches. She had hardly begun when she thought she heard someone shouting her name. "Miss Anna! Hey, Miss Anna!" She looked around, but, seeing the whole slope of the levee empty and no one on the deck of the Yacht Club except Gaines Williamson, the Negro bartender, she called the children back from the water's edge, toward which they had run as soon as the car stopped, and began to distribute the gear among them to carry down to the float.

Anna heaved the heavy cooler out of the car without much effort and untied the poles from the rack on the side of the car, talking as she worked. At thirty-six, she looked scarcely old enough to have three half-grown sons. Her high, round brow was unlined, her brown eyes were clear, and her strong, boyish figure in shorts and a tailored shirt looked almost like a child's. She wore her long sandy-brown hair drawn into a twist on the back of her head. Ralph and his friend Murray were ten; Steve was seven. Ralph's straight nose, solemn expression, and erect, sway-backed carriage made him look like a small preacher. Steve was gentler, with brown eyes like his mother's, fringed by a breathtaking sweep of dark lashes. They were beautiful children, or so Anna thought, for she regarded them with the most intense, subjective passion. Murray was a slender, dark boy with a closed face and a reserve that to Anna seemed impregnable. They were picking up the gear to move it down to the Yacht Club float when they all heard someone calling, and turned around.

"Ralph! Hey there, boys! Here I am, up here!" the voice cried.

"It's Estella, Mama," Ralph said. "There she is, over by the barges."

"Hi, Estella!" Steve shouted. He and Ralph put down the poles and cooler and ran along the rough, uneven slope of the levee, jumping over the iron rings set in the concrete to hold the mooring lines and over the rusty cables that held the terminal barges against the levee.

"Come on, Murray," Anna said. "Let's go speak to Estella. She's over there fishing off the ramp."

Sitting on the galvanized-iron walkway from the levee to the terminal, her legs dangling over the side of the walkway ten feet above the oily surface of the water, was Estella Moseby, a huge and beautiful Negro woman who had worked for the Glover family since the children were small. She had left them a few months before to have a child and had stayed home afterward, at James', her husband's, insistence, to raise her own family. It was the first time that Anna or the children had seen her since shortly after the child was born. Estella held a long cane pole in one hand and with the other waved toward Anna and the children. Her serene, round face was golden brown, the skin flawless even in the cruel light of the August sun, her black hair pulled severely back to a knot on her neck, her enormous dark eyes and wide mouth smiling with pleasure at the unexpected meeting. As the children approached, she drew her line out of the water and pulled herself up by the cable that served as a side rail for the walkway. The walk creaked under her shifting weight. She was fully five feet ten inches tall—at least seven inches taller than Anna—and loomed above the heads of the little group on the levee like an amiable golden giantess, her feet set wide apart to support the weight that fleshed her big frame. Her gaily flowered house dress, printed with daisies and morning-glories in shades of blue, green, and yellow, took on the very quality of her appearance, as if she were some tropical fertility goddess robed to receive her worshippers.

"Lord, Estella," Anna said. "Come on down. We haven't seen you in ages. How have you been?"

"You see me," Estella said. "Fat as ever." She carefully wrapped her line around her pole, secured the hook in the cork, and came down from her high perch to join the others on the levee. "Baby or no baby, I got to go fishing after such a fine rain," she said.

"We're going on a picnic," Steve said.

"Well, isn't that fine," Estella said. "Where is your brother?"

"Oh, he thinks he's too old to associate with us any more," Anna said. "He *scorns* us. How is the baby?"

The two women looked at each other with the shy pleasure of old friends long separated who have not yet fallen back into the easy ways of their friendship.

"Baby's fine," Estella said. "My cousin Bernice is nursing him. I said to myself this morning, 'I haven't been fishing since I got pregnant with Lee Roy. I *got* to go fishing.' So look at me. Here I am sitting on this ramp since seven this morning and no luck."

Steve threw his arms around her legs. "Estella, why don't you come *work* for us again?" he said. "We don't like *anybody* but you."

"I'm coming, honey," she said. "Let me get these kids up a little bit and I'll be back."

"Estella, why don't you go fishing with us today?" Ralph said. "We're going up to the north end of the lake and fish all day."

"Yes, come on," Anna said. "Come on and keep me company. You can't catch any fish around this old barge, and if you do they taste like fuel oil. I heard the bream are really biting in the upper lake—over on the other side, you know, in the willows."

Estella hesitated, looking out over the calm and shining dark water. "I ain't much on boats," she said. "Boats make me nervous."

"Oh, come on, Estella," Anna said. "You know you want to go."

"Well, it's the truth, I'm not catching any fish sitting here. I got two little no-'count bream on my stringer." Estella paused, and then she said, "*All* y'all going to fish from the boat? I'll crowd you."

"We're going to find a good spot and fish off the bank," Anna said. "We're already too many to fish from the boat."

"Well, it'll be a pleasure," Estella said. "I'll just come along. Let me get my stuff." She went up on the walkway again and gathered up her tackle where it lay—a brown paper sack holding sinkers, floats, hooks, and line, and her pole and a coffee can full of worms and dirt.

"I brought my gig along," Ralph said as they all trudged across the levee toward the Yacht Club. "I'm going to gig one of those great big buffalo or a gar or something."

"Well, if you do, give it to me, honey," Estella said. "James is really crazy about buffalo the way I cook it." Pulling a coin purse out of her pocket, she turned to Anna. "You reckon you might get us some beer in the Yacht Club? A nice can of beer 'long about eleven o'clock would be good."

"I've got two cans in the cooler," Anna said, "but maybe we'd better get a couple more." She took the money and, while Murray and Ralph brought the skiff around from the far side of the Yacht Club, where it was tied up, went into the bar and bought two more cans of beer. Estella and Steve, meanwhile, carried the fishing gear down to the float.

Gaines Williamson, a short, powerfully built man in his forties, followed Anna out of the bar and helped stow their gear in the little boat. The children got in first and then helped Estella in. "Lord, Miss Estella," he said, "you too big for this boat, and that's a fact." He stood back and looked down at her doubtfully, sweat shining on his face and standing in droplets on his shaven scalp.

"I must say it's none of your business," Estella said.

"We'll be all right, Gaines," Anna said. "The lake's smooth as glass."

The boys held the skiff against the float while Anna got in, and they set out, cruising slowly up the lake until they found a spot that Estella and Anna agreed looked promising. Here, on a long, clean sandbar fringed with willows, they beached the boat. The children stripped off their life jackets, pulled off the jeans they wore over their swimming trunks, and began to wade.

"You children wade here in the open water," Estella ordered.

"Don't go over yonder on the other side of the bar, where the willows are growing. You'll bother the fish."

She and Anna stood looking around. Wilderness was all about them. As far as they could see on either side of the lake, not even a road ran down to the water's edge. While they watched, two white herons dragged themselves awkwardly into the air and flapped away, long legs trailing. The southern side of the sandbar, where they had beached the boat, had no trees growing on it, but the edge of the northern side, which curved in on itself and out again, was covered with willows. Here the land was higher. Beyond a low hummock crowned with cottonwood trees, Anna and Estella discovered a pool, twenty-five yards long and nearly as wide, that had been left behind by the last rise, a few days before. Fringe willows grew all around it, and the fallen trunk of a huge cottonwood lay with its roots exposed on the ground, its whole length stretched out into the still water of the pool.

"Here's the place," Estella said decidedly. "Shade for us, and fringe willows for the fish. And looka there." She pointed to the fallen tree. "If there aren't any fish under *there* . . ." They stood looking down at the pool, pleased with their find.

"I'll go get our things," Estella said. "You sit down and rest yourself, Miss Anna."

"I'll come help you."

The two women unloaded the boat, and Anna carried the cooler up the low hill and left it in the shade of one of the cottonwood trees. Then they gathered the fishing tackle and took it over to a shady spot by the pool. In a few minutes, the children joined them, and Anna passed out poles and bait. The bream were rising to crickets, and she had brought a wire cylinder basket full of them.

"You boys scatter out, now," Anna said. "There's plenty of room for everybody, and if you stay too close together you'll hook each other."

Estella helped Steve bait his hook, then baited her own and dropped it into the water as close as she could get it to the trunk of the fallen tree. Almost as soon as it reached the water, her float began to bob and quiver.

"Here we go," she said in a low voice. "Take it under, now. Take it under." She addressed herself to the business of fishing with such delight and concentration that Anna stopped in the middle of rigging a pole to watch her. Even the children, intent on finding places for themselves, turned back to see Estella catch a fish. She stood over the pool like a priestess at her altar, all expectation and willingness, holding the pole lightly, as if her fingers could read the intentions of the fish vibrating through line and pole. Her bare arms were tense, and she gazed down into the still water. A puff of wind made the leafy shadows waver and tremble on the pool, and the float rocked deceptively. Estella's arms quivered with a jerk begun and suppressed. Her flowery dress flapped around her legs, and her skin shone with sweat and oil where the sunlight struck through the leaves across her forehead and down one cheek.

"Not yet," she muttered. "*Take* it." The float bobbed and went under. "Aaah!" She gave her line a quick, short jerk to set the hook; the line tightened, the long pole bent, and she swung a big bream out onto the sand. The fish flopped off the hook and down the slope toward the water; she dropped the pole and dived at it, half falling. Ralph, who had been watching, was ahead of her, shouting with excitement, grabbing up the fish before it could flop back into the pool, and putting it into Estella's hands, careful to avoid the sharp dorsal fin.

"Look, boys, look!" she cried happily. "Just look at him!" She held out the big bream, as wide and thick as her hand, marked with blue around the gills and orange on its swollen belly. The fish twisted and gasped in her hand while she got the stringer. She slid the metal end of the stringer through one gill and out the mouth, secured the other end to an exposed root of the fallen tree, and dropped the fish into the water, far enough away so that the bream's thrashing would not disturb their fishing spot.

"Quick now, Miss Anna," she said. "Get your line in there. I bet this pool is full of bream. Come on, boys, we're going to catch some fish today."

Anna baited her hook and dropped it in. The children scattered around the pool to their own places. In an hour, the two women had caught a dozen bream and four small catfish, and the boys had caught six or seven more bream. Then for ten minutes no one got a bite, and the boys began to lose interest. A school of minnows flashed into the shallow water at Anna's feet, and she pointed them out to Estella. "Bream are gone," she said. "They've quit feeding, or we wouldn't see any minnows."

Anna laid down her pole and told the children they could swim. "Come on, Estella," she said. "We can sit in the shade and watch them and have a beer, and then in a little while we can move to another spot."

"You aren't going to let them swim in this old lake, are you, Miss Anna?" Estella said.

"Sure. The bottom's nice and sandy here," Anna said. "Murray, your mama said you've got to keep your life preserver on if you swim." She said to Estella in a low voice, "He's not much of a swimmer. He's the only one I would worry about."

The children splashed and tumbled fearlessly in the water, Ralph and Steve popping up and disappearing, sometimes for so long that Anna, in spite of what she had said, would begin to watch anxiously for their blond heads.

"I must say, I don't see how you stand it," Estella said. "That water scares me."

"Nothing to be scared of," Anna said. "They're both good swimmers, and so am I. I could swim across the lake and back, I bet you, old as I am."

She fished two beers out of the Skotch cooler, opened them, and gave one to Estella. Then she sat down with her back against a cottonwood tree, gave Estella a cigarette, took one herself, and leaned back with a sigh. Estella sat down on a fallen log, and the two women smoked and drank their beer in silence for a few minutes. The breeze ran through the cottonwoods, shaking the leaves against each other. "I love the sound of the wind in a cottonwood tree," Anna said. "Especially at night when you wake up and hear it outside your window. I remember there was one outside the window of my room when I was a little girl, so close to the house I could climb out the window and get into it." The breeze freshened and the leaves pattered against each other. "It sounds cool," Anna said, "even in August."

"It's nice," Estella said. "Like a nice, light rain."

"Well, tell me what you've been doing with yourself," Anna said. "When are you going to move into your new house?"

"James wants to keep renting it out another year," Estella said. "He wants us to get ahead a little bit. And you know, Miss Anna, if I can hang on where I am we'll be in a good shape. We can rent that house until we finish paying for it, and then when we move we can rent the one we're in, and, you know, we own that little one next door, too. With four children now, we got to think of the future. And I must say, with all his old man's ways, James is a good provider. He looks after his own. So I go along with him. But, Lord, I can't stand it much longer. We're falling all over each other in that little tiny place. Kids under my feet all day. No place to keep the baby quiet. And in rainy weather! It's worse than a circus. I've gotten so all I do is yell at the kids. It would be a rest to go back to work."

"I wish you *would* come back to work," Anna said.

"No use talking about it," Estella said. "James says I've got to stay home at least until Lee Roy gets up to school age. And you can see for yourself I'd be paying out half what I made to get somebody to keep mine. But I'll tell you, my nerves are tore up."

"It takes a while to get your strength back after a baby," Anna said.

"Oh, I'm strong enough," Estella said. "It's not that." She pulled a stalk of Johnson grass and began to chew it thoughtfully. "I've had something on my mind," she said, "something I've been meaning to tell you ever since the baby came, and I haven't seen you by yourself—"

Anna interrupted her. "Look at the fish, Estella," she said. "They're really kicking up a fuss."

There was a wild, thrashing commotion in the water by the roots of the cottonwood tree where Estella had tied the stringer.

Estella watched a minute. "Lord, Miss Anna," she said, "something's after those fish. A turtle or something." She got up and started toward the pool as a long, dark, whiplike shape flung itself out of the water, slapped the surface, and disappeared.

"Hey," Anna said, "it's a snake! A snake!"

Estella looked around for a weapon and hastily picked up a short, heavy stick and a rock from the ground. Moving lightly and easily in spite of her weight, she ran down to the edge of the water, calling over her shoulder, "I'll scare him off. I'll chunk him. Don't you worry." She threw the rock into the churning water, but it had no effect. "Go, snake. Leave our fish alone." She stood waving her stick threateningly over the water.

Anna came down to the pool now, and they both saw the whiplike form again. Fearlessly, Estella whacked at it with her stick.

"Keep back, Estella," Anna said. "He might bite you. Wait a minute and I'll get a longer stick."

"Go, snake!" Estella shouted furiously, confidently. "What's the matter with him? He won't go off. Go, you crazy snake!"

Now the children heard the excitement and came running across the beach and over the low hill where Estella and Anna had been sitting, to see what was happening.

"A snake, a snake!" Steve screamed. "He's after the fish. Come on, y'all! It's a big old snake after the fish."

The two older boys ran up. "Get 'em out of the water, Mama," Ralph said. "He's going to eat 'em."

"I'm scared he might bite me," Anna said. "Keep back. He'll go away in a minute." She struck at the water with the stick she had picked up.

Murray looked the situation over calmly. "Why don't we gig him?" he said to Ralph.

Ralph ran down to the boat and brought back the long, barb-pointed gig. "Move, Estella," he said. "I'm gonna gig him." He struck twice at the snake and missed.

"Estella," Anna said, "I saw his head. He can't go away. He's swallowed one of the fish. He's caught on the stringer." She shuddered with disgust. "What are we going to do?" she said. "Let's throw away the stringer. We'll never get him off."

"All them beautiful fish! No, *Ma'am,*" Estella said. "Here, Ralph, he can't bite us if he's swallowed a fish. I'll untie the stringer and get him up on land, and then you gig him."

"I'm going away," Steve said. "I don't want to watch." He crossed the hill and went back to the beach, where he sat down alone and began to dig a hole in the sand.

Ralph, wild with excitement, danced impatiently around Estella while she untied the stringer.

"Be calm, child," she said. She pulled the stringer out of the water and dropped it on the ground. "Now!"

The snake had indeed tried to swallow one of the bream on the stringer. Its jaws were stretched so wide as to look dislocated; its body was distended behind the head with the half-swallowed meal, and the fish's head could still be seen protruding from its mouth. The snake, faintly banded with slaty black on a brown background, was a water moccasin.

"Lord, it's a cottonmouth!" Estella cried as soon as she had the stringer out on land, where she could see the snake.

A thrill of horror and disgust raised the hair on Anna's arms. The thought of the helpless fish on the stringer sensing its enemy's approach, and then of the snake, equally and even more grotesquely helpless, filled her with revulsion. "Throw it away," she commanded. And then the thought of the stringer with its living burden of fish and snake struggling and swimming away into the lake struck her as even worse. "No!" she said. "Go on. Kill the snake, Ralph."

Ralph paid no attention to his mother but stood with the long gig poised, looking up at Estella for instructions.

"Kill him," Estella said. "Now."

He drove the gig into the snake's body behind the head and pinned it to the ground, where it coiled and uncoiled convulsively, wrapping its tail around the gig and then unwrapping it and whipping it across the sand.

Anna mastered her horror as well as she could with a shake of her head. "Now what?" she said calmly.

Estella got a knife from the tackle box, held the dead but still writhing snake down with one big foot behind the gig on its body and the other on its tail, squatted, and deftly cut off the fish's head where it protruded from the gaping, fanged mouth. Then she worked the barbed point of the gig out of the body, picked the snake up on the point, and stood holding it away from her.

Ralph whirled around with excitement and circled Estella twice. "We've killed a snake," he chanted. "We've killed a snake. We've killed a snake."

"Look at it wiggle," Murray said. "It keeps on wiggling even after it's dead."

"Yeah, a snake'll wiggle like that for an hour sometimes, even with its head cut off," Estella said. "Look out, Ralph." She swept the gig forward through the air and threw the snake out into the pool, where it continued its aimless writhing on the surface of the water. She handed Ralph the gig and stood watching the snake for a few minutes, holding her hands away from her sides to keep the blood off her clothes. Then she bent down by the water's edge and washed the blood from her hands. She picked up the stringer, dropped the fish into the water, and tied the stringer to the root of the cottonwood. "There!" she said. "I didn't have no idea of throwing away all them—*those* beautiful fish. James would've skinned me if he ever heard about it."

Steve got up from the sand now and came over to his mother. He looked at the wiggling snake, and then he leaned against his mother without saying anything, put his arms around her, and laid his head against her side.

Anna stroked his hair with one hand and held him against her with the other. "It was a moccasin, honey," she said. "They're poison, you know. You have to kill them."

"I'm hungry," Ralph said. "Is it time to eat?"

Anna shook her head, gave Steve a pat, and released him. "Let me smoke a cigarette first and forget about that old snake. Then we'll eat."

Anna and Estella went back to the shade on the hill and settled themselves once more, each with a fresh can of beer and a cigarette. The children returned to the beach.

"I can do without snakes," Anna said. "Indefinitely."

Estella was still breathing hard. "I don't mind killing no snake," she said happily.

"I never saw anything like that before," Anna said. "A snake getting caught on a stringer, I mean. Did you?"

"Once or twice," Estella said. "And I've had 'em get after my stringer plenty of times."

"I don't see how you could stand to cut the fish's head off," Anna said, and shivered.

"Well, somebody had to."

"Yes, I suppose I would have done it if you hadn't been here." She laughed. "*Maybe.* I was mighty tempted to throw the whole thing away."

"I'm just as glad I wasn't pregnant," Estella said. "I'm glad it didn't happen while I was carrying Lee Roy. I would have been *helpless.*"

"You might have had a miscarriage," Anna said. She laughed again, still nervous, wanting to stop talking about the snake but not yet able to, feeling somehow that there was more to be said. "Please don't have any miscarriages on fishing trips with me," she went on. "I can do without that, too."

"Miscarriage!" Estella said. "That's not what I'm talking about. And that reminds me, what I was getting ready to tell you when we saw the snake. You know, I said I had something on my mind?"

"Uh-huh."

"You remember last summer when you weren't home that day, and that kid fell out of the tree in the yard, and all?"

"How could I forget it?" Anna said.

"You remember you spoke to me so heavy about it? Why didn't I stay out in the yard with him until his mama got there, instead of leaving him laying on the ground like that, nobody with him but Ralph, and I told you I couldn't go out there to him—couldn't look at that kid with his leg broke, and all—and you didn't understand why?"

"Yes, I remember," Anna said.

"Well, I wanted to tell you I was *blameless*," Estella said. "I didn't want you to know it at the time, but I was pregnant. I *couldn't* go out there. It might have *marked* my child, don't you see? I might have bore a cripple."

"Oh, Estella! You don't believe that kind of foolishness, do you?" Anna said.

"*Believe* it? I've seen it happen," Estella said. "I know it's true." She was sitting on the fallen log, so that she towered above Anna, who had gone back to her place on the ground, leaning against the tree. Now Estella leaned forward with an expression of intense seriousness on her face. "My aunt looked on a two-headed calf when she was carrying a child," she said, "and her child had six fingers on one hand and seven on the other."

Anna hitched herself up higher, then got up and sat down on the log beside Estella. "But that was an accident," she said. "A coincidence. Looking at the calf didn't have anything to do with it."

Estella shook her head stubbornly. "This world is a mysterious place," she said. "Do you think you can understand everything in it?"

"No," Anna said. "Not everything. But I don't believe in magic."

"All this world is full of mystery," Estella repeated. "You got to have respect for what you don't understand. There are times to be brave and times when you go down helpless in spite of all. Like that snake. You were afraid of that snake."

"I thought he might bite me," Anna said. "And besides, it was so horrible the way he was caught."

But Estella went on as if she hadn't heard. "You see," she said, "there are things you overlook. Things, like I was telling you about my aunt, that are *true*. My mother in her day saw more wonders than that. She knew more than one that sickened and died of a spell. And this child with the fingers, I know about him for a fact. I lived with them when I was teaching school. I lived in the house with that kid. So I'm not taking any chances."

"But I thought you had lost your head and got scared because he was hurt," Anna said. "When the little boy broke his leg, I mean. I kept thinking it wasn't like you. That's what really happened, isn't it?"

"No," Estella said. "It was like I told you."

Anna said no more, but sat quiet a long time, lighting another cigarette and smoking calmly, her face expressionless. But her thoughts were in a tumult of exasperation, bafflement, and outrage. She tried unsuccessfully to deny, to block out, the overriding sense of the difference between herself and Estella, borne in on her by this strange conversation so foreign to their quiet, sensible friendship. She had often thought, with pride both in herself and in Estella, what an accomplishment their friendship was, knowing how much delicacy of feeling, how much consideration and understanding they had both brought to it. And now it seemed to her that it was this very friendship, so carefully nurtured for years, that Estella had unwittingly attacked. With a few words, she had put between them all that separated them, all the dark and terrible past. In the tumult of Anna's feelings there rose a queer, long-forgotten memory of a nurse she had once had as a child—the memory of a brown hand thrust out at her, holding a greasy black ball of hair combings. "You see, child, I saves my hair. I ain't never th'owed away a hair of my head."

"Why?" she had asked.

"Bad luck to th'ow away combings. Bad luck to lose any part of yourself in this old world. Fingernail parings, too. I gathers them up and carries them home and burns them. And I sits by the fire and watches until every last little bitty hair is turned plumb to smoke."

"But why?" she had asked again.

"Let your enemy possess one hair of your head and you will be in his power," the nurse had said. She had thrust the hair ball into her apron pocket, and now, in the memory, she seemed to be brushing Anna's hair, and Anna remembered standing restive under her hand, hating, as always, to have her hair brushed.

"Hurry up," she had said. "Hurry up. I got to go."

"All right, honey. I'm through." The nurse had given her head one last lick and then, bending toward her, still holding her arm while she struggled to be off and outdoors again, had thrust a dark, brooding face close to hers, had looked at her for a long, scary moment, and had laughed. "I saves your combings, too, honey. You in my power."

With an effort, Anna drew herself up short. She put out her cigarette, threw her beer can into the lake, and stood up. "I reckon we better fix some lunch," she said. "The children are starving."

By the time they had finished lunch, burned the discarded papers, thrown the bread crusts and crumbs of potato chips to the birds, and put the empty soft-drink bottles back in the cooler, it had begun to look like rain. Anna stood gazing thoughtfully into the sky. "Maybe we ought to start back," she said. "We don't want to get caught in the rain up here."

"We're not going to catch any more fish as long as the wind is blowing," Estella said.

"We want to swim some more," Ralph said.

"You can't go swimming right after lunch," Anna said. "You might get a cramp. And it won't be any fun to get caught in the rain. We'd better call it a day." She picked up one of the poles and began to wind the line around it. "Come on, kids," she said. "Let's load up."

They loaded their gear into the skiff and dropped the stringer full of fish in the bottom. Anna directed Murray and Steve to sit in the bow, facing the stern. Estella got in cautiously and took the middle seat. Anna and Ralph waded in together, pushed the skiff off the sandbar, and then got into the stern.

"You all got your life jackets on?" Anna said, glancing at the boys. "That's right."

Ralph pulled on the recoil-starter rope until he had got the little motor started, and they headed down the lake. The heavily loaded skiff showed no more than eight inches of freeboard, and as they cut through the choppy water, waves sprayed over the bow and sprinkled Murray and Steve. Anna moved the tiller and headed the skiff in closer to the shore. "We'll stay close in going down," she said. "Water's not so rough in here. And then we can cut across the lake right opposite the Yacht Club."

Estella sat still in the middle of the skiff, her back to Anna, a hand on each gunwale, as they moved steadily down the lake, rocking with the wind-rocked waves. "I don't like this old lake when it's windy," Estella said. "I don't like no windy water."

When they reached a point opposite the Yacht Club, where the lake was a little more than a mile wide, Anna headed the skiff into the rougher open water. The wind, however, was still no more than a stiff breeze, and the skiff was a quarter of the way across the lake before Anna began to be worried. Spray from the choppy waves was coming in more and more often over the bow; Murray and Steve were drenched, and an inch of water sloshed in the bottom of the skiff. Estella had not spoken since she had said "I don't like no windy water." She sat perfectly still, gripping the gunwales with both hands, her paper sack of tackle in her lap, her worm can on the seat beside her. Suddenly a gust of wind picked up the paper sack and blew it out of the boat. It struck the water and floated back to Anna, who reached out, picked it up, and dropped it by her own feet. Estella did not move, although the sack brushed against her face as it blew out. She made no attempt to catch it. She's scared, Anna thought. She's so scared she didn't even see it blow away. And Anna was frightened herself. She leaned forward, picked up the worm can from the seat beside Estella, dumped out the worms and dirt, and tapped Estella on the shoulder. "Here," she said. "Why don't you bail some of the water out of the bottom of the boat, so your feet won't get wet?"

Estella did not look around, but reached over her shoulder, took the can, and began to bail, still holding to the gunwale tightly with her left hand.

The wind freshened, the waves began to show white at their tips, the clouds in the south raced across the sky, darker and darker. But still, although they could see sheets of rain far away to the south, the sun shone on them brightly. They were now almost halfway across the lake. Anna looked over her shoulder toward the quieter water they had left behind. Along the shore of the lake, the willow trees tossed in the wind like a forest of green plumes. It's just as far one way as the other, she thought, and anyhow there's nothing to be afraid of. But while she looked back, the boat slipped off course, no longer quartering the waves, and immediately they took a big one over their bow.

"Bail, Estella," Anna said quietly, putting the boat back on course. "Get that water out of the boat." Her mind was filled with one paralyzing thought: She can't swim. My God, Estella can't swim.

Far off down the channel she saw the Gay Rosey Jane moving steadily toward the terminal, pushing a string of barges. She looked at Murray and Steve in the bow of the boat, drenched, hair plastered to their heads. "Just sit still, boys," she said. "There's nothing to worry about. We're almost there."

The wind was a gale now, and the black southern sky rushed toward them as if to engulf them. The boat took another wave over the bow, and then another. Estella bailed mechanically with the coffee can. They were still almost half a mile out from the Yacht Club. The boat's overloaded, and we're going to sink, Anna thought. My God, we're going to sink, and Estella can't swim.

"Estella," she said, "the boat will not sink. It may fill up with water, but it won't sink. Do you understand? It is all filled with cork, like a life preserver. It won't sink, do you hear me?" She repeated herself louder and louder above the wind. Estella sat with her back turned and bailed. She did not move or answer, or even nod her head. She went on bailing frantically, mechanically, dumping pint after pint of water over the side while they continued to ship waves over the bow. Murray and Steve sat in their places and stared at Anna. Ralph sat motionless by her side. No one said a word. I've got to take care of them all, Anna thought. Estella kept on bailing. The boat settled in the water and shipped another wave, wallowing now, hardly moving before the labored push of the motor. Estella gave a yell and started to rise, holding to the gunwales with both hands.

"Sit down, you fool!" Anna shouted. "*Sit down!*"

"We're gonna sink!" Estella yelled. "And I can't swim, Miss Anna! I can't swim!" For the first time, she turned, and stared at Anna with wild, blind eyes. She stood all the way up and clutched the air. "I'm gonna drown!" she yelled.

The boat rocked and settled, the motor drowned out, another wave washed in over the bow, and the boat tipped slowly up on its side. An instant later, they were all in the water and the boat was floating upside down beside them.

The children bobbed up immediately, buoyant in their life jackets. Anna glanced around once to see if they were all there. "Stay close to the boat, boys," she said.

And then Estella heaved out of the water, fighting frantically, eyes vacant, mouth open, the broad expanse of her golden face set in mindless desperation.

Anna got hold of one of the handgrips at the stern of the boat and, with her free hand, grabbed Estella's arm. "You're all right," she said. "Come on, I've got hold of the boat."

She tried to pull the huge bulk of the Negro woman toward her and guide her hand to the grip. Estella did not speak, but lunged forward in the water with a strangled yell and threw herself on Anna, flinging her arms across her shoulders. Anna felt herself sinking and scissors-kicked strongly to keep herself up, but she went down. Chin-deep in the water, she threw back her head and took a breath before Estella pushed her under. She hung on to the grip with all her strength, feeling herself battered against the boat and jerked away from it by Estella's struggle. This can't be happening, she thought. We can't be out here drowning. She felt a frantic hand brush across her face and snatch at her nose and hair. My glasses, she thought as she felt them torn away. I've lost my glasses.

Estella's weight slid away, and she, too, went under. Then both women came up and Anna got hold of Estella's arm again. "Come *on,*" she gasped. "The *boat.*"

Again Estella threw herself forward, the water streaming from her head and shoulders. This time Anna pulled her close enough to get hold of the grip, but Estella did not try to grasp it. Her hand slid, clawing, along Anna's wrist and arm; again she somehow rose up in the water and came down on Anna, and again the two women went under. This time, Estella's whole thrashing bulk was above Anna; she held with all her strength to the handgrip, but felt herself torn away from it. She came up behind Estella, who was now clawing frantically at the side of the skiff, which sank down on their side and tipped gently toward them as she pulled at it.

Anna ducked down and somehow got her shoulder against Estella's rump. Kicking and heaving with a strength she did not possess, she boosted Estella up and forward so that she fell sprawling across the boat. "*There!*" She came up as the rocking skiff began to submerge under Estella's weight. "*Stay* there!" she gasped. "*Stay* on it. For God's . . ."

But the boat was under a foot of water now, rocking and slipping away under Estella's shifting weight. Clutching and kicking crazily, mouth open in a soundless prolonged scream, eyes staring, she slipped off the other side, turned her face toward Anna, gave a strange, strangled grunt, and sank again. The water churned and foamed where she had been.

Anna swan around the boat toward her. As she swam, she realized that Ralph and Steve were screaming for help. Murray floated in the water with a queer, embarrassed smile on his face, as if he had been caught at something shameful. "I'm not here," he seemed to be saying. "This is all just an embarrassing mistake."

By the time Anna got to Estella, the boat was a couple of yards away—too far, she knew, for her to try to get Estella back to it. Estella broke the surface of the water directly in front of her and immediately flung both arms around her neck. Nothing Anna had ever learned in a lifesaving class seemed to have any bearing on this reasonless two hundred pounds of flesh with which she had to deal. They went down. This time they stayed under so long, deep in the softly yielding black water, that Anna thought she would not make it back up. Her very brain seemed ready to burst out of her ears and nostrils. She scissors-kicked again and again with all her strength—not trying to pull loose from Estella's clinging but now more passive weight—and they came up. Anna's head was thrust up and back, ready for a breath, and the instant she felt the air on her face, she took it, deep and gulping, swallowing some water at the same time, and they went down again. Estella's arms rested heavily—trustingly, it seemed—on her shoulders. She did not hug Anna or try to strangle her but simply kept holding on and pushing her down. This time, again deep in the dark water, when Anna raised her arms for a strong downstroke, she touched a foot. One of the boys was floating above their heads. She grabbed the foot without a thought and pulled with all her strength, scissors-kicking at the same time. She and Estella popped out of the water. Gasping in the life-giving air, Anna found herself staring into Steve's face as he floated beside her, weeping.

My God, I'll drown him if he doesn't get out of the way, she thought. I'll drown my own child. But she had no time to say even a word to warn him off before they went down again.

The next time up, she heard Ralph's voice, high and shrill and almost in her ear, and realized that he, too, was swimming close by, and was pounding on Estella's shoulder. "Estella, let go, let go!" he was crying. "Estella, you're drowning Mama!" Estella did not hear. She seemed not even to try to raise her head or breathe when their heads broke out of the water.

Once more they went under and came up before Anna thought, I've given out. There's no way to keep her up, and nobody is coming. And then, deep in the lake, the brassy taste of fear on her tongue, the yielding water pounding in her ears: *She's going to drown me. I've got to let her drown, or she will drown me.* She drew her knee up under her chin, planted her foot in the soft belly, still swollen from pregnancy, and shoved as hard as she could, pushing herself up and back and Estella down and away. Estella was not holding her tightly, and it was easy to push her away. The big arms slid off Anna's shoulders, the limp hands making no attempt to clutch or hold.

They had been together, close as lovers in the darkness or as twins in the womb of the lake, and now they were apart. Anna shot up into the air with the force of her shove and took a deep, gasping breath. Treading water, she waited for Estella to come up beside her, but nothing happened. The three children floated in a circle and looked at her. A vision passed through her mind of Estella's body drifting downward, downward through layers of increasing darkness, all her golden strengh and flowery beauty mud-and-water-dimmed, still, aimless as a drifting log. I ought to surface-dive and look for her, she thought, and the thought of going down again turned her bowels to water.

Before she had to decide to dive, something nudged lightly against her hand, like an inquiring, curious fish. She grabbed at it and felt the inert mass of Estella's body, drained of struggle, floating below the surface of the water. She got hold of the belt of her dress and pulled. Estella's back broke the surface of the water, mounded and rocking in the dead man's float, and then sank gently down again. Anna held on to the belt. She moved her feet tiredly to keep herself afloat and looked around her. I can't even get her face out of the water, she thought. I haven't the strength to lift her head.

The boat was floating ten yards away. The Skotch cooler, bright red-and-black plaid, bobbed gaily in the water nearby. Far, far off she could see the levee. In the boat it had looked so near and the distance across the lake so little that she had said she could easily swim it, but now everything in the world except the boat, the children, and this lifeless body was unthinkably far away. Tiny black figures moved back and forth along the levee, people going about their business without a thought of tragedy. The whole sweep of the lake was empty, with not another boat in sight except the Gay Rosey Jane, still moving up the channel. All that had happened had happened so quickly that the towboat seemed no nearer than it had before the skiff overturned. Murray floated in the water a few yards off, still smiling his embarrassed smile. Steve and Ralph stared at their mother with stricken faces. The sun broke through the shifting blackness of the sky, and at the same time a light rain began to fall, pattering on the choppy surface of the lake and splashing into their faces.

All her senses dulled and muffled by shock and exhaustion, Anna moved her feet and worked her way toward the boat, dragging her burden.

"She's gone," Steve said. "Estella's drowned." Tears and rain streamed down his face.

"What shall we do, Mama?" Ralph said.

Dimly, Anna realized that he had sensed her exhaustion and was trying to rouse her.

"Yell," she said. "All three of you yell. Maybe somebody . . ."

The children screamed for help again and again, their thin, piping voices floating away in the wind. With her last strength, Anna continued to work her way toward the boat, pulling Estella after her. She swam on her back, frog-kicking, and feeling the inert bulk bump against her legs at every stroke. When she reached the boat, she took hold of the handgrip and concentrated on holding on to it.

"What shall we do?" Ralph said again. "They can't hear us."

Overcome with despair, Anna let her head droop toward the water. "No one is coming," she said "It's too far. They can't hear you." And then, from somewhere, dim thoughts of artificial respiration, of snatching back the dead, came into her mind and she raised her head. Still time. I've got to get her out *now,* she thought. "Yell again," she said.

"I'm going to swim to shore and get help," Ralph said. He looked toward his mother for a decision, but his face clearly showed that he knew he could not expect one. He started swimming away, his blond head bobbing in the rough water. He did not look back.

"I don't know," Anna said. Then she remembered vaguely that in an accident you were supposed to stay with the boat. "She's dead," she said to herself. "My God, she's dead. My fault."

Ralph swam on, the beloved head smaller and smaller on the

vast expanse of the lake. The Gay Rosey Jane moved steadily up the channel. They might run him down, Anna thought. They'd never see him. She opened her mouth to call him back.

"Somebody's coming!" Murray shouted. "They see us. Somebody's coming. Ralph!"

Ralph heard him and turned back, and now they saw two boats racing toward them, one from the Yacht Club and one from the far side of the lake, across from the terminal. In the nearer one they saw Gaines Williamson.

Thirty yards away, something happened to Gaines' engine; it raced, ground, and died. Standing in the stern of the rocking boat, he worked frantically over it while they floated and watched. It could not have been more than a minute or two before the other boat pulled up beside them, but every moment that passed, Anna knew, might be the moment of Estella's death. In the stern of the second boat they saw a wiry white man wearing a T shirt and jeans. He cut his engine when he was beside them, and, moving quickly to the side of the boat near Anna, bent over her in great excitement. "Are you all right?" he asked. He grabbed her arm with a hard, calloused hand and shook her as if he had seen that she was about to pass out. "Are you all right?" he asked again, his face close to hers.

Anna stared at him, scarcely understanding what the question meant. The children swam over to the boat, and he helped them in and then turned back to Anna. "Come on," he said, and took hold of her arm again. "You've got to help yourself. Can you make it?"

"Get this one first," she said.

"What?" He stared at her with a queer, concentrated gaze, and she realized that he had not even seen Estella.

She hauled on the belt, and Estella's back broke the surface of the water, rolling, rocking, and bumping against the side of the boat. "I've got somebody else here," she said.

He grunted as if someone had hit him in the stomach. Reaching down he grabbed the back of Estella's dress, pulled her toward him, got one hand into her hair, raised her face out of the water, and, bracing himself against the gunwale, held her there. Estella's peaceful face turned slowly toward him. Her mouth and eyes were closed, her expression was one of deep repose. The man stared at her and then at Anna. "My God," he said.

"We've got to get her into the boat," Anna said. "If we can get her where we can give her artificial respiration . . ."

"It's Estella," Steve said. "Mama had her all the time." He began to cry again. "Let go of her hair," he said. "You're hurting her."

The three children shifted all at once to the side of the boat where the man was still holding Estella, and he turned on them sternly. "Get back," he said "Sit *down.* And sit still."

The children scuttled back to their places. "You're hurting her," Steve said again.

"It's all right, son," the man said. "She can't feel a thing." To Anna, in a lower voice, he said, "She's dead."

"I'll push and you pull," Anna said "Maybe we can get her into the boat."

He shifted his position, bracing himself as well as he could in the rocking boat, rested Estella's head on his own shoulder, and put both arms around her. They heaved and pushed at the limp body, but they could not get her into the boat. The man let her down into the water again, this time holding her under the arms. A hundred yards away, Gaines still struggled with his engine.

"Hurry up!" the man shouted. "Get on over here. We can't lift this woman by ourselves."

"Fishing lines tangled in the screw!" Gaines shouted back. His engine caught and died again.

"We're going to have to tow her in," the man said. "That fellow can't start his boat." He reached behind him and got a life jacket. "We'd better put this on her," he said. They worked Estella's arms into the life jacket and fastened the straps. "I've got a rope here somewhere," he said. "Hold her a minute. Wait." He handed Anna a life jacket. "You put one on, too." While he still held Estella by the hair, Anna struggled into the life jacket, and then took hold of the straps of Estella's. Just then, Gaines got his engine started, raced across the open water, and drew up beside them.

The two boats rocked in the rough water with Anna and Estella between them. Anna, with a hand on the gunwale of each, held them apart while the two men, straining and grunting, hauled Estella's body up out of the water and over the gunwale of Gaines' boat. Gaines heaved her legs in. She flopped, face down, across the seat and lay with one arm hanging over the side, the hand trailing in the water. Anna lifted the arm and put it in the boat. Then the white man pulled Anna into his boat. As he helped her over the side, she heard a smacking blow, and, looking back, saw that Gaines had raised and turned Estella's body and was pounding her in the belly. Water poured out of her mouth and, in reflex, air rushed in.

The boats roared off across the lake toward the Yacht Club. The white man's was much the faster of the two, and he quickly pulled away. As soon as they were within calling distance, he stood up in the boat and began to yell at the little group gathered on the Yacht Club mooring float. "Drowned! She's drowned!" he yelled. "Call an ambulance. Get a resuscitator down here. Hurry!"

They drew up to the float. He threw a rope to one of the Negroes standing there and jumped out. Anna dragged herself to a sitting position and stared stupidly at the crowd of Negroes. Gaines Williamson pulled up behind them in the other boat.

"Give us a hand," the white man said. "Let's get her out of there. My God, she's huge. Somebody lend a hand."

To Anna it seemed that all the rest of the scene on the float took place above and far away from her. She saw legs moving back and forth, heard voices and snatches of conversation, felt herself moved from one place to another, but nothing that happened interrupted her absorption in grief and guilt. For the time, nothing existed for her except the belief that Estella was dead.

Someone took her arm and helped her onto the float while the children climbed up by themselves. She sat down on the splintery boards, surrounded by legs, and no one paid any attention to her.

"I saw 'em." The voice of a Negro woman in the crowd. "I was setting on the levee and I saw 'em. You heard me. 'My Lord save us, some folks out there drowning,' I said. I was up on the levee and I run down to the Yacht Club . . ."

"Did somebody call an ambulance?" the white man asked.

"I run down here to the Yacht Club, like to killed myself running, and . . ."

"How . . ."

"Gay Rosey Jane swamped them. Never even seen them. Them towboats don't stop for nobody. See, there she goes. Never seen them at all."

"Still got a stitch in my side. My Lord, I like to killed myself running."

"Anybody around here know how to give artificial respiration?"

"I was sitting right yonder on the terminal fishing with her this morning. Would you believe that?"

"God have mercy on us."

"Oh, Lord. Oh, Lord God. Lord God."

"Have mercy on us."

A young Negro in Army khakis walked over to where the white man and Gaines Williamson were trying to get Estella out of the bulky jacket. "We'll cut it off," he said calmly. He pulled a straight razor from his pocket, slit one shoulder of the life jacket, pushed it out of the way, and straddled Estella's body. "I know how," he said. "I learned in the Army." He arranged her body in position—lying flat on her stomach, face turned to the side and arms above her head—and set to work, raising her arms and then her body rhythmically. When he lifted her body in the middle, her face dragged on the splintery planks of the float.

Anna crawled through the crowd to where Estella lay. Squatting down without a word, she put her hands under Estella's face to protect it from the splinters. It passed through her mind that she should do something about the children. Looking around, she saw them standing in a row at one side of the float, staring down at her and Estella—no longer crying, just standing and starring. Somebody ought to get them away from here, she thought vaguely, but the thought left her mind and she forgot them. She swayed, rocked back on her heels, sat down suddenly, and then lay on her stomach, her head against Estella's head, her hands cradling the sleeping face.

Who's going to tell James, she thought. Who's going to tell him she's dead? And then, I. I have to tell him. She began to talk to Estella. "Please, darling," she said. "Please, Estella, breathe." Tears of weakness rolled down her face, and she looked up above the forest of legs at the black faces in a circle around them. "She's got four babies," she said. "*Babies.* Who's going to tell her husband she's dead? Who's going to tell him?" And then, again, "Please, Estella, breathe. Please breathe."

No one answered. The young Negro soldier continued to raise the limp arms and body alternately, his motions deliberate and rhythmical, the sweat pouring off his face and dripping down on his sweat-soaked shirt. His thin face was intent and stern. The storm was over, the clouds to the west had blown away, and the sun had come out and beat down bright and hot, raising steamy air from the rain-soaked float.

A long time passed. The soldier giving Estella artificial respiration looked around at the crowd. "Anybody know how to do this? I'm about to give out." He did not pause or break the rhythm of his motions.

A man stepped out of the crowd. "I can do it," he said. "I know how."

"Come on, then," the soldier said. "Get down here by me and do it with me three times, and then, when I stop, you take over. Don't break it."

"Please, Estella," Anna said. "Please."

"One . . . Two . . . "

She felt someone pulling at her arm and looked up. A policeman was standing over her. "Here, lady," he said. "Get up off that dock. You ain't doing no good."

"But the splinters will get in her face," Anna said. "I'm holding her face off the boards."

"It ain't going to matter if her face is tore up if she's dead," the policeman said. "Get up."

Someone handed her a towel, and she folded it and put it under Estella's face. The policeman dragged her to her feet and took her over to a chair near the edge of the float and sat her down in it. He squatted beside her. "Now, who was in the boat?" he said. "I got to make a report."

Anna made a vague gesture. "We were," she said.

"Who is 'we,' lady?"

"Estella and I and the children."

"Lady, give me the names, please," the policeman said.

"Estella Moseby, the Negro woman. She used to work for me and we *asked* her, we asked her—" She broke off.

"Come on, who else?"

Anna stared at him, a short, bald man with shining pink scalp, and drum belly buttoned tightly into his uniform. A wave of nausea overcame her, and she saw his head surrounded by the shimmering black spokes of a rimless wheel, a black halo. "I'm going to be sick," she said. Collapsing out of the chair onto the dock, she leaned her head over the edge and vomited into the lake.

He waited until she was through and then helped her back into her chair. "Who else was with you?" he said.

"My two children, Ralph and Steve," she said. "Murray McCrae. I am Mrs. Richard Glover."

"Where is this McCrae fellow? He all right?"

"He's a little *boy,*" Anna said. "A child. He's over there somewhere."

"You sure there wasn't nobody else with you?"

"No. That's all," Anna said.

"Now, give me the addresses, please. Where did the nigger live?"

"For God's sake," Anna said. "What difference does it make? Go away and let me alone."

"I got to make my report, lady."

Ralph tugged at Anna's arm. "Mama, hadn't I better call Daddy?" he said.

"Yes," she said. "Yes, I guess you had." Oh, God, she thought, he has to find out. I can't put it off. Everybody has to find out that Estella is dead.

Anna heard a commotion on the levee. The steadily increasing crowd separated, and two white-jacketed men appeared and began to work over Estella. Behind them, a woman with a camera snapped pictures.

"What are they taking *pictures* of her for?" Anna asked.

Then she heard her husband's voice shouting, "Get off the damn raft, God damn it! Get off. You want to sink it? Get back there. You want to drown us all?"

The policeman stood up and went toward the crowd. "What the hell?" Anna heard him say.

"And put that camera up, if you don't want me to throw it in the lake." Anna's husband was in a fury of outrage, and concentrated it for the moment on the woman reporter from the local newspaper, who was snapping pictures of Estella.

"You all right, Anna?" Richard asked her.

The people on the float were scuttling back to the levee, and the reporter had disappeared. Anna, who was still sitting where the policeman had left her, nodded, and opened her mouth to speak, but her husband was gone before she could say anything. She felt a wave of self-pity. He didn't even stay to help me, she thought.

Then, a moment or an hour later—she did not know how long—she heard a strange high-pitched shriek from the other end of the float. What's that, she thought. It sounded again—a long, rasping rattle and then a shriek. Does the machine they brought make that queer noise?

"She's breathing," somebody said.

"No," Anna said aloud to nobody, for nobody was listening. "No. She's dead. I couldn't help it. I let her drown. Who's going to tell James?"

The float was cleared now. Besides Estella and Anna, only the two policemen, the two men from the ambulance, and Gaines Williamson were on it. The man who had rescued them was gone. The crowd stood quietly on the levee.

"Where is Richard?" Anna said. "Did he leave?"

No one answered.

The long, rasping rattle and shriek sounded again. Gaines Williamson came over to where Anna was sitting, and bent down to her, smiling kindly. "She's alive, Mrs. Glover," he said. "She's going to be all right."

Anna shook her head.

"Yes, Ma'am. She's moving and breathing, and yelling like crazy. She's going to be all right."

Anna got up shakily. She walked over to where the men were working Estella onto a stretcher.

"What's she doing?" she said. "What's the matter with her?"

Estella was thrashing her arms and legs furiously, mouth open, eyes staring, her face again the mask of mindless terror that Anna had seen in the lake. The rattle and shriek were her breathing and screaming.

"She must think she's still in the water," one of the men said. "Shock. But she's O.K. Look at her kick."

Anna sat down on the float, her knees buckling under her, and someone pulled her out of the way while four men carried the stretcher off the float and up the levee toward the ambulance.

Richard reappeared at the foot of the levee and crossed the walkway to the Yacht Club float. He bent down to help her up. "I'm sorry I had to leave you," he said. "I had to get the children away from here and find someone to take them home."

"My God," Anna said. "She's alive. They said she would be all right."

Later, in the car, she said to her husband. "She kept pushing me down, Richard. I tried to hold her up, I tried to make her take hold of the boat. But she kept pushing me down."

"It's all right now," he said. "Try not to think about it any more."

The next day, when Anna visited Estella in the hospital, she learned that Estella remembered almost nothing of what had happened. She recalled getting into the skiff for the trip home, but everything after that was gone.

"James says you saved my life," she said, in a hoarse whisper, "and I thank you."

Her husband stood at the head of her bed, gray-haired and dignified in his Sunday suit. He nodded. "The day won't come when we'll forget it, Miss Anna," he said. "God be my witness."

Anna shook her head. "I never should have taken you out without a life preserver," she said.

"Ain't she suppose to be a grown woman?" James said. "She suppose to know better herself."

"How do you feel?" Anna asked.

"Lord, not a square inch on my body don't ache," Estella said. She laid her hands on the mound of her body under the sheet. "My stomach!" she said, with a wry laugh. "Somebody must've jumped up and down on it."

"I reckon that's from the artificial respiration," Anna said. "I had never seen anyone do it that way before. They pick you up under the stomach and then put you down and lift your arms. And then, too, I kicked you. And we must have banged you up some getting you into the boat. Lord! The more I think about it, the worse it gets. Because Gaines hit you in the stomach, too, as soon as he got you into the boat. That's what really saved your life. As soon as he got you into the boat, he hit you in the stomach and got rid of a lot of the water in your lungs and let in some air. I believe that breath you took in Gaines' boat kept you alive until we got you to the dock."

"You kicked me?" Estella said.

"We were going down," Anna said, feeling that she must confess to Estella the enormity of what she had done, "and I finally knew I couldn't keep you up. I kicked you in the stomach hard, and got loose from you, and then when you came up I grabbed you and held on, and about that time they saw us and the boats came. You passed out just when I kicked you, or else the kick knocked you out, because you didn't struggle any more. I reckon that was lucky, too."

Estella shook her head. "I can't remember anything about it," she whispered. "Not anything." She pointed out the window toward the smokestack rising from the opposite wing of the hospital.

"Seems like last night I got the idea there's a little man up there," she said. "He peeps out from behind the smokestack at me, and I'm afraid of him. He leans on the smokestack, and then he jumps away real quick, like it's hot, and one time he came right over here and stood on the window ledge and looked in at me. Lucky the window was shut. I said 'Boo!' and, you know, he fell off! It didn't hurt him; he came right back. He wants to tell me something, yes, but he can't get in." She closed her eyes.

Anna looked anxiously at James.

"They still giving her something to keep her quiet," he said. "Every so often she gets a notion somebody trying to get in here."

Estella opened her eyes. "I thank you, Miss Anna," she said. "James told me you saved my life." She smiled. "Seems like every once in a while I hear your voice," she said. "Way off. Way, way off. You're saying, 'I'll save you, Estella. Don't be afraid. I'll save you.' That's all I can remember."

A Tribute to The General

Charles East

SHE HAD BEEN in Richmond only once before, and that was in 1909, the year before The General died. She had gone with him when he went to address a Grand Encampment of United Confederate Veterans, and all across Virginia, sitting there in the chair car, The General was quiet. Sometimes he puffed at his cigar, but mostly he looked out of the train window, out onto the streets of Petersburg and the plains below Richmond, and when she said, "Billy," he didn't seem to hear. Maybe he heard. Maybe he heard the little boy who came up to him in the train station and said, "General, that charge you led . . . " Because that charge he led was now a part of history. If he hadn't led that charge, Lee would have had the men to turn the enemy's flank. If he hadn't led that charge, all those young men would not be dead now and all those widows would not be telling those stories on latticed galleries. But there were those who blessed The General's name and who said that because of his attack Lee was able to hold the field, and that was why The General looked out of that train window, and why, standing before the men in that abandoned hall, he wept. Not only because he was old, for he was in his seventies, but because that charge had settled nothing: if he had attacked sooner—or if he had not attacked at all—Lee might have turned the enemy's flank, and if Lee had turned the enemy's flank, his army might have won a smashing victory. And if that . . . The General wept for a succession of ifs and might-have-beens and probablys.

She did not know that then. She knew only that the war, and one day in the war, and a single hour, had broken his life in two. She would never know that other part of it. And so she watched The General (how grand he looked in his faded uniform!), and when he had finished and the men stood, she stood, and then he came down off the platform and moved among them, down to where she was. "Boys," he said, "my lady." And one of the men said, "Old Billy's lady." And they gave a cheer for her.

Miss Jenny remembered that, and those other cheers, long after

Billy's passing. And she remembered when the cheering stopped—the vacant years when she lived alone in the house The General built for her and when it seemed he was forgotten, except by the young professors who sometimes came to ask if they might see his letters, which she had kept, or the letters to him, which she had also kept. Angry letters. Bitter letters. Soldiers refighting old battles.

And then, long afterward, when she was in her seventies, it suddenly began again. A letter came, inviting her to speak before the United Daughters at a meeting in Montgomery. She went. She spoke briefly. "I am deeply honored, and I know this honor you bestow upon me is your tribute to The General . . ." It became, at last, a kind of ritual. Each year, once a year, sometimes twice, she performed the ritual. Alone, and always by train, she went, as she had come now, at ninety-one, to the gallant city of Richmond. But no longer alone, for at eighty-three her ankle gave way and she fell and broke her hip, and at eighty-four she declined an invitation to appear before a patriotic group in Nashville because the hip had never mended properly. After that, Maudy Bea accompanied her. "My eyes," she said. Her ears, too. A gentle woman. A gentle colored woman who lived in the house with her and rode the train with her, who helped her to her seat and sat there next to her. And a friend.

And so they rode into Richmond, the aged lady and her colored nurse, to perform again (perhaps for the last time) the solemn ritual. The ladies were at the station to welcome her, and they presented her with a corsage of sweetpeas which Maudy Bea took and pinned on her. One of them made a little speech and said, "We're just so proud you could come and be with us."

"She don't hear well," said Maudy Bea, and she heard that. She asked the ladies if this was the Richmond train station, and one of them said, "Yessum, it is," and she asked them if this was the train station that was here when she and The General were here, and the ladies asked her when was that. "Let's see," she said, and she had to think a while, "nineteen-o- . . . nineteen-o-nine." And Maudy Bea told her, "No, mam, Miss Jenny, I don't expect so."

Later, when they were seated in the hall where the Sons and Daughters of the Confederacy had gathered, she asked, too loud, if this was the hall where The General had given his address, and the ladies around her began to look at her, and Maudy Bea shook her head, and she asked, "Did I say something I oughtn't to have?" Maudy Bea patted her on the hand.

She didn't want me to come here noway, she thought—she's afraid I'm going to fall and break that hip again. Or my bladder's going to get too full and she's going to have to take me out of here. Then she remembered how thirsty she had been. Maudy Bea hadn't let her have a swallow of water since along about supper. Or was it dinner? "I got to have me some water," she said.

"It won't be long and I'll get you some water," said Maudy Bea, and she tried to whisper it.

"Well, if it won't be long," she said. She wondered why she had come here anyway. Out of some long habit. Memphis and Charleston and Jackson and Savannah. Because The General was gone and she was all that remained, all there was left of that legend. In a little while the man on the platform would stop talking and the regent or vice-regent would take his place, and whoever it was would begin to talk about The General and then they'd call her name and everybody would stand up and start to clap and then Maudy Bea would help her to her feet and whisper to her, "Wave. Wave now, Miss Jenny," and she would lift one hand and wave that little handkerchief, that little handkerchief that Billy had carried with him.

She knew whose handkerchief it was. Billy's first wife's—the girl he married back in Tennessee, a girl with hazel eyes and an oval face and weak lungs. She died at twenty-three, the first year of the war, and he grieved for her through the war and for a long time afterward, maybe forever. In those letters there was one from her, written in a childish hand. "Dear William, I send this by the boy Ned. You must come here Sunday if you can. Pa has bought me a bay mare and you can ride the little mare with the white feet, back to that place we found . . ." The place they found. Miss Jenny closed her eyes and saw that place, the way she had imagined it: a pine-straw path, a clearing in the woods, two horses, the riders leading them.

"The General's a fine man," her mother said, "but thirty years makes such a difference." It did not matter. She had known, from that evening on the gallery, that she would marry him. "Miss Jenny," he said, "I know it's presumptuous of a man my age to hope . . . " To hope! She was twenty-six; The General was then in his fifties. Already he had fought that fight a hundred times, the way

Longstreet had his, because they had lost and because losers are bitter. Already he had spoken in a hundred cities. And in other cities there were other generals. If Johnston had moved sooner . . . if Beauregard had pursued the enemy . . . if Jackson had lived . . .

"All those boys," The General would say. He would say that, and in his eyes she could see the smoke of distant battles. "The decision was mine. No one else's. The orders left it to my discretion."

"Billy . . ." she said.

"Do you think I was wrong?" he would say.

And she would tell him no. "No, Billy."

He went on fighting that fight, and she went on believing he was right, or at least that he was not wrong. They traveled about the country, sometimes when she wished that they were home again, and The General spoke, or marched, or listened for the cheers, that moment when suddenly, out of a crowd, a voice would cry out, "God bless you, Old Billy." But there were other moments, when small boys came up to him in railroad stations, or when the parade wended its way past a house and a porch and a woman in mourning who turned her face from him. And that night, late into the night, The General would sit there in the hotel room and she would try to talk to him. "Billy, I bet you were handsome as a young man." And he was. She had seen him in the photographs, a captain then, and his hair not white, and his eyes not blurred with smoke. But that was someone else, someone back before his memory. "What was it like?" she said.

He never answered her. Likely he was remembering that woman on the porch, her face away from him, or the girl whose handkerchief he had carried into battle. Her name was Rose. ROSE, BELOVED WIFE OF WILLIAM. And that child, and that child's grave, there beside the river. INFANT SON OF ROSE AND WILLIAM. The soldier's son, and the son of a mother with weak lungs, who lived but two days and who was buried there beside a river. The General's brother took her there, his younger brother, who believed his legend as she did, but who stayed on that farm and never fought. And when he had taken her there, to that graveyard, because she wanted to go, he rode her up the hill a ways to where there was part of a chimney still standing.

And she said, "The house?"

"Yes," he said. "The Yanks burned it."

And she remembered what The General said, maybe one of

those nights in one of those hotel rooms, after one of those parades. "Sometimes," he said, "I think we lost because we wanted to." Did it have to be, she thought, so terrible?

The man on the platform was eulogizing President Davis and the room was warm and for a few moments Miss Jenny dozed. She was dreaming of that place she never saw when a touch on the arm awakened her. "Is it time?" she said. She opened her eyes. Maudy Bea nodded.

One of the ladies was on the platform now and she was talking about The General. The old tributes. The spirit, the gallantry. And as she talked, Miss Jenny remembered him, his freckled hands, the mole on his chin and the smell of his cigars, but mostly his eyes, the smoke of distant battles. And she remembered how he looked there on that bed, as if, by some touch of the hand, those years had all been rolled away. She could hear his breathing. "Eh . . . eh . . ." And once she whispered, "Billy." And she saw him go, and thought again, Did it have to be so terrible?

They were standing now. They were singing "Dixie," and someone gave the Rebel yell. On the arm of Maudy Bea she rose, very slowly, remembering her broken hip, and carefully, before she remembered that she had drunk no water since the night before. Her throat was dry and she licked her lips. She could hear the cheers, so loud. Then she could hear, above the cheers, Maudy Bea telling her to wave. And so she waved, and she kept waving, and wondering, what it had been like, that time she never knew, before the fighting and the cheering, and wishing she had known him then, and had a son by him, and even that her name was Rose, buried by a river.

Barn Burning

William Faulkner

The store in which the Justice of the Peace's court was sitting smelled of cheese. The boy, crouched on his nail keg at the back of the crowded room, knew he smelled cheese, and more: from where he sat he could see the ranked shelves close-packed with the solid, squat, dynamic shapes of tin cans whose labels his stomach read, not from the lettering which meant nothing to his mind but from the scarlet devils and the silver curve of fish—this, the cheese which he knew he smelled and the hermetic meat which his intestines believed he smelled coming in intermittent gusts momentary and brief between the other constant one, the smell and sense just a little of fear because mostly of despair and grief, the old fierce pull of blood. He could not see the table where the Justice sat and before which his father and his father's enemy (*our enemy* he thought in that despair; *ourn! mine and hisn both! He's my father!*) stood, but he could hear them, the two of them that is, because his father had said no word yet:

"But what proof have you, Mr. Harris?"

"I told you. The hog got into my corn. I caught it up and sent it back to him. He had no fence that would hold it. I told him so, warned him. The next time I put the hog in my pen. When he came to get it I gave him enough wire to patch up his pen. The next time I put the hog up and kept it. I rode down to his house and saw the wire I gave him still rolled on to the spool in his yard. I told him he could have the hog when he paid me a dollar pound fee. That evening a nigger came with the dollar and got the hog. He was a strange nigger. He said, 'He say to tell you wood and hay kin burn.' I said, 'What?' 'That whut he say to tell you,' the nigger said. 'Wood and hay kin burn.' That night my barn burned. I got the stock out but I lost the barn."

"Where is the nigger? Have you got him?"

"He was a strange nigger, I tell you. I don't know what became of him."

"But that's not proof. Don't you see that's not proof?"

"Get that boy up here. He knows." For a moment the boy thought too that the man meant his older brother until Harris said, "Not him. The little one. The boy," and, crouching, small for his age, small and wiry like his father, in patched and faded jeans even too small for him, with straight, uncombed, brown hair and eyes gray and wild as storm scud, he saw the men between himself and the table part and become a lane of grim faces, at the end of which he saw the Justice, a shabby, collarless, graying man in spectacles, beckoning him. He felt no floor under his bare feet; he seemed to walk beneath the palpable weight of the grim turning faces. His father, stiff in his black Sunday coat donned not for the trial but for the moving, did not even look at him. *He aims for me to lie,* he thought, again with that frantic grief and despair. *And I will have to do hit.*

"What's your name, boy?" the Justice said.

"Colonel Sartoris Snopes," the boy whispered.

"Hey?" the Justice said. "Talk louder. Colonel Sartoris? I reckon anybody named for Colonel Sartoris in this country can't help but tell the truth, can they?" The boy said nothing. *Enemy! Enemy!* he thought; for a moment he could not even see, could not see that the Justice's face was kindly nor discern that his voice was troubled when he spoke to the man named Harris: "Do you want me to question this boy?" But he could hear, and during those subsequent long seconds while there was absolutely no sound in the crowded little room save that of quiet and intent breathing it was as if he had swung outward at the end of a grape vine, over a ravine, and at the top of the swing had been caught in a prolonged instant of mesmerized gravity, weightless in time.

"No!" Harris said violently, explosively. "Damnation! Send him out of here!" Now time, the fluid world, rushed beneath him again, the voices coming to him again through the smell of cheese and sealed meat, the fear and despair and the old grief of blood:

"This case is closed. I can't find against you, Snopes, but I can give you advice. Leave this country and don't come back to it."

His father spoke for the first time, his voice cold and harsh, level, without emphasis: "I aim to. I don't figure to stay in a country among people who . . ." he said something unprintable and vile, addressed to no one.

"That'll do," the Justice said. "Take your wagon and get out of this country before dark. Case dismissed."

His father turned, and he followed the stiff black coat, the wiry figure walking a little stiffly from where a Confederate provost's man's musket ball had taken him in the heel on a stolen horse thirty years ago, followed the two backs now, since his older brother had appeared from somewhere in the crowd, no taller than the father but thicker, chewing tobacco steadily, between the two lines of grim-faced men and out of the store and across the worn gallery and down the sagging steps and among the dogs and half-grown boys in the mild May dust, where as he passed a voice hissed:

"Barn burner!"

Again he could not see, whirling; there was a face in a red haze, moonlike, bigger than the full moon, the owner of it half again his size, he leaping in the red haze toward the face, feeling no blow, feeling no shock when his head struck the earth, scrabbling up and leaping again, feeling no blow this time either and tasting no blood, scrabbling up to see the other boy in full flight and himself already leaping into pursuit as his father's hand jerked him back, the harsh, cold voice speaking above him: "Go get in the wagon."

It stood in a grove of locusts and mulberries across the road. His two hulking sisters in their Sunday dresses and his mother and her sister in calico and sunbonnets were already in it, sitting on and among the sorry residue of the dozen and more movings which even the boy could remember—the battered stove, the broken beds and chairs, the clock inlaid with mother-of-pearl, which would not run, stopped at some fourteen minutes past two o'clock of a dead and forgotten day and time, which had been his mother's dowry. She was crying, though when she saw him she drew her sleeve across her face and began to descend from the wagon. "Get back," the father said.

"He's hurt. I got to get some water and wash his . . ."

"Get back in the wagon," his father said. He got in too, over the tail-gate. His father mounted to the seat where the older brother already sat and struck the gaunt mules two savage blows with the peeled willow, but without heat. It was not even sadistic; it was exactly that same quality which in later years would cause his descendants to over-run the engine before putting a motor car into motion, striking and reining back in the same movement. The wagon went on, the store with its quiet crowd of grimly watching men dropped behind; a curve in the road hid it. *Forever* he thought. *Maybe he's done satisfied now, now that he has . . .* stopping himself, not to say it aloud even to himself. His mother's hand touched his shoulder.

"Does hit hurt?" she said.

"Naw," he said. "Hit don't hurt. Lemme be."

"Can't you wipe some of the blood off before hit dries?"

"I'll wash to-night," he said. "Lemme be, I tell you."

The wagon went on. He did not know where they were going. None of them ever did or ever asked, because it was always somewhere, always a house of sorts waiting for them a day or two days or even three days away. Likely his father had already arranged to make a crop on another farm before he . . . Again he had to stop himself. He (the father) always did. There was something about his wolflike independence and even courage when the advantage was at least neutral which impressed strangers, as if they got from his latent ravening ferocity not so much a sense of dependability as a feeling that his ferocious conviction in the rightness of his own actions would be of advantage to all whose interest lay with his.

That night they camped, in a grove of oaks and beeches where a spring ran. The nights were still cool and they had a fire against it, of a rail lifted from a nearby fence and cut into lengths—a small fire, neat, niggard almost, a shrewd fire; such fires were his father's habit and custom always, even in freezing weather. Older, the boy might have remarked this and wondered why not a big one; why should not a man who had not only seen the waste and extravagance of war, but who had in his blood an inherent voracious prodigality with material not his own, have burned everything in sight? Then he might have gone a step farther and thought that that was the reason: that niggard blaze was the living fruit of nights passed during those four years in the woods hiding from all men, blue or gray, with his strings of horses (captured horses, he called them). And older still, he might have divined the true reason: that the element of fire spoke to some deep mainspring of his father's being, as the element of steel or of powder spoke to other men, as the one weapon for the preservation of integrity, else breath were not worth the breathing, and hence to be regarded with respect and used with discretion.

But he did not think this now and he had seen those same niggard blazes all his life. He merely ate his supper beside it and was already half asleep over his iron plate when his father called him, and once more he followed the stiff back, the stiff and ruthless limp, up the slope and on to the starlit road where, turning, he could see his father against the stars but without face or depth—a shape black, flat, and bloodless as though cut from tin in the iron folds of the frockcoat which had not been made for him, the voice harsh like tin and without heat like tin:

"You were fixing to tell them. You would have told him." He didn't answer. His father struck him with the flat of his hand on the side of the head, hard but without heat, exactly as he had struck the two mules at the store, exactly as he would strike either of them with any stick in order to kill a horse fly, his voice still without heat or anger: "You're getting to be a man. You got to learn. You got to learn to stick to your own blood or you ain't going to have any blood to stick to you. Do you think either of them, any man there this morning, would? Don't you know all they wanted was a chance to get at me because they knew I had them beat? Eh?" Later, twenty years later, he was to tell himself, "If I had said they wanted only truth, justice, he would have hit me again." But now he said nothing. He was not crying. He just stood there. "Answer me," his father said.

"Yes," he whispered. His father turned.

"Get on to bed. We'll be there tomorrow."

To-morrow they were there. In the early afternoon the wagon stopped before a paintless two-room house identical almost with the dozen others it had stopped before even in the boy's ten years, and again, as on the other dozen occasions, his mother and aunt got down and began to unload the wagon, although his two sisters and his father and brother had not moved.

"Likely hit ain't fitten for hawgs," one of the sisters said.

"Nevertheless, fit it will and you'll hog it and like it," his father said. "Get out of them chairs and help your Ma unload."

The two sisters got down, big, bovine, in a flutter of cheap ribbons; one of them drew from the jumbled wagon bed a battered lantern, the other a worn broom. His father handed the reins to the older son and began to climb stiffly over the wheel. "When they get unloaded, take the team to the barn and feed them." Then he said, and at first the boy thought he was still speaking to his brother: "Come with me."

"Me?" he said.

"Yes," his father said. "You."

"Abner," his mother said. His father paused and looked back—the harsh level stare beneath the shaggy, graying, irascible brows.

"I reckon I'll have a word with the man that aims to begin tomorrow owning me body and soul for the next eight months.

They went back up the road. A week ago—or before last night, that is—he would have asked where they were going, but not now. His father had struck him before last night but never before had he paused afterward to explain why; it was as if the blow and the following calm, outrageous voice still rang, repercussed, divulging nothing to him save the terrible handicap of being young, the light weight of his few years, just heavy enough to prevent his soaring free of the world as it seemed to be ordered but not heavy enough to keep him footed solid in it, to resist it and try to change the course of its events.

Presently he could see the grove of oaks and cedars and the other flowering trees and shrubs where the house would be, though not the house yet. They walked beside a fence massed with honeysuckle and Cherokee roses and came to a gate swinging open between two brick pillars, and now, beyond a sweep of drive, he saw the house for the first time and at that instant he forgot his father and the terror and despair both, and even when he remembered his father again (who had not stopped) the terror and despair did not return. Because, for all the twelve movings, they had sojourned until now in a poor country, a land of small farms and fields and houses, and he had never seen a house like this before. *Hit's big as a courthouse* he thought quietly, with a surge of peace and joy whose reason he could not have thought into words, being too young for that: *They are safe from him. People whose lives are a part of this peace and dignity are beyond his touch, he no more to them than a buzzing wasp: capable of stinging for a little moment but that's all; the spell of this peace and dignity rendering even the barns and stable and cribs which belong to it impervious to the puny flames he might contrive* . . . this, the peace and joy, ebbing for an instant as he looked again at the stiff black back, the stiff and implacable limp of the figure which was not dwarfed by the house, for the reason that it had never looked big anywhere and which now, against the serene columned backdrop, had more than ever that impervious quality of something cut ruthlessly from tin, depthless, as though, sidewise to the sun, it would cast no shadow. Watching him, the boy remarked the absolutely undeviating course which his father held and saw the stiff foot come squarely down in a pile of fresh droppings where a horse had stood in the drive and which his father could have avoided by a simple change of stride. But it ebbed only for a moment, though he could not have thought this into words either, walking on in the spell of the house, which he could even want but without envy, without sorrow, certainly never with that ravening and jealous rage which unknown to him walked in the ironlike black coat before him: *Maybe he will feel it too. Maybe it will even change him now from what maybe he couldn't help but be.*

They crossed the portico. Now he could hear his father's stiff foot as it came down on the boards with clocklike finality, a sound out of all proportion to the displacement of the body it bore and which was not dwarfed either by the white door before it, as though it had attained to a sort of vicious and ravening minimum not to be dwarfed by anything—the flat, wide, black hat, the formal coat of broadcloth which had once been black but which had now that friction-glazed greenish cast of the bodies of old house flies, the lifted sleeve which was too large, the lifted hand like a curled claw. The door opened so promptly that the boy knew the Negro must have been watching them all the time, an old man with neat grizzled hair, in a linen jacket, who stood barring the door with his body, saying, "Wipe yo foots, white man, fo you come in here. Major ain't home nohow."

"Get out of my way, nigger," his father said, without heat too, flinging the door back and the Negro also and entering, his hat still on his head. And now the boy saw the prints of the stiff foot on the doorjamb and saw them appear on the pale rug behind the machinelike deliberation of the foot which seemed to bear (or transmit) twice the weight which the body compassed. The Negro was shouting "Miss Lula! Miss Lula!" somewhere behind them, then the boy, deluged as though by a warm wave by a suave turn of carpeted stair and a pendant glitter of chandeliers and a mute gleam of gold frames, heard the swift feet and saw her too, a lady—perhaps he had never seen her like before either—in a gray, smooth gown with lace at the throat and an apron tied at the waist and the sleeves turned back, wiping cake or biscuit dough from her hands with a towel as she came up the hall, looking not at his father at all but at the tracks on the blond rug with an expression of incredulous amazement.

"I tried," the Negro cried. "I tole him to . . ."

"Will you please go away?" she said in a shaking voice. "Major de Spain is not at home. Will you please go away?"

His father had not spoken again. He did not speak again. He did not even look at her. He just stood stiff in the center of the rug, in his hat, the shaggy iron-gray brows twitching slightly above the pebble-colored eyes as he appeared to examine the house with brief deliberation. Then with the same deliberation he turned; the boy watched him pivot on the good leg and saw the stiff foot drag round the arc of the turning, leaving a final long and fading smear. His father never looked at it, he never once looked down at the rug. The Negro held the door. It closed behind them, upon the hysteric and indistinguishable woman-wail. His father stopped at the top of the steps and scraped his boot clean on the edge of it. At the gate he stopped again. He stood for a moment, planted stiffly on the stiff foot, looking back at the house. "Pretty and white, ain't it?" he said. "That's sweat. Nigger sweat. Maybe it ain't white enough yet to suit him. Maybe he wants to mix some white sweat with it."

Two hours later the boy was chopping wood behind the house within which his mother and aunt and the two sisters (the mother and aunt, not the two girls, he knew that; even at this distance and muffled by walls the flat loud voices of the two girls emanated an incorrigible idle inertia) were setting up the stove to prepare a meal, when he heard the hooves and saw the linen-clad man on a fine sorrel mare, whom he recognized even before he saw the rolled rug in front of the Negro youth following on a fat bay carriage horse—a suffused, angry face vanishing, still at full gallop, beyond the corner of the house where his father and brother were sitting in the two tilted chairs; and a moment later, almost before he could have put the axe down, he heard the hooves again and watched the sorrel mare go back out of the yard, already galloping again. Then his father began to shout one of the sisters' names, who presently emerged backward from the kitchen door dragging the rolled rug along the ground by one end while the other sister walked behind it.

"If you aint' going to tote, go on and set up the wash pot," the first said.

"You, Sarty!" the second shouted. "Set up the wash pot!" His father appeared at the door, framed against that shabbiness, as he had been against that other bland perfection, impervious to either, the mother's anxious face at his shoulder.

"Go on," the father said. "Pick it up." The two sisters stooped, broad, lethargic; stooping, they presented an incredible expanse of pale cloth and a flutter of tawdry ribbons.

"If I thought enough of a rug to have to git hit all the way from France I wouldn't keep hit where folks coming in would have to tromp on hit," the first said. They raised the rug.

"Abner," the mother said. "Let me do it."

"You go back and git dinner," his father said. "I'll tend to this."

From the woodpile through the rest of the afternoon the boy watched them, the rug spread flat in the dust beside the bubbling wash-pot, the two sisters stooping over it with that profound and lethargic reluctance, while the father stood over them in turn, implacable and grim, driving them though never raising his voice again. He could smell the harsh homemade lye they were using; he saw his mother come to the door once and look toward them with an expression not anxious now but very like despair; he saw his father turn, and he fell to with the axe and saw from the corner of his eye his father raise from the ground a flattish fragment of field stone and examine it and return to the pot, and this time his mother actually spoke: "Abner. Abner. Please don't. Please, Abner."

Then he was done too. It was dusk; the whippoorwills had already begun. He could smell coffee from the room where they would presently eat the cold food remaining from the mid-afternoon meal, though when he entered the house he realized they were having coffee again probably because there was a fire on the hearth, before which the rug now lay spread over the backs of the two chairs. The tracks of his father's foot were gone. Where they had been were now long, water-cloudy scoriations resembling the sporadic course of a lilliputian mowing machine.

It still hung there while they ate the cold food and then went to bed, scattered without order or claim up and down the two rooms, his mother in one bed, where his father would later lie, the older brother in the other, himself, the aunt, and the two sisters on pallets on the floor. But his father was not in bed yet. The last thing the boy remembered was the depthless, harsh silhouette of the hat and coat bending over the rug and it seemed to him that he had not even closed his eyes when the silhouette was standing over him, the fire almost dead behind it, the stiff foot prodding him awake. "Catch up the mule," his father said.

When he returned with the mule his father was standing in the black door, the rolled rug over his shoulder. "Ain't you going to ride?" he said.

"No. Give me your foot."

He bent his knee into his father's hand, the wiry, surprising power flowed smoothly, rising, he rising with it, on to the mule's bare back (they had owned a saddle once; the boy could remember it though not when or where) and with the same effortlessness his father swung the rug up in front of him. Now in the starlight they retraced the afternoon's path, up the dusty road rife with honeysuckle, through the gate and up the black tunnel of the drive to the lightless house, where he sat on the mule and felt the rough warp of the rug drag across his thighs and vanish.

"Don't you want me to help?" he whispered. His father did not answer and now he heard again that stiff foot striking the hollow portico with that wooden and clocklike deliberation, that outrageous overstatement of the weight it carried. The rug, hunched, not flung (the boy could tell that even in the darkness) from his father's shoulder struck the angle of wall and floor with a sound unbelievably loud, thunderous, then the foot again, unhurried and enormous; a light came on in the house and the boy sat, tense, breathing steadily and quietly and just a little fast, though the foot itself did not increase its beat at all, descending the steps now; now the boy could see him.

"Don't you want to ride now?" he whispered. "We kin both ride now," the light within the house altering now, flaring up and sinking. *He's coming down the stairs now,* he thought. He had already ridden the mule up beside the horse block; presently his father was up behind him and he doubled the reins over and slashed the mule across the neck, but before the animal could begin to trot the hard, thin arm came round him, the hard, knotted hand jerking the mule back to a walk.

In the first red rays of the sun they were in the lot, putting plow gear on the mules. This time the sorrel mare was in the lot before he heard it at all, the rider collarless and even bareheaded, trembling, speaking in a shaking voice as the woman in the house had done, his father merely looking up once before stooping again to the hame he was buckling, so that the man on the mare spoke to his stooping back:

"You must realize you have ruined that rug. Wasn't there anybody here, any of your women . . ." he ceased, shaking, the boy watching him, the older brother leaning now in the stable door, chewing, blinking slowly and steadily at nothing apparently. "It cost a hundred dollars. But you never had a hundred dollars. You never will. So I'm going to charge you twenty bushels of corn against your crop. I'll add it in your contract and when you come to the commissary you can sign it. That won't keep Mrs. de Spain quiet but maybe it will teach you to wipe your feet off before you enter her house again."

Then he was gone. The boy looked at his father, who still had not spoken or even looked up again, who was now adjusting the loggor head in the hame.

"Pap," he said. His father looked at him—the inscrutable face, the shaggy brows beneath which the gray eyes glinted coldly. Suddenly the boy went toward him, fast, stopping as suddenly. "You done the best you could!" he cried. "If he wanted hit done different why didn't he wait and tell you how? He won't git no twenty bushels! He won't git none! We'll gether hit and hide hit! I kin watch . . ."

"Did you put the cutter back in that straight stock like I told you?"

"No, sir," he said.

"Then go do it."

That was Wednesday. During the rest of that week he worked steadily, at what was within his scope and some which was beyond it, with an industry that did not need to be driven nor even commanded twice; he had this from his mother, with the difference that some at least of what he did he liked to do, such as splitting wood with the half-size axe which his mother and aunt had earned, or saved money somehow, to present him with at Christmas. In company with the two older women (and on one afternoon, even one of the sisters), he built pens for the shoat and the cow which were a part of his father's contract with the landlord, and one afternoon, his father being absent, gone somewhere on one of the mules, he went to the field.

They were running a middle buster now, his brother holding the plow straight while he handled the reins, and walking beside the straining mule, the rich black soil shearing cool and damp against his bare ankles, he thought *Maybe this is the end of it. Maybe even that twenty bushels that seems hard to have to pay for just a rug will be a cheap price for him to stop forever and always from being what he used to be;* thinking, dreaming now, so that his brother had to speak sharply to him to mind the mule: *Maybe he even won't collect the twenty bushels. Maybe it will all add up and balance and vanish—corn, rug, fire; the terror and grief, the being pulled two ways like between two teams of horses—gone, done with for ever and ever.*

Then it was Saturday; he looked up from beneath the mule he was harnessing and saw his father in the black coat and hat. "Not that," his father said. "The wagon gear." And then, two hours later, sitting in the wagon bed behind his father and brother on the seat, the wagon accomplished a final curve, and he saw the weathered paintless store with its tattered tobacco- and patent-medicine posters and the tethered wagons and saddle animals below the gallery. He mounted the gnawed steps behind his father and brother, and there again was the lane of quiet, watching faces for the three of them to walk through. He saw the man in spectacles sitting at the plank table and he did not need to be told this was a Justice of the Peace; he sent one glare of fierce, exultant, partisan defiance at the man in collar and cravat now, whom he had seen but twice before in his life, and that on a galloping horse, who now wore on his face an expression not of rage but of amazed unbelief which the boy could not have known was at the incredible circumstance of being sued by one of his own tenants, and came and stood against his father and cried at the Justice: "He ain't done it! He ain't burnt . . ."

"Go back to the wagon," his father said.

"Burnt?" the Justice said. "Do I understand this rug was burned too?"

"Does anybody here claim it was?" his father said. "Go back to the wagon." But he did not, he merely retreatd to the rear of the room, crowded as that other had been, but not to sit down this time, instead, to stand pressing among the motionless bodies, listening to the voices:

"And you claim twenty bushels of corn is too high for the damage you did to the rug?"

"He brought the rug to me and said he wanted the tracks washed out of it. I washed the tracks out and took the rug back to him."

"But you didn't carry the rug back to him in the same condition it was in before you made the tracks on it."

His father did not answer, and now for perhaps half a minute there was no sound at all save that of breathing, the faint, steady suspiration of complete and intent listening.

"You decline to answer that, Mr. Snopes?" Again his father did not answer. "I'm going to find against you, Mr. Snopes. I'm going to find that you were responsible for the injury to Major de Spain's rug and hold you liable for it. But twenty bushels of corn seems a little high for a man in your circumstances to have to pay. Major de Spain claims it cost a hundred dollars. October corn will be worth about fifty cents. I figure that if Major de Spain can stand a ninety-five dollar loss on something he paid cash for, you can stand a five-dollar loss you haven't earned yet. I hold you in damages to Major de Spain to the amount of ten bushels of corn over and above your contract with him, to be paid to him out of your crop at gathering time. Court adjourned."

It had taken no time hardly, the morning was but half begun. He thought they would return home and perhaps back to the field, since they were late, far behind all other farmers. But instead his father passed on behind the wagon, merely indicating with his hand for the older brother to follow with it, and crossed the road toward the blacksmith shop opposite, pressing on after his father, overtaking him, speaking, whispering up at the harsh, calm face beneath the weathered hat: "He won't git no ten bushels neither. He won't git one. We'll . . ." until his father glanced for an instant down at him, the face absolutely calm, the grizzled eyebrows tangled above the cold eyes, the voice almost pleasant, almost gentle:

"You think so? Well, we'll wait till October anyway."

The matter of the wagon—the setting of a spoke or two and the tightening of the tires—did not take long either, the business of the tires accomplished by driving the wagon into the spring branch behind the shop and letting it stand there, the mules nuzzling into the water from time to time, and the boy on the seat with the idle reins, looking up the slope and through the sooty tunnel of the shed where the slow hammer rang and where his father sat on an upended cypress bolt, easily, either talking or listening, still sitting there when the boy brought the dripping wagon up out of the branch and halted it before the door.

"Take them on to the shade and hitch," his father said. He did so and returned. His father and the smith and a third man squatting on his heels inside the door were talking, about crops and animals; the boy, squatting too in the ammoniac dust and hoof-parings and scales of rust, heard his father tell a long and unhurried story out of the time before the birth of the older brother even when he had been a professional horsetrader. And then his father came up beside him where he stood before a tattered last year's circus poster on the other side of the store, gazing rapt and quiet at the scarlet horses, the incredible poisings and convolutions of tulle and tights and the painted leers of comedians, and said, "It's time to eat."

But not at home. Squatting beside his brother against the front wall, he watched his father emerge from the store and produce from a paper sack a segment of cheese and divide it carefully and deliberately into three with his pocket knife and produce crackers from the same sack. They all three squatted on the gallery and ate, slowly, without talking; then in the store again, they drank from a tin dipper tepid water smelling of the cedar bucket and of living beech trees. And still they did not go home. It was a horse lot this time, a tall rail fence upon and along which men stood and sat and out of which one by one horses were led, to be walked and trotted and then cantered back and forth along the road while the slow swapping and buying went on and the sun began to slant westward, they—the three of them—watching and listening, the older brother with his muddy eyes and his steady, inevitable tobacco, the father commenting now and then on certain of the animals, to no one in particular.

It was after sundown when they reached home. They ate supper by lamplight, then, sitting on the doorstep, the boy watched the night fully accomplish, listening to the whippoorwills and the frogs, when he heard his mother's voice: "Abner! No! No! Oh, God. Oh, God. Abner!" and he rose, whirled, and saw the altered light through the door where a candle stub now burned in a bottle neck on the table and his father, still in the hat and coat, at once formal and burlesque as though dressed carefully for some shabby and ceremonial violence, emptying the reservoir of the lamp back into the five-gallon kerosene can from which it had been filled, while the mother tugged at his arm until he shifted the lamp to the other hand and flung her back, not savagely or viciously, just hard, into the wall, her hands flung out against the wall for balance, her mouth open and in her face the same quality of hopeless despair as had been in her voice. Then his father saw him standing in the door.

"Go to the barn and get that can of oil we were oiling the wagon with," he said. The boy did not move. Then he could speak.

"What . . ." he cried. "What are you . . ."

"Go get that oil," his father said. "Go."

Then he was moving, running, outside the house, toward the stable: this the old habit, the old blood which he had not been permitted to choose for himself, which had been bequeathed him willy nilly and which had run for so long (and who knew where, battening on what of outrage and savagery and lust) before it came to him. *I could keep on,* he thought. *I could run on and on and never look back, never need to see his face again. Only I can't. I can't,* the rusted can in his hand now, the liquid sploshing in it as he ran back to the house and into it, into the sound of his mother's weeping in the next room, and handed the can to his father.

"Ain't you going to even send a nigger?" he cried. "At least you sent a nigger before!"

This time his father didn't strike him. The hand came even faster than the blow had, the same hand which had set the can on the table with almost excruciating care flashing from the can toward him too quick for him to follow it, gripping him by the back of his shirt and on to tiptoe before he had seen it quit the can, the face stooping at him in breathless and frozen ferocity, the cold, dead voice speaking over him to the older brother who leaned against the table, chewing with that steady, curious, sidewise motion of cows:

"Empty the can into the big one and go on. I'll catch up with you."

"Better tie him up to the bedpost," the brother said.

"Do like I told you," the father said. Then the boy was moving, his bunched shirt and the hard, bony hand between his shoulder-blades, his toes just touching the floor, across the room and into the other one, past the sisters sitting with spread heavy thighs in the two chairs over the cold hearth, and to where his mother and aunt sat side by side on the bed, the aunt's arms about his mother's shoulders.

"Hold him," the father said. The aunt made a startled movement. "Not you," the father said. "Lennie. Take hold of him. I want to see you do it." His mother took him by the wrist. "You'll hold him better than that. If he gets loose don't you know what he is going to do? He will go up yonder." He jerked his head toward the road. "Maybe I'd better tie him."

"I'll hold him," his mother whispered.

"See you do then." Then his father was gone, the stiff foot heavy and measured upon the boards, ceasing at last.

Then he began to struggle. His mother caught him in both arms, he jerking and wrenching at them. He would be stronger in the end, he knew that. But he had no time to wait for it. "Lemme go!" he cried. "I don't want to have to hit you!"

"Let him go!" the aunt said. "If he don't go, before God, I am going up there myself!"

"Don't you see I can't?" his mother cried. "Sarty! Sarty! No! No! Help me, Lizzie!"

Then he was free. His aunt grasped at him but it was too late. He whirled, running, his mother stumbled forward on to her knees behind him, crying to the nearer sister: "Catch him, Net! Catch him!" But that was too late too, the sister (the sisters were twins, born at the same time, yet either of them now gave the impression of being, encompassing as much living meat and volume and weight as any other two of the family) not yet having begun to rise from the chair, her head, face, alone merely turned, presenting to him in the flying instant an astonishing expanse of young female features untroubled by any surprise even, wearing only an expression of bovine interest. Then he was out of the room, out of the house, in the mild dust of the starlit road and the heavy rifeness of honeysuckle, the pale ribbon unspooling with terrific slowness under his running feet, reaching the gate at last and turning in, running, his heart and lungs drumming, on up the drive toward the lighted house, the lighted door. He did not knock, he burst in, sobbing for breath, incapable for the moment of speech; he saw the astonished face of the Negro in the linen jacket without knowing when the Negro had appeared.

"De Spain!" he cried, panted. "Where's . . ." then he saw the white man too emerging from a white door down the hall. "Barn!" he cried. "Barn!"

"What?" the white man said. "Barn?"

"Yes!" the boy cried. "Barn!"

"Catch him!" the white man shouted.

But it was too late this time too. The Negro grasped his shirt, but the entire sleeve, rotten with washing, carried away, and he was out that door too and in the drive again, and had actually never ceased to run even while he was screaming into the white man's face.

Behind him the white man was shouting, "My horse! Fetch my horse!" and he thought for an instant of cutting across the park and climbing the fence into the road, but he did not know the park nor how high the vine-massed fence might be and he dared not risk it. So he ran on down the drive, blood and breath roaring; presently he was in the road again though he could not see it. He could not hear either: the galloping mare was almost upon him before he heard her, and even then he held his course, as if the very urgency of his wild grief and need must in a moment more find him wings, waiting until the ultimate instant to hurl himself aside and into the weed-choked roadside ditch as the horse thundered past and on, for an instant in furious silhouette against the stars, the tranquil early summer night sky which, even before the shape of the horse and rider vanished, stained abruptly and violently upward: a long, swirling roar incredible and soundless, blotting the stars, and he springing up and into the road again, running again, knowing it was too late yet still running even after he heard the shot and, an instant later, two shots, pausing now without knowing he had ceased to run, crying "Pap! Pap!", running again before he knew he had begun to run, stumbling, tripping over something and scrabbling up again without ceasing to run, looking backward over his shoulder at the glare as he got up, running on among the invisible trees, panting, sobbing, "Father! Father!"

At midnight he was sitting on the crest of a hill. He did not know it was midnight and he did not know how far he had come. But there was no glare behind him now and he sat now, his back toward what he had called home for four days anyhow, his face toward the dark woods which he would enter when breath was strong again, small, shaking steadily in the chill darkness, hugging himself into the remainder of his thin, rotten shirt, the grief and despair now no longer terror and fear but just grief and despair. *Father. My father,* he thought. "He was brave!" he cried suddenly, aloud but not loud, no more than a whisper: "He was! He was in the war! He was in Colonel Sartoris' cav'ry!" not knowing that his father had gone to that war a private in the fine old European sense, wearing no uniform, admitting the authority of and giving fidelity to no man or army or flag, going to war as Malbrouck himself did: for booty—it meant nothing and less than nothing to him if it were enemy booty or his own.

The slow constellations wheeled on. It would be dawn and then sun-up after a while and he would be hungry. But that would be tomorrow and now he was only cold, and walking would cure that. His breathing was easier now and he decided to get up and go on, and then he found that he had been asleep because he knew it was almost dawn, the night almost over. He could tell that from the whippoorwills. They were everywhere now among the dark trees below him, constant and inflectioned and ceaseless, so that, as the instant for giving over to the day birds drew nearer and nearer, there was no interval at all between them. He got up. He was a little stiff, but walking would cure that too as it would the cold, and soon there would be the sun. He went on down the hill, toward the dark woods within which the liquid silver voices of the birds called unceasing—the rapid and urgent beating of the urgent and quiring heart of the late spring night. He did not look back.

That Evening Sun

William Faulkner

I

Monday is no different from any other weekday in Jefferson now. The streets are paved now, and the telephone and electric companies are cutting down more and more of the shade trees—the water oaks, the maples and locusts and elms—to make room for iron poles bearing clusters of bloated and ghostly and bloodless grapes, and we have a city laundry which makes the rounds on Monday morning, gathering the bundles of clothes into bright-colored, specially-made motor cars: the soiled wearing of a whole week now flees apparitionlike behind alert and irritable electric horns, with a long diminishing noise of rubber and asphalt like tearing silk, and even the Negro women who still take in white people's washing after the old custom, fetch and deliver it in automobiles.

But fifteen years ago, on Monday morning the quiet, dusty, shady streets would be full of Negro women with, balanced on their steady, turbaned heads, bundles of clothes tied up in sheets, almost as large as cotton bales, carried so without touch of hand between the kitchen door of the white house and the blackened washpot beside a cabin door in Negro Hollow.

Nancy would set her bundle on top of her head, then upon the bundle in turn she would set the black straw sailor hat which she wore winter and summer. She was tall, with a high, sad face sunken a little where her teeth were missing. Sometimes we would go a part of the way down the lane and across the pasture with her, to watch the balanced bundle and the hat that never bobbed nor wavered, even when she walked down into the ditch and up the other side and stooped through the fence. She would go down on her hands and knees and crawl through the gap, her head rigid, uptilted, the bundle steady as a rock or a balloon, and rise to her feet again and go on.

Sometimes the husbands of the washing women would fetch and deliver the clothes, but Jesus never did that for Nancy, even before father told him to stay away from our house, even when Dilsey was sick and Nancy would come to cook for us.

And then about half the time we'd have to go down the lane to Nancy's cabin and tell her to come on and cook breakfast. We would stop at the ditch, because father told us to not have anything to do with Jesus—he was a short black man, with a razor scar down his face—and we would throw rocks at Nancy's house until she came to the door, leaning her head around it without any clothes on.

"What yawl mean, chunking my house?" Nancy said. "What you little devils mean?"

"Father says for you to come on and get breakfast," Caddy said. "Father says it's over a half an hour now, and you've got to come this minute."

"I aint studying no breakfast," Nancy said. "I going to get my sleep out."

"I bet you're drunk," Jason said. "Father says you're drunk. Are you drunk, Nancy?"

"Who says I is?" Nancy said. "I got to get my sleep out. I aint studying no breakfast."

So after a while we quit chunking the cabin and went back home. When she finally came, it was too late for me to go to school. So we thought it was whisky until that day they arrested her again and they were taking her to jail and they passed Mr Stovall. He was the cashier in the bank and a deacon in the Baptist church, and Nancy began to say:

"When you going to pay me, white man? When you going to pay me, white man? It's been three times now since you paid me a cent—" Mr Stovall knocked her down, but she kept on saying, "When you going to pay me, white man? It's been three times now since—" until Mr Stovall kicked her in the mouth with his heel and the marshal caught Mr Stovall back, and Nancy lying in the street, laughing. She turned her head and spat out some blood and teeth and said, "It's been three times now since he paid me a cent."

That was how she lost her teeth, and all that day they told about Nancy and Mr Stovall, and all that night the ones that passed the jail could hear Nancy singing and yelling. They could see her hands holding to the window bars, and a lot of them stopped along the fence, listening to her and to the jailer trying to make her stop. She didn't shut up until almost daylight, when the jailer began to hear a bumping and scraping upstairs and he went up there and found Nancy hanging from the window bar. He said that it was cocaine and not whisky, because no nigger would try to commit suicide unless he was full of cocaine, because a nigger full of cocaine wasn't a nigger any longer.

The jailer cut her down and revived her; then he beat her, whipped her. She had hung herself with her dress. She had fixed it all right, but when they arrested her she didn't have on anything except a dress and so she didn't have anything to tie her hands with and she couldn't make her hands let go of the window ledge. So the jailer heard the noise and ran up there and found Nancy hanging from the window, stark naked, her belly already swelling out a little, like a little balloon.

When Dilsey was sick in her cabin and Nancy was cooking for us, we could see her apron swelling out; that was before father told Jesus to stay away from the house. Jesus was in the kitchen, sitting behind the stove, with his razor scar on his black face like a piece of dirty string. He said it was a watermelon that Nancy had under her dress.

"It never come off of your vine, though," Nancy said.

"Off of what vine?" Caddy said.

"I can cut down the vine it did come off of," Jesus said.

"What makes you want to talk like that before these chillen?" Nancy said. "Whyn't you go on to work? You done et. You want Mr Jason to catch you hanging around this kitchen, talking that way before these chillen?"

"Talking what way?" Caddy said. "What vine?"

"I cant hang around white man's kitchen," Jesus said. "But white man can hang around mine. White man can come in my house, but I cant stop him. When white man want to come in my house, I aint got no house. I cant stop him, but he cant kick me outen it. He cant do that."

Dilsey was still sick in her cabin. Father told Jesus to stay off our place. Dilsey was still sick. It was a long time. We were in the library after supper.

"Isn't Nancy through in the kitchen yet?" mother said. "It seems to me that she has had plenty of time to have finished the dishes."

"Let Quentin go and see," father said. "Go and see if Nancy is through, Quentin. Tell her she can go on home."

I went to the kitchen. Nancy was through. The dishes were put away and the fire was out. Nancy was sitting in a chair, close to the cold stove. She looked at me.

"Mother wants to know if you are through," I said.

"Yes," Nancy said. She looked at me. "I done finished." She looked at me.

"What is it?" I said. "What is it?"

"I aint nothing but a nigger," Nancy said. "It aint none of my fault."

She looked at me, sitting in the chair before the cold stove, the sailor hat on her head. I went back to the library. It was the cold stove and all, when you think of a kitchen being warm and busy and cheerful. And with a cold stove and the dishes all put away, and nobody wanting to eat at that hour.

"Is she through?" mother said.

"Yessum," I said.

"What is she doing?" mother said.

"She's not doing anything. She's through."

"I'll go and see," father said.

"Maybe she's waiting for Jesus to come and take her home," Caddy said.

"Jesus is gone," I said. Nancy told us how one morning she woke up and Jesus was gone.

"He quit me," Nancy said. "Done gone to Memphis, I reckon. Dodging them city *po*-lice for a while, I reckon."

"And a good riddance," father said. "I hope he stays there."

"Nancy's scaired of the dark," Jason said.

"So are you," Caddy said.

"I'm not," Jason said.

"Scairy cat," Caddy said.

"I'm not," Jason said.

"You, Candace!" mother said. Father came back.

"I am going to walk down the lane with Nancy," he said. "She says that Jesus is back."

"Has she seen him?" mother said.

"No. Some Negro sent her word that he was back in town. I wont be long."

"You'll leave me alone, to take Nancy home?" mother said. "Is her safety more precious to you than mine?"

"I wont be long," father said.

"You'll leave these children unprotected, with that Negro about?"

"I'm going too," Caddy said. "Let me go, Father."

"What would he do with them, if he were unfortunate enough to have them?" father said.

"I want to go, too," Jason said.

"Jason!" mother said. She was speaking to father. You could tell that by the way she said the name. Like she believed that all day father had been trying to think of doing the thing she wouldn't like the most, and that she knew all the time that after a while he would think of it. I stayed quiet, because father and I both knew that mother would want him to make me stay with her if she just thought of it in time. So father didn't look at me. I was the oldest. I was nine and Caddy was seven and Jason was five.

"Nonsense," father said. "We wont be long."

Nancy had her hat on. We came to the lane. "Jesus always been good to me," Nancy said. "Whenever he had two dollars, one of them was mine." We walked in the lane. "If I can just get through the lane," Nancy said, "I be all right then."

The lane was always dark. "This is where Jason got scared on Hallowe'en," Caddy said.

"I didn't," Jason said.

"Cant Aunt Rachel do anything with him?" father said. Aunt Rachel was old. She lived in a cabin beyond Nancy's, by herself. She had white hair and she smoked a pipe in the door, all day long; she didn't work any more. They said she was Jesus' mother. Sometimes she said she was and sometimes she said she wasn't any kin to Jesus.

"Yes, you did," Caddy said. "You were scairder than Frony. You were scairder than T.P. even. Scairder than niggers."

"Cant nobody do nothing with him," Nancy said. "He say I done woke up the devil in him and aint but one thing going to lay it down again."

"Well, he's gone now," father said. "There's nothing for you to be afraid of now. And if you'd just let white men alone."

"Let what white men alone?" Caddy said. "How let them alone?"

"He aint gone nowhere," Nancy said. "I can feel him. I can feel him now, in this lane. He hearing us talk, every word, hid somewhere, waiting. I aint seen him, and I aint going to see him again but once more, with that razor in his mouth. That razor on that string down his back, inside his shirt. And then I aint going to be even surprised."

"I wasn't scaired," Jason said.

"If you'd behave yourself, you'd have kept out of this," father said. "But it's all right now. He's probably in St. Louis now. Probably got another wife by now and forgot all about you."

"If he has, I better not find out about it," Nancy said. "I'd stand there right over them, and every time he wropped her, I'd cut that arm off. I'd cut his head off and I'd slit her belly and I'd shove—"

"Hush," father said.

"Slit whose belly, Nancy?" Caddy said.

"I wasn't scaired," Jason said. "I'd walk right down this lane by myself."

"Yah," Caddy said. "You wouldn't dare to put your foot down in it if we were not here too."

II

Dilsey was still sick, so we took Nancy home every night until mother said, "How much longer is this going on? I to be left alone in this big house while you take home a frightened Negro?"

We fixed a pallet in the kitchen for Nancy. One night we waked up, hearing the sound. It was not singing and it was not crying, coming up the dark stairs. There was a light in mother's room and we heard father going down the hall, down the back stairs, and Caddy and I went into the hall. The floor was cold. Our toes curled away from it while we listened to the sound. It was like singing and it wasn't like singing, like the sounds that Negroes make.

Then it stopped and we heard father going down the back stairs, and we went to the head of the stairs. Then the sound began again, in the stairway, not loud, and we could see Nancy's eyes halfway up the stairs, against the wall. They looked like cat's eyes do, like a big cat against the wall, watching us. When we came down the steps to where she was, she quit making the sound again, and we stood there until father came back up from the kitchen, with his pistol in his hand. He went back down with Nancy and they came back with Nancy's pallet.

We spread the pallet in our room. After the light in mother's room went off, we could see Nancy's eyes again. "Nancy," Caddy whispered, "are you asleep, Nancy?"

Nancy whispered something. It was oh or no, I dont know which. Like nobody had made it, like it came from nowhere and went nowhere, until it was like Nancy was not there at all; that I had looked so hard at her eyes on the stairs that they had got printed on my eyeballs, like the sun does when you have closed your eyes and there is no sun. "Jesus," Nancy whispered. "Jesus."

"Was it Jesus?" Caddy said. "Did he try to come into the kitchen?"

"Jesus," Nancy said. Like this: Jeeeeeeeeeeeeeeesus, until the sound went out, like a match or a candle does.

"It's the other Jesus she means," I said.

"Can you see us, Nancy?" Caddy whispered. "Can you see our eyes too?"

"I aint nothing but a nigger," Nancy said. "God knows. God knows."

"What did you see down there in the kitchen?" Caddy whispered. "What tried to get in?"

"God knows," Nancy said. We could see her eyes. "God knows."

Dilsey got well. She cooked dinner. "You'd better stay in bed a day or two longer," father said.

"What for?" Dilsey said. "If I had been a day later, this place would be to rack and ruin. Get on out of here now, and let me get my kitchen straight again."

Dilsey cooked supper too. And that night, just before dark, Nancy came into the kitchen.

"How do you know he's back?" Dilsey said. "You aint seen him."

"Jesus is a nigger," Jason said.

"I can feel him," Nancy said. "I can feel him laying yonder in the ditch."

"Tonight?" Dilsey said. "Is he there tonight?"

"Dilsey's a nigger too," Jason said.

"You try to eat something," Dilsey said.

"I dont want nothing," Nancy said.

"I aint a nigger," Jason said.

"Drink some coffee," Dilsey said. She poured a cup of coffee for Nancy. "Do you know he's out there tonight? How come you know it's tonight?"

"I know," Nancy said. "He's there, waiting. I know. I done lived with him too long. I know what he is fixing to do fore he know it himself."

"Drink some coffee," Dilsey said. Nancy held the cup to her

mouth and blew into the cup. Her mouth pursed out like a spreading adder's, like a rubber mouth, like she had blown all the color out of her lips with blowing the coffee.

"I aint a nigger," Jason said. "Are you a nigger, Nancy?"

"I hellborn, child," Nancy said. "I wont be nothing soon. I going back where I come from soon."

III

She began to drink the coffee. While she was drinking, holding the cup in both hands, she began to make the sound again. She made the sound into the cup and the coffee splashed out onto her hands and her dress. Her eyes looked at us and she sat there, her elbows on her knees, holding the cup in both hands, looking at us across the wet cup, making the sound. "Look at Nancy," Jason said. "Nancy cant cook for us now. Dilsey's got well now."

"You hush up," Dilsey said. Nancy held the cup in both hands, looking at us, making the sound, like there were two of them: one looking at us and the other making the sound. "Whyn't you let Mr Jason telefoam the marshal?" Dilsey said. Nancy stopped then, holding the cup in her long brown hands. She tried to drink some coffee again, but it splashed out of the cup, onto her hands and her dress, and she put the cup down. Jason watched her.

"I cant swallow it," Nancy said. "I swallows but it wont go down me."

"You go down to the cabin," Dilsey said. "Frony will fix you a pallet and I'll be there soon."

"Wont no nigger stop him," Nancy said.

"I aint a nigger," Jason said. "Am I, Dilsey?"

"I reckon not," Dilsey said. She looked at Nancy. "I dont reckon so. What you going to do, then?"

Nancy looked at us. Here eyes went fast, like she was afraid there wasn't time to look, without hardly moving at all. She looked at us, at all three of us at one time. "You member that night I stayed in yawls' room?" she said. She told about how we waked up early the next morning, and played. We had to play quiet, on her pallet, until father woke up and it was time to get breakfast. "Go and ask your maw to let me stay here tonight," Nancy said. "I wont need no pallet. We can play some more."

Caddy asked mother. Jason went too. "I cant have Negroes sleeping in the bedrooms," mother said. Jason cried. He cried until mother said he couldn't have any dessert for three days if he didn't stop. Then Jason said he would stop if Dilsey would make a chocolate cake. Father was there.

"Why dont you do something about it?" mother said. "What do we have officers for?"

"Why is Nancy afraid of Jesus?" Caddy said. "Are you afraid of father, mother?"

"What could the officers do?" father said. "If Nancy hasn't seen him, how could the officers find him?"

"Then why is she afraid?" mother said.

"She says he is there. She says she knows he is there tonight."

"Yet we pay taxes," mother said. "I must wait here alone in this big house while you take a Negro woman home."

"You know that I am not lying outside with a razor," father said.

"I'll stop if Dilsey will make a chocolate cake," Jason said. Mother told us to go out and father said he didn't know if Jason would get a chocolate cake or not, but he knew what Jason was going to get in about a minute. We went back to the kitchen and told Nancy.

"Father said for you to go home and lock the door, and you'll be all right," Caddy said. "All right from what, Nancy? Is Jesus mad at you?" Nancy was holding the coffee cup in her hands again, her elbows on her knees and her hands holding the cup between her knees. She was looking into the cup. "What have you done that made Jesus mad?" Caddy said. Nancy let the cup go. It didn't break on the floor, but the coffee spilled out, and Nancy sat there with her hands still making the shape of the cup. She began to make the sound again, not loud. Not singing and not unsinging. We watched her.

"Here," Dilsey said. "You quit that, now. You get aholt of yourself. You wait here. I going to get Versh to walk home with you." Dilsey went out.

We looked at Nancy. Her shoulders kept shaking, but she quit making the sound. We watched her. "What's Jesus going to do to you?" Caddy said. "He went away."

Nancy looked at us. "We had fun that night I stayed in yawls' room, didn't we?"

"I didn't," Jason said. "I didn't have any fun."

"You were asleep in mother's room," Caddy said. "You were not there."

"Let's go down to my house and have some more fun," Nancy said.

"Mother wont let us," I said. "It's too late now."

"Dont bother her," Nancy said. "We can tell her in the morning. She wont mind."

"She wouldn't let us," I said.

"Dont ask her now," Nancy said. "Dont bother her now."

"She didn't say we couldn't go," Caddy said.

"We didn't ask," I said.

"If you go, I'll tell," Jason said.

"We'll have fun," Nancy said. "They won't mind, just to my house. I been working for yawl a long time. They won't mind."

"I'm not afraid to go," Caddy said. "Jason is the one that's afraid. He'll tell."

"I'm not," Jason said.

"Yes, you are," Caddy said. "You'll tell."

"I won't tell," Jason said. "I'm not afraid."

"Jason ain't afraid to go with me," Nancy said. "Is you, Jason?"

"Jason is going to tell," Caddy said. The lane was dark. We passed the pasture gate. "I bet if something was to jump out from behind that gate, Jason would holler."

"I wouldn't," Jason said. We walked down the lane. Nancy was talking loud.

"What are you talking so loud for, Nancy?" Caddy said.

"Who; me?" Nancy said. "Listen at Quentin and Caddy and Jason saying I'm talking loud."

"You talk like there was five of us here," Caddy said. "You talk like father was here too."

"Who; me talking loud, Mr Jason?" Nancy said.

"Nancy called Jason 'Mister,'" Caddy said.

"Listen how Caddy and Quentin and Jason talk," Nancy said.

"We're not talking loud," Caddy said. "You're the one that's talking like father—"

"Hush," Nancy said; "hush, Mr Jason."

"Nancy called Jason 'Mister' aguh—"

"Hush," Nancy said. She was talking loud when we crossed the ditch and stooped through the fence where she used to stoop through with the clothes on her head. Then we came to her house. We were going fast then. She opened the door. The smell of the house was like the lamp and the smell of Nancy was like the wick, like they were waiting for one another to begin to smell. She lit the lamp and closed the door and put the bar up. Then she quit talking loud, looking at us.

"What're we going to do?" Caddy said.

"What do yawl want to do?" Nancy said.

"You said we would have some fun," Caddy said.

There was something about Nancy's house; something you could smell besides Nancy and the house. Jason smelled it, even. "I don't want to stay here," he said. "I want to go home."

"Go home, then," Caddy said.

"I don't want to go by myself," Jason said.

"We're going to have some fun," Nancy said.

"How?" Caddy said.

Nancy stood by the door. She was looking at us, only it was like she had emptied her eyes, like she had quit using them. "What do you want to do?" she said.

"Tell us a story," Caddy said. "Can you tell a story?"

"Yes," Nancy said.

"Tell it," Caddy said. We looked at Nancy. "You don't know any stories."

"Yes," Nancy said. "Yes, I do."

She came and sat in a chair before the hearth. There was a little fire there. Nancy built it up, when it was already hot inside. She built a good blaze. She told a story. She talked like her eyes looked, like her eyes watching us and her voice talking to us did not belong to her. Like she was living somewhere else, waiting somewhere else. She was outside the cabin. Her voice was inside and the shape of her, the Nancy that could stoop under a barbed wire fence with a bundle of clothes balanced on her head as though without weight, like a balloon, was there. But that was all. "And so this here queen come walking up to the ditch, where that bad man was hiding. She was walking up to the ditch, and she say, 'If I can just get past this here ditch,' was what she say . . ."

"What ditch?" Caddy said. "A ditch like that one out there? Why did a queen want to go into a ditch?"

"To get to her house," Nancy said. She looked at us. "She had to cross the ditch to get into her house quick and bar the door."

"Why did she want to go home and bar the door?" Caddy said.

IV

Nancy looked at us. She quit talking. She looked at us. Jason's legs stuck straight out of his pants where he sat on Nancy's lap. "I don't think that's a good story," he said. "I want to go home."

"Maybe we had better," Caddy said. She got up from the floor. "I bet they are looking for us right now." She went toward the door.

"No," Nancy said. "Don't open it." She got up quick and passed Caddy. She didn't touch the door, the wooden bar.

"Why not?" Caddy said.

"Come back to the lamp," Nancy said. "We'll have fun. You don't have to go."

"We ought to go," Caddy said. "Unless we have a lot of fun." She and Nancy came back to the fire, the lamp.

"I want to go home," Jason said. "I'm going to tell."

"I know another story," Nancy said. She stood close to the lamp. She looked at Caddy, like when your eyes look up at a stick balanced on your nose. She had to look down to see Caddy, but her eyes looked like that, like when you are balancing a stick.

"I won't listen to it," Jason said. "I'll bang on the floor."

"It's a good one," Nancy said. "It's better than the other one."

"What's it about?" Caddy said. Nancy was standing by the lamp. Her hand was on the lamp, against the light, long and brown.

"Your hand is on that hot globe," Caddy said. "Don't it feel hot to your hand?"

Nancy looked at her hand on the lamp chimney. She took her hand away, slow. She stood there, looking at Caddy, wringing her long hand as though it were tied to her wrist with a string.

"Let's do something else," Caddy said.

"I want to go home," Jason said.

"I got some popcorn," Nancy said. She looked at Caddy and then at Jason and then at me and then at Caddy again. "I got some popcorn."

"I don't like popcorn," Jason said. "I'd rather have candy."

Nancy looked at Jason. "You can hold the popper." She was still wringing her hand; it was long and limp and brown.

"All right," Jason said. "I'll stay a while if I can do that. Caddy can't hold it. I'll want to go home again if Caddy holds the popper."

Nancy built up the fire. "Look at Nancy putting her hands in the fire," Caddy said. "What's the matter with you, Nancy?"

"I got popcorn," Nancy said. "I got some." She took the popper from under the bed. It was broken. Jason began to cry.

"Now we can't have any popcorn," he said.

"We ought to go home, anyway," Caddy said. "Come on, Quentin."

"Wait," Nancy said; "wait. I can fix it. Don't you want to help me fix it?"

"I don't think I want any," Caddy said. "It's too late now."

"You help me, Jason," Nancy said. "Don't you want to help me?"

"No," Jason said. "I want to go home."

"Hush," Nancy said; "hush. Watch. Watch me. I can fix it so Jason can hold it and pop the corn." She got a piece of wire and fixed the popper.

"It won't hold good," Caddy said.

"Yes, it will," Nancy said. "Yawl watch. Yawl help me shell some corn."

The popcorn was under the bed too. We shelled it into the popper and Nancy helped Jason hold the popper over the fire.

"It's not popping," Jason said. "I want to go home."

"You wait," Nancy said. "It'll begin to pop. We'll have fun then." She was sitting close to the fire. The lamp was turned up so high it was beginning to smoke.

"Why don't you turn it down some?" I said.

"It's all right," Nancy said. "I'll clean it. Yawl wait. The popcorn will start in a minute."

"I don't believe it's going to start," Caddy said. "We ought to start home, anyway. They'll be worried."

"No," Nancy said. "It's going to pop. Dilsey will tell um yawl with me. I been working for yawl long time. They won't mind if yawl at my house. You wait, now. It'll start popping any minute now."

Then Jason got some smoke in his eyes and he began to cry. He dropped the popper into the fire. Nancy got a wet rag and wiped Jason's face, but he didn't stop crying.

"Hush," she said. "Hush." But he didn't hush. Caddy took the popper out of the fire.

"It's burned up," she said. "You'll have to get some more popcorn, Nancy."

"Did you put all of it in?" Nancy said.

"Yes," Caddy said. Nancy looked at Caddy. Then she took the popper and opened it and poured the cinders into her apron and began to sort the grains, her hands long and brown, and we watching her.

"Haven't you got any more?" Caddy said.

"Yes," Nancy said; "yes. Look. This here ain't burnt. All we need to do is—"

"I want to go home," Jason said. "I'm going to tell."

"Hush," Caddy said. We all listened. Nancy's head was already turned toward the barred door, her eyes filled with red lamplight. "Somebody is coming," Caddy said.

Then Nancy began to make that sound again, not loud, sitting there above the fire, her long hands dangling between her knees; all of a sudden water began to come out on her face in big drops, running down her face, carrying in each one a little turning ball of firelight like a spark until it dropped off her chin. "She's not crying," I said.

"I ain't crying," Nancy said. Her eyes were closed. "I ain't crying. Who is it?"

"I don't know," Caddy said. She went to the door and looked out. "We've got to go now," she said. "Here comes father."

"I'm going to tell," Jason said. "Yawl made me come."

The water still ran down Nancy's face. She turned in her chair. "Listen. Tell him. Tell him we going to have fun. Tell him I take good care of yawl until in the morning. Tell him to let me come home with yawl and sleep on the floor. Tell him I won't need no pallet. We'll have fun. You member last time how we had so much fun?"

"I didn't have fun," Jason said. "You hurt me. You put smoke in my eyes. I'm going to tell."

V

Father came in. He looked at us. Nancy did not get up.

"Tell him," she said.

"Caddy made us come down here," Jason said. "I didn't want to."

Father came to the fire. Nancy looked up at him. "Can't you go to Aunt Rachel's and stay?" he said. Nancy looked up at father, her hands between her knees. "He's not here," father said. "I would have seen him. There's not a soul in sight."

"He in the ditch," Nancy said. "He waiting in the ditch yonder."

"Nonsense," father said. He looked at Nancy. "Do you know he's there?"

"I got the sign," Nancy said.

"What sign?"

"I got it. It was on the table when I come in. It was a hog-bone, with blood meat still on it, laying by the lamp. He's out there. When yawl walk out that door, I gone."

"Gone where, Nancy?" Caddy said.

"I'm not a tattletale," Jason said.

"Nonsense," father said.

"He out there," Nancy said. "He looking through that window this minute, waiting for yawl to go. Then I gone."

"Nonsense," father said. "Lock up your house and we'll take you on to Aunt Rachel's."

"'Twont do no good," Nancy said. She didn't look at father now, but he looked down at her, at her long, limp, moving hands. "Putting it off wont do no good."

"Then what do you want to do?" father said.

"I don't know," Nancy said. "I can't do nothing. Just put it off. And that don't do no good. I reckon it belong to me. I reckon what I going to get ain't no more than mine."

"Get what?" Caddy said. "What's yours?"

"Nothing," father said. "You all must get to bed."

"Caddy made me come," Jason said.

"Go on to Aunt Rachel's," father said.

"It won't do no good," Nancy said. She sat before the fire, her elbows on her knees, her long hands between her knees. "When even your own kitchen wouldn't do no good. When even if I was sleeping on the floor in the room with your chillen, and the next morning there I am, and blood—"

"Hush," father said. "Lock the door and put out the lamp and go to bed."

"I scared of the dark," Nancy said. "I scared for it to happen in the dark."

"You mean you're going to sit right here with the lamp lighted?" father said. Then Nancy began to make the sound again, sitting before the fire, her long hands between her knees. "Ah, damnation," father said. "Come along, chillen. It's past bedtime."

"When yawl go home, I gone," Nancy said. She talked quieter now, and her face looked quiet, like her hands. "Anyway, I got my coffin money saved up with Mr. Lovelady." Mr. Lovelady was a short, dirty man who collected the Negro insurance, coming around to the cabins or the kitchens every Saturday morning, to collect fifteen cents. He and his wife lived at the hotel. One morning his wife committed suicide. They had a child, a little girl. He and the child went away. After a week or two he came back alone. We would see him going along the lanes and the back streets on Saturday mornings.

"Nonsense," father said. "You'll be the first thing I'll see in the kitchen tomorrow morning."

"You'll see what you'll see, I reckon," Nancy said. "But it will take the Lord to say what that will be."

VI

We left her sitting before the fire.

"Come and put the bar up," father said. But she didn't move. She didn't look at us again, sitting quietly there between the lamp and the fire. From some distance down the lane we could look back and see her through the open door.

"What, Father?" Caddy said. "What's going to happen?"

"Nothing," father said. Jason was on father's back, so Jason was the tallest of all of us. We went down into the ditch. I looked at it, quiet. I couldn't see much where the moonlight and the shadows tangled.

"If Jesus is hid here, he can see us, cant he?" Caddy said.

"He's not there," father said. "He went away a long time ago."

"You made me come," Jason said, high; against the sky it looked like father had two heads, a little one and a big one. "I didn't want to."

We went up out of the ditch. We could still see Nancy's house and the open door, but we couldn't see Nancy now, sitting before the fire with the door open, because she was tired. "I just done got tired," she said. "I just a nigger. It ain't no fault of mine."

But we could hear her, because she began just after we came up out of the ditch, the sound that was not singing and not unsinging. "Who will do our washing now, Father?" I said.

"I'm not a nigger," Jason said, high and close above father's head.

"You're worse," Caddy said, "you are a tattletale. If something was to jump out, you'd be scairder than a nigger."

"I wouldn't," Jason said.

"You'd cry," Caddy said.

"Caddy," father said.

"I wouldn't!" Jason said.

"Scairy cat," Caddy said.

"Candace!" father said.

FROM
Shiloh

Shelby Foote

When I went to sleep the stars were out and there was even a moon, thin like a sickle and clear against the night, but when I woke up there was only the blackness and the wind sighing high in the treetops. That was what roused me I believe, because for a minute I disremembered where I was. I thought I was back home, woke up early and laying in bed waiting for pa to come with the lantern to turn me out to milk (that was the best thing about the army: no cows) and ma was in the kitchen humming a hymn while she shook up the stove. But then I realized part of the sound was the breathing and snoring of the men all around me, with maybe a whimper or a moan every now and again when the bad dreams came, and I remembered. We had laid down to sleep in what they call Line of Battle and now the night was nearly over. And when I remembered I wished I'd stayed asleep: because that was the worst part, to lie there alone, feeling lonely, and no one to tell you he was feeling the same.

But it was warm under the blanket and my clothes had dried and I could feel my new rifle through the cloth where I had laid it to be safe from the dew when I wrapped the covers round me. Then it was the same as if theyd all gone away, or *I* had; I was back home with my brothers and sisters again, myself the oldest by over a year, and they were gathered around to tell me goodbye the way they did a month ago when I left to join up in Corinth after General Beauregard sent word that all true men were needed to save the country. That was the way he said it. I was just going to tell them I would be back with a Yankee sword for the fireplace, like pa did with the Mexican one, when I heard somebody talking in a hard clear voice not like any of *my* folks, and when I looked up it was Sergeant Tyree.

"Roll out there," he said. "Roll out to fight."

I had gone to sleep and dreamed of home, but here I was, away up in Tennessee, further from Ithaca and Jordan County than I'd ever been in all my life before. It was Sunday already and we were fixing to hit them where they had their backs to the river, the way it was explained while we were waiting for our marching orders three days ago. I sat up.

From then on everything moved fast with a sort of mixed-up jerkiness, like Punch and Judy. Every face had a kind of drawn look, the way it would be if a man was picking up on something heavy. Late ones like myself were pulling on their shoes or rolling their blankets. Others were already fixed. They squatted with their rifles across their thighs, sitting there in the darkness munching biscuits, those that had saved any, and not doing much talking. They nodded their heads with quick flicky motions, like birds, and nursed their rifles, keeping them out of the dirt. I had gotten to know them all in a month and a few of them were even from the same end of the county I was, but now it was like I was seeing them for the first time, different. All the put-on had gone out of their faces—they were left with what God gave them at the beginning.

We lined up. And while Sergeant Tyree passed among us, checking us one by one to make sure everything was where it was supposed to be, dawn begun to come through, faint and high. While we were answering roll-call the sun rose big and red through the trees and all up and down the company front they begun to get excited and jabber at one another: "The sun of oyster itch," whatever that meant. I was glad to see the sun again, no matter what they called it.

One minute we were standing there, shifting from leg to leg, not saying much and more or less avoiding each other's eyes: then we were going forward. It happened that sudden. There was no bugle or drum or anything like that. The men on our right started moving and we moved too, lurching forward through the underbrush and trying to keep the line straight the way we had been warned to do, but we couldnt. Captain Plummer was cussing. "Dwess it up," he kept saying, cussing a blue streak; "Dwess it up, dod dam it, dwess it up," all the way through the woods. So after a while, when the trees thinned, we stopped to straighten the line.

There was someone on a tall claybank horse out front, a fine-looking man in a new uniform with chicken guts on the sleeves all the way to his elbows, spruce and spang as a gamecock. He had on a stiff red cap, round and flat on top like a sawed-off dice box, and he was making a speech. "Soldiers of the South!" he shouted in a fine proud voice, a little husky, and everybody cheered. All I could hear was the cheering and yipping all around me, but I could see his eyes light up and his mouth moving the way it will do when a man is using big words. I thought I heard something about defenders and liberty and even something about the women back home but I couldnt be sure; there was so much racket. When he was through he stood in the stirrups, raising his cap to us as we went by, and I recognized him. It was General Beauregard, the man I'd come to fight for, and I hadnt hardly heard a word he said.

We stayed lined up better now because we were through the worst of the briers and vines, but just as we got going good there was a terrible clatter off to the right, the sound of firecrackers mixed with a roaring and yapping like a barn full of folks at a Fourth of July dogfight or a gouging match. The line begun to crook and weave because some of the men had stopped to listen, and Captain Plummer was cussing them, tongue-tied. Joe Marsh was next to me—he was nearly thirty, middle-aged, and had seen some battle up near Bowling Green. "There you are," he said, slow and calm and proud of himself. "Some outfit has met the elephant." That was what the ones who had been in action always called it: the elephant.

They had told us how it would be. They said we would march two days and on the third day we would hit them where they were camped between two creeks with their backs to the Tennessee River. We would drive them, the colonel told us, and when they were pushed against the river we would kill or capture the whole she-bang. I didnt understand it much because what the colonel said was full of tactics talk. Later the captain explained it, and that was better but not much. So then Sergeant Tyree showed it to us by drawing lines on the ground with a stick. That way it was clear as could be.

It sounded fine, the way he told it; it sounded simple and easy. Maybe it was too simple, or something. Anyhow things didnt turn out so good when it came to doing them. On the third day we were still marching, all day, and here it was the fourth day and we were still just marching, stop and go but mostly stop—the only real difference was that the column was moving sideways now, through the woods instead of on the road. From all that racket over on the right I thought maybe the other outfits would have the Yankees pushed back and captured before we even got to see it. The noise had died down for a minute, but as we went forward it swelled up again, rolling toward the left where we were, rifles popping and popping and the soldiers yelling crazy in the distance. It didnt sound like any elephant to me.

We came clear of the woods where they ended on a ridge overlooking a valley with a little creek running through it. The ground was open all across the valley, except where the creek bottom was overgrown, and mounted to another ridge on the other side where the woods began again. There were white spots in the fringe of trees—these were tents, I made out. We were the left brigade of the whole army. The 15th Arkansas, big men mostly, with bowie knives and rolled-up sleeves, was spread across the front for skirmishers, advanced a little way in the open. There was a Tennessee regiment on our right and two more on our left and still another at the left rear with flankers out. Then we were all in the open, lined up with our flags riffling in the breeze. Colonel Thornton was out front, between us and the skirmishers. His saber flashed in the sun. Looking down the line I saw the other regimental commanders, and all their sabers were flashing sunlight too. It was like a parade just before it begins.

This is going to be what they promised us, I said to myself. This is going to be the charge.

That was when General Johnston rode up. He came right past where I was standing, a fine big man on a bay stallion. He had on a broad-brim hat and a cape and thigh boots with gold spurs that twinkled like sparks of fire. I watched him ride by, his mustache flaring out from his mouth and his eyes set deep under his forehead. He was certainly the handsomest man I ever saw, bar none; he made the other officers on his staff look small. There was a little blond-headed lieutenant bringing up the rear, the one who would go all red in the face when the men guyed him back on the march. He looked about my age, but that was the only thing about us that was alike. He had on a natty uniform: bobtail jacket, red silk neckerchief, fire-gilt buttons, and all. I said to myself, I bet his ma would have a fit if she could see him now.

General Johnston rode between our regiment and the Tennessee boys on our right, going forward to where the skirmish line was waiting. When the colonel in charge had reported, General Johnston spoke to the skirmishers: "Men of Arkansas, they say you boast of your prowess with the bowie knife. Today you wield a nobler weapon: the bayonet. Employ it well." They stood there holding their rifles and looking up at him, shifting their feet a little and looking sort of embarrassed. He was the only man I ever saw who wasnt a preacher and yet could make that high-flown way of talking sound right. Then he turned his horse and rode back through our line, and as he passed he leaned sideways in the saddle and spoke to us: "Look along your guns, and fire low." It made us ready and anxious for what was coming.

Captain Plummer walked up and down the company front. He was short, inclined to fat, and walked with a limp from the blisters he developed on the march. "Stay dwessed on me, wherever I go," he said. "And shoot low. Aim for their knees." All up and down the line the flags were flapping and other officers were speaking to their men.

I was watching toward the front, where we would go, but all I could see was that empty valley with the little creek running through it and the rising ground beyond with the trees on top. While I was looking, trying hard to see was anybody up there, all of a sudden there was a Boom! Boom! Boom! directly in the rear and it scared me so bad I almost broke for cover. But when I looked around I saw they had brought up the artillery and it was shooting over our heads towards the left in a shallow swale. I felt real sheepish from having jumped but when I looked around I saw that the others had jumped as much as I had, and now they were joking at one another about who had been the most scared, carrying it off all brave-like but looking kind of hang-dog about it too. I was still trying to see whatever it was out front that the artillery was shooting at, but all I could see was that valley with the creek in it and the dark trees on the flanks.

I was still mixed up, wondering what it all meant, when we begun to go forward, carrying our rifles at right shoulder shift the way we had been taught to do on parade. Colonel Thornton was still out front, flashing his saber and calling back over his shoulder: "Close up, men. Close up. Guiiide centerrrrr!" The skirmishers went out of sight in the swale, the same as if they had marched into the ground. When we got to where they had gone down, we saw them again, but closer now, kneeling and popping little white puffs of smoke from their rifles. The rattle of firing rolled across the line and back again, and then it broke into just general firing. I still couldnt see what they were shooting at, specially not now that the smoke was banking up and drifting back against us with a stink like burning feathers.

Then, for the first time since we left Corinth, bugles begun to blare and it passed to the double. The line wavered like a shaken rope, gaining in places and lagging in others and all around me they were yelling those wild crazy yells. General Cleburne was on his mare to our left, between us and the 5th Tennessee. He was waving his sword and the mare was plunging and tossing her mane. I could hear him hollering the same as he would when we did wrong on the drill field—he had that thick, Irish way of speaking that came on him when he got mad. We were trotting by then.

As we went forward we caught up with the skirmishers. They had given around a place where the ground was flat and dark green and there was water in the grass, sparkling like silver. It was a bog. We gave to the right to stay on hard ground and the 5th Tennessee gave to the left; the point of swampland was between us, growing wider as we went. General Cleburne rode straight ahead, waving his sword and bawling at us to close the gap, close the gap, and before he knew what had separated us, the mare was pastern-deep in it, floundering and bucking to get rid of the general's weight. He was waving his sword with one hand and shaking his fist at us with the other, so that when the mare gave an extra hard buck General Cleburne went flying off her nigh side and landed on his hands and knees in the mud. We could hear him cussing across two hundred yards of bog. The last I saw of him he was walking out, still waving the sword, picking his knees high and sinking almost to his boot-tops every step. His face was red as fire.

The brigade was split, two regiments on the right and four on the left, with a swamp between us; we would have to charge the high ground from two sides. By this time we had passed around where the other slope came out to a point leading down to the bog and we couldnt even see the other regiments. When we hit the rise we begun to run. I could hear Colonel Thornton puffing like a switch engine and I thought to myself, He's too old for this. Nobody was shooting yet because we didnt see anything to shoot at; we were so busy trying to keep up, we didnt have a chance to see anything at all. The line was crooked as a ram's horn. Some men were pushing out front and others were beginning to breathe hard and lag behind. My heart was hammering at my throat—it seemed like every breath would bust my lungs. I passed a fat fellow holding his side and groaning. At first I thought he was shot, but then I realized he just had a stitch. It was Burt Tapley, the one everybody jibed about how much he ate; he was a great one for the sutlers. Now all that fine food, canned peaches and suchlike, was staring him in the face.

When we were halfway up the rise I begun to see black shapes against the rim where it sloped off sharp. At first I thought they were scarecrows—they looked like scarecrows. That didnt make sense, except they looked so black and stick-like. Then I saw they were moving, wiggling, and the rim broke out with smoke, some of it going straight up and some jetting toward our line, rolling and jumping with spits of fire mixed in and a humming like wasps past my ears. I thought: *Lord to God, theyre shooting; theyre shooting at me!* And it surprised me so, I stopped to look. The smoke kept rolling up and out, rolling and rolling, still with the stabs of fire mixed in, and some of the men passed me, bent forward like they were running into a high wind, rifles held crossways so that the bayonets glinted and snapped in the sunlight, and their faces were all out of shape from the yelling.

When I stopped I begun to hear all sorts of things I hadnt heard while I was running. It was like being born again, coming into a new world. There was a great crash and clatter of firing, and over all this I could hear them all around me, screaming and yelping like on a foxhunt except there was something crazy mixed up in it too, like horses trapped in a burning barn. I thought theyd all gone crazy—they looked it, for a fact. Their faces were split wide open with screaming, mouths twisted every which way, and this wild lunatic yelping coming out. It wasnt like they were yelling with their mouths: it was more like the yelling was something pent up inside them and they were opening their mouths to let it out. That was the first time I really knew how scared I was.

If I'd stood there another minute, hearing all this, I would have gone back. I thought: Luther, you got no business mixed up in all this ruckus. This is all crazy, I thought. But a big fellow I never saw before ran into me full tilt, knocking me forward so hard I nearly went sprawling. He looked at me sort of desperate, like I was a post or something that got in the way, and went by, yelling. By the time I got my balance I was stumbling forward, so I just kept going. And that was better. I found that as long as I was moving I was all right, because then I didnt hear so much or even see so much. Moving, it was more like I was off to myself, with just my own particular worries.

I kept passing men lying on the ground, and at first I thought they were winded, like the fat one—that was the way they looked to me. But directly I saw a corporal with the front of his head mostly gone, what had been under his skull spilling over his face, and I knew they were down because they were hurt. Every now and then there would be one just sitting there holding an arm or leg and groaning. Some of them would reach out at us and even call us by name, but we stayed clear. For some reason we didnt like them, not even the sight of them. I saw Lonny Parker that I grew up with; he was holding his stomach, bawling like a baby, his face all twisted and big tears on his cheeks. But it wasnt any different with Lonny—I stayed clear of him too, just like I'd never known him, much less grown up with him back in Jordan County. It wasnt a question of luck, the way some folks will tell you; they will tell you it's bad luck to be near the wounded. It was just that we didnt want to be close to them any longer than it took to run past, the way you wouldnt want to be near someone who had something catching, like smallpox.

We were almost to the rim by then and I saw clear enough that they werent scarecrows—that was a foolish thing to think anyhow. They were men, with faces and thick blue uniforms. It was only a glimpse, though, because then we gave them a volley and smoke rolled out between us. When we came through the smoke they were gone except the ones who were on the ground. They lay in every position, like a man I saw once that had been drug out on bank after he was run over by a steamboat and the paddles hit him. We were running and yelling, charging across the flat ground where white canvas tents stretched out in an even row. The racket was louder now, and then I knew why. It was because I was yelling too, crazy and blood-curdled as the rest of them.

I passed one end of the row of tents. That must have been where their officers stayed, for breakfast was laid on a table there with a white cloth nice as a church picnic. When I saw the white-flour biscuits and the coffee I understood why people called them the Feds and us the Corn-feds. I got two of the biscuits (I had to grab quick; everybody was snatching at them) and while I was stuffing one in my mouth and the other in my pocket, I saw Burt Tapley. He'd caught up when we stopped to give them that volley, I reckon, and he was holding the coffee pot like a loving-cup, drinking scalding coffee in big gulps. It ran from both corners of his mouth, down onto the breast of his uniform.

Officers were running around waving their swords and hollering. "Form!" they yelled at us. "Form for attack!" But nobody paid them much mind—we were too busy rummaging the tents. So they begun to lay about with the flats of their swords, driving us away from the plunder. It didnt take long. When we were formed in line again, reloading our guns, squads and companies mixed every which way, they led us through the row of tents at a run. All around me, men were tripping on the ropes and cussing and barking their shins on the stakes. Then we got through and I saw why the officers had been yelling for us to form.

There was a gang of Federal soldiers standing shoulder to shoulder in the field beyond the tents. I thought it was the whole Yankee army, lined up waiting for us. Those in front were kneeling under the guns of the men in the second line, a great bank of blue uniforms and rifle barrels and white faces like rows of eggs, one above another. When they fired, the smoke came at us in a solid wall. Things plucked at my clothes and twitched my hat, and when I looked around I saw men all over the ground, in the same ugly positions as the men back on the slope, moaning and whimpering, clawing at the grass. Some were gut-shot, making high yelping sounds like a turpentined dog.

Smoke was still thick when the second volley came. For a minute I thought I was the only one left alive. Then I saw the others through the smoke, making for the rear, and I ran too, back toward the tents and the slope where we'd come up. They gave us another volley as we ran but it was high; I could hear the balls screech over my head. I cleared the ridge on the run, and when I came over I saw them stopping. I pulled up within twenty yards or so and lay flat on the ground, panting.

No bullets were falling here but everybody laid low because they were crackling and snapping in the air over our heads on a line with the rim where our men were still coming over. They would come over prepared to run another mile, and then they would see us lying there and they would try to stop, stumbling and sliding downhill.

I saw one man come over, running sort of straddle-legged, and just as he cleared the rim I saw the front of his coat jump where the shots came through. He was running down the slope, stone dead already, the way a deer will do when it's shot after picking up speed. This man kept going for nearly fifty yards downhill before his legs stopped pumping and he crashed into the ground on his stomach. I could see his face as he ran, and there was no doubt about it, no doubt at all: he was dead and I could see it in his face.

That scared me worse than anything up to then. It wasn't really all that bad, looking back on it: it was just that he'd been running when they shot him and his drive kept him going down the slope. But it seemed so wrong, so scandalous, somehow so un*religious* for a dead man to have to keep on fighting—or running, anyhow—that it made me sick at my stomach. I didnt want to have any more to do with the war if this was the way it was going to be.

They had told us we would push them back to the river. Push, they said; that was the word they used. I really thought we were going to push them—with bullets and bayonets of course, and of course I knew there were going to be men killed: I even thought I might get killed myself; it crossed my mind a number of times. But it wasnt the way they said. It wasnt that way at all. Because even the dead and dying didn't have any decency about them—first the Yankees back on the slope, crumpled and muddy where their own men had overrun them, then the men in the field beyond the tents, yelping like gut-shot dogs while they died, and now this one, this big fellow running straddle-legged and stone cold dead in the face, that wouldnt stop running even after he'd been killed.

I was what you might call unnerved, for they may warn you there's going to be bleeding in battle but you don't believe it till you see the blood. What happened from then on was all mixed up in the smoke. We formed again and went back through the tents. But the same thing happened: they were there, just as before, and when they threw that wall of smoke and humming bullets at us, we came running back down the slope. Three times we went through and it was the same every time. Finally a fresh brigade came up from the reserve and we went through together.

This trip was different—we could tell it even before we got started. We went through the smoke and the bullets, and that was the first time we used bayonets. For a minute it was jab and slash, everyone yelling enough to curdle your blood just with the shrillness. I was running, bent low with the rifle held out front, the way they taught me, and all of a sudden I saw I was going to have it with a big Yank wearing his coat unbuttoned halfway, showing a red flannel undershirt. I was running and he was waiting, braced, and it occurred to me, the words shooting through my mind: What kind of a man is this, would wear a red wool undershirt in April?

I saw his face from below, but he had bent down and his eyebrows were drawn in a straight line like a black bar over his eyes. He was full-grown, with a wide brown mustache; I could see the individual hairs on each side of the shaved line down the middle. I'd have had to say Sir to him back home. Then something hit my arm a jar—I stumbled against him, lifting my rifle and falling sideways. Ee! I'm killed! I thought. He turned with me and we were falling, first a slow fall the way it is in dreams, then sudden, and the ground came up and hit me: ho! We were two feet apart, looking at each other. He seemed even bigger now, up close, and there was something wrong with the way he looked. Then I saw why.

My bayonet had gone in under his jaw, the handguard tight against the bottom of his chin, and the point must have stuck in his head bone because he appeared to be trying to open his mouth but couldnt. It was like he had a mouthful of something bitter and couldnt spit—his eyes were screwed up, staring at me and blinking a bit from the strain. All I could do was look at him; I couldnt look away, no matter how I tried. A man will look at something that is making him sick but he cant stop looking until he begins to vomit—something holds him. That was the way it was with me. Then, while I was watching him, this fellow reached up and touched the handle of the bayonet under his chin. He touched it easy, using the tips of his fingers, tender-like. I could see he wanted to grab and pull it out but he was worried about how much it would hurt and he didnt dare.

I let go of the rifle and rolled away. There were bluecoats running across the field and through the woods beyond. All around me men were kneeling and shooting at them like rabbits as they ran. Captain Plummer and two lieutenants were the only officers left on their feet. Two men were bent over Colonel Thornton where they had propped him against a tree with one of his legs laid crooked. Captain Plummer wasnt limping now—he'd forgotten his blisters, I reckon. He wasnt even hurt, so far as I could see, but the skirt of his coat was ripped where somebody had taken a swipe at him with a bayonet or a saber.

He went out into the open with a man carrying the colors, and then begun to wave his sword and call in a high voice: "6th Mississippi, wally here! 6th Mississippi, wally here!"

Men begun straggling over, collecting round the flag, so I got up and went over with them. We were a sorry lot. My feet were so heavy I could barely lift them, and I had to carry my left arm with my right, the way a baby would cradle a doll. The captain kept calling, "Wally here! 6th Mississippi, wally here!" but after a while he saw there werent any more to rally so he gave it up. There were a little over a hundred of us, all that were left out of the four hundred and twenty-five that went in an hour before.

Our faces were gray, the color of ashes. Some had powder burns red on their cheeks and foreheads and running back into singed patches in their hair. Mouths were rimmed with grime from biting cartridges, mostly a long smear down one corner, and hands were blackened with burnt powder off the ramrods. We'd aged a lifetime since the sun came up. Captain Plummer was calling us to rally, rally here, but there wasnt much rally left in us. There wasnt much left in me, anyhow. I felt so tired it was all I could do to make it to where the flag was. I was worried, too, about not having my rifle. I remembered what Sergeant Tyree was always saying: "Your rifle is your best friend. Take care of it." But if that meant pulling it out of the man with the mustache, it would just have to stay there. Then I looked down and be durn if there wasnt one just like it at my feet. I picked it up, stooping and nursing my bad arm, and stood there with it.

Joe Marsh was next to me. At first I didnt know him. He didnt seem bad hurt, but he had a terrible look around the eyes and there was a knot on his forehead the size of a walnut where some Yank had bopped him with a rifle butt. I thought to ask him how the Tennessee breed of elephant compared with the Kentucky breed, but I didnt. He looked at me, first in the face till he finally recognized me, then down at my arm.

"You better get that tended to."

"It dont hurt much," I said.

"All right. Have it your way."

He didnt pay me any mind after that. He had lorded it over me for a month about being a greenhorn, yet here I was, just gone through meeting as big an elephant as any he had met, and he was still trying the same high-and-mightiness. He was mad now because he wasnt the only one who had seen some battle. He'd had his big secret to throw up to us, but not any more. We all had it now.

We were milling around like ants when their hill is upset, trying to fall-in the usual way, by platoons and squads, but some were all the way gone and others had only a couple of men. So we gave that up and just fell-in in three ranks, not even making a good-sized company. Captain Plummer went down the line, looking to see who was worst hurt. He looked at the way I was holding my arm. "Bayonet?"

"Yes sir."

"Cut you bad?"

"It dont hurt much, captain. I just cant lift it no higher than this."

He looked me in the face, and I was afraid he thought I was lying to keep from fighting any more. "All wight," he said. "Fall out and join the others under that twee."

There were about two dozen of us under it when he got through, including some that hadnt been able to get in ranks in the first place. They were hacked up all kinds of ways. One had lost an ear and he was the worst worried man of the lot; "Does it look bad?" he kept asking, wanting to know how it would seem to the folks back home. We sat under the tree and watched Captain Plummer march what was left of the regiment away. They were a straggly lot. We were supposed to wait there under the tree till the doctor came.

We waited, hearing rifles clattering and cannons booming and men yelling further and further in the woods, and the sun climbed up and it got burning hot. I could look back over the valley where we had charged. It wasnt as wide as it had been before. There were men left all along the way, lying like bundles of dirty clothes. I had a warm, lazy feeling, like on a summer Sunday in the scuppernong arbor back home; next thing I knew I was sound asleep. Now that was strange. I was never one for sleeping in the daytime, not even in that quiet hour after dinner when all the others were taking their naps.

When I woke up the sun was past the overhead and only a dozen or so of the wounded were still there. The fellow next to me (he was hurt in the leg) said they had drifted off to find a doctor. "Aint no doctor coming here," he said. "They aint studying us now we're no more good to them." He had a flushed look, like a man in a fever, and he was mad at the whole army, from General Johnston down to me.

My arm was stiff and the blood had dried on my sleeve. There was just a slit where the bayonet blade went in. It felt itchy, tingling in all directions from the cut, like the spokes of a wheel, but I still hadnt looked at it and I wasnt going to. All except two of the men under the tree were leg wounds, not counting myself, and those two were shot up bad around the head. One was singing a song about the bells of Tennessee but it didnt make much sense.

"Which way did they go?"

"Ever which way," one said.

"Yonder ways, mostly," another said, and pointed over to the right. The shooting was a long way off now, loudest toward the right front. It seemed reasonable that the doctors would be near the loudest shooting.

I thought I would be dizzy when I stood up but I felt fine, light on my feet and tingly from not having moved for so long. I walked away nursing my arm. When I reached the edge of the field I looked back. They were spread around the tree trunk, sprawled out favoring their wounds. I could hear that crazy one singing the Tennessee song.

I walked on, getting more and more light-headed, till finally it felt like I was walking about six inches off the ground. I thought I was still asleep, dreaming, except for the ache in my arm. And I saw things no man would want to see twice. There were dead men all around, Confederate and Union, some lying where they fell and others up under bushes where theyd crawled to keep from getting trampled. There were wounded men too, lots of them, wandering around like myself, their faces dazed and pale from losing blood and being scared.

I told myself: You better lay down before you fall down. Then I said: No, youre not bad hurt; keep going. It was like an argument, two voices inside my head and neither one of them mine:

You better lay down.

—No: you feel fine.

Youll fall and theyll never find you.

—Thats not true. Youre just a little light-headed. Youll be all right.

No you wont. Youre hurt. Youre hurt worse than you think. Lay down.

They went on like that, arguing, and I followed the road, heading south by the sun until I came to a log cabin with a cross on its ridgepole and a little wooden signboard, hand-lettered: Shiloh

Meeting House. It must have been some kind of headquarters now because there were officers inside, bending over maps, and messengers kept galloping up with papers.

I took a left where the road forked, and just beyond the fork there was a sergeant standing with the reins of two horses going back over his shoulder. When I came up he looked at me without saying anything.

"Where is a doctor?" I asked him. My voice sounded strange from not having used it for so long.

"I dont know, bud," he said. But he jerked his thumb down the road toward the sound of the guns. "Should be some of them up there, back of where the fighting is." He was a Texan, by the sound of his voice; it came partly through his nose.

So I went on down the road. It had been a line of battle that morning, the dead scattered thick on both sides. I was in a fever by then, thinking crazy, and it seemed to me that all the dead men got there this way:

God was making men and every now and then He would do a bad job on one, and He would look at it and say, "This one wont do," and He would toss it in a tub He kept there, maybe not even finished with it. And finally, 6 April 1862, the tub got full and God emptied it right out of heaven and they landed here, along this road, tumbled down in all positions, some without arms and legs, some with their heads and bodies split open where they hit the ground so hard.

I was in a fever bad, to think a thing like that. So there's no telling how long I walked or how far, but I know I came near covering that battlefield from flank to flank. It must have been a couple of hours and maybe three miles, but far as I was concerned it could have been a year and a thousand miles. At first all I wanted was a doctor. Finally I didnt even want that. All I wanted was to keep moving. I had an idea if I stopped I wouldnt be able to start again. That kept me going.

I didnt notice much along the way, but once I passed an open space with a ten-acre peach orchard in bloom at the far end and cannons puffing smoke up through the blossoms. Great crowds of men were trying to reach the orchard—they would march up in long lines and melt away; there would be a pause and then other lines would march up and melt away. Then I was past all this, in the woods again, and I came to a little gully where things were still and peaceful, like in another world almost; the guns seemed far away. That was the place for me to stop, if any place was. I sat down, leaning back against a stump, and all the weariness came down on me at once. I knew I wouldnt get up then, not even if I could, but I didnt mind.

I didnt mind anything. It was like I was somewhere outside myself, looking back. I had reached the stage where a voice can tell you it is over, youre going to die, and that is all right too. Dying is as good as living, maybe better. The main thing is to be left alone, and if it takes dying to be let alone, a man thinks: All right, let me die. He thinks: Let me die, then.

This gully was narrow and deep, really a little valley, less than a hundred yards from ridge to ridge. The trees were thick but I could see up to the crest in each direction. There were some dead men and some wounded scattered along the stream that ran through, but I think they must have crawled in after water—there hadnt been any fighting here and there werent any bullets in the trees. I leaned back against the stump, holding my arm across my lap and facing the forward ridge. Then I saw two horsemen come over, side by side, riding close together, one leaning against the other. The second had his arm around the first, holding him in the saddle.

The second man was in civilian clothes, a boxback coat and a wide black hat. It was Governor Harris; I used to see him when he visited our brigade to talk to the Tennessee boys—electioneering, he called it; he was the Governor of Tennessee. The first man had his head down, reeling in the saddle, but I could see the braid on his sleeves and the wreath of stars on his collar. Then he lolled the other way, head rolling, and I saw him full in the face. It was General Johnston.

His horse was shot up, wounded in three legs, and his uniform had little rips in the cape and trouser-legs where minie balls had nicked him. One bootsole flapped loose, cut crossways almost through. In his right hand he held a tin cup, one of his fingers still hooked through the handle. I heard about the cup afterwards—he got it earlier in the day. He was riding through a captured camp and one of his lieutenants came out of a Yank colonel's tent and showed him a fine brier pipe he'd found there. General Johnston said "None of that, Sir. We are not here for plunder." Then he must have seen he'd hurt the lieutenant's feelings, for he leaned down from his horse and picked up this tin cup off a table and said, "Let this be my share of the spoils today," and used it instead of a sword to direct the battle.

They came down the ridge and stopped under a big oak at the bottom, near where I was, and Governor Harris got off between the horses and eased the general down to the ground. He began to ask questions, trying to make him answer, but he wouldnt—couldnt. He undid the general's collar and unfastened his clothes, trying to find where he was shot, but he couldnt find it. He took out a bottle and tried to make him drink (it was brandy; I could smell it) but he wouldnt swallow, and when Governor Harris turned his head the brandy ran out of his mouth.

Then a tall man, wearing the three stars of a colonel, came hurrying down the slope, making straight for where General Johnston was laid out on the ground. He knelt down by his side, leaning forward so that their faces were close together, eye to eye, and begun to nudge him on the shoulder and speak to him in a shaky voice: "Johnston, do you know me? Johnston, do you know me?"

But the general didnt know him; the general was dead. He still looked handsome, lying there with his eyes glazing over.

FROM

Jordan County

SHELBY FOOTE

IN THE FALL following his sixth birthday Hector began to attend the Bristol public school. He still wore the serge knee-breeches, the ribbed stockings, and even the satin tie; the coachman drove him there every morning and called for him every afternoon. It was a new world, peopled with Lilliputians. There was a bell for everything, one to begin and one to end and one each for the many things that came between. First they had a morning prayer, asking God to make them good and thankful, then a song as they stood in the aisles: "Good morning, dear teacher, good morning to you." Then they sat, hands clasped on the desk tops, all eyes on the teacher who said solemnly, "Now we'll put on our thin-king caps," making a two-handed motion as if she were pulling a sack over her head, and all the children did the same; "Now we'll put on our thin-king caps!" they chanted, more or less in unison, performing that same curious head-in-sack motion, groping at the air beside their ears.

As a result of the reading lessons Mrs Wingate had given him every morning out of the primer he would use in school, Hector was far ahead of the other pupils. He could read straight through whole pages, moving glibly down lines of type that caused the others to falter and sweat and tangle their tongues in their teeth. Whenever a particularly difficult passage came up, one that prompted a general squirming and a hiding of eyes out of fear of being called on, the teacher assigned it to Hector, who not only read the words correctly but read them with expression as well, pausing for commas and inflecting the exclamation points and question marks like an actor arrived at his most effective speech. The other pupils turned in their desks and watched him with a certain awe, for sometimes like an orator he made gestures as he read. The teacher always smiled when he had finished and gave a little series of nods of approval. "Very good," she would say. "Very good, indeed. Why cant the rest of you do as well?"

At noon recess he sat apart and ate his lunch from a japanned box which the cook had packed according to his grandmother's instructions; Mrs Wingate had definite opinions about diet. He had a particular place where he sat to eat, on the side steps leading up to the principal's office, and a group of children always collected to watch. For them it was like Christmas morning, watching what came out of the fancy box, one good thing after another and always a surprise for dessert, a cookie with colored icing, a strawberry tart, or a gingerbread man with raisins for eyes and three more raisins in a row for the buttons on his coat. They stood at the foot of the steps, their eyes growing larger, their mouths gaping wider with each good thing that emerged. For Hector there was something embarrassing about having them stand that way, gawking. He thought they were probably hungry; they looked it. But once when he offered a boiled egg to one of the watchers (there was always a boiled egg, with two twists of waxed paper, one for salt and one for pepper; "They build bone," his grandmother said mysteriously) the boy put his hands quickly behind him, his eyes wide as he looked at the egg on Hector's palm, and backed away. "Go on, take it," Hector said. "I dont want it anyhow." The boy turned and ran.

Presently his brother, a big fourth-grade boy with a shock of yellow hair high on his head and a saddle of freckles across his nose, approached the steps. He came striding, then stopped with his face thrust close to Hector's and said in a gruff voice, "Keep your old done-up grub to yourself, Mister Fancy Pants."

"Well, I will," Hector told him.

"Well—all right," the boy said. He paused. Then, considering that this was a note perhaps not forceful enough to end the exchange on, he thrust his face closer and added still more gruffly, "You want to make something *of* it?" The freckles stood out large and brown, and his younger brother peeped around his shoulder.

"Well, no," Hector said. "I dont."

"Well—all right," the fourth-grader said. And deciding that this was probably forceful enough after all, he said no more. He just stood there, glowering and clenching his fists. All the watchers laughed and whooped until Miss Hobbs, the principal, came to the door at the top of the steps and scattered them.

"Hush this hubbub!" she cried, and they ran, exploding outward as if a bomb had gone off in their midst. She held a sheaf of papers in one hand and brandished a ruler in the other, a tall gray-haired woman wearing an alpaca skirt, streaked and splotched with chalk-dust, and a horn-rim pince-nez from which two strands of ribbon drooped to a gold pin at the breast of her shirtwaist. The ribbons fluttered in the breeze.

Hector returned to his lunchbox. He sat there eating as if nothing had happened. Miss Hobbs turned to go, then paused with one hand on the door knob, looking down at Hector. "Why didnt you stand up to them?" she asked. Her nippers glinted in the sunlight, vibrating with the flutter of the ribbons. "Even if that tow-headed one had hit you, it would have been lots easier than what they will do to you now." Hector stopped chewing. He looked at her, his jaw bulged with food. She watched him, not unkindly, waiting, but he only looked at her with that same vacant stare, eyes bland, expressionless. "Well, maybe you know best," Miss Hobbs said. She entered her office, closing the door behind her, and Hector resumed his chewing.

This ended that early, brief period during which the other children stood in awe of and even perhaps respected him. Now whenever the teacher assigned him a difficult passage they turned and watched as always, except that now their faces expressed not awe but derision. They smirked and sniggered at the way he dramatized the words, and sometimes when he made one of those oration gestures with a free hand to emphasize an action or a happy turn of phrase, the teacher had to rap smartly on the edge of her desk with her ruler to stop the catcalls of the boys and the giggles of the girls. It was as Miss Hobbs had foreseen.

Outside the classroom it was even worse. Beginning with the day of the boiled egg incident, it became part of the school life for a group to assemble at the carriage block for his arrival and departure. They would stand solemnly watching him climb into the carriage with the lunchbox under one arm and an oilcloth book satchel under the other. Then, as if by prearranged signal, at the moment when Samuel lifted the reins to flick the horses into motion, they would hoot and jeer, shouting "Fancy Pants! Mister Fancy Pants! Fancy Pants!" running alongside until the carriage picked up speed and left them behind. Hector kept his eyes to the front. High on the box Samuel muttered angrily, "Trash. Nothing but trash; thats all. White trash."

But that was not all, for soon it began to pale; it was not enough, and two weeks later a gang of boys waylaid him. He had seen them whispering behind their hands all morning, watching him out of the sides of their eyes. Obviously they were plotting something, but he did not discover what until that afternoon. The group at the carriage block, assembled to give him the jeering send-off, was much smaller than usual. He thought nothing of this, however, until the coachman slowed to turn a corner two blocks from the school and a band armed with barrel staves and lengths of lath came charging out of a clump of mulberry trees and began to beat on the sides of the carriage, cheering each other on and screaming their battle cries.

For a moment Hector was terrified by the din of sticks against the fenders and running-boards, the mass of wild, excited faces with open mouths and tossing hair. Then, drawing on some atavistic reserve—received perhaps from the man who fell near the apex of the V at Buena Vista—he stood on the seat, facing backward over the tonneau, and swung the oilcloth book satchel at their heads. He held it by the long carrying-strap and swung it with all his might. It was a gift from his grandmother, the latest model, with special compartments for books and tablets and a row of pencils stuck through little loops of elastic, each with his name stamped in gold on its shank near the rubber eraser. As he swung it he could hear the tablets and books slapping against each other and the dry, brittle sound of pencils breaking. Samuel looked back over his shoulder. "Give it to um, Little Mars!" he cried. "Give it to um!"

That was just what Hector was doing. The satchel made really an excellent counter-offensive weapon. But the first time it landed squarely against one of the upturned screaming faces, he felt the shock of resistance travel up the strap, the momentary give of flesh and then the solidity of bone beneath: whereupon, all of a sudden, there was a flutter at the pit of his stomach and a sour taste at the root of his tongue. He dropped the satchel onto the seat and, turning, sat for an instant with a stricken, dazed expression of revulsion on his face. Then he leaned deliberately foward, placing his head between his knees, and threw up on the floorboard of the carriage.

"What you want to quit for?" Samuel said, forlorn on the box. "You was just gitting going good."

The waylayers had been startled by the counterattack, as unexpected as it was violent, and when the satchel struck one of them they fell back. However, they recovered quickly—except the boy who had received the blow; he was nursing his face—and began to gather rocks and clods of dirt from the roadside and fling them after the carriage. One knocked Samuel's plug hat clean off; he barely managed to grab it before it rolled into the road. Another caught Hector above the left eye just as he was straightening up. These were the only two hits, though other clods and rocks continued to clatter against the rear of the carriage until it was out of range.

When they turned in at the house Mrs Wingate was standing in a rosebed beside the drive. She wore a heavy leather gauntlet as if for hawking, with a pair of snips in one hand and some dead stems in the other. First she saw the dent in the coachman's hat and then the cut above her grandson's eye. She took Hector up to her room, and when she had cleaned the wound with camphor she made him tell her what had happened, from the beginning. He had been all right up till then—in his mind at least, for the vomiting had resulted from an impulse in his stomach; it had nothing to do with his mind, he told himself—but now, as he stood in front of his grandmother, breathing the clean, medicinal smell of camphor, feeling it tingle the gash above his eye, and tried to tell about what had happened since the day of the boiled egg, he began to cry. And that was the greatest shame of all; it made him cry all the harder. When at length he had finished both the weeping and the telling, Mrs Wingate gave him his first lesson in the mysteries of human relationships.

"Now listen," she said. Placing both hands on his shoulders, she looked directly into his eyes and held him so that he had to look directly into hers. Whenever his eyes tried to wander or lose focus she gave him a shake that brought them back where they belonged. "There are really only two classes of people in this world, those who have and those who wish they had. When those of the second class . . . Mind what I'm telling you," she said sharply. She gripped him tighter, and when his eyes came back into focus she resumed. "When those of the second class begin to realize that they will never catch up with those of the first, they jeer. All right: listen. Those of the first class (which includes you," she said, releasing one shoulder to give him a prod, then grasping it again) "must realize that the jeering goes with the having. Besides, when you are older and able to strike back at them, by foreclosing their mortgages or causing them to be dismissed from their places of employment, they will not jeer where you can hear them. They wont dare to; no. And what is said behind your back cannot matter, first because you cannot hear it and second because it is a sort of underhanded compliment in the first place. It's a certain sign that they acknowledge your position, a proof of membership. You understand?"

"Yessum," he said, responding to another shake. But he did not.

That was his last day in a public school; he did not go back even to clean out his desk. Mrs Wingate engaged the mathematics and science teacher from Bristol High School to come to the house every afternoon and tutor him. This was Professor Rosenbach, a German with a dark brown beard and inward-slanting teeth: Professor Frozen Back he was called, for he walked with a stiff Prussian carriage as if he were pacing off the distance between barriers for a duel. However, there were those who said that he had left the fatherland as a youth to avoid military service in the war with France, and now he walked this way either to make up for it or to mislead suspicion. This may or may not have been true; in any event it was certainly malicious, being repeated mainly by pupils or former pupils who resented his stern classroom discipline and who could give first-hand testimony as to his zeal with the birch. But there was no doubt that he gave an impression of militarism. The seals on his watchfob made a little chinking sound wherever he went, reproducing in miniature the clink of a saber chain, and there was a cicatrice high on one cheek that might have been a dueling scar, direct from Heidelberg, except that it was rather small and neat and had been acquired in the high school chemistry laboratory when he was rinsing a beaker in which a careless or ingenious pupil had left a pellet of sodium.

The professor believed in memory work. It developed the mind, he said; he frequently referred to the mind in this manner, as if it were a muscle or a savings account or a combination of both. He sat in an armchair in the upstairs parlor during the lessons, holding the book on his knee and marking the place with a finger between the leaves, while Hector stood opposite him, arms straight at his sides, fists clenched, like a choir boy trying for a high note, and recited the multiplication tables or the rules of spelling and grammar. "Good. Very good," Professor Rosenbach would say, stroking the underside of his beard with the backs of fingers whose nails were filed straight across like those on the statues of Greek athletes. "We are making progress. Now give me the nine-times table." Then he would resume that curious rotary motion with his hand under the short dark beard, nodding his head in time to the chant of arithmetic, and when it was finished he would nod once more, with a sudden, ponderous motion, and shine his eyes. "Good. Good," he would say. "Very good, Master Hector."

At first it was queer, being at home all morning while the others were at school and only beginning his lessons after the others had finished. Some mornings he would think about them, the way they stood in the aisles beside their desks, heads bent, reciting the prayer, then lifting their heads and shuffling their feet and singing, "We're all in our places, With sunshiny faces; Good morning, dear teacher, Good morning to you," while the teacher beat time with her ruler and sang louder than anyone, wishing herself goodmorning. But after a while he seldom thought of them. The six weeks at the public school were a period far in the past; he might have dreamed it. Education was Professor Rosenbach, opposite him there in the armchair with the book held on one knee. If other children were herded together in an atmosphere of chalkdust and confusion, with a bell for this and a bell for that and bells for the hundred things that came between, obliged to chant in unison and wear invisible thinking caps, that was their misfortune. His grandmother had explained it, and though he did not understand the explanation, it was comforting at any rate to be told there was one.

When he was twelve and had completed a course of study roughly corresponding to the one covered by the local grammar school, he went away to boarding school in Virginia. By the time he was into his second year in the East, Bristol was secondary; he had come to think of it mainly as a place where he spent three more or less pleasant months doing nothing every summer. In dormitory conversations he dropped references to "our Mississippi plantation," saying the words with an off-hand, studied carelessness to imply that it was one of many, just as other boys up here said "our Newport place" or "our Pennsylvania holdings." It was that kind of school; Mrs Wingate had chosen it after a good deal of correspondence around the country. Bristol people (which included his mother and father, but not his grandmother) became a faraway conglomerate of faceless automatons who did not wear the clothes he wore or speak with the accent he spoke with or think the things he thought. It was rather as if they were all in a cage, provincial, and he was on the outside looking in.

The center spread in his American History book was a relief map of North America. On it he traced the Mississippi River from its source to a point where it made two sharp curves, like an S laid on its back, and that was Bristol (or at any rate it might have been, for the river had many such double bends); "Thats my home," he said, placing the tip of one finger on the lower curve. The map showed none of the man-made boundaries, only the natural formations, rivers and their tributaries, like lengths of string, and mountains like brown wrinkles on the page. It was strange, being able to point to this one spot out of all that veined and crinkled mass of brown and white, and tell someone "Thats my home" as if he owned it, river and all. He did not say it with any real conviction.

Christmas of 1892, when Hector was fourteen, he came home for the holidays for the first time in two years. He brought two classmates with him. They were out of Maryland, city boys from Baltimore, and when they had not understood what was said to them, they did not say Sir? or Maam? after the usage taught in Mississippi; they said Pardon? which would have made people think them abrupt and rude if they had not had such good manners otherwise and such expensive clothes and luggage. The highlight of their visit was the Christmas trip around the plantation. They went with Hector and Mrs Wingate in the carriage, and more than anything they were impressed with the way the tenants approached their mistress with their hats off, bobbing their heads and showing their teeth and saying, "Crissmus giff, Ole Miss: Crissmus giff! En you too, Little Mars: Crissmus giff!" and the way Mrs Wingate took silver dollars from a canvas sack on the seat beside her, handing them out one at a time with a stern expression and calling each of the Negroes by name as he stood bobbing and grinning above the hat he held in both hands like a basin.

"You wouldnt have believed it," the Maryland boys said afterwards. "It was like something out of the Middle Ages. It really was."

That was the way they told about their visit when they got back to school in Virginia. They had gone down there half expecting to find it one big swamp; they admitted now that they had had misgivings. But they had been wrong and they wanted to make amends.

Life in Mississippi—"the Delta, they call it, though it's not all the way down at the mouth of the river"—was fascinating (that was the word they used, back in Virginia) and Mrs Wingate was "a lady of the old school, one of the few that are left." Others listened while the travelers told about life on the plantation, especially the silver dollars distributed from a sack—"like something out of the Middle Ages. It really was"—and Hector's stock went up. They had never called him anything but Sturgis, yet now they began to use his first name and even abbreviate it. They called him Heck, a devil-may-care sort of nickname. It was almost as if he had made the varsity. Classmates who formerly had cut him dead now nodded to him on the quad. There was nothing really effusive about it, but all this was quite different from anything he had ever known before.

Also, now that it had brought him this, he began to see in his homeland values he had never sensed before. He saw it with new eyes, the eyes of strangers, and in a different light. It was indeed romantic, he saw now, where formerly he had thought of it as just the opposite. The Negroes, the overarching trees, the river, all the things he had taken for granted while he lived among them—even the giving of silver dollars out of a canvas sack, since that apparently had impressed the visitors most—now had an enchantment lent by distance and praise, and Hector told himself that when he got back home he would appreciate them. He would study them in this new light. Even his grandmother, whom he already admired to what he had thought were the limits of possibility, acquired an added value now that the Maryland boys had defined her singularity—"a lady of the old school, one of the few that are left." In her case, too, he told himself he would make a reassessment; he would appreciate her even more when they were together again.

It did not work out that way, however. They were never together again. The fever intervened.

Mrs Wingate wrote to him once a week, and that was how he learned of its return. First there were just a few scattered cases, nothing really unusual for the time of year. Then there were more, and more, until at last it had become an epidemic. He no longer had to wait for information from the letters. News of fever deaths was featured in all the papers. Yellow fever was general all down the Valley, and though it was not as serious as it had been fifteen years ago, in the season of Hector's birth, it was serious enough.

Then there was a week when no letter came. He told himself it was nothing. The authorities had quarantined the mails, or railroad workers had refused to handle anything out of the delta, even letters, or she was too busy to write. He told himself all these things and more, doing everything he could to keep one certain thought out of his mind. Then, when it passed from a notion to a conviction, he told himself not to think about it at all. It would work itself out; any day now he would get a letter in his grandmother's angular script explaining the lapse. What he finally got was a telegram signed by the family doctor, which put an end to wondering:

> GRANDMOTHER FATHER DEAD BUT MOTHER WILL LIVE
> I THINK. DO NOT COME HOME TIL EPIDEMIC PAST.

He had not believed Mrs Wingate would ever die. Sitting in the dormitory cubicle, the sheet of yellow flimsy in his hand, he could hear her speaking to him the way she had done through his childhood, telling him of Irish wheelbarrow laborers in the oldtime levee camps and of the two classes of people, the havers and the wishers, teaching him how to tell time with his dead grandfather's watch and how to blow his nose and tuck his shirttail, the long, involved, tortuous sentences grinding on, the convulsive syntax causing the language to turn back on itself like a snake devouring its tail. But she was dead now: dead, and so was his father: both were dead and probably buried, and he would never see them again. He kept saying it over and over in his mind, in order to accustom himself to thinking of them in the past tense.

It was difficult in his grandmother's case, for he could see her as clearly as if she were with him now in the cubicle, the mouth held a bit awry to hide the tooth-gap and the hair that was white because of the strange alchemy of bluing. But when he tried to think of his father he found that he could not shape the face. He could recall it in outline; his father had begun to get fat and his face was redder, too. But when he tried to fix the features, they faded and there was only the blank oval. He tried to remember words that his father had spoken to him, something, anything at all, but there was nothing. Then, as he had done before, he told himself not to think about it. It would work itself out in time, he told himself.

In mid-June there was an exchange of wires: SCHOOL IS OVER CAN I COME HOME NOW? and then the answer: FEVER STILL EPIDEMIC. DRAW ON BANK FOR FUNDS. It was signed MOTHER. So he went to Baltimore, returning the visit of the Maryland boys. He wrote home, telling where he was, and waited for an answer. For two weeks there was nothing. Then in the third week he got a letter, and when he saw the envelope his heart gave a leap. It was addressed in his grandmother's hand. But when he tore it open and looked at the foot of the single sheet (Mrs Wingate had always written at least three pages) the signature said *Mother.* It inclosed a check for a hundred dollars and instructed him to return the following week. That was all it said.

Previously the trainride had been one of the best things about coming home for the holidays. This time it was different, partly because there were no other young people on the train, but mainly because he was riding toward his first realization of death; he could not believe in his grandmother's death until he saw for himself that she was gone. He wired from Memphis and the carriage was waiting at the Bristol station, just as always except that Samuel was alone. During the ride to the house he observed that the town was expanding eastward toward the Wingate property. At last they were there, and when he saw that the house had not changed, that it even had a new coat of paint like the old one, he realized that he had expected to find it dilapidated, as if the epidemic would leave a path of destruction like Sherman or a cyclone. But the driveway gravel had been raked as neatly as ever and there were not even weeds in the rosebeds. Then, going up the steps, he saw Mrs Wingate's shawl folded over the arm of her rocker on the gallery.

The shawl was what did it, brought it into the open. When he saw the shawl he began to suspect, quite consciously, that this was all a hoax, an ugly joke prepared and staged to test him, to show him how much his grandmother meant to him. And now that he had begun to suspect quite consciously, it seemed to him that he had never believed in the absence of letters or even in the telegram that followed. She was not dead: they had only told him that. The feeling, the conviction grew as he entered the house. Upstairs, when he stopped with one hand on the newel post and peered through the twilight of the upper hall, into Mrs Wingate's room where the only light was what filtered between slats of the drawn blinds, he saw that his suspicions were true. She was propped up in bed, asleep, wearing one of her quilted jackets and a nightcap with frill as stiff as icing on a cake. Her hands rested outside the covers, the fingers half curled into fists. She lay so profoundly motionless that for a moment he thought they had saved her body, had postponed burial all these weeks until he got there to see her before she went down into the grave. Then, as he stood watching, her hands twitched in sleep, the rings glinting.

She was not dead: they had only told him that. But as he started forward, intending to waken her, he saw that she had indeed been sick. She was thinner, and even in that dim light he could make out new lines in her face. He looked at her carefully, closer now. Somehow the sickness had reduced her stature; her feet were a long way from the footboard. Then, without any preliminary flicker, the eyelids lifted. She was awake, looking at him, and her eyes had changed too. But it was only when she spoke to him, saying his name with the different inflection, that he saw his mistake. It was his mother.

The fever had wasted her, the ash-blonde hair gone to gray and the body under the counterpane was like a loosely tied bundle of sticks. She was convalescing now, allowed only the morning hours out of bed, but already she had assumed charge of the house. She had wanted the whip hand for so many years that as soon as it was hers she would not delay using it, not even for the fever. When she had passed the crisis and they told her Mrs Wingate was dead (she already knew about Sturgis, though they had moved him into the room where Hector dreamed of bears; she watched through the doorway while he died, and unlike the news of her mother's death—though it was true she was sicker at the time—it seemed not to affect her one way or the other) her reaction took the form of a violent impatience that would not be quieted until she was moved into the dead woman's room across the hall. The ravages of fever had caused her to resemble Mrs Wingate, or at least had heavily underlined a resemblance formerly made vague by the span of years between them, and she took pride in this, doing all she could to emphasize it. As soon as she was able to sit up in bed she began to wear the dead woman's clothes; she even held her mouth awry, irked and bitter-looking, though there was no gap to hide.

People were considerably taken aback at this manifestation of what they thought was grief and respect for the dead woman. They had rather supposed there was bad blood between them; they had not realized she loved her mother so. "It just goes to show," they said. "You never miss the water till the well runs dry. You cant tell about people, no way in the world." This was because they did not understand. What they called manifestations of grief and respect, and even love, was in fact the celebration of another victory, one by which all her others paled in comparison. She had not only outlived her enemy; she had assimilated her personality, her looks and character and actions, to the extent that the world would never know she was gone, much less miss her.

During the summer of her convalescence and afterwards, when Hector returned to the preparatory school, she extended her activities to include not only the running of the house but also the supervision of the plantation. Mrs Wingate had always watched the crops and checked the books and had weekly conferences with the manager, but Mrs Sturgis did more. She subscribed to and read periodicals on the new diversified agriculture, and in good weather or bad she rode the turnrows in her mother's carriage, taking the bows of the tenants, a small, bustling woman with a quick eye for a dollar and a sharp tongue for whoever crossed her. She had learned her lesson well and made her plans, and now she used them.

When Hector came home from his second year at the University of Virginia, a rather plump young man by then, wearing Eastern clothes and even a straw boater with a gaudy band and a shiny black, wet-looking length of string that drooped like fishline from its brim to the buttonhole at his lapel to keep it from blowing away, he discovered on his ride from the station that Bristol had indeed expanded eastward. The railroad no longer drew its noose about the limits of the town; a new, more fashionable residential district had sprung up beyond it. Mrs Sturgis had subdivided the West Hundred, a cut of buckshot bottomland where the crops had never been good, and people already were building houses there. Two years later, when he came home from graduation, a bachelor of arts, the new houses extended to within shouting distance of the Wingate house itself.

That was 1898. All down the seaboard, then westward through Atlanta and Birmingham, he had seen brass bands parading and lamp posts strung with bunting and cheesecloth lettered boldly lest people forget to remember the *Maine*. They were parading in Bristol, too, and when Captain Barcroft, who commanded the local volunteer company now being organized, approached him with the offer of a position as adjutant, Hector accepted. It carried the rank of lieutenant, and he was to be sworn in the following morning.

They were expecting marching orders any day, first to Jackson for field training with the regiment—the old Second Mississippi, in which his great-grandfather had fought and died, down in Mexico under Jefferson Davis—then to Cuba.

He did not tell his mother about it until that night when they were alone in the parlor after supper. He tried to make it casual in the telling.

"I'll be sworn in tomorrow," he said in conclusion.

Mrs Sturgis looked up sharply from her knitting. "I reckon not," she said. "This is no time for you to be gallivanting off, playing soldier." Her spectacles glittered in the gaslight. "Is that how you intend to use a fifteen thousand dollar education?"

"Noam. But I told Captain Barcroft—"

"So?" she said. "Well, you can just untell him."

When the volunteers entrained the following week at the Bristol depot, amid the hoarse shouts of old men and the fluttering handkerchiefs of the ladies, Hector Wingate Sturgis was not among them.

FROM

A Piece of My Heart

Richard Ford

I

In 1951 in the summer, they had driven in his father's Mercury from Jackson to Memphis, and on the first day he had sat with his mother in the Chief Chisca Hotel and looked out on Union Avenue and sighed, while his father went off in the heat to call on his accounts. And in the evening they went in the car as far on Union Avenue as there was a street to drive on and stopped at a white house with blue shutters where his father knew a man named Hershel Hoytt who sold raisins. In the house, the man was there and wore golfing shorts and carried a golf club and wore thick black glasses and had a face like a stork. They sat down at the round table in the kitchen and drank whiskey and laughed and sang and ate spaghetti with Vienna sausages, and he was shown to the bedroom where there was a wide bed with a white chenille cover, and told that he could go to sleep. At two o'clock he was asleep with the light on in the ceiling, when the door opened and his mother and father came and stood beside the bed and looked at him and said he was pretty (though he was awake by then) and gently moved him onto the pillows and lay across the bed themselves and went to sleep. And he lay in the bed, the three of them lying cross-wise in the tiny room with the fruit salad globe in the light, still shining over them, and he smelled their breath and listened to them breathing and remembered their singing, and listened to the strange house become quiet until he began to cry, and left the house.

On Union Avenue he walked back to town, walked back until he came to the chalky red bricks that sloped straight toward the river, and when he walked farther down toward where the water was, there was a terrible stink like oil and old cabbage, and he went back up the levee and over into town, and walked to the Peabody Hotel, where his father had said the rich people stayed when they came to Memphis. And in the upper lobby he went to sleep behind the notary public's desk.

In the morning at seven o'clock he waked up and looked down on the wide lobby from the mezzanine and saw people were standing at the circular fish pond in the middle of the wide room, holding tiny boxes of crackers and staring at the bank of elevators built into the wall with gilt mirrors for doors. And in a while the elevator door opened and a Negro wearing a white waiter's jacket came off followed by six mallard ducks, walking in a line behind him. And when the Negro had walked to the pond and stood beside it, the ducks all walked into the pond and began to float and quack and eat the crackers the people were holding for them, until the people were gone and there were small red and white cracker boxes floating on the water with the ducks, which the Negro later took away.

And his father said, when he had found them again in the Chief Chisca waiting, that they would never drink again, and that each day the Negro brought the ducks down precisely at seven o'clock, and precisely at five o'clock he came again and stood beside the pond and the ducks simply walked out and got on the elevator and rode it to the roof and got off and sat in their nests of straw and waited until he came again. Once, he said, a man from Arkansas came and fed one duck one tiny crystal of cyanide. And when the duck died, which wasn't very long, the others would not come down for a month. The Negro would ride the elevator to the roof and stand beside their nests and wait for them, but they wouldn't come. They simply quacked and quacked at him, as if he were the man who had betrayed them. Though after a month of quacking at the Negro and sitting on their nests all day getting fatter and fatter, the Negro came with a different colored coat and stood beside their cages, and they came along the way they always had. And before long, his father told him, sitting looking out the window at the Chief Chisca down on Union Avenue, the man went back to wearing his white jacket and the ducks could not remember they had thought he had betrayed them.

II

In the summer, in the tiny tourist cabin in Angola, he had sat with his father and stared out the door towards the prison, a wide, barbed wire compound visible by day, and only a ring of tiny lights at night. The day before, a brown panel truck had come down from Shreveport, with the electric chair, driven through the center of town, and made everyone stop in the sun and look. The state owned a single electric chair and delivered it to and fro wherever it was needed, from courthouse to courthouse all across the state wherever there was someone to electrocute. At midnight everyone in the town turned on their lights and stood at their windows and waited, and when the chair was turned on, all the lights in town went dim for a time, and all the glimmering lights at the prison went dim, and in the motel room with his father he lay in the bed and watched the ceiling fan turn slower and slower until it stopped. And in the morning he had gone with his father in his old Mercury to the gate of the prison, and through and along the well-paved macadam to the compound of long white barracks that looked like chicken houses. And in the lot his father had gotten out and gone inside to a man's office to sell him starch for the prisoners' laundry, and he had sat still in the car in the moistened heat of early morning and stared down the long rows of chalk barracks and wondered where the dead man was, wondered if he and the dead man, an unforgiving murderer named Walter L. Magee, were locked up there together, or if in the night they had taken him secretly out of the chair and carted him into town and left him in a room overnight to cool.

III

When he was twelve he had gone with his father and his mother to Biloxi, and they had stayed on the beach at a large, white hotel called the Buena Vista that had deep shady verandas and rows of white cottages in the back under the banana trees. His father went away in the day and came back in the evening, until Saturday when they went to visit a man his father had known in New Orleans, named Peewee McMorris, who had worked on oil derricks until another man had dropped an orange on his head accidentally from the top of the derrick, and after that he never worked again and was permanently stiff in his left leg and stayed in bed in his pink cottage in the palmettos behind Keesler Air Force Base near the V.A. His wife's name was Josephine, and when they arrived she made them all take tall drinks and took them out to visit Peewee, who was sitting on a nylon chaise in the back yard, putting down sprigs of St. Augustine grass from his chair, out of a peach basket he had beside him. Peewee was a small knuckly man with a long Italian jaw and was very glad to have a drink in the hot afternoon. When he had taken his first long sip of whiskey, Peewee smiled at him and asked him if he wanted to see a trick. When he said yes he would, Peewee jimmied himself off the chaise lounge and put his hand on the boy's shoulder and walked stiff-legged to the corner of the house to where Josephine had planted azaleas and forsythias to hide the water meter. Inside the largest azalea bush, which was blooming with violet pink petals, Peewee found a large wasp nest and pointed for him to see. He was afraid of wasps and did not like it, if that were to be the trick, and stood back. Peewee laughed, and when the last wasp had landed on the broad crusty hive and none were left flying around that he could see, he carefully put his hand into the nest and let the wasps light on him and walk around on his knuckly skin and try their stingers on his flesh, until it seemed they would reach the bone. Peewee, without shaking, began to laugh and laugh, and said that since the man had dropped the orange on his head he had not been able to feel pain in many parts of his body, and that his hand was one of the parts, and that a wasp could sting him until he was blue in the face and that it would not hurt. He drew back his hand with one wasp still clinging to his middle finger, his stinger sunk in Peewee's flesh. And Peewee laughed and flicked the wasp away like he would a match and left the stinger in place inside his hand. When he had looked at Peewee's hand for a long time, dangling beside his highball glass on the thick mat of St. Augustine, he told his mother he would like to go for a swim in the Gulf before he went to bed. And when he had stood in the brown brackish Gulf water for a long time and looked out along the Hotel's whitewashed pier at the old men dipping crab nets down toward the shallow water, he could see the blue Man o' Wars floating in on the tide, riding the lazy surf toward the beach, and he wondered if they would sting him if he mingled his legs among their straggling tentacles.

IV

In Jackson, Mississippi, in 1953, his father brought him downtown and left him in the lobby of the King Edward Hotel while he went away to the mezzanine to talk to a man about selling starch in Alabama. His mother was home in bed and too sick to watch him, so he sat in the lobby and watched the men standing against the fat pillars smoking cigars and shaking hands for minutes at a time. In a little while a midget came into the lobby wearing cowboy boots and a Texas hat, and attracted everyone's attention as he signed his name to the register and gave the bellboy a tip before he ever touched a bag. When he was ready to go to his room, the midget turned and looked around the pillared lobby into the alcoves and sconces as if he were looking for someone to meet him. And when he saw the boy sitting on the long couch, he came across in his midget's gait that made him look as if he were wearing diapers, and told the boy that his name was Tex Arkana, and that he was in the movies and had been the midget in *Samson and Delilah* and had been one of the Philistines that Samson had killed with the jaw-bone of a mule. He said he had seen the movie and remembered the midget fairly well. The midget said that in his bags he had all his movie photos and a long scrapbook with his newspaper clippings which he would be glad to show him if he cared to see. Most of the men in the lobby were watching the two of them sitting on the couch talking, and the midget kept watching them and talking faster. When the boy said he would care to see the scrapbook and the photos too, the midget got up and the two of them got on the elevator with the bellboy and went to the midget's new room which faced the street. When the bellboy had left, the midget took off his shirt and sat on the floor in his undershirt and opened the suitcase and went jerking through the clothes looking for the book while the boy sat on the chair and watched. In a little while the midget found the broad wooden-sided book and jumped on the bed, his cowboy boots dangling against the skirts and showed the boy pictures of himself in *Samson and Delilah* and in *Never Too Soon* and in a movie with John Garfield and Fred Astaire. There were pictures of the midget in the circus riding elephants and sitting on top of tigers and standing beside tall men under tents and in the laps of several different fat women who were all laughing. When they had looked at all the pictures and all the clippings, the midget said that he was sleepy after a long plane ride from the west coast and that the boy would have to go so he could go to sleep. The boy shook hands with the midget and the midget gave him an autographed picture of himself standing on a jeweled chariot with a long whip, being pulled by a team of normal sized men. And the boy left.

When he came back to the lobby his father was waiting for him, smoking a cigar, and he showed him the picture of the midget in the chariot, and his father became upset and tore up the picture, and went to the glassed-in office beside the front desk and had a long talk with the manager while the boy waited outside. In a little while his father came out and the two of them went home where his mother was sick. And late in the night he could hear his mother and father talking about the picture and about the midget with the cowboy boots on, and he heard his father say that the manager had refused to have the midget thrown out of the hotel, and in a little while he could hear his mother crying.

V

In the Roosevelt Hotel in New Orleans he went with his father out of their room and into the dark, shaded corridor to where the elevators were, to go have oysters in the Sazarac Bar. And in the corridor there were men piled up against a doorway, straining and staring inside at something he could not see, but that was the object of someone's flash camera inside the room. And when his father got to where the men were, he looked in over their shoulders and said, "Look here." And the men parted the way and he stepped up to the door and looked around the painted jamb and saw a young man in his thirties with short blond hair and a square meaty face, lying face down half on his bed and half off, with his feet sticking straight up into the air like flagpoles, holding a pistol. The room was cool and smelled like cheap soap, and the man looked strange to be lying in that particular way. And he said to his father, "What's this?" And all at once the dark man with the camera reached to move the young man who was half on and half off the bed, and his father said, "Listen, now listen, and you can hear him rattle in his throat." And he listened and when the man with the camera moved the man with his feet on the bed in such a way that he was no longer lying on his nose, there was a faint sound from somewhere, like someone in the room had caught a fly in his throat and tried to cough it up without making any noise, and his father said, "See? See? Did you hear it?" And he wasn't ever sure if he had heard it or not.

Revenge

Ellen Gilchrist

It was the summer of the Broad Jump Pit.

The Broad Jump Pit, how shall I describe it! It was a bright orange rectangle in the middle of a green pasture. It was three feet deep, filled with river sand and sawdust. A real cinder track led up to it, ending where tall poles for pole-vaulting rose forever in the still Delta air.

I am looking through the old binoculars. I am watching Bunky coming at a run down the cinder path, pausing expertly at the jump-off line, then rising into the air, heels stretched far out in front of him, landing in the sawdust. Before the dust has settled Saint John comes running with the tape, calling out measurements in his high, excitable voice.

Next comes my thirteen-year-old brother, Dudley, coming at a brisk jog down the track, the pole-vaulting pole held lightly in his delicate hands, then vaulting, high into the sky. His skinny tanned legs make a last, desperate surge, and he is clear and over.

Think how it looked from my lonely exile atop the chicken house. I was ten years old, the only girl in a house full of cousins. There were six of us, shipped to the Delta for the summer, dumped on my grandmother right in the middle of a world war.

They built this wonder in answer to a V-Mail letter from my father in Europe. The war was going well, my father wrote, within a year the Allies would triumph over the forces of evil, the world would be at peace, and the Olympic torch would again be brought down from its mountain and carried to Zurich or Amsterdam or London or Mexico City, wherever free men lived and worshiped sports. My father had been a participant in an Olympic event when he was young.

Therefore, the letter continued, Dudley and Bunky and Philip and Saint John and Oliver were to begin training. The United States would need athletes now, not soldiers.

They were to train for broad jumping and pole-vaulting and discus throwing, for fifty-, one-hundred-, and four-hundred-yard dashes, for high and low hurdles. The letter included instructions for building the pit, for making pole-vaulting poles out of cane, and for converting ordinary sawhorses into hurdles. It ended with a page of tips for proper eating and admonished Dudley to take good care of me as I was my father's own dear sweet little girl.

The letter came one afternoon. Early the next morning they began construction. Around noon I wandered out to the pasture to see how they were coming along. I picked up a shovel.

"Put that down, Rhoda," Dudley said. "Don't bother us now. We're working."

"I know it," I said. "I'm going to help."

"No, you're not," Bunky said. "This is the Broad Jump Pit. We're starting our training."

"I'm going to do it too," I said. "I'm going to be in training."

"Get out of here now," Dudley said. "This is only for boys, Rhoda. This isn't a game."

"I'm going to dig it if I want to," I said, picking up a shovelful of dirt and throwing it on Philip. On second thought I picked up another shovelful and threw it on Bunky.

"Get out of here, Ratface," Philip yelled at me. "You German spy." He was referring to the initials on my Girl Scout uniform.

"You goddamn niggers," I yelled. "You niggers. I'm digging this if I want to and you can't stop me, you nasty niggers, you Japs, you Jews." I was throwing dirt on everyone now. Dudley grabbed the shovel and wrestled me to the ground. He held my arms down in the coarse grass and peered into my face.

"Rhoda, you're not having anything to do with this Broad Jump Pit. And if you set foot inside this pasture or come around here and touch anything we will break your legs and drown you in the bayou with a crowbar around your neck." He was twisting my leg until it creaked at the joints. "Do you get it, Rhoda? Do you understand me?"

"Let me up," I was screaming, my rage threatening to split open my skull. "Let me up, you goddamn nigger, you Jap, you spy. I'm telling Grannie and you're going to get the worst whipping of your life. And you better quit digging this hole for the horses to fall in. Let me up, let me up. Let me go."

"You've been ruining everything we've thought up all summer," Dudley said, "and you're not setting foot inside this pasture."

In the end they dragged me back to the house, and I ran screaming into the kitchen where Grannie and Calvin, the black man who did the cooking, tried to comfort me, feeding me pound cake and offering to let me help with the mayonnaise.

"You be a sweet girl, Rhoda," my grandmother said, "and this afternoon we'll go over to Eisenglas Plantation to play with Miss Ann Wentzel."

"I don't want to play with Miss Ann Wentzel," I screamed. "I hate Miss Ann Wentzel. She's fat and she calls me a Yankee. She said my socks were ugly."

"Why, Rhoda," my grandmother said. "I'm surprised at you. Miss Ann Wentzel is your own sweet friend. Her momma was your momma's roommate at All Saint's. How can you talk like that?"

"She's a nigger," I screamed. "She's a goddamned nigger German spy."

"Now it's coming. Here comes the temper," Calvin said, rolling his eyes back in their sockets to make me madder. I threw my second fit of the morning, beating my fists into a door frame. My grandmother seized me in soft arms. She led me to a bedroom where I sobbed myself to sleep in a sea of down pillows.

The construction went on for several weeks. As soon as they finished breakfast every morning they started out for the pasture. Wood had to be burned to make cinders, sawdust brought from the sawmill, sand hauled up from the riverbank by wheelbarrow.

When the pit was finished the savage training began. From my several vantage points I watched them. Up and down, up and down they ran, dove, flew, sprinted. Drenched with sweat they wrestled each other to the ground in bitter feuds over distances and times and fractions of inches.

Dudley was their self-appointed leader. He drove them like a demon. They began each morning by running around the edge of the pasture several times, then practicing their hurdles and dashes, then on to discus throwing and calisthenics. Then on to the Broad Jump Pit with its endless challenges.

They even pressed the old mare into service. Saint John was from New Orleans and knew the British ambassador and was thinking of being a polo player. Up and down the pasture he drove the poor old creature, leaning far out of the saddle, swatting a basketball with my grandaddy's cane.

I spied on them from the swing that went out over the bayou, and from the roof of the chicken house, and sometimes from the pasture fence itself, calling out insults or attempts to make them jealous.

"Guess what," I would yell, "I'm going to town to the Chinaman's store." "Guess what, I'm getting to go to the beauty parlor." "Doctor Biggs says you're adopted."

They ignored me. At meals they sat together at one end of the table, making jokes about my temper and my red hair, opening their mouths so I could see their half-chewed food, burping loudly in my direction.

At night they pulled their cots together on the sleeping porch, plotting against me while I slept beneath my grandmother's window, listening to the soft assurance of her snoring.

I began to pray the Japs would win the war, would come marching into Issaquena County and take them prisoners, starving and torturing them, sticking bamboo splinters under their fingernails. I saw myself in the Japanese colonel's office, turning them in, writing their names down, myself being treated like an honored guest, drinking tea from tiny blue cups like the ones the Chinaman had in his store.

They would be outside, tied up with wire. There would be Dudley, begging for mercy. What good to him now his loyal gang, his photographic memory, his trick magnet dogs, his perfect pitch, his camp shorts, his Baby Brownie camera.

I prayed they would get polio, would be consigned forever to iron lungs. I put myself to sleep at night imagining their labored breathing, their five little wheelchairs lined up by the store as I drove by in my father's Packard, my arm around the jacket of his blue uniform, on my way to Hollywood for my screen test.

Meanwhile, I practiced dancing. My grandmother had a black housekeeper named Baby Doll who was a wonderful dancer. In the mornings I followed her around while she dusted, begging for dancing lessons. She was a big woman, as tall as a man, and gave off a dark rich smell, an unforgettable incense, a combination of Evening in Paris and the sweet perfume of the cabins.

Baby Doll wore bright skirts and on her blouses a pin that said REMEMBER, then a real pearl, then HARBOR. She was engaged to a sailor and was going to California to be rich as soon as the war was over.

I would put a stack of heavy, scratched records on the record player, and Baby Doll and I would dance through the parlors to the music of Glenn Miller or Guy Lombardo or Tommy Dorsey.

Sometimes I stood on a stool in front of the fireplace and made up lyrics while Baby Doll acted them out, moving lightly across the old dark rugs, turning and swooping and shaking and gliding.

Outside the summer sun beat down on the Delta, beating down a million volts a minute, feeding the soybeans and cotton and clover, sucking Steele's Bayou up into the clouds, beating down on the road and the store, on the pecans and elms and magnolias, on the men at work in the fields, on the athletes at work in the pasture.

Inside Baby Doll and I would be dancing. Or Guy Lombardo would be playing "Begin the Beguine" and I would be belting out lyrics.

Oh, let them begin . . . we don't care,
America all . . . ways does its share,
We'll be there with plenty of ammo,
Allies . . . don't ever despair . . .

Baby Doll thought I was a genius. If I was having an especially creative morning she would go running out to the kitchen and bring anyone she could find to hear me.

"Oh, let them begin any warrr . . ." I would be singing, tapping one foot against the fireplace tiles, waving my arms around like a conductor.

Uncle Sam will fight
for the underrr . . . doggg.
Never fear, Allies, never fear.

A new record would drop. Baby Doll would swoop me into her fragrant arms, and we would break into an improvisation on Tommy Dorsey's "Boogie-Woogie."

But the Broad Jump Pit would not go away. It loomed in my dreams. If I walked to the store I had to pass the pasture. If I stood on the porch or looked out my grandmother's window, there it was, shimmering in the sunlight, constantly guarded by one of the Olympians.

Things went from bad to worse between me and Dudley. If we so much as passed each other in the hall a fight began. He would hold up his fists and dance around, trying to look like a fighter. When I came flailing at him he would reach underneath my arms and punch me in the stomach.

I considered poisoning him. There was a box of white powder in the toolshed with a skull and crossbones above the label. Several times I took it down and held it in my hands, shuddering at the power it gave me. Only the thought of the electric chair kept me from using it.

Every day Dudley gathered his troops and headed out for the pasture. Every day my hatred grew and festered. Then, just about the time I could stand it no longer, a diversion occurred.

One afternoon about four o'clock an official-looking sedan clattered across the bridge and came roaring down the road to the house.

It was my cousin, Lauralee Manning, wearing her WAVE uniform and smoking Camels in an ivory holder. Lauralee had been widowed at the beginning of the war when her young husband crashed his Navy training plane into the Pacific.

Lauralee dried her tears, joined the WAVES, and went off to avenge his death. I had not seen this paragon since I was a small child, but I had memorized the photograph Miss Onnie Maud, who was Lauralee's mother, kept on her dresser. It was a photograph of Lauralee leaning against the rail of a destroyer.

Not that Lauralee ever went to sea on a destroyer. She was spending the war in Pensacola, Florida, being secretary to an admiral.

Now, out of a clear blue sky, here was Lauralee, home on leave with a two-carat diamond ring and the news that she was getting married.

"You might have called and given some warning," Miss Onnie Maud said, turning Lauralee into a mass of wrinkles with her embraces. "You could have softened the blow with a letter."

"Who's the groom," my grandmother said. "I only hope he's not a pilot."

"Is he an admiral?" I said, "or a colonel or a major or a commander?"

"My fiancé's not in uniform, Honey," Lauralee said. "He's in real estate. He runs the war-bond effort for the whole state of Florida. Last year he collected half a million dollars."

"In real estate!" Miss Onnie Maud said, gasping. "What religion is he?"

"He's Unitarian," she said. "His name is Donald Marcus. He's best friends with Admiral Semmes, that's how I met him. And he's coming a week from Saturday, and that's all the time we have to get ready for the wedding."

"Unitarian!" Miss Onnie Maud said. "I don't think I've ever met a Unitarian."

"Why isn't he in uniform?" I insisted.

"He has flat feet," Lauralee said gaily. "But you'll love him when you see him."

Later that afternoon Lauralee took me off by myself for a ride in the sedan.

"Your mother is my favorite cousin," she said, touching my face with gentle fingers. "You'll look just like her when you grow up and get your figure."

I moved closer, admiring the brass buttons on her starched uniform and the brisk way she shifted and braked and put in the clutch and accelerated.

We drove down the river road and out to the bootlegger's shack where Lauralee bought a pint of Jack Daniel's and two Cokes. She poured out half of her Coke, filled it with whiskey, and we roared off down the road with the radio playing.

We drove along in the lengthening day. Lauralee was chain-smoking, lighting one Camel after another, tossing the butts out the window, taking sips from her bourbon and Coke. I sat beside her, pretending to smoke a piece of rolled-up paper, making little noises into the mouth of my Coke bottle.

We drove up to a picnic spot on the levee and sat under a tree to look out at the river.

"I miss this old river," she said. "When I'm sad I dream about it licking the tops of the levees."

I didn't know what to say to that. To tell the truth I was afraid to say much of anything to Lauralee. She seemed so splendid. It was enough to be allowed to sit by her on the levee.

"Now, Rhoda," she said, "your mother was matron of honor in my wedding to Buddy, and I want you, her own little daughter, to be maid of honor in my second wedding."

I could hardly believe my ears! While I was trying to think of something to say to this wonderful news I saw that Lauralee was crying, great tears were forming in her blue eyes.

"Under this very tree is where Buddy and I got engaged," she said. Now the tears were really starting to roll, falling all over the front of her uniform. "He gave me my ring right where we're sitting."

"The maid of honor?" I said, patting her on the shoulder, trying to be of some comfort. "You really mean the maid of honor?"

"Now he's gone from the world," she continued, "and I'm marrying a wonderful man, but that doesn't make it any easier. Oh, Rhoda, they never even found his body, never even found his body."

I was patting her on the head now, afraid she would forget her offer in the midst of her sorrow.

"You mean I get to be the real maid of honor?"

"Oh, yes, Rhoda, Honey," she said. "The maid of honor, my only attendant." She blew her nose on a lace-trimmed handkerchief and sat up straighter, taking a drink from the Coke bottle.

"Not only that, but I have decided to let you pick out your own dress. We'll go to Greenville and you can try on every dress at Nell's and Blum's and you can have the one you like the most."

I threw my arms around her, burning with happiness, smelling her whiskey and Camels and the dark Tabu perfume that was her signature. Over her shoulder and through the low branches of the trees the afternoon sun was going down in an orgy of reds and blues and purples and violets, falling from sight, going all the way to China.

Let them keep their nasty Broad Jump Pit, I thought. Wait till they hear about this. Wait till they find out I'm maid of honor in a military wedding.

Finding the dress was another matter. Early the next morning Miss Onnie Maud and my grandmother and Lauralee and I set out for Greenville.

As we passed the pasture I hung out the back window making faces at the athletes. This time they only pretended to ignore me. They couldn't ignore this wedding. It was going to be in the parlor instead of the church so they wouldn't even get to be altar boys. They wouldn't get to light a candle.

"I don't know why you care what's going on in that pasture," my grandmother said. "Even if they let you play with them all it would do is make you a lot of ugly muscles."

"Then you'd have big old ugly arms like Weegie Toler," Miss Onnie Maud said. "Lauralee, you remember Weegie Toler, that was a swimmer. Her arms got so big no one would take her to a dance, much less marry her."

"Well, I don't want to get married anyway," I said. "I'm never getting married. I'm going to New York City and be a lawyer."

"Where does she get those ideas?" Miss Onnie Maud said.

"When you get older you'll want to get married," Lauralee said. "Look at how much fun you're having being in my wedding."

"Well, I'm never getting married," I said. "And I'm never having any children. I'm going to New York and be a lawyer and save people from the electric chair."

"It's the movies," Miss Onnie Maud said. "They let her watch anything she likes in Indiana."

We walked into Nell's and Blum's Department Store and took up the largest dressing room. My grandmother and Miss Onnie Mead were seated on brocade chairs and every saleslady in the store came crowding around trying to get in on the wedding.

I refused to even consider the dresses they brought from the "girls'" department.

"I told her she could wear whatever she wanted," Lauralee said, "and I'm keeping my promise."

"Well, she's not wearing green satin or I'm not coming," my grandmother said, indicating the dress I had found on a rack and was clutching against me.

"At least let her try it on," Lauralee said. "Let her see for herself." She zipped me into the green satin. It came down to my ankles and fit around my midsection like a girdle, making my waist seem smaller than my stomach. I admired myself in the mirror. It was almost perfect. I looked exactly like a nightclub singer.

"This one's fine," I said. "This is the one I want."

"It looks marvelous, Rhoda," Lauralee said, "but it's the wrong color for the wedding. Remember I'm wearing blue."

"I believe the child's color-blind," Miss Onnie Maud said. "It runs in her father's family."

"I am not color-blind," I said, reaching behind me and unzipping the dress. "I have twenty-twenty vision."

"Let her try on some more," Lauralee said. "Let her try on everything in the store."

I proceeded to do just that, with the salesladies getting grumpier and grumpier. I tried on a gold gabardine dress with a rhinestone-studded cummerbund. I tried on a pink ballerina-length formal and a lavender voile tea dress and several silk suits. Somehow nothing looked right.

"Maybe we'll have to make her something," my grandmother said.

"But there's no time," Miss Onnie Maud said. "Besides first we'd have to find out what she wants. Rhoda, please tell us what you're looking for."

Their faces all turned to mine, waiting for an answer. But I didn't know the answer.

The dress I wanted was a secret. The dress I wanted was dark and tall and thin as a reed. There was a word for what I wanted, a word I had seen in magazines. But what was that word? I could not remember.

"I want something dark," I said at last. "Something dark and silky."

"Wait right there," the saleslady said. "Wait just a minute." Then, from out of a prewar storage closet she brought a black-watch plaid recital dress with spaghetti straps and a white piqué jacket. It was made of taffeta and rustled when I touched it. There was a label sewn into the collar of the jacket. *Little Miss Sophisticate,* it said. *Sophisticate,* that was the word I was seeking.

I put on the dress and stood triumphant in a sea of ladies and dresses and hangers.

"This is the dress," I said. "This is the dress I'm wearing."

"It's perfect," Lauralee said. "Start hemming it up. She'll be the prettiest maid of honor in the whole world."

All the way home I held the box on my lap thinking about how I would look in the dress. Wait till they see me like this, I was thinking. Wait till they see what I really look like.

I fell in love with the groom. The moment I laid eyes on him I forgot he was flat-footed. He arrived bearing gifts of music and perfume and candy, a warm dark-skinned man with eyes the color of walnuts.

He laughed out loud when he saw me, standing on the porch with my hands on my hips.

"This must be Rhoda," he exclaimed, "the famous red-haired maid of honor." He came running up the steps, gave me a slow, exciting hug, and presented me with a whole album of Xavier

Cugat records. I had never owned a record of my own, much less an album.

Before the evening was over I put on a red formal I found in a trunk and did a South American dance for him to Xavier Cugat's "Poinciana." He said he had never seen anything like it in his whole life.

The wedding itself was a disappointment. No one came but the immediate family and there was no aisle to march down and the only music was Onnie Maud playing "Liebestraum."

Dudley and Philip and Saint John and Oliver and Bunky were dressed in long pants and white shirts and ties. They had fresh military crew cuts and looked like a nest of new birds, huddled together on the blue velvet sofa, trying to keep their hands to themselves, trying to figure out how to act at a wedding.

The elderly Episcopal priest read out the ceremony in a gravelly smoker's voice, ruining all the good parts by coughing. He was in a bad mood because Lauralee and Mr. Marcus hadn't found time to come to him for marriage instruction.

Still, I got to hold the bride's flowers while he gave her the ring and stood so close to her during the ceremony I could hear her breathing.

The reception was better. People came from all over the Delta. There were tables with candles set up around the porches and sprays of greenery in every corner. There were gentlemen sweating in linen suits and the record player playing every minute. In the back hall Calvin had set up a real professional bar with tall, permanently frosted glasses and ice and mint and lemons and every kind of whiskey and liqueur in the world.

I stood in the receiving line getting compliments on my dress, then wandered around the rooms eating cake and letting people hug me. After a while I got bored with that and went out to the back hall and began to fix myself a drink at the bar.

I took one of the frosted glasses and began filling it from different bottles, tasting as I went along. I used plenty of crème de menthe and soon had something that tasted heavenly. I filled the glass with crushed ice, added three straws, and went out to sit on the back steps and cool off.

I was feeling wonderful. A full moon was caught like a kite in the pecan trees across the river. I sipped along on my drink. Then, without planning it, I did something I had never dreamed of doing. I left the porch alone at night. Usually I was in terror of the dark. My grandmother had told me that alligators come out of the bayou to eat children who wander alone at night.

I walked out across the yard, the huge moon giving so much light I almost cast a shadow. When I was nearly to the water's edge I turned and looked back toward the house. It shimmered in the moonlight like a jukebox alive in a meadow, seemed to pulsate with music and laughter and people, beautiful and foreign, not a part of me.

I looked out at the water, then down the road to the pasture. The Broad Jump Pit! There it was, perfect and unguarded. Why had I never thought of doing this before?

I began to run toward the road. I ran as fast as my Mary Jane pumps would allow me. I pulled my dress up around my waist and climbed the fence in one motion, dropping lightly down on the other side. I was sweating heavily, alone with the moon and my wonderful courage.

I knew exactly what to do first. I picked up the pole and hoisted it over my head. It felt solid and balanced and alive. I hoisted it up and down a few times as I had seen Dudley do, getting the feel of it.

Then I laid it ceremoniously down on the ground, reached behind me, and unhooked the plaid formal. I left it lying in a heap on the ground. There I stood, in my cotton underpants, ready to take up pole-vaulting.

I lifted the pole and carried it back to the end of the cinder path. I ran slowly down the path, stuck the pole in the wooden cup, and attempted throwing my body into the air, using it as a lever.

Something was wrong. It was more difficult than it appeared from a distance. I tried again. Nothing happened. I sat down with the pole across my legs to think things over.

Then I remembered something I had watched Dudley doing through the binoculars. He measured down from the end of the pole with his fingers spread wide. That was it, I had to hold it closer to the end.

I tried it again. This time the pole lifted me several feet off the ground. My body sailed across the grass in a neat arc and I landed on my toes. I was a natural!

I do not know how long I was out there, running up and down the cinder path, thrusting my body further and further through space, tossing myself into the pit like a mussel shell thrown across the bayou.

At last I decided I was ready for the real test. I had to vault over a cane barrier. I examined the pegs on the wooden poles and chose one that came up to my shoulder.

I put the barrier pole in place, spit over my left shoulder, and marched back to the end of the path. Suck up your guts, I told myself. It's only a pole. It won't get stuck in your stomach and tear out your insides. It won't kill you.

I stood at the end of the path eyeballing the barrier. Then, above the incessant racket of the crickets, I heard my name being called. Rhoda . . . the voices were calling. Rhoda . . . Rhoda . . . Rhoda . . . Rhoda.

I turned toward the house and saw them coming. Mr. Marcus and Dudley and Bunky and Calvin and Lauralee and what looked like half the wedding. They were climbing the fence, calling my name, and coming to get me. Rhoda . . . they called out. Where on earth have you been? What on earth are you doing?

I hoisted the pole up to my shoulders and began to run down the path, running into the light from the moon. I picked up speed, thrust the pole into the cup, and threw myself into the sky, into the still Delta night. I sailed up and was clear and over the barrier.

I let go of the pole and began my fall, which seemed to last a long, long time. It was like falling through clear water. I dropped into the sawdust and lay very still, waiting for them to reach me.

Sometimes I think whatever has happened since has been of no real interest to me.

A Trip to Czardis

EDWIN GRANBERRY

IT WAS STILL DARK in the pine woods when the two brothers awoke. But it was plain that day had come, and in a little while there would be no more stars. Day itself would be in the sky and they would be going along the road. Jim waked first, coming quickly out of sleep and sitting up in the bed to take fresh hold of the things in his head, starting them up again out of the corners of his mind where sleep had tucked them. Then he waked Daniel and they sat up together in the bed. Jim put his arm around his young brother, for the night had been dewy and cool with the swamp wind. Daniel shivered a little and whimpered, it being dark in the room and his baby concerns still on him somewhat, making sleep heavy on his mind and slow to give understanding its way.

"Hit's the day, Dan'l. This day that's right here now, we are goen. You'll recollect it all in a minute."

"I recollect. We are goen in the wagon to see Papa——"

"Then hush and don't whine."

"I were dreamen, Jim."

"What dreamen did you have?"

"I can't tell. But it were fearful what I dreamt."

"All the way we are goen this time. We won't stop at any places, but we will go all the way to Czardis to see Papa. I never see such a place as Czardis."

"I recollect the water tower——"

"Not in your own right, Dan'l. Hit's by my tellen it you see it in your mind."

"And lemonade with ice in it. I saw——"

"That too I seen and told to you."

"Then I never seen it at all?"

"Hit's me were there, Dan'l. I let you play like, but hit's me who went to Czardis. Yet I never till this day told half how much I see. There's sights I never told."

They stopped talking, listening for their mother's stir in the kitchen. But the night stillness was unlifted. Daniel began to shiver again.

"Hit's dark," he said.

"Hit's your eyes stuck," Jim said. "Would you want me to drip a little water on your eyes?"

"Oh!" cried the young one, pressing his face into his brother's side, "don't douse me, Jim, no more. The cold aches me."

The other soothed him, holding him around the body.

"You won't have e're chill or malarie ache today, Dan'l. Hit's a fair day——"

"I won't be cold?"

"Hit's a bright day. I hear mournen doves starten a'ready. The sun will bake you warm. . . . Uncle Holly might buy us somethen new to eat in Czardis."

"What would it be?"

"Hit ain't decided yet. . . . He hasn't spoke. Hit might be somethen sweet. Maybe a candy ball fixed onto a rubber string."

"A candy ball!" Daniel showed a stir of happiness. "Oh, Jim!" But it was a deceit of the imagination, making his eyes shine wistfully; the grain of his flesh was against it. He settled into a stillness by himself.

"My stomach would retch it up, Jim. . . . I guess I couldn't eat it."

"You might could keep a little down."

"No . . . I would bring it home and keep it. . . ."

Their mother when they went to bed had laid a clean pair of pants and a waist for each on the chair. Jim crept out of bed and put on his clothes, then aided his brother on with his. They could not hear any noise in the kitchen, but hickory firewood burning in the kitchen stove worked a smell through the house, and in the forest guinea fowls were sailing down from the trees and poking their way along the half-dark ground toward the kitchen steps, making it known the door was open and that within someone was stirring about at the getting of food.

Jim led his brother by the hand down the dark way of yellow-pine stairs that went narrowly and without banisters to the rooms below. The young brother went huddling in his clothes, aguelike, knowing warmth was near, hungering for his place by the stove, to sit in peace on the bricks in the floor by the stove's side and watch the eating, it being his nature to have a sickness against food.

They came in silence to the kitchen, Jim leading and holding his brother by the hand. The floor was lately strewn with fresh bright sand, and that would sparkle when the daybreak got above the forest, though now it lay dull as hoarfrost and cold to the unshod feet of the brothers. The door to the firebox of the stove was open, and in front of it their mother sat in a chair, speaking low as they entered, muttering under her breath. The two boys went near and stood still, thinking she was blessing the food, there being mush dipped up and steaming in two bowls. And they stood cast down until she lifted her eyes to them and spoke.

"Your clothes on already," she said. "You look right neat." She did not rise, but kept her chair, looking cold and stiff, with the cloth of her black dress sagging between her knees. The sons stood in front of her, and she laid her hand on first one head and then the other and spoke a little about the day, charging them to be sober and of few words, as she had raised them.

Jim sat on the bench by the table and began to eat, mixing dark molasses sugar through his bowl of mush. But a nausea began in Daniel's stomach at sight of the sweet, and he lagged by the stove, gazing at the food as it passed into his brother's mouth.

Suddenly a shadow filled the back doorway and Holly, their uncle, stood there looking in. He was lean and big and dark from wind and weather, working in the timber as their father had done. He had no wife and children and would roam far off with the timber gangs in the Everglades. This latter year he did not go far, but stayed near them. Their mother stopped and looked at the man, and he looked at her in silence. Then he looked at Jim and Daniel.

"You're goen to take them after all?"

She waited a minute, seeming to get the words straight in her mind before bringing them out, making them say what was set there.

"He asked to see them. Nobody but God Almighty ought to tell a soul hit can or can't have."

Having delivered her mind, she went out into the yard with the man, and they spoke more words in an undertone, pausing in their speech.

In the silence of the kitchen Daniel began to speak out and name what thing among his possessions he would take to Czardis to give his father. But the older boy belittled this and that and everything that was called up, saying one thing was of too little consequence for a man, and that another was of no account because it was food. But when the older boy had abolished the idea and silence had regained, he worked back to the thought, coming to it roundabout and making it new and as his own, letting it be decided that each of them would take their father a pomegranate from the tree in the yard.

They went to the kitchen door. The swamp fog had risen suddenly. They saw their mother standing in the lot while their uncle hitched the horse to the wagon. Leaving the steps, Jim climbed to the first crotch of the pomegranate tree. The reddest fruits were on the top branches. He worked his way up higher. The fog was now curling up out of the swamp, making gray mountains and rivers in the air and strange ghost shapes. Landmarks disappeared in the billows, or half seen, they bewildered the sight and an eye could so little mark the known or strange that a befuddlement took hold of the mind, like the visitations sailors beheld in the fogs of Okeechobee. Jim could not find the ground. He seemed to have climbed into the mountains. The light was unnatural and dark, and the pines were blue and dark over the mountains.

A voice cried out of the fog:

"Are worms gnawen you that you skin up a pomegranate tree at this hour? Don't I feed you enough?"

The boy worked his way down. At the foot of the tree he met his mother. She squatted and put her arm around him, her voice tight and quivering, and he felt tears on her face.

"We ain't come to the shame yet of you and Dan'l hunten your food off trees and grass. People seein' you gnawen on the road will say Jim Cameron's sons are starved, foragen like cattle of the field."

"I were getten the pomegranates for Papa," said the boy, resigned to his mother's concern. She stood up when he said this, holding him in front of her skirts. In a while she said:

"I guess we won't take any, Jim. . . . But I'm proud it come to you to take your papa somethen."

And after a silence, the boy said:

"Hit were Dan'l it come to, Mamma."

Then she took his hand, not looking down, and in her throat, as if in her bosom, she repeated:

"Hit were a fine thought and I'm right proud . . . though today we won't take anything. . . ."

"I guess there's better pomegranates in Czardis where we are goen——"

"There's no better pomegranates in Czardis than right here over your head," she said grimly. "If pomegranates were needed, we would take him his own. . . . You are older'n Dan'l, Jim. When we get to the place we are goen, you won't know your papa after so long. He will be pale and he won't be as bright as you recollect. So don't labor him with questions . . . but speak when it behooves you and let him see you are upright."

When the horse was harnessed and all was ready for the departure, the sons were seated on a shallow bed of hay in the back of the wagon and the mother took the driver's seat alone. The uncle had argued for having the top up over the seat, but she refused the shelter, remarking that she had always driven under the sky and would do it still today. He gave in silently and got upon the seat of his own wagon, which took the road first, their wagon following. This was strange, and the sons asked:

"Why don't we all ride in Uncle Holly's wagon?"

But their mother made no reply.

For several miles they traveled in silence through their own part of the woods, meeting no one. The boys whispered a little to themselves, but their mother and their uncle sat without speaking, nor did they turn their heads to look back. At last the narrow road they were following left the woods and came out to the highway, and it was seen that other wagons besides their own were going to Czardis. And as they got farther along, they began to meet many other people going to the town, and the boys asked their mother what day it was. It was Wednesday. And then they asked her why so many wagons were going along the road if it wasn't Saturday and a market day. When she told them to be quiet, they settled down to watching the people go by. Some of them were faces that were strange, and some were neighbors who lived in other parts of the woods. Some who passed them stared in silence, and some went by looking straight to the front. But there were none of them who spoke, for their mother turned her eyes neither right nor left, but drove the horse on like a woman in her sleep. All was silent as the wagons passed, except the squeaking of the wheels and the thud of the horses' hoofs on the dry, packed sand.

At the edge of the town the crowds increased, and their wagon got lost in the press of people. All were moving in one direction.

Finally they were going along by a high brick wall on top of which ran a barbed-wire fence. Farther along the way in the middle of the wall was a tall, stone building with many people in front.

There were trees along the outside of the wall, and in the branches of one of the trees Daniel saw a man. He was looking over the brick wall down into the courtyard. All the wagons were stopping here and hitching through the grove in front of the building. But their Uncle Holly's wagon and their own drove on, making way slowly as through a crowd at a fair, for under the trees knots of men were gathered, talking in undertone. Daniel pulled at his mother's skirts and whispered:

"What made that man climb up that tree?"

Again she told him to be quiet.

"We're not to talk today," said Jim. "Papa is sick and we're not to make him worse." But his high, thin voice made his mother turn cold. She looked back and saw he had grown pale and still, staring at the iron-barred windows of the building. When he caught her gaze, his chin began to quiver, and she turned back front to dodge the knowledge of his eyes.

For the two wagons had stopped now and the uncle gotten down and left them sitting alone while he went to the door of the building and talked with a man standing there. The crowd fell silent, staring at their mother.

"See, Jim, all the men up the trees!" Daniel whispered once more, leaning close in to his brother's side.

"Hush, Dan'l. Be still."

The young boy obeyed this time, falling into a bewildered stare at all the things about him he did not understand, for in all the trees along the brick wall men began to appear perched high in the branches, and on the roof of a building across the way stood other men, all gaping at something in the yard back of the wall.

Their uncle returned and hitched his horse to a ring in one of the trees. Then he hitched their mother's horse, and all of them got out and stood on the ground in a huddle. The walls of the building rose before them. Strange faces at the barred windows laughed aloud and called down curses at the men below.

Now they were moving, with a wall of faces on either side of them, their uncle going first, followed by their mother who held to each of them by a hand. They went up the steps of the building. The door opened, and their uncle stepped inside. He came back in a moment, and all of them went in and followed a man down a corridor and into a bare room with two chairs and a wooden bench. A man in a black robe sat on one of the chairs, and in front of him on the bench, leaning forward, looking down between his arms, sat their father. His face was lean and gray, which made him look very tall. But his hair was black, and his eyes were blue and mild and strange as he stood up and held the two sons against his body while he stooped his head to kiss their mother. The man in black left the room and walked up and down outside in the corridor. A second stranger stood in the doorway with his back to the room. The father picked up one of the sons and then the other in his arms and looked at them and leaned their faces on his own. Then he sat down on the bench and held them against him. Their mother sat down by them and they were all together.

A few low words were spoken, and then a silence fell over them all. And in a while the parents spoke a little more and touched one another. But the bare stone floor and the stone walls and the unaccustomed arms of their father hushed the sons with the new and strange. And when the time had passed, the father took his watch from his pocket:

"I'm goen to give you my watch, Jim. You are the oldest. I want you to keep it till you are a grown man. . . . And I want you to always do what Mamma tells you. . . . I'm goen to give you the chain, Dan'l. . . ."

The young brother took the chain, slipped out of his father's arms, and went to his mother with it. He spread it out on her knee and began to talk to her in a whisper. She bent over him, and again all of them in the room grew silent.

A sudden sound of marching was heard in the corridor. The man rose up and took his sons in his arms, holding them abruptly. But their uncle, who had been standing with the man in the doorway, came suddenly and took them and went out and down through the big doorway by which they had entered the building. As the doors opened to let them pass, the crowd gathered around the steps pressed forward to look inside. The older boy cringed in his uncle's arms. His uncle turned and stood with his back to the crowd. Their mother came through the doors. The crowd fell back. Again through a passageway of gazing eyes, they reached the wagons. This time they sat on the seat beside their mother. Leaving their uncle and his wagon behind, they started off on the road that led out of town.

"Is Papa coming home with Uncle Holly?" Jim asked in a still voice.

His mother nodded her head.

Reaching the woods once more and the silence he knew, Daniel whispered to his brother:

"We got a watch and chain instead, Jim."

But Jim neither answered nor turned his eyes.

The Revolt of Brud Bascomb

LOYLE HAIRSTON

NOW WORD DONE GOT OUT that Bull Crawford were lookin for Pa too, that he aimed to have him flogged for quittin the sawmill. He told Gus Botley Pa owed him back credit for stuff he bought on time from the sawmill commi'sary store. Credit were Bull Crawford's reglar way of cheatin his work hands. Bein he never jotted down what you bought, you had to pay him whatever he said you owed; and if you wanted to keep your job you didn dare 'spute the lowdown snake. Mainly he robbed his colored hands. But Pa he wouldn bite, paid spot-cash for ever'thing he bought, down to his sack tobacco and cigarette paper. He swore he'd make a livin "sellin tadpole shit by the pound" before he'd do credit with a crook like Bull Crawford. Even the white folks knowed Pa warnt no common nigger.

When Pa didn turn up that week I got worried. And when word got out that Bull Crawford done sicked Moose Mallet on him, even Big Boy put on a extra frown. Though Ma tried not to let on, plain she were bothered. Ever' day she complained how the garden fence needed mendin; how the outhouse needed cleanin out; how the front gate needed fixin; and who was gon fetch the sack of shorts from uptown she done bought for the pig. There warnt no spark in her hymn singin and the more she prayed the more worser things got.

The Gang warnt allowed to come near our house, and me and Big Boy warnt allowed out of the yard after sundown. And she worked the tar out of us around the house. "A idle mind is the workshop of the devil," she always said anytime she caught us tryin to catch our breaths. And to top it off, we couldn go to bed at night till we done done ever' scrap of our lesson, no matter if we burnt a lamp of oil doin it. Bein uncommon thickheaded, poor Big Boy had a dismal time.

Before I went to sleep one night I done some powerful thinkin on Pa. I mean it didn seem right him not comin home on account of Moose Mallet. Even Squeench Eyes knowed Pa warnt scared of no white folks—not even Bull Crawford or Snake Thompson even. The next mornin I asked Ma on it. "Is a billygoat scared of a tick?" She said. "More 'n likely, he outin the woods somewhere with that buzzard, Poon Pendleton, makin whiskey!" I don't know how she knowed but word got out that it were mainly so. And in no time the gossip-hounds was hummin like bees on it, pilin on all kinds of whoppin lies as they went along.

Natural', Miz Lemander brung Ma ever scrap of gossip she could rake up. It were the only time she'd pay us a visit. "It's plumb scand'lous, Lula, what unGodly lies come outa niggers' mouths," she said one day. "The way folks just jump at the chance to smut up a body's good name. My land! I hate to tell you this: I don't blame you for shakin your head but—well it's a thing you ought to know. The Lord is my judge! Things like, 'Aint it a shame the way she treated that poor man.' 'She and her high-falutin airs.' 'If he a bootlegger, she drove him to it.' 'Forever houndin him about takin a little taste now and then when she'd drive our Holy Savior Hisself to the bottle.' D'you ever hear such dreadful lies? My land!

"But that aint hardly the half of it," she went on after takin a dip of snuff. "I 'spects old Lucifer done awready laid a place for heffers like Tille Jordan. D'you know what the hussy had the nerve to tell me? That Brud Bascomb he could put his boots out on *her* back porch *any*time. And that old Sadie Dudley—ever'body in town know she go with white mens—she just rolled her old whorish eyes back in her head and cackled, '*Honey hush!*' The lowclass thing. . . !"

Settin her sewin basket down, Ma got up from the porch swing and much obliged the old windbag for bringin her such a mess of news. "But if it aint too much trouble, Lemander Tutt," Ma snapped her, "I'd be much obliged if you'd spend more time min-din your own blessed bizness!" Miz Lemander went out of the yard in a huff and strutted across the street like she done paid up her ticket to heaven. Religion or not, Ma warnt a body to truck with. Generly she never paid nothin common niggers said no mind but it turned her damper up when she heard gossip about her and Pa. She said Pa were her business and when she got tired of 'tendin to it'd be time enough for the busybodies to "latch on to the big brute." Ma was a sight.

I reckon Miz Lemander upset her considerable cause she got more fractiouser ever' day. Beside workin our fingers to the bones, so to say, and makin us study till we was half blind, she started makin us read the blame Bible. And out loud. And bein the Bible's mainly done in parable riddles I got in trouble from the git-go. It were the part about Cain in the Adam and Eve story what done it. The Bible said God banished him from home for up and killin his brother, Abel. But in no time Cain done drummed up a wife and started hisself a spankin new family. Now ifn he and Adam and Eve, his momma and daddy, was the only bodies in the world back then—where in nation'd he rummage up a wife from?

Ma said in the first place it warnt none of my business; and in the second place, to even *think* such a notion was doin the devil's work. "You is your daddy's chile awright," she snapped me. "You little heathen. Go and wash your stinky behind and put your school clothes back on. I'm takin your little mannish butt to prayer meetin . . . you too, Big Boy. Settin there countin your fingers—boy, aint you learnt how to add and subtract yet? Mercy, Jesus! When your blessed daddy gets back—if he ever do—I think *I'm* gon run off. Now hurry up before I git my strop!" Comin home that night Big Boy promised to kill me the first chance he got.

That night the sapsucker most washed me out on the floor he flooded the bed so. On our way to school he shook his fist in my face and dared me to tell the Gang on him. So, natural', I done it—told Mutt and Squeench Eyes and Booker T soon's I seen 'em in the school yard. By the time we got to our room, even Miz Wadley knowed he done peed the bed. Big Boy up and thumped me when her back was turned but when I thumped him back she were lookin dead at me. On account of her rheumatisms she couldn whup me, so she marched me to 'Fessor Simpson's office and watched him whup the tar out of me.

But I didn cry a drop, doggonnit. And back at my desk I set down without flinchin though my hindparts was on fire. Miz Wadley shot me a hot look so I took my writin tablet and 'rithmetic book out of my sachel and opened 'em. But I warnt thinkin about no lesson. Then and there I started to jump out of the window and runoff from home, to find Pa and join up with him. And me and him we wouldn never come back to this old lowdown place. Never. Only I didn know where to even start out lookin for him, and that made me feel more madder even.

Miz Wadley done had fresh pi'tures plastered on the walls. The ones what showed big cities with tall skyscrapers and streets full of peoples caught my eye. Right off, I wished I was there, away from Miz Wadley and old 'Fessor Simpson and . . . and Ma too even. I'd quit school and get me a job makin a heap of money and I'd buy me some sporty clothes and a wrist watch. Ever' night I'd go to the pi'ture show, Sundays even and set downstairs smack amongst the white folks. Dip Cooley said he done it up North—and dared 'em to complain. I'd come home ever now and then to see Ma and Pa, and bring poor Squeench Eyes some clothes and things. And I'd drive the Gang round in my big fine car all up and down Main Street; and dare Moose Mallet to lock it up in the jailhouse yard like he done Buster Stokes and Dip Cooley once.

At recess time I asked Junior if he'wanted to come with me when I run off up North. "Shoot yeah!" He bust out. ". . . but I can't go till after Easter. Daddy awways give me five dollars for Easter . . ." Sometime I wonder how come Junior's folks ever let on he belong to them. The sapsucker snuck in the yard Saturday mornin while Ma was washin clothes out in back. "Guess what I found this mornin?" He whispered-like. "A raff."

"A what?"

A raff. It float on water . . . like a boat. A *raff.* Don't yall know what a raff is? It's out yonder on the creek. Yall wanta see it?"

Soon's we finished up our chores we picked up the rest of the Gang and went with Junior. The thing he found were a raff alright, made out of split logs and slab board plankin botched together. Junior hopped on it and jumped up and down to prove it wouldn sink. And he swore he didn swipe it, claimed he spotted it floatin down creek when he and Mr. Jim was settin their fishhooks that mornin. The Gang hopped on it and wanted to shove off for a run down creek then and there. But there warnt no paddles and even Squeench Eyes knowed you can't paddle a raff with your bare hands.

"We needs pitchpoles," I said. "Beside, we oughta camo'flag it so whoever it b'long to won't know it when they see us ridin it."

"Now how in shit you gon camoflag a raffboat?" Big Boy swoll up.

I thunk on it for a spell till a fetchin notion hit me. The Gang liked it and in no time we started roundin up rope and scrap lumber and wire and soda water signs and truck. By sundown we done botched up the holes and cracks in the floor, and built a first-rate cabin smack in the middle of the raff. And after Booker T and Squeench Eyes nailed a mast pole up in back of the cabin, we strung somebody's bedsheet on it for a sail. Then we unraveled a whoppin role of rope Junior swiped for the rail and riggin, and to use for our anchor "chain." And that Sunday he and Mutt paddled up in our skiffboat with a boatload of reglar plunder; namely—a old patched up inner-tube; a lantern; a rain hat and somebody's slicker; a window shade; a rusty old weather vane rooster; a tire boot; a airplane hat and goggles; a curtain rod; a nail keg; a tricycle wheel; a car fan; and a strip of black cloth. Junior said the cloth was for our flag. When we got done fixin her up our raff cut a fetchin sight. But it was too late to try her out on the creek so I told the Gang we'd do it the next day.

"But we hafta go to school tomorrow," Junior frowned up.

"Aw shoot!" I said, lookin at our raff rockin on the water like a regular shipboat. ". . . well, doggonnit, we just gon have to up and play hookey then!"

But Monday mornin Big Boy woke up scared. He said the very notion of Ma findin out we done played hookey from school drawed whelps on his hindparts. It done rained all night long and on our way to school it started pourin down again. We run under the part of the church what set high off the ground and I told Big Boy Miz Wadley wouldn say nothin to Ma. She'd just think the rain kept us home.

The Gang was in the raff cabin eatin up their school lunches when me and Big Boy got down to the creek. The rain done slacked to a light drizzle. And though the March wind was whippin through the trees it was uncommon warm. So we all took off our shirts and shoes, hung 'em up in the cabin, and rolled up our britcher legs to our thighs. Junior up and tied his buccaneer pirate rag round his head and strapped on his swode. But I told him we warnt no pirate rogues, blame his roguish hide.

"This is a whale boat ship!" I said and put on the rain hat and old raggedy slicker he brung. "We goin whale huntin, doggonnit—to catch that blame white whale runnin lose out yonder in the creek."

"What white whale?"

"Old Moby Dick, waterhead. The whale Mr. Jack told us about."

He told it to us most ever' time we went by to keep him company and eat up all his peanuts and "scaly barks." Even Big Boy liked the idear so I named myself Cap'n Ahabbe and named ever-'body else my mates and deck hands and harplooners. Except, Junior—I named him Starbuckles, my main mate next in line for Cap'n if I up and got drowned or somethin. Then I told 'em to take up their pitchpoles and shove off.

"Eevast, you lubbers and harlots!" I pumped out, standin in front of the cabin. "Up anchor and start turnin to on the fo'castle decks!"

And the Gang they all done it. Mutt and Booker T pulled the tree root anchor up out of the water and we started shovin off from the bank. And soon's we got out in the deep water the current sent us swoopin off down creek, our sheet sail bellyin out; and you could hear the flag Junior strung up flappin in the wind. The raff rolled and dipped all kind of ways, makin the churnin yeller water splash and splatter over the floor deck. And ever now and then the water'd come in such whoppin gushes it most washed us off our feets. We was havin a dandy time.

Thunder claps boomed like cannon guns; and bolts of lightnin lit up the thick black clouds what floated so low in the sky they most scraped the tree tops. It started rainin again, comin in sheets from the high wind and lashin us in drenchin squalls. But we was havin such a good time we warnt even scared of the lightnin. I walked to the front of the raff, gandered the creek up ahead and turned to Junior.

"Mr. Starbuckles," I said.

"Yessir, your Cap'n majesties."

"Give me the weather reports!"

Junior gandered the creek, water streamin down his ugly face. "There's a tycoon blowin off leeward boards, Cap'n sir!"

". . . then unhaul sail and tie it up and secure it. Hop to it, blubberheads!"

And most before I could bat a eye Squeench Eyes done run up the mast pole like a blame monkey and tore out the sheet sail.

"Eevast, thee monkey faced scalawopper!" I hollered him and then I turned to Big Boy. "Mr. Daggoons, will you fetch that little ape yonder to thine?"

When Squeench Eyes slid down the mast pole Big Boy grabbed him by his neck scruffs and brung him.

"Is thine a plumb moron, fool?" I said. "Don't you know better'n vandalate ship property like thus, swine hog *sow*!"

". . . I reckon I does, Cap'n A-rabbe sir," Squeench Eyes giggled. "But I slipped when I reached for the top of the sheet."

"Slip outa thine sight, snagglebutt!" I said. "Mr. Daggoons, lock this scalawopper up in hog irons and banish him to the skiffboat dungeon jailhouse stockades!"

Squeench Eyes followed Big Boy out to the skiffboat tied to the back of the raff and set down, lookin so dismal happy we all bust out laughin at him. It aint no common sight to see Squeench Eyes happy. When we passed Cap Harper's place it struck me how far we done floated down creek so I ordered the Gang to mind their watches and shake tail.

"Eehoy, lubbers!" I hollered 'em. "Now haul out your bowspits and whet up your harploon spears, thee think thou hear Moby Dick grumblin in the nearabouts off windboards!"

The rain started comin down hard again, beatin loud against our cabin. And you couldn hardly see the trees off the bank it done turnt so dark. Brush twigs and dry leafs and truck floated past us when we strayed out of the current. Mutt spotted a snake swimmin alongside a piece of tree limb, dove headlong in the creek for it and most drownded hisself when a dry log up and clunked him side his head. We throwed him the inner-tube and drug him back on the raff, the blame fool. Sometime Mutt give you the notion he aint too bright in the head.

All of a sudden a stinky smell hit me in the nose. I shedded my eyes from the rain and looked hard all around me. Round the bend you could see the city trash pile off the bank where they done piled a mountain of garbish and truck. Junior run up and saluted me three times.

"What ailin you, Mr. Starbuckles?" I said.

"Cap'n A-habbe sir."

"Thou?"

"Oughtn we put ashore to the bank and rummage up some supply stores and knick-knacks. . . ?"

"Straddle your appertites, Mr. Starbuckles. That's a garbish pile, not a commisary store, you blockhead! And leeboard garbish aint even fit for the deck hands to eat. Now get back to your watches before I have you flogged on the poopdecks!" Then I said to the Gang. "Well don't stand there gapin, blubberheads. Unbuckle your windlasses and navergate out to the open creek ocean. 'Cordin to the ship speedomiters, Moby Dick's breakin wind 'leven knots and a quarter 'mile up bowboard. So turn to and shake tail and nomore lollygaggin. You too, Squeench Eyes!"

Down the creek a old rotten tree done fell in the water blockin our way, so we took our pitchpoles and steered out of the deep water. Then we swung round another bend where they done built a levee along a considerable stretch of fields. And you could tell by the good fences and painted barns we seen that we was in old Enos Bilbone's neck of the woods. The current most peetered out now so we let the raff drift cause we was tired, and the blame rain was whippin the tar out of us. And Squeency Eyes complained he was gettin hongry.

"Mr. Starbuckles," I said to Junior, "take over the navergations—thou have to take a pee."

Junior done it and I up and peed off the side of the raff, then I went in the cabin where Booker T and Squeench Eyes was takin a rest from the dismal rain.

"Thar she blowin!" Junior hollered all a sudden.

"Which board, Mr. Starbuckles?" I poked my head out of the cabin.

"Over yonder board!"

I come out and looked where he was pointin but all I seen was old Rafe Perkins' haybarn. Junior wanted us to go ashore and rest up a spell till the rain slacked off. So we done it. While he and Big Boy parked the raff near a clump of bushes near the bank, me and Mutt and Booker T and Squeench Eyes run across the back barnyard into the old brokedown barn. It was most pitch dark inside but by and by we found a dry stall, piled in a stock of hay on the floor and set down to catch our breaths.

Junior and Big Boy come through the back door, draggin a snake they done found in the weeds down near the water. It was whoppin size. And though somebody done shot his head off, Mutt took the blame snake and patted it like it was his pet dog or somethin. Squeench Eyes clambed up in the loft and in a little while he hollered down to us, "Come here yall!"

From the front window up in the loft we looked down and seen a pile of scrap iron and 'luminum in the barnyard. Natural', Junior wanted us to swipe it but I told the Gang naw.

"That stuff b'long to Rafe Perkins, marblehead—the most low-downest redneck ever squatted behind two shoes."

"How in devil he gon know who took it?"

Which was so. But Rafe Perkins warnt no common pecker-wood—folks say he aint never got word Abraham Lincoln done freed the slaves. Still and all, with Easter just around the corner, so to say, we could use some spare spot-cash.

"Let's take all the 'luminum first," I said and started down the loft ladder. "Uncle Tut awways gip us on the scrap iron anyhow. Come on!"

Only we scarce got loaded up when all a sudden I heard horse hoofs come thunderin down on us. And before we could scoot out of the barnyard two little cracker boys, ridin two black horses, up and headed us off.

"Halt niggers!" One of 'em hollered out, pullin on his horse reins and makin his horses rare up and buck his head. Then the blame redneck pulled a double barrel pump BB-gun out of his saddle holster and aimed it at us. "Don't move a peg or I'll shoot you square in your stinky black asses." He said, "Ephriam, hop down and search them niggers."

And Ephriam he swung his leg over his horse and slid down off him like a reglar cowboy. He sidled over and made us put down the truck we was holdin then he patted us down and ordered us to take ever'thing out of our pockets.

"Aint you niggers got no better sense'n try'n rob Jeb Lee Perkins?" Jeb Lee Perkins said, slid down off *his* horse, slouched across the barnyard and waved his double barrel pump BB-gun on us. Squeench Eyes let out a squeak and started lookin round for runnin room. Mutt and Booker T looked like they was gon mess theirselfs. And Junior he up and turnt ashy in the rain. Even Big Boy was in a sweat.

". . . we aint robbin nobody." I up and said, scared as I was.

"Don't you reckon I got eyes to see with, nigger? D'you hear that, Ephriam? This little kinkyheaded nigger just called me a lie!"

"You callin white folks a lie, little kinkyheaded nigger?" Ephriam batted his old faded eyeballs at me.

"Naw. All I said was I—"

"Hush up your lyin mouth, nigger!" Jeb Lee barked out. "D'you think I'm gonna stand out here in the rain and put up with your sass? By God, Pa learnt me how to handle niggers like you. Ephriam—bring me my whup off my saddle yonder. I reckon we gonna have to take these roguish niggers in the barn and flog 'em. March, niggers!"

We done it cause plain these blame peckerwoods had the upperhand. I mean we was under the nutcut so you couldn blame the Gang for shakin in their boots, so to say. And it wouldn help none if we'd up and run away, bein these sapsuckers done seen who we was. But it was gettin late in the day and we *had* to be back in town by the time school let out. Else we'd be in more worser trouble even. So I put on my thinkin cap, so to say, and thought it around.

The rain started squallin down again, pourin through the roof and blowin through the gaps in the side walls. Jeb Lee made us stand in a stall till Ephriam went and brung their horses in out of the rain. But the blame roof leaked so bad he ordered us into another stall—the one we'd rested in before. Ephriam come back and he and Jeb Lee started squabblin over which one of 'em was gon do the floggin. Though it was uncommon dark inside, all a sudden I spotted that dead snake Junior and Big Boy drug in here from the creek bank. Mutt done curled it up on some hay in the corner of the stall, but it's tail most touched the back of Ephriam's rubber boot heels. Right off, it gived me a thumpin idea.

I nudged Junior, touchin the hatchet he wore in his belt, and went into action. "Don't move, Ephriam!" I bust out, pointin at his rubber boot heels. "Don't move a peg. Stop breathin even!"

"W-what?" Jeb Lee said, looked round at Ephriam and then back at me. "What's wrong with you, nigger?"

"A *snake!*" I kept pointin at Ephriam's rubber boot heels. "There! Curled up in back of Ephriam's feets—with his mouth wide open! Don't even twitch, Ephriam. Junior—give me the hatchet. Quick!"

Junior done it and I bolted across the stall and started hackin the tar out of that dead snake. In no time I done hacked him into little snake chips. Meantime, Ephriam done turnt whiter than a frog's belly, his eyeballs rollin back in his head till he looked most a sight worser than that chopped up snake even. By and by Jeb Lee brung him around. And he was so much obliged to me for savin his blame cousin's life, he gived us the whole batch of scrap iron and 'luminum for a reward.

On our way home the Gang most fell off the raff from laughin at how I outslicked them peckerwoods. Except Mutt. He done swoll to a boil cause I chopped up his poor dead snake but even Squeench Eyes didn pay him no mind he rolled and cackled so. The rain was comin down in bucketloads now, drenchin us and drillin the water like blazes. Thunderclaps boomed and rumbled through the low hangin black clouds what was rollin and billowin across the sky. We swung off in a vein of creek what headed back to town. Sheets of blowin rain most blinded us and splattered the tin walls of the raff cabin where Squeench Eyes and Booker T was hidin from the lightnin bolts.

When we got in sight of the depot water tanks juttin over a thick of trees I judged we'd make it back to town in time. But we still had considerable ways to go so we stayed with the current till it peetered out at the bend past the Bilbone Bridge. Then we used our paddles and pitchpoles to work our way down a wide stretch of shallow water. The rain slacked off a little and except for the thunder and lightnin scarin the tar out of Squeench Eyes and Booker T, we was havin a fetchin time.

Me and Junior was cipherin out how much Uncle Tut'd pay us for the scrap iron and 'luminum when all a sudden a boomin sound thumped my ears. Junior heard it too but he said it warnt no thunderclap. We listened till we heard it again and traced the sound to the shore. And when I seen somebody wavin at us from a thicket of high grass, I cupped my hands to my mouth and hollered out:

"Eehoy thar!"

"Ehoy my wet ass!" The voice boomed out. "Paddle that floatin trash pile over here and pick me up!"

I knowed the voice straight off. By jing it was *Pa!*

"*Pa!*" I most turned a somersault. "Is that you, Pa?"

". . . Napoleon. . . ? Boy—what the hell you doin—" A thunderclap up and drownded his voice out.

"Hey Gang," I said. "It's Pa. *Hotdangit!*"

"Which board, Cap'n?" Junior laughed.

"Larboard, Mr. Starbuckles." I said then barked out to the Gang.

"Now loose your scaly butts off the poopdecks and haul to on the sternboards. Then push lee'ards to the bank shore. Mr. Brudley Marshall Bascomb gon be our passenger rider. So shake tail!"

The Peaceful Eye

Martha Lacy Hall

THE PECAN LEAVES didn't crackle under her saddle oxfords as they might have on a warm, clear October morning. The rain last night had made them soggy. She felt a need for a crisp response beneath her shoes, and the little corner of her mind that was aware of these things told her that the magnolia leaves up in front of the Gatchell's would be crunchy. It took more than a night's rain to soften them, and this gave her a half-conscious comfort. They would jig-saw into little brown geometrics and lie there until barely larger than grit. She kicked a pecan, still in its bright green outer shell. It smacked sharply against a tree and glanced off into the gutter where it lay bruised and immature on the concrete.

I promised myself I'd never go to Miss Emma's again. I wish I could turn back. But Miss Scott would wonder why. And I'm the only one in the class who knows where her rooms are. She'd think I was crazy.

It was just after morning recess when Miss Scott asked her to run an errand. Civics class was about to begin, and Mary had spent recess memorizing the names of the President's cabinet: John Nance Garner, Henry Wallace, James Farley. . . . Mary gave no thought to what the errand might be. Miss Scott knew she liked to get out of class to do most anything except dust erasers.

She laid her yellow Mikado pencil in the long narrow slot on her desk with the point right at the J. of J. V. B. that someone had carved there long ago. Then she walked up to the teacher's desk with the envious eyes of twenty sixth-graders on her back.

"Mary, I forgot my grade book. Would you mind walking up to Miss Emma's to get it?"

"Yes ma'am. I mean no ma'am. I'll go. Where'll I find it?"

"Just look in my room on the bed or the dresser. I'm sure it's out where you'll see it. I'll appreciate it, Honey." She smiled.

Mary knew all about Miss Scott's apartment. Miss Emma Lamar's house was across the street from her own, and Mary knew where Miss Scott kept most of her things. She knew what books were in the book shelf, where the alarm clock sat beside the yellow breadbox on the oilcloth-covered table in the tiny kitchen, and how the three little fringed pillows were lined up on Miss Scott's bed that was covered with the white chenille bedspread. Mary's favorite thing in the whole apartment was a perfume bottle of delicate pink frosted glass that sat on the white linen, lace-edged dresser scarf. Miss Scott had once pulled out the long glass stopper and touched her white wrists, where the veins were blue. She assured Mary her beating pulse forced the scent into the air about her. Mary tried this with some of her mother's perfumes, and she felt that it worked, but she couldn't find a scent on her mother's crowded dressing table that was as heavenly as Appleblossom.

Miss Scott wasn't Miss Scott at all. She was Mrs. Fite. Last year she had married Billy Fite, a fat little meatcutter who had no education, and who cried and called his mother when it lightninged. Everyone in town knew about that. Billy was a butcher—a butcher! Everyone called him a meatcutter. It somehow sounded better—almost artistic. Billy wore a bloody apron, and Mary had watched him cleave the largest joint of a cow with one blow of that great axe-like knife. It was a splendid and terrifying performance, and Mary knew that Billy put his heart and soul into that blow. Afterward he would strike the surface of the huge square block of a tree that was his table and leave his meat axe vibrating while he wiped his hands on his blood-browned apron. He had a sweet shy smile.

Now Mary zigzagged so she could step on the big magnolia leaves and at the same time avoid the lines of the sidewalk.

"I hope Miss Emma's not at home, so I won't have to see her." Realizing she had spoken out loud, she looked around to see if anyone might have heard her, but no one was near. For a moment she walked straight, heedless of crackling leaves or the lines that would make her a rotten egg if she stepped on them.

Miss Scott had asked her why she never came to see her anymore. But Mary couldn't tell her why—that something too terrible to describe had happened between her and Miss Emma—that she felt she never could look at Miss Emma again, much less run the risk of talking to her.

Miss Scott was tall and looked like a Spanish queen. She wore her dark hair parted in the middle and pulled back into a low full bun on her neck. Not one bit of her ears showed, and her hair shone like Sunday shoes. She had a jaw line like Joan Crawford—square with sort of hollow cheeks. Her eyes were large and dark with thick, strangely straight black lashes that looked like starched fringe. Mary had studied them, and she'd decided that they were too stiff to yield to the eyelash curler that her sister used to turn up her light brown lashes. The most fascinating thing about Miss Scott's face was her dark moustache which could fill Mary with a mixture of revulsion and awe. Once, Miss Scott had bleached it only to have the most horrible yellow moustache glowing like a Mardi Gras joke on her proud face. But the moustache didn't really bother Mary.

Miss Scott had married Billy because she was thirty and figured he was her only chance. How many grown people had Mary heard say that? He was a foot shorter than she was, and he was a mamma's boy, but he did come from a nice family, and Miss Scott seemed happy with him. Mary wondered if Miss Scott had ever seen Billy at work at McGraw's Market, where he hacked and sawed and sliced his way through cow after cow and pig after pig.

Miss Emma's house was only four blocks from school, and Mary could have made the trip blindfolded because she walked to and from school twice every day—she went home for lunch. Everybody went home for lunch in Sweet Bay, only it was dinner in the middle of the day. Myrt cooked a big dinner every day, and at night Mary had a light supper. It was only when they stayed in a hotel in New Orleans that Mamma called the night meal "dinner." And that was because it *was* dinner. In New Orleans all meals were dinners, and Mamma and Daddy would try to be polite with their belching on the way home while Mary sat on the back seat of the car counting turtles on floating logs in the canal. Between La Place and Ponchatoula she would sometimes count over a hundred. After dark she counted one-eyed cars. The swamp road was wavy, and Daddy drove fast. She would stare ahead at the road lighted by the headlights trying not to think of the deep black water on either side of the highway.

Mary ran her hand along the tops of the fence pickets as she walked past Mrs. Gatchell's. Mrs. Gatchell was sitting on her front porch with a large blue and white enameled bowl on her lap. She was picking over mustard greens and rocking. Her heels came down rhythmically as she discarded the tough ends of the greens on a newspaper beside her chair. "Morning, Mary. Playing hookey?" Mary said no.

The Gatchells had a concrete platform in front of their gate on the edge of the street. It was made for stepping into a carriage or mounting a horse. Now it was just something to scratch the paint off a car door. It had a slab of white marble in the top of it with GATCHELL set in blue tile letters. Last Halloween some high school boys had painted out the GATC with green paint, leaving HELL. Mrs. Gatchell was outraged, and she found out that Bud Carnes and Mickey Beaumont did it and made them clean the paint off. Mary looked at it now. Faint traces of green paint showed in the concrete around the marble. Mary looked at Mrs. Gatchell and her blue bowl of greens and her funny skinny ankles that showed below her cotton print housedress. She liked to think of her out there standing over Bud and Mickey, threatening to call their parents if they didn't scrub and scrape harder. Mrs. Gatchell was tough, but she wasn't crazy. Miss Emma was. Mary liked a lot of old people in Sweet Bay whom she regarded as a little odd. Old Mr. Dickerson really believed his house was haunted by the man who built it before the Civil War. That was fun. But Miss Emma was something else.

Once, Mary had thought Miss Emma was merely a little mysterious, and she liked her. *My friend Miss Emma.* For one thing she was a Yankee, and the way she pronounced her r's made Mary think of biting hard candy that had been in the refrigerator. Mary used to spend hours in Miss Emma's porch swing, her toes barely scraping the clean gray-painted floor. As she swung gently back and forth, her fingers would travel up and down the links of chain, and she and Miss Emma talked about all sorts of things. The porch faced east and was lovely and shaded in the afternoons—in the spring fragrant with wisteria and magnolia fuscatas humming with bumblebees—in the fall when the air changed so mysteriously and the smell was of burning leaves and acorns, and the grassless spots under the big oak in front of the porch were traced with the finely combed trails of the leaf rake. She remembered the good croquet games they used to have. But all of this ended for Mary months ago.

Miss Emma's house was a quaint old two-story cottage with banistered porches upstairs and down. Her house sat to one side of the property, and she had a big side lawn that was flat enough for croquet. It sloped off near the street corner where there was a great cedar with the ground underneath covered with ivy and fern, and to Mary it had been a wonderful place. Miss Emma's yard was surrounded by a hedge—low boxwood up near the house but eight-foot-tall privet down by the cedar, to screen off Negro town which started right across the street.

The first Negro house belonged to Jim Cannon. Jim had a wooden leg and a moustache. He smoked a corncob pipe, and he was an expert at trimming hedges. He once told Mary that his shears were his "living." Mary had never forgotten, and after that she noticed he always carried his shears under his arm. His empty pants leg was packed in neat folds between the wooden leg and his *stump*. Jim's own hedge was as high on Miss Emma's side as hers was on his. His was very fancy in places with higher squares at the corners and at his gate. In one side he had sculptured a bench with arms, but you couldn't sit in it. Mary had tried. The sharp, stubby branches had pierced and scratched her when she sat on the soft looking green foliage. It was like jumping into a big pile of leaves expecting to plop down on a cushiony heap and landing with a shocking thud on the hard ground beneath. You couldn't tell how soft something was by looking at it.

Miss Emma was a Methodist and a widow. She walked to church every Sunday in good weather. When it rained she rode with Mary's family or with Miss Phaedra Mullins, another neighbor. Miss Emma was thin as a slat, with a pale little face, and she wore only white powder for make-up—no lipstick even. Mary always noticed that. She wore beige or brown, and in the summer she sometimes wore white. Now she reminded Mary of a dead mouse that she had seen in a trap, especially when she sang in the choir. Her mouth dropped open just like the mouse's had, chin receding. She was so like that mouse that lay dead on the storeroom floor. But Miss Emma hadn't been to church lately.

She used to play bridge almost every night except Sunday, which would have been a sin. She played with her two upstairs roomers, who, to Mary's puzzlement she had heard called "those two pansies." She had pictured the bridge foursome in Miss Emma's sitting room as Miss Emma and two large gold and purple velvet pansies and somebody else for a fourth—Miss Phaedra sometimes. Miss

Scott used to play with them before she married. Now she and Billy spent every night in their rooms with the shades down, and the mouse and the two pansies had to call someone—when they played, which was hardly ever now. Silky playing bridge didn't sound any sillier than two pansies. Silky was Miss Emma's golden spaniel.

Mary stopped and put her foot up on the red fire hydrant and tied her shoe. Silky was dead. She walked on.

When Miss Emma sang in the choir her lips never changed shape. Her jaw just worked up and down. She looked out over the congregation as though they weren't there, and she patted her foot, impatiently, to speed up the slow hymns. Her foot was the only one that moved in the row of shoes that showed under the short brown curtain that hung in front of the choir.

One day Silky had followed her into church; she went right up into the choir, and Miss Emma held her on her lap until the service was over. When it came time to stand and sing the offertory, Miss Emma stayed in her seat and patted her foot a little faster than the organ and sang with Silky on her lap.

Miss Emma had loved Silky better than anyone or anything. She brushed her and fussed over her and never let her run with the other dogs in the neighborhood. Last spring when it was discovered that Silky was going to have puppies, Mary thought Miss Emma might go crazy over it, she was so upset.

"I just don't know how this happened." Her mouth would clop, over and over, and tears would come in her eyes, and her little face would twitch. Then she quit mentioning it, and nobody else seemed to think much about it except Mary, who was excited and wanted one of the puppies.

One day she went over to Miss Emma's. She walked along the driveway on the narrow side of the yard, under the camphor trees that were planted too close to the house and had to lean out over the graveled paths.

At the back porch steps she called through the screened door. "Miss Emma." There was no answer so she opened the door and started in. Silky lay on her side on the rag rug that Miss Emma used to wipe her shoes when she came in from the yard. Mary knew at once that Silky was dead. There was something brown on her back legs, and her sides were strangely flat and empty looking.

Mary backed down the wood steps. She heard a faint chipping sound down near the cedar. She ran down and found Miss Emma under the tree trying to spade the hard ground.

"What happened? I saw her. What happened?"

"She's dead."

"I know. But what happened? What happened to the puppies?"

"They're dead."

"Oh." Mary pressed her fists to her cheeks.

"Can't I go get someone to come help you? Can't I *do* something? Where are the puppies?" Mary held a drooping cedar bough away from her face.

Miss Emma's face glistened with sweat. She was making little headway. Her small mouth hung open, and she pressed her foot on the shovel.

Mary turned and pushed through the high privet hedge. Jim was watering his flower beds. His shears lay on the porch.

"Jim! Come help Miss Emma dig a grave for Silky. She's dead from childbirth."

"Gawd. Limme git a box." He turned the water off at the nozzle, and the hose writhed in the grass like a snake that refused to die. Mary turned the water off at the hydrant, and the hose lay down and began to relax.

Jim looked around for a moment, then picked up a large pasteboard Grande Dame coffee box with a label on the top.

"What do you want?" asked Miss Emma. "I can do this."

"No'm," said Jim. "You gimme that shovel, now." And he began to dig. He was a powerful man and soon had a deep hole dug. He fitted the box into it, then took it out. "Now that'll jist about do it," he said. "Where the dog at, Miz Emma?"

Miss Emma said, "Show him, Mary. Wrap her in that rag rug."

Mary and Jim soon returned. The box was closed, but Miss Emma didn't even look at it. She just sat on the cold stone bench. The Grande Dame lady on top of the box looked straight ahead, her wavy hair parted in the middle and her little pink mouth prim. She had a peaceful eye. Jim threw the first spade of dirt into her blank, pretty face. Miss Emma rose. "Thank you, both." The cedar raked her hair. Mary heard the back porch door slam.

Jim beat the back of the spade down hard on Silky's grave, and then he stamped heavily on it with his big feet, to tamp the earth.

Mary thought of the picture of the Grande Dame coffee lady staring out forever, with her peaceful eye. And Silky—

Mary's eyes filled with tears.

"Ain't nothing but a dog, Miss Mary."

"I know it. Thanks a lot, Jim." And they left.

Later Mary found Miss Emma on her front porch. Mary leaned against the banister, feeling sorry for her.

"What happened to the puppies? How many were there?" She *had* to know.

"There were six," said Miss Emma. "They are all dead. They had slick short hair—black and white—terrible looking mongrels just like that beast that belongs to those nigras over there." She indicated the other end of the block by cutting her eyes to her left.

"What did you do with them?"

"I buried them behind the shed after you and the nigra left. The ground is softer back there. They were all born dead."

"Oh . . ."

"I'll go in now. You be careful crossing the street." Miss Emma left Mary, and Mary swung around the post and stepped off the front porch.

She found the fresh mound of earth just beyond the black pot where Sadie did Miss Emma's wash. On the bench under the shed was a galvanized tub half-filled with water. Mary put her hand on the clothesline and leaned forward. A white puppy with black spots floated there. Puppy hair floated on the water.

Mary heard her own breath sucked in. *She's drowned them. She lied. Drowned them—with her own hands—and she forgot to bury one.*

The spade leaned against the tub. Mary was about to reach for it when she heard a sound—a faint squeak. She froze. The squeak became a chorus. *No! Oh, no, no, no.* Dim baby cries came from the mound. She felt ill, as though she might faint or vomit. She dropped the spade, fell on her knees, and began clawing the damp earth. But she had barely felt the dirt under her nails when Miss Emma's voice, strange and harsh, rasped, "What do you think you are doing?"

"Please, Miss Emma! They aren't dead! I *hear* the puppies. Maybe we can save them." She lifted her hands from the dirt.

Miss Emma grasped Mary's arms roughly. "Go home immediately, young lady! This is none of your business."

In her own room Mary took a pillow and hid under her bed. She shut her eyes and beat her eyes with her palms to try to destroy the awful thing. She felt buried alive with the dying puppies under the dark, wet earth, squeaking out their last instinctive calls for help. She wrapped the soft pillow around her head and moaned.

It was almost dark when her mother waked her.

"Mary! What are you doing sleeping under the bed? A big girl nearly twelve years old! Come out from under there. Supper's almost ready."

Mary opened her eyes. Mamma had turned on the lamp, and she could see dust thick on the baseboard near her face. She felt the same dust lining her nostrils. She clutched her pillow, and crawled out and went to the front porch to look at Miss Emma's house. It had been no dream. And she was going to hear that terrible sound forever. If she couldn't dig them up, why hadn't she . . . but there was nothing she could do. Maybe . . .

She crossed the street. When she stepped behind Miss Emma's shed, she saw in the half-light that the galvanized tub had been emptied and hung on the wall—the molded rings in its bottom barely visible. She listened, one ear turned to the mound. There was no sound, and she felt some relief to know it was over.

Now she heard a soft rustle. She turned her head enough to know that Miss Emma was close behind her, and though she did not look at her, she knew so well what that face looked like.

"You forgot to bury one, and the others weren't dead."

"They are now. And they are *all* buried."

"How—*why* did you do it?"

"I thought they were dead. I held them under a long time—each one—till they quit squirming and were perfectly still and limp. I thought they were dead."

As she turned to look at Miss Emma, a picture of her flashed across Mary's mind—the pale hymn singer patting her foot impatiently in the church choir—Get on with it! Die! Die! I haven't got all day.

"You had done this before you buried Silky."

"This is what I planned to do all along. You forget, Mary, that these were my puppies to do what I please with. They were just mongrel puppies. They might have been cute for a while, but would have grown to be ugly dogs—mockeries of my poor Silky. Don't meddle, Mary, or I'll speak to your mother."

Mary knew she would speak to no one. She went home and sat down at the supper table. She slid her knees under the white cloth and began to push food around on her plate, but she couldn't eat.

As the months passed, she heard remarks about Miss Emma. "Emma was always peculiar. But here lately she seems hardly interested in *any*thing." "Emma used to play bridge regularly, but she never picks up a card now." "Emma's just *quit* the Missionary Society." Mary found it easy to avoid Miss Emma, and she learned to avoid pondering the things people were saying. *I don't care about Miss Emma one way or the other.* And in her bed at night when she thought of the sad little cries, she would turn on her lamp and read until she fell asleep. School started. She had for her teacher the Spanish queen who moved about in a pulsing mist of Appleblossom perfume, and for the first time in her life, she felt that she might be the favorite pupil in class. And this was a secret too dizzying to dare breathe to a soul. She was less troubled . . .

Miss Emma's apartment was on the right side overlooking the croquet lawn. Miss Scott and Billy lived on the left. She found, to her surprise, that Miss Scott's door was locked so she tried another farther down the hall. It was locked. Like it or not, she would have to ask Miss Emma to let her in.

She knocked at her door and got no answer. She rattled the white china knob and found the door bolted. Then she went into Miss Emma's kitchen from the back porch and called, "Miss Emma," into her bedroom. The room was neat and prim, the bed smoothly made, but there was no Miss Emma. Mary went no farther than the bedroom door; she returned to the kitchen and took Miss Emma's keys off the hook over the gas stove. She quickly found the one to open Miss Scott's apartment. The grade book lay on the bed. She locked up, replaced the keys, and hurried out of the house. This was her lucky day. She walked briskly back to school swinging the thin blue grade book by her side.

Coming home that afternoon, she noticed two cars in Miss Emma's driveway; also her father's car was home, parked in front of Mrs. Judge Griffith's and Mrs. Doctor Hough's cars. She went in the side door to avoid the living room, but her mother heard her and met her in her room. Something was wrong.

"Mary, Honey, something very unfortunate has happened. It's

Miss Emma." Mary tilted her head upward, and her eyebrows lifted slightly, questioning. Mamma's face had never looked quite like this before. There were fine little lines kind of stretched under her eyes, and there was a little shiver in her voice when she said, "She's dead, Mary."

Mary put her books on her desk. The big geography book fell to the floor, displaying a brown and green relief map of South America. Miss Emma was dead. She felt nothing. She tried to feel something. *What do I feel? Nothing.*

"What—when did she die? What happened to her?"

"Well, Miss Phaedra walked over there about eleven-thirty this morning, just to look in on her. She found her—dead."

"Found her? Dead at eleven-thirty? Where was she? What happened to her? Did she have a heart attack?"

"No, Mary. She found her lying on the floor beside her bed. She—Darling, she took her own life. Shot herself—Dr. Hough figures she did it about nine this morning."

Nine. Eleven-thirty. "What side of the bed was she on?"

"Why—she was on the side nearest her sitting room. You know—not on the kitchen side, the other side. What makes you ask that?"

"I just wondered—wondered where she—her body was."

"This is such a terrible thing to have to tell a little girl about her friend. I know it's shocking, Darling—something awful you've never had to even hear about—you and Miss Emma—friends since you were a baby . . . poor Darling. . . ." *Poor Mamma.*

She leaned her cheek against her mother's arm, and her mother hugged her close. *Poor Mamma.* "Poor Darling."

"I'm sorry, Mamma—I mean it really is terrible, isn't it? But don't worry—about me, I mean."

Her mother left her abruptly because she heard the two ladies—Mrs. Hough and Mrs. Griffith—leaving.

Mary put on her slacks, sneakers, and one of her brother's shirts. Later she looked into her mother's room. "Mamma, there are only about six blooms left in that nasturtium bed under your window. May I pull them up before frost gets them?"

Her mother looked surprised for only a moment. "I wish you would. That's very sweet, Mary." Mary was careful not to slam the screen door.

She dropped to her knees at the bed of annuals and began to pull up the spent summer plants.

"You never can tell about children." Her mother's voice. "Some little girls would have had hysterics." The voice drifted softly from the window. "Of course I didn't go into the bloody details. My Lord! Poor Phaedra, coming on that gruesome. . . ." The rich dark soil was cold. It made black arcs under the end of her nails. She crumbled handfuls and sifted it between her fingers letting it fill holes and depressions.

". . . why? God knows." Her father's voice. "Don't let it prey on your mind, Katherine. I'll have to help with the arrangements. Phaedra can't do it all."

"I know. I know. She took Emma's best beige silk down to the funeral parlor. And she's talked with the brother in Oklahoma; he'll be in tomorrow night on No. 4. He agreed on the phone that Emma of all people should be buried from her church. . . ."

"Well I told Phaedra I'd go out to the cemetery and see that the Lamar lot is trimmed up. I'll take Jim out there . . ."

A katydid struck its one-note song—not a song either, just a note with never a hurry or pause for breath. Katydids must not breathe.

The brittle nasturtiums had shallow roots and they came up as though they'd never had a grip on the earth. An agile, sherry-colored worm writhed frantically in the loose soil, then disappeared underground. She gathered the plants and broke off the bouquet of remaining blossoms—fragile gold and yellow petals. She added a few round green leaves with fine white throbless veins. Unfolding her body, a little stiffly, she knocked moist dirt from the knees of her pants.

In the kitchen she stood on a chair to reach a glass—the only one left of her grandmother's heavy old goblets with thistles on the sides, and she took it to the sink and filled it with water. Then she sank the pale, translucent stems into the water and walked to her mother's room. She set the flowers on the desk by the window—on an envelope so the glass wouldn't make a ring. She rubbed her hands back and forth on the hard smooth surface of the desk that warmed with the friction.

Looking out the window, she saw that Miss Emma's porch was shady and beginning to go lilac as it sometimes did when the sun sank lower in the evening. The swing was empty, and the fern baskets hung motionless over the banisters. The big oak tree laid a transparency of itself across the street and over half of Mary's yard. The croquet lawn was smooth and wicketless. She knew the wickets were stored neatly on the back porch with the mallets and balls, their bright-colored bands faded from years of use. The old house smelled of turkey carpets and mothballs. Silky lay beneath the dark cedar with the Grande Dame coffee lady whose face was so peaceful and unworried.

The nasturtiums glowed alive like sunshine, in the old goblet on the desk, and Mary felt the hotness of tears in her eyes.

Testimony of Pilot

Barry Hannah

When I was ten, eleven and twelve, I did a good bit of my play in the backyard of a three-story wooden house my father had bought and rented out, his first venture into real estate. We lived right across the street from it, but over here was the place to do your real play. Here there was a harrowed but overgrown garden, a vine-swallowed fence at the back end, and beyond the fence a cornfield which belonged to someone else. This was not the country. This was the town, Clinton, Mississippi, between Jackson on the east and Vicksburg on the west. On this lot stood a few water oaks, a few plum bushes, and much overgrowth of honeysuckle vine. At the very back end, at the fence, stood three strong nude chinaberry trees.

In Mississippi it is difficult to achieve a vista. But my friends and I had one here at the back corner of the garden. We could see across the cornfield, see the one lone tin-roofed house this side of the railroad tracks, then on across the tracks many other bleaker houses with rustier tin roofs, smoke coming out of the chimneys in the late fall. This was niggertown. We had binoculars and could see the colored children hustling about and perhaps a hopeless sow or two with her brood enclosed in a tiny boarded-up area. Through the binoculars one afternoon in October we watched some men corner and beat a large hog on the brain. They used an ax and the thing kept running around, head leaning toward the ground, for several minutes before it lay down. I thought I saw the men laughing when it finally did. One of them was staggering, plainly drunk to my sight from three hundred yards away. He had the long knife. Because of that scene I considered Negroes savage cowards for a good five more years of my life. Our maid brought some sausage to my mother and when it was put in the pan to fry, I made a point of running out of the house.

I went directly across the street and to the back end of the garden behind the apartment house we owned, without my breakfast. That was Saturday. Eventually, Radcleve saw me. His parents had him mowing the yard that ran alongside my dad's property. He clicked off the power mower and I went over to his fence, which was storm wire. His mother maintained handsome flowery grounds at all costs; she had a leafmold bin and St. Augustine grass as solid as a rug.

Radcleve himself was a violent experimental chemist. When Radcleve was eight, he threw a whole package of .22 shells against the sidewalk in front of his house until one of them went off, driving lead fragments into his calf, most of them still deep in there where the surgeons never dared tamper. Radcleve knew about the sulfur, potassium nitrate and charcoal mixture for gunpowder when he was ten. He bought things through the mail when he ran out of ingredients in his chemistry sets. When he was an infant, his father, a quiet man who owned the Chevrolet agency in town, bought an entire bankrupt sporting-goods store, and in the middle of their backyard he built a house, plain-painted and neat, one room and a heater, where Radcleve's redundant toys forevermore were kept—all the possible toys he would need for boyhood. There were things in there that Radcleve and I were not mature enough for and did not know the real use of. When we were eleven, we uncrated the new Dunlop golf balls and went on up a shelf for the tennis rackets, went out in the middle of his yard, and served new golf ball after new golf ball with blasts of the rackets over into the cornfield, out of sight. When the strings busted we just went in and got another racket. We were absorbed by how a good smack would set the heavy little pills on an endless flight. Then Radcleve's father came down. He simply dismissed me. He took Radcleve into the house and covered his whole body with a belt. But within the week Radcleve had invented the mortar. It was a steel pipe into which a flashlight battery fit perfectly, like a bullet into a muzzle. He had drilled a hole for the fuse of an M-80 firecracker at the base, for the charge. It was a grand cannon, set up on a stack of bricks at the back of my dad's property, which was the free place to play. When it shot, it would back up violently with thick smoke and you could hear the flashlight battery whistling off. So that morning when I ran out of the house protesting the hog sausage, I told Radcleve to bring over the mortar. His ma and dad were in Jackson for the day, and he came right over with the pipe, the batteries and the M-80 explosives. He had two gross of them.

Before, we'd shot off toward the woods to the right of niggertown. I turned the bricks to the left; I made us a very fine cannon carriage pointing toward niggertown. When Radcleve appeared, he had two pairs of binoculars around his neck, one pair a newly plundered German unit as big as a brace of whiskey bottles. I told him I wanted to shoot for that house where we saw them killing the pig. Radcleve loved the idea. We singled out the house with heavy use of the binoculars.

There were children in the yard. Then they all went in. Two men came out of the back door. I thought I recognized the drunkard from the other afternoon. I helped Radcleve fix the direction of the cannon. We estimated the altitude we needed to get down there. Radcleve put the M-80 in the breech with its fuse standing out of the hole. I dropped the flashlight battery in. I lit the fuse. We backed off. The M-80 blasted off deafeningly, smoke rose, but my concentration was on that particular house over there. I brought the binoculars up. We waited six or seven seconds. I heard a great joyful wallop on tin. "We've hit him on the first try, the first try!" I yelled. Radcleve was ecstatic. "Right on his roof!" We bolstered up the brick carriage. Radcleve remembered the correct height of the cannon exactly. So we fixed it, loaded it, lit it and backed off. The battery landed on the roof, blat, again, louder. I looked to see if there wasn't a great dent or hole in the roof. I could not understand why niggers weren't pouring out distraught from that house. We shot the mortar again and again, and always our battery hit the tin roof. Sometimes there was only a dull thud, but other times there was a wild distress of tin. I was still looking through the binoculars, amazed that the niggers wouldn't even come out of their house to see what was hitting their roof. Radcleve was on to it better than me. I looked over at him and he had the huge German binocs much lower than I did. He was looking straight through the cornfield, which was all bare and open, with nothing left but rotten stalks. "What we've been hitting is the roof of that house just this side of the tracks. White people live in there," he said.

I took up my binoculars again. I looked around the yard of that white wooden house on this side of the tracks, almost next to the railroad. When I found the tin roof, I saw four significant dents in it. I saw one of our batteries lying in the middle of a sort of crater. I took the bincoulars down into the yard and saw a blond middle-aged woman looking our way.

"Somebody's coming up toward us. He's from that house and

he's got, I think, some sort of fancy gun with him. It might be an automatic weapon."

I ran my bincoulars all over the cornfield. Then, in a line with the house, I saw him. He was coming our way but having some trouble with the rows and dead stalks of the cornfield.

"That is just a boy like us. All he's got is a saxophone with him," I told Radcleve. I had recently got in the school band, playing drums, and had seen all the weird horns that made up a band.

I watched this boy with the saxophone through the binoculars until he was ten feet from us. This was Quadberry. His name was Ard, short for Arden. His shoes were foot-square wads of mud from the cornfield. When he saw us across the fence and above him, he stuck out his arm in my direction.

"My dad says stop it!"

"We weren't doing anything," says Radcleve.

"Mother saw the smoke puff up from here. Dad has a hangover."

"A what?"

"It's a headache from indiscretion. You're lucky he does. He's picked up the poker to rap on you, but he can't move further the way his head is."

"What's your name? You're not in the band," I said, focusing on the saxophone.

"It's Ard Quadberry. Why do you keep looking at me through the binoculars?"

It was because he was odd, with his hair and its white ends, and his Arab nose, and now his name. Add to that the saxophone.

"My dad's a doctor at the college. Mother's a musician. You better quit what you're doing. . . . I was out practicing in the garage. I saw one of those flashlight batteries roll off the roof. Could I see what you shoot 'em with?"

"No," said Radcleve. Then he said: "If you'll play that horn."

Quadberry stood out there ten feet below us in the field, skinny, feet and pants booted with black mud, and at his chest the slung-on, very complex, radiant horn.

Quadberry began sucking and licking the reed. I didn't care much for this act, and there was too much desperate oralness in his face when he began playing. That was why I chose the drums. One had to engage himself like suck's revenge with a horn. But what Quadberry was playing was pleasant and intricate. I was sure it was advanced, and there was no squawking, as from the other eleven-year-olds on sax in the band room. He made the end with a clean upward riff, holding the final note high, pure and unwavering.

"Good!" I called to him.

Quadberry was trying to move out of the sunken row toward us, but his heavy shoes were impeding him.

"Sounded like a duck. Sounded like a girl duck," said Radcleve, who was kneeling down and packing a mudball around one of the M-80s. I saw and I was an accomplice, because I did nothing. Radcleve lit the fuse and heaved the mudball over the fence. An M-80 is a very serious firecracker; it is like the charge they use to shoot up those sprays six hundred feet on July Fourth at country clubs. It went off, this one, even bigger than most M-80s.

When we looked over the fence, we saw Quadberry all muck specks and fragments of stalks. He was covering the mouthpiece of his horn with both hands. Then I saw there was blood pouring out of, it seemed, his right eye. I thought he was bleeding directly out of his eye.

"Quadberry?" I called.

He turned around and never said a word to me until I was eighteen. He walked back holding his eye and staggering through the cornstalks. Radcleve had him in the binoculars. Radcleve was trembling . . . but intrigued.

"His mother just screamed. She's running out in the field to get him."

I thought we'd blinded him, but we hadn't. I thought the Quadberrys would get the police or call my father, but they didn't. The upshot of this is that Quadberry had a permanent white space next to his right eye, a spot that looked like a tiny upset crown.

I went from sixth through half of twelfth grade ignoring him and that wound. I was coming on as a drummer and a lover, but if Quadberry happened to appear within fifty feet of me and my most tender, intimate sweetheart, I would duck out. Quadberry grew up just like the rest of us. His father was still a doctor—professor of history—at the town college; his mother was still blond, and a musician. She was organist at an Episcopalian church in Jackson, the big capital city ten miles east of us.

As for Radcleve, he still had no ear for music, but he was there, my buddy. He was repentant about Quadberry, although not so much as I. He'd thrown the mud grenade over the fence only to see what would happen. He had not really wanted to maim. Quadberry had played his tune on the sax, Radcleve had played his tune on the mud grenade. It was just a shame they happened to cross talents.

Radcleve went into a long period of nearly nothing after he gave up violent explosives. Then he trained himself to copy the comic strips, *Steve Canyon* to *Major Hoople,* until he became quite a versatile cartoonist with some very provocative new faces and bodies that were gesturing intriguingly. He could never fill in the speech balloons with the smart words they needed. Sometimes he would pencil in "Err" or "What?" in the empty speech places. I saw him a great deal. Radcleve was not spooked by Quadberry. He even once asked Quadberry what his opinion was of his future as a cartoonist. Quadberry told Radcleve that if he took all his cartoons and stuffed himself with them, he would make an interesting dead man. After that, Radcleve was shy of him too.

When I was a senior we had an extraordinary band. Word was we had outplayed all the big A.A.A. division bands last April in the state contest. Then came news that a new blazing saxophone player was coming into the band as first chair. This person had spent summers in Vermont in music camps, and he was coming in with us for the concert season. Our director, a lovable aesthete named Richard Prender, announced to us in a proud silent moment that the boy was joining us tomorrow night. The effect was that everybody should push over a seat or two and make room for this boy and his talent. I was annoyed. Here I'd been with the band and had kept hold of the taste among the whole percussion section. I could play rock and jazz drum and didn't even really need to be here. I could be in Vermont too, give me a piano and a bass. I looked at the kid on first sax, who was going to be supplanted tomorrow. For two years he had thought he was the star, then suddenly enters this boy who's three times better.

The new boy was Quadberry. He came in, but he was meek, and when he tuned up he put his head almost on the floor, bending over trying to be inconspicuous. The girls in the band had wanted him to be handsome, but Quadberry refused and kept himself in such hiding among the sax section that he was neither handsome, ugly, cute or anything. What he was was pretty near invisible, except for the bell of his horn, the all-but-closed eyes, the Arabian nose, the brown hair with its halo of white ends, the desperate oralness, the giant reed punched into his face, and hazy Quadberry, loving the wound in a private dignified ecstasy.

I say dignified because of what came out of the end of his horn. He was more than what Prender had told us he would be. Because of Quadberry, we could take the band arrangement of Ravel's *Bolero* with us to the state contest. Quadberry would do the saxophone solo. He would switch to alto sax, he would do the sly Moorish ride. When he played, I heard the sweetness, I heard the horn which finally brought human *talk* into the realm of music. It could sound like the mutterings of a field nigger, and then it could get up into inhumanly careless beauty, it could get among mutinous helium bursts around Saturn. I already loved *Bolero* for the constant drum part. The percussion was always there, driving along with the subtly increasing triplets, insistent, insistent, at last outraged and trying to steal the whole show from the horns and the others. I knew a large boy with dirty blond hair, name of Wyatt, who played viola in the Jackson Symphony and sousaphone in our band—one of the rare closet transmutations of my time—who was forever claiming to have discovered the central *Bolero* one Sunday afternoon over FM radio as he had seven distinct sexual moments with a certain B., girl flutist with black bangs and skin like mayonnaise, while the drums of Ravel carried them on and on in a ceremony of Spanish sex. It was agreed by all the canny in the band that *Bolero* was exactly the piece to make the band soar—now especially as we had Quadberry, who made his walk into the piece like an actual lean Spanish bandit. This boy could blow his horn. He was, as I had suspected, a genius. His solo was not quite the same as the New York Phil's saxophonist's, but it was better. It came in and was with us. It entered my spine and, I am sure, went up the skirts of the girls. I had almost deafened myself playing drums in the most famous rock and jazz band in the state, but I could hear the voice that went through and out that horn. It sounded like a very troubled forty-year-old man, a man who had had his brow in his hands a long time.

The next time I saw Quadberry up close, in fact the first time I had seen him up close since we were eleven and he was bleeding in the cornfield, was in late February. I had only three classes this last semester, and went up to the band room often, to loaf and complain and keep up my touch on the drums. Prender let me keep my set in one of the instrument rooms, with a tarpaulin thrown over it, and I would drag it out to the practice room and whale away. Sometimes a group of sophomores would come up and I would make them marvel, whaling away as if not only deaf but blind to them, although I wasn't at all. If I saw a sophomore girl with exceptional bod or face, I would do miracles of technique I never knew were in me. I would amaze myself. I would be threatening Buddy Rich and Sam Morello. But this time when I went into the instrument room, there was Quadberry on one side, and, back in a dark corner, a small ninth-grade euphonium player whose face was all red. The little boy was weeping and grinning at the same time.

"Queerberry," the boy said softly.

Quadberry flew upon him like a demon. He grabbed the boy's collar, slapped his face, and yanked his arm behind him in a merciless wrestler's grip, the one that made them bawl on TV. Then the boy broke it and slugged Quadberry in the lips and ran across to my side of the room. He said "Queerberry" softly again and jumped for the door. Quadberry plunged across the room and tackled him on the threshold. Now that the boy was under him, Quadberry pounded the top of his head with his fist like a mallet. The boy kept calling him "Queerberry" throughout this. He had not learned his lesson. The boy seemed to be going into concussion, so I stepped over and touched Quadberry, telling him to quit. Quadberry obeyed and stood up off the boy, who crawled on out into the band room. But once more the boy looked back with a bruised grin, saying "Queerberry." Quadberry made a move toward him, but I blocked it.

"Why are you beating up on this little guy?" I said. Quadberry was sweating and his eyes were wild with hate; he was a big fellow now, though lean. He was, at six feet tall, bigger than me.

"He kept calling me Queerberry."

"What do you care?" I asked.

"I care," Quadberry said, and left me standing there.

We were to play at Millsaps College Auditorium for the concert. It was April. We got on the buses, a few took their cars, and were a big tense crowd getting over there. To Jackson was only a twenty-minute trip. The director, Prender, followed the bus in his Volkswagen. There was a thick fog. A flashing ambulance, snaking the lanes, piled into him head on. Prender, who I would imagine was thinking of *Bolero* and hearing the young horn voices in his band—perhaps he was dwelling on Quadberry's spectacular gypsy entrance, or perhaps he was meditating on the percussion section, of which I was the king—passed into the airs of band-director heaven. We were told by the student director as we set up on the stage. The student director was a senior from the town college, very much afflicted, almost to the point of drooling, by a love and respect for Dick Prender, and now afflicted by a heartbreaking esteem for his ghost. As were we all.

I loved the tough and tender director awesomely and never knew it until I found myself bawling along with all the rest of the boys of the percussion. I told them to keep setting up, keep tuning, keep screwing the stands together, keep hauling in the kettle-drums. To just quit and bawl seemed a betrayal to Prender. I caught some girl clarinetists trying to flee the stage and go have their cry. I told them to get the hell back to their section. They obeyed me. Then I found the student director. I had to have my say.

"Look. I say we just play *Bolero* and junk the rest. That's our horse. We can't play *Brighton Beach* and *Neptune's Daughter*. We'll never make it through them. And they're too happy."

"We aren't going to play anything," he said. "Man, to play is filthy. Did you ever hear Prender play piano? Do you know what a cool man he was in all things?"

"We play. He got us ready, and we play."

"Man, you can't play any more than I can direct. You're bawling your face off. Look out there at the rest of them. Man, it's a herd, it's a weeping herd."

"What's wrong? Why aren't you pulling this crowd together?" This was Quadberry, who had come up urgently. "I got those little brats in my section sitting down, but we've got people abandoning the stage, tearful little finks throwing their horns on the floor."

"I'm not directing," said the mustached college man.

"Then get out of here. You're weak, weak!"

"Man, we've got teen-agers in ruin here, we got sorrowville. Nobody can—"

"Go ahead. Do your number. Weak out on us."

"Man, I—"

Qaudberry was already up on the podium, shaking his arms.

"We're right here! The band is right here! Tell your friends to get back in their seats. We're doing *Bolero*. Just put *Bolero* up and start tuning. *I'm* directing. I'll be right here in front of you. You look at *me!* Don't you dare quit on Prender. Don't you dare quit on me. You've got to be heard. *I've* got to be heard. Prender wanted me to be heard. I am the star, and I say we sit down and blow."

And so we did. We all tuned and were burning low for the advent into *Bolero,* though we couldn't believe that Quadberry was going to remain with his saxophone strapped to him and conduct us as well as play his solo. The judges, who apparently hadn't heard about Prender's death, walked down to their balcony desks.

One of them called out "Ready" and Quadberry's hand was instantly up in the air, his fingers hard as if around the stem of something like a torch. This was not Prender's way, but it had to do. We went into the number cleanly and Quadberry one-armed it in the conducting. He kept his face, this look of hostility, at the reeds and the trumpets. I was glad he did not look toward me and the percussion boys like that. But he must have known we would be constant and tasteful because I was the king there. As for the others, the soloists especially, he was scaring them into excellence. Prender had never got quite this from them. Boys became men and girls became women as Quadberry directed us through *Bolero.* I even became a bit better of a man myself, though Quadberry did not look my way. When he turned around toward the people in the auditorium to enter on his solo, I knew it was my baby. I and the drums were the metronome. That was no trouble. It was talent to keep the metronome ticking amidst any given chaos of sound.

But this keeps one's mind occupied and I have no idea what Quadberry sounded like on his sax ride. All I know is that he looked grief-stricken and pale, and small. Sweat had popped out on his forehead. He bent over extremely. He was wearing the red brass-button jacket and black pants, black bow tie at the throat, just like the rest of us. In this outfit he bent over his horn almost out of sight. For a moment, before I caught the glint of his horn through the music stands, I thought he had pitched forward off the stage. He went down so far to do his deep oral thing, his conducting arm had disappeared so quickly, I didn't know but what he was having a seizure.

When *Bolero* was over, the audience stood up and made meat out of their hands applauding. The judges themselves applauded. The band stood up, bawling again, for Prender and because we had done so well. The student director rushed out crying to embrace

Quadberry, who eluded him with his dipping shoulders. The crowd was still clapping insanely. I wanted to see Quadberry myself. I waded through the red backs, through the bow ties, over the white bucks. Here was the first-chair clarinetist, who had done his bit like an angel; he sat close to the podium and could hear Quadberry.

"Was Quadberry good?" I asked him.

"Are you kidding? These tears in my eyes, they're for how good he was. He was too good. I'll never touch my clarinet again." The clarinetist slung the pieces of his horn into their case like underwear and a toothbrush.

I found Quadberry fitting the sections of his alto in the velvet holds of his case.

"Hooray," I said. "Hip damn hooray for you."

Arden was smiling too, showing a lot of teeth I had never seen. His smile was sly. He knew he had pulled off a monster unlikelihood.

"Hip hip hooray for me," he said. "Look at her. I had the bell of the horn almost smack in her face."

There was a woman of about thirty sitting in the front row of the auditorium. She wore a sundress with a drastic cleavage up front; looked like something that hung around New Orleans and kneaded your heart to death with her feet. She was still mesmerized by Quadberry. She bore on him with a stare and there was moisture in her cleavage.

"You played well."

"Well? Play well? Yes."

He was trying not to look at her directly. Look at *me,* I beckoned to her with full face: I was the *drums.* She arose and left.

"I was walking downhill in a valley, is all I was doing," said Quadberry. "Another man, a wizard, was playing my horn." He locked his sax case. "I feel nasty for not being able to cry like the rest of them. Look at them. Look at them crying."

True, the children of the band were still weeping, standing around the stage. Several moms and dads had come up among them, and they were misty-eyed too. The mixture of grief and superb music had been unbearable.

A girl in tears appeared next to Quadberry. She was a majorette in football season and played third-chair sax during the concert season. Not even her violent sorrow could take the beauty out of the face of this girl. I had watched her for a number of years—her alertness to her own beauty, the pride of her legs in the majorette outfit—and had taken out her younger sister, a second-rate version of her and a wayward overcompensating nymphomaniac whom several of us made a hobby out of pitying. Well, here was Lilian herself crying in Quadberry's face. She told him that she'd run off the stage when she heard about Prender, dropped her horn and everything, and had thrown herself into a tavern across the street and drunk two beers quickly for some kind of relief. But she had come back through the front doors of the auditorium and sat down, dizzy with beer, and seen Quadberry, the miraculous way he had gone on with *Bolero*. And now she was eaten up by feelings of guilt, weakness, cowardice.

"We didn't miss you," said Quadberry.

"Please forgive me. Tell me to do something to make up for it."

"Don't breathe my way, then. You've got beer all over your breath."

"I want to talk to you."

"Take my horn case and go out, get in my car, and wait for me. It's the ugly Plymouth in front of the school bus."

"I know," she said.

Lilian Field, this lovely teary thing, with the rather pious grace of her carriage, with the voice of imminent swoon, picked up Quadberry's horn case and her own and walked off the stage.

I told the percussion boys to wrap up the packing. Into my suitcase I put my own gear and also managed to steal drum keys, two pairs of brushes, a twenty-inch Turkish cymbal, a Gretsch snare drum that I desired for my collection, a wood block, kettle-drum mallets, a tuning harp and a score sheet of *Bolero* full of marginal notes I'd written down straight from the mouth of Dick Prender, thinking I might want to look at the score sheet sometime in the future when I was having a fit of nostalgia such as I am having right now as I write this. I had never done any serious stealing before, and I was stealing for my art. Prender was dead, the band had done its last thing of the year, I was a senior. Things were finished at the high school. I was just looting a sinking ship. I could hardly lift the suitcase. As I was pushing it across the stage, Quadberry was there again.

"You can ride back with me if you want to."

"But you've got Lilian."

"Please ride back with me . . . us. Please."

"Why?"

"To help me get rid of her. Her breath is full of beer. My father always had that breath. Every time he was friendly, he had that breath. And she looks a great deal like my mother." We were interrupted by the Tupelo band director. He put his baton against Quadberry's arm.

"You were big with *Bolero,* son, but that doesn't mean you own the stage."

Quadberry caught the end of the suitcase and helped me with it out to the steps behind the auditorium. The buses were gone. There sat his ugly ocher Plymouth; it was a failed, gay, experimental shade from the Chrysler people. Lilian was sitting in the front seat wearing her shirt and bow tie, her coat off.

"Are you going to ride back with me?" Quadberry said to me.

"I think I would spoil something. You never saw her when she was a majorette. She's not stupid, either. She likes to show off a little, but she's not stupid. She's in the History Club."

"My father has a doctorate in history. She smells of beer."

I said, "She drank two cans of beer when she heard about Prender."

"There are a lot of other things to do when you hear about death. What I did, for example. She ran away. She fell to pieces."

"She's waiting for us," I said.

"One damned thing I am never going to do is drink."

"I've never seen your mother up close, but Lilian doesn't look like your mother. She doesn't look like anybody's mother."

I rode with them silently to Clinton. Lilian made no bones about being disappointed I was in the car, though she said nothing. I knew it would be like this and I hated it. Other girls in town would not be so unhappy that I was in the car with them. I looked for flaws in Lilian's face and neck and hair, but there weren't any. Couldn't there be a mole, an enlarged pore, too much gum on a tooth, a single awkward hair around the ear? No. Memory, the whole lying opera of it, is killing me now. Lilian was faultless beauty, even sweating, even and especially in the white man's shirt and the bow tie clamping together her collar, when one knew her uncomfortable bosoms, her poor nipples. . . .

"Don't take me back to the band room. Turn off here and let me off at my house," I said to Quadberry. He didn't turn off.

"Don't tell Arden what to do. He can do what he wants to," said Lilian, ignoring me and speaking to me at the same time. I couldn't bear her hatred. I asked Quadberry to please just stop the car and let me out here, wherever he was: this front yard of the mobile home would do. I was so earnest that he stopped the car. He handed back the keys and I dragged my suitcase out of the trunk, then flung the keys back at him and kicked the car to get it going again.

My band came together in the summer. We were the Bop Fiends . . . that was our name. Two of them were from Ole Miss, our bass player was from Memphis State, but when we got together this time, I didn't call the tenor sax, who went to Mississippi Southern, because Quadberry wanted to play with us. During the school year the college boys and I fell into minor groups to pick up twenty dollars on a weekend, playing dances for the Moose Lodge, medical-student fraternities in Jackson, teen-age recreation centers in Greenwood, and such as that. But come summer we were the Bop Fiends again, and the price for us went up to $1,200 a gig. Where they wanted the best rock and bop and they had some bread, we were called. The summer after I was a senior, we played in Alabama, Louisiana and Arkansas. Our fame was getting out there on the interstate route.

This was the summer that I made myself deaf.

Years ago Prender had invited down an old friend from a high school in Michigan. He asked me over to meet the friend, who had been a drummer with Stan Kenton at one time and was now a band director just like Prender. This fellow was almost totally deaf and he warned me very sincerely about deafing myself. He said there would come a point when you had to lean over and concentrate all your hearing on what the band was doing and that was the time to quit for a while, because if you didn't you would be irrevocably deaf like him in a month or two. I listened to him but could not take him seriously. Here was an oldish man who had his problems. My ears had ages of hearing left. Not so. I played the drums so loud the summer after I graduated from high school that I made myself, eventually, stone deaf.

We were at, say, the National Guard Armory in Lake Village Arkansas, Quadberry out in front of us on the stage they'd built. Down on the floor were hundreds of sweaty teen-agers. Four girls in sundresses, showing what they could, were leaning on the stage with broad ignorant lust on their minds. I'd play so loud for one particular chick, I'd get absolutely out of control. The guitar boys would have to turn the volume up full blast to compensate. Thus I went deaf. Anyhow, the dramatic idea was to release Quadberry on a very soft sweet ballad right in the middle of a long ear-piercing run of rock-and-roll tunes. I'd get out the brushes and we would astonish the crowd with our tenderness. By August, I was so deaf I had to watch Quadberry's fingers changing notes on the saxophone, had to use my eyes to keep time. The other members of the Bop Fiends told me I was hitting out of time. I pretended I was trying to do experimental things with rhythm when the truth was I simply could no longer hear. I was no longer a tasteful drummer, either. I had become deaf through lack of taste.

Which was—taste—exactly the quality that made Quadberry wicked on the saxophone. During the howling, during the churning, Quadberry had taste. The noise did not affect his personality; he was solid as a brick. He could blend. Oh, he could hoot through his horn when the right time came, but he could do supporting roles for an hour. Then, when we brought him out front for his solo on something like "Take Five," he would play with such light blissful technique that he even eclipsed Paul Desmond. The girls around the stage did not cause him to enter into excessive loudness or vibrato.

Quadberry had his own girl friend now, Lilian back at Clinton, who put all the sundressed things around the stage in the shade. In my mind I had congratulated him for getting up next to this beauty, but in June and July, when I was still hearing things a little, he never said a word about her. It was one night in August, when I could hear nothing and was driving him to his house, that he asked me to turn on the inside light and spoke in a retarded deliberate way. He knew I was deaf and counted on my being able to read lips.

"Don't . . . make . . . fun . . . of her . . . or me. . . . We . . . think . . . she . . . is . . . in trouble."

I wagged my head. Never would I make fun of him or her. She detested me because I had taken out her helpless little sister for a few weeks, but I would never think there was anything funny about Lilian, for all her haughtiness. I only thought of this event as monumentally curious.

"No one except you knows," he said.

"Why did you tell me?"

"Because I'm going away and you have to take care of her. I wouldn't trust her with anybody but you."

"She hates the sight of my face. Where are you going?"

"Annapolis."

"You aren't going to any damned Annapolis."

"That was the only school that wanted me."

"You're going to play your saxophone on a boat?"

"I don't know what I'm going to do."

"How . . . how can you just leave her?"

"She wants me to. She's very excited about me at Annapolis. William [this is my name], there's is no girl I could imagine who has more inner sweetness than Lilian."

I entered the town college, as did Lilian. She was in the same chemistry class I was. But she was rows away. It was difficult to learn anything, being deaf. The professor wasn't a pantomimer—but finally he went to the blackboard with the formulas and the algebra of problems, to my happiness. I hung in and made a B. At the end of the semester I was swaggering around the grade sheet he'd posted. I happened to see Lilian's grade. She'd only made a C. Beautiful Lilian got only a C while I, with my handicap, had made a B.

It had been a very difficult chemistry class. I had watched Lilian's stomach the whole way through. It was not growing. I wanted to see her look like a watermelon, make herself an amazing mother shape.

When I made the B and Lilian made the C, I got up my courage and finally went by to see her. She answered the door. Her parents weren't home. I'd never wanted this office of watching over her as Quadberry wanted me to, and this is what I told her. She asked me into the house. The rooms smelled of nail polish and pipe smoke. I was hoping her little sister wasn't in the house, and my wish came true. We were alone.

"You can quit watching over me."

"Are you pregnant?"

"No." Then she started crying. "I wanted to be. But I'm not."

"What do you hear from Quadberry?"

She said something, but she had her back to me. She looked to me for an answer, but I had nothing to say. I knew she'd said something, but I hadn't heard it.

"He doesn't play the saxophone anymore," she said.

This made me angry.

"Why not?"

"Too much math and science and navigation. He wants to fly. That's what his dream is now. He wants to get into an F-something jet."

I asked her to say this over and she did. Lilian really was full of inner sweetness, as Quadberry had said. She understood that I was deaf. Perhaps Quadberry had told her.

The rest of the time in her house I simply witnessed her beauty and her mouth moving.

I went through college. To me it is interesting that I kept a B average and did it all deaf, though I know this isn't interesting to people who aren't deaf. I loved music, and never heard it. I loved poetry, and never heard a word that came out of the mouths of the visiting poets who read at the campus. I loved my mother and dad, but never heard a sound they made. One Christmas Eve, Radcleve was back from Ole Miss and threw an M-80 out in the street for old times' sake. I saw it explode, but there was only a pressure in my ears. I was at parties when lusts were raging and I went home with two girls (I am medium handsome) who lived in apartments of the old two-story 1920 vintage, and I took my shirt off and made love to them. But I have no real idea what their reaction was. They were stunned and all smiles when I got up, but I have no idea whether I gave them the last pleasure or not. I hope I did. I've always been partial to women and have always wanted to see them satisfied till their eyes popped out.

Through Lilian I got the word that Quadberry was out of Annapolis and now flying jets off the *Bonhomme Richard*, an aircraft carrier headed for Vietnam. He telegrammed her that he would set down at the Jackson airport at ten o'clock one night. So Lilian and I were out there waiting. It was a familiar place to her. She was a stewardess and her loops were mainly in the South. She wore a beige raincoat, had red sandals on her feet; I was in a black turtleneck and corduroy jacket, feeling significant, so significant I could barely stand it. I'd already made myself the lead writer at Gordon-

Marx Advertising in Jackson. I hadn't seen Lilian in a year. Her eyes were strained, no longer the bright blue things they were when she was a pious beauty. We drank coffee together. I loved her. As far as I knew, she'd been faithful to Quadberry.

He came down in an F-something Navy jet right on the dot of ten. She ran out on the airport pavement to meet him. I saw her crawl up the ladder. Quadberry never got out of the plane. I could see him in his blue helmet. Lilian backed down the ladder. Then Quadberry had the cockpit cover him again. He turned the plane around so its flaming red end was at us. He took it down the runway. We saw him leap out into the night at the middle of the runway going west, toward San Diego and the *Bohomme Richard.* Lilian was crying.

"What did he say?" I asked.

"He said, 'I am a dragon. America the beautiful, like you will never know.' He wanted to give you a message. He was glad you were here."

"What was the message?"

"The same thing. 'I am a dragon. America the beautiful, like you will never know.' "

"Did he say anything else?"

"Not a thing."

"Did he express any love toward you?"

"He wasn't Ard. He was somebody with a sneer in a helmet."

"He's going to war, Lilian."

"I asked him to kiss me and he told me to get off the plane, he was firing up and it was dangerous."

"Arden is going to war. He's just on his way to Vietnam and he wanted us to know that. It wasn't just him he wanted us to see. It was him in the jet he wanted us to see. He *is* that black jet. You can't kiss an airplane."

"And what are we supposed to do?" cried sweet Lilian.

"We've just got to hang around. He didn't have to lift off and disappear straight up like that. That was to tell us how he isn't with us anymore."

Lilian asked me what she was supposed to do now. I told her she was supposed to come with me to my apartment in the old 1920 Clinton place where I was. I was supposed to take care of her. Quadberry had said so. His six-year-old directive was still working.

She slept on the fold-out bed of the sofa for a while. This was the only bed in my place. I stood in the dark in the kitchen and drank a quarter bottle of gin on ice. I would not turn on the light and spoil her sleep. The prospect of Lilian asleep in my apartment made me feel like a chaplain on a visit to the Holy Land; I stood there getting drunk, biting my tongue when dreams of lust burst on me. That black jet Quadberry wanted us to see him in, its flaming rear end, his blasting straight up into the night at mid-runway—what precisely was he wanting to say in this stunt? Was he saying remember him forever or forget him forever? But I had my own life and was neither going to mother-hen it over his memory nor his old sweetheart. What did he mean, *America the beautiful, like you will never know?* I, William Howly, knew a goddamn good bit about America the beautiful, even as a deaf man. Being deaf had brought me closer to people. There were only about five I knew, but I knew their mouth movements, the perspiration under their noses, their tongues moving over the crowns of their teeth, their fingers on their lips. Quadberry, I said, you don't have to get up next to the stars in your black jet to see America the beautiful.

I was deciding to lie down on the kitchen floor and sleep the night, when Lilian turned on the light and appeared in her panties and bra. Her body was perfect except for a tiny bit of fat on her upper thighs. She'd sunbathed herself so her limbs were brown, and her stomach, and the instinct was to rip off the white underwear and lick, suck, say something terrific into the flesh that you discovered.

She was moving her mouth.

"Say it again slowly."

"I'm lonely. When he took off in his jet, I think it meant he wasn't ever going to see me again. I think it meant he was laughing at both of us. He's an astronaut and he spits on us."

"You want me on the bed with you?" I asked.

"I know you're an intellectual. We could keep on the lights so you'd know what I said."

"You want to say things? This isn't going to be just sex?"

"It could never be just sex."

"I agree. Go to sleep. Let me make up my mind whether to come in there. Turn out the lights."

Again the dark, and I thought I would cheat not only Quadberry but the entire Quadberry family if I did what was natural.

I fell asleep.

Quadberry escorted B-52s on bombing missions into North Vietnam. He was catapulted off the *Bonhomme Richard* in his suit at 100 degrees temperature, often at night, and put the F-8 on all it could get—the tiny cockpit, the immense long two-million-dollar fuselage, wings, tail and jet engine, Quadberry, the genius master of his dragon, going up to twenty thousand feet to be cool. He'd meet with the B-52 turtle of the air and get in a position, his cockpit glowing with green and orange lights, and turn on his transistor radio. There was only one really good band, never mind the old American rock-and-roll from Cambodia, and that was Red Chinese opera. Quadberry loved it. He loved the nasal horde in the finale, when the peasants won over the old fat dilettante mayor. Then he'd turn the jet around when he saw the squatty abrupt little fires way down there after the B-52s had dropped their diet. It was a seven-hour trip. Sometimes he slept, but his body knew when to wake up. Another thirty minutes and there was his ship waiting for him out in the waves.

All his trips weren't this easy. He'd have to blast out in daytime and get with the B-52s, and a SAM missile would come up among them. Two of his mates were taken down by these missiles. But Quadberry, as on saxophone, had endless learned technique. He'd put his jet perpendicular in the air and make the SAMs look silly. He even shot down two of them. Then, one day in daylight, a MIG came floating up level with him and his squadron. Quadberry couldn't believe it. Others in the squadron were shy, but Quadberry knew where and how the MIG could shoot. He flew below the cannons and then came in behind it. He knew the MIG wanted one of the B-52s and not mainly him. The MIG was so concentrated on the fat B-52 that he forgot about Quadberry. It was really an amateur suicide pilot in the MIG. Quadberry got on top of him and let down a missile, rising out of the way of it. The missile blew off the tail of the MIG. But then Quadberry wanted to see if the man got safely out of the cockpit. He thought it would be pleasant if the fellow got out with his parachute working. Then Quadberry saw that the fellow wanted to collide his wreckage with the B-52, so Quadberry turned himself over and cannoned, evaporated the pilot and cockpit. It was the first man he'd killed.

The next trip out, Quadberry was hit by a ground missile. But his jet kept flying. He flew it a hundred miles and got to the sea. There was the *Bonhomme Richard*, so he ejected. His back was snapped but, by God, he landed right on the deck. His mates caught him in their arms and cut the parachute off him. His back hurt for weeks, but he was all right. He rested and recuperated in Hawaii for a month.

Then he went off the front of the ship. Just like that, his F-6 plopped in the ocean and sank like a rock. Quadberry saw the ship go over him. He knew he shouldn't eject just yet. If he ejected now he'd knock his head on the bottom and get chewed up in the motor blades. So Quadberry waited. His plane was sinking in the green and he could see the hull of the aircraft carrier getting smaller, but he had oxygen through his mask and it didn't seem that urgent a decision. Just let the big ship get over. Down what later proved to be sixty feet, he pushed the ejection button. It fired him away, bless it, and he woke up ten feet under the surface swimming against an almost overwhelming body of underwater parachute. But two of his mates were in a helicopter, one of them on the ladder to lift him out.

Now Quadberry's back was really hurt. He was out of this war and all wars for good.

Lilian, the stewardess, was killed in a crash. Her jet exploded with a hijacker's bomb, an inept bomb which wasn't supposed to go off, fifteen miles out of Havana; the poor pilot, the poor passengers, the poor stewardesses were all splattered like flesh sparklers over the water just out of Cuba. A fisherman found one seat of the airplane. Castro expressed regrets.

Quadberry came back to Clinton two weeks after Lilian and the others bound for Tampa were dead. He hadn't heard about her. So I told him Lilian was dead when I met him at the airpot. Quadberry was thin and rather meek in his civvies—a gray suit and an out-of-style tie. The white ends of his hair were not there—the halo had disappeared—because his hair was cut short. The Arab nose seemed a pitiable defect in an ash-whiskered face that was beyond anemic now. He looked shorter, stooped. The truth was he was sick, his back was killing him. His breath was heavy-laden with airplane martinis and in his limp right hand he held a wet cigar. I told him about Lilian. He mumbled something sideways that I could not possibly make out.

"You've got to speak right at me, remember? Remember me, Quadberry?"

"Mom and Dad of course aren't here."

"No. Why aren't they?"

"He wrote me a letter after we bombed Hué. Said he hadn't sent me to Annapolis to bomb the architecture of Hué. He had been there once and had some important experience—French-kissed the queen of Hué or the like. Anyway, he said I'd have to do a hell of a lot of repentance for that. But he and Mom are separate people. Why isn't *she* here?"

"I don't know."

"I'm not asking you the question. The question is to God."

He shook his head. Then he sat down on the floor of the terminal. People had to walk around. I asked him to get up.

"No. How is old Clinton?"

"Horrible. Aluminum subdivisions, cigar boxes with four thin columns in front, thick as a hive. We got a turquoise water tank; got a shopping center, a monster Jitney Jungle, fifth-rate teenyboppers covering the place like ants." Why was I being so frank just now, as Quadberry sat on the floor downcast, drooped over like a long weak candle? "It's not our town anymore, Ard. It's going to hurt to drive back into it. Hurts me every day. Please get up."

"And Lilian's not even over there now."

"No. She's a cloud over the Gulf of Mexico. You flew out of Pensacola once. You know what beauty those pink and blue clouds are. That's how I think of her."

"Was there a funeral?"

"Oh, yes. Her Methodist preacher and a big crowd over at Wright Ferguson funeral home. Your mother and father were there. Your father shouldn't have come. He could barely walk. Please get up."

"Why? What am I going to do, where am I going?"

"You've got your saxophone."

"Was there a coffin? Did you all go by and see the pink or blue cloud in it?" He was sneering now as he had done when he was eleven and fourteen and seventeen.

"Yes, they had a very ornate coffin."

"Lilian was the Unknown Stewardess. I'm not getting up."

"I said you still have your saxophone."

"No, I don't. I tried to play it on the ship after the last time I hurt my back. No go. I can't bend my neck or spine to play it. The pain kills me."

"Well, *don't* get up, then. Why am I asking you to get up? I'm just a deaf drummer, too vain to buy a hearing aid. Can't stand to write the ad copy I do. Wasn't I a good drummer?"

"Superb."

"But we can't be in this condition forever. The police are going to come and make you get up if we do it much longer."

The police didn't come. It was Quadberry's mother who came. She looked me in the face and grabbed my shoulders before she saw Ard on the floor. When she saw him she yanked him off the floor, hugging him passionately. She was shaking with sobs. Quadberry was gathered to her as if he were a rope she was trying to wrap around herself. Her mouth was all over him. Quadberry's mother was a good-looking woman of fifty. I simply held her purse. He cried out that his back was hurting. At last she let him go.

"So now we walk," I said.

"Dad's in the car trying to quit crying," said his mother.

"This is nice," Quadberry said. "I thought everything and everybody was dead around here." He put his arms around his mother. "Let's all go off and kill some time together." His mother's hair was on his lips. "You?" he asked me.

"Murder the devil out of it," I said.

I pretended to follow their car back to their house in Clinton. But when we were going through Jackson, I took the North 55 exit and disappeared from them, exhibiting a great amount of taste, I thought. I would get in their way in this reunion. I had an unimprovable apartment on Old Canton Road in a huge plaster house, Spanish style, with a terrace and ferns and yucca plants, and a green door where I went in. When I woke up I didn't have to make my coffee or fry my egg. The girl who slept in my bed did that. She was Lilian's little sister, Esther Field. Esther was pretty in a minor way and I was proud how I had tamed her to clean and cook around the place. The Field family would appreciate how I lived with her. I showed her the broom and the skillet, and she loved them. She also learned to speak very slowly when she had to say something.

Esther answered the phone when Quadberry called me seven months later. She gave me his message. He wanted to know my opinion on a decision he had to make. There was this Dr. Gordon, a surgeon at Emory Hospital in Atlanta, who said he could cure Quadberry's back problem. Quadberry's back was killing him. He was in torture even holding up the phone to say this. The surgeon said there was a seventy-five/twenty-five chance. Seventy-five that it would be successful, twenty-five that it would be fatal. Esther waited for my opinion. I told her to tell Quadberry to go over to Emory. He'd got through with luck in Vietnam, and now he should ride it out in this petty back operation.

Esther delivered the message and hung up.

"He said the surgeon's just his age; he's some genius from Johns Hopkins Hospital. He said this Gordon guy has published a lot of articles on spinal operations," said Esther.

"Fine and good. All is happy. Come to bed."

I felt her mouth and her voice in my ears, but I could hear only a sort of loud pulse from the girl. All I could do was move toward moisture and nipples and hair.

Quadberry lost his gamble at Emory Hospital in Atlanta. The brilliant surgeon his age lost him. Quadberry died. He died with his Arabian nose up in the air.

That is why I told this story and will never tell another.

FROM

The Prisoners

EVANS HARRINGTON

HE WAITED UNTIL nearly dusk before he drove out to Camp Eight. There was no need to go earlier; he knew that Johnny would be with the Long Line in the fields, hoeing cotton. He was glad for the delay and at the same time impatient. It would not be nice; yet it hung over him all day, and he wanted to have it over.

Larkin was a huge, twenty thousand-acre ellipse set in a deep bend of the Mississippi River. On its west side was the long swelling green line of the levee, like a gigantic caterpillar which had burrowed in a semicircle under the thick river grass and the cypresses. On its east was the narrow-gauge, special railroad and the straight, flat ribbon of blacktopped highway, a state road which bordered the river a safe distance inside the flood area for the entire length of the state. On its north and south were huge ditches which marked the boundary between the prison, or Inside World, and the civilian plantations, or Free World, which extended in long rows of cotton or corn to the very edges of the ditches.

There were twenty-three camps spread over the area of Larkin, each a separate, virtually self-sustaining unit. The heart of the camps was what were known as the cage buildings, where the prisoners stayed when not in the fields. These buildings, usually big, one-story edifices, contained the actual cages, long barracks-like twin wings where the prisoners were kept behind bars and padlocks during the night; the central lobby which, between the two cages, served as office and sentry post for the camp officials; the mess hall which opened directly off the lobby and began the central shaft of the building's gigantic T shape; the trusty rooms and gun rooms, small wings bordering the mess hall; and finally the kitchen, which joined the mess hall at the back and completed the base of the T.

These buildings were set in wide squares of ground enclosed by fifteen-foot fences of reinforced steel mesh; the tops of the fences sloped inward on metal supports which braced three strands of barbed wire. There was only one entrance, a huge double gate at the front of the enclosure, guarded and operated by an armed trusty. Behind the main buildings there were secondary structures—barns, tool houses, stables—and at oblique angles on either side, small brick guard houses for use in emergencies only. The front area was usually devoted to sports—a basketball court, horseshoe pitching lanes, the infield of a baseball diamond. Outside the fence, usually across the road and a hundred yards or so removed from the camp, was the sergeant's home, brick too, normally, and often as spacious and well kept as a prosperous suburban residence.

The prisoners worked during the day in the fields or in the dairies and hog units, or in various capacities around the buildings. Their work day extended from sunrise until sunset every day except Saturday, when they were let off at midafternoon, and Sunday, when they were allowed to rest and have visitors. At night they were locked in the cages, but on Saturday afternoons and Sundays, and on some rainy days when they weren't able to work, they were allowed to move about freely within the fenced enclosure.

There were over twenty-seven hundred prisoners in all, from a hundred to a hundred and fifty in each camp. Over two-thirds of the total were Negroes, it seeming that Negroes were more criminal, or at least more often convicted, in the state; and, under the Deep South tradition of segregation rigidly adhered to at Larkin, there were twenty Negro camps and only three white ones. It had always been an item of interest to Walker that, in spite of the vaunted superiority of the whites (which the sergeants almost to a man would fight to uphold), every sergeant on Larkin coveted a Negro camp to administer. It was an established fact that the Negroes as a rule worked harder and more cheerfully, fought and feuded less often, co-operated more readily and more fully, and attempted far fewer revolts and escapes. In fact, of all the twenty-three camps, it was a white one, Camp Eight—where Walker was now going—that had the worst reputation for violence and disciplinary trouble. Which was a reason old Myers had always given for keeping Hiram Gwin in charge there: Gwin also had a reputation for handling, and even delighting in, the toughest situations he could find. It was his frequently announced opinion that there had never been anything wrong with a camp that a liberal use of Big Bertha, the leather lash, couldn't cure, and he had often taken measures to prove it. And Walker wondered, after what he had seen that morning, if Hoffman would stand by his order forbidding the lash.

Camp Eight was almost exactly in the center of the farm, six miles straight west from the administration area. After four years, Walker thought, swinging his pickup away from the administration building, he still hadn't become accustomed to the Delta's flatness. He drove slowly now along the straight, incredibly level strip of blacktop with the twin rows of gray, evenly spaced employees' houses on either side. He passed the dairy and the brickyard and the hospital, with its tall reinforced fence like those of the camp buildings. He moved on past the warden's home and Chaplain Thompson's newly remodeled brick bungalow.

Past the residences, he came to the end of the blacktop, and his pickup jolted firmly on the heavy gravel. The fields had started then, dark green in the dusk and stretching impossibly to the tiny black borders of cypress at the horizon on either side. From time to time he had to stop and pull over on the shoulder of the road to go around a work gang, a long triple file of sagging, ring-striped bodies, sweat-soaked, heavy-footed, their hoes slung carelessly over their shoulders. At a safe distance on either side, and also at the front and rear, there was a trusty with a stubby .30-30; these were the shooters, selected and trained to shoot quickly and well. They watched Walker as his car approached, their dark faces peering and suspicious until they recognized him; then they quickly took off their caps or sun hats and nodded respectfully (another holdover from Myers' training), still unsmiling and not actually respectful, Walker thought, only dutiful.

The cotton and corn on either side of him began to blur and the long V's of plowed earth between each row turned purple. The lights of the camps were springing up too, as he reached the crossroads where he turned off to Camp Eight; they seemed bright carnival clusters in the heavy dusk.

At Camp Eight the work gang from the field—the Long Line—had already returned and were putting up their hoes. Walker parked the truck beside the guard shack, and Bugger, a trusty, opened the big padlocked gate.

"Evening, Mr. Walker," he said, removing his cap and ducking his head quickly, his big round face vacantly eager.

"Evening, Bugger," Walker said, avoiding his face. "Is it hot enough for you?"

Bugger chuckled quick appreciation of the standard question.

"Just about, Mr. Walker," he crooned. The fawning and servility were something Walker had rebelled against when he first came to Larkin. It made him wince every time a prisoner snatched for his cap in the fearful, automatic gesture. He had even gone so far as to ask one or two of the men not to do it, but they simply looked at him blankly, distrustfully, and in a few cases contemptuously: it was clear that this revealed him as a tenderfoot who either would not last long or would learn his lesson and change quickly. It was one of the saddest problems of Larkin, Walker thought, that most of the men so quickly accepted the standards of the camps—the brutality, the coarseness, not to speak of the downright corruption: the perversion and graft. So he had accepted the custom of caps-off along with a hundred other little "traditions," like that of "taking Five," a means of settling disputes between prisoners by removing weapons from them and giving them five minutes to fight with no holds barred. It was a neat system, a sergeant had explained to Walker; in five minutes they hardly had time to kill each other, but they could come so close to it that neither of them would want to fight again soon. "Taking Five" was a favorite of sergeants and inmates; it was like boxing with more blood and a greater possibility of a killing; it was a cockfight with human cocks.

The camp building of Eight was typical of those all over the farm. It was very low and old-fashioned. All along the front the roof sloped down to form a wide gallery, supported every few feet with thick columns of red prison-made brick. The porch itself was concrete, as were the floors of the entire building. Walker passed the basketball court, a white, hard-packed rectangle with warped wooden goals at either end, passed the long beds of dismally sweet petunias thickly bordering the walk, and went up the two shallow steps.

Hiram Gwin sat tilted against the wall in a straight-backed chair. He was a tall, painfully thin man with narrow, stooping, high shoulders. His neck protruded forward, long and drooping, giving him with his hooked nose the look of a vulture. Walker wondered if his irascible nature might not be largely due to some illness, or glandular defect. His skin was an unhealthy sallow color even with his heavy tan, and his pale blue eyes were invariably yellow-whited. But illness, Walker thought, could never completely account for Hiram Gwin, or excuse him. Illness and ignorance and twenty-odd years of dealing with criminals could not completely account for

Gwin, though they did help. Gwin brought something of his own to the combination, something Walker didn't even care to explain or justify.

Gwin did not speak immediately. He sat, still propped in the chair and stared past Walker as though he wasn't there. Finally he said, "Hello, Walker." He did not get up and his gaunt, shadowed face did not alter.

"How are you?" Walker said. He was not disturbed by the coolness; this was standard procedure.

Gwin let him stand for a moment; then he said, "What for you?"

"Just dropping by," Walker said. "Want to see one of the men."

Gwin waited, but Walker did not go on.

"Which one?" Gwin said. "I got a lot of men here."

Walker moved over and sat in the swing. "Johnny Graves," he said at last. "I need to talk to him."

Gwin didn't answer. He might not even have heard. Walker took out a cigarette and lit it. Behind the building the drivers, civilian guards in charge of the Long Lines, were shouting formation orders. The prisoners would come before the long porch to be checked in.

When Gwin finally spoke he did not look at Walker; his face was turned down the porch toward the men. "Did you get that parole for the purty boy?" he said.

Walker drew on the cigarette, drew hard until the smoke became hot. He should have remembered that Gwin would undoubtedly know about his session with Hoffman, would know something about it if not the details. The grapevine was one of the sergeant's most important weapons on Larkin. He not only kept constant tab on what had happened at The Front but, often more important to him, prevented any leaks from seeping out of his own camp.

"I see your grapevine is working," he said finally; "maybe you can tell me if I did." As he spoke he realized he'd only made himself vulnerable.

Gwin's face twisted slightly in the shadows, grinning. "Maybe," he said. "But I'd like to hear it from you. After all, you're the assistant warden; it'll mean more coming from you."

He did know, Walker realized, and he was laughing at him. But how could he have found out so soon? There had been no one in the office but Hoffman and Miss Higgins and himself, and he didn't believe that either of them would have told it. It was the way of the grapevine, though; he sometimes wondered if anything happened anywhere on the farm that wasn't picked up immediately.

Gwin had turned to face him now; his grin had widened. "What happened to your man?" he said. "What happened to them new ideas?"

Walker drew again on the cigarette; it burned his fingers and he snapped it irritably out into the yard. "The kid will be paroled," he said. "I'm not through yet; he'll be paroled." It was a childish boast, he thought, worthy of Gwin himself. He had nothing to count on but the unpredictable reaction of John Kurt. But his anger drove him to it, anger not only at Gwin but at Carl Hoffman for having put him in this position. All of the sergeants must know it by now; and how they would gloat, not only over Walker himself but over the whole new administration.

Gwin was grinning and shaking his head elaborately. "That boy's no good," he said, "no good! There's a mean streak running clear through him."

"You've said that," Walker told him, "before. What is a mean streak anyway?" He kept his voice level.

Gwin looked at him. "It ain't in your books anywhere?" he said. "You don't have a test for it?"

He swung quickly around and went out to the walk. The prisoners were marching up in double files. "All right," he said. "Step it up! Goddamn! Y'all wanta take all night?"

The drivers lined them in twos and counted them.

"A hundred and three," McCrory said; he was the lead driver. "How many in the kitchen?"

"I've got that," Gwin said. "There's nine. Where's Graves? Where's Purty Boy?"

There was a moment's silence, with murmuring from the line.

"Graves!" McCrory bellowed. "Goddamn it, where are you?"

There was another murmurous silence; then a voice from the far end said, "He's down here, Cap."

"All right," Gwin told McCrory, "you can take the others in. Bring Purty Boy up here."

The men filed in through the entrance, removing their caps or sunhats as they passed before Gwin. Walker sat again in the swing.

Johnny stepped out from the end of the line and stood before Gwin. He had a baseball cap on his head and, when Gwin continued to look at him, he removed it slowly with his big brown, oversized hands. He had thick hair, dark brown and matted low on his short, square forehead. His eyes were wide and gray in a square, high-cheeked face. He was not heavily built, but his chest and shoulders in a tight sweat-stained t-shirt were broad and muscular. He held the cap in those big hands before him and looked at Gwin. He did not smile.

Gwin stood for a moment with his hands on his hips, as though undecided whether or not to speak to him. He took a step toward the door, but then he stopped. It was clear he couldn't resist it.

"Since when," he said, "did you forget your name?"

Johnny didn't answer; he just looked at him.

"Didn't you hear me call Purty Boy?" Gwin said. He glanced at McCrory, who had stopped behind Johnny. McCrory was grinning.

"Well, answer me," Gwin said. "Didn't you hear me?"

Johnny still looked at him. "I heard you," he said.

"Why didn't you answer then?" Gwin said. "Your name's Purty Boy; why didn't you answer?"

McCrory was grinning broadly now, and Gwin grinned too.

Walker got up from the swing, but sat back down almost immediately. If he couldn't fire Gwin, it would be best not to antagonize him further; he would only take it out on the boy when Walker left.

"Well?" Gwin told Johnny. "I'm waiting. What do you say?"

"My name is Graves," Johnny said. "Johnny Graves."

Gwin put his hands on his hips again and rocked back and forth. He opened his thin mouth wide, laughing. McCrory laughed too, even louder. Finally Gwin controlled himself with an effort, and bent again to face Johnny.

"Your name's Purty Boy," he said, still having trouble with his mirth, "just plain Purty Boy."

He turned, still laughing, and started toward the door. "Mr. Walker wants to advise with you," he said. "You won't mind, will you, Mr. Walker, if I send a trusty out to watch this boy? I'll tell him to stand way off."

So here it was, and it wasn't the best possible time for it, Walker thought. He got up as Johnny moved toward him, his big hands dangling now awkwardly. The boy wouldn't ask, he knew; he wouldn't even show his eagerness. Not that he meant to be surly, or aloof; he wasn't even conscious of it. It was something in him, the thing that antagonized Gwin: a composure, a self-containment, that made him stand a little too straight, that made him forget to remove his cap and do it a little too slowly when he did, that made him always a little too erect and a little too level of eye.

So he stood before Walker now, expressionless, waiting, in the faint light from the hall, and Walker thought of several ways to put it off, to hedge a little until the memory of Gwin's stupid laughter was less keen, but he gave them up before the level eyes and said it flat.

"I'm sorry, Johnny, not this time either."

Still there was no expression except a quick widening of the gray eyes in the shadow and a tightness that came about the mouth. Walker went on quickly, trying to distract him.

"But I'm not through yet," he said. "I still have one more chance. I'm going to see Mr. Kurt. I . . . think maybe he can help us." Still the boy did not speak, and a hardness was growing now in his face.

Walker said, "I think I can still get it; I know I can get it somehow. But it will take time." And then he realized that those were the words he had used before—a year before, a year and a half before—and they sounded stale even to him. He had no patience anyhow with this kind of thing—promises, weak little hopes—and he knew the boy hadn't either. This was one of the things they had in common.

"Look, Johnny," he said. "You're not a kid any longer. You're twenty-five, and you've been here a while. Suppose I can't get it. It's one of those things. You got off to a bad start; you were unlucky maybe in drawing Gwin, but you made things worse by . . . by your attitude. Oh, I know you were probably right, I know you had to take a lot of . . . things, but that's something else: you're old enough now to understand that just being right, just deserving something doesn't give it to you. A lot of right people have come out short."

He stopped but the boy didn't answer. One big hand raised and pushed at his cheek.

"And that's the point," Walker said; "that's what I'm trying to say. You've served five years, and that doesn't seem right; that *isn't* right. But it's still a fact, and if you get into trouble now, with just two years left—just two years now, less than half of five!—that wouldn't make sense, would it?"

He waited but still there was nothing except the white, expressionless hardness.

"Would it?" he said, wondering if Johnny had even heard.

"I don't know," Johnny said. His big hands shifted and grappled on his cap. "I don't know any more what makes sense. Is that all?" he said. "Are you through?"

Walker took out a cigarette and tapped it slowly on his thumb. He had begun to sweat in the thick June night, and his shirt was sticking to his arms. He lit the cigarette and drew on it deeply.

"Yes," he said finally, looking up at the boy. "Yes, I guess that's all for tonight. But, Johnny, don't do anything foolish."

He stood before him a moment longer, but he could think of nothing else to say. The whole thing didn't make sense.

Reluctantly he turned and went down the walk through the thick insistent sweetness of the petunias. He only hoped he could talk to Kurt, get something at least started before Johnny lost control completely. But it would have to be damn soon, he thought, remembering Johnny's white still face.

Johnny Graves was raised in Tucker County in the red-clay hills where there were pine trees, gallberry flats, and rutted gravel roads; where there were little white churches and little white schoolhouses under big oak trees, and graveyards and outdoor toilets and tables for dinner-on-the-ground; where there were watermelon cuttings and candy pullings and Sunday afternoon mule rides, even when the Fords and Chevrolets, the pickups and red farm-all tractors were filtering out from the towns; and where there were farming, blacksmithing, politicking, and even some unsanctioned crimes—but bootlegging was not one of these.

Johnny's father was killed in a lumber camp when Johnny was an infant. Johnny's mother raised Johnny and his older brother, Benny, on the farm which his father left—fifty acres of red clay with one five-acre bottom which would grow cotton.

Johnny's brother, six years older than Johnny, looked around when he was eighteen, made a decision concerning red clay, scrawny mules, and his equally scrawny, overaged mother, and went to work for a bootlegger.

By the time Johnny was twenty, they had moved into Olive, had a brick home, a Buick, and a "business" of their own with three trucks touring the country. Johnny was now a partner. It never occurred to him to question his brother's occupation; it never occurred to him to question his brother at all.

Which was all right until the Baptist preacher put on a drive and elected Viney Tolar sheriff. Johnny was driving one of the trucks the night Viney Tolar and two deputies stopped him. There was no need for his brother to come into it. Johnny wouldn't let him. And, though Viney Tolar offered Johnny a lighter sentence to tell everything (and later offered to beat him a little with a rubber hose, an offer he did not make good largely perhaps because he knew it would do no good) Johnny did not talk. He told Viney Tolar, and even the Baptist preacher, to go to hell.

There was something else, though. There was a girl who lived in Olive too. Her name was Lucille. She and Johnny went through high school together. She was blond and her skin was very fair; Johnny sometimes wondered that it did not bruise when he touched it. Her eyes were almost violet blue and her lashes were so long and black that Johnny could not believe them. And he did not want to undress her; he scarcely dared to touch her. He wanted to buy her the finest house there was in Beauregard—the only city he had ever been to—and put her in it on a satin pillow and just look at her. He told her this, and his lips trembled so that he could hardly say it. She cried and said she loved him and asked him to kiss her.

They would have been married then, except that her father was a prominent merchant in Olive and her mother a prominent matron and Johnny of course a bootlegger. So they met secretly for a year, and almost every time she cried, until finally they drove one night across the state line and lied about their ages.

It was six months before Johnny was arrested. They were very happy. Her mother and father wanted at first to have the marriage annulled, but were at last afraid to. If Lucille would go as far as she had, there was no predicting how far she might go; and as for Johnny—his whole blood was violent.

When Johnny was arrested, Lucille was hysterical for several days. But she visited him in jail, and told him that of course she would wait. When he was sent to Larkin she wrote to him every day at first and even came up twice on visiting Sundays. But then her letters grew less frequent and more and more strained, she did not come any more, and finally she stopped writing altogether.

Within six months after he came to Larkin, Johnny's mother was dead. A year later his brother was picked up in a neighboring state and sentenced to a term in that state's penitentiary. The charge was the same: bootlegging. . . .

Johnny didn't decide; it was like he had decided a long time before and was just waiting for Mr. Walker to say it. And he didn't hear the words at first, just the voice, the tight reluctant sound in the voice. By then the coldness had already started in his fingers and he was thinking, or not thinking, just feeling, knowing, *I've got to plan it, plan it!* Without ever really thinking, *I'll escape.*

But he couldn't plan it. He would see the road and the spot where he had thought before, *You could go in there; you could hit Miller with a shoulder block and if you were fast enough you could be in the corn before they could shoot.* But it was not really planning; it was just seeing it, seeing exactly as he had seen it so many times, with the tall Johnson grass on the bank and the ragged little gully in the middle that might trip you if you didn't pace it right, and with the others there too, behind him and beside him and in front of him, and Miller, the shooter, with the .30-30 in both hands like he was required to have it, but not watching really, his hot little blue eyes vacant, drowsing. But that was all it was, just seeing it, that one instant when he would lunge; and that wasn't a break, that wasn't planning it. And there were other places too, the one on the far side of the field they were working now, but you would just have to be lucky there, because it was ten yards or more from the end of the rows and even then there were just the trees, no heavy grass or underbrush.

And it was like that, just seeing it, feeling it almost, but then jumping to another place, and Mr. Walker's voice coming in too, reluctant still, but arguing now, and his steady blue eyes looking at Johnny like it was him that didn't get a pardon, like he knew what it meant. And Johnny wanted to tell him, *You'd do something else; there's something else you could do if it was you. Even the governor—you would even see him if it was you; and if he is crooked, there's the president.* But he didn't say it because it didn't matter now; he had already decided now, so it didn't matter.

Then Mr. Walker was winding up his little speech—Johnny could tell by the earnest way his voice dropped—and it was the same thing, of course, the same nice Free World logic: "It wouldn't make sense." The Free World liked making sense; that was a sort of game with them, like solitaire. It was fun on rainy days, and they made their own rules and played it by themselves, so if they lost they could cheat a little. Johnny didn't tell Mr. Walker that he'd forgotten how to play. Mr. Walker was a good man; he tried to help and he always gave it to you straight. But even he wouldn't understand. You had to go through it to understand. And anyway that didn't matter either. All that mattered was getting Mr. Walker to stop talking now so he could plan.

And finally he did; finally he left. But then it was even worse because, standing there in the dusk by himself, Johnny began to get Lucille into it too. Twice! Twice was all she came, and for over three years she hadn't even written! Then seeing her again the way she lay in the Doll House, the stiff hard whiteness of her face in the light from the little window, letting him go ahead but just lying there, and keeping her face turned away. . . .

The trusty was standing at the door. Johnny had forgotten him until he said, "You coming?" He was holding the door open.

"Yeah," Johnny said. "Yeah, I'm coming."

He stepped into the yellow light of the hall, and Gwin was looking at him. He told himself he'd better watch it, better put it away till later, when he was safe in the cage, but the coldness stayed in his fingers and it was hard to breathe.

He walked across the concrete floor of the wide lobby office, feeling Gwin's eyes still on him. He went into the long chow hall at the back and took his seat, telling himself to eat, to take the spoon and keep it moving, but he couldn't remember; his hand kept stopping and he would be sitting there staring, and suddenly he would look up and Gwin would be watching.

When they started to count in—shuffling in single file into the long barred cage, chanting their numbers, twenty-*one,* twenty-*two,* twenty-*three!* in hollow echoing cadence through the wide, high-ceilinged hall—Gwin called him out. His long face was scornful but there was a question in it, too; caution.

"You didn't get it," he said, "the parole."

"No," Johnny said, "I didn't get it."

"So?" Gwin said. He didn't want to ask it and Johnny didn't want him to.

"So," he answered, and tried to shrug.

Gwin looked at him thoughtfully, the scorn for a moment obscured, and his mouth moved, starting to ask it; but he could not force it out, and after a moment his thin lips twisted again.

"Don't try any crap," he said softly. "You hear me?"

Johnny waited a moment, watching him. "Is that all?" he said.

"That's all," Gwin said. "Just remember."

But it was not all, and it was just as well that, back on his bunk in the far end of the long barracks cage, with the sound of the guitars tinny and mournful in the thick, yellow light, Johnny couldn't plan. And later too, when the lights flickered, reminding him that he hadn't showered or even undressed, flickered three times warningly and after a minute went out—he could have saved the long, black sleepless hours when he could see her, was with her again, jumping the escape, the planning, everything, crazily, and seeing her standing as she had stood the first night behind the gym, the graduation dance and the music slow for the last number coming out thick and sweet behind them, and her skin too delicate even for the softness of the white gown closing smoothly just where her breasts swelled. And he would tremble again, as he had then, until he pulled himself away frantically, sweating cold in the darkness and telling himself that he never would get there, never would find out—why! why! had she stopped coming?

Like that, all night, and seeing the running too, passing the spot beside the road, and feeling his breath stop and the bright pink light over everything: the road, the corn, Miller, and holding his breath as he told himself, Now! Now! in midstep, as he passed the Johnson grass and then the bursting lunge with Miller's little blue eyes widening suddenly until Johnny caught him with his elbow, and the shouts from in front of the line as he timed it in one long stride across the little gully, ducking his head as the corn leaves came up slashing at his hands, and diving at an angle between the stalks, across the rows.

But that was all; that was as far as he got. The rest of it, the running, where he would go, how he would get clothes—it was too far away, too dim and shadowy, and his mind kept jumping it; and he would be already with her.

FROM

Hub

ROBERT HERRING

ACROSS THE MOUNTAIN COL, pushing back the lingering night shadows still edging the valley floor a thousand feet below. This time he had taken the boy with him—he was ten and it was his time: tall, a strong boy with hair the color of corn husks and eyes the pale green of mountain lichen. It was his first hunt.

They had been climbing since before dawn, following the deer trails along the lower slopes, then angling up through the somber rhododendron thickets, through the pitch pine and into the hardwoods, the ash and sourwood, yellow birch and buckeye, climbing steadily toward the heath bald, where he had placed the apples three days in a row, singeing each one with a handful of burning grasses to kill the man-scent even as he had fired the heavy wire snares he had set about the clearing. They were close now and he slipped quietly to his knees. The boy knelt behind him.

"Papa?"

"Sh-h. You're liable t'wooly 'em off."

"Yessir," the boy whispered.

"You foller right behind me," the boy's father said softly. "And did I say to, you shinny up a saplin'. Y'hear?"

"Yessir."

The boy looked into his father's steady eyes and nodded. Then the two of them crept forward through the dense myrtle, foxglove, and azaleas bordering up and over the rise thirty feet before them and beyond the last trees. The bald lay beyond the incline.

They had continued forward halfway to the crest, slipping easily through the mountain growth—

He's learnt well enough, his father thought, alert now for any sound and hearing none behind—

—when suddenly he stopped and crouched even lower, holding the twin-barreled shotgun just above the dew. He glanced back at the boy, then nodded toward a nearby low-limbed tree. He said nothing, and when the boy's lips moved to speak he drew his chin up sharply, again toward the tree, then back to his son. For a moment longer the boy returned his father's gaze, puzzled, when suddenly he too heard the choppy, abrupt snuffling just audible beyond the crest.

A rooshian! The boy had never seen one, imagining them only in the dark of his dreams, shaping them from the tales he had heard at Greenbrier, where sometimes the men of the cove gathered and where sometimes, too, his father took him when his mother needed the bottled yellow medicine he bought there for her cough—and he would listen, hearing of hounds gutted head to tail by a single slash of the upcurved tushes, and of men too who had been foolish or full of a moment's courage or just plain stupid who had come too close with two legs and who had forever thereafter walked on just one, if they had walked at all—tales of a boar built heavily forward like a buffalo yet agile as a deer, of the razor-sharp tushes the hunters of the cove prized more than the claws of a bear and which, around the soft coal-glow of their night fires, these men feared more than any creature in the forest depths from Cosby Knob to Tellico Plains—he would listen, wide-eyed, his knees drawn up snugly beneath his chin, and his freckled hands grown white-knuckled about his elbows.

"Boy," his father's whisper, low and urgent, and again the gesture toward the tree. He understood and angled away, trembling now as his father moved again forward, inching his way carefully up the slope, the gun still just above the grasses.

Both barrels! And pert' near in my pockets too when I shoot did I think to bring her down at all, his father thought, just beneath the crest now. A last thin wall of laurel stood along the border of the meadow and he eased up to it, gently parting the growth with the muzzle of the gun. She was there, twenty, perhaps twenty-five yards away, a two-hundred pounder he guessed, moving frantically back and forth between the two lifeless piglets snared and strangled, little furry sacks that she nudged in turn, rooting at them with her pointed snout as if to give them life, to wake them from some strange sleep which she could not understand and from which the piglets, after their brief throttled struggle, would never waken.

Well now, the man thought. She'd be they mama and the rest done moved on without her. He slipped both hands to the gun, resting his thumb and forefinger on the rabbit-eared hammers.

Ready. And with the toes of his boots he worried the earth beneath him until little cups gave him footholds in the embankment. Then he glanced once again back at his son, moving his head so slowly that the boy saw nothing until their eyes met. Satisfied, his father turned once more toward the clearing. A moment longer he waited, tensing, pressing the hammers back to that point just before which they would snap loudly into place, alerting the sow to his presence. But it must be now. The boy had reached the lower tree limbs and the wind was right, sweeping lightly across the bald and carrying away his scent and faint movement. Surprise would be his. He took a deep breath, steadied himself, then swiftly brought the rabbit ears into cocked firing position, and rose to his knees exposing his head and shoulders.

"Whoa!" he shouted, and the rooshian, startled, leaped into the air, whipping about even as she touched down, her tushes gleaming as her head dropped lowly to the grasses. Now you'll be a'comin', he thought, bringing the shotgun to his shoulder with deliberate slowness.

The creature charged, bolting forward, her narrow sharp hooves gouging out the laurel heath as she thundered toward him, the wedge-shaped head lower still and the small, pointed ears flattened.

"Shoot, Papa. Shoot it!" the boy yelled.

But still he waited, holding the gun steadily, his body motionless, his index and middle fingers curled about the twin triggers.

"Papa, shoot it, shoot it, shoot it," the boy's voice hysterical, echoing thinly out across the coombs and down the sawtooth ridges.

The sow's rapid breathing was audible to him now, closing, a frenzied intake and exhalation as its momentum mounted, a bristling ziggurat trailing a froth of saliva from its jaws.

Then it seemed to the boy that this was no animal at all, nothing fleshed and breathing and bone-structured but something delivered even of that which held all things to earth's surface in their time, for it seemed no longer in contact with the heath but somehow moving just above its surface, a black-brown blur as the tears sprang to his eyes, something fiercer still than all the wondrous tales he had heard at Greenbrier.

And when it was perhaps just a yard away, his father's hand

knotted abruptly and the roar of the gun shattered the mountain silence, reverberating thunderously down the green ridges. The boar slammed into the earth, kicked aimlessly with its hooves, and was still.

"Percy, I believe you could come down now did you want to," his father said quietly, reloading the gun with the same deliberate slowness, all the while still watching the sow.

"Yessir," the boy said, quickly drawing his shirt-sleeve across his eyes.

"I want you to touch it," his father said, only then turning away from the rooshian.

His son slipped lightly to the ground and moved up the slope to his father's side. Together they approached the lifeless creature.

"Papa?" the boy said.

"Jest touch it, son. You could do it with a toe."

"Yessir."

Then he moved to its hind parts and cautiously poked at the taut muscles down its leg. It did not move.

"Ain't nothin' but a old pig," his father said steadily.

"Yessir," the boy said. Then—"Papa, I wasn't afeared."

"I knowed that," his father said.

The boy continued then to worry the carcass as if to prove his words. His foot moved up the torso to the bloody stump where its head had been. The skull had caved in, crushed by the point-blank double-load of buckshot, and even the tushes were shattered. He withdrew his foot.

"Nothin' but a old pig," he said defiantly. Then he turned his eyes away and his voice lowered. "It was a mama," he said. He turned to his father, his lips apart as if to shape some question even he could not define.

"Percy."

"Yessir?"

"It's the way of things. You shouldn't ought to feel too bad."

And after a moment the boy nodded.

"Yessir," he said.

His father roughed his tousled hair. "Let's git 'em dresed out. Your ma's waitin'."

FROM

Blue Rise

Rebecca Hill

Family gatherings in rural Mississippi are sober to a fault in the absence of anyone who will come forward and risk changing iced tea into wine. When the Groves family gathers together, no exceptions arise. It is a certainty that iced tea will be drunk, just as it is a certainty that the men of the family will gather before the TV while the women cook and set the table and feed the children and call the men to come on and are themselves the last to sit down.

My mother and I are descended from a long line of such Groves women who take as their motto and creed *I suffer, therefore I am.* Well: The heart of Christianity is sacrifice, and these be Christian women. These be, in point of fact, Southern Baptist Christian women.

Groves women see to the men and the children and then proceed to take what is left of the fried chicken, fish the brown field peas from beneath the net of ham fat already beginning to congeal on the pot liquor, dig into the eroded mass of ambrosia salad and marvel in advance over Eola's pimento-cheese sandwiches and Bethany's baked beans and onions, and since the men have already taken their burdened plates back to the TV, they pull chairs up to the table with its company-best tablecloths of hand-crocheted lace over store-bought damask and eat, their plates wedged between the serving bowls. And then they clean the table, leaving half-empty bowls of food where they are in case some of the men or the children get hungry or want something else, and they wash the dishes and scrub the pots and exchange atrocity stories and trade vows of things they wouldn't do for love of children and Lord Jesus and family. They would never part with their children for more than a few days at most, they just couldn't, they love them so much. My cousin Felicia rinses soapsuds from her plump hands over the sink and wipes them on Aunt Lottie's embroidered dish towels.

She is saying, "Y'all remember when I tried taking that job at the post office. It just broke my heart to go off and leave Kimmy and that little ole Jason—left all day in some woman's house cryin' Momma—"

She stops here, and shakes her head.

A chorus rises from the women standing in the small fragrant kitchen.

"Pore-little-thangs, bless-their-hearts."

They just didn't know how anybody could do without their children. They just didn't know *how* I'd been able to come off down here for over a week without Laura. Wasn't she just five in April? How could I stand it?

Now. A word about those men in the other room. It has always been clear that the women in my mother's family go to some trouble to pick out deficient men to marry. I thought it probably was unconscious, the same way hostility escapes from them, but here I appear to be wrong. Consider the lineup: Aunt Lottie, married to a man thirty years her senior, thus guaranteed the long-term widowhood she is now living out. Aunt Bethany, married to a man who professes socialism and unemployment right here in the rural South. My own mother, married to a man who dealt in violence and who eventually won big. Aunt Lola, married to a man whose family ritually succumbs to heart disease before age forty, he himself picked up dead off the streets at forty-five, still in his jogging outfit. All these women are the daughters of a mother who was called in Jasper County "Widow Groves"—though her perfectly sound husband was off in the next county sawing logs. People saw her plowing the fields behind a horse alone, and when she went into town to buy feed, she drove her own team and hoisted her own sacks. She passed along her talent for choosing unsatisfactory husbands, and the trait survives all else, is virulent. Aunt Bethany's daughter Eola married a faithless charmer who deserted her and "her" three girls fifteen years ago. But Eola would be scandalized at the notion of divorce; after all, Delbert Charles is her Husband. That comes with a capital H in these parts. My cousins Berniece, Pauline and Felicia are the three daughters of that brief but consecrated union. They are nearly all into their twenties now and are married (respectively) to a pyromaniac, a drunkard and a cripple.

Mind you, I'm only citing the Groves women who were in attendance that day. As for myself, the fact that I am having trouble with my marriage would not make me fit in here. This is a shame of which one does not speak. Not speaking is itself a virtue. And I sense that my mother holds out some hope for me as we get into the car to go home. She still expects that I will become a mature woman, that I will yet grasp how it is that fulfillment is attained through selflessness.

So she says to me aloud what all the rest know by heart.

"That little Felicia," she says, speaking of my cousin who weighs some 240 pounds.

Obesity is another virulent family trait, and to my mind these traits are not unconnected.

"That little Felicia," she says again, securing my attention as she throws her gold Malibu into reverse on the soft sand of Aunt Lottie's driveway. "Isn't she just the sweetest thing you ever saw? She could have married anybody, but just think, who would have married James with his poor withered leg, if she hadn't?"

Momma takes the back roads past Gethsemane Baptist Church. The back roads are shaded and beautiful in the late June sun, but they command attention any time. Basically they are a one-lane track of packed red clay. When there has been a lot of rain, you avoid them, go the long way up to the Rise by the highway. When there hasn't been rain, you have a chance of telling when another car is on the road by the cloud of red dust that rises through the trees. Though the many curves and corners are absolutely blind, it is a matter of custom—faith in God, perhaps—that everybody drives fast and uses no horns. I understand that. At sixteen I attempted these roads on one of our annual visits "back Home." After I'd sounded the horn twenty times in the space of three miles, for no apparent reason other than cowardice, I, too, gave it up.

We get to the Blue Rise that way in silence. Blue Rise is the highest section of the clay ridge that stands above Gethsemane Valley. It gets the name from the way everything that can be seen from up here seems to turn blue with distance. More than that: At times a hazy bluish shimmer seems to hang in the very air.

Once we round Uncle Odell Hinton's place on the broad northern slope of the Rise, the house appears. Gray brick with white wood trim, tapered pillars bearing up a graceful portico. The effect is as trumped-up as all the other brick-with-white-trim Colonials that now litter the South. But this one does have in its favor excellent proportions. It looked good even when its only façade was tar paper, as it was for many years after my father built the house. For we moved North before the finish work was done. Sixteen years later when he and my mother returned here for his retirement, as they called it then, the place had been nearly ruined between rats and renters. That's when the renovation was done, capped by all these pillars and porticoes. When southerners return, they come all the way back.

But the result is handsome, as my father was in the habit of remarking at this point on the road. The house comes into view with its setting: bluish valley hues in the background, and in the foreground tree-fringed pastures, woods behind the house and barn, and my mother's front-yard profusions of flowers. And, these recent years, Uncle Odell's two mammoth chickenhouses beyond the garden. Not far enough beyond, as any breeze from the north testifies.

Today there is such a breeze awaiting us, and Momma grimaces, showing her molars and tightening the rigging of her neck in fresh disgust. "I hate that dirty chicken smell."

"The wind is wrong today."

"It isn't the wind. It's farming. Wait'll you get a noseful of that manure in my barn. In the middle of the day it will knock you speechless. That scent! It don't come out of your clothes, it don't come out of your hair—" She glances over at me. I am so innocent of familiar odors, so still. Though I am not a practicing Christian martyr, it is possible that I may have become that other thing: a lady. A thing she desires for me, fears in me. "Aren't you proud to have a farmer for a mother?"

"As a matter of fact, I am."

"Hunh. You must be worse off than I thought."

She turns the Malibu into the far end of the semicircular drive past the house. The near end has been closed off, piled with the sawn trunk and limbs of the old pecan tree. The tree died the same winter my father did, two years ago. It stood at the corner of the yard, and as children my brothers and I played there, fished in doodlebug holes between its roots and hid from each other in its branches. Its trunk and limbs are piled at one end of the driveway because Momma put them there. The spring after my father died, she herself sawed the old tree into the sections she needed. She herself pushed, pulled, lifted and dragged them into place. Teenagers in cars, she said. A widow alone, and all.

At sixty-five my mother is an extraordinary-looking woman. A pretty woman, the eyes arresting in that collapsed face, the teeth certainly passable. But it is not her face but the fierce vitality that plays through the face, through the still flexible, still mannishly strong body. The vitality is at times gentle, her beam turned low for radiance, for light rather than heat. But that is not to be depended upon. Better count on this woman for strength; count on the gentleness as you do the intervention of saints.

Her body has always been ten years younger than her face, and as she ages, the lag increases. Only a body like that could bear the dictates of her will, which has no relation to face, flesh or anything else mortal.

She brings the car to a stop at the center of the semicircle, in front of the white columns of the porch. While the dogs are still jumping at the car doors, I say, as though the idea is fresh, "Momma, think I'll go over and see Carrie Dean for a while."

Wordlessly Momma tosses me the keys and gets out.

She does speak to the dogs who, however foolishly and adoringly, are in her way. "Get on out of here," she says, and strides onto the porch and into the house.

The front door slams. The same momentum will carry her right through the place, through the dusty rose velvet and satin brocade in the parlor, through the magnanimously cluttered family room and kitchen, and out the back door to check on her animals, her garden. She will change her shoes on the back steps. My mother is never one to waste motion, words or much of anything else. Yesterday, after we drove in from the airport, we toured the flower beds in the front yard. Day lilies and infant crape myrtle were in vivid bloom around the birdbath, but something drew my eye to the petunias. The glazed white pot they were banked in.

"Mother, that isn't the old . . . ?"

The lifted chin gives hauteur to the reply. What you might call finality. "It's porcelain."

I slide into the driver's seat and start the car. My father had liked cars to have automatic transmissions; there had not been a stick shift in the family since the 1949 Hudson. Automatic transmissions spoke to my father of his executive days; they also covered his inveterate clumsiness with machinery of any kind. But after he died, Momma couldn't bear to drive his Pontiac Grand Prix; the purring automatic windows that were his pride, and also the pine tar matting up the carpet underneath the driver's feet, reminded her too much of him.

So she bought this gold Malibu, with four on the floor.

It wasn't that she was a racy driver, waiting to show her true colors. Lord knows she has nearly ground the gears into flywheels. This fancy car was a windfall of the sort that comes to those who only buy on sale. Occasionally they strike a deal for something enviable. If not exactly appropriate. But this car was gold, not red, so how was she to know? I can still hear her stricken tones over the telephone, the recent widow appealing to Larry and me in useless, far-off Iowa, "You don't mean to tell me I have bought *a sports car?*"

I turn the Malibu off Highway 24 onto the gravel of Carrie Dean's road, pausing an amateurish three seconds to find the gear low enough to get me up the hill. I can see Cal in this car on his stopovers Home, slipping from gear to gear with masculine accomplishment. My brother learned to drive on these roads at age ten, not unusual for a farm boy. I learned in the side streets of suburban Detroit at seventeen, sharing the controls with my high school's driver-training instructor.

But many things changed for us in that move North. Certainly religion, for even Baptists are northern in Detroit. We found ourselves exiled in a foreign culture, no longer interwoven among family like one lateral of a spider's web. In Detroit's Houghton Park we were rednecks; in Mississippi on those annual trips back Home, we talked funny. We belonged nowhere. My father, who was fond of the applications of molecular theory, told me we had become isotopes. An isotope is an element with the same character as another element in the periodic table. They occupy the same place, he explained, but the isotope can be distinguished in various ways. By differences in mass, for example, or radioactivity.

This notion seemed to satisfy him, and by junior high I could grasp most of what it meant. But it was not the kind of wisdom that counted on the playground.

At some point Sumrall Hinton found that neither exile nor executive privilege nor the elegance of molecular theory satisfied as well as drinking. One result was his dismissal—fifteen years in a sensitive research job earned him that many minutes to clear his desk and leave the factory complex. Northern industrial concerns are a different sort of spider's web. And so it was back Home to Mississippi for him and my mother. With the children grown, a retreat from the North at last, back home to the clay ridge, home to the house he had built and abandoned on Blue Rise, home to his daddy's land, home to the farm life he'd hated as a child and loved as a sentimental adult from a distance. Blood ties are slow to give up their knots.

This gravel road is the one I have traveled to Carrie Dean's house since childhood, although back then it wasn't really her house, any more than that chartreuse-trimmed ornament that now sits overlooking the highway is the same house that used to wait at the end of this drive. When we were growing up, the usual thing was for those big old wood-frame houses—they were big but often not as big as the families they held—to grow shabby and gray from lack of paint or improvements. Or maybe it was lack of conviction that things should be any different. For sooner or later a family would tear one house down and build another, often on the same spot. If the building had to go, the home place was permanent. By succession. Whatever was left of the old structure would be hauled several hundred yards away, and put to use as a barn or shed.

Both my grandmothers had got new houses in this way. As children my brothers and I spent hours playing in the old ones, diving into the mounds of soybean meal or sacks of cottonseed that occupied what had been Grandma Groves' living room, or Grandma Hinton's kitchen. Walking in the weeds between the new house and the old one, we had periodic finds of buttons, pencil stubs, a nickel or, less spectacularly, an embossed lid from one of Grandpa Hinton's tins of snuff.

When my father built our house on Blue Rise Road, Grandma Hinton's new place was one road over, around the next curve. As it is now. Renters live there. But Aunt Opal and Uncle Vinnie's house used to be there, too, right across the road between two pecan trees. Uncle Vinnie was my father's brother and when we moved to the house on the Rise I had my cousin Serene to play with. I was seven years old, and I thought life was not only perfect but permanent. Uncle Vinnie had a brain tumor, which meant only that we were to play quietly when we played at Serene's. Then we buried Uncle Vinnie; and, to my complete amazement, Aunt Opal moved their house. The very house! Men came and jacked it up, set it on blocks and then on log rollers, and shifted it onto a flatbed truck. Away down Blue Rise Road went the frame house, leaning perilously.

No new house was ever built in its stead, and the family was considered unfairly cut off, out of place. It was a kind of shame, just as it was for my father to take his college education off to Detroit all those years.

Serene grew up in the next county beside her other grandmother's place. After she left, I used to go up the road and play alone between the two pecan trees. Once I found a tiny square gold locket where the back steps had been. It must have belonged to Serene, but for some reason I got to keep it. It has since been lost again, out in the larger world of other people's houses and apartment buildings.

Carrie Dean Wentworth now lives in what was her mother's new house some twenty years ago. The Wentworth's old one had indeed been gray and weathered, but it was taken before its time by fire. Flames had run their tongues over the roof beams and licked out the eaves before Mr. Elmer Wentworth woke in his bed to a vision of fire and brimstone raining down like a judgment. He got his family to safety and was reaffirmed a Christian before the ashes cooled.

Mr. Elmer died later that year, and when her mother parceled up the Wentworth land among the children, Carrie Dean, as the only girl, was given title to the new house. The brothers by that time had built houses on their land for themselves and their families. The mailboxes along Highway 24 read in succession: R. W. Wentworth, Buford Wentworth, Tillis Wentworth, Harley Wentworth, Vernon Wentworth. Farther down the road are five or six more Wentworths who are Carrie Dean's uncles and cousins: Matthew Wentworth, Beulah Wentworth, Nelson Wentworth, and the rest. It's the same all over the community of Gethsemane, all over the whole rural South as far as I know. Roads of Wentworths give way to roads of Maxeys, roads of Groveses to roads of Drennans. Along Blue Rise Road mailboxes with Hinton printed on them in various uneven hands are strewn two miles in three directions.

Of course, Carrie Dean's name is not Wentworth anymore. The

mailbox at the foot of the road where gravel spills out over the blacktop says Parrish. And it is something unreasonably difficult for me to remember. Carrie Dean Parrish.

She sits waiting for me on the porch of the house with the chartreuse trim. She sits on the old porch swing, legs spraddled in a way that's characteristic. That swing is where we spent most of the summer when we were sixteen. My family's visit back Home that year came when school was out, and I was allowed to remain here and visit relatives, and to date when Carrie Dean did. The swing was the vantage point from which we paid careful attention to the cars on the highway below. To this day I can spot a light blue 1960 Ford Falcon a quarter of a mile away.

"There goes Billy Jim. By himself, no less. He still going with that Evans girl from Big Creek?"

Today Carrie Dean's eyes are trained not on the highway but on the five children playing on a gym-set on the sparse lawn. She shades her eyes and turns to grin in my direction when the car whines over the hill. When I get out, she rises in her loose irresolute way, bending forward as though part of her wanted to remain in the swing but hadn't the courage to argue.

I was raised in the Groves tradition of fierce huggers; Carrie Dean was not. As we hug each other—this day as in many days in our long past—I feel that her force goes to her joints rather than to her muscles. Muscles return value for value; joints give way. When we release each other, I am left feeling off-balance and presumptuous.

This problem is not one that arises up North. Up North hugging is not routine. Up North you aren't called on to hug anybody except in emergencies, such as for a Heimlich Maneuver. Intervention for safety is not to be confused with affection. When I married Larry, it was appropriate to exchange hugs with his immediate family. And I learned that they, too, had a family style of embracing. Theirs is the three-second hug. You clasp each other's arms and/or shoulders, draw your faces near for three seconds and break away in relief.

Probably Carrie Dean would have adapted to it better than I did.

"Can you tell which ones of that bunch belong to me?" She nods her head at the swarm of children now eddying toward us. "Not all of them do, you know. Just the prettiest ones."

The children reach us. They are all blond, freckled and openly curious.

"This is my friend Jeannine," she tells them officially. "She's a real honest-to-goodness Yankee now, but she didn't used to be."

Her pale eyes slide past mine in a knowing tease.

"And she doesn't bite that I know of, so come on up real close and shake her hand like the ladies and gentlemen you know how to be."

As the children twist their fingers and look at one another, Carrie Dean places a hand on the shoulder of the child nearest her.

"This is Victoria. She's mine."

A tiny hand is given and snatched away. Blue eyes stare up briefly.

"This is Garth, Junior. Enough said."

I shake the warm hand and see Garth, Sr.'s, solemn brown eyes in the eight- or nine-year-old face. Has it been that long?

"This is Tommy, that's Harley's oldest—give her your hand, Tommy—and his sister Nell, and the little dickens that just took off like a streak, that's Eliza, Tillis' girl. Three years old and all boy."

All the children turn and follow Eliza's lead, whooping and calling out each others' names as they run.

"Well!" Carrie Dean exclaims as they again cavort at the gymset. "That's not the end of the show, you know. My little one's in the house taking a nap. Thank goodness. You can see him afterwhile. Save the best for last," she grins, nudging me with a shoulder. There is such authority in the grin—it is the gapped teeth that do it, those marvelous free-standing teeth.

I nudge back. And grin, too. We turn together toward the house.

"I bet that little girl of yours is a sight by now, too. Where is she, again? Off visiting Granmaw?"

"Off visiting *other* Granmaw. A distinction there."

"Uh-huh."

We roll eyes at each other.

"Say, that's a good-looking bunch of kids, by the way, no matter which ones you say aren't yours."

"I already know that," she says. "Now come sit down and tell me what *you* know."

I think she means the porch, but she holds the screen door open for me, and I step up over the threshold and into the living room.

The negligent green of our girlhood has been banished. It is by no means the room I remember.

"You can quit looking," she says. "You've seen it all before."

"I have not! You only moved in two years ago, and you've put in this shag, paneled the walls—"

"And this is mine," she declares, collapsing into a rust corduroy sofa and hugging a matching pillow. "I had it ordered when we were still in the trailer. Momma says that's where it looks like it belongs. But I like it in here just fine."

The trailer Carrie Dean and Garth had in Biloxi until their third child was born encroaches on the side yard, some thirty feet from the southeast corner of the porch. I can see part of the aluminum buttress shape through the living room window. It is now the home of Carrie Dean's mother. Old Mrs. Wentworth had insisted upon the exchange, packing her clothes and dishes and announcing that it was time for them to move back Home.

"How much room does an old woman need?" she had put it, and no one had opposed her to her satisfaction. The Wentworth brothers viewed the plan as a matter of course; the house was always to be Carrie's, was it not?

"I liked my trailer house," Carrie Dean says to me pointedly, as though to stare down every pleated armchair and antimacassar in the room that surrounds us. "That was mine. It was on my lot in Biloxi and it was my house and I liked it just fine."

She shrugs a shoulder. "But I couldn't get anybody else to see it like I saw it."

"Was it hard on you, coming back?"

"It's my place to be here since Momma needs me."

"Well, anyway," I offer, unsure which way to go, "I'm glad you're back in Gethsemane so I get to see you."

Her gaze shifts and becomes intent. I pay attention to such looks, but I am unprepared for what comes next.

"Do you remember when we were in the primer together, and they found out you could read and I couldn't? They put you ahead to the first grade, and I felt so awful; I was just miserable. And you wouldn't even play with me when we had recess together. I bet you don't even remember."

And I don't. First grade: I can remember Miss Viola, and Cal threatening to beat up Davie Cahill if he tried to kiss me again. I can remember losing my snub-nosed school scissors and taking Jerry Comfort's. I remember getting restless in class and talking out loud, and being made to write "I will be quiet in school" a hundred times. It was such terrible labor that I quit and threw the paper in the wastebasket the second afternoon. I judged that I had been at it so long that Miss Viola would have forgotten. But the next morning the paper lay on my desk with red pencil in the upper-right corner. The message was succinct. It said "52 times."

I remember being in love with Cameron Wentworth, Carrie Dean's third cousin, who was in fourth grade. I remember the Kits and candy lipsticks we could buy in the school canteen at recess. I remember squatting on the toilet in the girls' bathroom, because my mother told me about germs and never sitting down.

Carrie Dean was not in my life at all. But I had been, she was telling me plainly, in hers.

"It hurt me so bad that you and me had always done everything together. I remember us drawing pictures together at your house."

Yes; we drew pictures of women. Women's faces, principally. For some reason I drew mine with U-shaped faces, the features gathered low in the U underneath a vast deep forehead. I thought my method entirely superior to Carrie Dean's, but when we asked my mother, *she* firmly preferred Carrie Dean's conventional O-shaped women.

"I liked drawing at your house," Carrie Dean resumes, "because you had crayons and I didn't."

Another surprise. I didn't dream that she had no crayons. At her house we played with creamy cool blond dominoes brought by one of her brothers from the war. I had coveted those dominoes with all my soul.

"You used to draw out the alphabet when we played. Your mother taught you all of your letters, but I didn't know what they were. I didn't want you to know it. I was ashamed not to know. I think I liked-to-never got over you not having anything to do with me at school the way you did."

She says this smilingly; her mouth has been smiling for some time, it now occurs to me. What else was there to do with pain so old and hopeless? But I have been looking not at the mouth but into the eyes, where suffering shows its sky-torn blue. I feel I have been spotted. Identified once again as the instrument of someone else's pain.

Something here is my fault, yet how could anything have been my fault? I was six years old and my life was playing jump boards and trying not to lick off my candy lipstick and being hopelessly in love with a fourth-grader. But I am the one in Carrie Dean's memory. Me; my wispy brown hair and baby teeth. If I do not remember, it is another fault of mine, and still more innocence is subtracted. What if I now must go into Jerry Comfort's feed store, and hear about those scissors? What of Davie Cahill, since Carrie Dean has told me he tried to kill himself twice in his teens over unrequited love? Will I meet him after Sunday Evening Prayer Service and hear how in first grade I set the course for his life?

Carrie Dean is saying, "What's your momma doing this afternoon? Why didn't she come with you?"

"She had some things to do. We have a Hinton family supper to go to this evening. You know my aunt Verlie?"

"The only ones of your daddy's people that I know are the ones that come to church. Garth went to school with a cousin of yours though." She goes still. "Drew, I think."

"Drew!" I brighten, anticipating, as ever the case with Drew, a story.

Carrie Dean lifts her tongue to the space between her front teeth, looks as though she will bring something to mind. But then her eyes snap to mine; she brings her spine erect. "Hey!" She shoves aside the cushion she has held. "Come on outside with me a minute. I want to show you something."

I hesitate, and she settles the matter in a tone that is more command than plea.

"Come on."

As girls we were both long-boned and slight, and pretty enough if the looking was kindly. Probably we both look better than we did, or perhaps that is giving style rather than youth its due. We have taken different paths to our looks, however; I am rather too thin these days, whereas I notice that Carrie Dean, when she rises from the sofa ahead of me, has gathered puddles of fat around her hips and belly. Childbearing fat, butter-bean fat.

We walk out of the house and down the porch steps in tandem, and Carrie Dean calls out to the children who have left off their playing to get some signal from her. We walk on up the drive past Mrs. Wentworth's trailer and into the garden.

"I want you to just see," Carrie Dean is saying.

The garden smells of sun beating on tomatoes. The air is heavy as a touch, and it smells of hot okra and bean blossoms. It smells of earth, and it sings with insect voices. The rows of broccoli, zucchini, carrots, peas, potatoes, tomatoes, beans and corn look like the rows of any well-kept garden. It could be the one Larry tends there in the back of the double lot we have in Des Moines. He is proud of it, the way Carrie Dean is. Often when he gets home at night, he leaves his car in the drive and goes directly to inspect his plants for signs of malfeasance in his absence, checking for weeds or worms, conducting a ritual harvest of one tomato or a bunch of scallions for our dinner salad.

Carrie Dean's garden looks like that, except that as we walk along the heady rows of plants, I begin to see that this "garden" extends all the way from the trailer to Tillis Wentworth's fence a quarter of a mile away. This garden is not a hobby; it consumes life. It is Carrie Dean's occupation. She feeds her family with it. She herself, with her hands in hot blanching baths and cold rinses, the kitchen ringing with canning lids and the clank of heat-proof jars on the counters. I know the scene from childhood. I have even echoed it in a fashionable way with a bushel of peaches or plums from a bargain at some rural market. But to live it—to provide for my family in this way!

I am diligent. I compliment Carrie Dean upon the beautiful array of plants. I exclaim over the fat hairy okras, the droop of tiny bell peppers hiding in their dark foliage. An odd look crosses Carrie Dean's face, and I understand how little like real garden talk all that sounds, know I cannot help it, am known for the stranger to country life I have become.

"I canned two hundred quarts of tomatoes last year, and just about that many green beans. And peas! You should have seen the field peas, I liked-to-never seen the end of them."

"Two hundred quarts—you mean your family eats all that?"

Carrie Dean stops and turns a tomato leaf over, exposing a green tomato worm.

"Well," she says with a short laugh, "it sure goes."

She picks up the worm's soft body between her thumb and forefinger, and pulls gently. The worm clings with its myriad feet, and she says, "Hateful things!"

The worm comes free and Carrie Dean grinds it into the loose earth with the toe of her sandal.

She shifts her weight more evenly and squints toward the house and the trailer by its side.

"Well, Momma likes to be able to give the boys something to take home with them every time they stop to see her. Wilson manages to stop about three times a week. 'Carrie Dean,'" she mimics, and the mourning-dove tones are as startlingly soft as her mother's, "'why don't you just find Wilson Earl some of those pole beans we put up last summer? They are the best beans, Wilson, you will love them. Now, Carrie Dean, don't be stingy. I won't be needing my share.'"

The long pause that follows embarrasses both of us. Carrie Dean has said more than she'd intended, more than is proper. This picture of old Mrs. Wentworth melodiously doling out the labor of this garden stuns me into silence. Outrage is out of place here; in the South, family is sacred. I cannot say what I think.

And so, in the hot silence between us, Carrie Dean thinks she hears what she expected to hear.

"Oh, I'm ashamed of myself for feeling the way I do. Don't pay any mind," she finishes flatly.

Turning on her heel to lead the way down the rows back toward the house, she waves one hand loosely at all that surrounds us.

"As you can see, I've got plenty."

There is a way to talk with close friends whom you happen not to have seen for ten years. I am certain that there is a way, and yet shyness or politeness or fear in some other form prevents Carrie Dean and me from finding it. I am sure that each of us keeps a book, and when we meet each other—whether it is a week or an hour or ten years that have come between us—each of us opens her book to the page where we left off. It is probably that simple. If we had the courage to seize the knowledge and proceed, our meetings and our partings would remain orderly. Instead, they are cluttered with overlays of other lives and passages of time and circumstance and the notion that we are somehow changed.

Here we are in Carrie Dean's garden, or on Carrie Dean's front porch or in Carrie Dean's living room sitting on Carrie Dean's mother's furniture, and the things I want to know start from childhood. "Do you still have the ivory dominoes?" I want to know. That is what I care about, not the details of Laura's birth or Victoria's ear operations, or Larry's career or the move to Des Moines.

Clearly Carrie Dean felt the same way. We had settled first grade, and now how about the boyfriends we had in our teens? "How could you marry Garth?" I wanted to ask her. "What did you ever do about the way you felt about Billy Jim?" In that way, on those foundations, we would soon be able to say to each other: "What do you think of this business of being grown up? How do you get through your life every day? How do you stand it, being wife-and-mother? If we could get hold of those books of ours, the recent ones where the marriages jolt and drone along, would you just as soon tear out the last few dozen pages? I would. Would you?"

We don't have that conversation. Perhaps it always works out that people simply don't. Not unless it is two women alone in a kitchen at eleven o'clock at night, the dishes done, the kids in bed, the man of the house gratefully someplace else.

But this is the middle of the afternoon, and life is in process. The garden reeking of it, the throng of children celebrating it. This is not the book but the movie, and we are both studying the ground, trying to find our marks without appearing to look for them.

I follow Carrie Dean down the rows.

"This is the most food I've ever seen in my life," I say, pushing my voice out to be heard over the several yards that now separate us.

"Your memory's failing you, Jeannine," she says over her shoulder.

It is some kind of opening, a lead. But I don't know where it points.

"What do you mean?" I call out.

She stops and faces me, her features open again, teasing.

"Did you grow up on Blue Rise Road? Was Cyrus Hinton your granddaddy? Did he used to sell peas and butter beans and corn to the Bayley markets?"

In an instant I see the old man, see his bald head and toothless mouth and the blood veins splayed over the crooked nose, see the rusty green pickup loaded with fruits and vegetables, its flapping tailgate wired shut.

My mother used to say that even the peaches smelled of beer. But she didn't say it when my father, or anybody else, was around.

I laugh.

"Must be this Mississippi sun," I call, as Carrie Dean again turns toward the house. "Must have fried my brains just like it did his."

"I'd be ashamed of myself, Jeannine Hinton." This from over her shoulder again.

"Well—I was supposed to think it; I just wasn't supposed to say it. That's the code, isn't it?"

"You're turning into a Yankee," she warns me.

One of These Mornings

Kenneth Holditch

Always the smell from the burning refuse hung about the shacks that clung like bats from the hills surrounding the dump. Five years before, the broad flat basin had been Gum Pond. In the early years of the century, the pond was a local resort with a boardwalk and a thick grove of gum trees, from which the site took its name. But with the acceleration of transportation, people abandoned the pond with its exiguous charms for state parks within a day's driving distance of the town. The boardwalk rotted and fell into the pond; caterpillars destroyed most of the gum trees; and the pond soon became a scrubby, unsightly place. As the Negro community of the town grew, surrounded on three sides by the white residential and business districts, it pushed out in the only direction available—toward the pond.

Even after the resort was only a memory, the pond was a good fishing spot, but the tornado of 1936 blew into the pond more than a dozen residents of the shacks lining the coliseum slopes. Although the pond was dragged to recover the victims, a legend grew to the effect that some of the bodies were never recovered, and as a result, most of the fishermen abandoned the place. Only the most penurious of the Negroes continued to supplement scanty incomes with their catches.

Ten years after the storm, tragedy again struck the faded resort; acids from the fertilizer plant north of the pond poisoned the water and killed all the fish. For weeks their bloated bodies floated, a silver-gray band around the edge of the pond. The stench from the decaying fish was almost unbearable. It was then that the board of aldermen decided to drain the old pond and convert it into a garbage dump.

With the water pumped out, the pond basin looked like a graveyard, the white knees of old cypress trees like primitive grave markers. With the first load of garbage came the eternal smell of decay and burning filth, unpleasant as the odor of the dead fish. Where gaily dressed ladies and their escorts had paraded along the boardwalk, where pleasure boats had glided as sedately as blossoms on the water, empty tin cans and old tires, paper and vegetable peelings, all the refuse of civilization lay, a graveyard to man's eternal struggles and hopes, a memorial to the transience of all things material.

The house in which Joe Edd lived with his parents and his three sisters hung on the rim of the west hill, as though preparing to dive headlong into the dump. The back door of the little three-room shack opened on Spring Street, but stepping out the front door, one found himself hard-put to resist the gravitational urge to run, slide, or fall down the slope into the pond basin below.

Joe Edd was only a little boy, and because he had never known anything else, he thought theirs was a lovely house. His mother had filled it with cast-off furniture from the homes of the various white families for whom she worked. She kept flowers in the front yard, and in the hard-packed earth where only small patches of scrub grass had grown before, her magic hand had coaxed into life hollyhocks and zinnias and princess feathers; from March to October, there was always some sort of blossoms there.

Joe Edd went to the grammar school three blocks from his home, and he loved his teachers, his classmates, his books. When school was in session, life was beautiful and perfect. But in the summer months, there was no school and no place to go. The town had no library or playground for his race, and only on rare occasions could the family afford to go to the Dixie Belle Theater for a Saturday night's entertainment. They had a radio and he loved listening to the music, but it was almost unbearably hot inside during the summer months; the sunlight on the tin roof converted the shack into an oven.

So from late May to early September, Joe Edd was usually fretful and unhappy. During the hot, protracted days, when both his parents and two of his sisters were at work (his father cleaned chickens for a poultry house; the women worked as cooks or maids), he and the youngest sister, Clairie May, played desultorily around the house or in the yard.

Only on two occasions during the day did Joe Edd have any fun.

In the afternoon, about three o'clock, he would put on his sunglasses (a broken pair he had found in the street), and holding Clairie May's hand, he would guide her down the precarious slope and in a semi-circle around the bottom of the basin to the grocery store. Clairie May was two years older than he, but something was wrong with her mind; she had to be cared for like a baby. That was his job during the day when everyone else was away from home. He always felt a little important as he scampered down the slope, holding carefully the little brown hand, and sauntered across the level ground to the store to spend the dime his mother gave him each morning.

Old Miss Maidie Leake owned the grocery store. She was a big fat white woman with a voice as deep as that of Joe Edd's father. There was a window fan in the store, and although it was not really cool there between the shelves of canned goods, boxes, and bottles, it was pleasant to feel the air stirring. There was a rich smell there, a relief from the odor of garbage: a compounding of all the scents of food and spices and fresh unsmoked tobacco. Joe Edd would have liked to remain in the store for a long time, leisurely deliberating on how to spend the dime. They could buy candy or cookies or their own individual choices of a half dozen kinds of cold drinks from a big red cooler in the front of the store. But Miss Maidie was a grumpy old lady, and if he and Clairie May stayed too long, she shouted things at them. Things like "What you niggers hanging around for?" She was very suspicious, and if the painfully intricate process of deciding between treats took more than a minute or two, she thought they were trying to steal from her. She would move her ample form around the counter, like an elephant set loose to find its way down the narrow lanes of a maze, and stand staring down at them. From Joe Edd's angle of vision, she looked an ogress, her beady, myopic eyes like black dots in a swollen mound of dough.

"What you nigger kids doing?"

Because of Miss Maidie's distrust and her bitter remarks that hurt like a slap in the face, Joe Edd always made up his mind on the way to the store and gently coaxed from Clairie May a statement of her preference. Thus their purchase could be made hastily, so that he would not have to spend too much time in the presence of the suspicious ogress.

Their daily dime spent, another day's decision safely receding into the past, Joe Edd and Clairie May would seat themselves on the top step of the porch and gaze out across the dump. If they had bought soda pop, the cold liquid would run cold down Joe Edd's throat and then burn exquisitely in his nose and eyes. Sometimes he was conscious of Miss Maidie's eyes peering through the dirty window full of signs advertising snuff and patent medicines. She was afraid they might try to steal her pop bottles; she was always warning him about that. He could feel her eyes, burning into the back of his head; he could imagine her face, a white circle ghostly against the cloudy glass. And when he knew she was there, the sweet liquid turned sour in his mouth and on his stomach.

Despite the suspicious old woman, however, Joe Edd enjoyed their trips to the store; he sat on the steps, relishing the burning sensation of cold pop or the sticky richness of a Baby Ruth, and watched Clairie May, who ate in little bites, making soft animal sounds as she swallowed. Before the store the blacktop road that meandered across the dump and climbed the hill toward town was soft as modelling clay. Sometimes a car passed, but usually the road was empty except for an occasional child who walked slowly by, eying enviously the treats being devoured by the boy and girl.

Across the road from the store was the weathered, gray shack in which Aunt Annie Beane lived; she was a midwife and a preacher in the sanctified church. Sometimes she would come out on her porch, a tall, bent woman dressed in white, wave at the children, then seat herself in a rocker and begin to sing.

Her voice was deep and rich, and it seemed to move beyond her house, to spread throughout the pond basin and up the hill and, Joe Edd sometimes thought, maybe even across town. On several occasions, Miss Maidie had stepped to the door of her store and shouted at Aunt Annie to cut out that noise, but the old woman had always gone right on singing, without missing a note, and after a while Miss Maidie would retire to the dark interior of her domain.

Joe Edd listened in amazement to the songs, some of them stories like the one about Jesus meeting the woman at the well or Joshua conquering Jericho. Sometimes he did not understand the words, but the songs were so sad and heavy that he felt tears come into his eyes:

> I been 'buked and I been scorned,
> I been 'buked and I been scorned,
> I been 'buked and I been scorned, children,
> Goin' to make this journey on.

Aunt Annie, after singing three or four songs, would stand up, wave to the children again, and then go back in her house. Even if he had finished his drink or his candy, Joe Edd would never leave until the old woman had completed her songs. Then he would walk home, holding Clairie May's hand, wondering what those white people way over town thought about that voice that came rolling out to them, plaintive and sad and strange.

This was one of the two pleasures for the boy in those long dull summer days.

The other pleasant time was in the morning, usually about ten o'clock, when the day's load of garbage was dumped by the city's white mechanical trucks. By the time the trucks arrived, there were usually a score or more children already gathered at the dumping site. They ranged in age from the noisy five-year-olds like Bubba Lester to the thirteen- and fourteen-year-old boys whose voices were either already deep or changing, sometimes bass, sometimes a high ludicrous squeak like an unoiled hinge. The older boys moved with assumed confidence and prowess among the group, boasting, shouting, hitting each other in the exuberance of youth.

"I going to find me a gun in there some day," one of them would say.

"Yeah! What you do with a gun?"

The boy with dreams would whip a dream pistol from his hip and mow down a row of the younger children, who stood gaping at him.

"I gonna find it, you wait and see."

They were a riotous, nervous group, and by the time the trucks came rumbling down the hill and across the flat land toward the present dumping site, there usually had been one or more fights. But the approach of the trucks was a signal for silence. When the first faint roar of the motors reached their ears, the children froze as if the sound marked the beginning of some religious observance. The big awkward vehicles with their white drivers and Negro crews would roll clumsily down the slope, speed up as they crossed the old pond bottom, turn, back up, and with a roaring sound, the large tanks would open up and empty their burden before the fascinated eyes of the children.

Whether from a slight sense of shame or perhaps from fear, none of the children would approach the newly dumped refuse until all the sanitation trucks had emptied their huge maws and roared away up the hill. Then in a mad scramble, as though released by signal for an Easter egg hunt, they rushed to the piles of refuse and began their search, scrambling without care among the rotting vegetable matter and filth heaped high in mounds. Later in the day city workers on graders would come to flatten out the little hills of garbage, for the city fathers had developed a plan to build up the level of the dump into firm high ground, suitable for business sites. But that was a dream of the future; now there was trash, thrown away by the white people of the town, and some of it was good, or at least usable.

Joe Edd scrambled about with the rest of them, always keeping an eye on Clairie May. She did not scavenge, but usually sat down under one of the old gum trees and sucked her thumb while the other children scampered and fought among the garbage like miners searching for gold nuggets. She stared in fascination at the process, her eyes big as saucers against the smooth brown skin. She was a beautiful child, and sometimes Joe Edd had seen his mother cry over her, and he could almost understand.

Meanwhile the frenetic search went on, amidst cries and shouts and a great deal of pushing and shoving.

Once Joe Edd found an egg beater for his mother, but she threw it out; it was broken beyond repair, his father said. He had almost cried when they threw away what he had thought to be a real treasure, but his mother hugged him and kissed him and said thank you, and then it was almost all right. Another time he found a doll with one arm missing and a badly scarred face; Clairie May still treasured it; she carried it to bed with her every night.

Usually he found nothing, for the bigger boys were faster than he. And even when the smaller children found something of value, it was more than likely snatched out of their small hands by the twelve- and thirteen-year-olds.

"You give me that back," was a frequent cry from the piping voice of a child, a cry greeted only by the deep vulgar laugh of the thief. Joe Edd always felt a sharp, physical stab of pity for the young children when this happened. He would be kind when he was grown. He would always be good to little children. Life was hard and sometimes sad. When he was five, his father had drawn him aside one day to tell him the difference between white people and Negroes, to tell him that he was a Negro and that because of this he had a delegated place in life and he must keep in that place. He had almost cried that day, because even though he did not understand all that his father said, he knew that being a Negro was somehow sad and a heavy burden, for his father's face was long and full of sorrow as he tried to explain to his son about life. And when

Joe Edd saw the smaller children deprived of their finds by the older boys, he felt sad and hurt.

They were a greedy, rebellious group of scavengers, and most of them were doomed to climb the slopes toward their homes without the treasures they had dreamed of the night before. Every day, Joe Edd looked forward with a strange mixture of anguish and anticipation to the new piles of debris, but when his search was over, he was sad, and sometimes, leading Clairie May back toward the house, he thought that he would not return on the following morning.

Then one day, quite unexpectedly, he found a real treasure. It was far away from the rest of the garbage, under the protective limbs of a willow tree near the road, as though it were waiting there for him. He had already given up hope of finding anything in the dump and was leaving, clasping tightly Clairie May's little hand, when he came upon it.

He saw first only a glint of metal, the sunlight striking the back fender; when he moved closer and lifted the willow limbs, his heart already quickened in anticipation, he saw the bicycle. The sight took his breath away, made tears in his eyes. He dropped the willow branches back into place and looked quickly over his shoulder to see if he were being observed. There was a tight stare of fear on his face. But the other children had already scattered; he could hear them far off in the distance, already climbing the slope, arguing among themselves.

Releasing Clairie May's hand, Joe Edd lifted the branches once more and pulled the bicycle cautiously from beneath the bush. It was battered, the seat was missing, but it was beautiful. It looked almost as good as Quincy's bicycle; Quincy was the son of the town's only Negro undertaker, a wealthy man who did not allow his children to mix with the scavengers. Quincy had everything, and most of the children envied him to the point of hatred.

"Look there, Clairie May," Joe Edd said when he had pulled the vehicle into view. "Jus' look."

Laughing and talking all the time to Clairie May who did not understand, he pushed his burden home with loving care, stopping at frequent intervals to examine it, to touch it as though to prove its reality, then looking around to see that none of the bigger boys had returned.

"Jus' look what I done found."

He knew all along that something would happen, that such intense joy could not go unchallenged. It was like the times when he was sitting in the shade of the store front, feeling that needly-burning sensation in his nose from the pop and feeling suddenly so happy he could burst, like an over-filled balloon, and then he would sense the beady black eyes of Miss Maidie Leake burning into the back of his head. It was like that. Everything in life was like that. Something would happen.

At the house, he deposited Clairie May on the porch with her mutilated doll.

"Now you stay right here, Clairie May. Right here on the po'ch. I going to try out this-here bicycle."

She stared up at him with the innocent half-smile that looked somehow very perceptive, her eyes as bright as any child's, her thumb in her mouth, and said not a word. She clutched the doll possessively to her breast, and Joe Edd knew that she would be waiting there, in the same place, as though she had not moved or even breathed, when he returned.

He stood in the front yard for a minute or two contemplating his treasure, holding it at arm's length, running his hand over the rusty metal. He knew there was no need to try the bicycle on the hill; no one, not even Quincy, could ride on that hill. So pushing the bike before him, as gently as though he were handling glass, he headed for the blacktop road that crossed the dump, the road built for the use of the garbage trucks and for the workers at the fertilizer plant.

The blacktop was hot and soft, and he pranced about until he had become accustomed to the heat against his bare feet. His first attempts to ride the bicycle failed. Since there was no seat, he had to stand up; one of the wheels was sprung and he kept veering to the right. Once he fell and skinned his knee and his forehead. But he persisted, and when he was started, he rode on down the street toward the store, going faster and faster. He was half afraid to continue in that direction; he did not want to pass the store and Miss Maidie or to see the other children. They still could take his treasure away. But he rode on, filled with an irresistible impulse to move, to go so fast it was not hot anymore. The air rushing past felt just like the breeze from the fan in the grocery store. He first smiled and then laughed and then shouted in his joy.

When he passed the store, he did not dare glance toward it, first of all because he did not want to see Miss Maidie, but also because it took all of his attention to keep the wobbly vehicle in the road. But she was there; he knew it. He could feel her eyes again, burning. Little black eyes, like those of an animal, trapped in that large white face, watching him and her bottles and now watching him and his bicycle. A chill ran through his body, as if someone had stepped on his grave (that was what his mother always said when a sudden, inexplicable shudder came over her). But he rode on, past the store, up the hill.

All day he rode, making periodic trips back to the house to check on Clairie May. He was tired and hot from his exertion, his clothes were drenched with sweat, but he rode on and on, faster and faster. And he was happy.

"Where'd you get that?"

Joe Edd stood in the yard, holding his treasure proudly before him; on the porch his father looked down at him, a dark scowl on his face, the question on his lips. His mother leaned tired against the door and watched with a blank stare.

"I found it," Joe Edd said, pointing down toward the dump. The garbage was burning now, and they could smell the smoke. "In the dump."

"You found it?" His father came slowly down the steps, his hands hanging at his sides; the scowl seemed permanently imprinted on his dark face. He took the bicycle from Joe Edd's hands and began to examine it. He mumbled something to himself, and Joe Edd watched, a tight knot of fear growing in his stomach; he felt the chill again, as he had felt it when he passed Miss Maidie's store. His father was always afraid, afraid of trouble, afraid of white men, afraid of everything. His father had been in the pen once, a long time ago, and he was afraid.

Now Joe Edd stood and watched as the big black hands moved about his treasure, and Joe Edd himself was afraid. When his father looked up at him, Joe Edd stepped back, and there were tears in his eyes.

"You didn't steal this, did you?" his father asked.

"Jack," his mother called from the doorway; she stepped onto the porch, but said nothing more, just her husband's name.

"Nawsir, I didn't steal it. I found it. Down there." He pointed again. "Ask Clairie May. She was with me. I found it."

"Where'd you find it? With the other junk down there?"

"Under some willow limbs. Over there, by the dump. I found it."

Jack continued his inspection of the bicycle; then, crouched down beside it, he looked up at his wife. "What you think, Flora?"

She answered quickly, as though she had only been waiting for an opportunity. "I know Joe Edd don't lie. I says he found it. I says it's junk, like everything else down there. It ain't got no seat an' it's rusted. Some white folks done throwed it away and bought they son a new one. I say it's his." Her voice, though tired, was firm and her husband listened. When she had finished, she turned and went back into the house. There was supper to be cooked, Clairie May to be looked after, and then bed. It was a hard life for all of them.

Joe Edd held his breath, waiting for his father's decision. After all, what could he do, return it to the dump, then watch one of his friends ride it around down there for years? What could he do? It was his, like his mother said. He found it, and it was his bike.

Standing up, his father leaned the bicycle toward Joe Edd. "You found it, boy, it's yours, I guess."

"You think can it be fixed, Daddy?" The words poured out, and he wanted to cry and laugh too, but he dared not; he still felt uneasy, even though his father had decided, even though the bicycle was his to keep.

"I don't know." Jack stood back inspecting the treasure. "I might find you a seat somewhere, borrow a hammer from Mr. Robert and try to straighten up that wheel. We see." He turned and climbed the steps, but at the top he turned to face Joe Edd again. "You be careful riding it, boy. You watch out for cars."

Laughing and mumbling to himself, trembling with delight at the fulfillment of his dreams, Joe Edd pushed the bicycle down the hill. He forgot about his supper. He was going to ride again. He was going to ride and ride and maybe never, never stop riding.

When the white man came for the bicycle the next day, Joe Edd was not really surprised. Hurt, yes, but not surprised. Ever since he found it, glistening in the sunlight beneath those willow boughs, he had been afraid, like his father, afraid something would happen. He had not known what form the tragedy would take: perhaps his father would refuse to let him keep it, or one of the big boys would take it away from him. But even in his moments of acutest pleasure, when he stood on the pedals, pumping furiously, fighting to keep the damaged wheel from careening to the right, there had lurked in his mind the eternal shadow of fear, the notion that all this joy could not last.

About six o'clock, when Joe Edd came out from his supper, hurrying, anxious to be back on the road, riding again, he found his father standing there in the yard, talking to the white man, and he knew.

"I been looking most of the afternoon," the white man said, "and then I went to Miss Leake's store, and she told me she saw your boy riding it, and I came up to . . . " He hesitated, turning a straw hat in his hands. He was a tall, slender man, his skin white as wax, his hands almost too small, as though they were artificial, had been added to his body, maybe just sewn on to the sleeves of his coat. He seemed nervous, self-conscious.

"The boy ain't done nothing wrong," Jack was saying. He spoke quietly, apologetically, the way he always talked to white men, ever since that time they sent him to the penitentiary. "He jus' found it down there." He too pointed toward the dump. "Kids, they always looking around down there for somethin'."

The white man looked toward the dump as though to find something there, something new and interesting. "I see," he said. He turned back to face Joe Edd's father. "I brought it down yesterday morning early, before I went to work. The boy, my son, had broke the seat off of it, and I'd been trying to fix it. I sprung the wheel somehow and couldn't get it straight." He turned the palms of his hands out in a helpless gesture, letting the hat hang pendulous from his forefingers. "I'm not much good at repairing things. I thought I'd buy him a new one, but my wife, she found out what I'd done, and she said to get it back, to get it fixed."

The white man looked nervously about him; he stared intently at Joe Edd on the porch, at the house, and then at Jack again. "You know how it is, I didn't know I could get it fixed, and . . . "

"Yessir."

Joe Edd just stood still; he did not cry or say anything, but only stared at the white man. He felt a little sick at his stomach, as though the collard greens and beans and fried meat he had just eaten were churning about down there, disagreeing with each other.

"I guess I better get the bike," the white man said. "I'm sorry . . . "

Jack interrupted him this time. "Yessir." He turned to Joe Edd. "Get the bicycle, boy," he said. Joe Edd hurried down the steps and around the house and was back in a few seconds, pushing his treasure before him.

"That's it," the white man said. "Yeah, that's it." He inspected the bicycle, then said, "Where's the seat? I threw it out there somewhere."

"There ain't no seat," Joe Edd said. "I didn't find none."

"Oh, I see. Well, I guess I can buy a new one." He took the bike from Joe Edd's hands. "I'm sorry about it, but my wife said maybe we could get it fixed and . . . " He looked down at the bicycle and stopped talking. The silence hung heavily about the three of them. Then the white man started to push the bike away, around the house toward the street. He stopped at the corner of the house, thrust his hand deep into his trousers pocket. He let the bicycle rest against the house and picked something out of the hand he had drawn from his pocket.

"Here, boy," he said, holding the something out to Joe Edd.

Joe Edd just stood there until his father touched him, gave him a gentle push, and then he walked over and took the half dollar the white man extended to him.

Joe Edd stood there quiet, holding the half dollar before him; he did not say anything until his father said, "What you say, Joe Edd?" and then Joe Edd said, "Thank you."

And the white man was gone, pushing the bicycle at his side, and that was the last Joe Edd ever saw of his treasure.

He never mentioned the bicycle again, and it was not mentioned in the house. The next afternoon, when he took Clairie May and went to the grocery store and old Miss Maidie said, "Well, I see you ain't got your bicycle anymore," he did not even answer.

Every morning, he went to the garbage dump, guiding Clairie May at his side, and he was thoughtful and quiet as they walked along. Two days later he got in a fight with a boy younger than he and snatched a battered hat from the child's hand. It was a dirty, useless hat, and he had to throw it away later. But he enjoyed taking it, and from then on he took what he wanted—and he wanted everything—from anyone who was small enough for him to whip.

An Open House

JAMES HUGHES

HE WOULD NOT come out of the bathroom. He'd been in there nearly all of Sunday. Dad and I, standing in the hallway with our faces almost flush against the bathroom door, wondered out loud whether he'd decided to take up permanent habitation in there. But we couldn't draw a laugh out of him, not even when Dad said, "Listen here now, Fig, you've been boxing old Buford long enough." This was a week after Fig's accident. I imagined him in there leaning into the bathroom mirror, wide-eyed, peeling back the gauze bandages and putting them in place and peeling them back again, but fixed quietly to the same spot and not even breathing loud enough for Dad and me to hear. What we were left with, out in the hall, was the sound of our own hearts and the yellow bathroom door that was screaming for a paint job and Mom's occasional sniffles from the study upstairs, where she was pretending to be grading papers.

This is not the way we usually spend our weekend afternoons around my house, but ever since my brother Fig got hurt we have all been on edge. It's true that Mom does a certain amount of schoolwork most weekends. She teaches freshman composition over at Hinds Junior in Raymond and also takes an assortment of self-help classes on weeknights, which means she has to grade papers Saturdays and Sundays. But back on that particular Sunday afternoon, with Fig's accident only seven days past, I knew she was only pretending to work; she might just as well have gone and had her cry in the bedroom, for all the good it was doing her to stay at her desk. And any other Sunday you would have found Dad stuck to the television set. We live in Mississippi, and, like a lot of other sports fans in our state, he follows the various pro teams of Houston, Atlanta, and most any other Southern neighbor grand enough to have such things as professional sports. Mississippi has a hard enough time just supporting its public schools and state colleges and keeping the chuckholes in its highways tarred over.

My brother Fig is in his senior year at Clinton High School. If he hadn't had the accident, late of a weekend afternoon he'd usually be out practicing with his band, Alleged Tumor, or up in his room playing his guitar. At eighteen, he is already one of the best-known electric guitarists in central Mississippi; I've heard him practically wring tears out of his black Les Paul. He's played all the better bars over in Jackson, the capital city, which lies ten miles to the east of our home in Clinton. He's got more money in the bank than I have and even more than Mom and Dad, I imagine—all from his playing at the senior proms of the richer local prep schools. The girls at Clinton High flock around him, and he doesn't seem to care or even notice. He's the family loan company, but he doesn't charge us interest. Whenever one of us in the family has a birthday, he takes us out to dinner at Le Fleur's and orders plates of Crabmeat Imperial all around. His Christian name is Lloyd, but he switched it to Fig—got the birth certificate fixed and everything—because he wanted to be called something more appetizing, he said. Actually, it was an old childhood nickname that stuck. He and I get along. We've only gotten into one fight; I messed up the cartilage in his nose after he struck me out four times in a Wiffle ball game, with several cousins from California watching, and later he came up to me, the black and blue forming under his eyes, and said, "I'm sorry I laughed when you kept striking out, but couldn't you hit me on the shoulder next time?"

We live in a small two-story house that Mom herself designed—an artsy natural-cedar structure, with sundecks jutting out from the upstairs study, and from Mom and Dad's bedroom and Fig's room, across the hall from them, and from the living room downstairs. My bedroom opens onto a stone patio, and so does the dining room. To Mom's thinking, it's just as important to have a comfortable living area out-of-doors as it is to make the house itself livable. Sitting in the living room downstairs, you can look up and survey just about the entire second floor, because the upstairs is one of those cutaway jobs with a balcony. Charm, I guess, was what Mom and the architect had in mind, but they didn't give much thought to privacy or economy of space. Through the cute but ineffective louvred doors of the study even the smallest sounds can pass, unhampered by wood or plaster, and then down through the living room and into the kitchen, the dining room, and my bedroom downstairs, and even into its corresponding bathroom across the hall. This was where my brother Fig had been hiding out since well before noon on that Sunday. By now the shadows of late afternoon were spilling into the house, and Dad and I stood with our ears pressed against the bathroom door like a pair of monkeys, listening for signs of life, but all we heard was Mom weeping in the study upstairs. Back there behind the locked door, Fig's stillness made you wonder whether he hadn't slipped away through some secret exit in the plumbing.

Finally, Dad and I made the mistake of turning our heads at the same time. He had a heavy beard—he doesn't have it anymore—but there was no mistaking the shared embarrassment I saw on his face now. There was nothing left for me to do but slam my fist on the door and say, "Damn it, Fig, you hear her up there! Now just come the hell out!"

He came out. He didn't look at us. I followed him across the hall into my bedroom. I guess Dad just sort of seeped into the carpet, because the next thing I knew he was gone and there was just the sound of his voice humming anxiously from someplace underground, it sounded like. I watched Fig fall back on my bed and look up at the ceiling. He raised his hands, the good one and the spoiled one, above him in the air, watching them as if they were some kind of abstract-art exhibit he figured he ought to admire. Mom's sobs and sniffles still filtered in, and now I could hear Dad, suddenly returned from the underworld, up there talking to her. I shut the door and slouched against it, hoping to strike a casual stance for Fig's benefit.

It's worth mentioning in her defense that Mom isn't your usual crybaby. She's kind but strong, and she's skilled in the various strategies of human relations—such as charm, assertiveness, and good looks—that people nowadays seem to think you can buy at your friendly neighborhood psychiatrist's office. For her, getting along with others isn't so much a skill as an art; it's part of her very nature. Her students love her. When she has to clean out her office at the end of every semester, she always brings home a carful of gifts and letters. Once, she brought home an entire *car*—a shabby but nice-looking M.G. convertible that an older student, a Vietnam veteran, gave her and refused to take back. She told us he stood in the parking lot as she was getting into her own worn-out Toyota and threatened to shoot himself in the head with a little .22 pistol he carried around if she didn't accept his gift. He said he wanted her to have it because she had encouraged him to the point where he thought it might be worth participating in life again. Mom said that half his foot had been blown away, but she is sort of gullible when it comes to appeals for sympathy; I saw him walking around the Hinds campus once, and he had on regular shoes and wasn't hindered by limp or stagger, as far as I could tell. The month after he gave her the M.G., we got a postcard from him out in Oregon, where he said he was picking apples and contemplating God's abundant creation with his new wife, Sukyo, who didn't have her visa yet but they were working on it. And speaking of cards, I remember another one to Mom, from an anorectic girl, that said, "Dear Mrs. Rembert"—Rembert being our family name—"Gosh, how can I thank you for all you did for me? I can look at food on the dinner table now and not feel like I have to eat all the leftovers. It's been three months now since I threw up my Sunday dinner, and I feel sure I'm over that habit. My weight is about normal. Friends and relatives tell me I look like Kitty from 'Gunsmoke,' do you know her? Thank you also for turning me on to William Golding and his 'Lord of the Flies.' As long as I stick to books like that, I'll never have to worry about having another one of those Krystal hamburger binges that used to haunt me so in the quiet moments when I tried to do something constructive. It makes me so happy to know I can now read books and listen to records and write letters in peace. Much much love (the true kind). Your friend and former student, Helen Skeet."

Mom has a large share of that vague, heroic quality called *mettle;* she's not given to fits of weeping. But because she's an attractive woman herself, with a keen eye for beauty and symmetry even in the lowest art forms—you should see the unusual towel racks in our house, for example—and loving her family as much as she does, Mom has had a harder time than any of us getting over Fig's injury. Fig himself, for all his hiding out behind locked doors, has most likely written the whole thing off to experience.

For a while, Fig wasn't what you'd call spunky. After Dad and I coaxed him out of the bathroom that Sunday, a week after the accident, I hopped nervously around the room, trying to appear busy so Fig wouldn't catch me looking at him. I put away records, books, pajamas, and dirty socks. I'd have made the bed, but Fig looked as if he was there to stay. He wouldn't say anything. He just lay there on his back, arms stretched full out, as in a scene from one of those Frankenstein-type movies where the doctor hasn't brought the monster all the way to life yet. The damaged finger on his left hand had layers and layers of gauze on it. I felt awful; I couldn't think of one worthwhile thing to say. Once, he opened his mouth a little, and I said, "What?" to encourage him in what I took to be his first speaking bid all day, but all that came out of him was one hard little sigh. Finally, I couldn't stand it anymore and I said, "Why don't we go out for a few beers?" Fig shrugged and followed me out to the car. It had quieted down upstairs by the time we stepped outside. It was dark by now, with no moon out; the air was heavy with humidity, and smelled of stale swamp water.

As I backed the VW, windows all open, out of the driveway, I hoped for rain, thinking Fig might feel better once it wasn't so hot and sticky. Later on, it came, a merciful downpour beating on the flat roof of the Red Bar, as Fig and I sat inside with our beers, talking about Fig's plans for graduation, only a month away. Fig had cheered up considerably since I got him out of the house. He likes the Red Bar. He's often said that some of his happiest memories are of all the times Dad used to bring us to the R.B. with him and treat us to pinball games and root beer and fried pickles, which are a house specialty.

"I don't think I'm gonna do the senior trip," said Fig now. "I played down in Panama City that time last summer, and Florida was the scum of the South. The band almost fell apart, we were so sick and miserable. We got food poisoning and nobody had the strength to leave the hotel. Come to think of it, that's when we changed our name from Erectosaur to Alleged Tumor. I feel so *old* all of a sudden. I just can't handle two weeks in Pensacola with all those redneck teen-agers."

It struck me then, looking at him, how bright my brother Fig is, and how pretty: thick head of shaggy brown hair, unobtrusive nose, fair skin—not like me, with my greenish skin, Lebanese beak, and capped teeth (from a car wreck I had three years ago). Also, at twenty-one, I am losing my hair.

"What is it?" I said to Fig. "The hand?"

His face reddened. "Don't start that crap," he said, and for a minute I thought he was going to throw his beer at me. Then he said, "No, you're right, I guess. Maybe by graduation night I might feel more like going."

"You deserve it. Twelve years of school without a break, except summers, and even then you always had summer school or that job bagging groceries at Jitney."

"I deserve it," said Fig.

I got up and bought us a couple more beers. When I came back to the table, Fig said, "What I really deserve is a break from Mom. She's driving me nuts."

"She's worried," I said.

"You're telling me." Fig slapped the table with his bandaged hand; he winced but kept talking. "She's eaten up with it. All that staring and crying, I mean. I can't stand it."

"Look," I said, "it's not like she's all worked up over nothing. She's got a right to be concerned."

"I know, I know," Fig said. "She's waiting for some God-almighty sign that I'm O.K.—that I haven't let this thing kill my lust for life and all that. Well, let me tell you something, brother. People don't lose their lust for life. Anybody who says they've lost it never had it in the first place. I know dozens of people not even out of high school yet who spend all their time feeling sorry for themselves. They think they know what grief is all about, but all they're really getting into is self-pity. Why can't they get their grieving done and then get the hell on with business? You know?"

I just nodded. It always embarrasses me a little when Fig goes off on one of his tangents. I find his logic hard to fault, but he has this way of making me feel like *I'm* the real teen-ager in the family.

Finally, I managed to say, "Fig, why have you been locking yourself in the bathroom all week?"

He looked at me for a few seconds. He drained his beer glass, belched, and made a funny noise in his larynx. "What do *you* think?" he said. "I'm trying to get used to looking at this thing before I have to unveil it to the world. You tell Mom I'll be just fine if she'll let me alone. All that crying bugs the hell out of me."

"Have you shown her what it looks like yet?" I said.

"You know she doesn't want to see it. Go start the car. I've gotta stop by the bathroom."

I finished my beer and went out and stood in the parking lot waiting for Fig. It had stopped raining. Spring rains in Mississippi tend to be torrential but brief, like a seizure of passion. The air smelled clean; it had cooled off some, and I was glad of it, though I knew it wouldn't last. Still no moon, but you had the feeling the remaining clouds might disintegrate at any minute and there you'd see it, close enough to touch. I walked over and sat on the fender of the VW. I thought of how, only a week ago, Fig and I had sat around the kitchen talking over beer and grilled-cheese sandwiches. He was supposedly on his way out to the strobe-lit Galaxy Disco to move among his high-school friends, and I had nothing to do, as usual. He didn't want to go. I knew this and I was trying to take advantage of it; I needed the company. I'd stopped out of college for a spell and didn't have a job. Summer was on its way, and I was consoling myself with the thought of going to Alaska, where I'd heard you could make big bucks working in the fish canneries. I thought I might even try to get on with one of the logging companies there. I knew that the smell of dirt and dead fish wouldn't really bother me.

I stood there at the stove, grilling up sandwiches and offering them to Fig, because I wanted him to stay and talk to me. I basked in the accumulation of smoke and grease. It was Sunday night, but Fig said the seniors fancied themselves big shots now, what with graduation coming up and all, so they were voicing their maturity to the parental world by staying out all night not just on Friday and Saturday but on school nights, too. He found that pretty amusing, but he didn't want to come off as a lily-white snob, he said, so he promised to join them in their revelry now and then. Tonight was supposed to be one of those times, but I knew Fig hated the Galaxy Disco, with its beer-soaked carpet and poisonous men's room and its mammoth, homicidal bouncers. I figured I was doing him a favor keeping him occupied at home. I plucked another Busch from the icebox and went to fixing myself a sandwich. Fig had eaten his last one and stood near the kitchen door, looking as if he might be ready to leave. I grabbed the sandwich off the spatula and tossed it to him on the counter, saying, "Wait! Wait! You haven't finished your supper yet!"

Fig shook his head. "My gut feels like an oil drum," he said. "But I was hungry."

"You were hungry," I said. "You needed something to go on. A person can't just go out dancing and drinking on an empty stomach."

I was wiping the grease splotches off the stove with a sponge when Fig plunked the car keys down on the counter and said, "I think I'm gonna stay here. My stomach hurts and it's going on nine already."

I offered him the roll of Tums I always carry around for heartburn.

"Nope," he said. "Here's the best medicine, right here, yes sir." He had got a lemon out of the box and commenced cutting it with a paring knife. "You really ought to get off those things," he said. "Here's the real sure-fire cure." He squeezed the juice of the lemon halves into a glass and held up the glass. "To life, and deliverance from the public schools!" he said, and downed the contents in one gulp. Then he grinned painfully and wiped his eyes on the sleeve of his shirt. "Good stuff, I'm telling you. You should try it."

I picked up one of the depleted lemon halves and dropped it in my shirt pocket, where some of the leftover juice seeped out and formed a small wet ring. "Gosh, thanks for the advice," I said to Fig. "Handy little items, aren't they?" This was the sort of dumb ironical episode Fig and I like to perform for each other's amusement.

"You smart-ass," he said, still grinning. "Give me that." And he went over to the sink and began stuffing the lemon remnants in the electric garbage disposal. Before he'd even got them in all the way, he flipped the switch and the motor started whirring, and I wish now with all my heart that I'd stopped him from doing the job backward like that—that I'd yelled, "No, Fig! Get it in all the way first and *then* turn the thing on." But I just stood there watching while the machine inside the drain made a snort and went on with its business, and Fig fell away from the sink saying "Heee" and leaned against the icebox for a moment. I watched him watch the blood spattering the floor, and then he hurried out of the kitchen and I heard a door slam.

He was only in the bathroom a couple of minutes. He'd tried to patch up the finger with a Band-Aid and Foille Ointment, and it hadn't done much good, of course. Dad came down and we wrapped Fig's hand up in a beach towel—it was the first thing I saw when I looked in the closet—and we drove right to Hinds General Hospital, where Dad nearly plowed the Impala through the emergency-room doors. There was so much blood we couldn't tell how serious the injury was, though we had a pretty good idea.

A garbage disposal isn't too skilled in matters of grace. I had a friend in school once who ate like that, all grunting, snarling mouth, and bits of food flying about the table.

In the waiting room, which was small and too bright and crowded with plastic plants, I felt numb, but Dad was pale and angry. He pulled at his beard as if he expected it to come off in his hand. He hollered at the receptionist, who kept shoving forms at him to fill out—I think he came close to slapping her—and when he and I were sitting alone over in a corner, he turned to me and said in a low, rasping voice, "You couldn't find the rest of it?"

His eyebrows were twitching, and I felt sort of hypnotized by them. "What rest?" I mumbled.

"Goddam it, didn't you *look?* You could have at least looked." He'd started shaking my arm. Just then, I noticed several other anxious faces across from us, and suddenly I felt responsible for the misfortunes of the whole world.

I stood up and moved a couple of steps away from him, but kept my voice low. "Dad, there's no way they could have saved anything. Think of what happened to Mom's wedding ring when it fell down in there."

"Don't you tell me about any goddam ring!" he shouted. "We're not talking about somebody's goddam ring here!" Then he jumped up and strode off toward the men's room.

When we finally got home from the hospital, Mom was back from her ballet class but she was still wearing her tights. We told her the news—the stupid accident, Fig's left index finger bitten down almost to the second knuckle; everything taken care of, though, everything O.K. They were keeping him at the hospital overnight to pump some blood back into him. Mom didn't bat an eye. She just went upstairs and came down with a little overnight bag and said she was going out there to stay with him. I told her they said he'd be all right by himself, or else Dad and I would've stayed with him and called from the hospital, but she was already out the door. Then Dad went up to his room, and I got in bed and lay there thinking about Mom and Fig, about how right it was for her to be the one who went to stay with him. Dad and I might have broken down and cried right in front of him while he was trying to rest. Mom and Fig were both strong; they were the doers of the family. Dad and I were the wimps.

Lying in bed, I thought of how he and I used that word—

wimp—to describe our former neighbor Mr. Hackett, who last year moved his family up to Connecticut to find a better school for his emotionally disturbed son, Larry. As far as I could tell, Mr. Hackett never held a job. He was always taking Larry off on long trips or coming over to bug Dad and me while we were working in the yard. We'd laugh at the old guy once he was out of earshot.

But lying in bed the night Fig got hurt, I felt sort of bad for ever having made jokes about Mr. Hackett. His view of what constitutes responsibility might be myopic, but I could not deny that he loves his son and would do anything in the world for him. I lay there thinking of Mom and Fig—of how they managed to do so well for themselves and still do a lot for others. It seemed to me they had both found their centers, as the saying goes, while Dad and I continued to thrash in a sea of disillusionment, Dad kidding himself that he was really going to leave the big, unsympathetic publishing company he's been with for fifteen years, and me a high-school—and now a college—dropout sitting around the house all day with nothing better to do than entertain big ideas of going off somewhere far away where, I tell myself, things will change, I will find my true calling, and everyone will say, "Yes, yes, we should have known he would become so great and do such remarkable things."

Dad and I were the true wimps. We were too helpless in our own lives to help anyone else. I kept thinking of Fig's accident and what an injury like that might have done to anyone (me or Dad, for instance) who didn't have Fig's—there's that word again—mettle. Before I fell asleep, I began to see that in the days to come it would be me and Dad who'd worry about Fig's guitar playing and self-esteem and the rest of it, while Fig himself would go on living his life without a lot of dumb self-pity. He might even end up better for the experience.

He came home from the hospital the next day, and, sure, his face was a bit drawn—he was in a fair amount of pain, after all—but somehow he was *all right.* Of course he was a bit moodier than usual, and he did spend those long periods locked in the bathroom, as I have said, but I knew already that what he told me the week after the accident, when we were sitting in the Red Bar, was true: he understood that he had to embrace this thing himself. This would take time and probably some long sober, private looks, with the bandages pulled back and nobody else around—but it would be only a matter of weeks, I knew, before he could wear his injury in front of the world. And I knew he meant to wear it without shame—not an easy thing, when you think of all the teen-age girls out there who'd wilt into the upholstery if the hand that pawed them in the back seat was missing half a finger.

I myself once shook hands with an amputee, an old Army friend of my father's who came for dinner with us. I recall noticing his hair, which was thick and unnaturally yellow, as he stood in the front hallway hugging Dad. Then he turned to me and said, "My God! This must be the oldest. When I last saw you, boy, you were still yelling and kicking in the high chair." He put out his hand. I was still interested in his hair and I just took his hand in an automatic fashion. Then I felt the clumsy grip, the odd contour of his hand. I looked down and saw that two of the three fingers were missing—middle and ring, the third and fourth digits. He wore a ring on the pinky. I didn't want to stare, but I couldn't help it. By this time, he'd withdrawn his hand; it hung by his side. I kept on staring and staring, and everybody just stood there in the hall noticing me notice the ruined hand. It reminded me of those dog-shaped shadows you make on the wall by holding out your hand and folding back your forefinger. My dad used to scare me with those hand shadows when I was a kid.

Anyway, I spent the rest of the day hiding out in my room, and I didn't come to the supper table until the friend left. Dad didn't speak to me at first, and when he did he said, "He's one of my oldest friends, and you have to go and make him feel like a crip. I didn't realize your mother and I had raised such an insensitive bastard." But later on that evening he knocked on my door and asked if I wanted to eat some popcorn and watch the Wednesday-night movie with him. They were showing Hitchcock's "The Birds," he said—one of our favorites.

Dad and I have had our share of squabbles, but there is a kindred feeling between us. Watching him sometimes, in all his petty cheerlessness—he never really seems to *enjoy* anything—I'm bothered by the notion that I'm glimpsing a sneak preview of my own adulthood. It also strikes me at times that when he observes me closely he's viewing home movies of when he was a kid. With Mom and me, it's more a case of mutual admiration, I guess. We're different, and I like to think it's the differences we respect each other for. She has a robust personality, while I have a sullen nature that tends to mark me as a social outcast but nonetheless buys me huge blocks of time to myself, which Mom envies. "Never enough privacy!" she often says. "Never enough time alone to get anything done." On the other hand, she is able to react emotionally in very decisive ways. She is angry, sad, happy, etc., without effort. Like Dad, I tend toward depression—depression, as I'd define it, being a confusion of emotions so severe as to leave you paralyzed, powerless to act. Mom doesn't have this problem, and, for that matter, neither does Fig.

But then, Fig is in a class by himself. He's able to hold back a reaction to something for a long time, without letting it muddle him up. He has a way of needing to get acquainted with a thing before he can decide how he feels about it. I've seen him withhold judgment about the most obvious fool and then, after you thought the verdict on the moron was widely agreed upon, he'll come out and say that person is truly all right. Other times, he'll call up a friend after an hour's deliberation and say he feels it's high time they terminate their relationship. As I've said, it was going to be just a matter of time before Fig learned to accept the mangled finger as just another part of his body. You may say half a finger isn't so much to lose, but I'm convinced it would be exactly the same if Fig had lost a whole hand, or even an arm or leg.

Driving home from the Red Bar that Sunday night, I asked Fig if he was worried about what might happen to his guitar playing. Without giving him time to answer, I said "Fig, you're such a goddam good player, this thing'll probably make you even better."

He said he hadn't even thought about it—"I take one thing at a time, don't you know that?"—and I knew he was telling the truth. "You're swerving all over the place," he said. "Pull over and let me drive." Then he reached over and turned the windshield wipers off. "You're wasted," he said gently.

"I am not," I said, but I pulled over. I always have to drink three times as many beers as Fig when we go out. It takes me that many to loosen up to where I can talk straight with him. Sober, I sometimes feel like an exposed lizard in his presence.

When we got home from the Red Bar, the house was all dark except for a lamp in the living room. I flipped on half a dozen downstairs lights and went to rummaging in the icebox; Fig sat down at the counter and watched. "Hey, hey," I said, offering him a pot of congealed-looking potato soup from a forgotten supper. "Want some?"

"God, no," said Fig. "Sh-h-h, wait. Hear that?"

Dad was snoring foghorns upstairs, as usual.

"That's pathetic," I said. "He's really gotten worse the last year or so."

"No. Listen." Fig's good hand was flapping, signalling for silence.

I set the pot on the counter and kept still a second. Then I heard it—Mom's voice above us, muted as though through a handkerchief.

"Oh, Christ, this is ridiculous," I said. "You think she's been crying ever since we left the house?"

"That's not crying I hear," said Fig. "Just listen a minute."

I went and stood in the dining room, looking at Fig through the doorway as I cocked an ear toward the ceiling.

Fig whispered, "Don't you hear it? She's saying something."

I heard her voice—the sound of the words—though I couldn't make out the actual words themselves. "Maybe she's on the phone," I said.

Fig's voice rose to a point between hoarse whisper and shout. "Man, that's *my* room! There's no phone up there."

Fig got to the top of the stairs first. He stopped and pointed toward his bedroom. The door was shut and there wasn't any light leaking out from under it—the way it usually looks when I can't sleep and go up to there to visit. He always keeps his door shut at night, and I can tell by the light if he's asleep or awake. One time, though, I did see the light on and went in and found him asleep in his clothes. He was lying half on, half off the bed, with beer on his breath. His mouth was partly open, and he was drooling all over the sheets. That was the only time I recall seeing him really wasted. I thought he looked positively graceful.

Fig was trying the knob. "Mom," he said keeping his voice low, slapping lightly at the door, "Mom, are you in there?"

I threw in my two cents' worth. "Mom? Is something wrong?"

Two cents was about all the effort I could afford to put into it; I was tired of all the crying and the locked doors. God damn it, I thought, everybody's hiding out around here except me. Fig I could forgive, but I could not understand this kind of behavior coming from Mom.

Now Fig rattled the door again, but there was no response. "Get a bobby pin and let's open it," he said.

I went and found one in a drawer in the bathroom. We got the door open and switched on the light. There wasn't anything unusual except for two open guitar cases sitting in the middle of the floor. Fig never left his guitars lying around when he went out. Fig was down on his hands and knees looking under the bed when I thought to open the closet door. It took a few seconds, but then I saw her, crouched among the boxes and hanging clothes, cradling a guitar in each arm. She was holding each one around the base of the neck—the black Les Paul and the sunburst Stratocaster—with a guitar resting against the outside of each knee and with the necks pointing up past her ears. The effect was of somebody trying to walk with stilts, only she was sitting down. A few of the boxes in the closet were open and old clothes and papers lay scattered around.

I bent down and slipped my arm around her and kissed her cheek. "Are you O.K.?" I said.

She just looked at me a moment. She hadn't been crying, as far as I could tell. By now, Fig had squeezed into the closet, crowding the party quite a lot, and he was yammering, "What the hell's going on? Mom, why don't you get up from there and talk to us? What kind of stunt is this?"

"Shut up," I said to Fig, pushing him out of the closet. Then I turned the closet light on and closed the door halfway. I was all worked up. I'd never seen Mom do anything this weird before. More than anything else, I guess, I was embarrassed for all of us. I took the guitars from her and slid them through the crack in the door. "Fig," I said, "get rid of these damn things." Then I turned back to Mom and said, "Ready to come out?"

Mom was holding on to my wrist. I thought she wanted me to help her up, but she pulled my face down next to hers and whispered, "Make him get rid of them, please. Maybe you could sell them?"

"What?" I said. I peeked out the closet door. Fig didn't seem to have heard. He was too busy trying to put his guitars away with one hand. I turned back to Mom.

She went on whispering. "I just can't stand the thought of him trying to play after what's happened," she said. "He'll never be any good again. It would break my heart to hear him groping. Oh, my baby!" Her voice was starting to crack.

Well, even all the crying incidents since the accident hadn't prepared me for this. For a minute there, I felt frightened, seeing my mother all unravelled. Then it changed, all at once, and her behavior seemed somehow to correspond with my own feelings. It was as if I was having some weird kind of shift. I helped her up from the floor and pressed my face in the crook of her neck. "Mom," I said (I was crying now), "I feel the exact same way. It's a terrible thing that's happened to Fig. It's permanent. Our family will never be the same."

Fig shoved his way into the closet. "What the hell are you two *doing* in here?" he said.

Mom fell upon him, making anguished sounds. Fig stood still and let her hug him, but he wore a pained expression. Then when he saw *I'd* been crying, he really looked disgusted. "Oh, God," he said. "Not you, too."

Mom said, "No, no," in a calmer voice. We'd drifted out of the closet by this time and she was standing in the middle of the room. Fig sat down on the bed. "No, Fig," Mom went on, "it's my fault. I was looking through your old clothes and school papers and I got all sentimental. It won't happen again."

"It got to me, too," I added. "Boy, Fig, you were a hell of a cute kid."

Fig got up again and announced he was going to bed. "I've had enough of this goddam crying," he said.

"Hold on, there," said Mom. She'd regained her composure, and now she was in-control Mom again. "Listen, kiddo," she said to Fig, "you haven't brushed your teeth yet. I smelled your breath when I hugged you." She kissed him on the forehead and motioned to me, and we left the room. Fig shut the door on us as soon as we got out in the hall. "Go to bed, you two," he called through the door. "Get some rest."

Mom and I stood there in the hall smiling at each other. "That smart-aleck, he's just as bad as ever," she said. I could hear the relief in her voice.

"He's a sweetheart, all right," I said.

I was hoping Mom might want to stay up awhile and talk. I still felt funny about what had just happened in Fig's room, but I think I felt somehow that it was too important to just throw it aside and forget about it. "Why don't I go down and make us some coffee?" I said.

Mom just touched my cheek and said, "Fix some for yourself if you want, honey. I've got conferences all day tomorrow and yoga class meets tomorrow night. Remind me to give your hair a little trim next weekend. It looks like a rat's nest. Tonight I told your dad how nice his beard looked, and he went in the bathroom and came out with it shaved off. Too much going *on* around here."

"Figures," I said.

Her face grew sad. "I think it was because of the gray. It wasn't there the last time he grew one—at least not so much of it—though I'm always saying I love salt-and-pepper beards best."

"Me, too," I said. I held a finger to my lips and nodded toward their bedroom door. "He's gotten worse, hasn't he?"

We stood there listening to Dad's labored breathing—snores you could measure with a seismograph—and for a moment we both smiled. Then Mom said, "You see how much weight he's put on this year. He can barely keep his jeans on, for the paunch. I tell him he ought to come to ballet with me sometimes, just for the warmup exercises, or at least yoga classes, but he laughs." She hugged me.

I drew back and leaned awkwardly on the balcony railing. There had been a last flicker of desperation in that hug—I could feel it—and now it made me self-conscious. The time for all that had passed; we'd both withdrawn to our regular old roles. I noticed that Mom's face still looked sad, but the strong jaw and confident eyes had been restored, and I knew there'd be no more awkward self-exposures that night. "Well," I said.

"Well, good night," she said. "Love you, dear."

"Love you," I said.

She went into the room and closed the door. I flipped off the hall lights and was about to go downstairs when I noticed the moon I'd hoped for had finally come out. There is a little cubbyhole on the landing, in which is fitted a bookcase and a tall, narrow window, and the whole little niche was so lit up that at first I wasn't entirely sure it was the moon's doing at all but maybe was caused by a new street light I hadn't noticed before. But I stood at the window and craned my neck around until I found the moon. It was partially hidden by some big pine trees in our yard but still visible—huge and white and verging on, but not quite, perfectly round, just about the way I'd imagined it. I almost decided to go sleep out on the deck, but when I put my hands on the glass I could feel the heat of the outdoors pulsing in my fingertips. It's not a pleasant sensation, the way a hot, still Mississippi night can make you aware of your own blood coursing through your limbs and pounding in your ears. Three years ago, when I was eighteen, I lay in bed at Hinds General Hospital for six weeks and had that feeling every night. I'd gotten messed up in that car wreck and I'd lost pints of blood and broken all kinds of bones, but, except for the capped teeth and a couple of small scars on my neck where they had to rebuild my jaw, I now look about the same as before. Just older.

Standing there between the closed doors of my brother's and parents' rooms, I tried to imagine how I would have stood up to a more obvious, permanent injury—an eye blinded, a lost finger, or a whole leg lost on the operating table, like the girl down the hall from me at Hinds General, who'd been in a much worse wreck and kept getting skin grafts for her busted-up leg. They took skin from the other, good leg, from her side, her upper arms, and even her buttocks, and they took pieces of bone from the most unlikely places, but the leg got infected and had to come off. She was a good-looking girl, a year or two younger than me; she'd been driving a Triumph Spitfire, and a cement truck ran a red light and hit her. She still sends me postcards sometimes, from her new home in Golden, Colorado.

I stood there on the landing, inside the narrow shaft of moonlight, and I tried to imagine carrying on if any part of me were mutilated. All I could conjure up was a bleak picture of me packing my bags and waving goodbye to the world of happy, ironical humans, and limping off to join the rest of my vegetal kind. No more beer and good talk with Mom and Dad and Fig outside on the deck in the summer; they would only look at me across the rims of their beer cans and realize that there were certain things—things pertaining to the world of whole, active humans—that I'd never be able to share with the rest of the family again.

But if there is another effect nighttime often has on you, it is to make you feel more helpless and cut off from everyone than you really are. Standing there, I could imagine Fig saying something like that—not calling me a coward or anything but merely scolding me for speculating so wildly on things I don't know much about. I could almost hear his voice saying, "Hey, I'm *telling* you, it's not nearly so awful as you make it out to be."

Oh, but isn't it, Fig, I thought.

The light was off in Fig's room now—he'd slipped off to bed without brushing his teeth—but for an instant I wanted to burst in on him and find him lying awake worrying about the things I felt he should be worrying about. It seemed that if I could catch him at it I'd be relieved and could sleep well myself. But I stayed fixed to my spot by the window, watching the moon move slowly out from behind the pine trees, and listening to the patterned rising and falling of Dad's absurd snoring, which sounded something like the cadence of life itself. I felt so lulled by these things that I almost stayed all night out on the landing, where I was. But at some point I heard something like the sound of a door closing and then the lock being turned, and I went to bed that night convinced—though I've never asked her—that Mom had been standing out in the hall watching me.

When the Morning Comes

Don Lee Keith

If you stand on the ledge in front of Choctaw Cave in the winter, when the trees are bare, and look across the creek bottom fields toward the west, you can see as far as our house, and if the wind is just right, sometimes a little smell of smoke from the chimney gets as far as the cave, nearly a mile away.

I spent all day yesterday in the cave, me and Azu Benton. His favorite thing in the world is cornbread with bacon grease. I took a fruit jar full for him, and three biscuits and sausage and two boiled eggs for me, and some matches.

Sometime in the late afternoon (I can't always tell sun time in the winter because the cold squeezes the daylight out of the days until there's not much left) I saw her coming across the bottom. Old Dora. I watched her from the time she got out of the plum thicket by the side of the smoke house, all the way, and it took her a long time. She had to be careful not to fall, picking through the dried-up cotton stalks and holding on to the silver-topped staff my grandpapa left her in 1937. And the closer she got, with the cold-purple clouds and icy sun behind her, the longer her shadow got.

I didn't want to see her, and I didn't want her to come, but I knew she would, all the time, and it was funny she had waited so long, knowing surely where I was. Once I thought about hiding in the cave, but it wasn't so deep she couldn't have found me, and besides, it was colder the farther back you went, away from my fire by the ledge. Last spring, I came across the carcass of a calf back there while I was hunting arrowheads. Must have froze to death, Old Dora said.

Everybody in and around Spinyarn calls her Old Dora. She's been old forever and tall as a pine sapling, and nearly as straight too, because she says when you start bending over in the back, your time is nigh, and her's ain't. She sleeps with a big board between the springs and mattress and won't have a featherbed, even when it snows and ices over. She's carried that silver-topped staff everywhere since Pappaw died four years ago, on my fifth birthday.

It's funny, how for all your life you like somebody, maybe you even say you love them when they ask you, and then all of a sudden, when you don't want to see anybody, not even them, and they come on when they know you feel like this, you suddenly don't like them even a little bit. And you wonder why you ever thought, much less said, you did. That's how I felt yesterday about her coming, and I knew she'd come, but when I looked out at the fields and there she was, I just didn't want her to be there. So I hugged Azu Benton tight. Dogs don't pester you and tell you things you don't want to know or bother you. Not Azu Benton.

Azu Benton and I found each other a winter three years ago, down by the railroad tracks that run alongside our place on the west. He had a broken leg. I figure somebody mean must have thrown him off the Rebel, which had just chugged past when I saw him. He didn't holler or bite when I picked him up and took him home, and when I tied a straight stick to his hurt leg with rags soaked in liniment, and made him stay in the wood bin for six days (Old Dora said that was enough), he didn't whimper. He's still got a little limp on that side.

When Old Dora was nearly to the ledge, the sun was getting ready to set, and it was shining on the ball of the staff, enough to blind abody, mainly because she keeps that silver ball rubbed with ammonia to make it shiny. She stopped and called up to me, but I didn't answer. Then she climbed up the steep path to the ledge and hollered again, "Kip, ooooohhh Kip." I didn't say a word. Her hollering made a little echo in the cave, and it caused Azu Benton to look around and fidget a little, but when she came up on the ledge, he just sat there in my lap and wagged his tail.

Then she started: "You've been out here all day long, Kip. One more death of cold you'll get if you don't mind. It's one thing to run off if it'll do any good, but it don't mean nothing when it's not helping the situation."

Situation is one of Old Dora's two big words and she uses it whenever she can. The other is diagnose.

Now that she was standing almost over me, the flickers from the dying fire made her eyes kind of sparkle, and her eyes seemed the only thing there was to her, since that was all you could see, she is so dark. Except the silver-topped staff. But I didn't say anything.

Old Dora doesn't wear glasses. Once a welfare woman came around, wanting her to go have her eyes checked in Bedford, saying the government would foot the bill. But Old Dora pointed to a barn roof sign a long ways down the road, and told the welfare woman to read it. When she couldn't, Old Dora, said "Jefferson Island Salt." Then the woman left. I know somebody had told Old Dora what the sign said, because she can't read in the first place. But she can see.

If Old Dora were a man, she would look like Goliath, except black. And she may be old, but she's strong. Last summer, a big Dominecker rooster tried to spur her in the leg when she went out to gather the eggs, and she took him up and wrung his neck right there in the yard.

By this time, she had reached down and was tugging at my shoulder. "Get up from there, boy. It's liable to snow tonight. Clouds look it. And it's about sundown already. Come on home. This place ain't no place to be when you've got a warm bed. Don't act like this."

But I wasn't going, didn't mean to. "Leave me alone," I said, and snatched my collar back.

She stood off a little and put one hand on her hip, the other holding the staff. "It ain't a purty thing for you to take, Kip, and it ain't hard for me to know that. Ain't hard for nobody to know it, but that's it. And it may be rough for me to throw it at you like that, but that's the only way of me letting you know. I spent the whole day slobbering 'round that house. I've done it, I've told you what happened, and now you've got to face up."

Suddenly I was screaming. I wanted her to hush, to go away, to leave me and Azu Benton alone. That's what I wanted. "Get away from me," I yelled. "Get on back to the house and leave me alone. You lied. Everything you say is a lie." It just came out like that, and I kept on. "You've always been a liar. You said my Easter ducks would hatch."

She took the hand off her hip and dug it into her apron pocket, for nothing. "Kip, it's about time you started acting like a man," she said.

Well, when she said that, something took hold of me, because that's the meanest thing anybody can say to you. So I thought of the meanest thing I could say, and said it. "Go on off in the woods, you nigger." I yelled it my loudest, and for a minute, the words just hung there in the air, like maybe they'd frosted over between her and me. Like something you could touch and look at, and I wanted right then to reach out and grab them. I really could hear them all over again and again, and I knew she could, because that was the first time I'd ever said anything like that.

And then the words faded, and I was sitting there with Azu Benton in my lap, and her staring down at me.

It might have been a few seconds, but then again, it might have been longer that I sat there with my fingers held still on Azu Benton's ears. He didn't move, and I didn't, and she didn't, but I knew she was looking at me.

The fire crunched, and one of the sticks shifted, sprinkling little orange-red coals out like a baby Roman candle on Christmas, and Old Dora said in her low, Bible voice, "Now Kip, I want you to hold yourself still. Don't move, and don't jump. Because over to your side there's a snake. He's come out for this fire, I guess. But hold still."

I tried not to move. Even though she says Azu Benton can't know what people are saying, he can. Because right then, he wheeled around in my lap and made a jump toward the ledge, between me and the snake. His little brown and white spotted hind leg gave way a little, but he jumped the same, and the snake, coiled up about two yards from us, slid out of its winding like a Chinese blow-out that whistles and coils back so you can puff again.

I just sat there, like when you're in a thunderstorm and lightning strikes a nearby tree, you're not sure if it's hit you or something else, so you sit there, not moving. And when you know you're not hit, you're alive again.

When I got my life back, Azu Benton was jumping in the air, turning flips and running sky-winding down through the field. Old Dora was going after that snake with the staff like it was about to bite Jesus, and when she swung, she usually hit. She nearly got me, even, when I ran out of the cave and into the field after Azu Benton.

It was the fastest I'd ever seen him run. Like he was doing, he could have won the dog races in West Memphis, just trotting. But he was flinching back his neck and throwing his body up sideways and then running a piece more, and every time I'd just about get to him, he'd go into another running fit and go faster than ever. I had to squint my eyes to see, it was getting so dark now, but his white spots would flare up from the rotting cotton stalks and he'd be gone again, with me right after him.

On and on he went, until he reached the creek. He didn't even pay attention to the bridge, which was in plain sight. He just gave one big flounce up and fell down on the creek bank, shivering like a live chill. When I got him in my arms, trying to cover him with my wool coat and tuck his tail inside, he'd break out in a shake for a minute, and then he was still as ice, not a hair or whisker moving, not grunting or growling like he sometimes does when he is asleep by me at night. And I thought when he was like that, so still, with me sitting there on the creek bank holding him, that he was gone, until he took another quivering spell.

The moon came up. I don't think it should have been there so early, but then I hadn't looked at the almanac. But it was there coming almost as fast as the sun had gone. Not real bright, like it is sometimes so you can go frog-gigging, but a soft light last night, almost like a candle with a round flame burning without flickering so you don't know it's a candle at all. That's the way it was.

Sometimes I'd pull open my coat to look at Azu Benton. His eyes would always be open, walled back in his head, and I'd pull them down and hold them shut, and hold him tighter to make sure he was breathing.

His nose, just where the hair begins at the top, had two little blood marks. I wiped them off with my chin.

Once I thought about praying. But I'd tried that yesterday morning.

Then, standing over me like a live oak, towering up like a church steeple, was Old Dora. She was wiping the silver knob of the staff on her petticoat, but she wasn't talking. She reached around with her free hand and untied her apron. I could see it was the calico one she made from quilt scraps, and she lowered it to me by one streamer. It went around Azu Benton twice.

Then we began the walk across the second half of the bottom, silent. Old Dora held her heavy coat together with one hand and made her way through the scratching, hard, empty-bolled stalks with the staff. I counted the steps and it seemed that every twenty or twenty-one steps I made, Azu Benton would take to jerking for a second. Not long, not nearly long, but enough to say he was still there, like just for the reason of letting me know.

Old Dora had begun to sing.

Bye and Bye, When the Morning Comes
When the Saints of God are Gathered Home,
We Will Tell the Story, How We've Overcome
We Will Understand it Better, Bye and Bye

I don't know if the song has other words. She sang the same ones over and over, but they always seemed to sound different. Her singing made it easier to walk. If you stepped every time you were supposed to, keeping time to the song, you got there faster it seemed, and so by the time she'd sung it six times, we were at the plum thicket.

When the winter night winds blow through the thicket and you're standing there, it sounds like an army of bamboo whistles all at once. Shrill, high-pitched. When I was little, they told me it was the heaven fairies dancing on the branches.

In the kitchen, where the big stove fire was beginning to die down, the windows were all fogged up, and little driplets of water ran down and into each other.

Once or twice, while I was holding Azu Benton in the rocking chair, he took a little jerking spell to say he was still there, but he didn't jump or care when we poured half a cup of meat grease down his throat. Old Dora says that will do the trick.

I wanted him to sleep in my bed, or at least in the house, but Old Dora said he wouldn't want to do that; being sick, he'd want to be out by himself. Nobody wants to have somebody else sleeping beside him when he's not feeling good.

She went and got a patchwork quilt out of the bottom of the hall tree (it was one of our best and newest and I didn't know how come she'd use it for a dog) and lit the light in the smoke house. I followed her out there and watched as she took all the stovewood out of one side of the wood bin, piling it some on the floor, and made a little bed.

After he was bedded down, not seeing backwards or forward, not even caring to, I knew we'd have to leave him, alone in the smoke house in the wood bin, the first time he'd been left there since he'd come to our house with his bad leg. And when I pulled the quilt up tighter and scratched his ears like I do every night at bedtime, he said good-bye by wagging his tail through the quilt.

Inside, near the big open hearth in the parlor, Old Dora sat in the big rocker, like she does every night, and she opened the big leather Bible. I've wondered why she does this. She knows that I know she can't read, and what she says is sometimes even made up.

I laid on the rug in front of the cracking fire that was slowly going under, and knew that I'd left Azu Benton's cornbread and bacon grease in the cave.

And yea, though I walk through the shadow of death
I shall fear no evil, for thou art with me,
thy rod and thy staff, they comfort me.
Thou preparest a table before me in the presence
of mine enemies . . .

And I saw again in the dim light, on the wall, in a frame, the sampler. Old Dora said it is done without a single mistake. My mother did it. It was the last thing she did. Did it, they said, while I was on my way. Tiny little stitches nobody but her could have seen to make.

Surely goodness and mercy
shall follow me all
the days of my life . . .

And there on the mantle was my daddy, framed with an oval and some song or prayer and a flag beneath the picture.

I was in Old Dora's lap then, like I was when I was younger, when there was no need to be a man, and I was remembering a poem the teacher read, about some boy and his mother. They had no money and were starving, and he was in her lap, being rocked, and it was getting colder and colder, and the wind like a wolf's head howled about the door. They burned up the furniture to stay alive.

The rocker had a creak when it went back and forth. Not a mean creak, but soft and nice and gentle, and when I closed my eyes, Old Dora's bosom was like a pillow.

When I woke up this morning, I was in my bed. Today is Tuesday. It must be, because yesterday was Monday in the cave, and the day before was Sunday. That was the day it happened.

This morning when I opened my eyes, it was way after sunup. Mrs. Oakley and Mrs. Turner woke me, talking in the kitchen. Mrs. Oakley said she'd brought a dozen stuffed eggs and Mrs. Turner a sweet potato custard. It's always struck me as funny, why people and neighbors always have to bring things to eat on times like this.

Old Dora was banging around the pans, not that she was cooking anything. But she always does that when anybody comes in. Opening cabinets, arranging skillets, banging pots together.

Then I heard Mrs. Oakley speak. Hushed, of course, but loud enough for me to hear. "I say, Old Dora, it's a pure shame and pity, all that before, and now all this."

And Mrs. Turner said, "What's to become? I told my husband this morning when I first heard it, what's to become?"

The sun is shining through the window on the carved wooden turtle on my dresser table. It has "Kip" carved on its back shell. My daddy sent it to me from Honolulu. He had a native carve it. And by the side of the mirror is a picture of his ship. Blue grey and shiny. He sent that too.

On the floor at the foot of my bed is a brown box, tied with heavy cord. It has funny looking stamps on it. Tomorrow is my birthday. Ninth. And on the box is written in black letters, "Do Not Open Until December 10."

I can hear Old Dora sighing loud now, like she does when she's burned a pie crust or scorched one of her petticoats on the ironing board. Like someone not near, she is talking to another someone far away, not those women in the kitchen. She said, "It's not only them across the waters, that's plenty. But now it's the dog, too."

I'm going to lock my door so nobody can get in, ever again.

Wild Rabbits

John Little

I DIDN'T START STUMP SITTING in the daytime until Mama whipped me for scaring her last Christmas. I didn't scare her on purpose. It was because Grandpaw wasn't there to be Santa Claus and read to us. Daddy said there wasn't no such thing as Santa Claus except for white children and gave us all a scout knife and told us to keep them sharp to cut polebean poles and didn't read us nothing. Then he took a drink and gave S T a rap across the legs and said next peep he heard out of us we'd get the same.

So I went around behind the shed and played dead. Pretty soon I heard Willie ask where I was and in a minute Mama was hollering for me but I just lay there. I peeped through the crack and saw Robert crawl up under the house looking for me, then Percy B was coming towards the shed. I shut my eyes thinking how sorry they would be that I was dead and how happy they would be when I wasn't. But Percy went on by and hollered after me in the woods.

Then the ground started getting cold and I had to move out of the shade. It was better in the sun and I wondered if Grandpaw felt this warm, but then the sand and weeds started itching my arms. I finally gave up and scratched and got the idea about the knife. I ran my thumb down the blade. It wasn't sharp but the point was. I stuck it through my shirt under my armpit and crawled out where they could find me with my mouth open in the sun thinking what they'd say. Once a chicken came by and gave my foot a peck but I just kept on being dead. I was thinking about how it'd be at the funeral with them crying and singing songs and talking about how I looked just like Grandpaw when I heard them come around the corner of the house. I opened one eye a little and saw Percy B and S T staring at me and closed it back.

"What's old clubfoot done now," Percy asked. S T didn't answer and I knew it was working. I heard them standing over me and shut my eyes tighter and stopped breathing.

"I don't see no blood," S T said in a minute. I had forgot about that.

"He's possuming," Percy said. "Stomp his foot."

I knew he'd pick my bad one and it was hard to keep from moving it but I didn't. But S T was barefoot too so it didn't hurt much and I just let my leg roll and my jaw go slack. They were quiet, then S T said we better get Mama. I was running out of air and took a deep breath when I heard the door slam. Then it slammed again and she was coming.

"George Byron Johnson, get yo self up off that ground before you catch yo death o cold." I kept dead.

"Byron?" she said, and I felt her hand on my arm and knew it was working. Then I heard Percy say move Mama and smelt the cow dookey and opened my eyes just before it hit me in the face. It was fresh and sticky and that's when I started coming here to stump sit in the daytime.

The stump is hollow and where I keep the powder and the letter. I remembered it from rabbit hunting and come a different way every time so I won't make a path that my brothers can follow to find me. She took my knife away after I hit Percy after he hit me with the dookey. It was the first time I ever hit anybody and made me sad. Not because he hit me back, because he hit me all the time. I hit him twice.

I used to like rabbit hunting because it was about the only time Daddy would ever be with all of us. Which wasn't for long because by the time we crossed two fields and a fence and a creek they'd be so far ahead I just could see the light. Sometimes I'd smell where they'd been by where they dumped the carbide. They never waited for me and I never knew why Daddy always made me come except he says when he takes his boys hunting he takes all his boys hunting. I love not being left out, but it seemed like a waste of walking for me since it was all I could do to catch up in time to limp behind them on the way back.

Not that there's any danger of them losing me because my brothers make such a racket tromping through the woods that both me and the rabbits can hear them a mile off. Which is most likely why we never kill any rabbits. Which don't seem to bother Daddy or my brothers. It's the spirit of the hunt that counts, Daddy says, him being out with his boys and such. Good soul-stuff, he'd say, and then say that was what black folk had to do with themselves because the white folk had forgotten how. And the only reason he always hunts by a melon patch or canebrake or neighbor's garden is because more rabbits feed there he says, but I didn't know at first what he meant by soul-stuff and thought it was the stuff we hauled out of the gardens and that was why he took us and what white folk had forgotten how. Mama said hush when I asked her.

We used to take the gun with us till Percy couldn't tell the cow's eye from a rabbit's and we might of lost a good neighbor if Daddy hadn't of made us drag it off and cover it with brush. And said he'd make it good the next day with Rody and maybe Simon. Rody is our plow mule and Simon was our dog.

Daddy named him like that. He named the other dogs Abe and Carver—like that. He was black and skinny, and Daddy named him Simon and gave him to me after he couldn't trade him because he was so skinny. And Simon is who got me started stump-sitting.

That was the best part of the hunt for me. After they'd get so far ahead I couldn't catch up I'd find this stump and sit and wait for them to come back and Simon would wait with me. And that's when the smells started coming. Daddy says I'm just lazy and next thing I'll be rooting around with my snout in the ground like our pigs. But that's not what I mean.

The kind of smelling I do is not with my nose. It's a feeling that comes when I close my eyes and breathe and smell the woods and the night and the carbide and the wild rabbits running, and I want to get up and run with 'em. Then I remember my foot and don't.

But I didn't start coming here in the daytime until Percy hit me with the dookey. Sometimes I just sit on the stump and look. I can see the pecan trees by the house from here but that always makes me think of Grandpaw so I usually get the letter and the powder out of the stump hole and lie down in the broom sage and read the letter and look at the powder. The writing is about worn off the bottle but I can still see Strychnine in red letters. And the skull with two bones crossed under it. One time I stuck my tongue to it and the powder got in my eyes when I breathed on it. It's brown and bitter.

But the letter is really why I stump sit in the daytime. It's worn too and faded brown from one time when the stump filled up with rain water but that doesn't matter because I can almost say it by heart. It's from Grandpaw to Daddy. After Daddy took him off.

Dear Son,

Sorry I haven't written till now but I wasn't sure you'd want to hear from me while I was convalescent. But that's historical now, I consulted to the Doctor last Wednesday and he was agreeable that I am improved enough to come home if you'll come after me. So I'm corresponding ahead so you and Molly can be getting my room ready. My same room with Byron and Baby John is all right by me since that's where my books and things are.

My room here is fine but it's not like home. The windowbars are crisscrossed and painted white like home windows but they don't fool me unless I'm playing. Which I do mostly now because I didn't like it here at first. But that was before I noticed the big pecan trees right outside my window when the wind was high and I could see the tops waving back and forth just like our orchard. I can stand on my tiptoes and pull up the window and interstice my elbows around the bars and suspend there and watch the squirrels playing in the boughs like I want to. My arms don't pain me like they did at first, and I've named the squirrels now, the big red fox squirrel after you and the little grey ones after the boys. I know it bothered you how I named the boys to be poets and it looks like I was wrong about them except Byron. That's why I named you Ben, too. But I won't bother you with that no more when I get back.

I can see the road from the window, too. The one you brought me here on. It's long and straight like a stretched-out black runner and the trees there are different. Water Oaks all the same height and lined up from each other on opposing sides like sentiments. Or sentinels. Sometimes my head gets fuzzy on words its been so long since I saw any and I don't have my dictionary here. Not a single squirrel nest in the oaks. Not fuzzy either, but old.

Looking at the road makes me dizzy and I have to lie down on my bunk but I still envision it and in a minute I'm right back up there staring at the road until they come sometimes and pry my hands loose and strap me to the bunk until I settle down in a little while and the Doctor comes and consults.

I don't mean to criticize, son, because I know you brought me here for my own betterment, but I can't help doubting how I'm different. I don't feel any different now than I ever did, just older. But when my neighbors have visitors, their families that come see them on Sundays—I used to wish for you to bring Byron but now that I am coming home I'm proud you didn't let him see me here and think you done right—they stop at my door and stare at me like Byron used to stare at the goldfish I brought him that stared back at him too. I can tell by their eyes they think I'm different and it makes a man sort of consider himself.

Like I used to catch myself sometimes in a conversation that had already happened. I'd be conversing along and suddenly it would come to me that I'd heard it all before but couldn't remember when or where. I'd concentrate but never be able to predict the next sentence but would recognize it as soon as it was conversed. Then, as soon as it hadn't bothered me long enough to forget it, the same conversation and sentence would happen again. I thought I was the only person in the world that could do it and when I asked Brother Pullium he looked scornful and said I was heathen if I believed in reincarnation.

All this might seem silly to you but the point is that just because a man thinks about reincarnation and poems don't mean he's different, does it? Think about how people must look to goldfish when they're staring at each other.

Anyway, that's all historical now. The Doctor told me on his rounds yesterday morning. I can come as soon as you come after me. I like the Doctor, he and the squirrels are my friends. He was almost to my room when this fellow across the hall in 202 that they just brought in last week shouts "Hey, Doc, look what I can do!" and jerks off his shoes and socks and counts his toes. I pitied the poor man, thinking he could prove his sanity by just counting. And then to make it worse he came out with nine. So imagine my indignity when the Doctor patted him on the head and said he was pleased with his progress and if he kept improving he could have ground privileges. Imagine that! All the time I'd spent telling the Doctor about myself and him telling me I'm improving. Then he ups and gives a complete nut ground privileges that can't even count. Well, I considered, if it works for him it should work for me.

I had my shoes off before he got there.

One, two, I started confidential . . .

three four five and changed feet . . .

six seven . . . slowing down to make it look good . . .

eightnineten I finished with flourishment.

He stood in the door with amazement on his face. So I asked him while he was still impressed if I could go home.

He nodded and started to pat me on the head but didn't and notated on his pad and smiled sadly when he left, like he hated to see me leave, and to tell the gospel, I'm probably going to miss him since he was the only real white folks that ever came to the colored ward.

But before I get there, I want you to know this is not the first time I've written you. But the other times it seemed like that conversation that had already happened. The Doctor says it's good therapeutics for me to write but truthfully I always feel worse but this is the first time I ever felt like finishing and mailing it. I just wanted you to know I don't hold it against you for bringing me here. And maybe if you knew these things you'd know none of us know how we look to each other, like goldfish. I'm not even sure that 202 didn't have a toe missing. So no hard feelings and the sooner you come after me the more I'd appreciate it.

Your father,
Coleman Johnson

P.S. Be certain to bring Byron with you. But let him wait at the road. Next Sunday is fine with me.

I always lie down in the broom sage after I read the letter. You can see little paths the rabbits make. Like tunnels. Sometimes I see rabbit pills where they stopped the night before where I lie down but I don't mind. Once a baby rabbit hopped right up to me and I could have caught it but I didn't.

Daddy doesn't know I have it or ever even read it. But I saw Grandpaw's writing soon as the mail rider left it and couldn't wait til Daddy got home to read it to us or let me read it or tell me what word he sent and how he was doing and when he was coming back to see us. But Daddy just sat there at the table with us standing around him and read it not looking up and walked outside and threw it in the garbage not saying a word and got mad and told me to hush when I asked when Grandpaw was coming.

But I got it after supper when I slopped the pigs and been coming here to read it ever since. At night sometimes I dream I'm a goldfish and a squirrel with yellow teeth gets after me but I play like a rabbit and outrun him. The saddest part I like best is when Grandpaw names the squirrels after us. He named me George Byron because of my foot. Daddy says it's a cleft foot like the Devil's but I consider it wouldn't be so bad if I wasn't always getting stone bruises from rabbit hunting. One time Grandpaw ordered me a special shoe but Daddy said I'd outgrow it in a year and need another and sent it back.

All of us are named like that. William Wordsworth and S. T. Coleridge and Robert Burns and Percy Bysshe on down to baby John Keats. Grandpaw did it because he was a teacher and wanted Daddy to write poems so he named him after one, but Daddy said word writing was all right for teachers but it didn't put meat on the table. So Daddy quit school and moved out here and married Mama and had us, then Grandpaw moved out here when he got old and started naming us to write poems.

He used to read his poem book to me more than my brothers because he said I was quicker in my head than on my feet. Daddy said nobody works with their feet anyway and he was going to put me up a shoe shine stand in Ludlow when I get big enough because everybody likes cripples. One time he called me a little nigger gimp when he caught me reading out of the poem book Grandpaw left when Daddy took him off.

He had a warm kind of smell. He'd get a croker sack and a poem book and me all in one arm and go to the orchard to gather pecans. And before the sack was half full he'd be sitting and reading with me in his lap. And when he was done, he wouldn't talk, just stare at the waving trees and squirrels until Daddy hollered at him.

And sometimes he still didn't hear until Daddy hit us with a pecan.

It's not the same when I read the book now. The words are still there, but the smell and the voice are gone. It's like one time when I saw our calf licking at a salt block that was all licked up, not getting any taste but not stopping because he knew the taste should be there. That's how it is now when I read. Because sometimes when Grandpaw read to me, I just smelled him and listened to his voice and not the words and knew I wasn't going to be traded or be a gimp nigger shoe shiner.

Daddy liked Grandpaw, Mama says. She knew by all the medicine he bought him when he started getting sickly.

Which is what I don't know.

Mama says Daddy took him off for his own betterment. But Grandpaw says he's just old and different. But Daddy got mad when I asked him and said it was because he was crazy and we couldn't afford the medicine anymore.

And what else I don't know is why we never did come see one another. Daddy said for a long time we'd go next Sunday. Then after we finally got the letter saying he was well Daddy would look mean when I mentioned it, and tell me I was getting as loony as Grandpaw and if I didn't quit reading his books he'd take me where he was when I got old enough. Which is when I started reading them more. But I didn't get old fast enough because before I did a letter came telling Daddy to come after him.

It was at the funeral where I first got the idea about the dog powder.

Not the powder either, but the feeling. He didn't have any smell there and still doesn't when I remember how he looked in the coffin with him not looking or talking or nothing, and now he's in the Pullium churchyard with not a sprig of grass growing, and knowing his voice won't be reading me poems anymore gave me the feeling.

But the reason I got the powder now is because of Simon. Mama said Daddy poisoned him because he sucked eggs, but all I know is that he was the only dog I ever liked and that was small enough to ride Baby John on. He had a good smell and was black and skinny and Daddy called him Simon and poisoned him because he sucked eggs and I liked him.

Anyway, when I found him with his throat all puffed and swollen, Mama pulled me away and said don't cry because he was going where Grandpaw was and would have golden eggs to suck. So that's why I got the rest of the powder down off the mantle and been keeping it in my stump: to take, so I can go where they are and be with them and maybe even run like wild rabbits.

The Great Speckled Bird

P. H. LOWREY

THE GOSPELERS APPEARED in Pochahontas on First Monday, though no one knew then what they were. This was June, the weather fine and hot, and ostensibly the three men came to hawk an herb remedy to the countrymen who gathered from four counties on the first Monday of each month to swap farm implements and hunting dogs and cows and worn-out shotguns and to socialize and lie a little. Niewatha Cardwell saw them when they turned their battered pickup and crazy lop-sided trailer into the square a little after seven in the morning. She always came in to do the week's shopping with her father, and while he was at the blacksmith's shop she waited for him in the only cool place in town, the shade of the courthouse elms. Not on the lounger's benches, where no lady would sit, but down on the retaining wall that ran square around the courthouse. Later cars would be nosed in here in a solid pack, and double parked, baking in the sun, but at that hour there were only a few. Niewatha sat quite still, content with the morning and the fine light breeze; maybe today her autographed photo of Ferlin Huskie would come. Because the pickup drew in only a few feet from her, when the two men climbed out stiffly it was her they asked where could they eat. They stood to stretch a little and look around at the sky, and though she watched them she did not think much about it then; except for the fact that neither of them was shaved they could have changed places with any of the men who were usually around the square. The older one finally walked over to where she sat, coming with a long easy spring, bending at the knees. He did not look at all like he did on the next Sunday, when they all three came stamping into the summer peace of Ebenezer Church, violating the shady cool like saints or avengers or an army; then they came striding as heavily as lions, with a curious and haggard light in their sea-blue eyes, singing their hymn to the harmonica and shouting volcanically and waving their rattlesnakes in the air like banners. But on that First Monday they looked like anybody.

"Hady," the tall man said, touching the brim of his black felt hat. "I wonder could you be kind enough to tell us what's a good place here to eat."

"The City Cafe's pretty good," she told him, and then, because he looked like her own people, added "but we mostly eat down at Miz Violet's." The man looked at her slowly and seemed to decide something.

"I reckon that'll be the place for us, then."

She told him how to go, pointing out the tiny tin sign that stuck out at right-angles from the small, steamy one-room store where Violet served boardinghouse style the same food she gave her husband: ham and bacon and biscuits and eggs set out in great platters on two wooden tables.

"I thank you right kindly," the man said, and touched his hat again. "We're right obliged to you." But he did not move away. Finally he said, "Hear tell you folks trade today." He had not looked directly at her since he first spoke.

"Yessir," she said, "down to the Jockey Yard, right across the highway. There's a sign there, and there'll be more men than to an election, nine or ten o'clock." But still he did not move away. He looked vaguely into the distance.

"You folks been gettin' good rain?" he asked after a minute.

"Too much, Daddy says. Says the weevils is already worse'n last year."

"Same further north," the man said, and turned to spit slow away from her, carefully. "Lord *will* arrange it His own way, though sometimes His way is hard to cipher out."

"Yessir, I reckon that's just it."

"I'm right obliged to you," he said again, and straightened, began to move. "I thank you kindly," nodding and touching his hat.

She stood and watched them climb back into the creaking pickup, the tall dark-haired one who had spoken to her having trouble getting all his legs in; the little pot-bellied, bald one moving fussily, like a woman. By that time some of the curious were standing watching as the tall one maneuvered the gaudy electric-blue trailer back out into the street. It was made up cleverly if not neatly out of two or three other trailers and looked a little drunken. Its roof had been silver once, but had been so daubed at with a tarbrush as to resemble an intricate map. The hitch to the pickup was none too good either, and the trailer took a direction all its own when it was backed. To get the whole rig straightened out and proper took a while. And was it then, Niewatha wondered after, that she saw—or did not see—for just a moment the obscure shadow of the third man, sharp-featured and grinning at her darkly from the trailer's smudged rear window. All she could see plainly in her mind's eye was the tipsy back of the bright blue contraption, swaying duck-like in the sun as it moved slowly off the square and down the hill toward the highway.

That night, when she and Charlene Weatherly were sitting on the front steps, Billy D., Charlene's brother, told her about the herb remedy and the snake-show and the one who was the talker. Billy D. would not have anything to do with them; he hunkered down ten feet away with a piece of grass in his teeth, trying to look like his father.

"Girl," Billy D. said, "he could talk the pictures off your wall. He had all kinds of tales, and when he starts sellin' right in the middle of it he stops and says to one of his helpers, 'Here son, separate that man from his dollar: that's what we come all the way down here for.' Laugh! There was one a minute. And he kept stringin' them along about how *after* he was gonna show 'em the pie-thon; was gonna show 'em how they milked the rattlesnake. 'And I take my sacred oath on the Holy Book, gentlemen,' he says, 'it ain't the same nor a cow, neither.' He was better'n that Fair last fall," Billy D. said, "all they had at that little ole Fair was chunk-the-cats and a shoot-'em-up. I tell *you,* the men was bunched in fifteen deep all around him, and wadn't a one of 'em leavin' there 'til he got that rattlesnake milked."

"How'd he do it?" Charlene said. Which of course she shouldn't have asked, only Billy D. was her brother. Niewatha looked away and said, "Which one did the talkin'. The little fat one or the tall one?"

"Neither one of *them,*" Billy D. said, "they only helped. It was the big red-headed one was the talker."

"How'd he milk it?" Charlene said. Niewatha only looked away again.

And then the news was that the trailer was parked down there, just beyond the Jockey Yard at the artesian well, only still nobody knew what they were. Some thought they might be oil-drillers because the red-headed one and the tall one drove around the county in the pickup like they were looking for something, asking questions. But others said they were just selling the herb remedy. The short fat one set up a little stand by the trailer, and for a quarter you could see the snakes and if you wanted buy four bottles of the remedy for a dollar, or soda-pop for a dime. There was a table of crockery dogs and wooden flamingoes and flower pots for sale too, but no one paid much attention to them. Then on Sunday morning out at Ebenezer, two miles from town, everybody found out for sure what they were. Gospelers.

They came without warning right after the first hymn; were just suddenly there, striding down the aisle. "There is a hap-py land," they sang fiercely, "faaar, faaar awaaay, where saints and angels stand—" singing at the tops of their voices with their snakes writhing and the harmonica going and their cast-iron feet raising the white country dust from the rough pine planking. The congregation spilled out of the church like water, some of them through the low open windows, the preacher along with the rest. Niewatha was socializing, there only as Charlene Weatherly's guest; later she saw it as a sign. When she was safe outside she recognized the older one, though he looked now like a prophet. He had climbed into the pulpit—the bald womanish one with steel spectacles was off to the right in front of him; the heavy red-headed one who had the harmonica strapped into a contraption that fitted around his neck was on the other side. They were all waving their snakes and chanting, and somewhere on the other side of the church a man was yelling—it sounded like Mr. Willy deShong—for somebody to God's sake phone up the Marshall, and off in the grove a woman still screamed faintly but steadily. Niewatha was too busy watching to mind.

"Friends!" the tall man was yelling in a high, nasal carrying voice. "Friends, attend unto me!" He looked the same as he had that first day, and not the same. He was hard-fleshed and brown from cropping and gaunted down from troubles and his dark hair was plastered neatly across his forehead like her father's, but he looked scary too; there was a glitter about him and his clothes seemed frosty and his chin stuck out as though he should have had a beard on it. His eyes were deep-set and blue for a wonder and did not seem to look at anything and his voice came high and steady with a little quaver in it. He was getting them told, all right.

"Standing in sin and corruption and the very stink of mortal fear," he sang out at them. He held his snakes aloft like hammers and roared it at them, telling them all the details of their hypocrisy and back-sliding, his face lined and hollow and his sharp adam's apple bouncing out of his collar like a fishing cork.

"Satan's own," he shouted, lifting his snakes, "Satan's very *own!* Spake to Eve and bid her eat!" The harmonica was chording lightly behind him and the bald-headed one kept up a steady chant of "Yes Lord! Tell hit!"

Pointing with his looping snakes, the tall one told them to fall on their knees. Told them that as proof of their faith the snakes would not harm them. "Oh ye of little *faith!*" he shouted, "ye have seen these rep-tiles do not harm us. No, *shall* not harm a hair on the head of his trusted servants, no, not a hair on the head of the least of these!" Told them how the Lord, through His mysterious ways, was willing to bring them back.

"Even through his deadliest rep-tiles," he sang, his voice draining now, as though something were sucking the marrow out of him. "Won't you come and pray!" he said. He was still moving his snakes but he was settling now, collapsing into the preacher's chair. "Halford," he said, raising his drooping head a little, "Halford's going to play for you. Going to lead you in 'The Great Speckled Bird.'"

And then the red-headed one was talking; talking all the while he was laying his sluggish snakes down on the front bench and taking off his harmonica. He lounged toward them, explaining, never going near the pulpit. Ferlin, something said to Niewatha, he's the One.

"Brothers and me," he said, "well, it's kinda like we was taken up for a mission, you might say." His voice was not slow and not fast, an easy hillman's voice, going on like he might be telling something in the store on Saturday afternoon. He grinned at them all and his dark red eyebrows bushed out over his amused china-blue eyes and hairs ran down to meet on the bridge of his sharp nose. His lean face never let go of the lopsided grin.

"Lord spake unto us one day," he said, "whilst we was settin', takin' our ease after croppin. Come in a bust upon us; come like a thunnerclap. Come like sudden hail on young corn. 'Boys' Lord said, 'Boys, go fetch you some of my rattlers, get you some of my deadliest rep-tiles.'" He ran his hand through his curling claybank hair and she shivered; she could feel that hair. Then he pulled another harmonica, a much larger one, from his hip-pocket and blew upon it once, tentatively, a sweet note. "Said, 'boys, I'm gonna take you up for a mission.' That was His Word. And He given us the power to speak in tongues, given us the Grace for the ministerin'. Given us deadliest rep-tiles, made tame as His sweet birds." Again he put the harmonica to his lips and blew the same sweet, sustained tone. "'Go to them as need,' Lord said, 'preach unto them.' That's what He said." He held the harmonica up slowly, his elbows out, and grinned. "And I 'spec you folks know," he said, "His Word travels a mite faster'n the Western Union."

He began to play, and listening, she could feel the electric shocks go all over her. The sound coming from the harmonica cradled in his big hands was loud, better than anything: it went into her toes. He cupped himself around that piece of metal, seemed to hunch down into it, as though it was God's breath he was blowing into it, and the alive sound filled the room like flowers and April and when it was done there was a silence.

"Won't you come on now, folks?" he said. Not grinning now; pleading. "Won't you come? I'm just gonna play the in-vite one more time now, and I hope you will all come." Then he was playing again, a tune more mournful that she didn't know, a thin questioning tune. 'Won't you come?' it said, 'why not fly!' She did not feel her feet begin to move.

"Here's a young lady now," he said when she came through the door, "she's settin' you the example." From one of the windows she could hear Mrs. Weatherly's voice was saying "Niewatha! You Niewatha Cardwell!" but it did not make any difference. He was signifying, looking right at her over the harmonica, and she was walking straight into the blue sea of his eyes. Him who could make reptiles still in his hand and bring a piece of metal to life by simply blowing into it with his breath.

"Maybe you could kinda get 'em started," he whispered to her when she stood in front of him, "you know, turn around to 'em and put out your hands like and testify."

She could see people and hear her own voice and her arms were cupped and yearning like the music; they would come now, surely. It surprised her to see coming down the aisle not Charlene or Mr. Weatherly or any of the others, but Georgie Bancroft, the town Marshall. Georgie, coming straight at her, unshaven and still wearing his old panama hat; his eyes were squinted a little and full of a glint that was like the glint of light on the barrel of the pistol he held in front of him.

"All right," Georgie said, "come on out of there quiet." They all heard the hammer on the pistol go back with a mean-sounding click.

"Mister," Halford said behind her, "we was only . . . "

"You get on up that aisle," Georgie said, "move." Then Georgie looked at her for the first time. "Niewatha, you get over here behind me. Wait'll I tell your Daddy, big grown girl like you."

When the men were halfway up the aisle Georgie stopped them.

"Wait a minute," he said, "hum-on back here and make sure all them snakes is tied up good."

And get your harmonica, she thought, the little one. But she could say nothing, her throat was so tight, and Georgie had them hustled up the aisle before she could do a thing. Georgie put handcuffs on them at the church door and loaded them into his Jeep. Halford and the bald-headed one he put in back; the older one climbed in front.

"It's Lord's work," he said. He looked sour and a little beaten, but he turned a shade of a grin to them all. "We been in jailhouses before," he said to no one in particular, "this is on you people's heads and hands."

"Shut up Taylor," Halford said, "you ain't doin' any good."

"All of you shut up," Georgie said and threw the Jeep in gear.

It was when they pulled away and she saw his face looking back at her through the eisenglass rear window that she wondered if she hadn't seen him on that First Monday too. His face looked dark and blurred, but she could see he was grinning at her and the goosepimples came again on her arms and the back of her neck. She turned and walked away from the crowd and went around the back of the church. The Weatherlys would think she was just going to the ladies'. After she got far enough out into the grove she pulled a red-oak leaf and put the stem in her mouth, thinking. He could touch me with his eyes, her quietening blood said. Then she slipped back to the church on the other side and climbed in a window and got the harmonica, still in its rack, and by folding it got most of it in her bag. She detoured back to the path from the ladies' and came around in front of the church and found Mrs. Weatherly looking like a cow about to hook.

"There she is," Mrs. Weatherly said, "Girl, what ever got *into* you! You brought up like you was with the Baptists!"

"Oh Mama, hush," Charlene said, "come on, Daddy's waitin'." But Mrs. Weatherly went right on, getting redder in the face.

"Well," she said, "if you was any girl of *mine,* even if you was near grown . . . " They had turned and headed for the Weatherly pickup; nobody listened to Charlene's mama much. When they were seated in back, leaning against the rear of the cab, they still couldn't speak because Mrs. Weatherly was talking out the window at them. Then the motor drowned her out.

"Well!" Charlene said, sounding a little like her mama, "You certainly do have to watch the quiet ones." She giggled and poked Niewatha. "Lord," she said, "I wish it had been me. He was just as *hand*some!" Niewatha looked straight out over the tailgate.

"I do believe you got a case," Charlene said.

"Maybe you don't know what it's like. Maybe you never been called."

"I reckon I have," Charlene said, laughing and punching her again. "Oh Lord yes. That red hair." But she was not studying Charlene. She sat in silence, watching the road spin away into the summer's dust behind them, and wondered how she was going to get the harmonica back to him.

All that afternoon it looked like nobody was going to give her any peace. There were people on the front porch half the time and the telephone hardly stopped a minute.

"I wouldn't even have got to see it," she would tell them with nothing in her face, "but I saw Charlene in the show Saturday night. And Charlene said 'come on home with us,' so I did, and that's how I was out at Ebenezer." Then she would tell it. "Well," the visitors would say when she was finished, "if that don't beat all," but they did not look satisfied. Then her Mama would always put in about how of course Niewatha wasn't moved by it, it must have been the heat or something. Listening to her mama she knew not one of them understood, and she figured she'd better be careful about getting it back to him.

Only when the time came, it was easy. On Tuesday she said she was going swimming, and it was simple enough to walk on out to the trailer from the pool, which was right on the highway. She was not sure they hadn't gone on, anyway; all she knew was that the Sheriff had held them one night on an open charge and then let them go. She walked slowly along the edge of the shimmering asphalt highway, so as not to perspire, and hoped no one would see her when she turned off. When she got beyond the last of the filling stations she breathed easier; she could see the gaudy blue of the trailer, partially hidden in the deep shade of a stand of sweet-gum. She knocked twice before anyone came, and then it was only the bald-headed one. He wore an apron and he had his spectacles pushed up on his forehead.

"Hal'd thank you kindly," he said when she gave him the harmonica, "he puts a store by that thing. Him and Taylor just gone up town for a minute; got to see the Sheriff again. Looks like them po-lice'd let a man alone," he said, "and him a-tryin' to help do for folks. But them po-lice. They're ever a trouble to us."

"There's some don't blame you," she said.

He put a toothpick into his small mouth and began to chew on it. "I'll make sure he gets the instrument," he said, "he'll appreciate you bringin' it."

"Tell him the one who testified," she said, "the one testified out at Ebenezer."

When she turned onto the pavement again she was empty, sure that what had brought them together had taken him again, that she had seen the last of him. Then she hadn't gone ten feet and there he was, turning down from town with his brother.

"Wellwellwell," he said grinning, "what in time you doing way up here on this old hot highway?"

"Somebody forgot their harmonica," she said, "I was just leavin' it."

"Well now," he said, "wadn't that sweet of her Taylor?" Taylor only looked sour. "I'd like you to make the acquaintance of my brother Taylor," he said, "Taylor Culbertson."

"We met already. Up on the square."

"Them up on that square," he said, "those jailhouse folks *still* tryin' to think up somethin' mean for us."

"The Lord will take care of it," Taylor said, "Lord wouldn't let us stay in that jailhouse. 'D smite the doors from the hinges."

"Taylor, he's got a strong belief," Halford said, flipping his head at his brother. "Believes a man oughtn't to worry none."

"I will not fret," Taylor said, "the Lord will provide."

"I tell him, a man he'ps his*self,* Lord will provide."

"Blasphemy," Taylor said, "you will turn the Lord's hand from us yet."

"May-be." He turned and grinned at her again. "You go on, Taylor," he said, "I'll just walk down to the traffic light with Miss . . ."

"Cardwell," she said, "Niewatha Cardwell."

"I'll just see Miss Cardwell down to the light, she's been so nice and all. That is," he said, ducking his head, "if Miss Cardwell don't mind."

"The Lord knows you," Taylor said, "knows your abominations."

"Don't mind him none," Halford said after Taylor stalked away. "He's still a little warm from talkin' to them po-lice. Down on me, too; he don't like my pickin' up the cash, playin' carnivals and fairs. Shoot, If I didn't bunko a little of Lon's medicine now and again we'd all starve. You don't hear him 'bominatin' the money though; just the cootchie dancers."

"Didn't know you all played carnivals."

"Suuuure," he said, "play anyplace they'll have us; trade days, churches, carnys, fairs. Anyplace. Snakes is always a good drawin' card."

They were across from the Kream Kup and he asked her wouldn't she like a milkshake. "I'd be right pleased if you'd drink with me," he said. They took the shakes over to a big hickory; the grass was nice there and the breeze got to them a little.

"Yessir," he said, "funny thing is, some of the things I could tell you about the Culbertson boys wouldn't bear repeatin'. You see plenty, travellin' around." He laughed. "Jailhouses, even, if you got Taylor with you." She felt his hand on her back, flat as though he might rub. "From the inside," he said, "which makes 'em look a sight different."

When she looked at him he was lying back in the grass, his head pillowed in the crook of his arm, and his eyes were laughing up at her from the covert of his eyebrows.

"You had a lady-bug back there," he said. He was chewing on a blade of bermuda grass, sucking at it through his strong white teeth. He looked different somehow, lying in the grass; taller. "Oh, I could tell *you*," he said.

"I got to get along," she told him. But before she left he made her promise to try to get out to Bethlehem Chapel, where they were going to put on the act again.

"This time we been invited," he said, "so there won't be no fuss. Usually somebody invites us, we get in the jailhouse once. It's good publicity."

"I'll try to make it."

"You try hard," he said, his eyes different again, squinted a little, "tomorrow night, prayer meetin'. Havin' a girl like you around is right smart of a help to a man."

"I'll see if some friends can bring me along," she said, and left him.

Neither she nor Charlene drove, so she had to ask Billy D. to take them. Charlene's mama objected to their using the pickup, but Charlene knew how to handle her Daddy. Riding out to Bethlehem Charlene wouldn't let her rest. She kept it up all the way to the Chapel, with Billy D. laughing at her from the driver's seat. Not that they could touch her.

"Don't tell *me*," Charlene said, "I think it's sweet and romantic, that's what." Billy D. guffawed, and Charlene kept on about how she *knew* something was going to happen on that Saturday night, because of all the shooting-stars. It was another thing, she thought.

"Don't you remember?" Charlene said, "coming home from the show? It was a *sign*." She could not remember and couldn't be bothered; she wanted to think about tonight, since it was going to be just Halford there. Lon and Taylor were in jail again; had got themselves booked this time, for leading a ragged little parade of people from the Primitive Church right into the Sheriff's office, all of them carrying placards.

"At least yours is got some sense," Billy D. said, "they say he argued with the other ones, *told* 'em they'd get theirselves arrested."

"Maybe he'll ask you to ride back with him," Charlene said happily. Her stomach went to ice. "Me and Billy, we'll just say we was riding around a little, after the Show." Billy D. hooted and zigzaged the pickup. It didn't make her feel any different. It was only when she saw Halford's red head under the bright light at the door of Bethlehem Chapel that she knew it was going to be all right. She stayed back in the shadows, though she could see that Halford was watching out for her.

When the service started, he saw her and grinned; she listened while he explained about Taylor and Lon, talking in that pleasant way like he had out at Ebenezer. He played and got the people to sing with him and handled the snakes a little. Then it was time for the special collection.

"I wouldn't ask none for myself," Halford said, "but for my

brothers in the jailhouse." When the plate came to her she put in the five silver dollars her Uncle Enon Gresham gave her for her fifteenth birthday. Then she sat with her hands quiet in her lap, and watched almost without blinking while he played 'The Great Speckled Bird' for the closing. In the darkness, by the cars afterwards, she was still hearing it when Halford found her.

"Here," he said, dropping the silver dollars back into her hand, "thought you was old enough to know better'n to try to guess which shell the pea is under."

"What?" she said.

"Ne'mine. Besides, even if it *wadn't* hanky-panky, Taylor *likes* to be in jail. You got to understand that. Come on, I already got the damn snakes in the trunk."

It went fast after that. She guessed she knew he was taking her back to the trailer, but she looked at him in wonder when he pulled up besides it. "I thought you might like to see the inside," he said. She couldn't say no, because she had wanted to see it right from the first day.

And she was right; it was different from any house she had ever seen. There was a hula skirt hanging from a ventilator, the walls were covered with souvenirs from the places they'd played, and every corner was stuffed with boxes and junk. Taylor's tracts, he told her, or Lon's Nature-Cure Remedy, things to sell. "Nuthin' in the Remedy but pure herbs, ma'am," he said grinning, "cleanses the liver just as *naturally*." The cotton stuffing was coming out of the sofa that stretched across the rear end, under the window; the bunks, which hung from the ceiling, were not made, and the kitchen was full of used pans and dirty dishes and the tag-ends of meals. There was a large guitar leaning against a lumpy objcct which was covered with an old army camouflage cloth, and above it a silvered cage with two lovebirds in it.

"You got to pardon the mess," he said, "things have been a little excitin'."

"Men can't do. It don't bother me." But she was thinking how she could straighten it all up in two hours.

"Now this here," Halford said, reaching for the camouflage cloth, "is the fourth Culbertson boy; he's afflicted, deef-an-dumb." He whipped off the cloth and she screamed: it was the statue of a man from the hips up, and it was bald and naked.

"Miss Cardwell, meet John Thomas," Halford said, "take out

your eye for the lady, John," and he pulled out the eye before she could cover her face. "Comes apart," he said, "a an-o-tom-i-cal dummy. Help sell a lotsa medicine." He began pulling off pieces of the dummy with both hands, calling them by long scientific names and throwing them on the couch. "Only trouble is," he said, "when you get to his liver *ever*'thing gives way," and she couldn't help laughing at the clatter of the rest of the dummy's insides bouncing all over the floor.

"Always gets a laugh," he said, "I've shoved a hunnerd boxes of the Remedy sometimes at carny, just on that one trick."

"Tell about carnivals," she said, shivering, "tell me."

He looked at her and did not say anything for a minute. Then he reached over and picked up the guitar and began to touch it with his fingers, softly.

"You wouldn't want to hear about carny," he said, "nice girl like you. Nice church-goin' girls ought not to want to hear about carny."

"Maybe I would."

"Nooooooo," he said, "*bad* folks around them places. You oughtn't to do with carny folk."

"Maybe I'd surprise you."

He looked at her again, his eyes different, changing, near to green.

"What you want to hear about," he said, turning the guitar, "strip-tease girls?" He was watching her, strumming. "No," he said finally, "I'll sing you a little church song instead. Some folks sing this one a different way. But these are the real words to it." He cocked the guitar on his knee, moving it only slightly, but she could see he had drawn himself up. Then he hit it, sure and hard, and it gave a big ringing sound. He watched her, letting the guitar play itself, and began to sing in his clear, sweet voice.

> Forgive me my sins, Lord, forgive me my wrong;
> I am lost and I lift up my heart in this song.
> Forgive me my sins, Lord, don't make me pay;
> Cleanse me with mercy for Judgement Day.
> Oh yes I am sinful, my sins are blood-red,
> But Jesus will make up my dyin' bed.

He sang three choruses, each with the same simple refrain. While she listened it was his hands stroking the guitar but making her sing, not the instrument. He held the last notes over the throbbing minor chords of the guitar, singing softly, with a break in his voice,

> Oh *yes* I am sinful, my sins are blood re-ed,
> But Jee-sus will make up my dy-e-ing bed.

She did not move when he leaned over and kissed her, and she made no motion when he slipped the guitar from between them.

Then it was a new world, in which she lived strangely, and did not live. Or there were two worlds, that she had dreamed of and the other, and she no longer knew which was real. The brightly-lit world of day, in which she stood in front of the stove and spoke to her parents and ate; the dark world of the pine grove below the pasture. Late in the nights, when she slipped away to see him, the pine needles were thick and soft and the stars pressed down in the warm velvet sky and he sang very softly in her ear. Between these were the times when she could see him in the day, going or coming in Pochahontas, or appearing in some little back-country church with his brothers and the snakes, when he looked different. Occasionally he met her at the Kream Kup to buy her a milkshake, and then they would sit under the hickory and he would talk to her, telling about the world, which he seemed to possess when he spoke. It was there one day, after a light shower, that she asked him.

"Halford," she said, "are you all going to stay here?"

"Stay?" he said. "In Pochahontas?" He was lying propped on one elbow, he rolled flat over on his back before he went on. "Nah," he said sleepily, "Taylor gets the call to stren'then the faith somewheres else, we'll be movin'." She could feel him stiffen. "Why?" he said. She could feel the slow, profound thud of her heart; she would never be able to say things right like him.

"I could take good care of you," she said, "I could keep the trailer lots better'n Lon." She could hear him letting his breath out long and slow.

"Taylor don't favor marryin'," he said, "you know that."

"Not marryin'," she said and waited, "just in the sight of the Lord."

"With *Taylor?*" His head snapped up. "Are you crazy?"

"But you need . . ."

"No," he said, and sat up. "Listen kid, I thought you knew." He watched her out of eyes that did not blink. "You know Taylor wouldn't allow none of that," he said more gently, "don't you get into no fuss about it now."

"We could ask him, though couldn't we?" And again she could hear him waiting. He stroked her arm softly, thinking.

"Weeeeelll," he said, "yeah, I guess we could ask him. You know *me*," and he grinned, "said yourself I could talk the Ford dealer into buyin' a Chivy. Maybe I could talk the lunkhead into it. He knows he can't get along without me."

"He'd learn to like it," she said, "I really can do around a house fine." But he was watching something else, abstracted. She looked where he was looking, seeing nothing. "What?"

"Little ole green-grass snake," he said, "see him? Ain't he pretty now?" It did look pretty, coming toward them, but it scared her.

"I used to catch them things all the time," he said, "had me a hunnerd of 'em when I's a shaver. Catch him."

She looked at him, and saw he did mean her. "I'd be scared to touch him," she said, "I can't do with snakes like you."

"You better learn, girl, you gonna be with me," he said. "I'll teach you. Watch now."

He got up easily and moved slowly toward the snake, which stopped and watched him. When he squatted down gently he was nearly on top of it. "All right," he said, "you come on around to the left. I got his eye." Halford watched the snake. "Get in close to him." When she was close he said "OK, pick it up quick right behind the head."

"No," she said, "I can't. You do it."

"You got to learn," he said, "everybody learns. Go on; he won't hurt you. Do it quick now." Slowly, fearfully, she put down her hand. The snake watched Halford, flicking its tongue at him occasionally. "Go *on*," he said, "it's just a snake." She grabbed and squealed as the snake writhed and slashed its head at her hand, and dropped him.

"Ah, what a dummy," Halford said, grabbing the snake expertly as it tried to slip away, "look." But she was looking at her hand. There were only the faintest marks; a scratch, as though she had brushed a thorn, and one tiny drop of blood.

"Here," Halford said, "Take him. Hold onto him this time."

"No," she said, "you told me . . ."

"I thought you wanted him," he said, "sure, he's got little ole bitty teeth, about like a nail-file. But they can't hurt you." He held the snake up and watched it writhing for a moment and then put it down in some tall grass. "Go on 'long there, then," he said, and pretty soon he had her laughing.

Before he left her at the traffic light they arranged it. He would try to soften Taylor up that night, and on Saturday she would come up and talk to Taylor with him.

"Taylor'll probably say it will just work out the Lord's way," he said, laughing, "and that may be." Looking first to see that no one was watching him, he gave her a quick kiss.

Saturday morning she slipped quiet out of the house and caught the Trailways to Pochahontas, though she could have gone up with ten different neighbors if she had wanted to. Being alone made her feel a little better braced for Taylor. It was as though she were still in the dream that was everyday, but it was changing now. She sang Halford's song as she watched the familiar fields slip by. Now she knew she would soon wake and feel good; the thought of Jesus making your dying bed made her think of making up the beds in the trailer. She would teach Taylor to like it, the bunks neat and the floor swept tidy and the kitchen clean. It was hot and she thought of the artesian well where the trailer was parked, and wanted a drink of the clean, cold water. Travellin' she thought, travellin' all around. She smiled to herself at the thought of Taylor's face when he saw how neat she would make it.

She got off at the traffic light and walked, keeping her eyes on the tops of the sweet-gums where they showed above the roof of the filling station, waving their star-shaped leaves to her in the bright morning sun. She went on past the station and then stopped. There was nothing under the sweet-gums: where the trailer had been there was nothing.

"They've gone to the jailhouse," she said, "to straighten things out," but she knew that was not true. She could feel the shaking in her legs and she wanted to sit down. "Maybe to get something fixed for going, maybe the trailer. . . ." She went into the shade of the sweet-gums, seeing the muddy ruts left by the wheels, and on to the artesian well. She sat gratefully on the concrete trough, listening to the cold sound of the water falling from its iron pipe, hearing the soft trickle where the overflow spilled and runneled away to the creek. Now she was shaking all over.

"There was signs," she said softly, "they'll be back in a minute," and folded her hands in her lap gently, like an old woman; it surprised her they were such good-looking hands. She raised her head and looked down the blank, shimmering highway, where the ribbons of heat-devils pulsed and quivered. She could hear the silence and the cool spill of water and the soughing of the gum leaves above her head. Then she looked at her foot. On her left shoe there was mud from the ruts, and she bent to clean it off. "It was only a scratch," she said. Now she knew she was into the real world; everything looked new and fresh. "You wouldn't even know it was there, tomorrow," she said, rubbing at the mud, watching the bright splash of tears off the top of her shoe.

FROM

Come Back, Lolly Ray

BEVERLY LOWRY

LOLLY

THE SUN AND RIVER were to the west, back over their shoulders on the other side of the levee. The main street of town—along which they waited, impatiently—dead-ended there, at the foot of the levee. Holding on to one another for support, they leaned out over the curb to see if she was coming yet and some even stepped into the street and stood hands cupped over their eyes in the middle of it, looking for a sign of her . . . until someone else shouted for them to get themselves back up on the sidewalk where everybody else was. Children, hot, played chase in and out of their parents' legs and pulled at their clothes and, wanting to get on with what they came for, gave notice if she wasn't here soon they were going home. Though by the calendar autumn had arrived, the day was still and hot, and no breeze at all came to dilute the heat pouring thick and heavy down on them. Even now, late afternoon, the sun persisted. Low, resting on the levee's crest like a sleeping baby's head, it seemed to want to see her too, and refused to sink behind. There was no sign yet of the north wind predicted to blow in that day and cool things off.

She wore a gold suit. Because the music was too far behind her, they would not hear it first, but awaited another clear and familiar signal. When the sun's light butted headlong into the bright gold thing she wore and was reflected off it: that quick flash of light. They watched for it. And just about the time the kids' squirming started turning into fistfights, the word passed that it had happened, the light had flashed and she was coming; she was on her way. Children screamed and pushed at each other for places to see from. The adults did not scream, but pushed. They couldn't see her distinctly at first because of the light bouncing back and forth. When she turned the corner at Hawthorne and came down Main toward them, all they could make out was a waving gold flash moving alone down the center of the street, boldly into the sun; as hot and bright as it was, braving it; coming down Main toward them and the river, directly into the Friday afternoon sun. The backs of their necks dripped with sweat as they kept their heads turned toward her.

At her middle, there were, in addition to the sun's reflection and her dazzling gold suit, yet two other bright things but these were silver, and moving. And when one of them went suddenly up to her face then past her head, people leaned out even farther and did what they could to help themselves see: they made awnings of their hands, or put spread fingers palm-out in front of their eyes, peering between them as if through blinds. The children pointed as the silver thing went farther and farther up over her, and screamed as it held there, a gleaming disc of silver which soon became pulled out into a starlike shape by the light of the sun. Heat waves rose up around her ankles and her body swam and turned under the silver star, like a goldfish in a pool of heat. Then as the silver started to come down, they held their breaths and followed it, waiting to see if it hit the street, wondering if it would, hoping it would, at the same time believing it would not, caught up in the excitement of both possibilities. Either way, they would have the exhilaration they came for. Then when it did not hit, when she stopped it at her waist where the other one was and moved them both one after the other quickly in succession behind her, around her, under her leg, around her neck, and finally back up over her so high the tallest old oaks lining Main could not with their topmost branches reach it, then the people released their breaths, sighed, clapped proudly, pounded their children on their backs, and said among themselves, "That Lolly . . . that girl! She never misses!"

She was their twirler, both in her time and after it, *the* town twirler, a title she could claim as surely as if she had been crowned, no matter who else was twirling while she was or continued to after she was through, because Lolly Ray Lasswell's name and legend would be passed on from generation to generation as the town of Eunola's own. Like Graham, the town drunk, like Booth Oates, the town idiot, and Alberta, the town whore, and even, though he was long gone, Sexton Cunningham, Eunola's comical and self-styled historical figure, Lolly would not be deposed by time, as they had not, the tales of their accomplishment now having been established outside time and ordinary human considerations. By the time Lolly was twirling, Sexton had been dead fifty-six years and Graham, seven. But Graham was still the town drunk, even though people in Eunola were a drinking community, and except for the hard-shelled Baptist refugees from Texas and the hills (those who always seemed to be squinting, sun or no, who waited Fridays not for Lolly but the band behind her), everybody thought it was all right to do it and most did. But there was not and had never been as far back as anybody could remember a drunk like Graham, who was above every other consideration in his life a drunk, who never merely *drank* but shaped his drinking as if it were an art: until it was his life itself. His capacities were sublime; his legend established; his place, unshakable. Because he transcended ordinary notions of ordinary limitations, he was exalted, and Lolly was no different from Graham.

As she got closer to the big crowd (which gathered about halfway up Main toward the levee because the big front-porched houses down toward Hawthorne and the railroad tracks were Eunola's oldest, and their inhabitants, also Eunola's oldest, prized their roses and camellias and didn't care for parade watchers trampling up the Bermuda grass), and they could see her better, their excitement grew. They became quieter, concentrating strictly on her now, unwilling to risk even a glance away in the chance it might be the moment when she did a special trick or, as noteworthy, dropped her baton. The promise of either kept them on edge, anticipating. She was shining now, coming closer, like a piece of the sun. Her uniform was made entirely of dime-sized solid gold overlapping sequins, each of which was attached at the top only so that when she moved the sequins shifted and swung a split second later and it looked as though either she was moving twice every time or that the uniform as it caught the sun and gave it back to them was moving on its own. It was a one-piece, sleeveless, legless costume, designed and made by Lolly herself, elasticized as far as it went, which in length was just far enough that arcs of her butt slipped out when she high-stepped. Her boots were silver up to her knees, tight, zippered, with two-inch heels and three gold tassels in a row swinging down the front. She was tiny, and thin. Her skin was pale; her hair the color of deep wet mud with an overlay of rust, glittering as the river was now with the sun almost in it, bouncing on her shoulders as if it had springs. As the band was still not in sight, she came alone, prancing by herself, though the sound of drums could now be heard approaching.

As she neared the last of the oak trees before the commercial part of downtown, the crowd, having waited so long, grew edgier. Children's screams thinned to squeals. They could see her face. People said . . . especially majorettes and majorettes' mothers . . . she was not *pretty*, not really. She was too pale, too thin, her features too large for the size of her face. And her nose . . . ! (Majorettes doted on the shape and length of Lolly's nose, which instead of turning up in the popular fashion, pointed down.) Curls of her thick coarse hair draped heavily about her face and half-covered her eyes, which, cool and blue, focused on something her fans could never determine the exact location or nature of. Certainly she never looked at them. Just like her daddy, some said. Never gives anybody the time of day unless he's pinned down and asked it.

She had two batons, which she turned like wheels in front of her, her arms straight out. Suddenly, about half a block from where they waited, she slapped them one over each arm and pranced straight ahead in a kind of goosestep, her arms in absolute and unshakable rhythm with her feet. As one baton went straight up beside her head, the other reached its position alongside her thigh. Alternating. Up . . . thigh, arm, baton . . . down. Locked in. Up . . . catching the sun again and again.

In the middle of the intersection just before the crowd's edge she stopped dead still, square in the center under the traffic light which blinked on and off, red, for the parade. Each thing she did was absolutely distinct from the next so that if afterward you had been asked you could have said she did this-then-this-then-this in clear succession with no overlap. She raised both arms, batons east-west, perpendicular to her arms, and pointed one toe toward the levee and one back toward the railroad tracks. Keeping her knees stiff and her head straight, her chin out toward the sun, she started easing her way down, sliding into a full split. And very slowly the batons began to turn in time with her sliding. The closer she got to the street, the faster the batons turned, until, when the tops of her thighs were within the heat of the concrete and she had thrown her head back, her eyes were facing the blinking light above, the tips of her hair were grazing her butt and the batons were speeding like crazy. She looked up . . . at the batons? The light? The sky? They wondered but could not tell. People in back leaned down on shoulders in front of them to see her going down and try to figure out what it was she saw, for Lolly never gave them everything they came for. As natural a dream as those that come in sleep, she let them grope for their own endings and explanations and slid on down then as easily as if on slick glass and when she was all the way down sat as if it were natural to be split apart one leg due east and one due west, naked against the hot street, facing the awful sun, toes pointed hard as street signs, her head still tilted.

On the sidewalk a little girl marched like Lolly's shadow, turning a circus baton in imitation. She, too, was on the concrete with her legs spread and as Lolly hopped gracefully back up on her feet and started off again, the little girl struggled to her feet. Unlike Lolly, the child acknowledged the applause and cheers. Lolly's eyes, still abstracted, disregarded them. But she did smile. Her teeth were large and straight, and with her head back shining, the smile held out promises.

About that time the band turned from Hawthorne down Main and the gaunt women in plain belted dresses, the teetotaling Baptists who had not looked at Lolly, or if they had, had looked quickly away as if it were sinful, clapped one hand stiffly against the other in recognition of the band's approach.

The line of majorettes across the front of the band (and no one referred to Lolly as a majorette except the majorettes themselves, who said the only difference between them was that Lolly wore a different uniform and could do a few more tricks) in their heavy chin-strapped, plumed tin soldier hats and standard white majorette boots and mid-thigh satin uniforms came red-faced into the threatening sun, marching as instructed, knee up groin high, toe pointed, to the music, keeping the line straight, and when the people got around to turning back and as an afterthought applauding them, it was little consolation. Being accompaniment for Lolly not only infuriated them, it made them even hotter in the afternoon sun than they might have been. And they could not, hard as they marched, catch up with her. Perspiring beneath the long sleeves of their white satin uniforms, the top fatty wedge of their thighs chafed and raw from constantly rubbing in the same place . . . same place . . . same place . . . against one another, they marched like hot little soldiers, trying not to see Lolly way ahead of them floating back and forth free as a dream, her hair shining and loose, jiving up and down and over and across potholed half-cobblestoned old Main Street, turning, flipping, kicking, leaping, twitching, sashaying her butt in their faces without a stumble or fall in her body.

Two Eunola residents were not at the parade, had in fact seen Lolly perform only one time on a Friday afternoon. Her father, Frank Lasswell, was back at the high school in his car, her school clothes draped over the seat next to him, waiting for her to get finished so he could take her home for dinner. Her mother was home in the trailer watching the last daytime television serial of the day.

"Can you believe it?" Sid Strunk said as if for the first time when Lolly passed his furniture and appliance store. "That girl was raised in a trailer house!" He said it every time she passed, every Friday of football season repeated those exact words. Part of the legend being the establishment of the language which, once done, remained impeccably unchanged. Part of the dream the astonishment that where she came from had not determined her destiny. That she had not become—like every other girl from the trailer park—a trailer tramp. That in his time as well Graham, a Cunningham, had rejected family advantage to go into the business of keeping a drunk on. That Booth Oates's family was a severely quiet and respectful one, who had yet produced one son, an idiot. Who, because he was *their* idiot, the town took care of. That their whore, Alberta, put on her hat and shopped with the best of them, demanding proper service, which was unhesitatingly given. All four outside regular social considerations, outside family and church . . . *outside.*

Two blocks before the levee, at the Delta Theater . . . known for its rats, B-grade black and white movies, and a pervert who sat against the left-hand wall waiting for colleagues and strangers . . . somebody yelled to Lolly to throw up her baton. She and the little girl on the sidewalk both did, and as Lolly leaned toward one knee, keeping a perfect balance between the strain of her body on the street and the silver stick moving against the force of its own inertia, she found her focus. Not on the baton itself but its aura, that stream of silver that when the baton was going fast enough caught up with itself and made a solid round of silver in the air. That dazzling exhaust; it kept her attention. Pure chance, from pure perfection. She thought concentrating on it would take her past where she was now, past all the ribbons and trophies she had already won, past being the substantiation of a dream for a town she disdained into being . . . the Lolly Ray Lasswell . . . of the *world,* somehow. She caught the baton and moved on, and the man who had called out for her to throw it beamed as if he had done it himself.

Behind the band another group turned from Hawthorne to Main. The Homecoming Court. It was Homecoming, and the queen and her six maids also trailed Lolly.

At the end of Main in front of the levee, the city had erected a statue in honor of its World War II dead. Some city fathers designed it, which, to Eunola's chagrin, was exactly what it ended up looking like, a statue designed by a committee. It was supposed to represent a warship. And you could tell it was a ship all right, but it looked more like one a child might draw than what any adult would design: trapezoid with top line longer than bottom, straight line sticking out the top, square attached to line, stars and stripes inside the square. If a child drew that, you'd say good, fine. But as a memorial, it was a monstrosity, an embarrassment. Which everyone saw every time he or she drove down Main toward the levee. It was made of white tile bordered in blue, and across the top of the memorial just under the border it had said for years now "TO T OSE WHO PROU LY ERV D IN ME RIAM." The missing letters had either fallen or been stolen and since the war by now had been pretty much relegated to past history and nobody wanted to fool with that memorial anyway, they had not been replaced. Listed under that message were the names of every white Eunolite who died in World War II.

When Lolly got close to the memorial, she tossed her hair out of her eyes and looked, for the first time, into the crowd. The statue stood directly in front of the levee, and as the levee blocked off the sun a little when she got close enough to it, she could look straight into the faces there. She was actually searching for a name on the memorial, Cecil Cyril DeLoach, against which he usually leaned. When she found it, he was not there. But he had never missed. Then she saw his wings glint, on the other side, to the left. There. He had moved; he was directly in front of Morris Leon Grizzanti, leaning on the second z. Morris' brothers and sisters now ran a pizza place near the trailer park. And the smile flooding over Lolly's face then was as pure as a baby's. Unclouded joy spread like a blush. He wore mirrored sunglasses and silver wings on his air force shirt, both of which picked up what sunlight they could from that angle and flashed it at her, just as she was flashing to the crowds up and down the street. That was what had caught her eye the first time, and while she hadn't been able to see his eyes for those strange silver glasses—and still hadn't—he had signaled her with a cocky two-finger salute, which, combined with the way he grinned at her and the slouchy way he leaned against the memorial, had established him in her mind as a collaborator. He knew what she was up to, it seemed, her contrivance and plans, and saw beyond what the others did. And saluted her for it. After that first time she looked for him every Friday there and acknowledged his presence with—besides that spectacular smile—a special heel-toe jiving dance step and an over-the-baton jump before turning left down River Road toward Court where she would turn left again and head, sun behind her, toward the high school she had started from.

Above the wings, though Lolly couldn't see it, a blue plastic tab announced her compatriot's name, which was Lt. James Blue. Lieutenant Blue came to see Lolly every Friday and never waited to see a single majorette.

Once the sun gave up and started sinking into the levee, the air cooled off a little and people felt a little easier standing on the concrete. Still, those lining Court had to look into the half-sun's blurred glow to see Lolly, and the majorettes still squinched their eyes up as they neared the end of Main. Lolly's performance never let up, but because the people on Court were a little less fanatic than those on Main, whose compulsion was not only to see her but to see her *first,* she gave them less. Some of the Mains came over to Court, however, and on the corners where they shouted to her she did a special trick, like bending herself backward until her head came down between her feet and all they could see was half her body with its head between its legs and two silver sticks turning beside it. Others went on home, some to prepare dinner and return to the stadium behind the high school, where she would twirl again at halftime. As it was Homecoming, crowds would be heavier than usual.

Frank Lasswell waited patiently for his daughter. From the sun's near disappearance he knew she'd be coming soon. Smoking, easing ashes off the end of his cigarette with his middle finger, he gave the impression of a tough and leathery, unapproachable old man. Parked over the railroad tracks in front of the school, he would see her just before she climbed the hump the tracks ran on, one split second where Court Street curved, then would lose her behind the hump. When she got high enough he would see her again, coming up like fireworks.

He neither understood nor liked what Lolly did. She had little idea what she risked, stirring people up, and little notion what they were capable of, once aroused. He didn't watch her in the parades because he couldn't stand to. He was vulnerable where she was concerned, and inside his stony chest his heart leaped and fell with her tricks and stunts. But she had worked so hard. He had seen her day after day from the time she was ten years old, turning first a broomstick then a baton around and around until her fingers ached. And when he had asked if she wanted to go to twirling camps and classes and she had refused and said she didn't need them, he had understood. Doing it on her own made her proud. It enabled her to have what she had worked for for herself, setting her off from the town. And so he said nothing of his skepticism, and helped her every way he knew how.

When he saw her on the tracks, her chin high, he thought she looked like Lucille . . . though Lucille had never done anything remotely similar to twirling a baton. When she hit the top of the tracks she turned around on one toe then stopped stock still between the ties. Her eyes were on Frank, her chin was out and up and long, her shoulders were back, and from up there she was looking out as if over a countryside that belonged exclusively to *her*. At that moment, she had the look of a Peavey. His wife's people. That fierce and uncontainable pride that bordered on hatred. If, that is, a Peavey had ever in his life owned anything to overlook besides his own delusions. It unnerved Frank.

At home, Lucille stirred the stew and checked the cornbread, which she was warming from lunch. Although she was not watching it, the television set filled the trailer with sounds of cartoon characters. The table was set for three, and every now and then Lucille ran a hand through her long curly graying hair and moaned softly. Her head hurt again.

After Lolly did her turn atop the railroad tracks, she was through

. . . the act was over . . . and when she ran like a child to her father and asked if she could please drive home, it was as if a mask had been taken off.

"No," he said briskly, "get in; we have to hurry." Not meaning to be short with her but still off-balance from seeing the Peavey in her.

But when she rounded the front of the car and coyly stuck her tongue out at him, looking across the car hood from the sides of her eyes, his face uncrinkled, he shot out a loving hand urging her to come take his place, and, bewitched, slid across.

She patted his leg softly when she got in, then pulled away from the curb. When they turned the corner just before the tracks, the majorettes were cresting the hump, perspiration running like rain from beneath their hats. Lolly glanced at them but did not wave or speak, and neither did they.

Behind the band and the Homecoming Court, the sun had finally dropped from sight. Only its fierce red and gold afterglow remained, its last gasp before sinking into the river and yielding to the north wind, which drew near. Clouds which had all day puffed and billowed themselves about like soap bubbles were now stretched out thin, and with the sun's light coming up through them their whiteness had turned into bright, hard colors, red, orange, and a violent pink. Like cheap teasing dimestore scarves they discreetly covered the sun's decline.

The Habits of Guineas

TOM MCHANEY

THAT SUMMER his father left for the little war, and in the winter they got word that he had died. The adults told him about the resurrection and the life everlasting. And they went into the country to live with his grandparents as soon as he had finished the first grade.

In the black prairie all he had to do at first was watch the trains. He waked to see the drab mail cars in the morning, moving along slowly like men returning reluctantly to work. After lunch, the silver passenger train flicked by and disappeared while the northbound freight lay on a siding and deferred to her silverness. The people in the sparkling coaches, some of them dining, never glanced at him from their blurred windows. Around midnight the last freight either waked him or gave him dreams, bawling and shrieking through the middle of the night, making the windows rattle and the bed shake. The trains came and departed as regularly as the moon and the stars. They marked the passing of each day but each day was the same. They kept no season: neither waxed nor waned. Though the days passed, time did not seem to progress. He grew sullen and bored.

Adam's grandfather was not a country man, but rather a displaced town dweller. He had failed in town; or, to be more exact, the town he had chosen and doggedly supported had failed out from under him, in one quick generation, thanks to the railroad. Aberdeen, where two rail lines crossed, became the market town. Muldon, the place where they lived, dried up. Many of the people who had settled there were drawn off to Aberdeen. Others died, and young people left never to return, except for Adam's mother. Muldon was a ruin: heavy concrete blocks lay like tombstones along the weed-choked, tree-lined lanes that had been streets. At the foot of a rusted railroad siding sprawled the twisted wreck of a cotton gin that had burned near the end of the town's heyday. Facing the main railroad track were more stones and three store buildings, two abandoned and picked at as if by ants, and a third that held in dusty suspension a ghostly horde of rope and leather and iron goods of interest to farmers and small boys. The store was his grandfather's, who opened it on call to the farmers of the region when they did not feel like driving their new pickup trucks the extra twelve miles to Aberdeen. His grandfather also owned the house they lived in and a recent model automobile that he used to deliver rural mail out of the post office in Aberdeen. He sold life and burial insurance in the county and collected for it as he brought the mail. He contracted to buy cotton and corn and beans at harvest time from the small farmers nearby. He spent his days on the road and never had much time for Adam.

So Adam had the town of Muldon to himself. He exhausted its physical possibilities in the course of one summer week, though he mildly puzzled again and again over the plentiful signs of mortality there. He also had the black prairie that lay so quiet and hot and unchanging between the distant Tombigbee and Sakatonchee rivers, and the railroad tracks with all that ran upon them. The only sign of life was the pig corn that grew in the field across the tracks. The only evidence of an outside world was the trains. Beyond this there was nothing, as if creation had stopped just at the point of making so much and waited to see what it would do next.

Therefore Adam had a great deal of time to think, and he tried to use it, but most of what was on his mind exhausted his capabilities quite as soon as he took it up. There was thinking what to do next, which failed. There was thinking about his father and the resurrection and the life everlasting, which made him frightened and sad and tightened up his mind until all thought stopped and he sat quietly blubbering on the back steps. There was thinking about the women in the house, but that failed too when he sat small and silent listening without comprehension to their strident voices. They went about household chores, the same every day, so fierce and persistent and bustling that, he thought, they did not seem to want him or anyone else to think.

Then his grandfather, about whom he had puzzled with an indefinable jealousy and a certain mystery, too, came home with the guineas. One lesson Adam had learned from hearing his grandmother and mother talk was that the grandfather did not know what to do with boys and that he was so busy eking out a living through his enterprises that he had no time to learn. But one day the old man brought home from Aberdeen a large paperboard carton containing six baby guinea hens and one guinea cock, fat, iridescent, gem-eyed guineas. His grandfather set the noisy box on the ground and tore it open and the guineas spilled out like buckshot: curious and abrupt, they chased away toward the house and Adam ran after them, trying to herd them back into a tight group. But he might as well have tried to herd the passing time, so quickly they eluded his grasp.

"What are they, granpaw?" he said. "What do they do?"

The old man told him what they were. "But they don't exactly do anything," he said, laughing. "They *are,*" he said. "They're God's creatures and they live and eat and sleep, like you and me. They're right pretty, too, don't you think?"

"Oh, yes," said Adam.

"But they're yours," his grandfather said. Adam stared his unbelief and then quickly broke into questions. His grandfather told him a few things and then said, "You'll have to learn a lot for yourself, though; you'll have to take care of them." Adam looked a trifle hopelessly from the scattering fowl to his grandfather. "I'll help you at first," the grandfather said. "We'll fix up the old hen house for them to live in, and you can raise 'em."

"Raise 'em?" Adam said.

As if they had heard the old man too, and also wondered what he meant, Adam's guineas stopped their flight and returned to the old man and the boy. They cocked their heads and peered at Adam's grandfather in a manner that caused him to laugh aloud. When he laughed, Adam also began, giggling foolishly, quite hard, and the women came running out of the house, scattering the guineas and standing in their places and making Adam and his grandfather laugh more, because the women were watching the man and the boy exactly as the guineas had done. Last of all, the guineas laughed too, a faint chuckling noise, and the cock chased a lady bug under the front porch and the rest pursued him madly.

"I'm going to raise them," Adam proclaimed. "Right now. Come on, guineas. Come on!" They paid no attention and he stooped to look under the porch and then turned disconsolately to the adults.

"It's all right, son," his grandfather said. "They'll come when it's time. Let's fix the house first. I'll show you. Then we'll give them some feed, and they'll come." He and the boy marched off toward the back of the house and Adam told his mother again, "*I* have to raise them. They're all mine." They set to work on the henhouse,

Adam fetching the hammer and getting in the way, mainly, while his grandfather stretched the wire and drove nails into the tin and wood and pried off broken hinges, replacing them with hardware taken from the miscellaneous stock of the store.

"Granpaw?"

"Hum?"

"How do I raise them?"

He put the hammer down and touched the boy's head. "Best way you can, son. And I guess that's by not worrying about it a whole lot. Things generally turn out. You just watch them. Get to know them and know what they like to do. Then make sure they don't get into something that can hurt them. Learn their habits."

"Oh," said Adam. "Their habits." He helped scoop some powdery seed from a bag his grandfather produced and they went to find the guineas. He spilled a few grains and the guineas rushed at him; he made them follow him back to the pen.

"What's 'habits'?" he said.

"What people get used to doing," his grandfather said. "What they like to do." He paused in thought. "Sometimes. What they get used to, anyway."

"Like what you do in the car," said Adam.

"I guess so."

"I see," said Adam. He led the guineas around by trailing the tiny seed before them. Then he opened the door of the chickenhouse and threw a handful of seed inside; headlong, the guineas raced to catch the grain and he closed the door, laughing.

In the days that followed, Adam pestered the guineas interminably. He fed them infinitesimal amounts of seed to make them squabble. He chased them up and down the narrow pen. He treated them as capriciously as he knew how, modeling his behavior on the adults who ruled him, including the schoolteacher from the year before, for which the guineas suffered most. And when they ignored him, he threatened them that he would go away and leave them forever in their pen. But they went right on with whatever they had been doing and after seven or eight days his grandfather found him, staring at the chickenhouse, disconsolate and bored.

"What's wrong, old man?" his grandfather said.

"I don't know."

"Have they been going out much?"

Adam admitted that he hadn't let them out. And sensing the disapproval that this disclosure brought, he stared apprehensively. "You mean you haven't let them out to forage?" his grandfather said. "You were going to study their habits. Have you learned anything?"

Adam admitted that he hadn't. He had ruled the guineas so fully by his own pleasure, they had kept a schedule very much like his own. He thought of them as little people.

"You ought to let them out," his grandfather said. "To forage during the day. It's cheaper. And it's what they like to do."

"They're mine, aren't they?" said Adam.

"They're your responsibility," said his grandfather. "But they're creatures, just like you and me."

"What if they go off and don't come back? If I let them out, they might not come back." His thoughts were whirling; he really wanted to end this interview, before he lost control of himself.

His grandfather waited a minute before he replied. "I believe they will," he said. "But you think about it. They're yours."

When his grandfather had gone, Adam went behind the chicken-house and started to cry. He thought about resurrection and the life everlasting. For a minute he felt very savage and if one of the guineas had gotten out and come to him, he knew he would have attacked it and done it harm, but he didn't know why. He spoke to them through the wall: "You old guineas! You old guineas!" The tears came hard.

But the next day he felt better. And as the mail train stumbled by he let his guineas out and for ten anxious hours he did not rest, pursuing them around the yard, under the house, into the mimosa tree. He began learning about guincas, and entertained the family that evening with all he had observed. Guineas ate apples; they loved to roam; they liked to fly into low tree branches and in the afternoon sun the feathers at their necks shone like dark jewels in the earth. His eyes were like sea-fire as he talked; and he gestured as his father had, so the family led him on, feeling a little more hope than usual in their lives. They could see the next year now, when before all they could do was look back. Adam wondered at the new way everyone treated him.

He and his grandfather became friends. Several times he rode with the old man on the mail route, and he helped put the letters and papers into the country boxes. His world enlarged. His grandfather stopped at country stores and bought him cold drinks and fruit, and he always saved a piece of apple or pear or, rarely, banana, to bring to the free and happy guinea hens. He had become so accustomed to the habits of his guineas that almost at any given moment he could walk to them with his eyes closed, for though with their little doll-like movements they seemed as erratic as blown paper, he had noted that they kept a schedule according to the heat or time of day. They sought shade or rest at the same hour daily, they foraged in particular parts of the yard as if they understood when the bugs would be there.

One afternoon, when he had been occupied with some repairs on the wire around their house, he had a sudden premonition that they were gone. He ran around the house, but he could not see or hear them. His grandfather was away, and he would not ask the women, so his only choice was to begin a search on his own, which he plied with increasing desperation in a widening circle away from the house. Finally, he reached the railroad tracks, which stretched to infinity either way he looked, expressing to him the emptiness of the moment and the limitlessness of his anguish. Then he saw them, like seven lumps of coal, foraging in the field that lay across the tracks. The pig corn had been harvested and the drying stalks had been turned already to make room for a winter vetch. He ran down on them, screaming, and chased them back to the house and put them in the pen and locked them up and sat on the back steps, livid, watching the chickenhouse as if he expected it to get up and walk away. His grandfather finally came home and he told him what had happened. The old man only looked at him, smiling.

"They changed their habits, that's all," he said. "Nothing to get excited about. Saw an opportunity and took it."

"They ran away," Adam repeated. "Across the tracks where I couldn't see them." And the next morning he didn't let them out, and, unexpectedly, his grandfather came home for lunch. He had another talk with Adam.

"What were they doing over there, yesterday?" his grandfather asked him. As if to emphasize the silence, the distant whistle of the afternoon freight, bound north but not on them yet, sounded and made Adam jump. "What were they doing?" his grandfather said again. Like water gathering, the train moved into view down the tracks, creeping forward.

"Eating," Adam said. He knew how adults argued; he knew he could only lose.

"Foraging," his grandfather said. "And what is that?" The freight had almost slipped past them, sounding like a bag full of dishpans being dragged up a metal stairway.

Adam told his grandfather what foraging was. Adults had all the words. The engine screamed for the brakeman to open the switch.

"They enjoy that, don't they," his grandfather said. "It's important to them. It's really one of their habits." While Adam was thinking, the train hunched backward against the line of empties and filled the siding with the noise of collapse.

"I guess so." While the freight made cooling noises on the siding, the questions went on. Adam was made to talk about what he liked to do, to admit his own habit of coming home for supper and bed, and the analogy his grandfather so laboriously led to was eventually completed. It reminded Adam of the conversations he had with his mother at night when he waked with bad dreams, but he let those memories drift out of his mind and concentrated on the train. His grandfather was concluding with a peroration:

"A guinea is a creature like you and me," the old man said, and paused so long that Adam flung in a defiant, "I know that, I know it!"

"A guinea's got his own ways," he continued. "Now if you have learned anything, it's that these guineas like you pretty well, and they always come back when it's time, just like you come back to me and gramma and mother when it's time. Isn't that right?"

Adam's face was red and he shook his head, yes; he felt like shouting, *What about the life everlasting?* but none of his thoughts cohered long enough to become speech. A keen sound speared the air and seemed to lead the silver bulk of the luxury passenger train across their vision; it flashed in the gaps between the freight cars and through their opened doors. Shortly after it was gone, the freight screamed, too, a frustrated cry, and gathered itself together and dragged off toward the north. Adam's grandfather made a funny noise in his throat, rubbed the boy's head, and went to the house. Adam went to the henhouse and scolded the guineas; he threatened to leave them again, but, finally, he told them also that they might forage across the tracks if they promised to be careful.

When he let them out the next day, they went back across the tracks as if someone over there had called them. Adam watched them anxiously, but he didn't interfere. He observed. He almost lost his nerve when he heard the afternoon freight and the guineas had not yet returned, but he spoke to himself manfully and stayed on his porch. After the passenger train and the freight had gone, almost while the cinders were whirling, he dashed to the roadbed. Over the track, shining like black and green beads in the lowering sun, the guineas bobbed upon the powdery earth. At dusk they bounced over the track, heads down and forward, and Adam threw into their pen an extra portion of seed. They chased it but didn't eat much.

The days were growing shorter, the guineas fatter. They began to think about nesting. Every evening after they had returned from their forage in the field, they sought places to roost. Adam was always chasing them from the mimosa or the peach tree near the house or off the railing on the porch. He wanted them to nest in boxes high up on the walls of their house.

In the middle of August, on a Wednesday, there was a train wreck about sixty miles north of Aberdeen; a switching engine hit a fuel tanker and killed a man. Traffic on the line was delayed for more than an hour. Consequently the passenger train was held back and the northbound freight had a longer wait than usual on the Muldon siding. Adam learned what had happened, and that a man had died, but he did not feel any particular emotion. He amused himself with planning the nesting boxes for his guineas, and it was only after the passenger train had hurtled through, an hour and twenty minutes late, that he recalled his hens in the field beyond the tracks. Now he saw that the freight still blocked the track, though it had uttered the despairing cry preparatory to the miracle of its launching forth again. He ran toward it hesitantly, then stopped, frozen. Below a boxcar with an open door were silhouetted the seven little guineas, bobbing and cocking their heads in great perplexity. The train was blocking their crosswalk. With a cry like that of the engine, Adam leaped forward, and just as he did, the guineas fathomed their situation and flew up out of danger into the open space in the empty car. Again Adam halted. But the guineas were apparently satisfied. They settled comfortably onto the wooden floor of the car, high and dry, and remarked to each other about the view. The cock strutted around his brood. As Adam watched, they moved off with the train, their heads bobbing complacently, framed fat and glistening against the sun in the open doorway.

For a long time after the train was gone, Adam stared into the bloody sun that dropped behind the tracks. His mother called him to eat and he entered the house by the front door, something he had not done in a long time. All the talk at supper was about the wreck. The adults did not notice what or how he ate or that he seemed strangely absorbed.

After supper his grandfather was reading the paper and, as usual, calling the news to the women busy in the kitchen. Adam waited beside the chair until he had finished giving the local news.

"The train goes north, doesn't it?"

"Which one?" his grandfather said.

"The freight in the afternoon."

"That's right. The midnight freight goes south."

"The other way?"

"Yes."

"At midnight?"

"At eleven forty-eight," his grandfather said, smiling.

"It comes from the other way?"

"Uh huh. The north."

"Thank you," Adam said.

When the house was quiet, the others in bed, and when he believed it was reasonably close to the proper time for that train, Adam dressed and crept out and made his way to a dark spot by the tracks, settling on the hard ground. He sat facing north, his ankles aching underneath him, and stared into the faint silver infinity of the track. His thoughts tried to go between the twin snail's trace, but they scattered at random. His mind was full of the phrases the adults had been using on him for the last year. And finally, to keep from crying, he brought up the only prayer he knew and began reciting it, bobbing a little in the cold air, waiting for the returning train. He did not really believe the prayer and so he was not very hopeful.

The Lonesomes Ain't No Spring Picnic

BIRTHALENE MILLER

ME AND CANDY sitting in the swing, pumping it slow and easy, floating out in air so full of spring that if we close our eyes, we can smell the grass growing. We're counting together, aiming on going up to a thousand. For no reason at all, except to show Jeffrie and Jimmie and Rhodie that there is one more thing we can do that they can't. Just letting the devil git ahold of our souls, Grandpop would say. We stop when he come out into the yard.

He's got on his best dark-blue, marking-for-death suit, and he carry his pearl-handled walking stick in one hand and the Bible in the other. Candy and me cross our fingers and watch him walk down the street. When he's out of sight, I open my mouth and my breath comes popping out like soap bubbles, I'm that relieved.

I look at Candy and she's shaking. "Why you still scared?" I say. "He done gone past your house."

Candy say, "I hear a screech owl last night right outside my window."

"You hold your wrist and choke it til you make it quit hollering and tell it to go away and mark somebody else for bad luck or dying?"

"Yeah, but what if the devil git me alive for doing it the way your grandpop always preaching?"

"I druther the devil git me alive than he git me dead," I say, but I whisper it so that Rhodie can't tattle-tale it the way she do everything, even the time she catch me and Candy with our hands on each other doing a thing that Grandpop say is an admonition to the Lord and eternal damnation to our souls. We still do it sometimes. We try not to, though, cause we're scared of what God'll do to us if He catch us.

Candy is thinking of that now, I know, cause she look worried and I start worrying, too. We start up the swing again but there's no joy in it now. The world that smell so clean and green and sweet just smell sad like funerals now, and we git down and go into the kitchen.

Grandma is baking custard pies. She's got a streak of flour, white as death's pale horse, smeared across her face. She's looking towards us but her eyes are going on through us, and she's mumbling to herself.

"Grandma?" I ask. "Grandma, who is it going to die?"

Grandma don't answer but start in rolling out the dough and I see she's mad or upset from the heavy way she is leaning on the dough roller.

"Grandma, who is it going to die?" I say again, and Grandma look at me finally and say, "Ain't nobody going to die, if the Lord be merciful." But her eyes got that look of her body being here and her mind over yonder someplace, like she's two people at once. Make a chill run up and down my spine. What Miz Rose call a possum walking over my grave. But I don't want to think about no graves now, especially my own, and I grab Candy's hand.

We just the other side of the door when Grandma start in mumbling again. "Lord, pore little Sue Ellen. . . . Lord, all alone and scared."

"Sue Ellen?" Candy ask, but I can't answer because of the catball that's suddenly caught in my throat. We go out and set on the front steps. Just quiet and holding hands. It is the first time we ever know Grandpop to mark someone so young for dying. Sixteen.

After a long while Candy ask, "Why'd he want to go and do that to her?"

I say, "He don't do the choosing. The Lord do that. Grandpop just points out them that the Lord say to."

Candy say, "I wonder what she dying from?"

"I know," Rhodie say, crawling out from under the steps beneath us. "She dying from forcation."

"What?" me and Candy say together, and then I say, "Look here, Rhodie, Grandpop is going to git you for saying ugly words like that."

Rhodie say, "He say it hisself."

"That's different. Preachers have got to say what the Lord tell them to and if He tell them to say a bad word, they gotta say it."

Rhodie plops the bottle against her doll's painted lips and asks, "Why is forcation a bad word?"

"Cause . . . just cause it is," I say, trying to sound knowing. "And another thing, if you keep telling them lies, Grandpop is gonna strap you."

"What lies?" Rhodie cry, looking like she don't even know what I'm talking about. Sometimes I wonder how she can be my sister, she's so dumb.

I say, "Them lies you tell about Sue Ellen dying from—"

"Ain't lies," Rhodie say. "Sue Ellen dying from forcation. Deacon Riddell say it hisself and she his own daughter—"

"Niece," I say. "Just cause she live with them don't make them her parents. And the word is fornication, dummy. Don't nobody die from it."

"Do too. Grandpop and Deacon both say Sue Ellen dying from it."

"When they say that?" I ask.

"A few minutes ago. When they come up the street. They in the church now."

I can see the church door open. "What else they say?"

"Deacon tell Grandpop he raised her up in the straight and narrow, and he never allowed her to smoke or drink or paint her face or wear short skirts or mess around with boys."

I wonder again how Sue Ellen stayed so gay and friendly living with two people what always go round like their mouths stuck full of straight pins and they afraid to smile for fear they swallow one.

I see Grandpop and Deacon come out of the church and go into the cemetery.

"Picking out a spot for the grave," Candy say.

"Don't have to pick one. They'll put her beside her mama and daddy," I say, but the two men walk past Sue Ellen's parents' graves and on to the far corner of the cemetery. Deacon bend down and start driving down the burial stake.

There ain't no graves at all in that section and I think of Sue Ellen with her pretty face and smile being put off all by herself and my eyes run over with tears and Candy keeps asking over and over, "Why they putting her there, Mary Ann? Why they putting her there?"

She look at me and see I'm crying and she start crying, too. We don't want to watch no more, and we go round the house and set on the bench beneath the bare wisteria vines that crook over into themselves like they got a hurt, too, like me and Candy has. I got a worry, also, that keep gnawing at me. I say, "Don't see how Sue Ellen . . . I mean, how she can . . . what with her not going with no boys."

"And no men, neither."

"Lizzie Beth Collins . . . she all the time with her. She the one. Got to be."

Me and Candy look at each other. Then we both move down the bench as far away as we can from each other and Jeffrie and Jimmie sneak up behind us and start shouting, "Bang! Bang! You dead!"

They stop hollering suddenly and I look up and see Grandma standing on the steps. She say, "For shame . . . Lord, as if there ain't enough killing and dying in this world without you two play-acting it. You, Jeffrie, you Jimmie, throw them sticks down right now!"

Grandma ain't quite five feet tall, not much more'n me and Candy and we eight—or almost—years old. But Grandma's voice got ten feet of do-what-I-say in it, and the boys throw the gun-sticks down quicker'n they be red hot coals.

Grandma say, "Candice, your mama want you and the boys to go home now, and Mary Anne, you and Rhodie's dinner is on the table. Pearl and me are taking some pies over to Miz Rose's and the Deacon's.

After Rhodie finally git through dawdling over dinner, I go outside and Candy come over. We set on the steps but far apart. After awhile, Grandma and Miz Pearl come back. As they coming up the walk, Grandma saying, "But Lord, a coat hanger!"

Miz Pearl look at me and Candy, and she poke Grandma in the ribs. They go up the steps past me and Candy. They set down in the rockers and Miz Pearl say, "That Deacon Riddell . . . expecting any minute for the corpse to be brought back from the undertaker, and all he can talk about is the disgrace." Her and Grandma whisper to each other.

When they hush whispering, Grandma say, "You see what I see? Two cats so full of curiosity that they going to bust open in a minute. Friday and the last spring holiday from school and you two waste it just setting around eavesdropping."

"We ain't eavesdropping. We watching them dig Sue Ellen's grave."

"And they digging it in the far corner," I add.

"Mary Anne, what you talking about? Her parents buried in the middle."

"Yes'm, I know but. . . ."

"They burying her in the new ground they take in. Way over at the far end of it," Candy burst in ahead of me.

Miz Pearl and Grandma both get up and look.

Grandma say, "Lord, they right, Pearl. That pore motherless. . . ." She moan and press her hands against her belly like she got a pain in it somewhere.

Grandpop come into the yard and up the steps like he don't even see Grandma or Miz Pearl or me or Candy, though we got to quick jerk back to keep his death-marking clothes from touching us.

"Mr. Robinson, may I have a word with you, please?" Grandma say, low and respectful, like Grandpop preach in the pulpit that it's the duty of a woman to be that way cause she neath her husband, being only his rib and he got to all the time stand with his shadow between her and God.

"Speak ahead, woman," Grandpop say.

"Private. Please," she say.

"All right, but it will have to be fast," Grandpop say. His eyes have that look they always git when he's working on one of his pulpit-thumping, window-rattling, hell-fire-breathing sermons.

Grandma shut the door behind her and Grandpop. We can't hear what she saying but we hear him plenty good through the open window.

"Fitting? Fitting? A fornicator and a murderer. What would be a more fitting place for us to bury her? Less'n we bury her outside the cemetery altogether?"

"But just a child." Grandma talking louder now. "What if it was Mary Anne or Rhodie? In a few years they will be young ladies. . . ."

"And it will be the church's duty to make them and all other young folks know that the wages of sin is death everlasting."

"Mr. Robinson!" Grandma cry. "You're not fixing to preach a hell damnation sermon over that poor girl's body, are you?"

"The Lord puts the words in my mouth. I only say them."

"But. . . ."

"Enough, woman. I got to be about the Lord's work."

Grandpop come back out and go across to his church. After awhile we hear Grandma talking on the phone. She's on the phone a long time, forever it seem, and the warm spring afternoon run quickly towards cold sunset. The air so still and so heavy with flower smell and sunshine and wet, I feel like I'm looking through glass. Lying on my side in a goldfish bowl and looking across the yard and the cemetery at the grave diggers and the water so quiet and heavy over me that I can hear the thud-thump of the hard shovels against clay and the far-off distant sound of Grandma talking.

When she finally come out, her eyes shining with mad. She say, "Lord! Men! The tribulation of them." She walk up and down the porch. And down and up it. She moan as she walk. "Lord . . . that pore . . . Lord, that lily-livered woman wanting to do better but always obeying that rock-hearted man of hers."

She stop pacing finally and stand staring at the church. "Lord, why you lay such a burden on womenfolks by putting that obeying thing in?"

After awhile, she turn and go into the house and start rattling the pots, and Miz Pearl tell Candy to come along and help her get supper, cause afterwards they all going over to the Riddell's. Candy look at me and I see how bad she hating the thought of going. I reach out my hand to her. Our hands are all but touching when we remember and jerk them back.

I watch her go and the loneliness is a boil inside me aching to pop itself. I go inside. Grandma hears mine and Rhodie's prayers and tucks us into bed. I ain't sleepy and I git up and go to the bathroom. When I pass the opened door of Grandpop's and Grandma's room, I peep inside and see Grandma sitting all alone and quiet and reading the Bible.

Seeing her like that gives me a bad case of the lonesomes. But everywhere is going to be lonesome from now on without Candy, I think, and I crawl under the quilt beside Rhodie. I think of Sue Ellen and the lonesomeness of her grave off by itself. I think of all the lonesomeness in the world. Then I think of dying and hellfire and I throw the covers back and pull my gown up and look at my body. I expect to see the red flickering of flames on it but the streetlights coming in through the shades make it look green. And I think that maybe it's poisonous for me or anybody else to touch ever again.

In the morning, Grandma and Grandpop don't say nothing to each other. After we all dress up in our funeral-going clothes, we set in the living room and wait for the hearse to bring the corpse. Grandma set with her black purse in one hand and her Bible in the other and with the quiet all around her. Grandpop keep looking at her. Finally he say, as if he can't stand it no more, "Idie, what is it? What's ailing you?"

Grandma set on as though she don't even hear him, even though

I know she do and even though she always before pay heed to every word he say, like the Bible says to. That's the reason I decided I ain't never going to git married but just always have lots of boyfriends.

Grandpop ask, "Is it the grave?"

Grandma don't say nothing and Grandpop say, "Idie, you know that I got to say and do the things the Lord tell me to."

"And I got to do and say the things He tell me to," Grandma speaks at last.

Grandpop open his mouth wide to say something but just then he see the hearse coming and he grab his hat up and run out.

Grandma follow him and me and Rhodie follow Grandma. Candy join me in the church yard and we follow the people inside. When we all seated, I look up and see Grandpop standing at one end of the casket and Grandma standing at the other end. I don't understand that, cause everybody but the preacher is supposed to be setting. And I don't understand it even more when Grandpop go up into the pulpit and Grandma go up behind him and stop in front of the pulpit stand so she between Grandpop and the congregation. Everybody look at her, not understanding. Everything so quiet you could drop a straight pin point down and hear it hit.

Grandma open her mouth and speak and her voice is as quiet and peaceful as winter rain dripping past a bedroom window. She say, "I know that most, maybe even all of you, think it sinful for a woman to speak in church. Preacher"—she nod over her shoulder at Grandpop—"Reverend Robinson say it and I respect him as my husband and my preacher. But there is somebody else I respect, too. Some people. Though many say they don't need or deserve respect. I say they do. I say until they git their respect this world going to go on being messed up."

People look at Grandma and some begin to shift around and clear their throats, small noises grating against the quiet, cracking the thick hull of it.

Grandma look at the crack in the quiet and she draw the quiet closer around herself. She say, "Women—that's who I'm talking about. Women all the time git blamed for every sin done under the sun. Some we do. Some we don't. But nearly always the sin we do we don't do alone. There's a man do it with us and he just as guilty. Only he, being a man, don't git the blame heaped on him like us women do."

She look down into the slowly widening crack and she say,

"There's someone, a man, or a boy what think he's a man, who ain't one bit less guilty than Sue Ellen. But I don't see nobody pointing him out, accusing him of his sins. And he, more'n likely, setting right here among us."

The people turn slowly from looking at Grandma and begin alooking at each other and I see them wondering as I am. A boy or a man, I think—and not Lizzie Beth Collins. The worry that has been corked up inside me comes spewing out like half-frozen Coke.

Grandma say, "Sue Ellen in years scarcely more than a child. But she die the death of a woman. If there be any woman here today what can love or pity her because of, or despite of, what she did, I invite that woman to step forward and help me in burying this, our dead sister."

Grandma stand waiting in the quietness that is so thick that I feel I can reach out and touch it, so soft and deep that I can put my whole hand in it. Grandpop still standing behind her, and he look like he don't know what to do or say, and the people all look at Grandma and nobody move. Then suddenly Miz Pearl git up quick and go stand beside Grandma. Lizzie Beth and several other girls and some women go up. Me and Candy go up, hand in hand.

Deacon Riddell jump up. The frowns in his face so deep you could plant a turnip patch in them. He cry, "Preacher, I object to such unorthodox proceedings."

Grandpop don't say nothing, and Grandma go down and stand at the head of the casket. We follow her and I look down at Sue Ellen's face. It look as calm and peaceful and quiet as Grandma's. And so beautiful. The beautifulest face I ever see. Except Grandma's now with the softness on it like light. She say, "Let us pray."

After the service, Miz Pearl and five other women act as pallbearers. They start to carry the casket towards the red mound of dirt in the far corner of the graveyard, but Grandma stop them. She pick Miz Riddell out of the crowd following along behind us. She say, "You, Lucille. You Sue Ellen's only blood kin. You decide where you want her buried—alongside her parents, or way off in the corner by herself." She point to the two mounds of dirt—one that we see yesterday and a new one in the middle of the cemetery. I stare at the nearest mound and Miz Riddell and everybody else stare at it. All except Grandma, who look as if there ain't nothing unusual about a grave gitting dug all by itself in the middle of the night.

Miz Riddell look at the grave. "Please," she say. "She has been a daughter to me for twelve years." Tears come running down her face.

"An admonition unto the Lord," Deacon interrupt. "I say she is to be buried in the grave I pick for her."

"No!" Miz Riddell say. She say it low at first. Then she say it louder. "No!" And her sobbing overtakes her.

Deacon say, "The Bible says wives obey their husbands."

"The Bible says it all right," Grandma say. "But it say a lot of other things, too, like love and mercy and he without sin casting the first. . . ."

"Right in God's own Book. It say wives obey their husbands and. . . ."

"Maybe it say that just cause it's written there by men," Grandma say.

Deacon's face quiver like there is water under it boiling. "Heresy!" he screech. "Preacher! A heretic!"

Grandpop been standing back in the crowd. He step forward now and lay a big hand upon Deacon's shoulder. He say, "No member of my church going to call no other member a heretic. Especially no one going to call my wife one." He look around at the crowd and then back down at Deacon. "The women have taken it upon themselves to conduct this funeral. Let us let them carry on with it," he say and turn and walk slowly out of the cemetery and into his church.

Deacon stare after Grandpop. Then he spit upon the ground and march out of the cemetery, too.

When we pass the church after finishing burying Sue Ellen, I see Grandpop setting in his study. Even after it is dark out and the spring air is thick with a misting of rain, I still see him setting alone and lonesome looking.

I lay awake a long time thinking of the day and Grandma and the strange ways of women and men. Rhodie flops over towards me and abandons her pillow and burrows into mine. I start to push her away but don't. I lay breathing her breath and it smell warm and rich and sweet like the hot chocolate Grandma give us before putting us to bed. I think of Candy and, with the secret fear and guilty worry that Sue Ellen's death brought gone, the thought of her is warm and gentle and sweet again in my mind.

To Pass Him Out

William Mills

"Come in, come in Mabel. And who's that you have with you?" she asked in a violent whisper. A ten-year-old boy followed Mabel Bauman in off the front gallery and through the hall.

"This is Tommy, my sister Julie's child. Tommy's visiting with us this summer. Wanted to see what country life was like. Say hello, Tommy," demanded Mabel Bauman, following her friend into the front parlor.

"Hello ma'am," Tommy chimed automatically. The house had funny smells. Everything was old.

"Miz Fanny," said Aunt Mabel, then hesitating to give weight, "how is Mr. Tillman? We've been so worried."

Aunt Mabel didn't know Mr. Tillman very well, but Uncle Jack had said Mr. Tillman owned a big farm out of Bethel. That he took sick way back in the woods on his place and there was nobody to take care of him but a pack of niggers living on the place. Mrs. Fanny told some of the ladies in the church to bring Mr. Tillman to her house (even if he didn't want to come) and she'd take care of him.

"Just hanging on, Mabel, just hanging on. He had a troublesome night. I just don't know how he does it. The poor dear is so weak, but he's got a will, you know. You can just see it in his eyes. I remember my second husband, Mr. Steele, before he went to his reward. His eyes seemed so quiet"—she paused, her eyes looking off to see the scene, "quiet with acceptance. But now Emmett Tillman is a different man."

Then she suddenly turned her attention to the boy. "How would you like a glass of cold buttermilk, young man?"

"Now, Miz Fanny, he doesn't need a thing. Don't you bother yourself. I just wanted to visit a minute and maybe sneak a few lilies for the church. That's such a fine bed you have out front."

"Help yourself to anything you see, Mabel. But it's no bother at all to get this young man a glass of buttermilk. I'll get you some shears and you can be doing that while I go to the kitchen."

No one had bothered getting the boy's answer; did he want some buttermilk?

Mrs. Fanny trudged down the hall to the back of the house. The boy's aunt took the shears and went out to cut flowers, leaving him suddenly alone with Mrs. Fanny. She hummed a fragment of a hymn as she opened the icebox. Taking a gallon crock from inside, she poured the frothy buttermilk into a big glass. He watched the yellow flecks of butter swirl around as she placed the glass in front of him and said, "There." As she did so she leaned close to him and the inside of her dressing gown folded open just enough so part of her breast showed. It was whiter than the brown, freckled skin of her throat and there were little blue veins near the nipple, but he could not see the nipple.

Tommy swallowed his saliva as she drew away, no sign that she knew he had seen, no sign that she even cared whether he had seen. She said, "That ought to hold you. There's more if you want it."

"Yessum." He started to drink, tasting it gingerly. He had never drunk buttermilk before and was not prepared for the sour acrid taste. He wrinkled his nose.

"It's a little sour. Is that the way it's supposed to taste?" he asked.

"Let me see," and picked up his glass, taking a taste. "Why sure. That's good and fresh."

He took the glass and held it, she still looking, but he was thinking about where her old lips had touched the glass, marked harshly by the drying buttermilk.

"It'll do you good, besides being good," she said, he not believing.

"Well, now, it's time for Mr. Tillman's medicine," she announced. "You just go right ahead and drink your buttermilk," she insisted. She opened a wooden cabinet over the sink and took down two bottles of pills, then poured one red and two yellow ones. She took a glass from another cupboard, and placed all of this on a silver tray.

He had decided while she was doing this that the only way was to drink this buttermilk like he would milk of magnesia. Block out as much taste, smell, sight as possible, scrunch up the inside of your head until your ears rang like the wind was blowing. Then gulp, trying to will no feeling in your mouth. And he did.

Mrs. Fanny turned around carrying the tray just as he set the glass on the table.

"My, my. You must of been thirsty," she said, putting the tray down again. "Let me get you some more."

"No ma'am. I'm filled up." Oh don't make me drink anymore, please, please.

"All right," said Mrs. Fanny.

She shuffled out of the kitchen and down the hall to Mr. Tillman's room. He got up from the table and took his glass to the sink and rinsed it out. Just like his mother. Have to drink this. Have to eat kidney stew. Ugh.

He saw an ancient picture in the big hall through the kitchen door and walked over to it. It was an old man in a high white collar and gold rimmed glasses.

The hall floor was unvarnished in the middle from years and years of walking to the bathroom at the end of the hall and the kitchen. This great hall had a high ceiling. Its wallpaper was no longer snug against the wall, but hung like the loose flesh on a fat woman's arms. Brown, liver-looking water spots all over the ceiling and walls were now like permanent decorations that seemed to belong with the brown-yellowness and thick musty air. The house smelled almost like a funeral home he had visited once. These were special smells like some other houses he'd visited in this town.

The pine boards creaked as Mrs. Fanny came from the bedroom. She was humming a Methodist hymn as she carried a white enamel bedpan in front of her. Long used to the odor of urine and human feces, she did not wrinkle her nose. The smell lingered on her waddling train of air. Cleaning noises came from the bathroom and then she came out.

"I'll be through in a minute, son. Soon as I fix up Mr. Tillman," she said, noticing him looking at the picture.

"Who is this?" he asked.

"That's a picture of Dr. Waterson, my husband," she replied, as she reentered the room.

He puzzled about that. Waterson? Why was her name Steele?

When she came out she said, "I was his nurse in the hospital in New Orleans and we got married there." She paused half-pensively, "That was many years ago. There's just me doing the nursing now."

He was faintly embarrassed by some of this conversation, but he said, "Yessum."

"Why don't you say hello to Mr. Tillman? He doesn't get to see many people now cause he sleeps so much and he'd enjoy it. He won't be able to say much, though," and she ushered him into the room.

The shades were drawn but there was still enough light to see. There in the bed lay the old man, his head propped up high enough that the immense oak headboard seemed to frame his gray-covered skull. His eyes flickered with interest as the boy followed Mrs. Fanny.

"Tommy, this is Mr. Tillman. Emmett, this is Mabel's nephew. He's visiting us in Bethel this summer," said Mrs. Fanny.

The old man croaked out, "Hello . . . boy," and moved his hand as if to shake hands. The boy reached and took it in his own and shook it once. The knuckles were big and the hand was bent in the peculiar way of arthritis.

"How do you do, sir," answered Tommy. He didn't know what to say.

The old man tried to urge something else out, but the boy couldn't understand.

"Sir?" embarrassed.

"What's that Emmett?" demanded Mrs. Fanny, louder than Tommy thought necessary.

Mr. Tillman's chest began to heave convulsively. "Huuh . . . huuh." His yellow eyes began rolling wildly and he coughed, racking his thin body, barely visible underneath the crocheted coverlet. Some of the phlegm in his eyes caught in his eyelashes. Mrs. Fanny reached over with her fingers to wipe them and then wiped the phlegm on her dressing gown.

The coughing subsided a moment and she said, "Come on, son, let's let Mr. Tillman rest." Mr. Tillman looked at him forlornly Tommy thought, as if the old man didn't want him to leave, as if he had something to tell him.

Mrs. Fanny was fingering the coverlet. "I crocheted this a long time ago. Do you like it?" she asked Tommy, apparently no longer interested in the man.

"Yessum."

"Come see the one on my bed," and led the way into the hall and into the adjoining room. There was a door between the two, but on Mrs. Fanny's side, there was an old armoire blocking the way.

"This one took me long hours to do, but I've always liked it," she said, moving her palm over the coverlet, caressing it.

On one wall near the foot of her tester bed was a picture that the boy looked at briefly. It hung so that it could be seen if someone was lying in the bed. There were two figures, a young man and a young woman. They were in postures of affectionate adoration. The young woman had a misty face, hard ivory cheeks with a rouged blush of innocence, and long blond hair hung to her bosom at which point the man's head, covered with blond ringlets, rested in divine repose.

Above the head of the bed a picture of Jesus hung so that no one could see it lying down in bed. It was on a calendar and one of those views of Jesus with a bright red valentine heart that glistened on his outer garments. The year of the calendar caught the boy's attention because it was before he was even born.

Mrs. Fanny had big hands and wrists. They looked out of place as she picked up some little porcelain figurines and showed them to him.

"These are some from my house in New Orleans."

He turned them over in his hands and nodded. He wished he was back over at the service station talking to Gene, his friend. His daddy ran the service station and Gene worked there on Saturday. The big cow trucks and farm tractors pulled in for gas and oil. Gene's daddy said it was all right for him to help put the gas in and wipe the windshields. A lot of the men parked their pickups near the station and came in just to talk. There were several Coke cases to sit on and one chair near the Coke machine. Some of the men shot long streams of tobacco juice near the stove that wasn't working. Tommy wished he were there watching them. He felt uneasy.

The back door slammed and he could hear his Aunt Mabel in the kitchen. Mrs. Fanny looked very slightly annoyed but said, "Let's go see what your aunt has got." She put her arm around his shoulder and walked by him to the kitchen. He thought he would die, but then he remembered her breast and even though he was uncomfortable, he felt pleasingly warm. He insisted to himself, however, that he wanted to get away. She dropped her arm before they came to Aunt Mabel.

"Oh, Miz Fanny, everything was so fresh and beautiful, I just hated to cut anything. But just look at them. Aren't they nice?" She had an arm load of white lilies spread out on newspaper on the kitchen table. The yellow pollen was dusted over the big round insides and made Tommy almost heady as Mrs. Fanny offered one for him to smell. He took the one she offered him and the juicy sap stained his hand. It was sticky and a little perplexing. He wanted to wipe his hands on his pants, but he couldn't and so it dried there. Most of the other thick stems were together and looked like asparagus in a glass jar.

"Let me help you put them in water, Mabel," and the two women busied themselves with their chore.

Again he thought of the service station. While he was there this morning, before Aunt Mabel came and got him, he had told Gene he had to go with his aunt to Mrs. Fanny's. Some of the men sitting around the station had heard him and started talking about her among themselves. He had overheard them discuss all the land she had around the country and every once in a while they would laugh quietly. The men had mentioned Mr Tillman, too, but they had said something Tommy didn't understand, something about *passing him out*. He didn't know what that meant.

"Well, now, they'll look real nice for Easter services, won't they, Miz Fanny," commented Aunt Mabel. "You're going to be able to come, aren't you?"

"It doesn't look like it, Mabel, honey. Mercy me, I'll have to be here with Emmett. And I know everyone is going to be there, too. But I just don't see how. But my lilies will be there anyway.

"Well, don't you fret. I'll mention you to everybody," she said and then turned to Tommy. "So, youngun, let's us go. Take some of the flowers." He did as he was told.

"Thank Miz Fanny for the buttermilk."

"Thank you for the buttermilk and everything," he murmured.

"You come back and see me, you hear," and she pressed his thin shoulder with her arm.

He and his aunt walked along the gravel street to their house. He waved across the railroad track to Gene at the service station, and hoped he didn't look too sissified carrying a vase of flowers walking by his aunt.

The Organ Piece

BERRY MORGAN

I HAD LIVED right here on this plantation on to fifty-odd years and never had had a bit of confusion with white or colored. Lots of times when I started to King's Town with my vegetables, Mama would tell me watch out for people's mean tricks, or not carry my collards to a particular lady's, but I went right on, because our Lord said "Let not your heart be troubled" and mine wasn't. The only thing I ever got into that it looked like I might not get back out of again was listening at an organ piece, and I didn't want to do that.

The cause of my going to hear it was Laurance Ingles. He was a white boy that grew up out there by himself in the big house with nobody to notice him but the cook, because his family went away to New Orleans and forgot about him. And Laurance was a good boy—*meant* to be good—but he was hard to cross. Mama said that was because he was birthed backwards—hind end before—and maybe so, but whatever it was from you couldn't hardly go against what Laurance said you had to do. He was fine though.

Laurance used to come by every Sunday to see Mama and me. If the weather was too bad to keep him on the porch, Mama would let him come in and sit by the curtain to her bed and they would talk a little. "You don't notice my china jar, do you Laurance?" Mama would ask him, trying to get on to how much she made me sun it, and he would say no ma'am, not at all, until it got to be a little foolishness we counted on.

About the piece, I already knew Laurance played the piano because we could hear it in the summertime all the way from his house, but I didn't know he was practicing on the organ too. And he was. One Sunday when he came by, Mama and I both noticed he was acting mighty pleased over something—he must have been about fourteen then—and fixing to start up about it.

First he asked Mama how her head was. She had those terrible sick headaches and you never knew. But while she was trying to tell him, he reached in his pocket and brought up something that looked like a fancy key. And then it came out it was to the organ at the white Church and he had got permission to practice on it and had a piece by heart that he could play straight through.

I looked at Mama. She didn't keep but a little slit of curtain open by her bed because she couldn't stand the light, but even through this I could see her look *that way* at me. Well, I went to the kitchen right quick to make some Kool-Aid, so I could give her time to veer him off. Because already, bless her heart, she had seen him heading toward getting me to go to the Church with him and listen at the piece. You see nothing made a bit of difference to him—no kind of argument that the Church was white, or anything.

"It's such a nice invitation," I said when I got back, "and I appreciate it to the highest, and furthermore I know the Church is beautiful on the inside and the piece would be a real treat, but I am colored."

Mama didn't give him a chance to beat this down. "Don't you lead Roxie into trouble," she said. But like I knew he would, Laurance went right on—we could go when there was nobody in the Church and I could listen at him that once and then leave—like he never heard a word.

Mama sat up in bed then, which she is not supposed to on account of it rushing her heart. "And what am I going to do," she asked him, "lying helpless from I don't know how many strokes, and Roxie in the jailhouse?"

"For what?" Laurence wanted to know. "What would she be in the jailhouse for?"

And then Mama pulled the curtain to and pinned it and told Laurance to run along. He had set off her head with his wild talk.

I started to rub her feet—that's what she liked the best—and after a while she was getting sleepy. I made myself respectful, all the while thinking about how lonesome Laurance was, with only us colored to know, and there he had gone to all the pains of learning a piece, and it did look like I ought to be willing to leastways go and listen. After a while an idea came to me of dusting. If any rightful members happened by and found me in the Church, I could say I'd come to dust it, after he played, because I helped Laurance's cooks off and on—especially when they're putting up—and it sounded true.

After I got Mama to sleep, I couldn't stop myself—I changed into my good dress and got my gloves and an old handkerchief that

I wouldn't mind using to dust and started to walk up to the big house. And sure enough there was Laurance waiting in the place's truck, so he must have expected all the time that I'd give in. On the way to town, I made him promise over and over he would never tell, that he would never say a word to Mama.

But as soon as we were in the Church, I forgot all about my cause for worriment. The stained colored windows reached all the way to its roof and a tall gold cross was at one end, and things seemed to gleam from a special dark and I could hardly catch my breath. I followed Laurance on up to where the organ was and sat down in back of him. Right by me and handy to look out of was a clear spot in Jesus's robe that I could use—not so much to spy on any rightful member that was coming, just to be a little bit careful.

And then the music started. It seemed to come from every which way at once. There was no way to make it stand back, and I saw my whole life passing right in front of me in the organ piece. At the end of it I was crying, because this might be something like God's face on Judgment Day was going to be.

I had forgotten all about the hole in Jesus's robe and watching out. And when the music stopped, a light shined on us and the front door had come open. Two ladies were standing there with flowers in their arms. One was a friendly, white-haired lady I clean floors for just before Christmas every year, but the other one I didn't know—an old shaky-headed lady that I found out later was the first one's cousin and on a visit to her from Columbia. I got out my handkerchief and started on the plan while Laurance closed the organ up. All the time the two of them were tiptoeing up the aisle—they had dropped the flowers—and finally I thought it wasn't right to not say something and I told them good evening.

"Roxie," the one who was my friend said, like she was brokenhearted, "don't you know this is God's house?"

"Yes ma'am," I said, and something made my stomach dodge, but I went on. "I was just dusting for Mr. Laurance here and he has permission to practice on it."

Well, the two of them stood there and looked at us and you would have thought they were witnessing a sight. "I've heard about this boy and his cook," the one who was my friend said to the other one, "and now he's using the Church."

Laurance started down the aisle then, and I followed him, and we stepped over the big-headed summer flowers that had fallen when they saw us. And as soon as we got to the truck and started home, all I could think of was that they would send the Sheriff after me and put me in jail and ruin the good names of Mama and her father, the Reverend Isaac Stoner, who was sanctified in Grace. But I had sense enough left not to taint a child with my worry and I didn't let on a thing to Laurance—just told him over and over again how much I loved the piece.

That night I couldn't sleep at all. Every time Mama wanted me I was sitting there waiting for the headlights of the law, but thank our Heavenly Father none came—there was only the soft moon, waning, and a few whippoorwills. And I began to hope the ladies had felt sorry for me after all, and overlooked telling the Sheriff. Or maybe they told him and he liked me so much he refused to come after me, even for mixing, because one time he said something about me raising the finest okra he ever ate. I didn't know.

By morning I had given God a solid promise that if Mama didn't find *this* out, and have to suffer shame on my account, I would never mix again. And when she woke up and I started my work, I kept looking at her from around corners, but she hadn't noticed a thing and was clearing her throat like she does.

By the time I'd finished up for her and gone outside to hoe in my cucumbers that were grown up in Johnson grass, here was Laurance coming down the cattle path. He had on the same clothes he'd worn to the Church, and when he got up close I saw his eyes were red, like he'd been crying. But he didn't say a thing except asked again how had I liked the piece, and I mustered all the heart I could and bragged some more.

"It's a good thing you heard it when you did," he said, after he'd watched me skin grass awhile. "Or else you never would of. They needed back the key." And he went on to tell how two deacons had gotten through his dogs and made the cook wake him up after dark to take it back, and now he could never play the organ piece again.

I wanted to fall on my knees right in the cucumbers. To think of what little faith I had when the Almighty spent the same night I was so worried steering the whole thing around to keep Mama from ever finding out.

They were bound to do something, I told him. And that was about the least they could do when they caught me in there with you. But I saw he didn't care or understand about that, he wanted me to sorrow for *him* over it, and I did—or anyway I tried to.

FROM

Good Old Boy

WILLIE MORRIS

WHEN I WAS FIVE my mother took me by the hand into the two-story brick schoolhouse on Main Street, and left me in the care of Miss Bass, a stern old lady who looked as if she would bite. Bubba Barrier was in my room. Someone was supposed to get me after the first day was out, but failed to come. Bubba and I were frightened, but finally we walked hand in hand away from the school, along the bayou, up Grand Avenue and home. Such adventure befitted a boy's stature as a first grader in the Free Public School System of Yazoo County, Mississippi.

The school was a big old structure with white columns, iron fire escapes, and tall old-fashioned windows. It was set in a large plot of three or four acres; the public library was at one end of the lot, and at the other, in the farthest corner of the grounds, the gray Confederate monument. On top of the monument about thirty feet from the ground were two statues: a lady holding a Confederate flag in front of her, and a soldier with a rifle in one hand, his other hand slightly raised to accept the flag—but a little shyly, as if he did not want to go around all day holding both a flag and a gun, particularly with a ten-inch bayonet attached.

Inside, the school building was all long, shadowy halls, smelling always of wax. On the wall near the front door were portraits of George Washington and Jefferson Davis. Downstairs was a large basement, where we met to wait for the morning bell to ring on rainy days and where, at noon, we took our lunch. It was a dark, eerie place; I was to have a nightmare of those years. I am trying to climb out of the sunless basement through a small, narrow window to the playground outside. The window is not big enough. My trouser legs are caught in it, nothing can budge me. The bell rings, everyone goes upstairs, and I am left alone. Some rainy gray mornings, waiting in that concrete chamber with its one light bulb in the peeled ceiling casting strange shadows, I could hardly bear the time until the bell rang. The room was attached to the boys' toilet, and from it came the echoes of the toilets flushing. Off to the side, in a kind of wired-in room, was the lunch hall, where lunches sold for a dime apiece and where the teachers, with shouts and sometimes slaps, would make us finish all our wieners and sauerkraut or bologna and black-eyed peas. It was our small contribution to the "war effort," eating everything on our plate. It might have been easier to lose the war.

All this was in the early 1940s, and the Second World War was on to defend democracy, as our teachers told us. They told us we were in school to help democracy, to strengthen our country and our God, and to learn enough so we could make good money for ourselves. In the assembly hall upstairs, where we marched in every Friday with the music teacher playing the March from *Aida* on the spinet piano, the American flag on the right of the stage and the Confederate flag on the left, the speaker would tell us of the man he once knew who could have been President of the United States, except that when the time came for him to be chosen, some of his friends felt honorbound to tell everybody that he had been lazy, lied a great deal, and had taken to liquor when he was young; so he never got the chance to be President. Quite frankly, I did not believe this story, and neither did Bubba Barrier.

I had a friend named Spit McGee who lived far out in the country. Spit was something of a lone wolf. He wore khaki clothes and did not come to school except when the mood was upon him. He was long and skinny, with a red face and a nose that should have belonged with somebody else's face. His given name was Clarence, but he concealed that fact; he could spit farther than anyone else, and with unusual accuracy.

Spit lived in the swamps, and he was a hunter and fisherman. Foxie Tompkins might bring an apple to school for the teacher, but not Spit. If he brought her anything it would be a catfish, or a dead squirrel for frying. Rivers Applewhite was often the recipient of the most beautiful wild swamp flowers, which Spit brought into town in the spring. One day he brought the teacher a dead chicken snake in a burlap sack, and a chicken was still inside the snake's belly (or whatever snakes call bellies); but the teacher made him bury it behind the Confederate monument. Later she caught him chewing tobacco near the snake's grave and gave him an F in Conduct. When she caught him smoking a Camel two weeks later she sent a note to Spit's mother, but Spit told me he wasn't worried because his mother couldn't read.

One day during recess Spit reached into his pockets and pulled out a dead grubworm, a live boll weevil, a wad of chewed-up bubble gum, four leaves of poison ivy which he said he was not allergic to, two shotgun shells, a small turtle, a rusty fish hook, the feather from a wild turkey, a minnow, the shrunken head of a chipmunk, and a slice of bacon. Spit may not have been smart in the ways of books, but he was diligent and resourceful, with a wisdom that came straight from the swamps. He claimed that he had taken an old useless .12 gauge shotgun and made it into a pellet gun, manufacturing his own bullets from rusty tin cans and soaking them in a mixture of frog's blood, burnt moss, dust from rattlesnake rattles, cypress juice, and mashed black widow spiders. When a victim was hit by one of these pellets, he said, it would not kill him, but knock him completely unconscious for three hours. He even said he had tried it once on his father, who was drunk in a willow tree, and that his father, not knowing what hit him, had not only been knocked out for six hours but once he did awaken gave up whiskey for three months.

We were envious of him not merely because of the bounty he carried in his pockets, but because he came to school barefooted whenever he felt like it, while we had to wear shoes that pinched our big toes and made our feet itch. He also claimed he could predict when it would rain from an ache he got in his arm, which he had broken falling out of a chinaberry tree. To my knowledge he was not wrong on a single rainfall. He further claimed that he was the great-great-nephew of Joe Bob Duggett—the boy who had discovered the witch in 1884—that he had once spent the night sleeping on an old blanket on the witch's grave in the cemetery, that he had dug up a grave in a Baptist cemetery on a plantation near the River, and that he had not taken a bath since the previous Easter. On the first three points we felt he was lying, but we believed him on the fourth.

At noon recess one day, when we were in third grade, Spit said he was going to play a prank on our teacher. Then he took off mysteriously for the bayou with a big box under his arm. When the bell rang half an hour later and we filed into our room, I saw a sight such as I will never forget. About three dozen crawdads, in all postures and movements, were crawling around the room. Five or six of them were on the teacher's desk, and one had gotten into her purse. The teacher was in a state of considerable anger, and she demanded to know who had done this horrible deed. For a while there was silence, and then Foxie Tompkins and Edith Stillwater, the teacher's pets, shouted almost at once. "It was Spit McGee!" Poor Spit got three paddlings: one from the teacher, one from the principal, and one from the superintendent of city schools, the last one being the worst because the superintendent had a paddle with air holes in it to make bigger blisters.

The next day there was revenge on a massive scale. Since I had taken Edith Stillwater to two war movies at the Dixie Theater (*Guadalcanal Diary* and *Flying Leathernecks*), spending ten cents each on her, I demanded the return of my twenty cents. (She only gave me back a dime.) She was giving a piano recital at the Baptist Church that afternoon before about fifty proud and cooing relatives and friends; we sneaked into the church early and got the piano out of tune, scraped some fresh cow manure onto the piano pedals, and placed a stray alley cat inside the piano and put the top back down. Then, led by Spit, we cornered Foxie Tompkins and marched him off to our official meeting place, the chicken shed behind Henjie Henick's house. After borrowing a rope from Henjie, Spit tied one end to the rafter and made a hangman's noose with the other. Then we put Foxie on a wooden box, tightened the noose around his neck, and told him to apologize fifty times in a row, but that he had better do it quickly because the box was shaky and if it fell over, that would be the end of Foxie's fine career, both in school and otherwise. We retired from the chicken coop and closed the door. From outside we heard Foxie apologizing rapidly, in a determined but squeaky voice. Just at that moment a funeral came by on Grand Avenue, and we went over to watch it. We forgot about Foxie. Luckily for his career, Henjie Henick's mother went back to feed the chickens and found Foxie balancing on his toes just as the box was beginning to fall over.

At the Baptist Church, we were told later, the cat squealed as Edith Stillwater started her off-key étude, ruining the recital. All that remained was to take the crawdads, which the teacher had returned to Spit, back to the bayou. As a celebration, Spit led us to the chicken snake's grave and we dug it up, to find that the snake had rotted but the chicken was still there.

This list of my schooltime favorites, Bubba, Spit, and all the rest, would not be complete without the one I think of the most: Rivers. Rivers Applewhite. She was without doubt the most beautiful girl in our class, but she was not a demure kind of beauty. Not at all. She wore her dark brown hair short (sometimes the way the models did in *Harper's Bazaar*) to offset her fine willowy grace, and she had deep green eyes, and in spring and summer she was always brown as a berry from all the time she spent in the sun. I am also pleased to say that she was not a tomboy; who in his proper senses would want a girl to kick a football farther than he could, or outrun him in the 50-yard dash? She was smart as could be—much smarter than Edith Stillwater, even though Edith got better grades—and she got Spit McGee through final exams in the third grade by bribing him, with the lemon pies she always was baking, to practice his long division and memorize poems. (Spit McGee once recited Browning: "Oh to be in April, Now that England's here.") She was also partial to Old Skip, my dog, and would bring him bones and cotton candy, so Skip was a regular old fool over Rivers Applewhite, sidling up to her with his tail wagging, putting his wet black nose against the palm of her hand, jumping and gyrating in her presence like the craziest creature alive. Unlike some of the other girls, especially Edith Stillwater, she would never so much as consider telling the teacher on anybody, and to this day I cannot recall a traitorous or deceitful act on her part. Kind, beautiful, a fount of good fun and cheer, she was the best of all feminine symbols to the wild and unregenerate boys of Yazoo. All of us, dogs and boys alike, were a little bit in love with Rivers Applewhite.

I remember her in a white summer dress, one day shortly before Christmas in Yazoo, walking up a sidewalk of Main Street under the bright holiday tinsel. As always, we were riding in Bubba's old red Ford, and we saw her from a half a block away, recognizing her from behind by the way she walked, half on her toes and half on her heels. As we got up close behind her near Kuhn's Nickel and Dime Store, I noticed that she *rippled* along that sidewalk, and that when she passed by people coming her way, just smiling calmly and being her jaunty self, they got a smile on their faces too.

There was terror for me in that school. Miss Abbott was my fourth grade teacher, and for the first time my grades were bad and my conduct report worse.

Miss Abbott had a pink nose and came from a small town in

South Mississippi. The only book she ever read through and through, she told us, was the Bible, and you lived to believe her, and to feel bad about the day she got hold of that book. I myself liked the Bible. I had my own private friendship with God, which included the good old hymns and quiet mumbled prayers and holy vengeance when it was really deserved, and in that town and in that age you took God so much for granted that you knew he was keeping a separate book on you as part of His day's work.

But Miss Abbott's religion was one of fear and terror—it got you by the hind end and never let go. It was a thing of long, crazy speeches; she wanted you to believe she herself was in telephone contact with the Lord, and had hung the moon for Him on day number four. She played a little plastic flute which she had bought at Woolworth's for a quarter, and she would play us rousing hymns and marches, paying no attention to the saliva trickling down the instrument to the floor. She would not drink Coca-Cola, she said, because of the liquor hidden in it. She would preach to us every day: if God ever caught us doing something wrong, she said, we would surely go to hell before the next sunrise.

Twice a day, early in the morning and in the afternoon after lunch, she would call on each of us to pray. We would all begin by blessing our soldiers and then ripping into the Germans and the Japs. Once Spit began his prayer by saying, "Dear Lord, thank you for the bombs that ain't fallin' on us," and then stopped. "What's wrong?" the teacher asked, and he said, "I just can't think of nuthin' else to say." Then would come the Bible verses. For two hours each morning she would make us recite the verses she had assigned us to learn by heart. When we forgot a verse, she would rap our palms with a twelve-inch ruler. Then out would come that flute again, and if she caught you drowsing while she piped away on some song, or scratching your weary tail, she would go to her conduct book, and with a slight little flourish write down a "5."

I made the mistake of correcting her one day, during one of the rare hours in which we were doing schoolwork. The capital of Missouri, she said, was St. Louis. I held up my hand.

"What is it, Willie?" she asked.

"Miss Abbott, the capital of Missouri is Jefferson City."

"No, it's St. Louis."

"I bet it's Jefferson City," I said, and then immediately wished I hadn't said it because the Bible was against gambling.

"Kay King," she snapped, "look in the book and show him it's St. Louis."

The girl looked in the book and turned red. "Well," she said, "it says here Jefferson City," but frightened, like everyone else in that ill-fated class, she added, "But Miss Abbott ought to—"

"We'll see," Miss Abbott growled, and changed the subject. Later, during "silent study," I caught her glowering at me. Why couldn't those wretched people in Missouri have settled on St. Louis? Then Rivers Applewhite sent a note over to me that said: "I'm proud of you. Someday you will be Governor of Mississippi."

At noon recess that spring, while the teacher sat on the grass with a group of fawning little girls around her who fetched things for her and scratched her back when it itched, gave her little compliments and practiced their Bible verses, held her hand and looked for four-leaf clovers to put behind her red ears, we were playing softball nearby. Honest Ed Upton hit a lazy foul that went high into the air behind third base. From shortstop I watched it come down with mounting interest, with an almost fanatic regard, as the ball drifted earthward and smacked Miss Abbott on the head. She sprawled on the ground, with a moo like a milk cow's—out cold. *Oh joy of joys!* The other teachers picked her up and carried her away in a car. In our room later, with the principal looking out for us, all the little girls cried—silent little bawls—and even Honest Ed Upton shed tears. The boys scratched their heads and fiddled with their pencils; such was the fear in that room, they dared not look into one another's eyes. All except Spit McGee. He caught a glance of mine and puckered up his lips, and before long a note in pencil came over from him—*i wich she got hit with a hardbal insted.* I prayed that she would die.

But back she came, risen on the third day. One Friday afternoon, when she had stepped out of the room, I made a spitball and threw it over two rows at Kay King. "*Willie!*" The sound of Miss Abbott's voice sent terror to my soul. Each afternoon during that wonderful spring I had to stay in, two hours a day for six weeks, working long division. Miss Abbott would sit at her desk, reading the Bible or *Reader's Digest,* while the shadows got longer and the sound of the boys' voices wafted in through the open window. And when that year ended, with a C on my report card in math, I had crossed, waded, swum the Sea of Galilee, and joyously entered the city limits of old Jerusalem.

The Sin Eater

Lewis Nordan

LATER, WHEN THE CHILD would go over these events in his mind, he would imagine the old woman, Mrs. Tremble, as she would have appeared a moment before she heard the sound of the ambulance. The peacocks, living wild in the cottonwoods, descendants of birds that once strutted tame across this property, would have heard the siren first. Their shrieks and shrill comedy might have alerted her, their thunderous bustle and flutter across pastures and into the deeper woods. The slave-built house, with its spacious porch and gently sagging roofline, visible from the child's bedroom if he had thought to look a hundred yards across the goat pasture, would have sat bright and unchanged in the late-morning sun. Inside the house would have sat Mrs. Tremble, by a small fire in her living room. Her high windows would be closed, as would the drapes, against the first chill of the Mississippi autumn. A floor lamp, with a brass base and a tasseled shade, would be her only light. When the sound of the siren reached her, she would remove her glasses from their place on her nose and lay aside the needlepoint motto on which she had been working. "What on earth can it be?" she might have said, in her ridiculous, grandmotherly way. "I swan." She would have put aside the pipe that she was smoking.

The child who would imagine her was ten years old, named Robert McIntyre. In his bedroom, in this more modest house, he saw the green bottle, which he had filled with kerosene. He saw it touch the lips of his baby brother. Like a kiss, he thought, even as the oily fluid flowed over the lips and off the infant's chin. Even as the little head jolted backwards. The eyes rolled up and became white and senseless. The baby had drunk the kerosene Robert was hiding. The kerosene he had thought even a parent could not find.

But Robert did not move, not yet. He could not. His brother, already unconscious but not yet fallen, weaved drunkenly, like a comic actor on a television screen. Who was that actor, Robert thought. The child fell, and the bottle clattered against the floor. The kerosene darkened the wood, and Robert saw the future. He knew his brother would not live. As soon as he knew that, he screamed.

He lifted his brother's head. With his too-short fingers he reached into the narrow throat to call back the kerosene and cause the accident not to have happened. An oily froth covered Robert's fingers, warmly. The pupilless eyes were still open. Then, in revulsion, he jerked away. He stood above his brother and scrubbed his fingers against his pants.

He saw the objects of his house, and the sounds and persons, as if they were old, recognizable photographs. There was his mother on the telephone. There was the empty bottle, the stain on the floor. There was a voice, his mother's voice, and there were his own words, like mice, scuttering and scurrying and contemptible. A white ambulance was in the driveway, surrounded by the peacock's cries, and, immediately, his father's car also. Robert noticed two patches of rust on the roof of the car and found that he hated his father for them.

His father's voice said, "Robbie, listen. Go to Mrs. Tremble's. Tell Mrs. Tremble what happened. I'll call from the hospital." When his mother came back into the room, Robert realized he had been seeing her all these years only in miniature, as if he looked at a dense concentration of the woman and not, perhaps, as everyone else had already seen her. She seemed now to be a tree, one of the ancient sycamores in the back pasture, silver-blue and enormous. A redtailed hawk swooped near but did not light, balancing upon the wind.

When the ambulance was gone, Robert was alone. He stared at the bottle, which was no longer there, because his father had taken it in the ambulance, but which he could still see, the bottle he had filled and hid. The kerosene he planned to use for—he didn't know what. Games, on the lakebank. Little fires.

Before the sound of the words reached him, or any sound, he knew Mrs. Tremble was in the room. Kindly fat rich ancient shaky-hands old Mrs. Tremble, with the white hair and wild peacocks and the gaseous aroma of pipe tobacco and face powder. Her breath preceded her like a messenger of lightning and thunder. "Robert," said her voice. "What on earth has happened, child? I saw the ambulance." Robert turned to face her, since doing so was unavoidable. Because of her concern, perhaps, she had become even more of what she had always been, old and quiet and kind and repulsive and grandmotherly, and somehow frightening now as well. She had thin, pale lips, which seemed always to be chapped. In them were tiny vertical lines that looked painful, and her breath, which could travel long distances without diminution of effect, stank like a pipe-smoker's. Though she was never actually known to smoke a pipe, it was never doubted by any child who drew within her considerable range that she did so and that the pipe, should it ever be discovered, would be of briar and grotesque of shape and deadly poison. "Whatever in the world has happened, child?"

In Mrs. Tremble's living room, Robert became very small. By magic, he had shrunk, as soon as he walked through the front door. He sat as far forward as possible in a blue brocaded chair, but still his feet would not touch the floor. His elbows, no matter how hard he strained, would not rest comfortably on the chair arms. He had been in this room many times, but it had never shrunk him before. The colors had never been so bright, nor the ceilings so high. Long-necked golden birds shrieked at him from the Chinese carpets. There was a tiny fire in the fireplace, though it was only October and not really cold yet, and there was a smell, sulfurous and sickening, which Robert believed must be the moist, solid residue of Mrs. Tremble's breath, growing and reproducing in the rugs and drapes and upholstered chairs.

Mrs. Tremble fussed around the room, out again and back again, monstrously cheerful. Everything would be fine, she said, just fine. Her breath streaked around the room like a laser, rebounding from the walls and floors and ceiling. Robert watched it and stayed out of its path. What Robert must do, she said, must *promise* her right this minute he would do, was not worry. Worry was by far the worst thing in the world he could do right now. His little brother was going to be fine, yes siree, just you wait and see. Robert was afraid she might hug him, but she stayed her distance. Her breath idled between them like an engine.

There was to be a choice: Lemonade, or hot chocolate, or spiced tea. Now which would it be? she wanted to know. Which do you choose? He could have a cinnamon stick with the tea, she promised. For a moment a strange feeling passed through his body. He believed he might be a character in a book that somebody else was reading. He looked at Mrs. Tremble, and at her breath. It was the spiced tea that made him wonder. He tried to see Mrs. Tremble as he had seen his mother, the larger tree in which her miniature was contained. But nothing changed. He could see nothing differently. "No, thank you, Mrs. Tremble," he said. "Nothing for me, thanks."

So he waited. He moved from the brocaded chair to the fire and looked into the little wreckage of coals. Even the fire had an odd smell, a little too sweet, as if she might be burning applewood. The firescreen was black and large, with tiny brass handles at either side. The poker and shovel and tongs were also heavy and black. When he tried to think of his brother's dying, he found that he could not. He remembered Jack and the Beanstalk, disobedient child of a grieving mother. The harp and hen and golden eggs. The race downward through vegetation, the ax, the collapse and fall and death of the giant. The green breath streaked suddenly over his right shoulder and made the fire blaze up. Sparks crackled and shot up the chimney. "Do you like the fire, Robert?" said the words that came trailing in the wake.

He struggled not to flinch. He thought of Hansel in the wooden cage. He saw Gretel stare deep into the oven. He braced himself but could not force himself to turn and meet her unbelievable, cheery eyes, or risk breathing her fumes. "Yes m'am," he said, into the fire. Did he like the fire? What might such a question mean? "Yes, it's nice," he said. "A nice little fire."

There had been a grass fire once, set accidentally by his father in the back pasture. Robert helped fight it with rakes and wet rugs. The smoke burned his chest when he breathed it, but Robert had not minded. When it spread to the edge of the woods, tractors plowed lanes around the flames. His father, riding one of the tractors, was the handsomest man in the world that day. His eyes had streamed with tears in the smoke. There was a gasoline fire too, another day, set by a child Robert's age. It caught the child's clothes and burned his jeans and boots into the flesh. Robert had not seen it; only, later, the grafted skin. He had seen it in his dreams, though. He had smelled the flesh and rubber in his dreams. There was a house too that burned, a shack. He remembered the pathetic few pieces of furniture someone had saved. They sat beside the smoking ashes and standing chimney, a chair, a wooden table, a dark wardrobe. They sat in the weather, long after the ashes had cooled and washed away. They whitened and rotted and finally were gone. There would have been his own little fires, on the lakebank. The kerosene. Burning ships, forts surrounded by Indians, volcanoes, human sacrifice. He wondered if kerosene felt like fire in the baby's throat. He wondered how people died.

Once, in a museum, he had thought of dying. He saw a stiff brown hunk of contorted clay in a glass case, and he learned it was a mummified child. This was the first time he ever thought he might die. He had seen his father kill wild dogs, the packs that sometimes came out of the woods and took down a goat, or larger stock. Brass shell casings would leap from the rifle, and the animals would scatter and drop. Sometimes they were only wounded, and his father would close their clear eyes at closer range.

He went outside the house. A noisy, noxious rocket of pipesmoker's breath streaked past his ear and struck a fencepost deep in the pasture. It crumbled and collapsed into ashes, and the six gauge barbed wire fell slack in that section. The voice said, "Robert. Oh, Robert dear. Won't you need a coat, child?" Beds of fireants crackled and burned and lay silent and gray and motionless. "Please don't go far. Promise you won't, Robert. If anything happened to you, I'd . . ." What would she do? he thought. Would she die? He tried not to wish that she would die. He tried not to wish that he would die. "I'm sorry," he prayed.

He was deep in the back pasture now. A she-goat was stuck by her horns, like small scimitars, in the squares of fence wire, where she had tried to reach a sweeter clump of grass. He walked to the crying animal and released the horns. He crossed the fence and walked toward the lake and woods.

It was afternoon now, and the air had more chill than he had thought. He could not go back for his jacket. What kind of person would call a boy "Robert dear" or "child"? What kind of person would have pipesmoker's breath and shaky hands and be named Mrs. Tremble?

The trees had begun some subtle change. The black-green lushness of September had become a lighter, friendlier green. The persimmons were ripe on the trees, and sullen wasps staggered fat and gorged in the pink-gold sweetness of the fallen fruit. Here and there he noticed hardwoods in which some of the leaves were already brown, but most were still green and, every so often, in a spreading oak or maple, a bouquet of red and yellow leaves appeared like decorations. The squirrels were busy; acorns were thick underfoot.

To his left, from a thicker brake of trees and cane, emerged first the movement and then the head and then the entirety of a large dog. A fear rippled through him and caused him to forget the afternoon chill. He did as his father had taught him. He kept an eye on the wild dog and, at the same time, scanned the woods to see whether there was a pack. He started a slow movement backwards, trying to put distance, a tree or two, if possible a fence, between them. He kept looking. He could not find a pack, not another dog, no movement in the woods or cane. The dog before him was long-legged and black and thin. The long muscles seemed almost to show through the matted hair.

He backed away. The dog had not yet really looked at him, not directly. It sniffed the ground and raised its chin to the breeze. It did not look, but it was aware of him. Robert looked hard at the dog and thought he saw something, something like himself and other than himself. He was distracted by a noise that, at first, he thought belonged to the wind.

"Robert, oh Robert dear." Pipesmoker's breath blazed through the trees and pasture, killing leaves and grass, setting fire to old birdnests. The surface of the lake was choppy and uneven. The wind increased and raised chillbumps on his bare arms. He remembered the years he had been the only child in his family. He remembered the fear and the envy he felt when his father came to his room. "Robbie," he had said, "son. You're going to be a big brother. Can you believe it? Mama's going to have a baby." He remembered the loathing. He looked at the two of them, mother and father, and imagined the cloying sexuality, vague and terrible, the dominance of his father upon his mother's nakedness. "It's the gift of life," his father had said. Afterwards, Robert held the child and began to love it. He gave him its bottle and was thankful his mother had not breast-fed. He brought friends home from school and showed them the baby. He taught them to hold its head. He learned to forget the baby and, in that way, to love it more. He went to fourth grade and learned to play two songs on a plastic recorder; he kissed Melissa Townley outside the skating rink. He helped his father bale alfalfa for the goats; he took pictures with his father's reflex camera and learned to read a light meter. "Oh, Robert dear. Telephone."

He turned from the dog and walked through the pasture, deliberately not running, but walking fast and, twice, almost falling. He looked back. The dog had lain down and was licking a paw. The goats bleated and fanned away. "Here I am, Mrs. Tremble," he said. "I'm coming."

The telephone was on the wall, a boxy, old-fashioned instrument that only Mrs. Tremble would have owned. The earpiece was shaped like a bell and was separate from the mouthpiece, which was part of the wooden box.

His father had not meant to tell him on the phone, but Robert asked the question directly and made him answer. The answer was no surprise: the child, Robert's brother, was dead. Robert had known. All through himself, inside as well as outside, Robert felt a pain, like that that seemed so constant in Mrs. Tremble's split, chapped lips. Then the silence was over. "These will be lonely, bad days, son," the voice said, his father. It was impossible to imagine a voice so kind or so tired. "But it's no one's fault."

"I love you, Daddy."

"I love you."

"Tell Mama . . ."

When he had hung up, Robert remembered a movie he had seen on television, a western, filmed in Utah and full of wide desert and red buttes. A faint cold fear thrilled through him. He thought of graves and of museums with large bottles filled with fetuses, two-headed sheep and piglets with human faces. He felt responsible for each one. No warmth, he thought. No breath. He tried to pray for museums. He asked forgiveness for Siamese twins and freak shows. No tears came to him, and he was dry all through.

A meteor of Mrs. Tremble's breath struck the gold-colored drapes on the west windows and exploded into light like the sun. "It will be better with them open," she might have said. She pulled the tasseled cord hanging beside the windows and made the light from the floor lamp unnecessary. Robert watched her carefully, knowing that she knew. But she did not try to hug him or kiss him. She moved slowly through the room and seemed older than ever. Robert didn't know what to do. "He's dead," he told her, having nothing else to say.

Without answering him, Mrs. Tremble moved to a table that sat in the sunlight near the windows. It was a large table, round and topped with creamy rose-veined marble. She opened one of its several shallow drawers and removed a pipe and a pouch of tobacco.

The pipe was not at all what he imagined. Its bowl should have been black and shaped like the head of a wild horse or an African woman with tight kinky hair and swollen lips and a gold nosering, or it should have been chalk-white, the face of a madman or a coolie, or it should have had no shape at all, formless and chaotic. It was not a large pipe, very ordinary-looking, a light reddish-brown in color. When she had sat in her chair before the little fire, she filled the pipe with tobacco from the pouch and lighted it with a kitchen match. It smelled like chocolate, cooking on a stove. Robert sat in the upholstered chair with blue brocade and did not notice whether he felt large or small. Grief was everywhere, but it was hard to form a mental picture of the dead child. He remembered skinning a catfish with his father. With the fish still alive they cut a circle around the head and pulled off the skin, strip by strip, with a pair of pliers. He prayed forgiveness, or tried, and did not feel forgiven. He wanted to be alone. He didn't want to be here with Mrs. Tremble. But if he went back home, across the pasture to his own house, he would be too much alone. He was afraid of what he might do, or become. Mrs. Tremble was talking. He tried not to listen, but it was impossible.

She stopped and puffed at the pipe and struck a new match to goad it to life again. "That was a long time ago," she said. "I was younger then than you are now. That year—one of those years—a man came, an old man, and camped out, right in the middle of town, not so far from my family's house. We called them hoboes back then. There were more of them then, it seems to me. He put up a tepee-like affair, made from—oh, you know—one thing and another. Packing crates, scraps of lumber, an old door from no-telling-where. Right beneath the old railroad trestle." Mrs. Tremble's voice was odd. There was something in it, like pain, but that was only a part. There was old-lady nostalgia, and obsession, and senility, and yet none of these exactly. Robert believed that later she might not even remember saying these words, telling this tale. Now and then he saw the green bottle, the stain on the floor. He wondered how he could continue to live, knowing he had killed his brother. He wondered what his father must be feeling. For the first time he thought of suicide.

"Everyone talked about the hobo," Mrs. Tremble went on. "Children sometimes slid down the clay embankment to his tepee and sat with him. I did so myself. He was kindly, and he stank, of course. I think now he must have stolen food to stay alive. I'm not really sure. People might have given him things. He called himself a 'Sin Eater.' No one knew what he meant, or cared, I suppose. There were so many odd ones . . ." She blew a long stream of smoke through the firescreen, and the hot coals flamed up and danced.

"Someone died not long after, a few weeks after we first noticed him. It was a woman, some old woman. I don't even remember her name, I only remember it was the first funeral I ever went to.

"It was held in the old lady's home. That was the way then, the corpse laid out—'decently,' was the expression—for viewing. People came and brought things. There were covered dishes of food, and a bottle of bourbon in the linen closet. The men drank from it—discreetly they must have imagined. Afternoon changed to dusk, and dusk to night, and most of us were still there.

"There was a knock at the kitchen door. It was not a thing you would expect. Persons either come to a wake or they don't, you know. No one comes so late, or to the back door. When someone finally heard and went to answer it, it was the hobo, the man who called himself the Sin Eater. His face was yellow-looking, probably from jaundice; so many of the old-time ones were sick, or alcoholic. He was wearing a dark coat of some kind, and probably nothing else. His legs and feet were bare. He stank terribly, an odious, leathery old man. But something about him—something about the outrage of his coming to that house, at such a time—caused my father and the rest not to send him away just then. They opened the screened door and he came in."

Mrs. Tremble let out a small, mirthless laugh, bewildered almost, and bewildering. Robert was careful not to be struck by her breath. "The house grew quiet," she went on. "He came farther in, and the crowd parted to let him pass. Food was spread along a makeshift counter in the kitchen, put together out of boards and saw horses. Butterbeans and crowder peas and fried squash, all the rest, a typical wake in a little southern town. Somebody had brought a ham.

"The Sin Eater looked at the food. He had a quiet, ordinary voice. We had not expected that, somehow, even those of us who had talked with him. 'Put some in a bowl, please'm,' he said, almost shy, 'a wood bowl if you have it.' One of my aunts, a large-breasted woman with her slip always showing, did as he said. She put a little of each food, one thing right on top of another, in a big maple salad bowl. I thought he was just begging. Everybody thought so, probably. We were all terribly embarrassed, even outraged, I suppose. All we wanted was for him to be gone and for this to be over. But you couldn't help feeling sorry for him.

"The food, all the juices, mingled together in the bowl. My aunt tried to hand it to him, but he turned and wouldn't take it. He walked through the house, big as Ike and twice as natural, and went in the living room, where the old woman lay in her coffin. It was no more than a pine box, with the lid not yet nailed down. 'I'd be proud to receive it now,' he said, meaning the bowl of food. He wanted it handed across the corpse. I'll never forget his quaint, countrified way of speaking. He'd be 'proud to receive it.' Some of us children giggled behind our hands.

"He took the bowl from my aunt and held it over the corpse, just for a moment. He placed the bowl upon the dead woman's breast. Why on earth he was allowed to do such a thing, I will never understand. Old men like him were never really welcome in town, certainly not in our homes. Why didn't someone say, 'Well, now, wait just one minute here'? Some red-faced man, maybe, like my father. No one said anything, though. Not a word. Then, with no utensil except his filthy hands, he ate the food, every morsel, right over the woman's corpse. Can you believe such a thing? When he had finished, he burned the bowl in the fireplace with fat pine. We just stood there, men, women, and children. It was all we could do, just stand there looking like fools. All of a sudden he was speaking again. It was still the same countrified, untutored voice but different now, not affected at all but slightly more distant, more formal and yet more filled with passion. 'I am the Sin Eater,' he said. 'I am the propitiation for your sins. I have taken unto my flesh all the sin and guilt of these here assembled, and especially those of the woman who lies dead before me. I am unclean with them. I feel them. They burn inside me. Despise me, and beware of me. Touch nothing of me, neither of my body nor of my clothing. Azazel rages inside me. I am the Sin Eater, and I am doomed.'

"By now, of course, the outrage could not be ignored. Several men—probably most of them had drunk an extra share at the linen closet by now—ushered him roughly out the back door and warned him not to show his face around here again. Maybe he had better get moving, get on out of town, they told him. The next day he was not in the tepee, the little hovel he had set up beneath the trestle. When he still failed to show up that night, the tepee was dismantled and burned."

Mrs. Tremble lighted the pipe again and blew out the match with smoke. A sickening cloud of her effluvium seemed to have formed in the air of the room. It was not the pipesmoke itself; that smelled good, like candy. It was something from inside herself, a malodorous, personal stench, that stank up whatever space she occupied. She puffed deeply on the pipe, again and again. Sky rockets of her fetid breath detonated about his head, fulminated in the air. The paint on the walls blistered and cracked and fell away. Plaster crumbled to dust and sifted down into his hair. He was determined to think of his dead brother. The death-pale face, the rolled-up eyes. This beastly old woman! Her boring spew of boring childhood!

Suddenly, he was taken off guard. He had not been looking at her, and while his attention was away, she had moved from her chair and was standing directly above him. Her breath, her filthy, stinking breath, covered him like a sour, damp blanket. He was sick; he began to retch. "I just want you to know how sorry I am, child," she said. "I swan." She bent over and took him in her arms and kissed him with her split, chapped lips. "I'm just so sorry, child."

"Get away from me!" he screamed. He struggled and kicked and flung his arms. He dug his nails into the brocade of the chair and squirmed free, squirting from her bewildered grasp and almost knocking her over. "I hate you!" he screamed. "I hate you! I hate you!" He ran from the room and burst out the back door into the yard. When he had crossed the fence into the pasture, he stopped and looked back. She was at the back door, looking as if she had aged a hundred years in the last sixty seconds. "You stink!" he screamed. "Your breath stinks, and I hate you!"

He turned and ran toward the lake. Goats parted, bleating, fanning out before him. There was a stitch in his side when he stopped, and his breathing was raw and painful. He fell to his knees and gasped for breath. He got up again and ran again until he fell, this time near the lake. He cried, so loud and so strenuous, he wished he could see himself in a mirror. He had never heard such crying. He hated that damned old stinking woman. He hated her.

Later, when he was finished crying, he could not remember having stopped. He may have slept. He was very tired, and he wished his father would come home. He felt the back pocket of his jeans for a handkerchief, but did not have one. He blew his nose with his fingers and wiped his hand on his pants.

He was embarrassed at what he had said to Mrs. Tremble, but he was not sorry. He did hate her. He wondered why he had put up with her for so many years, and why his mother and father had forced her on him. Later, he would apologize, just to keep everyone happy. But he wouldn't mean it, and she would know he didn't.

As he was trying to decide whether to go on and get that part of it over, or whether to sneak across the pasture to his own house, he noticed something in a patch of cane to his right. It was the partly eaten carcass of a baby goat. And there was something else as well—a glimpse of the black dog he had seen earlier. It sank out of sight, into the woods. He was not afraid, exactly, since he knew the dog had eaten; there would be no reason for it to attack. But he did not feel safe enough to stay alone any longer either. He walked up the pasture toward Mrs. Tremble's house.

It was odd, he thought, feeling the cockleburrs and beggars' lice collecting in his socks. It was odd that nothing was changed. It was not like in stories, where people always seem to change. He felt different, of course, emptier, because he had cried; but nothing had really changed. He had learned nothing that would make him, overnight, grow into a man, the way people did in stories. He was not better, or wiser. A brother was dead: that was true. But not even that loss, that diamond of pain and emptiness, could be transformed to abstraction, to innocence, or its loss. The marvel was, in fact, that everything could be so much the same, that what his father said could be true: no blame, no guilt. Life was not a dream, he thought, or a story; the persons you meet are not fabulous, or enchanted. Mrs. Tremble was no witch. The wonder, whether you liked it or not, was the choppy surfaces of lakes and the mounds of fireants and the wild peacocks in the trees. The miracle was the hunger of wild dogs and the availability and vulnerability of goats.

Revive Us Again

Gloria Norris

"How I ever let you talk a lifelong Methodist like me into going to a Baptist revival on a night like this I'll never know," I told Irma right off in the car. "This is like stepping into an oven." It turned out one of those stifling August nights when people would die if they couldn't keep saying Hot enough for you? or Can we stand another one like this? Driving up the first hill with Lamar shifting the gears slow, we had to gasp for breath.

"Whoo-whee," Lamar said, wiping his handkerchief over his face and grinning at me across Irma with his lips shut—he has bad teeth. "Hot enough for you, Sister?"

"Can we stand another one like this?" Irma cut in mechanically. She was fanning us all three with a cardboard fan showing Abraham leading Isaac off through the desert on the front and on the back saying *Courtesy of Revell Furniture, Your Friendly Furniture Dealer.*

"Will you stop fanning so hard, Irma," I said. "I guess nobody'd look at an old-maid schoolteacher if she came out naked, but I don't see any need to have my hair standing on end." With all her weight she's hot-natured. She's always been the fat talky sister, me the smart skinny one.

Irma said all innocent: "Why I thought you'd like to finish your visit with us with a little outing, Sister. And we just couldn't not go a single night, Methodists or not, and hurt little Brother Bobby's feelings. Sister, he's the new young Baptist preacher and the nicest they ever had—just so sweet and sincere and dedicated. Not like a Baptist at all. We went to hear him preach two Sundays ago when our preacher was out of town."

Now I realized why she was dragging us out was this nice-looking preacher. Just be a young man and smile at Irma and remember her name and she'll be glad to go out and catch a wild horse for you. Always been a positive fool over anything in pants.

"But I hear this visiting preacher . . ." Irma broke off, shaking her pretty gray curls. "Or was it three Sundays ago we went to hear Brother Bobby? Lamar, was it three Sundays ago?"

"Believe it was."

"No, you're wrong. It was *two* Sundays ago, because *last* Sunday Sister came."

"That's right, that's right."

Papa would have said a man like Lamar didn't have sense enough to come in out of the rain and wasn't worth going after to bring in. Irma should have done better. But she didn't and she thinks that's better than not doing at all like I did.

"Well, what about this visiting preacher?" I said, impatient with all their repeating.

"Oh, I hear he's a regular Holy Roller. Shouts and cries and gets on his knees. But he's got twenty converts this week."

"Well," I said, "if you'd told me you were dragging me to a Holy Rolling, I would have said No, thank you." Lamar laughed, shaking his head and slapping the steering wheel. But I was honestly peeved. I can't stand any of that Church of God carrying-on. It's all right for poor ignorant country people, but it's an insult to my intelligence.

I should have known Irma was saving something up. "Well, Missy, you may be mighty glad I had you come. I have it on good authority that somebody you were once mighty sweet on is going to show up tonight and surprise everybody. You would have killed yourself if you missed it."

Irma's all I have left in the world, so I put up with her. Every August just before school starts and I have to buckle down again to teachers' meetings and lunch money and geography lessons, I spend two weeks visiting her and Lamar. They live in the same big old house that Irma and I were born in and that poor Mama and Papa and Brother all died in, and Lamar runs Papa's old store.

Well, Alcoma's no Memphis, but I know everybody around there, and I find out who's having a baby and who's running around on his wife and whatever else has kept tongues from going out of use since the year before.

We couldn't remember when we'd seen so many pickups and cars parked around the Alcoma Baptist Church. It's an old white frame building sinking on its cement blocks, the walls leaning in like they might fall any minute. We climbed the rickety steps from the dark and came to the double open doors and saw the church was just bursting with people and hot lights. The little children had to sit sweating on their mamas' laps, and every pew was filled and spilling people onto folding chairs in the aisles. A Baptist crowd, ladies with home-permanent hair and men that would never look at home in a white shirt, even without a tie. They were all fanning with Revell fans, but all the faces were glistening under the bare ceiling lights. Five-hundred-watt bulbs the fools had up there, no shade a-tall, moths circling around them. Brother used to say they have revivals in the hottest time of year to put people in mind of what Hell will be like. And the Baptists go one better by putting those hot bare lights on so you think you've got a toe in there for trial.

Well, I told myself, I guess the worse that can happen is you'll have a heat stroke and they'll have to carry you out.

Then I got a look at the visiting preacher.

He was sitting up front on the choir platform behind the altar, his face turned up to the ceiling and his eyes squeezed closed. Meditating. He was just a short, bald, fat little man, with a fringe of gray hair around his shiny scalp and little white hands and little feet in high-cut shiny black shoes. Little low-set eyes, and his cheeks sagged down and ran into a dewlap. But deep lines sunk down each side of his mouth and made him look like he meant business. Just as we stood there, a snatch of laughing came from the choir room behind, and he snapped open his eyes and frowned back mean at them. He meant business, all right.

Of course there weren't three seats together, so Irma sent Lamar up front to sit in a little space by Harvey Giles, the next-to-richest man in Alcoma. Harvey was in the same grade with me at school and used to be Methodist, but he couldn't get along at our church with Mr. Fallbriar, who is the richest man in Alcoma, so Harvey moved over to the Baptist church, got himself immersed, and runs things on the strength of his tithe. He's Mr. Big Baptist.

Irma and I squeezed into two folding chairs at the far right, and we all sat there sweating like Trojans, feeling that preacher warming up, while all through the quiet crowd an uneasiness was running through the heat and babies' squalls. Like lambs penned up while the slaughter fires are lit.

Because we all knew that little fat preacher could wind up the biggest man in the place and run him around like he was nothing but a child's hoop. How? By knowing how to stir him up. And to tell the truth, that's what they had come for. Hardworking people that are God-fearing and keep their self-respect by living by the Commandments and caring for themselves and tending their own sick and old folks. That doesn't leave much room for stirring up of other kinds but coming to church and hearing some visiting preacher scare you about Hell.

But I'm against that. What is it when you get all wrought up and come down crying to the preacher and let him fall on your neck shouting "Bless you, bless you, you've made the right decision"? It sure dudn't look like religion to me. It looks like people losing their heads. And if the Lord gave us one unmixed blessing, it's our heads, and losing your head, I say, is just throwing away the best thing you got. So seeing that fat preacher getting set to make everybody do just that, I got a headache right off.

Well, be durn if Irma didn't hit me with something else. She jabbed me in the side. "See who just walked in? I *told* you. Bet this is the first time he's darkened the door of a church in forty years. They say the doctor's told him his liver can't last more than six months."

Who should be standing uncertain at the open doors but Gene Paul Prescott! He'd got so old and dried up, I had to look twice to know him. Gone plumb white-headed and wearing gold-rimmed glasses like I'd never imagined on him. Everybody else was craning around at him too—he ducking his head to one side from all that staring. Then he saw a little space in the middle of a pew halfway down and squeezed in and stuck his face in a hymnbook without saying a word to a soul.

Well, sure didn't make any difference to *me* if he wanted to show up at the Baptist church. But he was the last person I'd expect—a drunk but besides that he's from one of the oldest families in town and raised rich and Presbyterian. Not that his coming was the slightest concern of mine. I'd rather not ever set eyes on him again. I've got my pride.

The choir came in from behind the altar, singing self-conscious in a single marching line and looking like they'd just been anointed in the choir room by Jesus personally. The young preacher followed them—he *was* better looking than the visiting preacher—and announced the first hymn. It was a loud old foot-thumping song, and naturally the singing was loud enough to wake the dead out back.

Revive us again!
  Fill each heart with Thy love
Let each soul be rekindled
  With fire from above . . .

Windy Diker's big horse-face grinned from the choir while he thundered the bass in the chorus.

Hallalujah! sang the sopranos.

THINE THE GLORA, sang Windy loud as all them put together.

Hallalujah!
ARMEN
Halla*lu*jah!
THINE THE GLORA

and all together . . .

REVIVE US AGAIN!

We kept on sweating and got through the scripture and the hymns and offertory until the nice-looking young preacher sat down and the fat one—Brother Benson was his name—got up and came to the altar, walking surprisingly light for a fat man in those high-cut shiny black shoes. He looked out over us a minute, narrowing his eyes, until the little coughs and stirring stopped right quick. With everybody quiet and watching, he took out his pocket watch and laid it to the side of the altar.

"*Brethern and sistern,*" he said in a loud, carrying voice. "I understand some of the membership don't like the way I been preaching."

Some of the ladies squirmed around. Harvey Giles sat up real straight.

The preacher smiled at the rest of us and started in telling that old joke about the negro preacher that gets up and says "Everybody ought to quit cussing," and the little old negro woman on the front row says "Amen," and the preacher says "Everybody ought to quit drinking," and she says "Amen" again. That goes on till he gets down to "Everybody ought to quit dipping snuff." And the little old negro woman, with her lip full of snuff, says "*Now he's quit preachin' and gone to meddlin'.*"

A big wave of laughing rose up when he said the last, like everybody hadn't heard it at every revival since time began.

As the last laughing died, Brother Benson raised a hand like he was calming a flood. "Call me a meddler if you want to. But let me tell you, if you had seen some of the sad sights I have, you'd be on your knees up here beside me, begging, pleading with all the poor sinners to repent . . .

"Just last week I was holding a meeting up in Tennessee, and I went out to see a farming man who'd broke away from God. I talked with him and I prayed with him and finally I thought he was about to make a commitment. But the Devil got aholt of his heart again, and he says not today, Brother, I got too much to think about today, I got my crops to think about today, maybe next week, not today. But my dear friends, the *Lord* don't wait till *you* say you're ready. Next week was too late for that man. That very night he took a pain in his side and was *dead* by morning. Oh, brother! oh, sister! how my heart bleeds for that sinner, cast out into eternal darkness, into the *ee*-ternal fires of Hell!"

His voice broke off high and loud, and he was quiet while he walked around to the front of the pulpit, his head hanging down like he couldn't stand the thought of that poor man burning in Hell.

You could have heard a pin drop. A lot of folks drew their arms down tight over their sides like they'd just remembered having a pain there like that Tennessee man.

When Brother Benson started talking again, his eyes looked out over us through the open doors at the dark sky, his hands folded together like a undertaker's. His voice went quiet but threatening too.

"*Revive us again* . . . while I was sitting there," he jerked his head backward toward the choir, "meditating on that wonderful old hymn, I heard God talking to me. He said: 'Son, there's somebody here that needs to get right with Me tonight, somebody that had better make it right with Me 'cause he don't have much time left.' *No!*"—he was back to shouting and shaking his finger so you felt God's wrath—"he don't have much time left! Now, brothers, I don't know who that man or that woman is, and I don't know what your sin is, friend; but I do know you better make it right with God this very night. You better accept Jesus Christ tonight!"

He walked back behind the pulpit letting that sink in, and everybody hung there like just when the doctor looks down and away from you before giving you the bad news, suddenly you're scared sick and all alone with the bad news hanging over you about to fall. We all hung onto that preacher's eyes, wondering Does he know something I've done that I don't? Oh, you start thinking of lots of little things you shouldn't of done, but which one is my big sin? Does he know something that is keeping me from God? And what if I should be taken right now tonight—nobody knows when his hour will come. Is there something that will keep me from going to His home when I die, cast me back into that awful black *nothing*ness that we come out of and so quick go back to forever unless someone has the mercy and the power to save us? It's what you push out of your mind every day, that last minute when you're facing eternity and the end of yourself, lying weak and helpless with your family already so far away, no way for them to help you, it's you dying, not them. You know you will be terrified, falling helpless into that dark nothingness. It's that realizing at revivals that that time *will be* for you, and you know you've been oh! so careless, that moment is so awful you must live every minute in your life preparing for it.

That devilish preacher had me going right along with the rest, what with his eyes boring right into me and his voice sliding from loud to soft. But when he got back behind the pulpit he changed again so quick I saw through him. He wasn't really worrying about that Tennessee man burning in Hell or about the person here about to die. He was cool as ice inside while he was stirring us up.

I trembled inside before I got control. There's enough fools I meet every day, I said, that I don't need to be made one of by you. If the world was made just like everybody thinks it should be—to go *his* way—then you could allow yourself to get stirred up. You could just be soft, like women especially want to be, and let yourself ride along where your feelings lead you and you'd come to no harm. But you come to find out that the world isn't made anywhere like it should be. The only way you can stand up to it is to steel yourself and hold on and hold on some more, more than you ever thought you could.

It's what I been doing all these years. One weary day after another at school and thinking plenty of days I can't make myself get up and do it one single more day. And knowing, oh, since way back there was no need to let myself dream about anything but putting up with children's runny noses and jealous mamas and grumpy principals, all just to live alone in the rented back apartment of some old widow. Oh, if you want to get married, I'll give you some free advice: Don't be a Mississippi schoolteacher. Whether you're pretty or not pretty, like me, the men shy away. Like they'll be put in the shade just because you know some algebra and where Cape Horn is! And then when I'd accepted that, Mama and Papa and Brother all taken within two years . . . until I wondered who was ruling in Heaven. So steeling yourself is the only way to get through, and even then—and this I threw back to that fat preacher—it gets so hard you stop being afraid of dying. When every year you lose something else, and you don't see anything ahead . . . It was Brother's death finally made me realize that one by one things will go and the only thing left is steeling yourself.

So I told that fat preacher that had everybody else sweating and leaning toward him out of their pews while he waved his little hands and opened them up to Heaven like he was talking to God, if I have lived through all that without breaking, I don't have to worry about somebody who has no particular business with me stirring me up so *he* can feel righteous and claim God sends messages down direct to him about who is saved and who isn't. If he has got messages from God, I've talked to Ulysses S. Grant.

But that Benson could read my mind as plain as those lighted headlines that run flickering at night around the Sterick building in Memphis. That devil fired back, "Brethern, God told me there was one here tonight I might be privileged to save, one who wasn't going to have another chance. And I *aim* to find that man tonight!" He was looking straight at Gene Paul.

I had forgot all about him. I peeped over and the sight could break your heart. His head was popped out in big drops of sweat; his pinched-in old-man's lips were pulled up scared, like a rabbit trapped by the dogs and knowing it's caught and is afraid even to squirm this way or that. He looked at me and I said to him, looking right back at him so he could read my eyes: "Are you going to let this fat preacher take you in?" And then I thought, well, it would be just like you. And it was like watching a fire blazing at your house with everything you have in the world inside and praying it will stop, and then you see the roof go up.

Because Gene Paul hadn't ever done anything in his life like you would have expected him to, just looking at him. Who would ever have thought when we were young he would turn into what he is—a drunk that even little children make jokes about. Living in the Prescotts' old cookhouse while his big two-story house in front sits closed-up, and seeing nothing except rough hill-men, the scrapings of the earth, and drinking rotgut with them at a still in the woods, a wonder he hadn't gotten himself killed by their likes, and most days for the past thirty years getting so liquored up he can't walk straight.

But that isn't enough to shame you, I said. And shame me that was once fool enough to care about you. Now you want to go down to the altar for this Benson to gloat over, tears coming down your old cheeks for everybody to gape at, and within three weeks you'll be back to drinking with that much more reason to be shamed. Can't you see for once what *is* and act accordingly?

No, he never did anything like a mother would hope for him. When we were growing up he was always doing things nobody else had the nerve to. Went over the waterfall once in a barrel and come over it, the Lord only knows how, without killing himself. All through high school, he never had one particular girl, although he dated them all. Oh, all the girls chased him, and fell in love with him, fine-looking and devil-may-care as he was. He was polite to all, even me the bookworm, but never got serious about anyone. To me none of the other boys came up to his level with their roughness and no brains. But when Mr. Pescott sent him off to Ole Miss (he was the only one of the Alcoma boys that got to go back then with so little money around in the town), Gene Paul dropped out after the first semester. I can still see Irma's letter to me—I was going to Normal in Moorehead then: "Guess who you were sweet on once has quit Ole Miss and is off traveling in Texas. Hint: Mrs. P. is fit to be tied."

It was 1916, my second year of teaching, that Irma wrote me Gene Paul had come home and brought a wife with him. Some woman with dyed blonde hair and bad grammar. Poor Mrs. Prescott. He got a house on the corner below his mother's and went into Mr. Prescott's drugstore, driving two nights a week the thirty miles over to Ole Miss to get his pharmacy degree.

Well, it came as a blow. I was working in this little poor Delta town, hardly making enough to stay alive and nobody there my age, day in and out the same thing with my pupils. I was impatient then. Well, one night Gene Paul comes home early from Oxford and finds his wife is entertaining an old boyfriend in the house (*where* in it, I'm not prepared to say).

Harvey Giles next door heard the ruckus and came running over.

As he told it, Gene Paul had gone for his shotgun but the other man got it away from him and knocked Gene Paul on the floor and was holding the gun on him. Gene Paul was sitting helpless with the blood coming out of his mouth, looking up at the man that took his wife and now was holding a gun on him. Harvey shouted for them to break it up, and Gene Paul got up real slow, wiping his mouth with the back of his hand. And then, looking shamed as a man could, he just walked out, turning once at the door to look back at his wife. Harvey followed him, afraid he'd be back with another gun. But all Gene Paul did was walk up the street to his mother's. The wife and the boyfriend ran off that night, although maybe you couldn't call it running off since nobody tried to stop them.

A few days later Mrs. Prescott closed down the empty house and had her negro move the new furniture to her storehouse, and Gene Paul moved out to the Prescotts' old cookhouse where he's lived ever since.

Oh, why does a man throw his life away when any fool could tell him not to! Like you didn't have any *reason* to start drinking. He kept on at the drugstore, and one morning Mr. Prescott didn't wake up, so Gene Paul took over the business complete. When I was home that summer, I went in every day and he wouldn't look me straight in the eye, him a fine-looking young man that had been so devil-may-care, and now he just kept his eyes down on his hands when he gave me whatever I asked for. I thought he'd be able to tell by the way I spoke to him he wasn't shamed as a man just because of that one no-good woman. That was a summer, well, it seemed to me—I was still young—that something *had* to happen to me in the years going by.

Something *did* happen. We got so I could tease him a little when I'd be looking around the drugstore and nobody else was in there. It was cool and smelled from where he stood behind the counter of iodine and tinctures and camphor and things I couldn't recognize but that he must know like the palms of his hands, able to mix and heal folks with. That was the way I saw him, able to be strong and heal others if he would.

"I guess you're making a lot of money, getting rich, Gene Paul," I would tease him when he rang up that cash register, while somebody shut the front door that tinkled.

He would shoot a look over going by me, but grinning one-sided, handsome as could be. "Looks to me like you're buying an awful lot of headache powders, BC's and all. Maybe you got school-teacher's headaches and need to change your line of work? Maybe you ought to go to pharmacy school; you were always smart."

Didn't sound like that dead voice he talked to everybody else with, but more like the boy I'd known. I got to feeling he looked for me every morning.

One July morning I went in, not really anything I needed to buy, and I looked over the boxes of candy up front while he waited on this one and that one. I knew he was busy, and I didn't even notice when everybody went out.

"Buying some candy for your sweetie?" he said sudden behind me, and I jumped ten feet. He'd never stood without the counter between us.

I guess I blushed blood-red. Then I caught myself and teased, "I just might. But I need a mighty big box, he's a mighty big man."

And he looked like I slapped him.

"I'm just joking, Gene Paul. You know that," I blurted out. I couldn't stand to see him hurt if that was what he was.

He looked at me like he never had, like he needed something but couldn't say what it was.

"Is it something you want to say, tell me?" I said after the time ticked by, him looking at me naked with whatever it was. Nothing like this had happened to me, I didn't know men's hearts, what he could be thinking. I didn't know how not to be a lady, wait for a man to say what he wanted. And he said it, grinned with one side of his mouth going up higher than the other, so my heart jumped just to see that grin.

"You be home tonight, because I'm coming over to see you." I was as excited as I've ever been. I took my time getting dressed and then about dark I went out and sat on the front porch. I waited thinking about that one-sided grin, and trying not to imagine what would happen. Daddy told Irma to quit meddling, but she couldn't keep from sticking her head out every half-hour. And then every fifteen minutes until I asked her to please refrain. It got later and I began to strain at every noise in the yard. Well, that was a long night. Inside they all went to bed. But it wasn't until about mid-night, when I saw the last of the moon slide off the other side of the porch, that I let myself cry.

Next morning, when I went for the mail, everybody downtown

was just buzzing over how Gene Paul was wild drunk in the streets last night and the sheriff had to take him home.

I kept hope for a few days, but I never heard one word from him. I had to face the truth. Either he'd already been drunk out of his mind when he said he was visiting me, or else he was having a good joke on the old maid. Take your pick, either way I was a fool.

After that everybody could notice him smelling of whiskey every day, getting worse all the time, until one day he shut up the drugstore and gave himself over to full-time drinking. He stopped caring a-tall what people thought, and some said it was that that killed Mrs. Prescott, although goodness knows she was eighty-eight when she finally died, so it took a while. But after a spell, one spring led to one cotton-ginning time and that to one more spring until time got by and nobody ever thought about how Gene Paul had wasted himself—it just didn't bear remarking on, like a lot of things about yourself that you put away from your mind and can't grieve about if you are to keep going, and you don't remark on any more, except once in a blue moon when something brings it back fresh.

And now we're not so far from the end of our road, and the only thing to be proud of is that you have looked at things straight as you could and called them what they were, hard as they were to admit, and now that you're old you at least don't act like a fool any more and you can walk along to your end with dignity.

That fat preacher was marching back and forth behind the pulpit on his little feet. Yelling that we were all sinners, all guilty of original sin. Oh, he could just taste that Presbyterian drunkard-convert in his mouth, like a cat with a canary.

Suddenly Gene Paul stirred in his seat. My Lord, he was ready to jump up and go down, not even wait for the invitation! I glared right at him, and he looked right back. *Please don't make a fool of yourself,* my eyes begged him.

And he leaned back, his pinched old-man's lips fallen apart. But the preacher was closing in, shouting "Won't you accept Him, friend? It's so easy to believe on Him. The Bible says 'Believe on the Lord Jesus Christ and *thou shalt be saved.*' Won't you trust Him? As the choir sings the invitational, won't you come up here to the altar and say *Yes,* I accept, *yes,* I'm through with sinning, *yes, Jeez*us is my Savior . . ."

The choir started the slow begging first verse of *Just As I Am Without One Plea,* and the preacher said "Won't you come, brother? Just put your hand in His as the choir sings. Won't you come? Not only you lost, but those that need to rededicate their lives, all you church members come too to rededicate. Won't you come?" He held out his hands over us like he was Jesus Christ and if I was going to die of a stroke, I would have then . . .

You would have thought he was giving away money down at the altar. Harvey Giles started down and the whole church nearbout followed. The noise was loud from all over the church of people coming, even a loud *bang* once. Somebody hurrying so fast he knocked a hymnbook down, I figured. All I could do was look at the floor and not let anybody see my face. The choir went on singing *Just As I Am* and Benson was gloating. "Welcome, brother, praise the Lord, welcome, sister . . ."

Down front the crush of people were crying and confessing things and hugging in that heat that was about to take us all over into a faint, and I looked away, not able to bear seeing him in that Benson's hands. I told Irma, who was dabbing her eyes, I'd meet her at the car. I walked out into the dark down the gravel road.

I heard somebody coming behind me on the gravel, and being in no mood to exchange remarks, I stepped out of sight between two pickups. It was a man walking brisk. He stopped, his face in shadows but not so much I couldn't see who it was.

Gene Paul held his suit jacket out like it was wet. Threw some broken pieces of glass on the gravel. A strong raw smell hit my nose—the *nerve* of him, bringing a pint of whiskey right into church in his jacket pocket! And then it came clear—that loud bang I heard was Gene Paul breaking his whiskey bottle on the pew when he hurried to get to that Benson. To think *that* had brought him to his senses!

Gene Paul said something to himself in an unsteady old drunk's voice like "Safe until next year." Well, that will be all right with me, buddy, I thought—join the Baptists when they got somebody besides Benson that thinks he is God's messenger. And Gene Paul walked off whistling *Revive Us Again,* all jazzed up, like he never heard of liver trouble.

I stepped along that gravel road and a little breeze blew my headache away good as a BC powder. I sat in the car, enjoying the little breeze and smelling sweet honeysuckle. When Irma and

Lamar came up, she picked up her fan and said "Sister, what did you think of the revival?" and I said, feeling that breeze and smiling to myself out the window, "Oh, it was just fine. Guess we're all good and revived for this year."

Lamar, cranking the car, sings out "Amen."

FROM

The Moviegoer

Walker Percy

My half brothers and sisters are eating crabs at a sawbuck table on the screened porch. The carcasses mount toward a naked light bulb.

They blink at me and at each other. Suddenly they feel the need of a grown-up. A grown-up must certify that they are correct in thinking that they see me. They all, every last one, look frantically for their mother. Thérèse runs to the kitchen doorway.

"Mother! Jack is here!" She holds her breath and watches her mother's face. She is rewarded. "Yes, Jack!"

"Jean-Paul ate some lungs." Mathilde looks up from directly under my chin.

My half brother Jean-Paul, the son of my mother, is a big fat yellow baby piled up like a buddha in his baby chair, smeared with crab paste and brandishing a scarlet claw. The twins goggle at us but do not leave off eating.

Lonnie has gone into a fit of excitement in his wheelchair. His hand curls upon itself. I kiss him first and his smile starts his head turning away in a long trembling torticollis. He is fourteen and small for his age, smaller than Clare and Donice, the ten year old twins. But since last summer when Duval, the oldest son, was drowned, he has been the "big boy." His dark red hair is nearly always combed wet and his face is handsome and pure when it is not contorted. He is my favorite, to tell the truth. Like me, he is a moviegoer. He will go see anything. But we are good friends because he knows I do not feel sorry for him. For one thing, he has the gift of believing that he can offer his sufferings in reparation for men's indifference to the pierced heart of Jesus Christ. For another thing, I would not mind so much trading places with him. His life is a serene business.

My mother is drying her hands on a dishcloth.

"Well well, look who's here," she says but does not look.

Her hands dry, she rubs her nose vigorously with her three

middle fingers held straight up. She has hay fever and crabs make it worse. It is a sound too well known to me to be remembered, this quick jiggle up and down and the little wet wringing noises under her fingers.

We give each other a kiss or rather we press our cheeks together, Mother embracing my head with her wrist as if her hands were still wet. Sometimes I feel a son's love for her, or something like this, and try to give her a special greeting, but at these times she avoids my eye and gives me her cheek and calls on me to notice this about Mathilde or that about Thèrése.

"Mother, I want you to meet Sharon Kincaid."

"Well now!" cries Mother, turning away and inserting herself among the children, not because she has anything against Sharon but because she feels threatened by the role of hostess. "There is nobody here but us children," she is saying.

Sharon is in the best of humors, rounding her eyes and laughing so infectiously that I wonder if she is not laughing at me. From the beginning she is natural with the children. Linda, I remember, was nervous and shifted from one foot to the other and looked over their heads, her face gone heavy as a pudding. Marcia made too much over them, squatting down and hugging her knees like Joan Fontaine visiting an orphanage.

Mother does not ask how I happen to be here or give a sign that my appearance is in any way remarkable—though I have not seen them for six months. "Tessie, tell Jack about your class's bus trip."—and she makes her escape to the kitchen. After a while her domesticity will begin to get on my nerves. By the surest of instincts she steers clear of all that is exceptional or "stimulating." Any event or idea which does not fall within the household regimen, she stamps at once with her own brand of the familiar. If, as a student, I happened to get excited about Jackson's Valley Campaign or Freud's *Interpretation of Dreams,* it was not her way to oppose me. She approved it as a kind of wondrous Rover boy eccentricity: "Those? Oh those are Jack's books. The stacks and stacks of books that boy brings home! Jack, do you know everything in those books?" "No'm." Nevertheless I become Dick Rover, the serious-minded Rover boy.

It is good to see the Smiths at their fishing camp. But not at their home in Biloxi. Five minutes in that narrow old house and dreariness sets into the marrow of my bones. The gas logs strike against the eyeballs, the smell of two thousand Sunday dinners clings to the curtains, voices echo round and round the bare stairwell, a dismal Sacred Heart forever points to itself above the chipped enamel mantelpiece. Everything is white and chipped. The floors, worn powdery, tickle the nostrils like a schoolroom. But here on Bayou des Allemands everybody feels the difference. Water laps against the piling. The splintered boards have secret memories of winter, the long dreaming nights and days when no one came and the fish jumped out of the black water and not a soul in sight in the whole savannah; secrets the children must find out and so after supper they are back at their exploring, running in a gang from one corner to another. Donice shows me a muskrat trap he had left last August and wonder of wonders found again. They only came down this morning, Mother explains, such a fine day it was, and since the children have a holiday Monday, will stay through Mardi Gras if the weather holds. With Roy away, Mother is a member of the gang. Ten minutes she will spend in the kitchen working with her swift cat-efficiency, then out and away with the children, surging to and fro in their light inconstant play, her eyes fading in a fond infected look.

Thèrése is telling about her plans to write her Congressman about the Rivers and Harbors bill. Thèrése and Mathilde are something like Joan and Jane in the Civics reader.

"Isn't that Tessie a *case?*" my mother cries as she disappears into the kitchen, signifying that Tessie is smart but also that there is something funny about her precocity.

"Where's Roy? We didn't see a car. We almost didn't walk over."

"Playing poker!" they all cry. This seems funny and everybody laughs. Lonnie's hand curls. If our arrival had caused any confusion, we are carried quickly past by the strong current of family life.

"Do you have any more crabs, Mother?"

"Any more crabs! Ask Lonnie if we weren't just wondering what to do with the rest. You haven't had your supper?"

"No'm."

Mother folds up the thick layer of newspapers under the crab carcasses, making a neat bundle with her strong white hands. The whole mess comes away leaving the table dry and clean. Thèrése spreads fresh paper and Mathilde fetches two cold bottles of beer and two empty bottles for hammering the claws and presently we have a tray apiece, two small armies of scarlet crabs marching in neat rows. Sharon looks queer but she pitches in anyhow and soon everybody is making fun of her. Mathilde shows her how to pry off the belly plate and break the corner at the great claw so that the snowy flesh pops out in a fascicle. Sharon affects to be amazed and immediately the twins must show her how to suck the claws.

Outside in the special close blackness of night over water. Bugs dive into the tight new screen and bounce off with a guitar thrum. The children stand in close, feeling the mystery of the swamp and the secrecy of our cone of light. Clairain presses his stomach against the arm of my chair. Lonnie tries to tune his transistor radio; he holds it in the crook of his wrist, his hands bent back upon it. Once his lip falls open in the most ferocious leer. This upsets Sharon. It seems to her that a crisis is at hand, that Lonnie has at least reached the limit of his endurance. When no one pays any attention to him, she grows fidgety—why doesn't somebody help him?—then, after an eternity, Mathilde leans over carelessly and tunes in a station loud and clear. Lonnie turns his head, weaving, to see her, but not quite far enough.

Lonnie is dressed up, I notice. It turns out that Aunt Ethel, Roy's sister, was supposed to take him and the girls to a movie. It was not a real date, Mother reminds him, but Lonnie looks disappointed.

"What is the movie?" I ask him.

"*Fort Dobbs.*" His speech is crooning but not hard to understand.

"Where is it?"

"At the Moonlite."

"Let's go."

Lonnie's head teeters and falls back like a dead man's.

"I mean it. I want to see it."

He believes me.

I corner my mother in the kitchen.

"What's the matter with Lonnie?"

"Why nothing."

"He looks terrible."

"That child won't drink his milk!" sings out my mother.

"Has he had pneumonia again?"

"He had the five day virus. And it was bad bad bad bad bad. Did you ever hear of anyone with virus receiving extreme unction?"

"Why didn't you call me?"

"He wasn't in danger of death. The extreme unction was his idea. He said it would strengthen him physically as well as spiritually. Have you ever heard of that?"

"Yes. But is he all right now?"

She shrugs. My mother speaks of such matters in a light allusive way, with the overtones neither of belief nor disbelief but rather of a general receptivity to lore.

"Dr Murtag said he'd never seen anything like it. Lonnie got out of bed in half an hour."

Sometimes when she mentions God, it strikes me that my mother uses him as but one of the devices that come to hand in an outrageous man's world, to be put to work like all the rest in the one enterprise she has any use for: the canny management of the shocks of life. It is a bargain struck at the very beginning in which she settled for a general belittlement of everything, the good and the bad. She is as wary of good fortune as she is immured against the bad, and sometimes I seem to catch sight of it in her eyes, this radical mistrust: an old knowledgeable gleam, as old and sly as Eve herself. Losing Duval, her favorite, confirmed her in her election of the ordinary. No more heart's desire for her, thank you. After Duval's death she has wanted everything colloquial and easy, even God.

"But now do you know what he wants to do? Fast and abstain during Lent." Her eyes narrow. Here is the outrage. "He weighs eighty pounds and he has one foot in the grave and he wants to fast." She tells it as a malignant joke on Lonnie and God. For a second she is old Eve herself.

Fort Dobbs is good. The Moonlite Drive-In is itself very fine. It does not seem too successful and has the look of the lonesome pine country behind the Coast. Gnats swim in the projection light and the screen shimmers in the sweet heavy air. But in the movie we are in the desert. There under the black sky rides Clint Walker alone. He is a solitary sort and a wanderer. Lonnie is very happy. Thèrése and Mathilde, who rode the tops of the seats, move to a bench under the projector and eat snowballs. Lonnie likes to sit on the hood and lean back against the windshield and look around at me when a part comes he knows we both like. Sharon is happy too. She thinks I am a nice fellow to take Lonnie to the movies like this. She thinks I am being unselfish. By heaven she is just like the girls in the movies who won't put out until you prove to them what a nice unselfish fellow you are, a lover of children and dogs. She holds my hand on her knee and gives it a squeeze from time to time.

Clint Walker rides over the badlands, up a butte, and stops. He dismounts, squats, sucks a piece of mesquite and studies the terrain. A few decrepit buildings huddle down there in the canyon. We know nothing of him, where he comes from or where he goes.

A good night: Lonnie happy (he looks around at me with the liveliest sense of the secret between us; the secret is that Sharon is not and never will be onto the little touches we see in the movie and, in the seeing, know that the other sees—as when Clint Walker tells the saddle tramp in the softest easiest old Virginian voice: "Mister, I don't believe I'd do that if I was you"—Lonnie is beside himself, doesn't know whether to watch Clint Walker or me), this ghost of a theater, a warm Southern night, the Western Desert and this fine big sweet piece, Sharon.

A good rotation. A rotation I define as the experiencing of the new beyond the expectation of the experiencing of the new. For example, taking one's first trip to Taxco would not be a rotation, or no more than a very ordinary rotation; but getting lost on the way and discovering a hidden valley would be.

The only other rotation I can recall which was possibly superior was a movie I saw before the war called *Dark Waters.* I saw it in Lafitte down on Bayou Barataria. In the movie Thomas Mitchell and Merle Oberon live in a decaying mansion in a Louisiana swamp. One night they drive into the village—to see a movie! A repetition within a rotation. I was nearly beside myself with rotatory emotion. But *Fort Dobbs* is as good as can be. My heart sings like Octavian and there is great happiness between me and Lonnie and this noble girl and they both know it and have the sense to say nothing.

FROM

The Last Gentleman

Walker Percy

He was a young man of a pleasant appearance. Of medium height and exceedingly pale, he was nevertheless strongly built and quick and easy in his ways. Save for a deafness in one ear, his physical health was perfect. Handsome as he was, he was given to long silences. So girls didn't know what to make of him. But men liked him. After a while they saw that he was easy and meant no harm. He was the sort whom classmates remember fondly; they liked to grab him around the neck with an elbow and cuff him around. Good-looking and amiable as he was, however, he did not strike one as remarkable. People usually told him the same joke two or three times.

But he looked better than he was. Though he was as engaging as could be, something was missing. He had not turned out well. There is a sort who does well in school and of whom much is heard and expected and who thereafter does less and less well and of whom finally is heard nothing at all. The high tide of life comes maybe in the last year of high school or the first year of college. Then life seems as elegant as algebra. Afterwards people ask, what happened to so and so? And the answer is a shrug. He was the sort who goes away.

Even now he made the highest possible scores on psychological aptitude tests, especially in the area of problem-solving and goal-seeking. The trouble was he couldn't think what to do between tests.

New York is full of people from small towns who are quite content to live obscure lives in some out-of-the-way corner of the city. Here there is no one to keep track. Though such a person might have come from a long line of old settlers and a neighborhood rich in memories, now he chooses to live in a flat on 231st Street, pick up the paper and milk on the doorstep every morning, and speak to the elevator man. In Southern genealogies there is always mention of a cousin who went to live in New York in 1922 and not another word. One hears that people go to New York to seek their fortunes, but many go to seek just the opposite.

In his case, though, it was part of a family pattern. Over the years his family had turned ironical and lost its gift for action. It was an honorable and violent family, but gradually the violence had been deflected and turned inward. The great grandfather knew what was what and said so and acted accordingly and did not care what anyone thought. He even wore a pistol in a holster like a Western hero and once met the Grand Wizard of the Ku Klux Klan in a barbershop and invited him then and there to shoot it out in the street. The next generation, the grandfather, seemed to know what was what but he was not really so sure. He was brave but he gave much thought to the business of being brave. He too would have shot it out with the Grand Wizard if only he could have made certain it was the thing to do. The father was a brave man too and he said he didn't care what others thought, but he did care. More than anything else, he wished to act with honor and to be thought well of by other men. So living for him was a strain. He became ironical. For him it was not a small thing to walk down the street on an ordinary September morning. In the end he was killed by his own irony and sadness and by the strain of living out an ordinary day in a perfect dance of honor.

As for the present young man, the last of the line, he did not know what to think. So he became a watcher and a listener and a wanderer. He could not get enough of watching. Once when he was a boy, a man next door had gone crazy and had sat out in his back yard pitching gravel around and hollering out to his enemies in a loud angry voice. The boy watched him all day, squatted down and watched him, his mouth open and drying. It seemed to him that if he could figure out what was wrong with the man he would learn the great secret of life.

Like many young men in the South, he became overly subtle and had trouble ruling out the possible. They are not like an immigrant's son in Passaic who decides to become a dentist and that is that. Southerners have trouble ruling out the possible. What happens to a man to whom all things seem possible and every course of action open? Nothing of course. Except war. If a man lives in the sphere of the possible and waits for something to happen, what he is waiting for is war—or the end of the world. That is why Southerners like to fight and make good soldiers. In war the possible becomes actual through no doing of one's own.

But it was worse than this in his case. It was more than being a Southerner. For some years he had had a nervous condition and as a consequence he did not know how to live his life. As a child he had had "spells," occurrences which were nameless and not to be thought of, let alone mentioned, and which he therefore thought of as lying at the secret and somehow shameful heart of childhood itself. There was a name for it, he discovered later, which gave it form and habitation. It was *déjà vu,* at least he reckoned it was. What happened anyhow was that even when he was a child and was sitting in the kitchen watching D'lo snap beans or make beaten biscuits, there came over him as it might come over a sorrowful old man the strongest sense that it had all happened before and that something else was going to happen and when it did he would know the secret of his own life. Things seemed to turn white and dense and time itself became freighted with an unspeakable emotion. Sometimes he "fell out" and would wake up hours later, in his bed, refreshed but still haunted.

When he was a youth he had lived his life in a state of the liveliest expectation, thinking to himself: what a fine thing it will be to become a man and to know what to do—like an Apache youth who at the right time goes out into the plains alone, dreams dreams, sees visions, returns and knows he is a man. But no such time had come and he still didn't know how to live.

To be specific, he had now a nervous condition and suffered spells of amnesia and even between times did not quite know what was what. Much of the time he was like a man who has just crawled out of a bombed building. Everything looked strange. Such a predicament, however, is not altogether a bad thing. Like the sole survivor of a bombed building, he had no secondhand opinions and he could see things afresh.

There were times when he was as normal as anyone. He could be as objective-minded and cool-headed as a scientist. He read well-known books on mental hygiene and for a few minutes after each reading felt very clear about things. He knew how to seek emotional gratifications in a mature way, as they say in such books. In the arts, for example. It was his custom to visit museums regularly and to attend the Philharmonic concerts at least once a week.

He understood, moreover, that it is people who count, one's relations with people, one's warmth toward and understanding of people. At these times he set himself the goal and often achieved it of "cultivating rewarding interpersonal relationships with a variety of people"—to use a phrase he had come across and not forgotten. Nor should the impression be given that he turned up his nose at religion, as old-style scientists used to do, for he had read widely among modern psychologists and he knew that we have much to learn from the psychological insights of the World's Great Religions.

At his best, he was everything a psychologist could have desired him to be. Most of the time, however, it was a different story. He would lapse into an unproductive and solitary life. He took to wandering. He had a way of turning up at unlikely places such as a bakery in Cincinnati or a greenhouse in Memphis, where he might work for several weeks assaulted by the *déjà vus* of hot growing green plants.

A German physician once remarked that in the lives of people who suffer emotional illness he had noticed the presence of *Lücken* or gaps. As he studied the history of a particular patient he found whole sections missing, like a book with blank pages.

Most of this young man's life was a gap. The summer before, he had fallen into a fugue state and wandered around northern Virginia for three weeks, where he sat sunk in thought on old battlegrounds, hardly aware of his own name.

FROM

The Second Coming

WALKER PERCY

NOW HE STOOD ALONE in the glade after slicing out-of-bounds on eighteen. He was holding the three-iron, not like a golf club or a shotgun now, but like a walking stick. Its blade resting on a patch of wet moss sank slightly of its own weight and the weight of his hand. Tiny bubbles of air or marsh gas came up through the moss next to the metal of the iron.

Once he was in the pine forest the air changed. Silence pressed in like soft hands clapped over his ears. Not merely faint but gone, blotted out, were the shouts of the golfers, the clink of irons, the sociable hum of the electric carts. He listened. There was nothing but the sound of the silence, the seashell roar which could be the *ee*ing and *oh*ing of his own blood or the sound of cicadas at the end of summer which seems to come both from the pines and from inside one's head.

Then he heard a chain saw so faraway that he could not make out its direction yet close enough to register the drop in pitch as the saw bit into wood and the motor labored.

The golf carts were going away. They had crossed a rise in the fairway. Through the trees he could see their white canopies move, one behind the other, as silently as sails.

He turned his head. Beyond the glade the pine forest was as dark as twilight except for a single poplar which caught the sun. Its leaves had turned a pale gold. Though the air was still in the forest, one leaf shook violently. Beyond the aspen he made out a deadfall of chestnuts. A flash of light came from the chestnut fall. By moving his head he could make the light come and go. It was the reflection of sunlight from glass.

Above him the branches of the pines came off the trunks at intervals and as regularly as the spokes of a wheel.

Lifting the three-iron slowly and watching it all the while, once again he held it like a shotgun at rest, club head high between his chest and arm, shaft resting across his forearm. Now, carefully, as if he were reenacting an event not quite remembered, as if he had forgotten something which his muscles and arms and hands might remember, he swung the shaft of the iron slowly to and fro like the barrel of a shotgun. He stopped and again stood as still as a hunter. Now turning his head and stooping, he looked back at the fence.

But he had not forgotten anything. Today for some reason he remembered everything. Everything he saw became a sign of something else. This fence was a sign of another fence he had climbed through. The hawk was a sign of another hawk and of a time when he believed there were fabulous birds. The tiger? Whatever he was, he was gone. Even the wheeling blackbirds signified not themselves but a certain mocking sameness. They flew up, flustered and wheeling and blown about by the same fitful wind just as they had thirty, forty years ago. There is no mystery. The only mystery is that nothing changes. Nothing really happens. Marriages, births, deaths, terrible wars had occurred but had changed nothing. War is not a change but a poor attempt to make a change. War and peace are not events.

Only one event had ever happened to him in his life. Everything else that had happened afterwards was a non-event.

The guitar sound of the fence wire stretched above him and the singing and popping of the vines against his body were signs of another event. Stooping now, he was trying to make his body remember what had happened. Suddenly it crossed his mind that nothing else had ever happened to him.

The boy had gone through the fence first, holding the new Sterlingworth Fox double-barreled twenty-gauge ahead of him, while the man pulled up the top strand of barbed wire. He had gone through the fence, but before he could stand up, the man had grabbed his shoulder from the other side of the fence in a grip that surprised him not so much for the pain as for the suddenness and violence and with the other hand grabbed the gun up and away from him, swung him around and cursed him. *Goddamn you, haven't I told you how to go through a fence with a loaded shotgun? Don't you know what would happen if*—suddenly the man stopped.

Now on the golf links years later he recognized the smell. It was the funky tannin rot of the pin-oak swamp as sharp in his nostrils as wood smoke.

The boy, who had already gotten over the pain but not the

surprise, stood looking at the man across the fence holding the two shotguns, still too surprised to feel naked and disarmed without his gun. Nothing would ever surprise him again. Once the surprise was gone and his heart slowed, he began to feel the first hint of the coolness and curiosity and watchfulness of the rest of his life. Is it possible that his eyes narrowed slightly (he wasn't sure of this) as he put his empty hands in his pockets (he was sure of this) and said:

If what?

They had gone into the woods after singles. The dog had run over the covey instead of pointing it, and the covey had flushed too soon and too far away for a shot, the fat birds getting up with their sudden heart-stop thunder, then angling off tilt-winged and planing into the trees. The man, whitefaced with anger, cursed the guide, shot the dog instead of the birds, to teach the dog never to do that again, he said, not to hurt the dog bad what with the distance and the number-eight bird shot. The dog and the guide disappeared.

When the man handed the shotgun back to him, his eyes glittered but not in the merry way they did when a hunt went well. He had given the boy the new shotgun for Christmas and he had just finished trying an important lawsuit in Thomasville close by and this was the very place, the very woods where he, the man, once had had a great hunt, perhaps even a fabled hunt, with his own father. But this hunt had gone badly. The Negro guide was no good. The dog had been trained badly. The lawsuit was not going well. They, the man and the boy, had spent a bad sleepless night in an old hotel (the same hotel where the man had spent the night before the great Thomasville hunt). The hotel was not at all as the man had remembered it.

Here, said the man, handing him the shotgun and stretching up the top strand of barbed wire. The wire creaked. *I trust you now.*

Thank you. The boy was watchful as he took the gun.

Do you trust me? asked the man.

Yes. No.

You have to trust me now.

Why?

I'm going to see to it that you're not going to have to go through what I am going through.

What's that?

You'll just have to trust me, okay?

Okay, said the boy, eyes wary and watchful. The man sounded almost absentminded and his glittering eye seemed to cast beyond him to the future, perhaps to the lawsuit Monday.

Come over here a minute.

What?

Here. Over here by me.

Oh.

Now, as the boy stood beside him, the man gave him a hug with the arm not holding the gun. He felt the man's hand giving him hard regular pats on the arm. He was saying something. The boy, no longer surprised, did not quite hear because he was reflecting on the strangeness of it, getting an awkward hug from his father, as they stood side by side in their bulky hunting clothes in the wet cold funk-smelling pin-oak swamp. He couldn't remember being hugged before except at funerals and weddings, and then the hugs were perfunctory and the kisses quick cheek kisses and that was all right with him, he didn't want to be hugged or kissed then or now.

And now, standing in the glade with the three-iron, he was wondering idly. *Why?* Why is it that I would not wish then or now or ever to kiss my father? Why is it that it was then and now a kind of violation, not the violation of the man grabbing him across the fence but a violation nevertheless, and a cheapening besides. Italians and Frenchmen and women hugged and kissed each other and what did it signify?

What? asked the boy.

The man pulled him close and turned his face down toward him and the boy smelled the heavy catarrh of his breath with the faint overlay of whiskey from the night before. His father was understood to suffer from "catarrh" and all night long, while the boy lay still, watchful and alert, the man had tossed and breathed out his heavy catarrh-and-whiskey breath.

Two singles went in here. I'll take one and you the other. But the man didn't let him go, held him still and gave him regular hard pats.

The man liked to go after singles after the covey was flushed, veering from the fields and open woodlands which the dogs had quartered and plunge backward into thickets and briars where not even the dogs would go, turning and using his body as entering wedge, the vines singing and popping against the heavy duck of his pants and jacket. When a single got up and he shot it and found it (no thanks to the dogs), and held the bird in his hand for a moment before stuffing it into the game pocket, his eyes would grow merry as if he had set himself an impossible quest and won, had plunged into the heart of the darkness and disorder of the wet cold winter woods and extracted from it of all things a warm bright-eyed perfect bird.

But now the man was standing still, eyes glittering, holding the gun oddly and gazing down at it, the stock resting on ground, the barrel tilted just back from the vertical and resting lightly in the crotch of thumb and forefinger.

You and I are the same, said the man as if he were speaking to the gun.

How?

You are like me. We are two of a kind. I saw it last night.

Here come the pats again, hard, regular, slow, like a bell tolling.

Saw what?

I saw the way you lay in bed last night and slept or didn't sleep. You're one of us, I'm afraid. You already know too much. It's too bad in a way.

Us? Who's us?

You'd be better off if you were one of them.

Who's them?

The ignorant armies that clash by night.

The boy was silent.

We have to trust each other now, don't we?

Yes, said the boy, rearing slightly so he could see the man better.

We're buddies, aren't we?

Yes. No. You're wrong. We're not buddies. I don't want to be anybody's buddy.

Okay. Let's go. There are two of them. You take the one on the right.

Okay.

Oh shit, said the man. Last hard pat, sock, wham, on the shoulder. *I'm sorry.*

The boy looked up not surprised but curious. He had never heard the man say *shit* before.

Now standing with the three-iron in the glade, he was thinking: he said that one and only *shit* in exactly the same flat taped voice airline pilots use before the crash: *We're going in. Shit.*

Now the man was looking more like himself again, cheeks ruddy, cap pushed back on his head as if it were a summer day and he needed the air, though it was very cold. It was his regular chipper look but when the boy, going forward, looked at him sideways he noticed that his eyes were too bright.

They kicked up two singles but the birds flew into the trees too soon and there was no shot. The birds angled apart and the man and the boy, following them, diverged. A lopsided scrub oak, dead leaves brown and heavy as leather, came between them. A ground fog filled the hollows like milk. As the boy moved ahead silently on the wet speckled leaves, his heart did not beat in his throat as it used to before quail are flushed. Then it came, on the man's side of the tree, the sudden tiny thunder of the quail and the shot hard upon it and then the silence. There was not even the sound of a footstep but only a click from the Greener. Now the boy was moving ahead again. He heard the man walking. They were clearing the tree and converging. Through the leathery leaves and against the milkiness he caught sight of a swatch of khaki. Didn't he hear it again, the so sudden uproar of stiff wings beating the little drum of bird body and the man swinging toward him in the terrific concentration of keeping gunsight locked on the fat tilt-winged quail and hard upon the little drumbeat the shocking blast rolling away like thunder through the silent woods? The boy saw the muzzle burst and flame spurting from the gun like a picture of a Civil War soldier shooting and even had time to wonder why he had never seen it before, before he heard the whistling and banging in his ear and found himself down in the leaves without knowing how he got there and even then could still hear the sound of the number-eight shot rattling away through the milky swamp and was already scrambling to get up from the embarrassment of it (for that was no place to be), but when he tried to stand, the keening in his ear spun him down again—all that before he even felt the hot wetness on the side of his face which was not pressed into the leaves and touched it and saw the blood. It was as if someone had taken hold of him and flung him down. He heard the *geclick* and *gecluck* of the Greener's breech opening and closing. Then he heard the shot. He waited until the banging and keening in his head stopped. He did not feel cold. His face did not hurt. Using the gun as a prop, he was able to get to his knees. He called out. It had been important to get up before calling. Nobody, not him, not anybody, is going to catch me down here on the ground. When there was no answer, he waited again, aware only of his own breathing and that he was blinking and gazing at nothing in particular. Then, without knowing how he knew, he knew that he was free to act in his own good time. (How did he know such a thing?) Taking a deep breath, he stood up and exhaled it through his mouth *sheeew* as a laborer might do, and wiping blood from his lip with two fingers he slung it off as a laborer might sling snot. Twelve years old, he grew up in ten minutes. It was possible for him to stretch out a hand to the tree and touch it, not hold it. He walked around the tree before it occurred to him that he had forgotten his shotgun. At first he didn't see the man, because both the jacket and the cap had a camouflage pattern which hid him in the leaves like a quail and because the bill of the cap hid his face. The man was part lying, part sitting against a tree, legs stretched out and cap pulled over his face like a countryman taking a nap and there was the feeling in the boy not that it was funny but that he was nevertheless called upon to smile and he might even have tried except that his face suddenly hurt. He did not see the man's gun, the big double-barreled twelve-gauge English Greener. For some reason which he could still not explain, he went back to look for his own gun. It was not hard to walk but when he bent to pick up the gun his face hurt again. When he came back he saw the dark brown stock of the Greener sticking out from the skirt of the man's jacket.

Now the boy was squatting (not sitting) beside the man. He pushed his own cap back as if it were a hot day. He pulled the man's cap off. He was not smiling and his eyes were closed but his face looked all right. His cheeks were still ruddy.

He put his hand under the man's jacket but the Greener got in the way. He pulled the shotgun out by the butt and put his hand under the jacket again and against the man's chest. The heart beat strongly. But his hand was wet and something was wrong. The fabric of shirt and underwear was matted into flesh like burlap trodden into mud.

Now squatting back on his heels beside the man he took his handkerchief from his pocket with his dry hand and carefully wiped the blood from the other hand. Then he pushed his cap back still farther because his forehead was sweating. He blew into both hands because they were cold and began to think.

What he was thinking about was what he was going to do next but at the same time he noticed that he did not feel bad. Why is it, he wondered, that I feel that I have all the time in the world to figure out what to do and the freedom to do it and that what is more I will do it? It was as if he had contracted into the small core of curiosity and competence he had felt within himself after the man had grabbed him across the fence, spun him around, cursed him, and took his gun away. Now he was blowing into his hands and thinking: This is a problem and problems are for solving. All you need to do anything is time to do it, being let alone long enough to do it and a center to do it from. He had found his center.

The guide doesn't live far from here. We passed the cabin. The Negro boy ran home when the man cursed him and shot the dog.

Now he was standing up and looking carefully around. He even made out a speckled quail lying in the speckled leaves. As he waited for the dizziness to clear, he watched the man.

Don't worry, I'm going to get us both out of here. He knew with certainty that he could.

Later, after it was over, his stepmother had hugged them both. *Thank God thank God thank God* she said in her fond shouting style. *You could have both been killed!*

So it had come to pass that there were two accounts of what had happened, and if one was false the other must be true; one which his stepmother had put forward in the way that a woman will instantly and irresistibly construe the world as she will have it and in fact does have it so: that the man had had one of his dizzy spells—he knows with his blood pressure he shouldn't drink and hunt!—and fell; that in falling he discharged the double-barrel, which wounded the boy and nearly killed the man. The boy almost came to believe her, especially when she praised him. *We can thank our lucky stars that this child had the sense and bravery to know what to do. And you a twelve-year-old*—mussing up his hair in front in a way she thought of as being both manly and English—*We're so proud of you. My fine brave boy!*

But it was not bravery, he thought, eyes narrowing, almost smiling. It was the coldness, the hard secret core of himself that he had found.

The boy and his father knew better. With a final hug after he was up and around and the boy had recovered, except for a perforated and permanently deafened left middle ear and a pocked cheek like a one-sided acne, the man was able to speak to him by standing in the kitchen and enlisting D'Lo the cook in the conversation and affecting a broad hunter's lingo not at all like him: *I'm going to tell yall one damn thing*—Yall? He never said *yall.* Talking to D'Lo, who stood at the stove with her back to them? *I'm getting rid of that savage.* He nodded to the Greener on the pantry table. *I had no idea that savage had a pattern that wide! So wide it knicked you—did you know that, D'Lo?* Hugging the boy, he asked D'Lo. D'Lo must either have known all about it or, most likely, had not been listening closely, for she only voiced her routine but adequate *hnnnonnhHM! Now ain't that something else!*—which was what the man wanted her to say because this was the man's way of telling the boy, through D'Lo, what had happened and soliciting and getting her inattentive assent to the routineness and even inevitability of it. Such things happen! *And I'll tell you something else,* the man told D'Lo. *When a man comes to the point that all he can think about is tracking a bird and shuts everything out of his mind to the point of shooting somebody, it's time to quit!* D'Lo socked down grits spoon on boiler rim. *You right, Mister Barrett!* Was she even listening? And now the man finally looking down his cheek at him hugged alongside: *Right?*

Yes sir. He waited only to be released from the hug.

There was silence. They spoke no more of it. We know, don't we, the silence said, that the man was somehow wounded by the same shot and there is nothing to be said about it.

But how did he miss the bird? How did he wound himself?

While the sheriff was taking care of the man in the swamp, the guide brought the two shotguns, a dead quail, and three empty shells into the dark clean room smelling of coal oil and newspaper and flour paste where the Negro woman was washing his face. She dried it and patted something light and feathery—spiderwebs?—on his cheek. He didn't feel bad but his ear still roared. "*Here dey,*" said the black youth. *They yours and hisn.* He looked down at the kitchen table at the two shotguns, the three empty Super-X shells, and the dead quail. This black boy was no guide. What guide would pick up empty shotgun shells? *You didn't see the other bird?* he asked the guide. *Ain't no other bird,* said the black boy. The white boy said: *There were two singles and he shot twice and he never misses.* The black boy said: *Well he done missed this time.* The white boy heard himself saying: *You just didn't find the bird,* and getting angry and wondering: Why am I worrying about the second bird? *Nawsuh,* said the woman, whose black arms were sifted with flour. *John sho find your bird if he was there. Look, he even found your bullets. Must have been the dogs got him.*

He looked at the Greener on the kitchen table in the shotgun cabin, sat down, broke the breech, and took out the one empty shell and set it next to the shells the guide had found. As he gazed he put one hand to his cheek, which had begun to bleed again, and covered his roaring ear.

Now in a green forest glade near a pretty pink-and-green golf links, he touched his deafened ear. Did it still roar a little or was it the seashell roar of the silence of forest? Holding the three-iron in both hands he tested the spring of its steel shaft.

It was as if the thirty years had passed and he had not ever left the Negro cabin but, strange to say, had only now got around to saying what he had not said for thirty years. Again he smelled the close clean smell of kerosene and warm newspaper.

Now in Carolina in a glade in the white pines he said aloud: *There was only one shell in the Greener,* for some reason smiling a little and examining the three-iron closely as if it had a breech which could be broken, revealing the missing shell. But he only saw the green Winchester Super-X with its slightly wrinkled cylinder smelling of cordite. *What happened to the other shell?* Nothing. There was no other shell. I broke the breech of the Greener and there was only one shell. Why? Because he reloaded after the first shot. He shot the first single. Then there was a pause. It was then that I heard the *geclick* of the Greener breech opening and the *gecluck* of its closing. But why reload with one good shell left? That was all he needed for the second single if I missed it. Because he always liked to be ready. He liked to shoot quick and on the rise. And why, after the second shot, did he reload with only one shell?

Because—He smiled at the three-iron which he held sprung like a bow in front of him.

Because when he reloaded the last time, he knew he only needed one shot.

But why reload at all? He had reloaded before the second shot. After the second shot, he still had a good shell in the second chamber.

Wait a minute. Again he saw the sun reflected from something beyond the chestnut deadfall.

What happened? Here's what happened.

He fired once at the first single. Geclick. Eject one shell and replace it. Gecluck.

He fired the second time at the second single and also hit me. Geclick. Reload. Gecluck.

Why reload if he knew he only needed one more shot? He still had a good shell in the second chamber.

In the Carolina pine forest he closed his eyes and saw green Super-X shells lined up on the clean quilt in the Negro cabin.

There were *four* shells.

Faraway the golfers were shouting, their voices blowing away like the killdeer on the high skyey fairways. It was close and still in the glade. He was watching the three-iron as, held in front of him like a divining rod, it sank toward the earth. *Ah, I've found it after all. The buried treasure,* he thought smiling.

Strange to say, there rose in his throat the same sweet terror he had felt long ago when his father's old bitch Maggie (not the sorry pointer dog his father shot at Thomasville) pointed, bent like a pin, tail quivering, and they went slowly past her to kick up the covey, knowing as certainly as you can know anything that any second it would happen again, the sudden irruption at one's very feet, the sudden heart-stop thunder from the very earth where one stood.

Ah then, so that was it. He was trying to tell me something before he did it. Yes, he had a secret and he was trying to tell me and I think I knew it even then and have known it ever since but now I know that I know and there's a difference.

He was trying to warn me. He was trying to tell me that one day it would happen to me too, that I would come to the same place he came to, and I have, I have just now, climbing through a barbed-wire fence. Was he trying to tell me because he thought that if I knew exactly what happened to him and what was going to happen to me, that by the mere telling it would not then have to happen to me? Knowing about what is going to happen is having a chance to escape it. If you don't know about it, it will certainly happen to you. But if you know, will it not happen anyway?

The Shadow of an Arm

Thomas Hal Phillips

Peane sat on a stool beside the compress and watched the cotton, like a stream of snow, slide down into the baler. In his right hand he held a short hickory rod, now worn sleek, with which he stirred the cotton so that the chute would not choke. He could not see Mr. Sid and Mr. Clark, standing on the weighing platform behind him, but he could hear them; and Mr. Clark was saying: "But Papa, that's old-timey business. If I'm going to keep books I want to pay everybody with a check every Saturday night. And if they say I never paid, then I'll have a record."

"All right," Mr. Sid said. "All right. But nobody yet ever told me I didn't pay them. Let's go on up to the house and you can write the checks."

Above the sound of the gin Peane heard Mr. Sid walking toward him. He knew Mr. Sid's walk. Then he felt the hand touch his shoulder and Mr. Sid said: "We're going to dinner. We'll be back in a little while."

"Yessuh," Peane said. He heard them go down the ladder. Then he looked around to see that Mr. Clark was the last to disappear below. He hoped Mr. Sid wouldn't let Mr. Clark start writing checks on payday. Having a check was not the same as having the bills, even the wrinkled bills; and that was another thing Mr. Clark didn't understand. But Mr. Sid did.

Peane reached out his right hand and jerked the cotton down. Sometimes he did not use the stick at all. He liked to feel the cotton just before it went into the bale. It was warm and soft then. He smiled a little. His hands and arms always looked blacker against the white blanket sliding downward. He half-closed his eyes and pictured every wheel that quivered now in a long, steady drone. He knew everything about the gin: he and Mr. Sid had built it. He knew more about it than Mr. Roy Drew, who was only the ginner. He thought of Mr. Roy because he heard laughter. It came from the suction platform at the front of the gin, and he knew it was Mr. Roy talking to Mr. Albert. They were ginning Mr. Albert's bale now, and in a few minutes Mr. Albert would come back to the compress and joke about how much his bale was going to weigh.

After a while he heard the steps he expected but he did not look up at that moment, for the chute was filling. His left hand reached out for the lever; slowly the presser went down. Then he released the lever, and with a hiss of steam the presser jolted upward again.

"Peane?"

"Yessuh." He turned. It was Mr. Albert. He was tall and heavy and red-faced now. Peane could remember when he was tall and slender and the bottoms of his trousers always struck above his ankles.

"Where's Sid?"

"At the house. For dinner." His left hand worked hard at the lever again.

"When you gonna quit monkeying with this old gin and come over to my place to grow cotton?"

"I don't know, suh." Peane laughed. Mr. Albert was a lot like Mr. Sid.

"Well, hell. I feed my hands. It's nearly one o'clock."

"Yessuh. Mr. Sid'll be back now, any time. Then I go eat."

"Has Clark come home from school to run his daddy's farm next year?"

"I don't know. Mr. Sid didn't say yet. But Mr. Clark's here." Peane let the press down and up again. A light cloud of steam covered his hand.

"What's it gonna weigh?"

Peane laughed. "About 490."

Mr. Albert looked over into the baler. "Now when the hell have you weighed a bale for me that didn't push the pè beyond five hundred?"

Peane reached out with the stick, for the chute was filling again. He let the presser down and the compress creaked. Mr. Albert grunted. "I'll be damned, Peane. If I brought you and Sid a six-hundred-pound bale your old compress would bust wide open. You ought to get a new all-electric outfit, like the one in Raymond. Just touch a button there and a button here . . ." They turned to the sound of steps behind them.

Mr. Sid was climbing the gin's back ladder. His big arms and shoulders were just above the gin's floor. A healthy red always showed across his face.

"Sid," Mr. Albert said. "Did you hear what I said?"

Mr. Sid was standing straight now. He was big, not fat. "No. What?"

"If you don't jack up this damned gin and put a new electric outfit under it, I'm gonna start hauling my cotton to Raymond."

Mr. Sid grinned and came on to where Peane sat. He put his hand on Peane's shoulder. "He can't tell a good gin when he sees one, can he?"

Peane laughed. Mr. Sid turned toward Mr. Albert. "You want those fancy suction motors to shoot your cotton through and cut it all to pieces? Hell no."

"I know," Mr. Albert said. "I know they shoot it through so fast it looks like it's sprinkled with pepper. And cut it up too."

"Now you're talking," Mr. Sid said. He took the hickory stick from Peane's hand. "Reckon this bale will touch five hundred, Peane? Or is this another one of those shirttail bales of Albert Bynum's?"

"A dollar on it," Mr. Albert said. "A dollar that it tips five hundred."

Mr. Sid laughed. "You better go on and get something to eat, Peane."

Peane walked toward the house with the November chill close about him. He wondered what it would be like if Mr. Clark took over the gin, though he did not believe Mr. Sid would let him change anything. He remembered Mr. Clark saying: "But you ought to switch over to electricity, Papa. You could save on cordwood, and belts, a dozen things, and cut out half the work. . . ." And Mr. Sid had said: "I'm sixty-two years old. I'm not going to tear up something I built just to do away with a little work. That's the trouble with the world. People trying to get out of work when it's the best thing I know of to keep a man happy—plenty of work and a good wife."

"But it's foolish not to switch."

"Someday, Clark," Mr. Sid had said, "it'll belong to you and Elizabeth and Karen. Then you can put in electric motors and push buttons—mirrors, if you want to."

Mr. Clark did not understand.

But Peane understood. It was something you felt, and not something to talk about. He looked back for a moment to the gin which he and Mr. Sid had built thirty years ago: the high tin top, the tall smokestack, and the silver suction pipes. He turned and hurried on toward the house.

He passed his own small house and then Etta's house at the edge of the garden. He did not see anyone nor any smoke from Etta's chimney. It seemed like a day when everything had stopped. Something was waiting.

On the back steps, at the big house, he stopped. He did not remember the first time he had gone into that house. He remembered being seven and Mr. Sid six, and together they had sometimes slept on the same pallet. Then Mr. Sid was suddenly grown—all too soon. His face was big and red, and the ridges leaped on his arms when he lifted any weight. The farm was all his. But he did not make Peane work in the fields. Together they had built the gin—though a few of the field hands helped now and then. That was why Mr. Sid didn't want the gin changed. Mr. Clark could never understand.

Peane went into the kitchen. When he did not see Etta, he called to her. He heard only a voice in the living room, and he knew it was Mr. Clark. "Mother, what time did Elizabeth and Karen go to Vicksburg?"

"While you were at the gin. They didn't know you wanted to go. And besides, they're going to be at the high school all afternoon." That was Miss Annie. Then she said: "Peane? Is that you?"

"Yes, ma'am."

"Etta's in the garden. She put you a plate in the warming closet."

"Yes, ma'am."

The moment his hand touched the warming closet of the stove he heard the gin's whistle, and in his mind he could see clearly the long blasts of steam rising above the boiler. His heart leaped but he did not move. His hand seemed glued to a platter. Mr. Clark's voice was quick in the living room. "Mother, something is wrong at the gin. That damned old dilapidated boiler, I guess."

Peane wanted to turn, to say the whistle wouldn't blow if there was anything wrong with the boiler. But his hand still clutched the platter.

"Peane?"

Suddenly his hand jerked to his side and he was hurrying toward Mr. Clark.

"Let's see what's the matter. I've been telling Papa that something was going to happen. . . ."

They ran out of the house toward the gate and the car. Peane sat in the back seat as they raced down the driveway and turned into the road toward the gin. Mr. Clark's lips kept moving: "Damned old thing ready to fall in on his head and Papa won't change it. No telling what's happened now."

The car lurched from the gravel road on to the sawdust-covered gin yard. Peane's hands reached out and pressed against the seat when the car came to a stop near the scales. He ran behind Mr. Clark toward the ladder of the gin.

At the head of the ladder Mr. Albert towered above them. He reached down and caught Mr. Clark's arm, helping him up the last few rungs. "Over here, Clark. . . ."

Peane pulled himself up quickly to the gin's floor. His short breath was like a quick heartbeat. Mr. Sid was lying beside the compress, his bloodstained arm folded across his chest. His sleeve was hardly torn, like little rips from barbed wire. A small streak of blood crossed his lips.

"You can't stop the blood," Mr. Albert said. "Too much in the shoulder. You'll have to take him to Raymond. You can't get to Vicksburg in time."

"But there's nothing at Raymond—a two-by-four clinic."

"We can't get to Vicksburg."

Mr. Clark was kneeling. His own face was turning white. Mr. Albert reached down and pulled him up. "Go on. Go on down, Clark. Get the car started. Peane's stout. He can lift him and I'll hold his arm and shoulder."

"Where's Roy?" Mr. Clark said. His breath was fast.

"Gone after you. Go on now. . . ." He shoved Mr. Clark toward the ladder.

Peane stooped and lifted Mr. Sid, who opened his eyes and closed them again.

"Peane?"

Peane could not answer. Mr. Sid was too heavy. Mr. Albert had the injured arm and shoulder and he was saying: "Easy, Peane. You'll have to carry him down the ladder by yourself—not room for us both."

Peane's foot touched the top rung. He inched downward. His shoulders touched either side of the ladder opening. He wanted to look up, as if suddenly everything was reversed and he couldn't ask God for anything unless he looked up. He was almost saying: "God, you know I can't think of nothing with all this weight. . . ."

Then he was in the car and they were moving. Mr. Clark's right hand was cotton-white upon the steering wheel, and Mr. Albert was holding the shoulder and whispering: "You made it, Peane, and that damned ladder sagging with all your weight. . . ." And still Peane wanted to look up but he could not, he thought, for the weight in his arms. It was all a little like the times they used to wrestle—and he could throw Mr. Sid. He wanted to touch Mr. Sid's face, to wipe the streak of sweat and blood away.

Mr. Sid did not open his eyes. He said: "The press caught my shoulder. It stuck. The lever. You know how it does . . . sometimes . . . Peane. . . ."

Peane did not move though the weight was getting heavier and heavier. He wished Mr. Sid was six or seven. He could hold him then. It would be all right. For a moment Peane seemed to close his own eyes. Then the car was stopping. His body came to life again, beneath the weight.

He put Mr. Sid on the white table in the clinic. Then, without saying anything, he turned and went back to the car. He wanted to look up and say something, now that the weight was gone, but he was sick—low inside him. He got into the back seat. Then he saw the blood and got into the front seat, put his head down into his hands, and tried not to think of the dripping from the cotton which Mr. Albert had held beneath the torn sleeve. He sat a long time.

Somebody tapped him on the shoulder. "They want you in there," Mr. Albert said. "And hurry. I have to leave—to go to Vicksburg after Elizabeth and Karen."

In the hall of the clinic Peane saw the doctor and Mr. Clark and the nurse. They were in a little group. Peane knew the doctor: he was Mr. Edgeworth's boy and not much older than Mr. Clark.

"Can't we do something else?" Mr. Clark was saying. "Can't we wait until Karen and Elizabeth get here?"

"Yes," the doctor said. "We can wait. But the sooner he gets the blood the better. And they're not likely to have AB, since you didn't. He can't wait long for a transfusion."

Mr. Clark kept looking at the doctor, not at his face, but at the mask hanging around his neck. Then slowly he turned to Peane. His face was very white. "Would you give Papa a transfusion—if you're the right type?"

Peane could not answer; he had not expected Mr. Clark to ask him anything. He nodded, and again he was beginning to be sick, low in his stomach. Mr. Clark caught his arm lightly and said: "Go with the nurse." It was the first time Peane ever remembered Mr. Clark's touching him. He nodded again, and then he followed the nurse. He was trying to think about his hat, trying to remember where it was.

The room was white and the smell was sharp. The nurse took the forefinger of his right hand and washed it with alcohol. "Hold still," she said.

"Is he going to be all right?" Peane said.

"We don't know."

"Sometimes it gits stuck," he said. "The lever at the compress."

"Clench your fist, then open it."

He was afraid.

"It stuck with Mr. Sid. Then the press comes down . . ."

"Open it. Your hand."

"But it always comes down slow and you can git out of the way. Only this time it must . . ."

She pricked his finger. "Now lean back and rest awhile." She went away and he closed his eyes.

In a few minutes he was lying on a white table with the needle in his arm. It was the thought of the needle that hurt. He kept his eyes closed and tried to think that it was only somebody pinching him—like Mr. Sid poking fun.

"It was the right kind," the nurse whispered, but she did not seem to be talking to him. And he was afraid to ask anything; even his asking might make things go wrong.

After a few minutes he heard: "I'm all through now. You just lie there and rest awhile."

He lay there, trying not to remember, and the nurse went out. But the smell and the quietness did not make him afraid any more. He felt as if he had touched something he had always wanted to touch, had held something he had always wanted to hold. It was a long time before the nurse came back into the room. He was glad when she came.

"They're moving Mr. Walters now. He's awake. The doctor wants you to lift him onto the bed. They're all sick. Everybody but the doctor. Some people can't look at blood."

Peane nodded slowly. He got up.

"You know where room two is? Down the hall?"

"No, ma'am."

"Come on. I'll show you."

She went down the hall ahead of him and turned into a room. He reached the doorway of the room and stopped. His hand clutched the facing. Then he knew that Mr. Sid's arm was gone.

"Here," the doctor said. "Can you lift him by yourself?"

Peane pulled his hand away from the facing. Slowly he walked toward the bed.

"Stand between the roller and the bed," the nurse said. "And turn his head that way."

Slowly Peane nodded. He was numb with the feeling that he might drop Mr. Sid. His whole body seemed unable to stand. Then his hands moved under Mr. Sid's shoulders and under his thighs. His arms against the white sheet were darker now—like their being against the stream of cotton in the compress. He closed his eyes, lifted, and turned. Something hurt in his stomach. Mr. Sid's shoulders touched the bed. He opened his eyes and for a moment stared. Then his lips moved slowly. "Peane . . . did you give me the blood?"

"Yessuh."

"You shouldn't be lifting me."

"You're all right now," the nurse said quickly. "You're going to be all right." Her hands moved along the sheet beside his good right arm.

Mr. Sid kept looking at Peane. "You know how that damned lever sometimes sticks. . . ."

"Yessuh," Peane said.

"You rest now," the nurse said. She motioned Peane quietly toward the door.

Peane walked home. He knew that he did not have to walk: it was something he wanted to do. He had walked for a long time when he realized that it was beginning to rain. The wind seemed to whip the low clouds down into his face. He had been thinking that Mr. Sid would be all right.

When he came within sight of the gin he thought of Mr. Clark there, so he turned and cut across the pasture and went past the barn toward the house which was dark now. When he passed the big house he wished that somebody had been there: he wanted to tell somebody something. It was a strange feeling, as if nothing had happened to Mr. Sid, but the day itself had died.

In the damp darkness inside his room he lay on his bed and waited. He did not sleep, but sometimes he would feel his arms, as if to make certain that nothing had happened to them. A little while later he heard the sound of a car, and he got up. Then he saw the light from the big house. He crossed the yard to the back door and went into the kitchen. He was not hungry. He only wanted to tell somebody something—that everything was gone and he could never go back to the gin again.

He could hear voices in the living room. Then suddenly Mr. Clark was saying: "Peane? Is that you?"

"Yessuh." He was trying hard to think how to tell Mr. Clark—he would take over the gin now.

"Did you want something, Peane?"

Peane could not answer. He could not say anything.

"Oh, you want your pay." Mr. Clark turned back into the living room. The house was silent, more lifeless than Peane ever remembered. Then Mr. Clark was returning across the dining room toward the kitchen. He held out a check before him. Still Peane could not move nor say anything. Mr. Clark reached out and pushed the check into his coat pocket, and then he quickly drew two twenty-dollar bills from his wallet. "Here's something for you, Peane. And if you don't mind, I wish you wouldn't tell anybody about giving the blood." They did not say anything else to each other. After a minute Mr. Clark went back into the living room. Peane stood and watched until the light went off in the dining room. Slowly he turned and went out into the night. He looked across the yard toward the gin, and beyond the gin toward Mr. Albert Bynum's place. But for a while he did not move. He took the check and the bills and tore them piece by piece and let the rain wash the pieces out of his hand and onto the ground. Then he began to walk, for he knew that Mr. Sid would understand. And he was thinking that he would not take all of himself: he would leave something behind.

Mighty Long Time

STERLING D. PLUMPP

EBENEZZER SMITH up and hit Sonny Boy side the head; said the boy was doing things the wrong way. No way to hold a harp. You can't blow the right sounds if you don't pick it up right. It was that way every time we was over at their house; Sonny Boy would grab the harmonica and start playing something and then Ebenezzer Smith wouldn't say nothing but would come over and hit him side the head, knocking the harp out his mouth.

"You, allright, Sonny Boy" Boopee said.

"Un-huhn" grunted Sonny Boy rubbing his head.

"Maybe we outhta git our slingshots and look for birds" I said.

"Won't show'em how to blow no harp right" Ebenezzer Smith said.

We never said nothing back to him. Just got up and walked outside then went running toward the woods. Octobers was a good time to look for woodpeckers up high in trees knocking a hole in one for his winter house. If you tipped lightly you could get right under one knocking away and have your slingshot's sling drawn way back and boom!—you got him before he knowed a thing. It was funny with birds and slingshots; sometimes you could almost get close enough to grab them and yet miss them when you shot and others you could shoot at one that is flying and git'em. I got my first one when once I seed a fat robin bouncing up and down by the barn pecking every now and then at something the horses done left behind. When I got to the spot I had shot at his body was there and his head a little farther away.

"Look, there's a rabbit" Boopee said.

"Yeah, must be a jack rabbit" Sonny Boy said.

"Rascal, sure is big" I said.

"Wish, I had my rifle" Thomas Berry said.

"What?" Boopee said.

"Nigger, ain't got no rifle" Sonny Boy said.

"Yeah, I is" Thomas Berry said.

"You lying" Sonny Boy said.

"Git offa my back and keep that juke harp in your mouth" Thomas Berry said.

"What you say, nigger?" Sonny Boy asked.

But by the time they squared off Boopee stepped between them and from way off in the distance we heard dogs; we was hunting down behind Teet Spann's fields over by the road that led to Mound Hood Church. We had to watch out cause sometimes no-good rednecks would hunt and look for trouble; they might wanna kill anything black they seed. We headed in direction of the big creek cause the rednecks probably hunting birds and would stay close to the hills. No need us finding out if they evil or not cause we been told more than once how mean they is. Folks talked about Squirrel was killed by them though he was found floating in Walter Money's pond. They said Squirrel would look lightning in the eye and they must've met him one night and when he didn't bow down they hit him in the head and chunked him in the pond where he drown.

"Sonny Boy" I said.

"Un-Huhn" he said.

"Why don't you go off somewhere by yourself and blow" I said.

"Ain't like that" he said.

"How come?" I said.

"You oughta" Boopee said.

"That's right" Thomas Berry said.

"I can blow the harp—just can't blow blues out it. Not like eating, this blues-playing—you can't just use your own spoon to clean your plate—gotta dip from somebody else's too. Ebenezzer got them blues—had'em most his life. Took me in, they say when my momma died with pneumonia and I was three years old. Been with him and Miss Mae ever since; she the only momma I knowed and he my daddy. Miss Mae say ain't nobody never can blow the blues like Ebenezzer Smith; say he could stop folks from playing baseball at a picnic. Then one night in a honky-tonk in Vicksburg he blowed so low folks broke down and cried like they at a revival. He was the best til they took him away. Some no-good nigger said Ebenezzer Smith was in with him in stealing cotton; when all he'd done was help some fella load cotton one night up in Clarksdale—"

"Look—a thrash" Thomas Berry said, pointing at a red oak.

"You git'em" Boopee said.

"What happened, Sonny Boy?" I said.

"Judge say he was guilty, too. Give him twenty years and a day. They let him go after fifteen years on good behavior and he ain't played right since. He was fifty three when I was took in thirteen years ago. Now all he do is make four or five bales of cotton, raise hogs, and plenty corn. Never go nowhere 'cept to town and hunting. I wanna play harp since Miss Mae told me bout him" Sonny Boy said.

No matter how often we went hunting for birds or went fishing we always wound up listening to Sonny Boy. He telling bout how the blues was something inside you that you had to know to make the harp bring out. Telling us that Ebenezzer Smith had been the best at doing it. Telling us it was his basket catch in life. Yet we couldn't understand Sonny Boy always picking up the harp and gitting hit side the head in front of us.

"Ain't right" Ebenezzer would say. "Nobody never done blowed that harp right 'less he done felt right inside and done holded it right when blowing. Like trying to pick a juicy berry that's surrounded by thorns—you gotta want it mighty bad and you gotta hold your hand just right, stay outta way of the thorns. Can't never be no man 'less you do things right. We's born cause things done right, we lives cause things done right, and we dies when things go wrong yet we lives after death if things done right. Boy gotta live in that harp like he live his life. No two ways bout it."

Then I ain't seed Sonny Boy in a month. Nowhere. Not even at school after the crops been harvested. I been over his house a time or two and one time Miss Mae say he ain't there and the other Ebenezzer Smith say the same thing but in a meaner way. After while Thomas Berry say Mister Timmy Robinson say that Miss Ollie Smith say she seed him riding that ol' white mule toward Clinton with what looked like a sack of corn across its back to be ground into meal at Johnson's Mill. They say it was reckly after the first frost when hogs was killed the Friday after Thanksgiving—about eight days ago. I got to find out for myself what going on with Sonny Boy cause if I don't I won't be able look him in the eye when I see him again. With me being his best friend I gotta try and find out more bout him or listen to his mouth: "Don't expect much from

Boopee—but he allright—but ain't knowed him that long; and that lying Thomas Berry ain't won't nothing but a bottle of home brew'—can't hardly look after hisself, let alone somebody else. You don't like me no more, T-Man." Sonny Boy never let things git cold fore he said his say on them. But again maybe I oughta mind my own business cause seem like Ebenezzer Smith live in one world and Sonny Boy in another and he trying to put a spell on Sonny Boy and drag him in his world. Ain't no needa me gitting all tangled up in family stuff. Then again maybe something happened to him that done been kept quiet; he coulda done something and had to leave or had something done to him.

I pretend I going possum hunting. Don't wanna bother Momma cause she worry if I go out at night but Poppa don't mind cause he feel a man gotta do man things. Boopee, Thomas Berry, and me hunt sometimes now since it is late fall. But I gotta know if Sonny Boy really around cause if Thomas Berry say somebody say they seed him, then I don't know what to think. But Miss Ollie and Mister Jimmy both church folks and don't take no part in lies. Sonny Boy and them live, near the swamps bout two miles from us down past Lake Kickapoo way off the gravel road that goes to Bolton right near that big bend. I got my twelve gauge and can walk through the woods cross Mister Charlie Johnson's fields down back of Mister Jack Greer's and cut through Old Man Randolph's pasture and hit the road that way; the bend where I turn off ain't far from there. Ain't good to stay on roads at night. Rednecks and the law might mess with you any time. They say that what happened to Mister Roger Berry, Thomas Berry's daddy, who was found lying in a ditch; his head done been cut off and was facing his foots. That was way back bout time I was born and Thomas Berry was two. They say white folks did away with him cause he wouldn't tell them where his stills was and who was in it with him or give them any money.

Don't look like nothing strange going on but I gotta cut through the garden and come up at the side of the house; that way Ol' Black, that mean coon hound, won't start barking and carrying on like the devil and his family is having a ball cause he'll be on the other side and to the back. No way you can come up to the front door without having him act up. I gotta crawl under the house and ease up by the front window; I can count the brick pillars til I get there. It's right by the second one. Sure is dark but I can't use this flashlight. Funny how you tote something you need but can't use it when you have to.

I hear something coming through the floor. Sound like somebody crying or moaning. Hope that crazy Ebenezzer Smith ain't done something to Sonny Boy and now he singing it or playing it away. Folks say people who can sing can sing troubles outta their souls—like the women you see in church on Sundays jumping up, shaking like a chill done got them, and moving slow like a spider web you can't see is holding onto them, and opening their mouths wide but nothing coming out you can hear; they trying to git rid of something hurting them so bad they can't go on 'less they git it outta them. That's what sound like happening here; a little floor shaking from a foot, a little crying, and sound of a harp. I bet that strange old man done killed Sonny Boy and is now gitting rid of the trouble from his soul. I see Sonny Boy—that he blowing the harp. Ain't hardly moving, just sitting in that chair with his eyes closed and his hands going together and apart and moving up and down on the harp—that harp in his mouth like it something to give him breath. Now he open his mouth a little and say something while Miss Mae sit in that rocker moving slowly and clapping her hands a little; every time he open up his hands and say something she throw her hands up and cry—she might be saying: "Lord, have mercy." I can tell from the way she throw her hands up, say something, then drop them back down again and keep on rocking. But Sonny Boy is blowing that harp and singing and Ebenezzer is sitting by the fireplace before a small fire and looking straight ahead; every now and then he nod his head a little up and down, then when Sonny Boy sings something or suck in a high note, he laugh a little and stomp first his right foot and then his left—it like he dancing when all he doing is sitting in a rocking chair, nodding his head up and down, laughing, and patting his foots loud. He ain't hitting Sonny Boy side the head no more; ain't even looking at him, just staying in the rocker, nodding, laughing, and patting his foots.

Ain't easy, stay way from crime
ain't easy, stay way from crime,
but, thank God, my days a mighty long time

I can stray away from the road
yes, walk way off the road

trying to tote some evil load

but before the sun go down
yes, before the evening sun go down
I still be righteous bound

cause it ain't easy, stay from crime
yes lord, ain't easy stay from crime
but, thank God, I had a mighty long time

I ease from the window, falling on the ground. I don't want to cause that old dog to bark and I gotta make my way back home through the thickets of darkness. Sonny Boy allright; he got that harp blowing out the blues that Ebenezzer Smith had so bad that he can't blow them no more. Look like he blowing more the life of Ebenezzer Smith than hisself. But still I gotta go . . .

Alvira, Lettie, and Pip

Jessie Schell

I FIRST BEGAN to understand Aunt Lettie during a freshman English course at college. We were studying *Moby Dick* and Dr. Rosenblatt lounged before us on the desktop, her weight on one elbow, spread out like an odalisque with only her mauve lips moving.

"Pip finds God at the bottom of the sea," she said, hitching her slip strap up under the stretched material at her shoulder, "and rises from the ocean mad with his vision."

I was drunk with *Moby Dick*, and at the time, coming directly from Mississippi as I had, I tended to believe intensely, with absolute conviction, whatever words were thrown me at this North Carolina women's college. I felt that I had swum up from the ocean's depths myself, fleeing north to school, where Yankees talked breathlessly fast, where, unweighted with the thick, lush smell of magnolias and cape jasmine, the very air I swallowed was bright and frosty with truth. I had emerged from the watery shadows under Mississippi oaks into this rarefied air, not crazed but visionary, and Dr. Rosenblatt, with her sensuous attitude towards learning, was fleshly proof of the journey.

All I needed to do was remember Miss Cluett from Greenlove High School with her support hose and her tack-on lace collar, with her hair screwed back from her forehead and jabbed together with mother-of-pearl hairpins, her legs eternally amputated beneath the wooden desk she seemed to wear like a great box-skirt. She had taught us books like *The Scarlet Letter* and *Silas Marner* and once had sent me home to my father with a note when she found me reading D. H. Lawrence behind my classroom copy of *Ethan Frome.*

In comparison, Dr. Rosenblatt had a positively sexual relationship with words. She draped herself before us and her hands swam in the air like long white snakes as she spoke about Melville and Conrad, her provocative shoulders shrugging suggestively for punctuation, her voice jaded and weary with knowledge.

But Dr. Rosenblatt has little to do with my discovery about Aunt Lettie, except that she acted as a kind of conduit, her languid musing on *Moby Dick* and Pip left to smolder like hot coals in my head. And it does not matter that it only took me two months to discover that North Carolina was not north at all, only a hilly version of the flat, Delta farmland I thought I was escaping. They grew tobacco in North Carolina instead of cotton, and they allowed a token Negro or two in each graduating class (this was all back in the prehistoric fifties), but otherwise it was the same old story. I did manage to meet the handful of New Yorkers who had been sent south to a girls' college for some inexpensive "finishing," and they made all the difference. And I did get myself worked up enough, thinking I inhaled the heady air of truth, to discover what had always been puzzling me about Aunt Lettie. That is what I want to talk about.

Every family has its black sheep. My father always said it depended on the shade of black, how interesting the family really was. I, for example, was considered my generation's black sheep amongst all my cousins for crossing three states to go to college when the entire football team at Ole Miss was just waiting to be dated. That only shows you how genes get watered down from parent to child if you let yourself get complacent like all my aunts and uncles did, and it supports a theory my father always held about children revolting in every way possible from their parents. Because he and all his brothers, sisters and cousins had married ordinary men and women, husbands and wives as drab as bleached laundry, smooth lumps of quiet flesh that never caused embarrassment or commotion, who never wore anything more fashionable than a drip dry suit, a paisley dress, who never, in short, resembled in any way their generation before them, and that generation was chiefly my great aunt Lettie and my grandmother Alvira.

Alvira we all knew well, for she lived in the same town with her two sons, Harry and my father, Luke. Her daughter Mollie had managed to stretch herself as far away as St. Charles, La., across the river, but Alvira operated from a great yawning brownstone whose grounds had once contained a fruit orchard, a rose garden and even a small stable, but which was now eaten away by concrete parking lots, a Jiffy-Serve drugstore, and even a small luncheonette called DewCumIn—all because she allowed Uncle Harry to manage the family estate.

Harry was the oldest son, and to Alvira, that meant Harry's primal duties were legislated from the start. It did not matter that his brain was vanilla pudding or that Alvira herself had to pay off two cousins from Vicksburg to take his final exams at Ole Miss. She forgot the incident entirely. It had not ever happened. For it was only the exercise of sovereign family tradition that was sacred to Alvira. Form, rules, mandates—Alvira would, in any other family, even in the fifties, be considered a black sheep for her line of thinking, but my father and his generation preferred to call her eccentric, reserving the black sheep title, with all its rattling closet bones, for her sister Aunt Lettie.

Alvira moved among the thick marble busts, the horsehair love seats, the milkglass bric-a-brac of her home like an empress frozen outside time. From her bed, lying underneath the turgid swirl of air from the ceiling fan, she telephoned her family, issuing command invitations, reminding them all of Cousin Josh's birthday next week, "Don't forget to send a card," advising a niece by long distance collect to Little Rock that "Your daughter was here last week with her teeth half chewed out with decay. I've made an appointment with Dr. Hinshaw for next week—What do you *mean* you prefer Dr. Young there. Hinshaw pulled my wisdom teeth ten years ago and he can see as well as you or I."

Sometimes when the phone rang at our house (always during supper), my father would catch Mother's arm as she started to rise from the table.

"Let it ring," he'd say. "I would like to know what food tastes like hot."

"Luke," my mother sighed. "You have to be tolerant with Alvira. Think how your father's illness wears at her."

Father forked a brussels sprout as if he were spearing an enemy.

"She doesn't even care about Pa," I'd mutter indignantly. "It only irritates her. She doesn't want to pay for that nurse she has to have because she won't nurse him herself, and she has to put up with his fishing friends coming in and smelling up the back room."

Alvira and I had never been on good terms. She knew a black sheep when she saw one, and had had me pegged from the day she found me, at the age of eight, sashaying up and down the front walk in Aunt Lettie's red velvet cloak.

"What the devil are you doing? Where did you find that thing?" She yanked me by my elbow into the concealing shade of the hibiscus bush and her quick hands tore at the cloth I had pinned together with a rhinestone brooch from her jewelbox. "Half the town must be driving round the block looking at you," she cried and her cheeks went waxen like the Italian statues in her living room, her eyes as vacant. "Common little thief," she spluttered, jerking my neck forward as she pulled at the brooch's rusted catch.

"I'm not," I said and stamped my foot accidentally on her open-toed sandals. She jumped back from me and her eyes came to life again. "I didn't steal a thing. This old brooch is nothing but cut glass and the cape belongs to Aunt Lettie. I found it in the attic."

She ignored the brooch theft. "There *is* no Aunt Lettie," she thundered instead, then lowered her voice, remembering the shallow protection her grounds afforded her, what with the Dew-CumIn patrons travelling through what used to be a grape arbor. "Lettie is dead," she hissed dramatically and stalked off to the house with the cape tucked under her arm like bedclothes.

I ran the four blocks home that afternoon and sat on the front steps waiting for my father to finish work at the paper. He took me in his arms when he came and shook me until my teeth clicked against each other, making me laugh, and wiped the dirt stains from my cheeks where I had cried rivers.

"Aunt Lettie isn't dead," he said easily. "She's just away, she's not well. Alvira was only being eccentric."

"What's eccentric," I asked, "mean and ugly?"

"No," he said and tickled me under my bony arm until I squirmed with joy.

But I wouldn't forget so easily. "Then what?"

"She has her little ways," he said. "She lives in her own world."

That night at supper, while the phone continued to ring so long that my father gave up spearing brussels sprouts and stared wistfully at the quiet twilight outside the windows, my mother shook her head at me disapprovingly, her soft, placid face ruffled into unfamiliar emotion.

"No, dear," she corrected. "Alvira's just eccentric, you know that. She cares in her own way." She tilted her fork hazily over her plate, taking in my father's black expression. "Go answer the phone," she'd whisper then, like a shy child, and I would throw down my napkin and walk to the phone that fairly jumped with irritation.

"Hello, Alvira," I'd say, powerful in my certainty that it would be she. Then I would hold the phone four inches from my ear to save my hearing and to conserve energy. This way everyone got the message from the horse's mouth and I need not repeat it over my cold food.

Alvira was at her best when she got me on the phone. I think she resented the soft, sighing voices that offered meagre resistance to her latest injunction. She had nothing if not imagination, and she worked at these commands creatively. No wonder the scanty returns provided little pleasure. She tossed boulders into the tranquil lakes of her family's days and seldom witnessed splash or ripple for her effort. On me her imagination and logic were honed to a fine edge. I could almost hear the blood beating in her arteries at the sound of my voice.

"Ah, Antonia," she'd say and I would feel my own pulse quickening behind my ears.

"Tony," I asserted routinely for the hundredth time that month.

"How common. Is your father home?"

I looked towards the table with the phone streched out from my ear like a conch shell. My father shook his head, no.

"No." I crossed one foot over the other and leaned my head against the wall.

"What are you doing?" The voice airy and light, enjoying the chase.

"Eating supper."

"Without your father? I suppose the poor dear has his supper warmed up and dried out."

Mother's face went blank and helpless.

"As a matter of fact," I said, "he's on a diet. Obesity runs in his family, you know."

There was a short pause while Alvira considered the counterattack, although it must be said that my remark was misguided, an emblem more of rage than of any icy cunning on my part. At this young age I had only an endless well of sarcasm from which to draw, and by the time I was old enough to know how to win, it was too late to want to try.

"Your grandfather's family was all pudgy, that's quite astute of you, Antonia," she said, rolling the vowels of my name around her tongue like gumdrops. "Now where's Margaret? I want her to pick up a hat for me at Goldsmith's when she's in Memphis next week."

My mother's eyes widened and her head shook "no" at me

mutely. Father turned his face towards the disembodied voice crashing out of the receiver, poised for the news.

"Mother's not going to Memphis," I said.

"Yes, she is, dear. And I hope you will not wear that repulsive lip glob when you see Dr. Kremshaw."

"Who is Dr. Kremshaw and if you mean lipstick, I'm thirteen and it's only a Natural, no color at all."

"That's funny," she said. "I saw it quite clearly Wednesday when you were here and it was a most peculiar shade of purple." Then, before I could retort, "Dr. Kremshaw is an orthodontist. He will be fitting braces on your front teeth."

I stared at the receiver, then turned urgently to my father, since my mother seemed to be flattened to the back of her chair, waiting out the conversation the way one sits through a weather disaster report.

Father smiled at me tiredly and said in a normal voice that carried, "Don't worry. We can't afford it."

"We can't afford it," I repeated quickly.

"Who was that speaking? You don't have to afford it. Harry has just closed a deal with a Mexican corporation and he assures me Mama's estate dividends will double. Therefore, I am donating what I can to correct your unfortunate overbite."

I held the phone in front of me like a snake I had caught and strangled the receiver with both hands, but then Father's face pulsed into my vision. He was pale and rigid with disbelief and his curly eyebrows bristled over darkening eyes.

"What Mexican corporation and what collateral?" he distinctly bellowed and gripped the linen tablecloth in his hands.

I repeated his question, the message carried up through my toes like electrical current. I could already feel the steel bands inside my tender upper lip.

"What *is* that voice shouting? It's a Mexican typewriter manufacturer, if you must know, and I *do* think you're precocious for knowing words like collateral. Harry put up some of the land, of course."

"Of course," my father and I said in unison, and then we actually heard what she had said. Mexican typewriters.

"I have to go now, Alvira," I said.

My mother's eyes were closed in a closed face and my father had let go the tablecloth but was heading fast towards the liquor cabinet.

"Next Friday then, dear. Have your poor mother call me later tonight for the details." There was a calculated pause. "About the hat and your teeth."

"Goodbye, Alvira."

"And tell your father. . . ."

"Goodbye, Alvira."

And that was how the rose garden was sold to the UWasheria Laundromat. Alvira transplanted all the roses into family lawns, each rooting turned into a dedication ceremony to her largesse. We got the Queen Juliana (pink) and the Austrian Love Bloom (yellow), and my mother almost had a breakdown nursing them back from the shock of being moved.

It was not simply that Uncle Harry was imbecilic, Father said. It was that everyone in the southwestern United States knew it. But of course, the appointment for my braces fell before Alvira learned that the Mexican government had never heard of the Arríba Typewriter Corporation, and I was dutifully driven to Memphis and to Dr. Kremshaw's hairy fists the following week. Money for the weight of metal in my mouth, for the straight line of tamed and tortured teeth, was simply deducted from my portion of Alvira's will. But, in the end, none of that mattered: not the braces or having to buy my own discomfort. I would gladly endure it all again for the sake of that one Memphis trip.

Mother and I had been to Dr. Kremshaw's and to Goldsmith's for Alvira's hat and were sitting in the coffee shop of the Peabody Hotel over cokes when it happened. That is to say, I looked up at the ordinary room and beheld the most startling apparition of my life.

I had seen movie stars who came down to Mississippi for location shooting on some film about the decadent South. I had watched the Harlem Globetrotters and their antics in the Atlanta Coliseum. I had even shaken hands with a Russian countess whose bosom was punctured by diamonds, like stickpins in a cushion. (She was a refugee trying to make a career in this country as a medium and Alvira had had her to tea.) I had met Eleanor Roosevelt. But the woman I saw floating through the Peabody Hotel Coffee Shop was more awesome than these.

Flowing through the crush of pinstriped businessmen, of cotton merchants' wives wearing pillbow hats like stoppers on their heads, past truculent children exhausted by department stores, this woman shone iridescent. It was as if a gypsy queen had sailed into the Wednesday Brass Polishing Circle at the Episcopal Church.

She came in with her head poised high on a long swan's neck. Her hair was dyed an unnatural black and glowed in the muted light. The tendrils flicked around her shoulders like tongues. She wore heavy pearl pendants in her ears that dragged at the scruffy lobes and an anklelength black dress of old crushed velvet, with a fuchsia silk scarf thrown over her arms and around that narrow length of neck, Isadora Duncan style. Over one thin wrist hung a gold sequin purse, and on the other hand large knobby rings clustered over each finger—lumps of color: green, gold, crimson.

But more than the dress, more too than the jewels, there was on her face a kind of charmed light. She came into the shop with that delicate head bobbing on its stalk, a white lily, and it was as if she had entered a royal court. If conversation lowered suddenly like a stage curtain, then surged up again to mask her entrance into the sane light of morning, then this she seemed to take as a sign of eloquent deference. She nodded to the faces strained away from her, she touched the top of a child's head who stared wide-eyed, voice plugged with a thumb, at her scarlet mouth. The mouth itself bloomed in a white field of powder, below eyes that Cleopatra might have conjured.

"Mother, look," I whispered in awe, and my mother glanced up from digging in her purse for a tip. Her eyes widened for an instant in confusion, and then a beatific smile washed over her face. My mother has an ordinary face, her features so regular and symmetrical that I often have trouble remembering her expression when I'm away. But the smile she wore now transformed her with delight, and I think I will never forget what she looked like at that moment.

It's been such a long time," she sighed.

"What did you say?"

But the pendant earrings swayed closer. All the glittering heaps of finger rings were rising in a graceful arc of the hands, and the gypsy's vaguely gracious expression now concentrated itself on us. I bit into my Coke straw and clutched the glass with trembling fingers, but the woman swept towards us quickly and was standing with her hands outstretched towards my mother. *My* mother.

"My dear," the woman cried and clasped my mother's hands in hers. Mother kissed the floured cheek the woman offered and I caught the sad scent of lilacs as she bent towards us.

"How are you, darling?" Mother asked. I had never heard my

mother use the word 'darling' before but it was sincere and it jolted me so that I bit through the straw and into my bottom lip. "How have you been?"

The woman squeezed my mother's hands tightly in hers and shook them in the air. "The stars have been erratic," she said, tilting her head back on that long, white neck.

She released Mother's hands, swung the fuchsia scarf around her shoulders. I was staring at the tiny ribbing wrinkles formed in her neck and on her hands. Great blue veins lay close under the surface of her skin, fragile and somehow insubstantial, like seeing the thin ivory bones in a bird's wing held to the light.

Mother nodded as if she'd made perfect sense, and I began to squirm in my chair. It was not so much that people had turned to stare as that I was being totally ignored at my own table. I had always dreaded meeting Mother's friends on similar trips, suffering introductions and the dreary conversations that followed, but this was different. And for once, Mother seemed to forget she knew me at all. I might have been a stranger who occupied the next seat, even though she absently handed me her change purse to hold when the gypsy approached us.

"I'm sorry to hear that," she said sympathetically now, making a little *tss*king noise with her tongue. "Tell me, how are your investments?"

I noticed now that the gypsy carried a folded newspaper under one arm like a businessman. She whisked it out now, tossing her wild black hair, and lowered herself onto the tip of the seat opposite us.

"My dear, I am delighted you visited me today. My horoscope said this morning that under no circumstances should business be conducted unless a loved one made contact. And I so wanted to sell Sperry-Rand for IBM. You've done me a great service." She fanned her face with the folded paper and a little puff of white rained out.

The talk turned generally then to Dow-Jones averages, common stock, and Merrill-Lynch.

"My, my," was Mother's only comment when the woman leaned back from her precarious perch at the chair's edge to look down her nose between stock quotations.

Then, quite suddenly, the gypsy turned a startled, flaming smile to me as if I had made a sudden noise. Actually, I had sat through the entire conversation in a buzzing trance, hypnotized by the earrings the woman wore. They swung before me, heavy crystallized milkdrops smudged with white face powder where they knocked against her cheek.

"You do resemble your father," she pronounced emphatically, then turned to Mother again. "And how is the lieutenant? Still sailing the high seas and sinking U-boats?"

My mother's smile fixed itself more permanently around her lips. "Oh, yes," she said, "lots of heavy fire."

"Good," the woman said and whacked the table with her newspaper. "Next time you write, you tell him I said 'well done.'" She gathered her paper and golden bag and rose like a dark wave from the sea, her gown and scarf billowing around her. "And when are you expecting, my dear?" she whispered, and bent her white face down on its long neck.

My mother's smile tightened, but she straightened her shoulders inside her linen suit jacket. The little bones in her back stuck out like hidden wings. "Very soon," she said.

"Umm. What will you name it?"

"Antonia," Mother said, and I watched a small pink circle forming itself in the center of her cheek.

The woman threw back her head and closed her eyes, testing the sound of the name. "Antonia—that's a nice, round sound. Very good," and she held her jewelled hand out, the stones blinking and winking like stoplights. "So good of you to drop in," she said, giving us a smile that flashed. "I'm late for the Exchange." And Mother took the hand gently in her own, then released her to the humming room.

I held my breath until the tip of fuchsia scarf sailed out the doorway, then I pinched my mother's arm, crinkling the cool linen. "Sweet Jesus, Mother, who *was* that?"

And, of course, she answered mildly, still smiling sweetly towards the door, "Why, that's just your Aunt Lettie, dear." Then she looked down at my sweaty palm clutching her sleeve and disentangled my grip. "And don't be profane," she added.

"What do you mean, 'just your Aunt Lettie.' I thought Aunt Lettie was tucked away in some sanitorium, coughing up blood."

We were driving the long, straight road sliced into cottonfields, the road I had counted telephone poles on for as many dull trips as my mind could hold. But there was no time, no need for such distraction now. The thick green fields blurred past my vision, red combines and swooping gull-like cotton dusters nervous, irritated movements outside my attention.

"Whatever gave you that idea?" Mother asked absently. Her hands, as usual, gripped the top of the steering wheel, as though without the steady pressure of each wrapped finger, the car might swerve, on its own, into the nearest field. "We never said that."

"You never said anything. You just said Aunt Lettie was away being ill. What did you expect me to think?"

"I suppose I expected you to find out about Aunt Lettie the same way you discovered all the family secrets *I* never knew until you told me." Her round knuckles whitened as she pressed the wheel and slid around a tractor. "Usually in front of company, I might add."

"Well, I didn't. I thought she was lying in a frilly bedjacket in some mountain hospital, consumptive. I even thought she might be locked up in an asylum somewhere, a nice one maybe, crazy as a loon."

Mother smiled into the windshield. "Well, she is, dear. Crazy, I mean. Not locked up."

That night at supper, Father smiled and nodded while Mother told him of the meeting. I had grown angry since the surreal conversation in the car and sat pushing the food around my plate with a fork until Mother finished. Then Father turned to me and said, "You must never tell Alvira who you saw today."

This was too much. I threw down my fork and pushed my chair back from the table. "I'll put it in the *Greelove Democrat Times* unless somebody tells me what's going on."

"Don't threaten your father," Mother said. "Pass the potatoes around."

I thrust the bowl at her without looking and waited for my father to finish chewing.

"I wonder what hot food tastes like," he mumbled, that old refrain, but turned to me anyway, sighed, and told me the story. Even at that, it wasn't nearly enough. It was like being given a blurred photograph. Locked inside those wavy lines, that mass of grey, was a likeness, a face, something you could outline with the tip of your finger. What I got was watery and pale, teasing with half-light.

It seems Alvira and her older sister Letticia were unusually pretty and popular girls. There were only two years between them, and they entered society together in the Gay Nineties and drove for miles each summer night to dances in plantation halls, in lake mansions, even to Memphis and Jackson to the Grand Mask balls at harvest time.

"But they never got along," Father said, "from what I can gather. They were too close in age, you know, sharing dresses and shoes—whatever girls share—even boys. Neither was prettier or more popular, but it was only because they worked at it with a vengeance, never letting the other catch them resting. One thing and another, there were always spats over flirting with each other's dates, and whose turn it was to wear your great-grandmother's pearls. When Pa came to town to run the paper, they stuck to him like syrup on a fly."

"Pa," I hooted, thinking about the quiet, round man who had never so much as acknowledged Alvira's running commentary as long as I had known him. She got plenty of nods from him and sometimes a grunt, but all I knew of Pa was that he smelled of bream and catfish, that he spent each day from dawn until suppertime out fishing on the river, since his retirement, that he gave me quarters and heavy fifty cent pieces with a wink when Alvira's back was turned. He had never been a verbal man, not only with Alvira, but with his children and grandchilren, though Father assured me he had been eloquent in print. I had looked up some of his old editorials in the musky light of the library basement, and sure enough, this fishy, silent man, with his round smile and his round blue eyes faded the color of old denim, this sweet and almost invisible Pa had been vividly assertive. His typewriter must have smoked with the fire of his convictions, the words rolling onto the page like thunder—against segregation, against misusing the land, against Hoover. Maybe, I thought now, he had once been charming, dashing, a man to quarrel over, one with a gleam in his eye.

I thought this over while Father was absorbing my outburst, then he went on carefully.

"He took one of them out one night, the other the next. Things must have got awful hot in that house, and your great-grandparents decided it was time the girls began their Grand Tours—people were still doing that then, you know, sailing off their girls to Europe like clockwork, and when the girls got back they all thought they were Queen Victoria. Well, Lettie was the oldest, so she was to go first. They thought it best not to send them both at once, feeling a kind of cooling-off period between them might ease things up a bit.

"She fought it to the bitter end, thinking Alvira would have a corner on the market by the time she returned, but her parents insisted, and Alvira gloated, and Lettie was seen off at the New Orleans dock on June 8th, 1900. She was nineteen."

He paused then and lit a cigarette while my mother took his cold food away and slipped a steaming coffee cup between his hands. And he stirred the silver spoon inside the coffee and stared at the liquid churning there in silence.

"And what? What then?" I prodded him.

Father took a deep drag on the cigarette and rubbed his eyes. "Then a wire came from Calais. It said someone should come and fetch Lettie, she was being kept in a hospital. And Pa and Alvira sailed on the next ship to bring her home."

"For Pete's sake, why? Why?"

"Don't push your father, dear," my mother said.

"Somehow, somewhere, during that crossing, Lettie just—lost her mind," he sighed in a voice still full of wonder at the words.

I felt the air sink out of my lungs, my ribs pushed against my skin as I caught my breath. "But what happened?"

Father shook his head, then shook it again, as if clearing it of sleep. Then as though he were truly waking from a dream, he moved suddenly in his chair and picked up the coffee cup, sipped, sighed again. "No one remembers anything unusual. Only one morning, one night, in the middle of a calm, quiet ocean, Lettie just lost her sanity. As if she dropped it overboard. No one knows why," he said again.

"Eat your apple tart," Mother urged softly.

Later that evening, huddled on the front steps into the sounds of insects beating against the dark air, I thought of Lettie. I saw her ringed fingers dancing before me, heard Alvira insist, "*Lettie is dead.*"

Father came out into the thick night air. "Let's go for a walk," he said and took my hand.

We walked in silence away from the house. I could feel the soft, fat leaves lapping my arms, the pavement still warm under my bare feet, but my mind revolved like a top around the questions in my head.

"Why does Lettie live in Memphis?" I asked him. "Why does

Alvira say she's dead? Does she hate her that much still, after everything?" My voice rose helplessly, I could hear the thin, childish sound it made.

"Alvira doesn't hate Lettie, she never did. They're sisters—oh, you should have had a sister. You'd know then."

He was quiet and the insects swelled and throbbed around us. Then he said, "They arranged for her to live at a Home in Memphis and she seemed better there. But she kept running away, and it looked like she would have to be moved to a state hospital to keep her safe. But then Alvira said 'Let her out in the daytime, let her do as she wants—she'll stay then.' And sure enough, the minute they started letting her go her way in the daytime, she calmed down. She always came back at night."

"But why?" I insisted, filled suddenly with anger at Alvira. "Why couldn't she stay at home with Alvira if she could traipse around in broad daylight without harming anyone?" It seemed to me Alvira was hiding Lettie away like the black sheep she was, wishing her dead to keep the family secret safe from gossip, to preserve the family name in all its traditional rules and outlines, like a neat hopscotch game laid out on the sidewalk for all to witness and marvel over.

But Father said Alvira and Pop wanted to keep Lettie with them—they'd decided to get married by then. Only Lettie got worse at home, ran away more than ever. "It broke Alvira's heart, watching her sister sink back to silence each time she was brought home. Pop had a hard time persuading her Lettie was happier in Memphis. She seemed so much saner there. Not exactly crazy, you know—she was more eccentric in Memphis than crazy."

"Like Alvira," I whispered, and knew that wasn't really true. For an instant I saw Lettie again in the dark air that hung before me. "Only Alvira's nothing like that. Oh, Daddy, you should have *seen* her," reverting to my childhood name. And I couldn't even wipe away the tears that fell down my face and blurred my vision. I couldn't even lift a hand to move the hair they plastered to my cheek.

My father hugged me to him with one arm and let me cry for a minute, then he dug in his pocket and stuck his handkerchief, still pressed and folded crisp from the laundry, into my face. "Wipe up and blow," he said and stopped walking while I did. His arm still hugged me to him as we bumped down the deserted sidewalk.

"Now she wasn't so bad was she? Of course not! You saw her: she's happy, she's got her own interests, she's even quite charming. Like Alvira, only stretched out, exaggerated."

"I guess so," I admitted, and blew my nose hard. "Only when I *think* about it—Daddy, she knew Mama when I was going to be born." I shook my head at the stars swimming into focus again. "How does she know about you at all, much less anticipating me?"

Father smiled up at the lion's blank face which guarded the First National Bank's front door. "Pop took us to meet her during the war," he said. "She was having a particularly clear day and it's stuck in her mind all this time. Your mother was six months pregnant then. But she sees her from time to time now on her trips to Memphis. Lettie seems to favor the Peabody Coffee Shop and Mother sometimes runs into her there, once a year or so."

We were circling the block now and automatically stopped at the Penny Scales outside Knight's Hardware. I stood on the raised scale while Father dropped the coin inside. The ticket popped out of its metal slot with a whirr.

"You will enjoy the fruits of the mind, 102 pounds," I read, forgetting the fortune as soon as I stepped off the rubbery scale to let Father climb up.

His penny clinked inside and the machine sighed again. "Expect a tall, dark stranger to come into your life, 170 pounds." Father held his ticket out. "Let's swap."

"Does Alvira never see her?" I asked as we turned the corner onto Main Street.

"Never," Father said. "She once asked me a few years back if I visited Lettie. 'Only once or twice,' I said. And Alvira said, 'I never got to apologize to her for all those silly quarrels.' And that was all she's ever said to me about the subject."

"Then how do you know all this? Who told you?"

"Pop told me. He wanted to be sure somebody took care of Lettie if anything happened to him."

"It's so confusing," I said. "It's so sad and strange."

"Yes and no," Father answered. "One day you'll understand better, I think." He paused on the sidewalk by a hibiscus bush. "You know, I never will forget meeting Lettie. She was one of the most delightful women I've even seen and, in her own way, one of the happiest." He looked down at me. "She and Alvira are still very much alike," he said. "You'll see that one day."

"Luke," Alvira called then, and I noticed for the first time where we had stopped. Alvira's tiny figure was tucked into a porch rocker. She swayed back and forth underneath the ceiling fan, her diamond choker blinking like a chain of lightning bugs around her throat.

I followed my father up the front walk and stood before her, noticing too, for the first time, how small she had grown, how large I had become. Her feet barely touched the porch floor, and her quick hawk's eyes glittered inside a delicate face.

"I brought your hat, from Margaret," he said, holding out a round-lidded box I had not seen before either.

"Ah," she breathed and reached out for it with fingers delighted into motion. "How sweet of you." She pulled the hat out of its tissue, all crisp, green feathers, and held it in her hands like a nest. "Go pour yourself a gin and tonic and say hello to Pa," she instructed Father, and he tipped his hand to his forehead in a salute and went inside the vast, dark front rooms behind her.

Alvira looked me over from head to foot, the hat settled into her lap now. "That color is bad for you," she said, shaking her head so the diamonds glistened around her neck. "It turns you pale in the moonlight. And barefoot to boot—where are your manners? How dare your mother let you out of the house that way?"

I stood strangely silent before her and she cocked her head at my pursed lips.

"Well, come and sit down," she said, patting the rocker next to her, "and tell me all about Memphis."

It was only then that I could force myself to speak. "Dr. Kremshaw has halitosis," I said. And Alvira, rocking in the moonlight, began to smile.

Five years later, scuffing through maple leaves in North Carolina with Dr. Rosenblatt's throaty voice caught in my ears, I began to understand about Aunt Lettie and Alvira and what my father had tried to say that night. Wrenched from that fertile crescent of land, from Alvira's suppertime calls and the astonishing presence of Lettie drifting through city streets only ninety miles away, I could see them both in perspective—small, manageable figures held in the bowl of my mind like a vision glimpsed through the wrong end of a telescope.

Try as I might—Melville, Conrad, Lawrence put to hard use—I

saw I could never believe that some dark, evil experience had swallowed Lettie on the waters. What was there, after all, in this small world that could so transform a simple, lovely Southern girl on the calm and glassy seas? I would never know what had actually transpired aboard that ship. But whatever it was, I was convinced it could not have been horrifying—bizarre, perhaps, other-worldly. Private, certainly. But not damaging to the soul or to the heart.

As for Alvira, her patchwork of rules and mandates, her jerking us around like so many puppets, was not only forgivable but totally understandable: surely, through controlling us as best she could, she was only taking out insurance against the loss of another. Her devotion to life's trivia, to dress and tradition, to strict propriety and the right dentist—this was her stronghold against the stray casualties of chance, her levee pushed against whatever dark waters of fear she acknowledged for us all.

It no longer confused me that she should refuse to visit Lettie. I will not say that Lettie, like Pip, saw the face of God. I do not make that connection. But I find in that fictional experience a touchstone, a mark: whatever Lettie read in those green depths, whatever came upon her in the unrimmed night, was beyond what we can bear to see who are left behind. Alvira could not stand to witness it on her sister's face, could not sustain losing that sister to whatever vision it was that claimed her. She castled her instead under the glass bell of her memory, and preferred to call her dead.

There is one more chapter to this story, one last puzzling piece to a puzzle which will never really be finished. I don't even know where this piece fits, or if it does at all.

When Lettie died, my senior year at college, I did not attend the funeral. No one did except my parents and the doctor at her Home. Sweet, silent Pa had died two years before, and Alvira, of course, would not grace any function after the fact. For her, Lettie had died and been buried at sea.

But my father wrote me a letter and told me what happened when a Memphis lawyer drove down to read Lettie's will, for she had one. The lawyer insisted that Alvira be present, and she consented, knitting, my father wrote, through most of the procedure with a condescending smile on her face. It was, he said, as if she were waiting through the ninth performance of a bad play which she had been required, through politeness, to observe.

It seems that Lettie's clear moments had endured throughout her life and had fixed almost entirely on her business dealings. Her stock market conversation with my mother in the Peabody Hotel Coffee Shop had been the one crisp evidence of a mind still functioning, not only in sanity, but shrewdly.

Lettie left Alvira upwards of half a million dollars in stocks and bonds, bequeathing to her parents, long dead, and to my father, the lieutenant, various wildly imagined real-estate holdings such as the Taj Mahal and half of the Vieux Carré. The stocks and bonds—Bell Telephone, U.S. Steel, Standard Oil—these were as real as the ivory bond they were written on. Alvira was a wealthy woman.

Lettie willed Alvira the bloom of her assets, Father wrote she had testified, "because she is my only sister and has never argued with me through the years over anything more trifling than a bauble or a boy."

I telephoned home the night Father's letter arrived. "What did Alvira do? What did she say?"

"She wants to know what Alvira said," my mother repeated to Father, who was trying to begin his supper.

Over the crackling wire I heard his chair scrape, and then the sigh as he took the receiver. But when he spoke, his voice was elastic with delight. It stretched all the way to North Carolina past the feeble Greenlove telephone system without needing to shout.

"Tony?" he asked, "Tony—she just stopped knitting with the yarn still wrapped over her finger and cocked her head at that lawyer. Then she said to no one in particular, 'Lettie always was more tolerant than I,' and started up her needles again."

"What?" I gasped. "That was it?"

"Should there be more?"

The long distance wire sang between us for a moment, humming all the way from Mississippi.

"Of course not," I admitted then, allowing myself at last to be stitched into the embroidered family myth, to become another strengthening thread in that absurdly tangled pattern. "It's only that Alvira's so eccentric," I said.

FROM

Forever Island

Patrick D. Smith

Timmy had been the most depressed of all by the news of the land development and the necessity to move. He thought that this would separate him forever from his grandfather, and he feared the unknown that was to come. His father had kept him busy gathering fronds for the chickee they were building, but on this morning he had slipped away and come down to his grandfather's camp.

One log had been left after Charlie had carved the little dugouts which were sold to the souvenir stands, and he was making this last canoe for Timmy. He was driving chips from the center of the log when Timmy trotted down the dirt path and dropped down beside him on the ground.

Charlie looked up from his work and noticed that the constant smile was missing from Timmy's face. He said, "I am making this dugout for you."

"Really, Granpappa?" Timmy said without the expected enthusiasm. "When can I have it?"

"In a day or so. We will see how fast I can finish it." He then put the log aside, looked at Timmy again and said, "I think it is time you climbed the big tree."

When he said this, Timmy became very excited. He asked quickly, "Can we leave now, Granpappa?"

"Yes, we will go now so there will be plenty of time. It is a long climb to the top of the sky."

Any thought Timmy had of ever leaving the swamp vanished completely as they drifted along this stream he loved so much. It was now only he and his grandfather and the trees and the vines and the birds and the turtles, and it would be so forever. No other thing existed as they moved deeper into the swamp, no trucks passing his house and no saws humming and no bulldozers moving about like huge angry tortoises. It seemed all too soon to him before they had crossed the ponds and the sloughs and were at the tree.

He asked his grandfather, "Can I see Forever Island? Which way do I look, Granpappa?"

"It is far away and to the south, but look hard enough and you may find it."

Charlie poled the dugout as far as he could into the thick knees, then Timmy got out and waded through the dark water to the base of the tree. He looked upward and it seemed to him that the tree had no end.

"Climb slowly and with a firm grip," Charlie cautioned. "Do not look down until you reach the top."

Timmy climbed the slanted base and reached the first rung, then one by one he moved upward, gripping one rung and stepping up, gripping another and moving upward again, feeling the wind grow stronger and stronger as he moved steadily upward toward the open sky. He was aware when he passed the roof of the swamp and there were no longer trees to the right and left of his climb, but he dared not look down. He felt his arms and legs tremble as he touched the last rung and knew he had reached the top.

The part of the trunk where the top branches forked out formed a small flat platform, and Timmy stepped onto this and steadied himself against a limb. It was only then that he really opened his eyes, and he suddenly felt as if he had left the earth and joined a flight of egrets high above the swamp. He was fifty feet above the tops of the other trees, and the roof of the swamp looked like a long flat meadow punctured by stalks of dandelions which were the royal palms. He imagined that he could spread his arms and sail outward and upward, swooping and dipping and circling like a hawk. He looked to the south, and the River of Grass was a velvety brown mass moving endlessly, spotted with the green clumps of the hammocks, and when the wind blew, the strands of sawgrass swayed and weaved and tumbled. It seemed to Timmy that this was the world of the Great Spirit or God, and it would endure. Then he moved his eyes further south to seek the island, but the horizon was hidden from view. A solid wall of smoke drifted upward from the land and into the clouds, forming a link between earth and sky.

Timmy would have chosen to stay forever on this platform above the swamp had he not finally heard his grandfather calling from below. When he reached the base of the tree and stepped into the cool water he had to grasp a cypress knee and steady himself from the dizziness before he could cross to the dugout.

The trip back into the swamp was an anticlimax, and Timmy thought that surely he had just returned from a place where no one else had ever before been, and that he had seen things no one else had ever seen or would ever see. He lay in the bottom of the dugout and closed his eyes, and the things he had witnessed came back just as vividly as he had seen them from the top of the tree. It was a moment before he realized the canoe had stopped.

He sat up and watched as his grandfather chased crawfish up and down a shallow slough. Charlie was putting them into a tin bucket he had brought along. When he had all that he wanted he came back to the dugout and stuffed tree moss into the bucket to cover the flouncing captives. "I have enough this time for us and Gumbo too," he said. "Your grandmother will make us a feast when we return."

As Charlie got back into the dugout, Timmy suddenly reached out and struck at a swarm of dragonflies. His grandfather said, "Do not kill the creatures unless you have need of them. When you kill them without need you destroy a part of yourself."

"They're nothing but pesky old dragonflies," Timmy said.

"They are eating the mosquito," Charlie said to him. "Then the bird will eat the dragonfly, and the bird will help spread the seeds of the plants and trees. The deer will eat the plants, and then we will eat the deer. We all have need of each other, and I have told you this before."

"I didn't know that anything would eat an old mosquito for its meal," Timmy said. "I thought they were only to bite us."

"The minnow will eat the mosquito also," Charlie said. "The bass and the turtle will eat the minnow, and we will eat both of them. The snake will also eat the fish, and the alligator will eat the snake. Many years ago we used the hide of the alligator to make our war shields, and we ate the flesh of its tail. All things in the swamp are important, Timmy, and you should not kill without need."

"Then why are the men with the machines killing the swamp?" Timmy asked.

For a moment Charlie didn't answer; then he said, "Billy Joe says that it is because they will build houses."

"Nothing can eat a house," Timmy said, not satisfied with the answer.

Charlie could not explain to Timmy a thing that he did not understand himself, so he pushed the dugout away from the slough and continued toward the creek.

When they reached the landing Charlie carried the bucket up to Lillie and then took some of the crawfish to Gumbo. He dropped them on the ground and Gumbo grabbed them one at a time, scurrying in and out of the storage chickee to eat them out of sight. He bounded back and forth to the hut until there was no more, then he climbed onto Charlie's shoulder and scratched at his head. "Stop that, Gumbo," Charlie said, putting the 'coon back on the ground. "Go down to the creek and catch a fish if you are still hungry. You have not forgotten how to hunt for youself." As if he understood, Gumbo rambled off down to the water's edge and paced up and down the bank.

Lillie chopped okra, tomatoes, peppers, and bay leaves into the pot with the crawfish, and put the pot over the fire to simmer. She would also fry halves of bananas over which they would pour wild honey. Charlie and Timmy sat at the table and waited patiently as Lillie whipped the corn meal into a batter to make the hot pone.

Timmy was still reeling from his climb into the tree, but he was disappointed by the smoke wall that blocked his view to the south. He said, "Tell me about Forever Island, Granpappa." He had heard the story once before but he could listen to it again and again.

"Not now, Timmy," Charlie said. "It is a long tale, and we will speak of it some other time."

"Have you seen the island?" Timmy asked.

"I am not sure," Charlie answered. "I could have been born there, but I am not sure of this. I have heard my father tell of the island many times. He knew it well."

"Will you take me there someday, Granpappa?"

"It is possible. Maybe we will go there together someday."

Timmy looked anxious for a moment; then he said, "Will the men take the machines to the island, Granpappa?"

"No, they will not do this," Charlie said. "The island is too far in the marsh for the machines to reach. They will never take the machines to the island."

By then the crawfish bisque was almost done, and the aroma was drifting over to man and boy. Timmy got up and stuck his head close to the pot, sniffing deeply. "Is it ready now, Granmamma?" he asked.

"It is done enough for you," she said, stopping the sewing machine. "Sit at the table and I will bring it to you."

The distant hum of the power saws went unnoticed as Lillie crossed from the platform to the grill.

The Day Before

Elizabeth Spencer

When I started to school, my grandfather and the old maid next door and her two old bachelor brothers took a great interest in the event, so important in my life, and tried to do everything they could think of for me. One bought me a lunch basket; another planned just what should be put in it, and Miss Charlene Thomas, the old maid, made me a book satchel out of green linen with my initial embroidered on it in gold thread. Somebody even went uptown to the drugstore where the school books were sold and got me a new primer to replace an old one, still perfectly good, which had belonged to my cousin. And there was a pencil box, also green, with gilt lettering saying PENCILS, containing: three long yellow Ticonderoga pencils, an eraser—one end for ink, the other for lead—a pen staff, two nibs, and a tiny steel pencil sharpener. My grandfather laid the oblong box across his knees, unsnapped the cover, and carefully using the sharpener he began to sharpen the pencils. After doing one of them and dusting off his trousers, he took out his pen knife, which had a bone handle, and sharpened the other two in the manner which he preferred. Then he closed up the box and handed it to me. I put it in the satchel along with the primer.

Mr. Dave Thomas, one of the two bachelor brothers of Miss Charlene, having made a special trip uptown in the August heat, came in to say that copy books were not yet on sale as they had not arrived, but could be bought for a nickel from the teachers on opening day. "Here's a nickel right now," said Mr. Dave, digging in his trousers' pocket. "*I'll* give her one," said my grandfather. I was spoiled to death, but I did not know it. Miss Charlene was baking ginger cakes to go in my lunch basket. I went around saying that I hated to go to school because I would have to put shoes on, but everybody including the cook laughed at such a flagrant lie. I had been dying to start to school for over a year.

My grandfather said that the entire family was smart and that I would make good grades, too. My mother said she did not think I would have any trouble the first year because I already knew how to read a little (I had, in fact, already read through the primer). "After that, I don't know," she said. I wondered if she meant that I would fail the second grade. This did not fill me with any alarm, any more than hearing that somebody had died, but made me feel rather cautious. Mr. Ed, Mr. Dave's brother, called me all the way over across the calf lot to his house to show me how to open a new book. I stood by his chair, one bare foot on top the other, watching him while he spread the pages out flat, first from the center, then taking up a few at a time on either side and smoothing them out in a steady firm way, slowly, so as not to crack the spine, and so on until all were done. It was a matter, he said (so they all said), of having respect for books. He said that I should do it a second time, now that he had showed me how. "Make sure your hands are clean," he said, "then we can go eat some cold watermelon." I remember still the smell of that particular book, the new pages, the binding, the glue, and the print as combining to make a book smell—a particular thing. The pencil box had another smell altogether, as did the new linen of the satchel. My brown shoes were new also, a brand called Buster Brown. I did not like the name, for it was invariably printed above a picture of a little round-faced boy with straight bangs and square-cut hair who was smiling as though he was never anything but cheerful. I did not know what I looked like especially, but I knew I did not look like that, nor did I want to. I asked to be allowed to wear new tennis shoes to school, and if not new ones, then old ones. My mother said I could not wear tennis shoes of any description to school and when I said I wanted to go barefoot then, she said I was crazy. I told my grandfather but he only said I had to mind her. I felt that he would have let me do as I liked and was only saying what he had to. I felt that my parents were never as intelligent as my grandfather, Mr. Dave, Mr. Ed, and Miss Charlene.

After dinner that day it was very hot and when everybody lay down and quit fanning themselves with funeral parlor fans because they had fallen sound asleep, some with the fans laid across their chests or stomachs and some snoring, the two Airedales that belonged to Mr. Dave had running fits. If a relative was visiting, or any stranger to our road, which was a street that didn't go anywhere except to us and the Thomas house, they were liable to get scared to death by those Airedales because the way they sometimes tore around in hot weather it looked as if they had gone mad. It was something about the heat that affected their brains and made them start running. It all happened silently; they would just come boiling out of nowhere, frothing at the mouth, going like two balls of fire, first around Miss Charlene's house, then up and down the calf lot between their house and ours, then all around our house, finally tearing out toward the field in front of the house, where, down among the cotton and the corn, they would wear it all out like the tail of a tornado. Eventually the foliage would stop shaking and after a long while they would come dragging themselves out again, heads down and tongues lolling, going back to where they belonged. They would crawl under the house and sleep for hours. We had got used to their acting this way, and though it was best, we agreed, to keep out of their way, they did not scare us. The Negro children used to watch them more closely than anybody did, saying "Hoo, boy, look a-yonder." White people had sunstrokes or heatstrokes or heat exhaustion—I did not ever learn quite what the difference in these conditions was, and don't know yet. Dogs had running fits instead.

The Airedales were named Pet and Beauty, and only Mr. Dave, who owned them, could tell them apart. He took their fits as being a sort of illness, and as he loved them, he worried about them. He gave them buttermilk out of dishes on the floor and got them to take cobalt blue medicine out of a spoon, holding their jaws wide with his thumb, pouring in the medicine, then clamping the jaws shut tight. It must have tasted awful, for the dogs always resisted swallowing and tried to fight free, their paws clawing the ground, head lashing around to get away and eyes rolling white and terrible. They could jump straight up and fight like wild ponies, but he always brought them down, holding on like a vise and finally, just when it seemed they weren't ever going to, they would give up and swallow. Then it was all over. I never knew if the medicine did them any good or not.

They had one of their fits that very afternoon, the day before school started. We had a friend of my aunt's from out in the country who had stopped by and been persuaded to stay for dinner and she saw them out her window and woke everybody up out of their nap. "Those dogs!" she cried. "Just look at those dogs!" "It's all right!" my father hollered from down the hall. "They've just got running fits, Miss Fannie," my mother cried. "It's not rabies," she added.

"At least they don't bark," said my grandfather, who was angry because she had waked him up. He didn't care much for her anyway and said she had Indian blood.

I don't know what I thought school was going to be like. It was right up the road, only about twenty minutes' walk, just a little too far to come home for dinner, and I had passed the building and campus all my life, since I could remember. My brother had gone there, and all my cousins, and still were recognizable when they returned home from it. But to me, in my imagination beforehand, it was a blur, in the atmosphere of which my mind faltered, went blank, and came to with no clear picture whatsoever.

After I got there it was all clear enough, but strange to the last degree. I might as well have been in another state or even among Yankees, whom I had heard about but never seen. I could see our house from the edge of the campus, but it seemed to me I was observing it from the moon. There were many children there, playing on the seesaws, sliding down the sliding board, drinking at the water fountains, talking and running and lining up to file inside to the classrooms. All of them seemed to know each other. I myself did not recognize any of them except occasionally one of the older ones who went to our tiny Sunday School. They stopped and said, "Hey," and I said, "Hey." One said, "I didn't know you were starting to school." And I said, "Yes I am." I went up to a child in my grade and said that I lived down that street there and pointed. "I know it," she answered. She had white-blonde hair, pale blue eyes and very fair skin, and did not look at me when she spoke. The way she said "I know it" gave me to understand that she probably knew just about everything. I have seen sophisticated people since, and at that time I did not, of course, know the word, but she was, and always remained in my mind, its definition. I did not want to go away and stand by myself again, so I said, "I live next door to Miss Charlene Thomas and Mr. Dave and Mr. Ed Thomas." "I know it," she said again, still not looking at me. After a time she said, "They feed their old dogs out of Havilland china." It was my turn to say I know it, because I certainly had seen it happen often enough. But I said nothing at all.

I had often lingered for long minutes before the glass-front china cabinet on its tiny carved bowed legs, the glass, not flat, but swelling smoothly forward like a sheet in the wind, and marvelled to see all the odd-shaped matching dishes—"Syllabub cups," Miss Charlene said, when I asked her. "Bone dishes," she said, "for when you eat fish." There were tiny cups and large cups, sauce bowls and gravy boats, and even a set of salt holders, no bigger than a man's thumb, each as carefully painted as a platter. It was known to me that this china, like the house itself and all the fine things in it, the rosewood my mother admired, the rose taffeta draperies and gilt mirrors, had belonged to the aunt of the three Thomases, a certain Miss Bedford, dead before I was born, who had been highly educated, brilliant in conversation, and whose parrot could quote Shakespeare. I did not find the words to tell any of this to the girl who knew everything. The reason I did not was because, no more than I knew how to do what she so easily accomplished in regard to the dogs' being fed out of Havilland china—which had often been held up to the light for me and shown to be transparent as an eggshell—I did not know what value to give to what I knew, what my ears had heard, eyes had seen, hands had handled, nor was there anything I could say about it. I did not think the child was what my grandfather meant by being smart, but I did know that she made me feel dumb. I retreated and was alone again, but a day is a long time when you are six and you cannot sit opening and closing your new pencil box forever. So I went up to other children and things of the same sort continued to happen. In the classroom I did as I was told, and it was easy. I must have realized by the end of the week that I would never fail the second or any other grade. So everything would be all right.

From then on, life changed in a certain way I could not define, and at home in the afternoons and on weekends I did not feel the same. I missed something but did not know what it was. I knew if I lived to be a thousand I would never do anything but accept it if an old man fed his dogs out of the best china or if a parrot could quote Shakespeare. At home when I looked up, I saw the same faces; even the dogs were the same, named the same, though they, as was usual, had stopped having fits once the nights got cooler. Everybody, every single person, was just the same. Yet I was losing them; they were fading before my eyes. You can go somewhere, anywhere you want—any day now you can go to the moon—but you can't ever quite come back. Having gone up a road and entered a building at an appointed hour, there was no way to come back out of it and feel the same about my grandfather, ginger cakes, or a new book satchel. This was the big surprise, and I had no power over it.

Life is important right down to the last crevice and corner. The tumult of a tree limb against the stormy early morning February sky will tell you forever about the poetry, the tough non-sad, non-guilty struggle of nature. It is important the way ants go one behind the other, hurrying to get there, up and down the white-painted front-porch post. The nasty flash and crack of lightning, striking a tall young tree, is something you have got to see to know about. Nothing can change it; it is just itself.

So nothing changed, nothing and nobody, and yet having once started to lose them a little, I couldn't make the stream run backward, I lost them completely in the end. The little guilt, the little sadness I felt sometimes: was it because I hadn't really wanted them enough, held on tightly enough, had not, in other words, loved them?

They are, by now, nearly every one dead and buried—dogs, parrot, people, and all. The furniture was all either given away or inherited by cousins from far away, the house bought by somebody and chopped up into apartments; none of this can really be dwelt on or thought of as grievous: that is an easy way out.

For long before anybody died, or any animal, I was walking in a separate world; our questions and answers, visits and exchanges no more communicated what they had once than if we were already spirits and flesh and could walk right through each other without knowing it.

Years later, only a few months ago, when home for a visit, I was invited to play bridge with some friends and on the coffee table saw a box of blue milk glass, carved with a golden dragon across the lid, quite beautiful. "That came out of the old Thomas house," my friend said. She had got it in a devious way, which she related, but had never been able to open it. I picked it up, not remembering it, and without even thinking my finger moved at once to the hidden catch, and the box flew open. It wasn't chance; I must have once been shown how it worked, and something in me was keeping an instinctive faith with what it knew. Had they never been lost then at all? I wondered. A great hidden world shimmered for a moment, grew almost visible, just beyond the breaking point of knowledge. Had nothing perhaps ever been lost by that great silent guardian within?

A Southern Landscape

ELIZABETH SPENCER

IF YOU'RE LIKE ME and sometimes turn through the paper reading anything and everything because you're too lazy to get up and do what you ought to be doing, then you already know about my home town. There's a church there that has a gilded hand on the steeple, with the finger pointing to Heaven. The hand looks normal size, but it's really as big as a Ford car. At least, that's what they used to say in those little cartoon squares in the newspaper, full of sketches and exclamation points—"Strange As It Seems," "This Curious World," or Ripley's "Believe It or Not." Along with carnivorous tropical flowers, the Rosetta stone, and the cheerful information that the entire human race could be packed into a box a mile square and dumped into Grand Canyon, there it would be every so often, that old Presbyterian hand the size of a Ford car. It made me feel right in touch with the universe to see it in the paper—something it never did accomplish all by itself. I haven't seen anything about it recently, but then, Ford cars have got bigger, and, come to think of it, maybe they don't even print those cartoons any more. The name of the town, in case you're trying your best to remember and can't, is Port Claiborne, Mississippi. Not that I'm *from* there; I'm from *near* there.

Coming down the highway from Vicksburg, you come to Port Claiborne, and then to get to our house you turn off to the right on State Highway No. 202 and follow along the prettiest road. It's just about the way it always was—worn deep down like a tunnel and thick with shade in summer. In spring, it's so full of sweet heavy odors they make you drunk, you can't think of anything—you feel you will faint or go right out of yourself. In fall, there is the rustle of leaves under your tires and the smell of them, all sad and Indian-like. Then in the winter, there are only dust and bare limbs, and mud when it rains, and everything is like an old dirt-dauber's nest up in the corner. Well, any season, you go twisting along this tunnel for a mile or so, then the road breaks down into a flat open run toward a wooden bridge that spans a swampy creek bottom.

Tall trees grow up out of the bottom—willow and cypress, gum and sycamore—and there is a jungle of brush and vines—kudzu, Jackson vine, Spanish moss, grapevine, Virginia creeper, and honeysuckle—looping, climbing, and festooning the trees, and harboring every sort of snake and varmint underneath. The wooden bridge clatters when you cross, and down far below you can see water, lying still, not a good step wide. One bank is grassy and the other is a slant of ribbed white sand.

Then you're going to have to stop and ask somebody. Just say, "Can you tell me where to turn to get to the Summerall place?" Everybody knows us. Not that we *are* anybody—I don't mean that. It's just that we've been there forever. When you find the right road, you go right on up through a little wood of oaks, then across a field, across a cattle gap, and you're there. The house is nothing special, just a one-gable affair with a bay window and a front porch—the kind they built back around fifty or sixty years ago. The shrubs around the porch and the privet hedge around the bay window were all grown up too high the last time I was there. They ought to be kept trimmed down. The yard is a nice flat one, not much for growing grass but wonderful for shooting marbles. There were always two or three marble holes out near the pecan trees where I used to play with the colored children.

Benjy Hamilton swore he twisted his ankle in one of those same marble holes once when he came to pick me up for something my senior year in high school. For all I know, they're still there, but Benjy was more than likely drunk and so would hardly have needed a marble hole for an excuse to fall down. Once, before we got the cattle gap, he couldn't open the gate, and fell on the barbed wire trying to cross the fence. I had to pick him out, thread at a time, he was so tangled up. Mama said, "What were you two doing out at the gate so long last night?" "Oh, nothing, just talking," I said. She thought for the longest time that Benjy Hamilton was the nicest boy that ever walked the earth. No matter how drunk he was, the presence of an innocent lady like Mama, who said "*Drinking?*" in the same tone of voice she would have said "*Murder?*," would bring him around faster than any number of needle showers, massages, ice packs, prairie oysters, or quick dips in December off the northern bank of Lake Ontario. He would straighten up and smile and say, "You made any more peach pickle lately, Miss Sadie?" (He could even say "peach pickle.") And she'd say no, but that there was always some of the old for him whenever he wanted any. And he'd say that was just the sweetest thing he'd ever heard of, but she didn't know what she was promising—anything as good as her peach pickle ought to be guarded like gold. And she'd say, well, for most anybody else she'd think twice before she offered any. And he'd say, if only everybody was as sweet to him as she was. . . . And they'd go on together like that till you'd think that all creation had ground and wound itself down through the vistas of eternity to bring the two of them face to face for exchanging compliments over peach pickle. Then I would put my arm in his so it would look like he was helping me down the porch steps out of the reflexes of his gentlemanly upbringing, and off we'd go.

It didn't happen all the time, like I've made it sound. In fact, it was only a few times when I was in school that I went anywhere with Benjy Hamilton. Benjy isn't his name, either; it's Foster. I sometimes call him "Benjy" to myself, after a big overgrown thirty-three-year-old idiot in *The Sound and the Fury,* by William Faulkner. Not that Foster was so big or overgrown, or even thirty-three years old, back then; but he certainly did behave like an idiot.

I won this prize, see, for writing a paper on the siege of Vicksburg. It was for the United Daughters of the Confederacy's annual contest, and mine was judged the best in the state. So Foster Hamilton came all the way over to the schoolhouse and got me out of class—I felt terribly important—just to "interview" me. He had just graduated from the university and had a job on the paper in Port Claiborne—that was before he started work for the *Times-Picayune,* in New Orleans. We went into an empty classroom and sat down.

He leaned over some blank sheets of coarse-grained paper and scribbled things down with a thick-leaded pencil. I was sitting in the next seat; it was a long bench divided by a number of writing arms, which was why they said that cheating was so prevalent in our school—you could just cheat without meaning to. They kept trying to raise the money for regular desks in every classroom, so as to improve morals. Anyway, I couldn't help seeing what he was writing down, so I said, "'Marilee' is all one word, and with an 'i,' not a 'y.' 'Summerall' is spelled just like it sounds." "Are you a senior?" he asked. "Just a junior," I said. He wore horn-rimmed glasses; that was back before everybody wore them. I thought they looked unusual and very distinguished. Also, I had noticed his shoulders when he went over to let the window down. I thought they were distinguished, too, if a little bit bony. "What is your ambition?" he asked me. "I hope to go to college year after next," I said. "I intend to wait until my junior year in college to choose a career."

He kept looking down at his paper while he wrote, and when he finally looked up at me I was disappointed to see why he hadn't done it before. The reason was, he couldn't keep a straight face. It had happened before that people broke out laughing just when I was being my most earnest and sincere. It must have been what I said, because I don't think I *look* funny. I guess I don't look like much of any one thing. When I see myself in the mirror, no adjective springs right to mind, unless it's "average." I am medium height, I am average weight, I buy "natural"-colored face powder and "medium"-colored lipstick. But I must say for myself, before this goes too far, that every once in a great while I look Just Right. I've never found the combination for making this happen, and no amount of reading the makeup articles in the magazines they have at the beauty parlor will do any good. But sometimes it happens anyway, with no more than soap and water, powder, lipstick, and a damp hairbrush.

My interview took place in the spring, when we were practicing for the senior play every night. Though a junior, I was in it because they always got me, after the eighth grade, to take parts in things. Those of us that lived out in the country Mrs. Arrington would take back home in her car after rehearsal. One night, we went over from the school to get a Coca-Cola before the drugstore closed, and there was Foster Hamilton. He had done a real nice article—what Mama called a "writeup." It was when he was about to walk out that he noticed me and said, "Hey." I said "Hey" back, and since he just stood there, I said, "Thank you for the writeup in the paper."

"Oh, that's all right," he said, not really listening. He wasn't laughing this time. "Are you going home?" he said.

"We are after 'while," I said. "Mrs. Arrington takes us home in her car."

"Why don't you let me take you home?" he said. "It might—it might save Mrs. Arrington an extra trip."

"Well," I said, "I guess I could ask her."

So I went to Mrs. Arrington and said, "Mrs. Arrington, Foster

Hamilton said he would be glad to drive me home." She hesitated so long that I put in, "He says it might save you an extra trip." So finally she said, "Well, all right, Marilee." She told Foster to drive carefully. I could tell she was uneasy, but then, my family were known as real good people, very strict, and of course she didn't want them to feel she hadn't done the right thing.

That was the most wonderful night. I'll never forget it. It was full of spring, all restlessness and sweet smells. It was radiant, it was warm, it was serene. It was all the things you want to call it, but no word would ever be the right one, nor any ten words, either. When we got close to our turnoff, after the bridge, I said, "The next road is ours," but Foster drove right on past. I knew where he was going. He was going to Windsor.

Windsor is this big colonial mansion built back before the Civil War. It burned down during the eighteen-nineties sometime, but there were still twenty-five or more Corinthian columns, standing on a big open space of ground that is a pasture now, with cows and mules and calves grazing in it. The columns are enormously high and you can see some of the iron-grillwork railing for the second-story gallery clinging halfway up. Vines cling to the fluted white plaster surfaces, and in some places the plaster has crumbled away, showing the brick underneath. Little trees grow up out of the tops of columns, and chickens have their dust holes among the rubble. Just down the fall of the ground beyond the ruin, there are some Negro houses. A path goes down to them.

It is this ignorant way that the hand of Nature creeps back over Windsor that makes me afraid. I'd rather there'd be ghosts there, but there aren't. Just some old story about lost jewelry that every once in a while sends somebody poking around in all the trash. Still, it is magnificent, and people have compared it to the Parthenon and so on and so on, and even if it makes me feel this undertone of horror, I'm always ready to go and look at it again. When all of it was standing, back in the old days, it was higher even than the columns, and had a cupola, too. You could see the cupola from the river, they say, and the story went that Mark Twain used it to steer by. I've read that book since, *Life on the Mississippi,* and it seems he used everything else to steer by, too—crawfish mounds, old rowboats stuck in the mud, the tassels on somebody's corn patch, and every stump and stob from New Orleans to Cairo, Illinois. But it does kind of connect you up with something to know that Windsor was there, too, like seeing the Presbyterian hand in the newspaper. Some people would say at this point, "Small world," but it isn't a small world. It's an enormous world, bigger than you can imagine, but it's all connected up. What Nature does to Windsor it does to everything, including you and me—there's the horror.

But that night with Foster Hamilton, I wasn't thinking any such doleful thoughts, and though Windsor can be a pretty scary-looking sight by moonlight, it didn't scare me then. I could have got right out of the car, alone, and walked all around among the columns, and whatever I heard walking away through the weeds would not have scared me, either. We sat there, Foster and I, and never said a word. Then, after some time, he turned the car around and took the road back. Before we got to my house, though, he stopped the car by the roadside and kissed me. He held my face up to his, but outside that he didn't touch me. I had never been kissed in any deliberate and accomplished way before, and driving out to Windsor in that accidental way, the whole sweetness of the spring night, the innocence and mystery of the two of us, made me think how simple life was and how easy it was to step into happiness, like walking into your own rightful house.

This frame of mind persisted for two whole days—enough to make a nuisance of itself. I kept thinking that Foster Hamilton would come sooner or later and tell me that he loved me, and I couldn't sleep for thinking about him in various ways, and I had no appetite, and nobody could get me to answer them. I half expected him at play practice or to come to the schoolhouse, and I began to wish he would hurry up and get it over with, when, after play practice on the second night, I saw him uptown, on the corner, with this blonde.

Mrs. Arrington was driving us home, and he and the blonde were standing on the street corner, just about to get in his car. I never saw that blonde before or since, but she is printed eternally on my mind, and to this good day if I'd run into her across the counter from me in the ten-cent store, whichever one of us is selling lipstick to the other one, I'd know her for sure because I saw her for one half of a second in the street light in Port Claiborne with Foster Hamilton. She wasn't any ordinary blonde, either—dyed hair wasn't in it. I didn't know the term "feather-bed blonde" in those days, or I guess I would have thought it. As it was, I didn't really think anything, or say anything, either, but whatever had been galloping along inside me for two solid days and nights came to a screeching halt. Somebody in the car said, being real funny, "Foster Hamilton's got him another girl friend." I just laughed. "Sure has," I said. "Oh, Mari-leee!" they all said, teasing me. I laughed and laughed.

I asked Foster once, a long time later, "Why didn't you come back after that night you drove me out to Windsor?"

He shook his head. "We'd have been married in two weeks," he said. "It scared me half to death."

"Then it's a mercy you didn't," I said. "It scares *me* half to death right now."

Things had changed between us, you realize, between that kiss and that conversation. What happened was—at least, the main thing that happened was—Foster asked me the next year to go to the high-school senior dance with him, so I said all right.

I knew about Foster by then, and that his reputation was not of the best—that it was, in fact, about the worst our country had to offer. I knew he had an uncommon thirst and that on weekends he went helling about the countryside with a fellow that owned the local picture show and worked at a garage in the daytime. His name was A. P. Fortenberry, and he owned a new convertible in a sickening shade of bright maroon. The convertible was always dusty—though you could see A. P. in the garage every afternoon, during the slack hour, hosing it down on the wash rack—because he and Foster were out in it almost every night, harassing the countryside. They knew every bootlegger in a radius of forty miles. They knew girls that lived on the outskirts of towns and girls that didn't. I guess "uninhibited" was the word for A. P. Fortenberry, but whatever it was, I couldn't stand him. He called me into the garage one day—to have a word with me about Foster, he said—but when I got inside he backed me into the corner and started trying it on. "Funny little old girl," he kept saying. He rattled his words out real fast. "Funny little old girl." I slapped him as hard as I could, which was pretty hard, but that only seemed to stimulate him. I thought I'd never get away from him—I can't smell the inside of a garage to this good day without thinking about A. P. Fortenberry.

When Foster drove all the way out to see me one day soon after that—we didn't have a telephone in those days—I thought he'd come to apologize for A. P., and I'm not sure yet he didn't intend for me to understand that without saying anything about it. He certainly put himself out. He sat down and swapped a lot of Port Claiborne talk with Mama—just pleased her to death—and then he went out back with Daddy and looked at the chickens and the peach trees. He even had an opinion on growing peaches, though I reckon he'd given more thought to peach brandy than he'd ever given to orchards. He said when we were walking out to his car that he'd like to take me to the senior dance, so I said O.K. I was pleased; I had to admit it.

Even knowing everything I knew by then (I didn't tell Mama and Daddy), there was something kind of glamorous about Foster Hamilton. He came of a real good family, known for being aristocratic and smart; he had uncles who were college professors and big lawyers and doctors and things. His father had died when he was a babe in arms (tragedy), and he had perfect manners. He had perfect manners, that is, when he was sober, and it was not that he departed from them in any intentional way when he was drunk. Still, you couldn't exactly blame me for being disgusted when, after ten minutes of the dance, I discovered that his face was slightly green around the temples and that whereas he could dance fairly well, he could not stand up by himself at all. He teetered like a baby that has caught on to what walking is, and knows that now is the time to do it, but hasn't had quite enough practice.

"Foster," I whispered, "have you been drinking?"

"Been *drinking?*" he repeated. He looked at me with a sort of wonder, like the national president of the W.C.T.U. might if asked the same question. "It's so close in here," he complained.

It really wasn't that close yet, but it was going to be. The gym doors were open, so that people could walk outside in the night air whenever they wanted to. "Let's go outside," I said. Well, in my many anticipations I had foreseen Foster and me strolling about on the walks outside, me in my glimmering white sheer dress with the blue underskirt (Mama and I had worked for two weeks on that dress), and Foster with his nice broad aristocratic shoulders. Then, lo and behold, he had worn a white dinner jacket! There was never anybody in creation as proud as I was when I first walked into the senior dance that night with Foster Hamilton.

Pride goeth before a fall. The fall must be the one Foster took down the gully back of the boys' privy at the schoolhouse. I still don't know quite how he did it. When we went outside, he put me carefully in his car, helped to tuck in my skirts, and closed the door in the most polite way, and then I saw him heading toward the privy in his white jacket that was swaying like a lantern through the dark, and then he just wasn't there any more. After a while, I got worried that somebody would come out, like us, for air, so I got out and went to the outside wall of the privy and said, "Foster, are you all right?" I didn't get any answer, so I knocked politely on the wall and said, "Foster?" Then I looked around behind and all around, for I was standing very close to the edge of the gully that had eroded right up to the borders of the campus (somebody was always threatening that the whole schoolhouse was going to cave in into it before another school year went by), and there at the bottom of the gully Foster Hamilton was lying face down, like the slain in battle.

What I should have done, I should have walked right off and left him there till doomsday, or till somebody came along who would use him for a model in a statue to our glorious dead in the defense of Port Claiborne against Gen. Ulysses S. Grant in 1863. That battle was over in about ten minutes, too. But I had to consider how things would look—I had my pride, after all. So I took a look around, hiked up my skirts, and went down into the gully. When I shook Foster, he grunted and rolled over, but I couldn't get him up. I wasn't strong enough. Finally, I said, "Foster, Mama's here!" and he soared up like a Roman candle. I never saw anything like it. He walked straight up the side of the gully and gave me a hand up, too. Then I guided him over toward the car and he sat in the door and lighted a cigarette.

"Where is she?" he said.

"Who?" I said.

"Your mother," he said.

"Oh, I just said that, Foster. I had to get you up someway."

At that, his shoulders slumped down and he looked terribly depressed. "I didn't mean to do this, Marilee," he said. "I didn't have any idea it would hit me this way. I'm sure I'll be all right in a minute."

I don't think he ever did fully realize that he had fallen in the gully. "Get inside," I said, and shoved him over. There were one or two couples beginning to come outside and walk around. I squeezed in beside Foster and closed the door. Inside the gym, where the hot lights were, the music was blaring and beating away. We had got a real orchestra specially for that evening, all the way down from Vicksburg, and a brass-voiced girl was singing a nineteen-thirties song. I would have given anything to be in there with it rather than out in the dark with Foster Hamilton.

I got quite a frisky reputation out of that evening. Disappearing after ten minutes of the dance, seen snuggling out in the car, and gone completely by intermission. I drove us away. Foster wouldn't be convinced that anybody would think it at all peculiar if he reappeared inside the gym with red mud smeared all over his dinner jacket. I didn't know how to drive, but I did anyway. I'm convinced you can do anything when you have to—speak French, do a double back flip off the low diving board, play Rachmaninoff on the piano, or fly an airplane. Well, maybe not fly an airplane; it's too technical. Anyway, that's how I learned to drive a car, riding us up and down the highway, holding off Foster with my elbow, marking time till midnight came and I could go home without anybody thinking anything out of the ordinary had happened.

When I got out of the car, I said, "Foster Hamilton, I never want to see you again as long as I live. And I hope you have a wreck on the way home."

Mama was awake, of course. She called out in the dark, "Did you have a good time, Marilee?"

"Oh, yes, Ma'am," I said.

Then I went back to my shed-ceilinged room in the back wing, and cried and cried. And cried.

There was a good bit of traffic coming and going out to our house after that. A. P. Fortenberry came, all pallid and sober, with a tie on and a straw hat in his hand. Then A. P. and Foster came together. Then Foster came by himself.

The story went that Foster had stopped in the garage with A. P. for a drink before the dance, and instead of water in the drink, A. P. had filled it up with grain alcohol. I was asked to believe that he did this because, seeing Foster all dressed up, he got the idea that Foster was going to some family do, and he couldn't stand Foster's family, they were all so stuckup. While Foster was draining the first glass, A. P. had got called out front to put some gas in a car, and while he was gone Foster took just a little tap more whiskey with another glassful of grain alcohol. A. P. wanted me to understand that Foster's condition that night had been all his fault, that instead of three or four ounces of whiskey, Foster had innocently put down eighteen ounces of sheer dynamite, and it was a miracle only to be surpassed by the resurrection of Jesus Christ that he had managed to drive out and get me, converse with Mama about peach pickle, and dance those famous ten minutes at all.

Well, I said I didn't know. I thought to myself I never heard of Foster Hamilton touching anything he even mistook for water.

All these conferences took place at the front gate. "I never saw a girl like you," Mama said. "Why don't you invite the boys to sit on the porch?"

"I'm not too crazy about A. P. Fortenberry," I said. "I don't think he's a very nice boy."

"Uh-*huh*," Mama said, and couldn't imagine what Foster Hamilton was doing running around with him, if he wasn't a nice boy. Mama, to this day, will not hear a word against Foster Hamilton.

I was still giving some thought to the whole matter that summer, sitting now on the front steps, now on the back steps, and now on the side steps, whichever was most in the shade, chewing on pieces of grass and thinking, when one day the mailman stopped in for a glass of Mama's cold buttermilk (it's famous) and told me that Foster and A. P. had had the most awful wreck. They had been up to Vicksburg, and coming home had collided with a whole carload of Negroes. The carnage was awful—so much blood on everybody you couldn't tell black from white. They were both going to live, though. Being so drunk, which in a way had caused the wreck, had also kept them relaxed enough to come out of it alive. I warned the mailman to leave out the drinking part when he told Mama, she thought Foster was such a nice boy.

The next time I saw Foster, he was out of the hospital and had a deep scar on his cheekbone like a sunken star. He looked handsomer and more distinguished than ever. I had gotten a scholarship to Millsaps College in Jackson, and was just about to leave. We had a couple of dates before I left, but things were not the same. We would go to the picture show and ride around afterward, having a conversation that went something like this:

"Marilee, why are you such a nice girl? You're about the only nice girl I know."

"I guess I never learned any different, so I can't help it. Will you teach me how to stop being a nice girl?"

"I certainly will not!" He looked to see how I meant it, and for a minute I thought the world was going to turn over; but it didn't.

"Why won't you, Foster?"

"You're too young. And your mama's a real sweet lady. And your daddy's too good a shot."

"Foster, why do you drink so much?"

"Marilee, I'm going to tell you the honest truth. I drink because I like to drink." He spoke with real conviction.

So I went on up to college in Jackson, where I went in for serious studies and made very good grades. Foster, in time, got a job on the paper in New Orleans, where, during off hours, or so I understood, he continued his investigation of the lower things in life and of the effects of alcohol upon the human system.

It is twenty years later now, and Foster Hamilton is down there yet.

Millions of things have happened; the war has come and gone. I live far away, and everything changes, almost every day. You can't even be sure the moon and stars are going to be the same the day after tomorrow night. So it has become more and more important to me to know that Windsor is still right where it always was, standing pure in its decay, and that the gilded hand on the Presbyterian church in Port Claiborne is still pointing to Heaven and not to Outer Space; and I earnestly feel, too, that Foster Hamilton should go right on drinking. There have got to be some things you can count on, would be an ordinary way to put it. I'd rather say that I feel the need of a land, of a sure terrain, of a sort of permanent landscape of the heart.

Weep No More, My Lady

JAMES STREET

THE MOONLIGHT SYMPHONY of swamp creatures hushed abruptly, and the dismal bog was as peaceful as unborn time and seemed to brood in its silence. The gaunt man glanced back at the boy and motioned for him to be quiet, but it was too late. Their presence was discovered. A jumbo frog rumbled a warning and the swamp squirmed into life as its denizens scuttled to safety.

Fox fire was glowing to the west and the bayou was slapping the cypress knees when suddenly a haunting laugh echoed through the wilderness, a strange chuckling yodel ending in a weird "gro-o-o."

The boy's eyes were wide and staring. "That's it, Uncle Jess. Come on! Let's catch it!"

"Uh, oh." The man gripped his shotgun. "That ain't no animal. That's a thing."

They hurried noiselessly in the direction of the sound that Skeeter had been hearing for several nights. Swamp born and reared, they feared nothing they could shoot or outwit, so they slipped out of the morass and to the side of a ridge. Suddenly, Jesse put out his hand and stopped the child, then pointed up the slope. The animal, clearly visible in the moonlight, was sitting on its haunches, its head cocked sideways as it chuckled. It was a merry and rather melodious little chuckle.

Skeeter grinned in spite of his surprise, then said, "Sh-h-h. It'll smell us."

Jesse said, "Can't nothing smell that far. Wonder what the durn thing is?" He peered up the ridge, studying the creature. He had no intention of shooting unless attacked, for Jesse Tolliver and his nephew never killed wantonly.

The animal, however, did smell them and whipped her nose into the wind, crouched and braced. She was about sixteen inches high and weighed twenty-two pounds. Her coat was red and silky and there was a blaze of white down her chest and a circle of white around her throat. Her face was wrinkled and sad, like a wise old man's.

Jesse shook his head. "Looks som'n like a mixture of bloodhound and terrier from here," he whispered. "It beats me—"

"It's a dog, all right," Skeeter said.

"Can't no dog laugh."

"That dog can." The boy began walking toward the animal, his right hand outstretched. "Heah. heah. I ain't gonna hurt you."

The dog, for she was a dog, cocked her head from one side to the other and watched Skeeter. She was trembling, but she didn't run. And when Skeeter knelt by her, she stopped trembling, for the ways of a boy with a dog are mysterious. He stroked her, and the trim little creature looked up at him and blinked her big hazel eyes. Then she turned over and Skeeter scratched her. She closed her eyes, stretched and chuckled, a happy mixture of chortle and yodel. Jesse ambled up and the dog leaped to her feet and sprang between the boy and the man.

Skeeter calmed her. "That's just Uncle Jess."

Jesse, still bewildered, shook his head again. "I still say that ain't no dog. She don't smell and she don't bark. Ain't natural. And look at her! Licking herself like a cat."

"Well, I'll be a catty wampus," Skeeter said. "Never saw a dog do that before." However, he was quick to defend any mannerism of his friend and said, "She likes to keep herself clean. She's a lady and I'm gonna name her that, and she's mine 'cause I found her."

"Lady, huh?"

"No, sir. My Lady. If I name her just plain Lady, how folks gonna know she's mine?" He began stroking his dog again. "Gee m'netty, Uncle Jess, I ain't never had nothing like this before."

"It still don't make sense to me," Jesse said. But he didn't care, for he was happy because the child was happy.

Like most mysteries, there was no mystery at all about My Lady. She was a lady, all right, an aristocratic Basenji, one of those strange barkless dogs of Africa. Her ancestors were pets of the Pharaohs and her line was well established when the now proud races of men were wandering about Europe, begging handouts from Nature. A bundle of nerves and muscles, she would fight anything, and could scent game up to eighty yards. She had the gait of an antelope and was odorless, washing herself before and after meals. However, the only noises she could make were a piercing cry that sounded almost human and that chuckling little chortle. She could chuckle only when happy and she had been happy in the woods. Now she was happy again.

As most men judge values, she was worth more than all the possessions of Jesse and his nephew. Several of the dogs had been shipped to New Orleans to avoid the dangerous upper route, thence by motor to a northern kennel. While crossing Mississippi, My Lady had escaped from the station wagon. Her keeper had advertised in several papers, but Jesse and Skeeter never saw papers.

Skeeter said, "Come on, M'Lady. Let's go home."

The dog didn't hesitate, but walked proudly at the boy's side to a cabin on the bank of the bayou. Skeeter crumbled corn bread, wet it with pot likker and put it before her. She sniffed the food disdainfully at first, then ate it only when she saw the boy fix a bowl for his uncle. She licked herself clean and explored the cabin, sniffing the brush brooms, the piles of wild pecans and hickory nuts, and then the cots. Satisfied at last, she jumped on Skeeter's bed, tucked her nose under her paws and went to sleep.

"Acts like she owns the place," Jesse said.

"Where you reckon she came from?" The boy slipped his overall straps from his shoulders, flexed his stringy muscles and yawned.

"Lord knows. Circus maybe." He looked at M'Lady quickly. "Say, maybe she's a freak and run off from some show. But they'd give us two dollars for her."

Skeeter's face got long. "You don't aim to get rid of her?"

The old man put his shotgun over the mantel and lit his pipe. "Skeets, if you want that thing, I wouldn't get shed of her for a piece of bottom land a mile long. Already plowed and planted."

"I reckoned you wouldn't, 'cause you like me so much. And I know how you like dogs, 'cause I saw you cry when yours got killed. But you can have part of mine."

Jesse sat down and leaned back, blowing smoke into the air to drive away mosquitoes. The boy got a brick and hammer and began cracking nuts, pounding the meat to pulp so his uncle could chew it. Skeeter's yellow hair hadn't been cut for months and was tangled. He had freckles too. And his real name was Jonathan. His mother was Jesse's only sister and died when the child was born. No one thereabouts ever knew what happened to his father. Jesse, a leathery, toothless old man with faded blue eyes, took him to bring up and called him Skeeter because he was so little.

In the village, where Jesse seldom visited, folks wondered if he were fit'n to rear a little boy. They considered him shiftless and no-count. Jesse had lived all of his sixty years in the swamp and his way of life was a torment to folks who believed life must be lived by rules. He earned a few dollars selling jumbo frogs and pelts, but mostly he just paddled around the swamp, watching things and teaching Skeeter about life.

The villagers might have tried to send Skeeter to an orphanage, but for Joe (Cash) Watson, the storekeeper. Cash was a hard man, but fair. He often hunted with Jesse, and the old man had trained Cash's dogs. When there was talk of sending Skeeter away, Cash said, "You ain't agonna do it. You just don't take young'uns away from their folks." And that's all there was to it.

Jesse never coveted the "frills and furbelows of damn-fool folks" and yearned for only two things—a twenty-gauge shotgun for Skeeter and a set of Roebuckers for himself, as he called store-bought teeth. Cash had promised him the gun and the best false teeth in the catalogue for forty-six dollars. Jesse had saved $9.37.

"Someday I'm gonna get them Roebuckers," he often told Skeeter. "Then I'm gonna eat me enough roastin' ears to kill a goat. Maybe I can get a set with a couple of gold teeth in 'em. I seen a man once with six gold teeth."

Once Skeeter asked him, "Why don't you get a job with the W.P. and A. and make enough money to buy them Roebuckers?"

"I don't want 'em that bad," Jesse said.

So he was happy for Skeeter to have M'Lady, thinking the dog would sort of make up for the shotgun.

The boy cracked as many nuts as his uncle wanted, then put the hammer away. He was undressing when he glanced over at his dog. "Gosh, Uncle Jess. I'm scared somebody'll come get her."

"I ain't heard of nobody losing no things around here. If'n they had, they'd been to me 'fo' now, being's I know all about dogs and the swamp."

"That's so," Skeeter said. "But you don't reckon she belonged to another fellow like me, do you? I know how I'd feel if I had a dog like her and she got lost."

Jesse said, "She didn't belong to another fellow like you. If'n she had, she wouldn't be so happy here."

Skeeter fed M'Lady biscuits and molasses for breakfast, and although the Basenji ate it, she still was hungry when she went into the swamp with the boy. He was hoping he could find a bee tree or signs of wild hogs. They were at the edge of a clearing when M'Lady's chokebore nose suddenly tilted and she froze to a flash point, pausing only long enough to get set. Then she darted to the bayou, at least sixty yards away, dived into a clump of reeds and snatched a water rat. She was eating it when Skeeter ran up.

"Don't do that," he scolded. "Ain't you got no more sense than run into water after things? A snake or a gator might snatch you."

The Basenji dropped the rat and tucked her head. She knew the boy was displeased, and when she looked up at him her eyes were filled and a woebegone expression was on her face.

Skeeter tried to explain, "I didn't mean to hurt your feelings. Don't cry." He stepped back quickly and stared at her, at the tears in her eyes. "She is crying! Be John Brown!" Skeeter called her and ran toward the cabin, where Jesse was cutting splinters.

"Uncle Jess! Guess what else my dog can do!"

"Whistle?" the old man laughed.

"She can cry! I declare to goodness! Not out loud, but she can cry just the same."

Jesse knew that most dogs will get watery-eyed on occasion, but, not wanting to ridicule M'Lady's accomplishments, asked, "What made her cry?"

"Well, sir, we were walking along and all of a sudden she got a scent and flash pointed and then—" Skeeter remembered something.

"Then what?"

Skeeter sat on the steps. "Uncle Jess," he said slowly, "we must have been fifty or sixty yards from that rat when she smelled it."

"What rat? What's eating you?"

The child told him the story and Jesse couldn't believe it. For a dog to pick up the scent of a water rat at sixty yards simply isn't credible. Jesse reckoned Skeeter's love for M'Lady had led him to exaggerate.

Skeeter knew Jesse didn't believe the story, so he said, "Come on. I'll show you." He whistled for M'Lady.

The dog came up. "Hey," Jesse said. "That thing knows what a whistle means. Shows she's been around folks." He caught the dog's eye and commanded, "Heel!"

But M'Lady cocked her head quizzically. Then she turned to the boy and chuckled softly. She'd never heard the order before. That was obvious. Her nose came up into the breeze and she wheeled.

Her curved tail suddenly was still and her head was poised.

"Flash pointing," Jesse said. "Well, I'll be a monkey's uncle!"

M'Lady held the strange point only for a second, though, then dashed toward a corn patch about eighty yards from the cabin.

Halfway to the patch, she broke her gait and began creeping. A whir of feathered lightning sounded in the corn and a covey of quail exploded almost under her nose. She sprang and snatched a bird.

"Partridges!" Jesse's jaw dropped.

The child was as motionless as stone, his face white and his eyes wide in amazement. Finally he found his voice, "She was right here when she smelled them birds. A good eighty yards."

"I know she ain't no dog now," Jesse said. "Can't no dog do that."

"She's fast as greased lightning and ain't scared of nothing." Skeeter still was under the spell of the adventure. "She's a hunting dog from way back."

"She ain't no dog a-tall, I'm telling you. It ain't human." Jesse walked toward M'Lady and told her to fetch the bird, but the dog didn't understand. Instead, she pawed it. "Well," Jesse said. "One thing's certain. She ain't no bird hunter."

"She can do anything," Skeeter said. "Even hunt birds. Maybe I can make a bird dog out'n her. Wouldn't that be som'n?"

"You're batty. Maybe a coon dog, but not a bird dog. I know 'bout dogs."

"Me too," said Skeeter. And he did. He'd seen Jesse train many dogs, even pointers, and had helped him train Big Boy, Cash Watson's prize gun dog.

Jesse eyed Skeeter and read his mind.

"It can't be done, Skeets."

"Maybe not, but I aim to try. Any dog can run coons and rabbits, but it takes a pure D humdinger to hunt birds. Ain't no sin in trying, is it?"

"Naw," Jesse said slowly. "But she'll flush birds."

"I'll learn her not to."

"She won't hold no point. Any dog'll flash point. And she'll hunt rats."

"I'm gonna learn her just to hunt birds. And I'm starting right now," Skeeter said. He started walking away, then turned. "I seen a man once train a razorback hawg to point birds. You know as good as me that if a dog's got pure D hoss sense and a fellow's got bat brains, he can train the dog to hunt birds."

"Wanta bet?" Jesse issued the challenge in an effort to keep Skeeter's enthusiasm and determination at the high-water mark.

"Yes, sir. If I don't train my dog, then I'll cut all the splinters for a year. If I do, you cut 'em."

"It's a go," Jesse said.

Skeeter ran to the bayou and recovered the rat M'Lady had killed. He tied it around his dog's neck. The Basenji was indignant and tried to claw off the hateful burden. Failing, she ran into the house and under a bed, but Skeeter made her come out. M'Lady filled up then and her face assumed that don't-nobody-love-me look. The boy steeled himself, tapped M'Lady's nose with the rat, and left it around her neck.

"You done whittled out a job for yourself," Jesse said. "If'n you get her trained, you'll lose her in the brush. She's too fast and too little to keep up with."

"I'll bell her," Skeeter said. "I'm gonna learn her ever'thing. I got us a gun dog, Uncle Jess."

The old man sat on the porch and propped against the wall. "Bud, I don't know what that thing is. But you're a thoroughbred. John dog my hide!"

If Skeeter had loved M'Lady one bit less, his patience would have exploded during the ordeal of training the Basenji. It takes judgment and infinite patience to train a bird dog properly, but to train a Basenji, that'll hunt anything, to concentrate only on quail took something more than discipline and patience. It never could have been done except for that strange affinity between a boy and a dog, and the blind faith of a child.

M'Lady's devotion to Skeeter was so complete that she was anxious to do anything to earn a pat. It wasn't difficult to teach her to heel and follow at Skeeter's feet regardless of the urge to dash away and chase rabbits. The boy used a clothesline as a guide rope and made M'Lady follow him. The first time the dog tried to chase an animal, Skeeter pinched the rope around her neck just a bit and commanded, "Heel!" And when she obeyed, Skeeter released the noose. It took M'Lady only a few hours to associate disobedience with disfavor.

The dog learned that when she chased and killed a rat or rabbit, the thing would be tied around her neck. The only things she could hunt without being disciplined were quail. Of course, she often mistook the scent of game chickens for quail and hunted them, but Skeeter punished her by scolding. He never switched his dog, but to M'Lady a harsh word from the boy hurt more than a hickory limb.

Jesse watched the dog's progress and pretended not to be impressed. He never volunteered suggestions. M'Lady learned quickly, but the task of teaching her to point birds seemed hopeless. Skeeter knew she'd never point as pointers do, so he worked out his own system. He taught her to stand motionless when he shouted "Hup!" One day she got a scent of birds, paused or pointed for a moment as most animals will, and was ready to spring away when Skeeter said "Hup!"

M'Lady was confused. Every instinct urged her to chase the birds, but her master had said stand still. She broke, however, and Skeeter scolded her. She pouted at first, then filled up, but the boy ignored her until she obeyed the next command, then he patted her and she chuckled.

The lessons continued for days and weeks, and slowly and surely M'Lady learned her chores. She learned that the second she smelled birds she must stop and stand still until Skeeter flushed them. That she must not quiver when he shot.

Teaching her to fetch was easy, but teaching her to retrieve dead birds without damaging them was another matter. M'Lady had a hard mouth—that is, she sank her teeth into the birds. Skeeter used one of the oldest hunting tricks of the backwoods to break her.

He got a stick and wrapped it with wire and taught his dog to fetch it. Only once did M'Lady bite hard on the stick, and then the wire hurt her sensitive mouth. Soon she developed a habit of carrying the stick on her tongue and supporting it lightly with her teeth. Skeeter tied quail feathers on the stick, and soon M'Lady's education was complete.

Skeeter led Jesse into a field one day and turned his dog loose. She flashed to a point almost immediately. It was a funny point and Jesse almost laughed. The dog's curved tail poked up over her back, she spraddled her front legs and sort of squatted, her nose pointing the birds, more than forty yards away. She remained rigid until the boy flushed and shot, then she leaped away, seeking and fetching dead birds.

Jesse was mighty proud. "Well, Skeets, looks like you got yourself a bird hunter."

"Yes, sir," Skeeter said. "And you got yourself a job." He pointed toward the kindling pile.

The swamp was dressing for winter when Cash Watson drove down that day to give his Big Boy a workout in the wild brush.

He fetched Jesse a couple of cans of smoking tobacco and Skeeter a bag of peppermint jawbreakers. He locked his fine pointer in the corncrib for the night and was warming himself in the cabin when he noticed M'Lady for the first time. She was sleeping in front of the fire.

"What's that?" he asked.

"My dog," said Skeeter. "Ain't she a beaut?"

"She sure is," Cash grinned at Jesse. Skeeter went out to the well and Cash asked his old friend, "What the devil kind of mutt is that?"

"Search me," Jesse said. "Skeets found her in the swamp. I reckon she's got a trace of bloodhound in her and some terrier and a heap of just plain dog."

M'Lady cocked one ear and got up and stretched; then, apparently not liking the company, turned her tail toward Cash and strutted out, looking for Skeeter.

The men laughed. "Som'n wrong with her throat," Jesse said. "She can't bark. When she tries, she makes a funny sound, sort of a cackling, chuckling yodel. Sounds like she's laughing."

"Well," Cash said "trust a young'un to love the orner'st dog he can find."

"Wait a minute," Jesse said. "She ain't no-count. She's a bird-hunting fool."

Just then Skeeter entered and Cash jestingly said, "Hear you got yourself a bird dog, son."

The boy clasped his hands behind him and rocked on the balls of his feet as he had seen the men do. "Well, now, I'll tell you, Mr. Cash. M'Lady does ever'thing except tote the gun."

"She must be fair to middling. Why not take her out with Big Boy tomorrow? Do my dog good to hunt in a brace."

"Me and my dog don't want to show Big Boy up. He's a pretty good ol' dog."

"Whoa!" Cash was every inch a bird-dog man and nobody could challenge him without a showdown. Besides, Skeeter was shooting up and should be learning a few things about life. "Any old boiler can pop off steam." Cash winked at Jesse.

"Well, now, sir, if you're itching for a run, I'll just double-dog dare you to run your dog against mine. And anybody who'll take a dare will pull up young cotton and push a widow woman's ducks in the water."

Cash admired the boy's confidence. "All right, son. It's a deal. What are the stakes?"

Skeeter started to mention the twenty-gauge gun he wanted, but changed his mind quickly. He reached down and patted M'Lady, then looked up. "If my dog beats yours, then you get them Roebuckers for Uncle Jess."

Jesse's chest suddenly was tight. Cash glanced from the boy to the man and he, too, was proud of Skeeter. "I wasn't aiming to go that high. But all right. What do I get if I win?"

"I'll cut you ten cords of stove-wood."

"And a stack of splinters?"

"Yes, sir."

Cash offered his hand and Skeeter took it. "It's a race," Cash said. "Jesse will be the judge."

The wind was rustling the sage and there was a nip in the early-morning air when they took the dogs to a clearing and set them down. Skeeter snapped a belt around M'Lady's neck and, at word from Jesse, the dogs were released.

Big Boy bounded away and began circling, ranging into the brush. M'Lady tilted her nose into the wind and ripped away toward the sage, her bell tinkling. Cash said, "She sure covers ground." Skeeter made no effort to keep up with her, but waited until he couldn't hear the bell, then ran for a clearing where he had last heard it. And there was M'Lady on a point.

Cash almost laughed out loud. "That ain't no point, son. That's a squat."

"She's got birds."

"Where?"

Jesse leaned against a tree and watched the fun.

Skeeter pointed toward a clump of sage. "She's pointing birds in that sage."

Cash couldn't restrain his mirth. "Boy, now that's what I call some pointing. Why, Skeeter, it's sixty or seventy yards to that sage."

Just then Big Boy flashed by M'Lady, his head high. He raced to the edge of the sage, caught the wind, then whipped around, freezing to a point. Cash called Jesse's attention to the point.

"That's M'Lady's point," Skeeter said. "She's got the same birds Big Boy has."

Jesse sauntered up. "The boy's right, Cash. I aimed to keep my mouth out'n this race, but M'Lady is pointing them birds. She can catch scents up to eighty yards."

Cash said, "Aw, go on. You're crazy." He walked over and flushed the birds.

Skeeter picked one off and ordered M'Lady to fetch. When she returned with the bird, the boy patted her and she began chuckling.

Cash really studied her then for the first time. "Hey!" he said suddenly. "A Basenji! That's a Basenji!"

"A what?" Jesse asked.

"I should have known." Cash was very excited. "That's the dog that was lost by them rich Yankees. I saw about it in the paper." He happened to look at Skeeter then and wished he had cut out his tongue.

The boy's lips were compressed and his face was drawn and white. Jesse had closed his eyes and was rubbing his forehead.

Cash, trying to dismiss the subject, said, "Just 'cause it was in the paper don't make it so. I don't believe that's the same dog, come to think of it."

"Do you aim to tell 'em where the dog is?" Skeeter asked.

Cash looked at Jesse, then at the ground. "It ain't none of my business."

"How 'bout you, Uncle Jess?"

"I ain't telling nobody nothin'."

"I know she's the same dog," Skeeter said. "On account of I just know it. But she's mine now." His voice rose and trembled. "And ain't nobody gonna take her away from me." He ran into the swamp. M'Lady was at his heels.

Cash said, "Durn my lip. I'm sorry, Jesse. If I'd kept my big mouth shut he'd never known the difference."

"It can't be helped now," Jesse said.

"'Course she beat Big Boy. Them's the best hunting dogs in the world. And she's worth a mint of money."

They didn't feel up to hunting and returned to the cabin and sat on the porch. Neither had much to say, but kept glancing toward the swamp where Skeeter and M'Lady were walking along the bayou. "Don't you worry," he said tenderly. "Ain't nobody gonna bother you."

He sat on a stump and M'Lady put her head on his knee. She wasn't worrying. Nothing could have been more contented than she was.

"I don't care if the sheriff comes down." Skeeter pulled her onto his lap and held her. " I don't give a whoop if the governor comes down. Even the President of the United States! The whole shebang can come, but ain't nobody gonna mess with you."

His words gave him courage and he felt better, but for only a minute. Then the tug-of-war between him and his conscience started.

"Once I found a Barlow knife and kept it and it was all right," he mumbled.

But this is different.

"Finders, keepers; losers, weepers."

No, Skeeter.

"Well, I don't care, She's mine."

Remember what your Uncle Jess said.

"He said a heap of things."

Yes, but you remember one thing more than the rest. He said, "Certain things are right and certain things are wrong. And nothing ain't gonna ever change that. When you learn that, then you're fit'n to be a man." Remember, Skeeter?

A feeling of despair and loneliness almost overwhelmed him. He fought off the tears as long as he could, but finally he gave in, and his sobs caused M'Lady to peer into his face and wonder why he was acting that way when she was so happy. He put his arms around her neck and pulled her to him.

"My li'l' old puppy dog. Poor li'l' old puppy dog. But I got to do it."

He sniffed back his tears and got up and walked to the cabin. M'Lady curled up by the fire and the boy sat down, watching the logs splutter for several minutes. The he said, almost in a whisper, "Uncle Jess, if you keep som'n that ain't yours, it's the same as stealing, ain't it?"

Cash leaned against the mantel and stared into the fire.

Jesse puffed his pipe slowly. "Son, that's som'n you got to settle with yourself."

Skeeter stood and turned his back to the flames, warming his hands.

"Mr. Cash," he said slowly, "when you get back to your store, please let them folks know their dog is here."

"If that's how it is—"

"That's how it is," Skeeter said.

The firelight dancing on Jesse's face revealed the old man's dejection, and Skeeter, seeing it, said quickly, "It's best for M'Lady. She's too good for the swamp. They'll give her a good home."

Jesse flinched, and Cash, catching the hurt look in his friend's eyes, said, "Your dog outhunted mine, Skeets. You win them Roebuckers for your uncle."

"I don't want 'em," Jesse said, rather childishly. "I don't care if'n I never eat no roastin' ears." He got up quickly and hurried outside. Cash reckoned he'd better be going, and left Skeeter by the fire, rubbing his dog.

Jesse came back in directly and pulled up a chair. Skeeter started to speak, but Jesse spoke first. "I been doing a heap of thinking lately. You're sprouting up. The swamp ain't no place for you."

Skeeter forgot about his dog and faced his uncle, bewildered.

"I reckon you're too good for the swamp too," Jesse said. "I'm aiming to send you into town for a spell. I can make enough to keep you in fit'n clothes and all." He dared not look at the boy.

"Uncle Jess!" Skeeter said reproachfully. "You don't mean that. You're just saying that on account of what I said about M'Lady. I said it just to keep you from feeling so bad about our dog going away. Gee m'netty, Uncle Jess. I ain't ever gonna leave you." He buried his face in his uncle's shoulder. M'Lady put her head on Jesse's knee and he patted the boy and rubbed the dog.

"Reckon I'll take them Roebuckers," he said at last. "I been wanting some for a long, long time."

Several days later Cash drove down and told them the man from the kennels was at his store. Skeeter didn't say a word, but called M'Lady and they got in Cash's car. All the way to town, the boy was silent. He held his dog's head in his lap.

The keeper took just one look at M'Lady and said, "That's she, all right. Miss Congo III." He turned to speak to Skeeter, but the boy was walking away. He got a glance at Skeeter's face, however. "Hell," he muttered. "I wish you fellows hadn't told me. I hate to take a dog away from a kid."

"He wanted you to know," Cash said.

"Mister"—Jesse closed his left eye and struck his swapping pose—"I'd like to swap you out'n that hound. Now, course she ain't much 'count—"

The keeper smiled in spite of himself. "If she was mine, I'd give her to the kid. But she's not for sale. The owner wants to breed her and establish her line in this country. And if she was for sale, she'd cost more money than any of us will ever see." He called Skeeter and offered his hand. Skeeter shook it.

"You're a good kid. There's a reward for this dog."

"I don't want no reward." The boy's words tumbled out. "I don't want nothing, except to be left alone. You've got your dog, mister. Take her and go on. Please." He walked away again, fearing he would cry.

Cash said, "I'll take the reward and keep it for him. Someday he'll want it."

Jesse went out to the store porch to be with Skeeter. The keeper handed Cash the money. "It's tough, but the kid'll get over it. The dog never will."

"Is that a fact?"

"Yep. I know the breed. They never forget. That dog'll never laugh again. They never laugh unless they're happy."

He walked to the post where Skeeter had tied M'Lady. He untied the leash and started toward his station wagon. M'Lady braced her front feet and looked around for the boy. Seeing him on the porch, she jerked away from the keeper and ran to her master.

She rubbed against his legs. Skeeter tried to ignore her. The keeper reached for the leash again and M'Lady crouched, baring her fangs. The keeper shrugged, a helpless gesture.

"Wild elephants couldn't pull that dog away from that boy," he said.

"That's all right, mister." Skeeter unsnapped the leash and tossed it to the keeper. Then he walked to the station wagon, opened the door of a cage and called, "Heah, M'Lady!" she bounded to him. "Up!" he commanded. She didn't hesitate, but leaped into the cage. The keeper locked the door.

M'Lady, having obeyed a command, poked her nose between the bars, expecting a pat. The boy rubbed her head. She tried to move closer to him, but the bars held her. She looked quizzically at the bars, then tried to nudge them aside. Then she clawed them. A look of fear suddenly came to her eyes and she fastened them on Skeeter, wistfully at first, then pleadingly. She couldn't make a sound, for her unhappiness had sealed her throat. Slowly her eyes filled up.

"Don't cry no more, M'Lady. Ever'thing's gonna be all right." He reached out to pat her, but the station wagon moved off, leaving him standing there in the dust.

Back on the porch, Jesse lit his pipe and said to his friend, "Cash, the boy has lost his dog and I've lost a boy."

"Aw, Jesse, Skeeter wouldn't leave you."

"That ain't what I mean. He's growned up, Cash. He don't look no older, but he is. He growed up that day in the swamp."

Skeeter walked into the store and Cash followed him. "I've got that reward for you, Jonathan."

It was the first time anyone ever had called him that and it sounded like man talk.

"And that twenty-gauge is waiting for you," Cash said. "I'm gonna give it to you."

"Thank you, Mr. Cash." The boy bit his lower lip. "But I don't aim to do no more hunting. I don't never want no more dogs."

"Know how you feel. But if you change your mind, the gun's here for you."

Skeeter looked back toward the porch where Jesse was waiting, and said, "Tell you what, though. When you get them Roebuckers, get some with a couple of gold teeth in 'em. Take it out of the reward money."

"Sure, Jonathan."

Jesse joined them, and Skeeter said, "We better be getting back toward the house."

"I'll drive you down," Cash said. "But first I aim to treat you to some lemon pop and sardines."

"That's mighty nice of you," Jesse said, "but we better be gettin' on."

"What's the hurry?" Cash opened the pop.

"It's my time to cut splinters," Jesse said. "That's what I get for betting with a good man."

The Horse in the Bedroom

CHESTER SULLIVAN

WHEN THE WAR came along some Mississippi people wanted to go to it and some didn't. Then things got worse and worse until a number of men who didn't want to fight hid out in Choctaw County and down in the Piney Woods. Jim Shuler shot himself to keep from going, and Joel Harvey said in church, "When they were instigating this war they didn't call on the churches to pray them into it, and now they needn't call on us to pray them out of it!"

Wild Tom was seventy in the third year of the war. At Eastertime he told his children and nephews and nieces and grandchildren to bring their children and all to his house for dinner. Bright and early Easter Sunday Aunt Sally hid some hen eggs along the east slope, carefully bending dewy grass to cover them. She put two in a corner of the rail fence that separated the east slope from the meadow below it, and while she was doing that she frequently looked down to the treeline below the meadow. Being only fifty, she insisted that all of the children call her aunt instead of grandmaw—she was too young to be called grandmaw. This morning she knew that her favorite grandson, Turnel, would be down there in the treeline. If he felt it was safe he would slip up to the house for dinner. He was in the trees, but she saw no sign of him.

Turnel watched Aunt Sally hide the eggs. Then he waited while the sun warmed the meadow, and while he waited he thought about his grandfather's axe-shaped hams and about how his grandfather would slice down through one across the grain and then work off thin shavings, like he was whittling more for the good looks of his monumental ham than for the serving portions that he was cutting off, all the while expounding on a matter of politics or the Gospels. Turnel sat beside the fuzzy black horse he called Roger looking up at the porch and the people who had begun gathering there. They were somewhat clean, he imagined. He stunk like pine smoke. He was ravenously hungry. Breathing deeply, he watched the hill beyond the house, trying to sense the mistake before he bit it, trying to smell the taint, knowing for sure that there was someone somewhere in the green curving world who did not love him and wish him well.

Then he saw Ruthie come onto the porch with his daughter in her arms. They were followed by her husband, who was wearing a suit. Although Turnel couldn't see it at the distance he'd been told there was a heavy-linked gold chain hanging across the front of that suit. The children were compelled to wait on the porch until Wild Tom gave his signal, and Turnel imagined the things they were saying. He decided there was nothing wrong at the house. It had no conscriptors inside, nor would the man in the suit gain anything by betraying him because everybody knew all about Ruthie and Turnel and their new baby girl, just like everybody knew why that man had come here and involved himself with their sprawling, lawless, notorious family. The man had met Ruthie on the Short Dog, and like every man who had ever seen her, he'd desired her. Ruthie's attraction derived from her bearing and speech and coloring and manner, and nobody had ever succeeded at describing it—other than to say that she was wonderful or that she was beautiful—because her attraction was a combination of things that simply made people feel good being around her. What Ruthie saw in the stranger, however, was a different matter. He was from far away, and he talked to her like no one ever had before. Of course, it was clear to him on the train that Ruthie would soon bear a child. When he asked her friendly questions about her family, about her husband, she told him openly to his face that the baby's father was her cousin and they weren't married. Then she took up with him. Thereafter people referred to him as the Mister Man that Ruthie met on the Short Dog, and everybody knew all about it.

Roger picked at the grass as if he were looking for a biddy to eat. The children wouldn't listen long to the story about Ruthie meeting a man on the Short Dog. It didn't interest them. They had stories of their own like, "One time Roger chewed through his halter rope and, wandering around loose in the yard, stretched out his skinny neck and nipped up one of Aunt Sally's biddies. He raised his head, chewed up the biddy, and swallowed it." The event was witnessed by a number of trustworthy children who promptly gave Roger the reputation for being a chicken eater. They knew that anybody would kill an egg-sucking dog, but Wild Tom just whistled in amazement when they tattled on Roger for eating that biddy.

When the time came for Turnel to hide out he took a wagonload of stuff off down to the Cohay bottoms and buried part of it and hung the rest of it up in the trees. He took blankets and cornmeal and whiskey and bacon, and he pulled the wagon with the little chicken-eating horse that could run through briars and vines like a dose of salts or stand flatfooted and jump a fence or maybe even climb a tree if it felt so inclined. Turnel would ride him bareback through tangles so thick, "You couldn't drag a bridle through them," the children heard him say. He also said, "I'll run, I'll hide, I'll steal, I'll lie if I get caught, but I won't burden myself with a gun. I wouldn't shoot somebody else just to keep from going to the army myself." His nonchalant salute and the way he drove off in that one-way wagon appealed to the children's imaginations, making them tell brave stories about what they'd do if they were hiding out in the woods with Turnel. Despite their brave stories, however, the children feared Turnel like they feared his shaggy black horse. Unlike their parents, they saw no jealous connection between him and the man Ruthie met on the Short Dog.

Then Turnel swung up on Roger, giving him a moderately hard kick in the flank. He rode out of the trees and up the rise toward his grandfather's house. When he got to the rail fence he slid off Roger. He looked at the porch and saw that the children had all been told for the last time to shut up about the eggs. They were sullen and impatient. Then Wild Tom came down the porch steps and walked cross the yard until he looked up and saw Turnel standing there. He stopped and beckoned to the children, who surged down the steps and swirled past him. One of them squealed, "Turnel's here!" A boy in a long-tailed shirt said, "That Roger, he'll bite you!" Someone else said, "Naw he won't, but he'll eat our eggs."

"How've you been?" Tom said when he got to Turnel.

"All right." He quickly took the eggs that he knew were in the fence and cracked them. He shelled one out and ate it whole.

"Lowrey caught and hung some men at Quaker's Neck. He's got dogs."

While he nodded, Turnel watched Ruthie on the porch. The children were aware of him, and they kept their distance.

"People say you had on a dress down at Ellisville. Just walked out of town, went into a stranger's house, took off your dress, and walked out the back door." Tom's voice brightened while he talked.

"Yeah, I did that. You want me to wear my dress to dinner?"

"Naw. The children would giggle."

Turnel shelled the second egg.

"You wouldn't fool any conscriptors, not with all the kids laughing at you." Tom let a silence pass. "I've put Joe Ray up in the loft. If he sees somebody coming he'll tell us. You can sneak out the back."

"I reckon if they come they'll come from the back."

"Well then—" the old man chuckled, "you'll have to go out the front—"

Children were finding eggs, stepping on some in the process. There was trading going on and crying too, but the people stayed on the porch and let the children peck it out for themselves.

Wild Tom drew his pocket knife, opened it, and tested the blade against his thumb. Then he said softly, "You don't want to make trouble for Ruthie."

"What does that sonofabitch do, anyway!"

"Hell if I know. He doesn't sweat. He wears nice clothes and talks about railroads. I suppose he's like everybody else—waiting for the war to end to see how things turn out."

"I could tell him how things will turn out. This country and most everybody in it is going to suffer. We will all suffer for years to come."

"I imagine you're right. There's been thousands—"

"Don't tell me. Do you think it would make trouble for Ruthie if I went up there and saw my baby?"

"No. The man said if it was a boy she must name it after you. He's being decent."

"Has she named it yet?"

"Baby." He folded the pocket knife. "Here, you need a knife?" He offered it to Turnel.

"No, Grandpaw. I've got one."

"Then," Tom eyed him closely, "let's drop knives for luck."

Exchanging knives by dropping was a game that boys played, gambling that the knife they got would be better than the one they gave. Turnel took his knife from his pocket, concealing it inside his closed hand according to the custom. At the same time he held his left hand out palm up. While Tom did likewise, and each man dropped his knife into the other's hand. Turnel said, "By the feel of it, I've owned this blade before." The old man said, "It's plenty sharp."

The children had tallied up their eggs and were demanding of

Aunt Sally how many she'd hidden. She told them a number, and a boy, Turnel's nephew, said, "There's two more here somewheres."

Another child said, "If Roger didn't eat them."

"At least he ought to wait until they hatch," the boy said, cutting his eyes at Turnel. Then Turnel looked at his grandfather closely and saw that in the last months Wild Tom had become an old man. His eyes were teary. He waved his hand as if he were trying to dismiss the children. Turnel wheeled at them and yelled, "Give me those eggs! You git the hell away from here! Git to the house!"

They fled.

Tom said, "That's a hard way to treat your kinfolk—"

"Well, you wanted them gone, didn't you?"

"Yeah—I did. I'm a pudding anymore. I don't know which is which—Can't tell the boys from the girls—Can't imagine why anybody'd go to the trouble of making one." Turnel looked away. "I've lost my teeth—Losing my brains—A pudding—It takes all my faculties to imagine how you feel down in the swamps, scared and cold, wanting to take Ruthie's clothes off and roll her up in your blankets. What's your favorite part, the wing or the neck? I can't even remember the last time I ate chicken." He thought for a moment. "Aunt Sally only has five hens now. Everything in Mississippi has gone to hell."

Then Turnel smiled at his grandfather. He said, "You're trying to pull a fast one on me. I'm gonna ask Aunt Sally if you are a pudding." Then he took up Roger's reins, shook them once, dropped them loose, and said, "Jump!" The horse hopped over the fence. Turnel caught him up and grinned as he asked the old man, "You trying to get me to shed a tear, or are you worried that I might not succeed to make a fool of myself without your help?"

"No son. I am trying to share a confidence with you, sympathize with you, tell you that I love you and hope you don't get killed and thrown in the Cohay with none of us there to pull you out. I'm sorry about you and Ruthie, too."

"Oh—I've forgotten that stuff."

"So have I—That's what I was trying to explain to you, about eating chicken."

"And I'm gonna tell Aunt Sally you've been talking nasty!"

Turnel, leading his horse, walked with his grandfather up to the porch, where he nodded and spoke to everyone, especially Ruthie's husband.

Nobody had to tell the children to keep clear of Roger's head and feet.

"I heard about how you got out of Ellisville," the man said cordially, opening with a safe topic.

Turnel nodded and said, "You're doing well?"

"Tolerable. In these bad times. The railroads are all soldier now. Torn up."

Turnel glanced at Ruthie's eyes. "How's your baby?" he asked her.

"She finds things to complain about. But she's a good baby. You want to hold her?"

Turnel wiped his palms on his trousers. After a pause he said, "Yeah, I'd like that." He reached out, and Ruthie handed him the baby, who immediately began to cry. She stiffened her back, kicked her legs, and tried to squirm from his grasp, but he held her tight and pulled her to his chest with an impulse to set her up on Roger and give her a quick ride. Instead he rocked her twice and then handed her back to Ruthie. "She's pretty, like you," he said. Ruthie smiled at him, and he knew that she had been turning over in her mind the clever things she might say to him but then had decided to say nothing.

It was a two-crib log house, facing south, with a long porch across the front. It had a straight, overhanging roof and a chimney at either end. The large oaks in the front yard had yet to leaf out. The west crib was the bedroom, the east crib the living room, and the kitchen was a lean-to on the back off the living room. A dinner table was set up for the children in the dogtrot between the two cribs. Aunt Sally stood beside it, and Turnel bowed slightly upon seeing her, smiled, and said, "Hello, Aunt Sally."

She smiled at him, her eyes wet with tears.

"I suppose you've cooked a lot today?"

"A right smart," she said, "but no biscuits. We can't get flour."

"And you managed to save up some eggs for the children—"

"Yes."

"Well now—I'm going to ask you a crazy thing."

"What?"

"I want to bring my horse in the house."

"Yes."

"It's these bad times, Aunt Sally, and he's gentle as a pet coon."

"Pet coon, is he? I've heard he's the meanest thing in Creation!"

Then Turnel climbed the steps and pulled sharply on the bridle reins, and Roger without excessive walling of his eyeballs followed Turnel's lead up the steps, across the porch, and down the dogtrot to the bedroom door. He balked at the doorway, stamped the floor a couple of times, and then allowed Turnel to lead him into the dark bedroom. In a moment Turnel came out and closed the door.

"Well—" Ruthie's husband started speaking again, keen on being friendly. "I've heard that you Piney Woods people are originals! But allow me to remark that I've never seen a horse so handily stabled!"

Turnel moved to reply, and Billy and the aunts were uncomfortable. Turnel said, "These are original times, Sir. We have in the State of Mississippi what is called the Twenty Negro Rule—But I don't own twenty Negroes, so if Mr. Lowrey and as few as six men under his authority come here—and catch me—they have the authority to hang me. I shall have dinner with my Aunt Sally and if we are interrupted during our dinner I shall run back to the Cohay swamps—where I have been for quite some time."

Wild Tom came to the children's table. He said, "Now—this is all going to be fine. We'll just leave the horse in the bedroom like that's the way we usually do. If Turnel needs him all of a sudden, he'll have him handy. I want you and you and Billy and me to go in the living room and close the door. I want everybody else to act natural, and I want you children to all go down in the yard and play you some play—and if you don't play good I'll come down there and play with you!" Then he went into the living room, and the men he'd designated followed him.

In his living room Tom raised a floor plank and took out a clear glass jug, putting it on the side table where they kept the water bucket and dipper. He got the dipper half full of water, filled it on up with whiskey, and swirled it. Then he took a long, slow sip and passed it to Billy. Billy drank and gave the dipper to Mister Man, who drank and gave it to Turnel. Then Billy lifted the jug with his one hand and took a shallow nip directly from it. There were only a couple of inches of liquor in the jug.

"Now," Wild Tom said, "we'll have a nice dinner after a while. Then maybe we'll all take a nap."

Billy grinned and said, "Turnel's horse is in your bedroom, Papa." Amused by his own wit, Billy laughed and looked at the other men to see how they took it.

"Then we'll sleep in here. Just stretch out on the floor," Wild Tom said.

"How are you managing to keep out of the army?" Turnel asked abruptly. The question did not catch Mister Man by surprise. He gestured to Billy that he wanted the jug. Taking it in both hands, he swirled it at arm's length, starting at the clear liquid like a Gypsy would a crystal ball. Then he raised it slowly and took a drink. He set it down softly on the table. He wiped his mouth with a handkerchief. Then he said, "The army? There is no army. It's all soldier. I'm an engineer from New York. You would be surprised the way things turn out." He passed the jug to Wild Tom. Then he said, "This here is sanity. This is what I like. Ruthie told me stories about her grandfather, Wild Tom. She said he once put a sheriff's neck in a rail fence, and I liked hearing it."

Tom nodded, acknowledging the story from his youth.

The man asked Turnel, "Have you ever seen an army? It's a terrible thing. Nobody in it does what he thinks is right. It's all soldier. I left after a week." Then he patted his chest pocket. "I've got a certificate says I'm blind beyond six feet—that way they can't catch me with the flinch test. But every time I've shown it I've used bribe money."

Billy, fascinated by the idea of such a certificate, asked, "Why would you pay bribe money if you've got that certificate?"

"Once because they were going to make me their cook. They said I could see as far as the stew pot. Another time I had to pay a bribe because I let it slip that I could write. They said that my arm certainly was shorter than six feet."

Then Joe Ray heard the soldiers. It was later argued (because of a mark on the sergeant's horse, but in the war horses changed hands like everything else, so that was weak evidence) that they were Southern cavalry in Yankee uniforms. At any rate, Joe Ray didn't have time to beat them to the house, so he stayed where he was. Aunt Sally whispered through the living room door that soldiers were all around the house. Wild Tom moved the loose floor plank, and Turnel rolled over its wooden lip into darkness. Tom replaced the plank, took the glass jug into the crook of his arm, and lay down on the plank to open his mouth and snore. Billy needlessly unrolled his empty sleeve to let it swing freely by his side.

Then, suddenly, Ruthie's Mister Man decided he would do well to go under the floor with Turnel. "Pssst!" he said, nudging Wild

Tom. Tom peeped open one eye and saw Mister Man on all fours, his gold watch chain swinging until it almost touched the floor. "Pssst—" He whispered again, "is there room down there for me, too?"

"Yes, but it's dusty under the house," Tom said.

"I think the time has come for me to retire my certificate," Mister Man said.

Billy hunkered down, joining their discussion while voices were heard in the yard. Billy gestured to Mister Man, fluttering his fingers as if he were unfolding a piece of paper with his one hand. While Tom slowly lifted the plank, Mister Man pinched the certificate from his coat pocket and gave it to Billy. Billy took it gratefully. Then he realized that he'd better talk quick before one of the people outside said something that would reveal Mister Man's presence. He jumped up and walked to the door. He jerked it open and stomped onto the dogtrot saying, "There ain't no men on the place but me and my old drunk Daddy, and I got blowed to pieces at—" He saw the blue uniform—Hell! It don't matter where—" He shoved the paper deep into his pants pocket.

The sergeant sat his horse at the steps, the flap unfastened on his pistol holster. "Were you a soldier?" he asked.

"Yes, Sergeant," Billy said. "I was. But I'm through with this war. I got blowed to pieces—"

"Then you won't begrudge us some food?"

The children, like people will, all remembered that question exactly—the intonation—and they all could imitate the sergeant's voice years later because it was their food he was talking about. "Then, yew woant bee grudge us some feud—" They would say.

The soldiers had closed on Wild Tom's place like a noose. While the sergeant talked the others searched the outbuildings and then tightened the circle, closing in on the house. Of course they found Joe Ray in the barn, but he was only twelve. Then the soldiers at the back of the house came in through the dogtrot, and the sergeant gestured for them to search the east crib. They brought out Wild Tom, so drunk he could hardly walk, his glass jug, and two hams that they'd found hanging from a rafter. Then the sergeant swung his hand to the left, and the soldiers went to the bedroom. The first soldier to enter, frightened by Roger's shifting bulk in the darkness, yelled, "God dern! There's a dern horse in the bedroom!" Then the sergeant got hot and asked tough questions about why there was a horse in the bedroom, and Aunt Sally told him it was because whiskey had made her husband drunk at breakfast and Roger was all the remembrance he had of his grandson, who'd been taken away by conscriptors, and because he was drunk, and because it was Eastertime, he'd brought Roger into the house to be part of the family. Years later when the children remembered it they said Aunt Sally's story was so drawn out and pitiful it made the counterfeit sergeant cry. Then one of them, a five-year-old, stood up on the bench behind the table wearing nothing but a long-tailed shirt, it was a boy child, people remembered, and he proclaimed, "That horse in there is one mean horse! He eats chickens! Don't you boys go in there without you got yourself a big stick!"

After the soldiers finished their dinner they rode away taking Roger, all the ham, the remaining inch of liquor in Wild Tom's jug, and a tale of Piney Woods people who lay drunk and kept horses in their house. Turnel and Ruthie's Mister Man went to the Cohay swamps and stayed there a long time together. Then Mister Man came out of hiding and took Ruthie and her baby to New York where they lived all their lives. Turnel married Jo Anderson, and they lived in Wild Tom's log house and raised nine children. When he was an old man Turnel liked to tell funny stories about the times he had with Ruthie's Mister Man in the Cohay swamps and the jokes they played on one another. His favorite story was that the first night they spent in the bottoms he and Mister Man were huddled on a little board platform thirty feet up a gum tree. Turnel had left a jug of whiskey hidden up there, so he and Mister Man got to drinking it and after a while they began talking about how pretty Ruthie was and how sweet the baby was—when they heard slow, heavy footsteps sloshing toward them—there was a half a foot of water on the ground. It was pitch black, and the footsteps came right up to their tree. Turnel and Mister Man heard a long sigh, like somebody had come miles and was out of breath and was waiting for them to speak first. Turnel and Mister Man froze where they were, almost afraid to breathe. After a long time the moon came up and cast its dim light. Then they slowly peeped over the edge of the platform to see who had them.

Below them they saw someone dressed all in white sitting on a big black horse. He sat there for an hour, it seemed, until Turnel could stand it no longer and said, "Who's there?" But the ghostly figure would not answer him. After another hour Mister Man found the courage to ask the specter, "Are you Death?" But he got no reply either. They didn't say another word to it, just huddled there until the tiny birds started singing and daylight made its soft way through gray limbs and budding twigs. Then Turnel peeked over the side again and saw that it was not a ghost sitting on a black horse. It was Roger with a hundred-pound sack of precious flour tied across his back and his lead rope chewed in two.

FROM

Roll of Thunder, Hear My Cry

MILDRED D. TAYLOR

"LITTLE MAN, would you come on? You keep it up and you're gonna make us late."

My youngest brother paid no attention to me. Grasping more firmly his newspaper-wrapped notebook and his tin-can lunch of cornbread and oil sausages, he continued to concentrate on the dusty road. He lagged several feet behind my other brothers, Stacey and Christopher-John, and me, attempting to keep the rusty Mississippi dust from swelling with each step and drifting back upon his shiny black shoes and the cuffs of his corduroy pants by lifting each foot high before setting it gently down again. Always meticulously neat, six-year-old Little Man never allowed dirt or tears or stains to mar anything he owned. Today was no exception.

"You keep it up and make us late for school, Mama's gonna wear you out," I threatened, pulling with exasperation at the high collar of the Sunday dress Mama had made me wear for the first day of school—as if that event were something special. It seemed to me that showing up at school at all on a bright August-like October morning made for running the cool forest trails and wading barefoot in the forest pond was concession enough; Sunday clothing was asking too much. Christopher-John and Stacey were not too pleased about the clothing or school either. Only Little Man, just beginning his school career, found the prospects of both intriguing.

"Y'all go ahead and get dirty if y'all wanna," he replied without even looking up from his studied steps. "Me, I'm gonna stay clean."

"I betcha Mama's gonna 'clean' you, you keep it up," I grumbled.

"Ah, Cassie, leave him be," Stacey admonished, frowning and kicking testily at the road.

"I ain't said nothing but—"

Stacey cut me a wicked look and I grew silent. His disposition had been irritatingly sour lately. If I hadn't known the cause of it, I could have forgotten very easily that he was, at twelve, bigger than I, and that I had promised Mama to arrive at school looking clean and ladylike. "Shoot," I mumbled finally, unable to restrain myself from further comment, "it ain't my fault you gotta be in Mama's class this year."

Stacey's frown deepened and he jammed his fists into his pockets, but said nothing.

Christopher-John, walking between Stacey and me, glanced uneasily at both of us but did not interfere. A short, round boy of seven, he took little interest in troublesome things, preferring to remain on good terms with everyone. Yet he was always sensitive to others and now, shifting the handle of his lunch can from his right hand to his right wrist and his smudged notebook from his left hand to his left armpit, he stuffed his free hands into his pockets and attempted to make his face as moody as Stacey's and as cranky as mine. But after a few moments he seemed to forget that he was supposed to be grouchy and began whistling cheerfully. There was little that could make Christopher-John unhappy for very long, not even the thought of school.

I tugged again at my collar and dragged my feet in the dust, allowing it to sift back onto my socks and shoes like gritty red snow. I hated the dress. And the shoes. There was little I could do in a dress, and as for shoes, they imprisoned freedom-loving feet accustomed to the feel of the warm earth.

"Cassie, stop that," Stacey snapped as the dust billowed in swirling clouds around my feet. I looked up sharply, ready to protest. Christopher-John's whistling increased to a raucous, nervous shrill, and grudgingly I let the matter drop and trudged along in moody silence, my brothers growing as pensively quiet as I.

Before us the narrow, sun-splotched road wound like a lazy red serpent dividing the high forest bank of quiet, old trees on the left from the cotton field, forested by giant green-and purple stalks, on the right. A barbed-wire fence ran the length of the deep field, stretching eastward for over a quarter of a mile until it met the sloping green pasture that signaled the end of our family's four hundred acres. An ancient oak tree on the slope, visible even now, was the official dividing mark between Logan land and the beginning of a dense forest. Beyond the protective fencing of the forest, vast farming fields, worked by a multitude of share-cropping families, covered two thirds of a ten-square-mile plantation. That was Harlan Granger land.

Once our land had been Granger land too, but the Grangers had sold it during Reconstruction to a Yankee for tax money. In 1887, when the land was up for sell again, Grandpa had bought two hundred acres of it, and in 1918, after the first two hundred acres had been paid off, he had bought another two hundred. It was good rich land, much of it still virgin forest, and there was no debt on half of it. But there was a mortgage on the two hundred acres bought in 1918 and there were taxes on the full four hundred, and for the past three years there had not been enough money from the cotton to pay both and live on too.

That was why Papa had gone to work on the railroad.

In 1930 the price of cotton dropped. And so, in the spring of 1931, Papa set out looking for work, going as far north as Memphis and as far south as the Delta country. He had gone west too, into Louisiana. It was there he found work laying track for the railroad. He worked the remainder of the year away from us, not returning until the deep winter when the ground was cold and barren. The following spring after the planting was finished, he did the same. Now it was 1933, and Papa was again in Louisiana laying track.

I asked him once why he had to go away, why the land was so important. He took my hand and said in his quiet way: "Look out there, Cassie girl. All that belongs to you. You ain't never had to live on nobody's place but your own and long as I live and the family survives, you'll never have to. That's important. You may not understand that now, but one day you will. Then you'll see."

I looked at Papa strangely when he said that, for I knew that all the land did not belong to me. Some of it belonged to Stacey, Christopher-John, and Little Man, not to mention the part that belonged to Big Ma, Mama, and Uncle Hammer, Papa's older brother who lived in Chicago. But Papa never divided the land in his mind; it was simply Logan land. For it he would work the long, hot summer pounding steel; Mama would teach and run the farm; Big Ma, in her sixties, would work like a woman of twenty in the fields and keep the house; and the boys and I would wear threadbare clothing washed to dishwater color; but always, the taxes and the mortgage would be paid. Papa said that one day I would understand.

I wondered.

When the fields ended and the Granger forest fanned both sides of the road with long overhanging branches, a tall, emaciated-looking boy popped suddenly from a forest trail and swung a thin arm around Stacey. It was T. J. Avery. His younger brother Claude emerged a moment later, smiling weakly as if it pained him to do so. Neither boy had on shoes, and their Sunday clothing, patched and worn, hung loosely upon their frail frames. The Avery family sharecropped on Granger land.

"Well," said T.J., jauntily swinging into step with Stacey, "here we go again startin' another school year."

"Yeah," sighed Stacey.

"Ah, man, don't look so down," T.J. said cheerfully. "Your mama's really one great teacher. I should know." He certainly should. He had failed Mama's class last year and was now returning for a second try.

"Shoot! You can say that," exclaimed Stacey. "You don't have to spend all day in a classroom with your mama."

"Look on the bright side," said T.J. "Jus' think of the advantage you've got. You'll be learnin' all sorts of stuff 'fore the rest of us. . . ." He smiled slyly. "Like what's on all them tests."

Stacey thrust T.J.'s arm from his shoulders. "If that's what you think, you don't know Mama."

"Ain't no need gettin' mad," T.J. replied undaunted. "Jus' an idea." He was quiet for a moment, then announced, "I betcha I could give y'all an earful 'bout that burnin' last night."

"Burning? What burning?" asked Stacey.

"Man, don't y'all know nothin'? The Berrys' burnin'. I thought y'all's grandmother went over there last night to see 'bout 'em."

Of course we knew that Big Ma had gone to a sick house last night. She was good at medicines and people often called her instead of a doctor when they were sick. But we didn't know anything about any burnings, and I certainly didn't know anything about any Berrys either.

"What Berrys he talking 'bout, Stacey?" I asked. "I don't know no Berrys."

"They live way over on the other side of Smellings Creek. They come up to church sometimes," said Stacey absently. Then he turned back to T.J. "Mr. Lanier come by real late and got Big Ma. Said Mr. Berry was low sick and needed her to help nurse him, but he ain't said nothing 'bout no burning."

"He's low sick all right—'cause he got burnt near to death. Him and his two nephews. And you know who done it?"

"Who?" Stacey and I asked together.

"Well, since y'all don't seem to know nothin'," said T.J., in his usual sickening way of nursing a tidbit of information to death, "maybe I ought not tell y'all. It might hurt y'all's little ears."

"Ah, boy," I said, "don't start that mess again." I didn't like T.J. very much and his stalling around didn't help.

"Come on, T.J.," said Stacey, "out with it."

"Well . . ." T.J. murmured, then grew silent as if considering whether or not he should talk.

We reached the first of two crossroads and turned north; another mile and we would approach the second crossroads and turn east again.

Finally T.J. said, "Okay. See, them Berrys' burnin' wasn't no accident. Some white men took a match to 'em."

"Y-you mean just lit 'em up like a piece of wood?" stammered Christopher-John, his eyes growing big with disbelief.

"But why?" asked Stacey.

T.J. shrugged. "Don't know why. Jus' know they done it, that's all."

"How you know?" I questioned suspiciously.

He smiled smugly. "'Cause your mama come down on her way to school and talked to my mama 'bout it."

"She did?"

"Yeah, and you should've seen the way she look when she come outa that house."

"How'd she look?" inquired Little Man, interested enough to glance up from the road for the first time.

T.J. looked around grimly and whispered, "Like . . . death." He waited a moment for his words to be appropriately shocking, but the effect was spoiled by Little Man, who asked lightly, "What does death look like?"

T.J. turned in annoyance. "Don't he know nothin'?"

"Well, what does it look like?" Little Man demanded to know. He didn't like T.J. either.

"Like my grandfather looked jus' 'fore they buried him," T.J. described all-knowingly.

"Oh," replied Little Man, losing interest and concentrating on the road again.

"I tell ya, Stacey, man," said T.J. morosely, shaking his head, "sometimes I jus' don't know 'bout that family of yours."

Stacey pulled back, considering whether or not T.J.'s words were offensive, but T.J. immediately erased the question by continuing amiably. "Don't get me wrong, Stacey. They some real swell kids, but that Cassie 'bout got me whipped this mornin'."

"Good!" I said.

"Now how'd she do that?" Stacey laughed.

"You wouldn't be laughin' if it'd've happened to you. She up and told your mama 'bout me goin' up to that Wallace store dancin' room and Miz Logan told Mama." He eyed me disdainfully then went on. "But don't worry, I got out of it though. When Mama asked me 'bout it, I jus' said ole Claude was always sneakin' up there to get some of that free candy Mr. Kaleb give out sometimes and I had to go and get him 'cause I knowed good and well she didn't want us up there. Boy, did he get it!" T.J. laughed. "Mama 'bout wore him out."

I stared at quiet Claude. "You let him do that?" I exclaimed. But Claude only smiled in that sickly way of his and I knew that he had. He was more afraid of T.J. than of his mother.

Again Little Man glanced up and I could see his dislike for T.J. growing. Friendly Christopher-John glared at T.J., and putting his short arm around Claude's shoulder said, "Come on, Claude, let's go on ahead." Then he and Claude hurried up the road, away from T.J.

Stacey, who generally overlooked T.J.'s underhanded stunts, shook his head. "That was dirty."

"Well, what'd ya expect me to do? I couldn't let her think I was goin' up there 'cause I like to, could I? She'd've killed me!"

"And good riddance," I thought, promising myself that if he ever pulled anything like that on me, I'd knock his block off.

We were nearing the second crossroads, where deep gullies lined both sides of the road and the dense forest crept to the very edges of high, jagged, clay-walled banks. Suddenly, Stacey turned. "Quick!" he cried. "Off the road!" Without another word, all of us but Little Man scrambled up the steep right bank into the forest.

"Get up here, Man," Stacey ordered, but Little Man only gazed at the ragged red bank sparsely covered with scraggly brown briars and kept on walking. "Come on, do like I say."

"But I'll get my clothes dirty!" protested Little Man.

"You're gonna get them a whole lot dirtier you stay down there. Look!"

Little Man turned around and watched saucer-eyed as a bus bore down on him spewing clouds of red dust like a huge yellow dragon breathing fire. Little Man headed toward the bank, but it was too steep. He ran frantically along the road looking for a foothold and, finding one, hopped onto the bank, but not before the bus had sped past enveloping him in a scarlet haze while laughing white faces pressed against the bus windows.

Little Man shook a threatening fist into the thick air, then looked dismally down at himself.

"Well, ole Little Man done got his Sunday clothes dirty," T.J. laughed as we jumped down from the bank. Angry tears welled in Little Man's eyes but he quickly brushed them away before T.J. could see them.

"Ah, shut up, T.J.," Stacey snapped.

"Yeah, shut up, T.J.," I echoed.

"Come on, Man," Stacey said, "and next time do like I tell ya."

Little Man hopped down from the bank. "How's come they did that, Stacey, huh?" he asked, dusting himself off. "How's come they didn't even stop for us?"

"'Cause they like to see us run and it ain't our bus," Stacey said, balling his fists and jamming them tightly into his pockets.

"Well, where's our bus?" demanded Little Man.

"We ain't got one."

"Well, why not?"

"Ask Mama," Stacey replied as a towheaded boy, barefooted and pale, came running down a forest path toward us. The boy quickly caught up and fell in stride with Stacey and T.J.

"Hey, Stacey," he said shyly.

"Hey, Jeremy," Stacey said.

There was an awkward silence.

"Y'all jus' startin' school today?"

"Yeah," replied Stacey.

"I wishin' ours was jus' startin'," sighed Jeremy. "Ours been goin' since the end of August." Jeremy's eyes were a whitewashed blue and they seemed to weep when he spoke.

"Yeah," said Stacey again.

Jeremy kicked the dust briskly and looked toward the north. He was a strange boy. Ever since I had begun school, he had walked with us as far as the crossroads in the morning, and met us there in the afternoon. He was often ridiculed by the other children at his school and had shown up more than once with wide red welts on his arms which Lillian Jean, his older sister, had revealed with satisfaction were the result of his associating with us. Still, Jeremy continued to meet us.

When we reached the crossroads, three more children, a girl of twelve or thirteen and two boys, all looking very much like Jeremy, rushed past. The girl was Lillian Jean. "Jeremy, come on," she said without a backward glance, and Jeremy, smiling sheepishly, waved a timid good-bye and slowly followed her.

We stood in the crossing gazing after them. Jeremy looked back once but then Lillian Jean yelled shrilly at him and he did not look back again. They were headed for the Jefferson Davis County School, a long white wooden building looming in the distance. Behind the building was a wide sports field around which were scattered rows of tiered gray-looking benches. In front of it were two yellow buses, our own tormentor and one that brought students from the other direction, and loitering students awaiting the knell of the morning bell. In the very center of the expansive front lawn, waving red, white, and blue with the emblem of the Confederacy emblazoned in its upper left-hand corner, was the Mississippi flag. Directly below it was the American flag. As Jeremy and his sister and brothers hurried toward those transposed flags, we turned eastward toward our own school.

The Great Faith Elementary and Secondary School, one of the largest black schools in the county, was a dismal end to an hour's journey. Consisting of four weather-beaten wooden houses on stilts of brick, 320 students, seven teachers, a principal, a caretaker, and the caretaker's cow, which kept the wide crabgrass lawn sufficiently clipped in spring and summer, the school was located near three plantations, the largest and closest by far being the Granger plantation. Most of the students were from families that sharecropped on Granger land, and the others mainly from Montier and Harrison plantation families. Because the students were needed in the fields from early spring when the cotton was planted until after most of the cotton had been picked in the fall, the school adjusted its terms accordingly, beginning in October and dismissing in March. But even so, after today a number of the older students would not be seen again for a month or two, not until the last puff of cotton had been gleaned from the fields, and eventually most would drop out of school altogether. Because of this the classes in the higher grades grew smaller with each passing year.

The class buildings, with their backs practically against the forest wall, formed a semicircle facing a small one-room church at the opposite edge of the compound. It was to this church that many of the school's students and their parents belonged. As we arrived, the enormous iron bell in the church belfry was ringing vigorously, warning the milling students that only five minutes of freedom remained.

Little Man immediately pushed his way across the lawn to the well. Stacey and T.J., ignoring the rest of us now that they were on the school grounds, wandered off to be with the other seventh-grade boys, and Christoper-John and Claude rushed to reunite with their classmates of last year. Left alone, I dragged slowly to the building that held the first four grades and sat on the bottom step. Plopping my pencils and notebook into the dirt, I propped my elbows on my knees and rested my chin in the palms of my hands.

"Hey, Cassie," said Mary Lou Wellever, the principal's daughter, as she flounced by in a new yellow dress.

"Hey, yourself," I said, scowling so ferociously that she kept on walking. I stared after her a moment noting that she *would* have on a new dress. Certainly no one else did. Patches on faded pants and dresses abounded on boys and girls come so recently from the heat of the cotton fields. Girls stood awkwardly, afraid to sit, and boys pulled restlessly at starched, high-buttoned collars. Those students fortunate enough to have shoes hopped from one pinched foot to the other. Tonight the Sunday clothes would be wrapped in newspaper and hung for Sunday and the shoes would be packed away to be brought out again only when the weather turned so cold that bare feet could no longer traverse the frozen roads; but for today we all suffered.

On the far side of the lawn I spied Moe Turner speeding toward the seventh-grade-class building, and wondered at his energy. Moe was one of Stacey's friends. He lived on the Montier plantation, a three-and-a-half-hour walk from the school. Because of the distance, many children from the Montier plantation did not come to Great Faith after they had finished the four-year school near Smellings Creek. But there were some girls and boys like Moe who made the trek daily, leaving their homes while the sky was black and not returning until all was blackness again. I for one was certainly glad that I didn't live that far away. I don't think my feet would have wanted that badly for me to be educated.

The chiming of the second bell began. I stood up dusting my bottom as the first, second, third, and fourth graders crowded up the stairs into the hallway. Little Man flashed proudly past, his face and hands clean and his black shoes shining again. I glanced down at my own shoes powdered red and, raising my right foot, rubbed it against the back of my left leg, then reversed the procedure. As the last gong of the bell reverberated across the compound, I swooped up my pencils and notebook and ran inside.

A hallway extended from the front to the back door of the building. On either side of the hallway were two doorways, both leading into the same large room which was divided into two classrooms by a heavy canvas curtain. The second and third grades were on the left, the first and fourth grades on the right. I hurried to the rear of the building, turned to the right, and slid into a third-row bench occupied by Gracey Pearson and Alma Scott.

"You can't sit here," objected Gracey. "I'm saving it for Mary Lou."

I glanced back at Mary Lou Wellever depositing her lunch pail on a shelf in the back of the room and said, "Not any more you ain't."

Miss Daisy Crocker, yellow and buckeyed, glared down at me from the middle of the room with a look that said, "Soooooooo, it's you, Cassie Logan." Then she pursed her lips and drew the curtain along the rusted iron rod and tucked it into a wide loop in the back wall. With the curtain drawn back, the first graders gazed quizzically at us. Little Man sat by a window, his hands folded, patiently waiting for Miss Crocker to speak.

Mary Lou nudged me. "That's my seat, Cassie Logan."

"Mary Lou Wellever," Miss Crocker called primly, "have a seat."

"Yes, ma'am," said Mary Lou, eyeing me with a look of pure hate before turning away.

Miss Crocker walked stiffly to her desk, which was set on a tiny platform and piled high with bulky objects covered by a tarpaulin. She rapped the desk with a ruler, although the room was perfectly still, and said, "Welcome, children, to Great Faith Elementary

School." Turning slightly so that she stared squarely at the left side of the room, she continued, "To all of you fourth graders, it's good to have you in my class. I'll be expecting many good and wonderful things from you." Then addressing the right side of the room, she said, "And to all our little first grade friends only today starting on the road to knowledge and education, may your tiny feet find the pathways of learning steady and forever before you."

Already bored, I stretched my right arm on the desk and rested my head in my upraised hand.

Miss Crocker smiled mechanically, then rapped on her desk again. "Now, little ones," she said, still talking to the first grade, "your teacher, Miss Davis, has been held up in Jackson for a few days so I'll have the pleasure of sprinkling your little minds with the first rays of knowledge." She beamed down upon them as if she expected to be applauded for this bit of news, then with a swoop of her large eyes to include the fourth graders, she went on.

"Now since there's only one of me, we shall have to sacrifice for the next few days. We shall work, work, work, but we shall have to work like little Christian boys and girls and share, share, share. Now are we willing to do that?"

"YES'M, MIZ CROCKER," the children chorused.

But I remained silent. I never did approve of group responses. Adjusting my head in my hand, I sighed heavily, my mind on the burning of the Berrys.

"Cassie Logan?"

I looked up, startled.

"Cassie Logan!"

"Yes, ma'am?" I jumped up quickly to face Miss Crocker.

"Aren't you willing to work and share?"

"Yes'm."

"Then say so!"

"Yes'm," I murmured, sliding back into my seat as Mary Lou, Gracey, and Alma giggled. Here it was only five minutes into the new school year and already I was in trouble.

By ten o'clock, Miss Crocker had rearranged our seating and written our names on her seating chart. I was still sitting beside Gracey and Alma but we had been moved from the third to the first row in front of a small potbellied stove. Although being eyeball to eyeball with Miss Crocker was nothing to look forward to, the prospect of being warm once the cold weather set in was nothing to be sneezed at either, so I resolved to make the best of my rather dubious position.

Now Miss Crocker made a startling announcement: This year we would all have books.

Everyone gasped, for most of the students had never handled a book at all besides the family Bible. I admit that even I was somewhat excited. Although Mama had several books, I had never had one of my very own.

"Now we're very fortunate to get these readers," Miss Crocker explained while we eagerly awaited the unveiling. "The county superintendent of schools himself brought these books down here for our use and we must take extra-good care of them." She moved toward her desk. "So let's all promise that we'll take the best care possible of these new books." She stared down, expecting our response. "All right, all together, let's repeat, 'We promise to take good care of our new books.'" She looked sharply at me as she spoke.

"WE PROMISE TO TAKE GOOD CARE OF OUR NEW BOOKS!"

"Fine," Miss Crocker beamed, then proudly threw back the tarpaulin.

Sitting so close to the desk, I could see that the covers of the books, a motley red, were badly worn and that the gray edges of the pages had been marred by pencils, crayons, and ink. My anticipation at having my own book ebbed to a sinking disappointment. But Miss Crocker continued to beam as she called each fourth grader to her desk and, recording a number in her roll book, handed him or her a book.

As I returned from my trip to her desk, I noticed the first graders anxiously watching the disappearing pile. Miss Crocker must have noticed them too, for as I sat down she said, "Don't worry, little ones, there are plenty of readers for you too. See there on Miss Davis's desk." Wide eyes turned to the covered teacher's platform directly in front of them and an audible sigh of relief swelled in the room.

I glanced across at Little Man, his face lit in eager excitement. I knew that he could not see the soiled covers or the marred pages from where he sat, and even though his penchant for cleanliness was often annoying, I did not like to think of his disappointment when he saw the books as they really were. But there was nothing that I could do about it, so I opened my book to its center and began browsing through the spotted pages. Girls with blond braids and boys with blue eyes stared up at me. I found a story about a boy and his dog lost in a cave and began reading while Miss Crocker's voice droned on monotonously.

Suddenly I grew conscious of a break in that monotonous tone and I looked up. Miss Crocker was sitting at Miss Davis's desk with the first-grade books stacked before her, staring fiercely down at Little Man, who was pushing a book back upon the desk.

"What's that you said, Clayton Chester Logan?" she asked.

The room became gravely silent. Everyone knew that Little Man was in big trouble for no one, but no one, ever called Little Man "Clayton Chester" unless she or he meant serious business.

Little Man knew this too. His lips parted slightly as he took his hands from the book. He quivered, but he did not take his eyes from Miss Crocker. "I—I said may I have another book please, ma'am," he squeaked. "That one's dirty."

"Dirty!" Miss Crocker echoed, appalled by such temerity. She stood up, gazing down upon Little Man like a bony giant, but Little Man raised his head and continued to look into her eyes. "Dirty! And just who do you think you are, Clayton Chester! Here the county is giving us these wonderful books during these hard times and you're going to stand there and tell me that the book's too dirty? Now you take that book or get nothing at all!"

Little Man lowered his eyes and said nothing as he stared at the book. For several moments he stood there, his face barely visible above the desk, then he turned and looked at the few remaining books and, seeming to realize that they were as badly soiled as the one Miss Crocker had given him, he looked across the room at me. I nodded and Little Man, glancing up again at Miss Crocker, slid the book from the edge of the desk, and with his back straight and his head up returned to his seat.

Miss Crocker sat down again. "Some people around here seem to be giving themselves airs. I'll tolerate no more of that," she scowled. "Sharon Lake, come get your book."

I watched Little Man as he scooted into his seat beside two other little boys. He sat for a while with a stony face looking out the window; then, evidently accepting the fact that the book in front of him was the best that he could expect, he turned and opened it. But as he stared at the book's inside cover, his face clouded, changing from sulky acceptance to puzzlement. His brows furrowed.

Then his eyes grew wide, and suddenly he sucked in his breath and sprang from his chair like a wounded animal, flinging the book onto the floor and stomping madly upon it.

Miss Crocker rushed to Little Man and grabbed him up in powerful hands. She shook him vigorously, then set him on the floor again. "Now, just what's gotten into you, Clayton Chester?"

But Little Man said nothing. He just stood staring down at the open book, shivering with indignant anger.

"Pick it up," she ordered.

"No!" defied Little Man.

"No? I'll give you ten seconds to pick up that book, boy, or I'm going to get my switch."

Little Man bit his lower lip, and I knew that he was not going to pick up the book. Rapidly, I turned to the inside cover of my own book and saw immediately what had made Little Man so furious. Stamped on the inside cover was a chart which read:

PROPERTY OF THE BOARD OF EDUCATION
Spokane County, Mississippi
September, 1922

CHRONOLOGICAL ISSUANCE	DATE OF ISSUANCE	CONDITION OF BOOK	RACE OF STUDENT
1	*September 1922*	*New*	*White*
2	*September 1923*	*Excellent*	*White*
3	*September 1924*	*Excellent*	*White*
4	*September 1925*	*Very Good*	*White*
5	*September 1926*	*Good*	*White*
6	*September 1927*	*Good*	*White*
7	*September 1928*	*Average*	*White*
8	*September 1929*	*Average*	*White*
9	*September 1930*	*Average*	*White*
10	*September 1931*	*Poor*	*White*
11	*September 1932*	*Poor*	*White*
12	*September 1933*	*Very Poor*	*nigra*
13			

The blank lines continued down to line 20 and I knew that they had all been reserved for black students. A knot of anger swelled in my throat and held there. But as Miss Crocker directed Little Man to bend over the "whipping" chair, I put aside my anger and jumped up.

"Miz Crocker, don't, please!" I cried. Miss Crocker's dark eyes warned me not to say another word. "I know why he done it!"

"You want part of this switch, Cassie?"

"No'm," I said hastily. "I just wanna tell you how come Little Man done what he done."

"Sit down!" she ordered as I hurried toward her with the open book in my hand.

Holding the book up to her, I said, "See, Miz Crocker, see what it says. They give us these ole books when they didn't want 'em no more."

She regarded me impatiently, but did not look at the book. "Now how could he know what it says? He can't read."

"Yes'm, he can. He been reading since he was four. He can't read all them big words, but he can read them columns. See what's in the last row. Please look, Miz Crocker."

This time Miss Crocker did look, but her face did not change. Then, holding up her head, she gazed unblinkingly down at me.

"S-see what they called us," I said, afraid she had not seen.

"That's what you are," she said coldly. "Now go sit down."

I shook my head, realizing now that Miss Crocker did not even know what I was talking about. She had looked at the page and had understood nothing.

"I said sit down, Cassie!"

I started slowly toward my desk, but as the hickory stick sliced the tense air, I turned back around. "Miz Crocker," I said, "I don't want my book neither."

The switch landed hard upon Little Man's upturned bottom. Miss Crocker looked questioningly at me as I reached up to her desk and placed the book upon it. Then she swung the switch five more times and, discovering that Little Man had no intention of crying, ordered him up.

"All right, Cassie," she sighed, turning to me, "come on and get yours."

By the end of the school day I had decided that I would tell Mama everything before Miss Crocker had a chance to do so. From nine years of trial and error, I had learned that punishment was always less severe when I poured out the whole truth to Mama on my own before she had heard anything from anyone else. I knew that Miss Crocker had not spoken to Mama during the lunch period, for she had spent the whole hour in the classroom preparing for the afternoon session.

As soon as class was dismissed I sped from the room, weaving a path through throngs of students happy to be free. But before I could reach the seventh-grade-class building, I had the misfortune to collide with Mary Lou's father. Mr. Wellever looked down on me with surprise that I would actually bump into him, then proceeded to lecture me on the virtues of watching where one was going. Meanwhile Miss Crocker briskly crossed the lawn to Mama's class building. By the time I escaped Mr. Wellever, she had already disappeared into the darkness of the hallway.

Mama's classroom was in the back. I crept silently along the quiet hall and peeped cautiously into the open doorway. Mama, pushing a strand of her long, crinkly hair back into the chignon at the base of her slender neck, was seated at her desk watching Miss Crocker thrust a book before her. "Just look at that, Mary," Miss Crocker said, thumping the book twice with her forefinger. "A perfectly good book ruined. Look at that broken binding and those foot marks all over it."

Mama did not speak as she studied the book.

"And here's the one Cassie wouldn't take," she said, placing a second book on Mama's desk with an outraged slam. "At least she didn't have a tantrum and stomp all over hers. I tell you, Mary, I just don't know what got into those children today. I always knew Cassie was rather high-strung, but Little Man! He's always such a perfect little gentleman."

Mama glanced at the book I had rejected and opened the front cover so that the offensive pages of both books faced her. "You say Cassie said it was because of this front page that she and Little Man didn't want the books?" Mama asked quietly.

"Yes, ain't that something?" Miss Crocker said, forgetting her teacher-training-school diction in her indignation. "The very idea! That's on all the books, and why they got so upset about it I'll never know."

"You punish them?" asked Mama, glancing up at Miss Crocker.

"Well, I certainly did! Whipped both of them good with my hickory stick. Wouldn't you have?" When Mama did not reply, she added defensively, "I had a perfect right to."

"Of course you did, Daisy," Mama said, turning back to the books again. "They disobeyed you." But her tone was so quiet and noncommittal that I knew Miss Crocker was not satisfied with her reaction.

"Well, I thought you would've wanted to know, Mary, in case you wanted to give them a piece of your mind also."

Mama smiled up at Miss Crocker and said rather absently, "Yes, of course, Daisy. Thank you." Then she opened her desk drawer and pulled out some paper, a pair of scissors, and a small brown bottle.

Miss Crocker, dismayed by Mama's seeming unconcern for the seriousness of the matter, thrust her shoulders back and began moving away from the desk. "You understand that if they don't have those books to study from, I'll have to fail them in both reading and composition, since I plan to base all my lessons around—" She stopped abruptly and stared in amazement at Mama. "Mary, what in the world are you doing?"

Mama did not answer. She had trimmed the paper to the size of the books and was now dipping a gray-looking glue from the brown bottle onto the inside cover of one of the books. Then she took the paper and placed it over the glue.

"Mary Logan, do you know what you're doing? That book belongs to the county. If somebody from the superintendent's office ever comes down here and sees that book, you'll be in real trouble."

Mama laughed and picked up the other book. "In the first place no one cares enough to come down here, and in the second place if anyone should come, maybe he could see all the things we need—current books for all of our subjects, not just somebody's old throwaways, desks, paper, blackboards, erasers, maps, chalk . . ." Her voice trailed off as she glued the second book.

"Biting the hand that feeds you. That's what you're doing, Mary Logan, biting the hand that feeds you."

Again, Mama laughed. "If that's the case, Daisy, I don't think I need that little bit of food." With the second book finished, she stared at a small pile of seventh-grade books on her desk.

"Well, I just think you're spoiling those children, Mary. They've got to learn how things are sometime."

"Maybe so," said Mama, "but that doesn't mean they have to accept them . . . and maybe we don't either."

Miss Crocker gazed suspiciously at Mama. Although Mama had been a teacher at Great Faith for fourteen years, ever since she had graduated from the Crandon Teacher Training School at nineteen, she was still considered by many of the other teachers as a disrupting maverick. Her ideas were always a bit too radical and her statements a bit too pointed. The fact that she had not grown up in Spokane County but in the Delta made her even more suspect, and the more traditional thinkers like Miss Crocker were wary of her. "Well, if anyone ever does come from the county and sees Cassie's and Little Man's books messed up like that," she said, "I certainly won't accept the responsibility for them."

"It will be easy enough for anyone to see whose responsibility it is, Daisy, by opening any seventh-grade book. Because tomorrow I'm going to 'mess them up' too."

Miss Crocker, finding nothing else to say, turned imperiously and headed for the door. I dashed across the hall and awaited her exit, then crept back.

Mama remained at her desk, sitting very still. For a long time she did not move. When she did, she picked up one of the seventh-grade books and began to glue again. I wanted to go and help her, but something warned me that now was not the time to make my presence known, and I left.

I would wait until the evening to talk to her; there was no rush now. She understood.

FROM

Child Ellen

Frank Trippett

Clifton Sharpe (Cliff) Worth:

As soon as he heard footsteps ascending the creaky stairs within four minutes after he himself had gotten not to work but merely to his office, he knew who it had to be, because, on arriving and parking on the main street down below, he had glimpsed who it had to be sitting with his legs propped up on his desk like two blunt cannon in the window of the *Mirror* office across the street, and knew that he himself of course had been glimpsed by who it had to be, and so was so little surprised when the stocky young man with the hairless globe-like head and the collarless patterned shirt loomed in and barged eagerly through his private doorway, that he neither had to ask nor hear what T. C. Horris wanted but instead silently gestured him into the chair opposite and began talking even as he poured him a cup from the quart thermos of coffee that he had brought in with him under his arm.

He said:

Broadly, it was like escaping from time, like stumbling into some kind of proceeding that might just possibly have occurred accidentally somewhere back before the invention of law. Possibly the very kind of proceeding that might have so impacted on the minds of men as to convince them suddenly and utterly of the absolute necessity either to formulate that mystical fiction we call jurisprudence or else abandon all hope of ever arriving at an understanding or agreement as to who should do the talking, and who should do the listening, and hence all hope of ever resolving any conflict of any nature whatsoever by any means other than incantation or combat.

In short, it seemed, at the outset, like a proceeding without procedure, with those who had called on me as counsel all but physically assaulting the magistrate from one side, while the honorable adversaries of my dear clients assaulted him from the other, not physically but with such a clamor that, had I been he, I would have jailed the lot on the spot with strong recommendations against any subsequent show of mercy or amnesty.

Maybe the closest thing to it I have ever been privileged to witness was the trial and conviction, by forcible exile, of a West African witch doctor who had been accused by his tribe of being a fraud, and who, when I last saw him, was sprinting into the jungle hotly pursued by the jury of tribesmen who, by the very act of the defendant's flight, had become his peers. There were two or three hundred of them in pursuit, flinging spears and knives and axes and stones at the defendant, along with samples of a certain kind of nut that grows to the size of a baseball. Their theory of law was that if he were indeed a witch doctor he would by his powers emerge from the jungle unscathed, and, if not, would be perhaps overwhelmingly tempted not to emerge at all, in which case he might just possibly enjoy life to a ripe old age somewhere else and the tribe, meanwhile, could see to the selection of a dependable witch doctor. Upon close examination, their theory turns out to be exquisitely sound and literally pregnant with the fine juices of both justice and mercy, and possibly even amnesty, which is the most merciful juice of all.

At the moment I got there, to thc jail, the receiving room where the deputies had already more or less collapsed in hysteria, it seemed that the magistrate, the honorable one-eyed Charlie d'Iberia, had fallen into the role of witch doctor, with my clients and their adversaries more or less taking the part of the tribesmen, and certainly with none of them showing an inordinate respect for the dignity of a half-blind judge who had just torn himself away from his postprandial cups to answer a call to duty. The whole pack of them, Matt and Mark on one side, and Henry, too, and Jim and Jack Burcell on the other, looked like they had just come in from a street riot that had not quite ended yet. All told, they were as bloody and disheveled looking a bunch as I have seen since a certain untoward event in Singapore. Bruises. Black eyes. Cuts. Splits. Contusions. Lumps. Shredded shirts. You know, the kind of cosmetic effect you can expect when you apply your makeup with tire irons, brass knuckles, pistol barrels, and even plain unvarnished fists and feet. They looked awful, horrible even, though our beloved medical examiner Amos McCall had come in and poured iodine all over them and patched gauze here and there, as well as temporarily binding up Henry's right hand, which, I was a long time learning, he evidently broke in two or three places in exchange for a fascinating new profile that he achieved in the hitherto unblemished nose of everybody's favorite roughneck, Jack Burcell.

I was personally happy to see that Amos was still hanging around when I got there, since my first thought was that his services might be further needed, and this in fact seemed an eventuality that he was prepping for by periodically pouring himself little drinks out of a paperbagged pint into a paper cup that kept dripping down his shirt front. Which Amos kept on doing, and the cup too, even though His Honor, good old Charlie d'Iberia, would look over from time to time, no doubt more out of envy than for the sake of decorum, and caution that there would be no drinking tolerated in this courtroom. To which Amos countered each time by raising the drippy paper cup in a toast and saying: "This is not a courtroom, Your Honor."

Which, after the third or fourth time, prompted His Honor Charlie to personally march all of us out of the receiving office of the jailhouse and across the street and into a courtroom, where he didn't assume the bench but, instead, sat at the counsel's table along with everybody else. Amos McCall came along, too, with his brown bag and cup, and now when His Honor Charlie cautioned him that no drinking would be tolerated, Amos raised up his drippy cup and said, "It's a prescription drug, your honor. I prescribed it myself."

Meanwhile, Sonny Grindell had come in wearing a brand new plaid vest to bolster the case of his clients, the Burcell boys, but was having as little luck in quieting them down as I was with mine, my clients, or at least Matt and Mark, since the Rust boy didn't need quieting down, as he evidently was suffering an anomalous case of good manners. But to shorten it all down, some crude semblance of order finally obtained after I finally managed to catch His Honor Charlie's bloodshot eye and ear and, with as much volume as I could manage, employed a little known defense technique by moving that the court, instantum, find everyone present including counsel guilty of contempt and sentence us all to the county jail until sunrise the following day or until total silence should prevail among us, whichever might come first. At the word "motion," however, Sonny Grindell stopped staring down at his new plaid vest and jumped to his feet to object, and did this in such a magnificent voice that it produced just sufficient silence to permit His Honor Charlie d'Iberia to observe, with admirable clarity, that he wasn't about to entertain any objection simply because he wasn't there to entertain any motion that might be objected to, and in fact was not conducting a session of court nor even sitting as a court but was present only as the magistrate required by State Statute 109.11 to participate at the issuance of any warrants charging a capital felony.

Evidently this was the first moment during which Sonny Grindell quite realized that his clients were in danger of the electric chair, and this brought him once again to his feet, with his coat held apart and his vest well displayed, saying: "Capital? What capital offense?"

"Kidnapping, to name just one," said His Honor Charlie, "and conspiracy to commit murder, to name another. But sit down Mr. Vest—uh, Mr. Grindell—sit down and shut up and let's start at the be-goddam-ginning, and maybe we will be lucky enough to discover several others as we go along, and maybe I will even find out what happened along with all the instruction in law that the complainants and putative defendants have variously been giving me."

And, sure enough, to my astonishment, but not necessarily to my relief, they did—start at the be-goddam-ginning, that is. Up to now, all His Honor Charlie had heard was that long and ever-growing list of charges that the Burcell boys wanted to place against my clients, and those ever-more-imaginative charges that my clients, having had the disadvantage of past association with a lawyer, wanted to prosecute against them. As to what had happened to give rise to all the fury and wounds and recriminations, His Honor Charlie d'Iberia had even less of an idea than I, and I had none at all that was worthy of the name idea, since, on the phone, all Matt had told me that had now been substantially verified was, "Cliff, we're down at the goddam jail with the goddam Burcells, and they're trying to charge us with attempted homicide, et cetera et cetera." But once His Honor Charlie got them started at the be-goddam-ginning, at least some rudimentary outline of the prior and moving events began to emerge.

"Let me hear one side at a time," His Honor Charlie said, and of course, at that, Matt and Mark and Jim and Jack Burcell all began yelling again, but not with their prior force and velocity, and they soon fell silent after His Honor Charlie stopped up his ears with his two index fingers, which, at this dramatic show of respect—the silence—he removed, and then flipped an imaginary coin and pointed toward my clients.

"Let's hear your account of what happened," His Honor Charlie said, and, when Matt and Mark both started talking at once, left it to me to mediate between them and select a spokesman, which I did by applying the seniority rule and designating Matt, who is of course the elder by some very few minutes.

Whereafter we were all ennobled by an account wherein it appeared that Matt and Mark Worth were present at these proceedings first and foremost, and indeed only, as civic-minded defenders of law and order, a role that Matt was enabled the better to intimate by the fact that nobody was under oath, nor was to be put under oath. His Honor Charlie proclaimed, until he had got the stories and until he had decided whether anybody or everybody was entitled to swear out warrants certifying to all the felonies mentioned so far.

Naturally, Matt didn't begin quite at the beginning. He began by describing how he and his brother had merely been cruising about in their decapitated limousine before supper, going no place in particular, just passing the time, when they had driven down the street where their friend Henry Rust happens to live, and had seen parked thereon two suspicious looking characters sitting in a car with overload springs and a pair of oversized dice hanging from the mirror, two characters who on closer inspection chanced to be Jim and Jack Burcell. Well, having decided that for the good of the community and the safety of the neighborhood they should inspect the situation more closely, they had circled a block and come back the other way down said street, and had got back to it just in time to see the Burcell car pull forward toward some approaching citizen who, as it turned out, was their friend Henry Rust. And then, to their astonishment, they saw the Burcell car stop alongside Henry Rust, and saw Jack Burcell get out and, as it appeared to them, force their friend to get in the car, which then drove off.

Well, naturally, as Matt told it, they thought they had eyewitnessed a possible kidnapping, a capital felony if there ever was one, and a crime any citizen is obligated to take note of and act on in some reasonable way. And so, to investigate further, they had tailed the Burcell car, keeping it under surveillance as it turned off of Henry's street and onto the main drag, bearing east, and following it hence out the highway east of town, their suspicions growing all the while, to crystallize when they observed the Burcell car turn left onto a dirt road that everybody who got around at all knew was seldom used by traffic engaged in normal law-abiding business. All their suspicions were enhanced, of course, by the fact that the Burcells had Henry Rust sitting between them on the front seat at a time when the rear seat of the car would have been more comfortable for him as well as more convenient for the driver and his kindred companion.

Thus my clients decided that the moment had come for them to do their duty and act on their suspicions in a reasonable way, and so they gunned their decapitated limousine and drove up alongside said Burcell vehicle and, with Matt at the wheel and Mark doing the calling out, had ordered Jack Burcell, operator of the object car, to stop forthwith. It seems that said Jack Burcell answered this reasonable request not with compliance but with some common abusive oath, and it was at that moment that my clients invoked the whole body of the law in the behalf of their mission and decency and forthwith informed Mr. Burcell that he was under arrest.

They were executing, you see, a citizen's arrest, evidently the first recorded in the legal history of the county, according to His Honor Charlie, whose grasp of legal history abides with him even amidst certain other lapses. Jack and Jim Burcell, however, did not gracefully surrender at once, and in fact kept driving onward down the dirt road, all the while addressing my clients in provocative, abusive, and even threatening language, to their dismay.

At last, when it seemed that Jack Burcell, as well as talking bad, was leaning forward as though to retrieve from its holster the deadly weapon everybody knew was usually carried in his car, Matt and Mark were obliged to make one of those split-second decisions that are forced on citizen arresters, evidently, as well as conventional officers of the law. Matt swerved in such a way as to encourage the Burcell vehicle to come to a halt, and, in fact, it came to a halt with its front wheels in the shallow ditch that runs alongside that particular road. My clients, of course, immediately leaped out to make the arrest, but were confronted with totally uncooperative suspects as well as what they felt they reasonably construed as grave danger.

Just as they leaped from the limousine, in fact, a revolver held in Jack Burcell's hand came sticking out the window of his car, and in fact it was discharged, but fortunately only after Henry Rust, from his place in the front seat, had yanked Jack Burcell from behind, causing the shot to go askew.

"And then," as Matt put it, "the trouble started, Your Honor."

The young, of course, have no sense whatever of beginnings. Even today, Matt likely would resist the notion that the trouble started not then, nor when they saw the Burcell boys, nor when the Burcell boys took Henry Rust into their car, nor even in this epoch, and not even with the birth of the principals in the case, but in some no-time back there when some mysterious nothing on earth was caused for unknown reasons to begin tending toward the occurrence of human life on this peculiar planet.

Of course, the trouble Matt was talking about was that which evolved as the pistol's owner followed the pistol out of the car, and as his brother Jim Burcell, exiting from the other side, leaped over the hood of their car with a tire iron that he planted on Mark's cheekbone. Obviously, the story here must be fragmented, but, as Matt pieced it together, it seems that while Mark was dealing with Jim Burcell, Matt and Henry had their hands full with Jack. That is, while the tire iron befell Mark, Jack whipped his pistol back against Henry's face, after which Matt, with a providentially accurate punt kicked the pistol out of Jack's hand.

Jack's hand had no sooner lost the pistol, which went skeetering down the road, than it dipped into his coat pocket and reappeared dressed with metal knuckles, with which he began chopping into Matt's face, even as Henry, from behind, tried to restrain him with a stranglehold. Which didn't hold, since, as Matt and Mark now admit, and Henry too, the Burcell boys are not putting up a false front when they travel on their reputation for strength and meanness.

For awhile, in fact, Jack, with the help of the knucks, was better than holding his own against Matt and Henry. And, meanwhile, Mark was being spun around like a ballet dancer grasping onto the end of the tire iron that Jim Burcell was of course trying to shake him loose from so as to put it back into productive use. Jim did shake him loose, unfortunately for Mark, and got in two fast clouts on the collarbone and skull. But this, as Matt put it, caused Mark to lose his temper. Yes, to lose his temper so thoroughly that he kicked Jim Burcell where it hurts real bad, which kick, in this instance, caused Jim Burcell to lose all interest in the tire iron, which he dropped, and which Mark deftly retrieved and used to eliminate the possibility of suffering further harm at the hands of this adversary. He knocked him unconscious, in short, and evidently at almost the same time that Matt had leaped down the road and picked up the pistol, which, as chance had it, was at precisely the same moment that Henry connected with a lucky haymaker that demolished Jack Burcell's nose, and presumably his will to resist arrest, as well as Henry's own guitar-picking right hand.

And so it came to pass that, while peace-loving folk everywhere were either contemplating or enjoying or finishing up supper, two deputy sheriffs, both of them quite likely on the private payroll of the Burcell boys, looked up from their domino game in the receiving room of the jail and saw Jim and Jack Burcell marched in at the point of their own gun, it held by the hand of my client Matt Worth, with Mark following close at hand holding a tire iron, and Henry holding the knuckles, all of which items they hoped and intended to introduce as evidence upon the trial of these defendants, whom they announced they had apprehended as citizens acting under State Statute 219.87 as amended in 1891. And against whom, they informed the deputies, they were lodging charges of kidnapping, felonious assault, attempted homicide, disorderly conduct, illegal use of firearms, threatening and abusive language, et cetera et cetera et cetera, and of course, resisting arrest.

I don't have to describe for you the hysterical dilemma of the deputies faced by a demand that they book and incarcerate their moonlight employers, nor the reaction of Matt and Mark when they heard the Burcell boys begin to describe *themselves* as the actual complainants, and when they saw the deputies actually listening, paying attention, with respect, as Jack and Jim began charging *them* with kidnapping, attempted homicide, et cetera et cetera. Which is, of course, where I came in, or where I was brought in by their phone call.

So now, after Matt had done, His Honor Charlie listened to the Burcell side of the story, as told by Jack, according to whose account they had not forced Henry Rust to get in their car, they had only *asked* him to go with them to talk something over, he being an old family friend. Said they were only driving him out to their country house which is in fact just down that country road. Said they had not even got around to talking in the car when, lo and behold, these two maniac kids in the decapitated limousine roared up beside them and told them to get the hell over and turn Henry loose. Said, actually, they would have cheerfully turned Henry loose, if that had been the point, but that the point was, nobody on earth except an officer of the law had any right to drive up alongside them and order them to do a goddam thing. And said naturally they hadn't stopped, and when the Worth kids swerved into them, naturally they had come out fighting. Said, as for the gun, well, he wouldn't have fired it at all if their friend Henry hadn't panicked behind him and, for some reason, shook him up, because he had only intended to use the gun to scare these kids and keep them from trespassing on their rights.

When he had done, His Honor Charlie d'Iberia thought a second or two and then seemed to catch the Burcells off guard. His Honor said, "What'd you want to talk to him about?"

And Jack Burcell said, "Talk to him about? What's that got to do with it?"

And His Honor said, "What'd you want to talk to him about?"

And Jack said, "That's private business, judge."

And His Honor said, "Not any more. What did you want to talk to Henry Rust about?"

Well, the Burcells started to squirm, and Sonny Grindell, with his thumbs in his plaid vest, started to say something, but His Honor Charlie raised a brusque hand to silent him and said, "It's not a trial, Mr. Grindell." And then he turned to Henry, who was sitting there beside me, and said, "Henry, what did they want to talk to you about?"

And Henry said, "Well, all they, or rather Jack, said to me was, 'Carol's talked to us, and you and me's got some talking to do.'"

And His Honor said, "Would that be Carol Burcell?"

And Henry said, "Yes, sir."

And His Honor said, "Did you know what they meant?"

And Henry said, "I didn't know what they had in mind."

And His Honor said, "No, of course not. Did they force you to get in the car?"

And Henry said, "Well, not exactly, Jack just said, 'Get in the goddam car.'"

And His Honor said, "And you got in."

And Henry said, "Yes, sir, I got in."

And His Honor said, "I see." And his bloodshot eye confirmed that he did. And then he turned to the Burcells again and said,

"Okay, boys, let's hear about the talking you wanted to do with this young man."

And Jack Burcell said, "Your Honor, we can't talk about that, it was strictly a private matter." They were both squirming good now, with Jim sitting there picking at some shred of his blood-stained shirt, doing that while His Honor Charlie *slowly* got up from his seat at the center of the table, and told everybody to sit still, and went out, and down the hall, and soon came back, and said sit still a little longer, which we all did for about fifteen minutes during which we didn't know what was up.

We didn't have the slightest hint until the deputy ushered her in the door. Actually, I saw her brothers' faces before I saw her, and after seeing them knew that when I turned around I was going to see her, and did. The deputy brought her down the aisle and up to the table facing Charlie d'Iberia, and she stood there trembling, more or less aghast at the sight of her brothers and the others, and soon not looking at anybody at all but keeping her eyes fixed down on the table top while Charlie explained to her, talking very softly, that at the moment he was not holding a trial, but was only trying to find out one thing, and that was what her brothers had wanted to talk to Henry Rust about, and that her brothers wouldn't say, and that it would be unfair to ask Henry Rust to guess, and that she didn't have to say anything at all, but that her name had been brought up in connection with it, and so, if she could and would enlighten him, he would be much obliged and maybe could then proceed to resolve this whole complicated mess if not to everybody's satisfaction at least his own. He let her stand silent and shaking for a long time and then merely spoke her name very softly—"Carol?"—and then waited again, and pretty soon she spoke up in a barely audible voice.

She said, "Well, I told them I was in trouble, and I guess they wanted to talk to him about that."

And Charlie said, "You mean pregnant."

And she said, "That's what I told them."

And Charlie said, "And you told them it was Henry."

And she said, "Well, they knew we used to go together."

And Charlie said, "Used to."

And she said, "We don't any more."

And Charlie said, "Did you tell Henry?"

And she said, "Henry?"

And Charlie said, "Did you tell him you were in trouble?"

And she said, "No, sir."

And Charlie said, "You didn't tell Henry? You told your brothers?"

And she said, "Yes, sir."

And Charlie said, "If he was the one, why didn't you tell Henry?"

And she said, "I don't know, sir."

Well, by now the Burcell boys were studying their sister as though she were the defendant and they part of the prosecution team, silently, of course, because by now everybody had fallen absolutely quiet, Henry inscrutably quiet, sitting there beside me at the end of the table, his eyes glancing from her, to his hands, to Charlie d'Iberia, who suddenly turned our way and spoke.

Charlie said, "Henry, you have anything to say?"

And Henry peered at Charlie for a couple of seconds and then looked directly toward her who was still standing there facing Charlie, still standing and no doubt still owning the same devastating shape she's owned for the last couple of years but at the moment looking strangely crumpled or deflated or something, as you can imagine. And it was not His Honor but to her that he spoke, Henry, quietly and with some immense calm and certainty and earnestness that surely caught me by surprise and obviously everybody else, too, including her.

He said, "Carol, if you're pregnant I'll marry you."

Well, at that, she looked not merely astonished but shocked, and the Burcell boys commenced to muttering betwixt themselves as though they were thinking of inviting *her* to go for a talk on some country road, and Matt and Mark at first gaped and then took on that peculiar look to suggest that they actually knew what was going on, and Charlie d'Iberia suddenly squinted his thick little eyebrows together and peered with that bloodshot eye at Henry as either somebody who had just offered him a thousand dollars tax free or maybe had just confessed to some hitherto unsolved atrocity, staring at him, in other words, with the profoundest perplexity and incredulousness until he finally thought of what was on his mind.

And then His Honor Charlie said, "You *mean* that, son?"

And Henry said, "Sure, I mean it."

Well, maybe it was Henry's own cool, calm, perfectly serene and certain tone of voice that all of a sudden crystallized what His Honor had probably already begun thinking, as some of the rest of us certainly had after observing Carol and taking note of her wordings. In any event, His Honor now looks not at Carol, whose face is the picture of arrested consternation and regret, but past her out among the benches where Amos McCall is still sitting, there with his prescription drug dripping out of the paper cup that he had stuck over the one that was previously dripping.

And Charlie says, now very briskly and formally, "Dr. McCall, how quickly can you do an examination on this young woman?"

And Amos, startled to attention, says, "Examination?"

And all but simultaneously the girl is shouting out, "I'm not going to take a damn examination!"

And all of a sudden her words are hanging there in the room as clear and distinct as a single cloud in a summer sky. And His Honor Charlie just lets them hang there for what seemed a long time to me and must have seemed an eternity to Carol Burcell. Charlie just sat gazing at her now, not like a magistrate at all, but like a loving uncle perhaps, disappointed in a favorite niece, just sat watching her sympathetically and giving her time to discover for herself the meaning of what she had just said, and the implication of it in the light of what Henry had just said. We all sat watching now in utter stillness, until frankly even I felt an impulse to go take her in my arms, and not out of resurgent lechery but out of a feeling kin to that which continued to show on the face of old Charlie d'Iberia. Charlie waited until she had actually begun to sob, had let the tears come running, and still waited, and then just as she began to sob, just as what was inside her demanded to come out more than she could any longer demand that it stay in, until she was sobbing and then sagging into that immemorial slumped posture of regret wherein every human being somehow resembles a question mark, only then did he speak up in the quietest and kindliest possible voice.

Charlie said, "Carol, are you—"

But she didn't let him finish. She said, "I thought I was yesterday, but—No, sir, I'm not." And then she started sobbing and shouting at once. She said, "But I thought I was! I thought I was! I swear I thought I was."

And then all of a sudden her whole upper half fell forward on the table, with her arms in her face, and Charlie pointed a finger at

Jack Burcell and said, "Take your sister to a seat and then on home after we finish up, and try to be understanding, you hear me? She's hurtin' enough. In fact, everybody here is hurtin' enough for one day." And while Jack Burcell was coming over and getting her, His Honor Charlie more or less wrapped it up, with a decision that won't but ought to go down in the history not of jurisprudence, which it wasn't, but of humaneness and common sense, which it indubitably was.

He said, "Now, having heard the complaints and preliminary reports in the cases variously of Matt Worth and Mark Worth and Henry Rust and Jim Burcell and Jack Burcell, it is the decision of the magistrate that if *any single one* of the multitudinous charges involved is to be pressed, then all such charges and countercharges will be certified for grand jury action and all defendants incarcerated and held without bail pending possible indictment, and in the event of indictment, pending trial and final disposition. Now is the appropriate time for either any complainant or counsel for same to let it be known whether any single charge is to be pressed."

Well, Sonny Grindell and I both vigorously shook our heads in the negative at once, and then everybody tensed as though to rise, but were signaled to sit fast for one more moment by His Honor, who had only a few more words to say.

Charlie said, "So be it, then, and let all preliminary accusations be expunged from the records, let the matter be forgotten, and let peace and order and goodwill be resumed. And now the court requests that Dr. Amos McCall repair with him to chambers for an examination of the evidence in the case of the prescription drug."

More coffee, son?

FROM

Jubilee

MARGARET WALKER

> When Israel was in Egypt's land—
> Let my people go.
> Oppressed so hard they could not stand—
> Let my people go.

"VYRY, WAKE UP CHILD, wake up so's we can make haste and git along."

Mammy Sukey shook the sleeping child and she stirred in her sleep.

"Wake up, wake up! Sun's up, and us got a far ways to travel. Git up, now, git up and make haste, I says."

Vyry was seven, and the old crone, Mammy Sukey, was all the mother she had ever known or could remember. Today was special. When Vyry remembered, she jumped up from her pallet, rubbing her eyes with her fists and nudging her legs and feet together.

"Today I'm going to the Big House to stay!" she thought to herself.

"What you gone say when you sees Big Missy?" and Mammy Sukey's words shook her out of her reverie. Vyry bowed herself and crossed her legs in an elaborate curtsey, and with a solemn face and soft voice said, "I'm gone say, 'Morning to yall, Missy.' "

"What you gone say to Marster?"

"Morning to yall, Marster."

"And the young Missy Lillyum?"

"Morning, Missy!"

"And young Marster John?"

"Morning, Marster!"

After the slow and serious rehearsal Mammy Sukey nodded approval.

"That's good. That's good. That's just like I showed you. Mind your manners good, and be real nice and polite. You a big gal now, but you ain't gone be no field hand and no yard nigger. You is gone wait on Quality and you got to act like Quality. Go to now—eat your vittles."

While she talked she fixed their breakfast, pulling out of a flour sack two tin plates. She went outside her cabin and from the smoldering fire, dying away into ashes, she brought a hoecake of bread and scraps of fried salt meat. Together they ate, after Mammy Sukey muttered a blessing over the food. The child mixed the bread and the sweet thick syrup with her fingers as she had long watched the toothless old woman do, and together they washed down the food with a gourd dipper of cold water, Mammy Sukey drinking first, and then Vyry.

When they started down the Big Road toward Marse John's Big House, nearly five miles away as the crow flies, dew was still on the grass, but the rising sun was already beaming down on Vyry's bonnet and on Mammy Sukey's head rag. At first the cool, damp grass and the moist earth felt squishy under Vyry's bare feet, but soon they were on a hot dusty clay road. Occasionally she felt pebbles and roots roughen her way so that she stubbed her toes, and sometimes she stumbled.

Ever since she could remember Mammy Sukey had been bringing her along this dirt road, taking her to the Big House many times. Sometimes they picked a pail of blackberries early in the morning before the sun was high. Sometimes they went fishing and caught catfish for their supper. Most times they ambled along just enjoying the summer and the Georgia countryside—butterflies and will-o'-the-wisps, and pretty pink flowers with deep cups of gold pollen that grew along the wayside, or scarlet-colored cardinals and blue jays chattering and screeching and flying over their heads.

But today was different. Today they were in a big hurry, and Mammy Sukey held her hand so tightly it felt hot and sweaty, and her fingers felt cramped. The old woman muttered to herself, and sometimes she seemed to forget the little girl who was trudging along beside her.

"Ain't make a speck of difference nohow. Politeness and cleanness and sweet ways ain't make no difference nohow. She gone stomp her and tromp her and beat her and mighty nigh kill her anyhow." And the child listening was puzzled and troubled, but she did not question Mammy Sukey.

She had been to the Big House many times and she knew what to expect. Marse John was always kind to her when he was around. He would tell the little Missy to share when he brought bananas and oranges and other goodies. "Give Vyry some, too," he would tell her and Miss Lillian would do as her father said. The two little girls often played together making mud pies, or running over the hillside playing hide-and-go-seek and playhouse under the big live oaks and shouting and laughing in fun. On a hot summer's day Vyry had sometimes seen inside the Big House and stood in awe at the dark coolness inside and the richness of the lavish furnishings. In Big Missy's bedroom there was a great oaken bed whose headboard nearly touched the high ceiling and the high mountain of feather mattresses always was covered with a snow-white counterpane. In young Missy Lillian's there was a tester bed with a canopy of sprigged pink and white cotton while the Marster and young Marster had rooms with massive dark furniture with silk furnishing in dark greens and reds and blues. Vyry would go from room to room, tiptoeing in awe and not daring to touch all the wonderful things she saw and the beauty of the rooms that seemed endless. Now, when she thought about it, she wondered why she did not feel happy about going to the Big House to stay.

She vaguely felt, however, that neither young Marster John nor his mother, Big Missy Salina, liked her very much. They were never kind and Mammy Sukey was always trying to keep her out of their way. Why this was true Vyry did not understand, and she did not ask. It was not her place to ask and Mammy Sukey taught her never to get out of her place.

There was that time when Big Missy had company from Savannah and Vyry was at the Big House playing in the yard with Miss Lillian. She heard the lady ask Big Missy, "My, but those children look so much alike, are they twins?" Vyry jumped when she heard the question and dared not turn her burning face in Big Missy's direction. Big Missy's cold angry voice hastened to correct the mistake. "Of course not. Vyry's Lillian's nigger maid. John brought her here to be a playmate to Lillian because they're around the same age, and Lillian has nobody else to play with. I must say they're near the same size, but I never have seen where they look alike at all."

The woman must have realized what a terrible mistake she had made, for she fumbled with the ivory fan that hung around her neck, at the same time changing color and muttering incoherent phrases in half-apologetic and half-frightened tones. But Vyry had a staunch champion in Miss Lillian. In those early years the little

Missy did not mind saying to anyone, "Yes, Vyry's my sister, and I love her dearly, and she loves me, too, now don't you, Vyry?" And Vyry would mumble, "Yes, Missy, I reckon I does." But that was child's talk and had nothing to do with their elders, Big Missy and Marse John.

Marse John was forty years of age and slowly settling into a man of serious purpose. At this time of morning he was just getting out of bed. His little daughter, Lillian, still in her long white batiste nightdress with insertions of pink ribbon and lace, ran in to kiss him good morning and confide happily. "Vyry's coming today!"

"Oh, is she? I guess that means making mud pies all day?"

"Oh, no, she's coming to stay. She's going to be my own individual maid all the time, isn't she, Mama?" And Lillian clapped her hands in happy anticipation. Marse John dropped one of the heavy riding boots he was about to put on and turned a questioning look on his wife, Salina, who was standing before a large and ornate mirror arranging her hair.

"What the devil is the child talking about?"

"What she said. The nigger Vyry starts working today as Lillian's maid. Run along now, Lillian, and let Caline get you dressed and comb your hair. Breakfast ought to be ready in a little while."

He put on his boot and then stood fully dressed except for his riding coat. As soon as the child was out of earshot he turned on his wife, "What in hell is going on around here? Why the devil wasn't I told about what's happening in my own house?" His voice was pitched low and well controlled to keep the slaves in the upstairs hall from hearing him, but his face bespoke his deep hostility and anger.

"Because you were either not here when I made the decision, what with all your new political notions and hunting all night in the swamps—if that is what you are really doing all night—or else you were too drunk to notice. And anyway, the house is my affair. I run things here as I please. Unless you change your ways overnight, which isn't likely, I'll have to run the whole plantation. Everything's going to rack and ruin, what with all your nigger-loving ways. You were going to bring her in here anyhow when you got good and ready, just like you've brought all your other bastards. I just beat you to it, and you've got the nerve to be angry."

For a full moment they eyed each other without speaking, and then in an oddly controlled voice he said, "I'm riding over to the

Smith Barrow and Crenshaw plantations. They've got some horses and dogs for sale that I want to see."

"You going before breakfast?"

"I don't want any breakfast."

"Humph, well remind them about the dinner party, will you?"

"I will not. That is really your affair, so you attend to it yourself." And grabbing up his riding cap he rushed out of the room slamming the door behind him.

Downstairs, out of the house, and on his way to the stables his mind was busy with a half-dozen things, the confusion of the morning, his abrupt leave of Salina, Vyry and Lillian, and the dead girl, Hetta, and his growing political ambitions. Already it was a warm August morning and the sun was hot. Sweat popped out on him and he mopped his face and brow more than once before spying Grandpa Tom.

"Morning, Tom. Saddle my horse and be quick about it. I'm riding over to the Barrow and Crenshaw plantations, and I'm in a powerful big hurry."

"Yassah, Marster, morning to yall. Ain't you riding kind of early, sah?"

"Not early enough. This blasted sun'll cook me before I get halfway there."

"Yassah, yassah, I reckon so. Hope you'll find it cooler before you starts back home."

John Morris Dutton, sitting astride his chestnut bay horse, threw his head back and laughed. "Now, how'd you know I won't be home soon? Evening or cooler weather, hanh?"

"Nice to see you then, Marster. Nice to see you then."

And as the horse and his rider went trotting down the path to the Big Road, old Grandpa Tom laughed to himself and scratched the bald top of his head.

When Marse John rode away from his house, Vyry and Mammy Sukey were well on their way toward the Big House. At the same time the slave driver, Grimes, who was Marse John's overseer on the plantation, was returning home with six new slaves he had purchased two days before at the slave market in Louisville. They were all field hands, or supposed to be, and they had brought a high price in the market. But Grimes was a little uneasy. He had been on his way since sunup, and since he was already in the swamp bottoms near Marse John's place he hoped to be home soon after breakfast or close around breakfast time. But the youngest of his chattel purchases, a boy in his early teens who was supposedly seventeen but who acted and looked more like fourteen, kept slowing down the journey by falling on the ground and tugging at the line of rope on which the six were strung. Grimes prodded him on with his horse whip by hitting him a lick or two. Both times the boy got up and staggered forward only to drop again in a half-hour or three-quarters of an hour's time. The sun was hot, and they had not had much water, but Grimes was beginning to suspect that the boy was not just suffering from heat and fatigue, he was sick. The auctioneer had cheated him and sold him a sick slave in the lot. He swore softly under his breath, and then yelled, "Hey you, there! Move along there now! You act like you got lice falling off you. We ain't got all day."

Uneasy as he was, he rode along lazily on his old gray nag not wanting to push the horse too hard. He was tired sitting in the saddle, and the butts of his pistols rubbed against his flesh uncomfortably. The Negroes were glum. When they first started out they talked among themselves. Each night when they stopped to make camp, they had sung their mournful songs while sitting in the darkness before lying down to sleep. Grimes kept them tied together even at night for fear of a runaway, and he hardly dared doze despite the loaded pistols he was wearing. In the morning light the boy's eyes looked glazed and sick. Jack, the big brawny slave standing six feet in his bare feet, put his hand on the boy's forehead as if to determine whether he had fever. Two of the others, Ben and Rizzer, gave the child their water, and he drank thirstily, but he would not eat anything. He vomited once and cried out during the night in his sleep.

Grimes looked up at the early morning sky where buzzards circled high above the trees, and he wished he were already home.

The six slaves, all male, were naked to the waist. Their one piece of clothing was a pair of ragged and faded cotton breeches cut off at the knees and tied around their waists with small ropecord. To this was attached the long piece of rope stringing them together in single file. Their bare legs and feet moved carefully through the swampy ground and the thickets of briers and weeds, heedless of scratches or cuts, while their quick eyes were ever watchful for snakes. Around their faces and feet buzzed flies, gnats, and mosquitoes, which they constantly tried to brush away with their manacled hands. Sweat glistened on all the bodies but the boy's. He looked dry and parched and his thin body was bony. Across his face was a long scar like a cut, and across his back and shoulders a huge welt, which had healed, still stood out prominently. The boy groaned constantly, making a wheezing and delirious sound that was first a moan then a whine mixed with a high-pitched, babbling, sing-song cry. Annoyed by this, Grimes started to hit him again, and thought better of it. They couldn't have much farther to go.

Grimes was a short, thick-set man, his shoulders big and round like a barrel and his heavy thighs like the broad flanks of a big boar with short, stocky legs and short but powerful arms. His watery blue eyes were as small as pig eyes, and when he was angry they turned a fiery red, though not exactly the same red as his thin carrot-colored hair and the dull red freckles that peppered his face and mottled his neck and arms. Even his upper lip and stubby chin were covered with a day's growth of red bristles which also stuck out of his nostrils and ears. His squinting eyes darted right and left, watching carefully for every turn of the road, and keeping the Negroes well in front of him. He was chewing tobacco and when he spat he stained the creases around his mouth and dropped dabs of the brown juice on his blue cotton-linsey shirt. His collar was open enough to show the red bristles on his chest, for the perspiration rolled off him, and where his cotton breeches were stuck in his fine leather boots they were soaking wet to the skin. He used his boots to nudge his nag and urge the beast along. When a horse has trotted nearly a hundred miles without much fancy attention a little easy nudge is in order. Of course, he never did have a good horse. John Morris Dutton kept all the fine thoroughbreds for hunting and carriage pulling and riding, while he gave Grimes all the nags and mules for work horses. Grimes did not think this was exactly right, but then what can you expect from a nigger-loving man like Dutton when it comes to treating poor white people right?

Now his wife's different. She's a lady, Missy Salina Dutton is, a fine, good lady. She nurses the sick far and wide, white and black. She knows how to handle niggers and keep a big establishment; how to set a fine table, and act morally decent like a first-class lady. She's a real Christian woman, a Bible-reading, honest-dealing, high-quality lady who knows and acts the difference between niggers and white people. She ain't no nigger-loving namby-pamby like that s.o.b. pretty boy she's married to. She knows how to lay the law down to niggers and keep her business to herself. Deep down in their hearts, a lot of people might feel sorry for the way her husband mistreats her, carrying on with nigger wenches, and even stooping so low as to raise whole families by them, shaming a good wife and a decent white woman of Quality. Not that she ever gives a sign like she knows about his goings-on. She is always strictly business-like and matter-of-fact. She acts so unconcerned you have to admire her for her guts. Of course people know and folks can't help talking about it, anyhow. Then too, it wouldn't be so bad if she wasn't so all-fired good-looking, but she is a beautiful woman. He sometimes wished his Jane Ellen had the kind of quality looks Missy Salina Dutton had. Of course Janey has had a hard time. She come from the pine barrens and her folks is awful poor, so poor they eat dirt, and sometimes, like right now while Janey is expecting (this'll be number eight), she craves dirt like her Maw done before her and that's why she eats so much snuff. But Janey was once real nice-looking too, before all these younguns, and when her blonde hair was real light colored and not so stringy as it is now, and she wasn't so careless, like walking around in a dirty dress with her feet stomp barefooted like she come in the world. But they is one sure thing, by God, she is a true, good wife and she don't have no nigger-loving husband like that trashy John Morris Dutton.

Most folks would never guess how he longed some day to have a farm of his own. He knew darn well how to run a farm, and he wouldn't be running off all the time leaving the work to somebody else. A lot of people think running a farm and handling nigras is nothing, but that ain't so; it's hard work. Managing a farm and keeping a pack of evil, black slaves in line ain't no child's play, but he knew how to do it. That's what he told Mister Dutton when he hired him, and he, Ed Grimes, was tough and hard enough a man to prove it. Of course you got a lot of things against you, things to contend with like the weather, for an instance. Rain slows the work down and niggers always hollering, "more rain, more rest." You got to keep a firm hand on niggers, else they won't hit a lick of the snake. Half the time they make out like they sick and got the rheumatiz or the whooping cough or just plain misery, and half the time they is just putting on. You can't pay them no mind, because they are the biggest liars God ever made—that is, if God made them. Sometimes it seems like a fact for certain that niggers is the work of the devil, and cursed by God. They is evil, and they is ignorant, and the blacker they is the more evil; lazy, trifling liars, every one of them. The Marster, Mister Dutton, indulges niggers cause he thinks they are helpless and childish, and they ain't got no mind, but the truth is they is just plain evil and stubborn and hard-headed. Best thing to keep a nigger working and jumping is a good bull whip. All you got to do is flick that whip, and believe you me, they jumps. I ought to know. And Missy Salina knows, too, you can't give niggers no rope, do and they'll hang you, give em an inch and they'll take a mile. You can't let up on a niggah if you wanta be a good driver, and that's what I am, a first class A-number-one good driver.

Vyry and Mammy Sukey walked into the back yard of the Big House just in time to see a big commotion. All the house servants and yard hands were crowded around Mister Grimes, the overseer, who had brought six slaves into the back yard and was cutting the rope and unlocking the chains holding them together. Big Missy Salina was standing in the back door of the Big House. Mammy Sukey turned to Vyry and said, "Go ask Aunt Sally for a washpan so's you can wash your footses fore you goes inside." And just at that moment when Vyry ran to obey, the sick black boy fell sprawling face down in the dust. Mammy Sukey pushed forward into the group around Grimes, and then her eyes widened in horror. She yelled, "Lord, have mercy, all you niggers get back! Send for Granny Ticey fast and tell Missy get the doctor quick. I clare fore God this nigger's got the plague."

Vyry pushed open the back door to the one-room, lean-to kitchen-house and saw Aunt Sally bending over the brick oven in the large fireplace chimney where she did all of Marster's cooking. For a minute Vyry stood there in the hot kitchen inhaling the smell of biscuits still baking, of fried ham with the smell still hanging on the air, and bubbling coffee. It seemed a long time since she and Mammy Sukey had eaten.

"Shucks, child, you scared me so I like to blistered myself with this here coffeepot. What you doing here?"

"I come to stay in the Big House with Miss Lillyum, and Mammy Sukey say give me a pot, please ma'am, so I can wash my footses fore I mess up Big Missy's pretty clean house, and they's a nigger outen there laying on the ground, Mammy say he got the plague . . ."

All her words came out in the rush of one breath. Aunt Sally stood looking through her for another long minute before she seemed to understand about the washpan the child was seeking.

"Got the plague? Oh, my Lord have mercy! Look-a-yonder hanging on the back porch and get that water bucket. You can set out there and wash yourself. I gotta see what's going on outside."

Vyry took the wooden bucket and went to the rain barrel to get water. But all that first day she could scarcely understand what was going on outside or inside. First, Big Ben and Rizzer moved the sick boy to one of the empty slave cabins where Big Missy kept all her medicines and where sick slaves went when they were bad off enough to need the doctor or stay on their pallets and need nursing, and then, as Mammy Sukey said, they had better be sick enough to die and prove it. Granny Ticey and Mammy Sukey took charge because Big Missy said she wasn't fooling with no niggers who had the plague, and she shooed all the rest of the slaves, including Aunt Sally, back to their work. When Big Ben and Rizzer saw that the sick boy was dying they stayed to help the two old women. Twenty-four hours later Ben and Rizzer dug a fresh grave. By their second evening that first new grave was filled. The dead boy was put naked into a feed sack, and then into a pine box in which he was hastily buried. Lime was spread liberally inside the grave, over, and around it.

That first night away from Mammy Sukey, lying on a strange pallet at the foot of Miss Lillian's bed, Vyry trembled for a long time before she could go to sleep. All day long she had gone back and forth from the kitchen to the springhouse, back to pull the dinner bell, then to gather eggs, to help feed the chickens, to fetch Miss Lillian a glass of water, and everything she had done and said was wrong. Twice Big Missy slapped her in the mouth with the back of her hand, and once Vyry barely escaped the foot of her mistress kicking her. Once she yelled to the startled child, "You stupid bastard, if you break airy one of my china dishes, I'll break your face."

If Vyry's first day was confusing, because Mammy Sukey was too busy to get her off to a good start in the Big House, it was increasingly confusing in the days that followed. Big Missy, Aunt Sally, and Caline kept explaining what to do next, and before many hours had passed Vyry sensed that her days here were not going to be what she had thought. There was no more time for mud pies. Miss Lillian was studying book lessons after breakfast. While Caline combed and brushed Miss Lillian's hair into curls Vyry stood by and she said, "Can I have curls, too?"

But Miss Lillian laughingly said, "Niggers don't wear curls, do they Caline?" And Caline watching Vyry's stricken face said, "Naw Missy, they sure don't."

Toward the end of the third day Vyry slipped away from the Big House twice to find Mammy Sukey, and twice she was sent back to her work and threatened with a whipping. Vyry told Aunt Sally she would rather die than catch a whipping. But the next day, fearing something she could only sense, she could not stay away, and she tried again to speak through the barred door of the cabin where Mammy Sukey still was. But the old woman's voice was now tired and troubled and she spoke a final admonition to the child:

"Gone back to the Big House, child, don't come here no more unlessen Aunt Sally sends you. Be good, and mind your manners like I told you and let Aunt Sally see after you . . ." and the familiar voice the child loved trailed off weakly.

That was the day Vyry forgot to empty Miss Lillian's chamber pot. Every morning when Caline and Jim, the houseboy, emptied slop jars, Vyry was told to empty Miss Lillian's little china chamber pot and see that it was washed outdoors and dried in the sun and brought in before bedtime and put under Miss Lillian's bed, but in her distress over being separated from Mammy Sukey, whom she dared not believe was sick, she forgot the chamber pot. That night when she heard Big Missy calling her from her supper in the kitchen with Aunt Sally she jumped up like she was shot. Trembling with fear of the whipping she knew she was going to get she stood before Big Missy, who was standing in the doorway of the kitchen and holding the pot of stale pee in her hand. Instead of whipping her, she threw the acrid contents of the pot in Vyry's face and said, "There, you lazy nigger, that'll teach you to keep your mind on what you're doing. Don't you let me have to tell you another time about this pot or I'll half-kill you, do you hear me?"

"Yas'm."

Early the next morning Vyry started toward the forbidden cabin again. When she saw them bringing out the stiff dead body of

Mammy Sukey she began screaming and crying as if she could never stop. She cried all day, but after that evening when she knew Mammy Sukey would never take her down the Big Road any more she hushed her tears and determined not to cry any more.

For five days there was a new grave every day. But Vyry bent her back to Big Missy's hatred and struggled hard to please her. She lost track of the days and she could not know she had been there two weeks when she broke one of Missy's china dishes. This time she knew Big Missy was going to whip her. Vyry saw Big Missy standing with the leather strap in her hands, and she looked up impassive and resigned, then she clasped her hands tightly, bowed her head and closed her eyes, tensely waiting for the first terrible lick, but Missy Salina laughed and said, "Do you think I'm going to hurt myself whipping you? Open your eyes and come here to me." Too startled to feel relieved, Vyry looked up and saw her mistress holding a closet door open. She hooked the strap to a nail, then, snatching up Vyry, she crossed her hands and caught them securely with the strap. Vyry's toes barely touched the floor of the closet. Suddenly Big Missy slammed the door behind her and left Vyry hanging by her hands there in the darkness. Terribly frightened, the child did not whimper. At first she was terrified in the dark, but after such a long time, with her arm-pits hurting so bad, she lost consciousness of everything and did not know how long she hung there in torture.

Two weeks after his early morning encounter with his wife, Marse John was returning home. Riding along the edge of his vast home properties he was savoring the pleasant air of a bright September morning. His mind was not on the pedigreed hunting hounds he bought from Barrow, nor the good whiskey he drank with Crenshaw. His neighbors were coming to his house for a hunting party as soon as the weather was cold enough. That would mark the beginning of his political campaign. Things ought to stack up in his favor as a candidate from Terrell County for the legislature. He expected to win hands down since he owned Terrell County and most of what was left of Lee County, too. His drivers were already his deputy sheriffs. Law and order in the county were gradually taking shape under his hands with political organization as his ultimate goal. He owned enough slaves to give him a large number of votes. For every five slaves he could count three votes. The only trouble was it took so much time, and he needed more time to spend covering the state. Rural traveling wasn't fun, and the weather determined everything. This trip had not been extended enough to visit his lands in Bainbridge and Newton counties for these bordered the Alabama line on one side, and the Florida line on another end. He would like to go more often traveling out of the state, but Salina never wanted to go anywhere except Augusta and Savannah. Once, before he was married, he spent a carnival season in New Orleans; pretty nearly spent the winter there. He surely enjoyed the lavish balls and gay social affairs in that exotic city. He even toyed with the idea of setting up one of those colored gals who had taken his fancy at the Quadroon balls. My God, but they were pretty! Only very rich white men were sought for them; they were bred only for the purpose of being some white man's mistress. But he decided it was foolish, a waste of good money, and too far from home to be convenient. Besides, at that time, he still had Hetta. Anyway, when he came home to Georgia, he came to God's country, and no other place on earth could be half so fine.

Here on his plantation between the Flint and Chattahoochee rivers was the land he remembered as a boy, where he had grown to manhood. What good times he had in these very woods when he was just a slip of a lad and his father took him coon hunting at night with the hounds, slaves, patter-rollers, and all! He laughed loudly just remembering.

Once they were coming along this same stretch of swampland with a pack of dogs hot on the scent of a possum or coon or something, and they ran smack-dab through the tangled briars and sticky thickets of vines following the yelping dogs who were barking up a helluva lot of noise. His father, excited, kept edging the dogs on, calling them by name, Queenie and Bessie, while they moaned and hollered, leading them into the thickest and deepest part of the woods. There the dogs barked like bedlam, the hunters hollered, "She's treed him." And they gathered around a big live oak tree. It was midnight and no moon, and they almost ran into the tree before his father flashed his lantern, and he, a young boy, stood gaping with the rest of the party, a tattered and tired bunch, with his father still breathing hard from running, when suddenly there was a dead hush. The light flickered at the base of the huge tree. The dogs tucked their tails, whined, and drew back. Against the dark bark of the tree stood a very large and glittering rooster.

He appeared to be all of two feet high. His red and green and black feathers were gleaming like satin. His coxcomb was a bright, bristling red. But his eyes were fantastic. They looked like the eyes of a human being. He was wide-eyed and unblinking, and stared back at them unruffled, calm, and steadily. Finally his father said in a tired voice, "Call off your dogs, boys, let's go home." Disappointed, he said, "But why, Poppa? Where's our game? We ain't got no coon yet."

"Ain't no game, son, leastwise not tonight. When did you ever see a chicken this far from roost this time of night?"

And the wide-eyed slave boys shook their heads and whispered among themselves.

"Sho ain't no coon!"

". . . and sho ain't no possum!"

". . . and it sho ain't no rooster neither."

Yes, this was his land, and this was home. His mother's holdings and his father's father's land had become his. They made him one of the seven richest planters in the center of Georgia. They kept him on the go so much he had to trust most of the running of the plantations to his drivers, even though Salina accused him of leaving the home place in her hands. He couldn't be in two or three places at the same time. On one plantation alone, the last time he had it surveyed, he owned three thousand acres. In addition to the rivers, his broad fertile lands in the river valleys were also watered by the Kinchafoonee and the Muckalee creeks. It was here in the marshy thickets and lush swamps of many meandering streams and treacherous bogs that a number of slaves had tried to run away to freedom. Most of them were caught by the patter-rollers and brought back for a flogging, in order to teach them a lesson and set an example for the others. Once when he was a half-grown boy he had gone on a searching party after a runaway slave. They gave the hounds the scent of his clothes. It sickened him now to remember. Flogging wasn't necessary that time because the dogs tore the fellow to pieces. Even now he could see the hideous bloody sight. His father was fighting mad. Runaway or no runaway, slaves cost money and mangling expensive property didn't please him one little bit, no sir-ee!

Sometimes Grimes overstepped his authority now, but they really had to depend upon him. He had a reputation of knowing how to handle nigras. Perhaps Salina was correct when she accused her husband of being a weak disciplinarian and not firm enough with his slaves. He preferred to leave the stern punishing of all his black labor in Grimes's hands as long as he didn't go too far.

Like an ancient lord in a great feudal, medieval castle surrounded by water and inaccessible except by a drawbridge over a moat (before one entered the fortified dwelling), he lived in a most inaccessible section of Georgia—deep in the forest, miles from the cities, and impossible distances to travel on foot. It was fully a half-day's journey from the old Wagon Road, where the stage coaches once traveled the Big Road, to the long oak-lined avenues leading up to the stately white manor of his own Shady Oaks. When he turned off the Wagon Road he had to travel ten or twelve miles on this narrow road that was overhung with great live oaks and towering virgin pine trees that touched the sky. From the live oak trees hung the weird gray veils of Spanish moss waving wildly in the wind, and trailing like gray tresses of an old woman's hair, lost from the head of some ghost in the wilderness. Often during daylight hours the sky was completely obscured by an archway of these trees. Here in the stillness of the forest one was cut off from reality and lost in a fantastic world of jungle. In this world of half-darkness and half-light he had often felt as though eyes were watching him.

After the twelve miles the road led along the path of the Kinchafoonee Creek where the swampy woods were full of cypress, so dense and dank and dark that it seemed as if the sky were overcast and a shadow hung over the day, sending a shiver creeping along his spine in the eerie atmosphere. Though the summer was waning, the air was fragrant with exotic sub-tropical flowers mingling with the pungent smell of pine. The colorful pink and orange bougainvillea and the royal purple wisteria hung in thick grape-like and trumpeting clusters. They grew in wild profusion, while the undergrowth was tangled with blue morning glory vines and running bushes of the climbing Cherokee rose. Yellow flickers, blue jays, thrashers, kildeers, brown wrens, speckled field larks, and scissor tails darted back and forth through the brush and through the trees, screeching with merriment, while here and there a chattering school of crows made their caw-caw noise. Gradually the swampy woods disappeared and Marse John came at last to his broad fields which were under cultivation on both sides of the road. Now the cotton was white with harvest, and as always his slaves were working in the fields, filling long croker sacks with the fluffy yield.

On his way to the house he passed the cemetery, the family plot where his parents and his grandparents were buried, where he too, in time, would be laid beside them. Fresh mounds of earth drew his quick attention and he got down off his horse to investigate. Six new graves in two short weeks? Name of God, who could they be? The rough wooden boards told him they were slaves but only two bore names, Granny Ticey and Mammy Sukey! From the plentiful sprinkling of lime he knew very well the deaths were due to something contagious.

Sorrowful now, he remounted and went to the house where such a stillness seemed unnatural. Chickens pecking around the back kitchen house and well were a familiar sight. Curtains were drawn against the heat and he was relieved to have his daughter Lillian run to meet him. She whispered in his ear, "Oh, Poppa, come quick, Vyry's hanging by her thumbs in the closet and I do believe she's dead."

He lost no time running up the stairs where Salina sat in her room with a basket of mending in her lap as though nothing were unusual, but when she saw him bound for the closet she jumped up. Quickly he caught the child, Vyry, whose feet barely touched the floor, and he saw she was only in a dead faint.

"What you trying to do, Salina, kill her?"

"Yes. I reckon that's what I oughta do. Kill her and all other yellow bastards like her. Killing's too good for her."

"Well, don't you try it again, d'ye hear me? Don't you dare try it again! She's nothing but a child, but someday she'll be grown-up and worth much as a slave. Then you'll be sorry."

"Humph! Are you talking to me? I'll never be sorry. Never, d'ye hear? How much do you expect me to put up with? Here in this very house with my own dear little children. And my friends mortifying me with shame! Telling me she looks like Lillian's twin. Don't you dare threaten me, John Morris Dutton, don't you dare threaten me. So far as killing her, I ain't even hurt her. I oughta kill her, but I ain't got the strength to kill a tough nigra bastard like her."

FROM

The Redneck Poacher's Son

Luke Wallin

THE NEXT MORNING Aunt May gave them a breakfast of scrambled eggs with wild onion and garlic chives. As she was cleaning up they saw a man walking out of the woods, on the overgrown logging road.

It was the sheriff, Potts Riggins. He was tall, with a pouchy face and belly, and big tatooed arms. He wore khaki work pants and short-sleeved shirt, and except for his badge and pistol he looked like a mill worker.

"Riggins!" Paw cried with a smile. "You forgot what I told you!"

The sheriff stopped twenty yards from them and looked uncertain of his next move.

"I ain't forgot nothin, Twaint. I come to tell you somethin you need to know."

"Yes," Paw said loudly and pleasantly, "you slipped up and forgot."

Riggins wiped his mouth nervously.

"Now listen, Watersmith," he said irritably, "ain't no man got the right to say the law can't walk up on him."

"But I said it, didn't I?"

"Yes, I reckon you said it. But you ain't got a phone. How we supposed to get hold of you?"

"I guess you ain't!" Paw laughed and laughed, and Jesse waited to see what was next.

"Never mind that," Riggins said, "I got somethin to tell you."

Twaint's smile faded. He stared at the sheriff and waited.

"They're gearing up in town for another election."

"You in trouble?"

"Well, I ain't got it made, that's for sure. Preacher's against me, tellin everybody I'm in with the moonshiners."

Paw laughed suddenly in his throat. "Everybody knows that."

"Yeah, Twaint, but I don't have to tell you that even them *drinkin* Baptists will vote against me if I'm too much out in the open."

"Damn hypocrites."

"Now that's so, that's so. But it's a real old system, that you and me ain't gonna change."

Paw looked around and rubbed his palm on his leg.

"Anyway," Riggins said, "folks want a dry county, with moonshine available. Only thing, preacher's got em about half convinced the sheriff who *gives* em that is an outlaw. Twisted as that sounds, you know and I know it's how they are."

"They want their whiskey, I know that."

"Yeah, but I got to ask you to slow it down until after the votin. That ain't long."

"How long?"

"Two months."

Paw spit on the ground.

"If you keep makin runs," Riggins said, "I'm gonna look mighty bad."

"That's your neck."

The sheriff was dark-faced now.

Paw smiled. "You won't have no more job, will you?"

They stared at each other for a long silence in which two jaybirds squawked at each other in a tree.

"Long and the short of it is this, Twaint," Riggins finally said, "if I was to lose this election, you boys would have to talk to a *new* sheriff."

"Yes, indeed."

"*But,* that there new sonofabitch might want more money, or he might rather just put you out of business."

"I'll tell you what," Paw snapped, walking toward Riggins, "I've put me a many a sheriff out of business, is who's put somebody out of business."

The man seemed to wilt under Paw's stare. He looked at the ground.

"Twaint," he said in a tired and patient voice, "all I'm askin for is two months."

"Well, now," Paw said, "*Askin* sounds a lot more like it."

"Sho, Twaint, that's all."

"Well, me and my sons will discuss the matter."

"Go right ahead."

"We'll let you know."

"Ain't necessary," Riggins said, regaining his composure a little, "if I see Robert Elmer and Bean makin them deliveries, or if I don't, either way I'll know."

"Very well then," Paw said, sounding pleased with himself.

"Good day," Riggins said.

"Sho."

When the deputy was gone everybody was busy, avoiding Paw. Bean chopped stovewood for Aunt May without being asked. He set the dry sections of oak on end, swung the axe high and tilted it expertly at the last second, making a fine pistol shot sound and sending the pairs of logs spinning.

Robert Elmer took the five-gallon canvas bag and went off to the spring. And Jesse got a hammer and set about resetting tent stakes loosened by the previous evening's wind.

But Paw himself seemed strangely good-humored. He got out his sharpening stone and his skinning knife, and squatted on the balls of his feet near the woodpile. He smiled as he studied his blade, pulling it carefully first one side then the other, stopping every few strokes to moisten the stone with a few drops of oil from a bent can.

"Boys," Paw finally said.

Bean stood still and Jesse walked over to the woodpile.

"You heard it just like I did."

"Yes, sir," Bean said.

"It ain't good news, but we ain't gonna let it get us down."

He kept scraping the knife.

"I been gettin a good price on venison. Best cuts goin to the cafes, and the rest goin for dog food. Dog food prices are flyin, so what the hell," Paw said. "Really. I mean, they can stop us from one thing, but they can't stop us from another, can they?"

"No, Paw," Jesse said. He was grateful Paw wasn't drinking.

"We'll just kill a few more deer, right Bean?"

"Uh, yeah Paw."

"And catch a few more skins for the fall. Jesse, you got another week or two."

Paw looked out across the clearing before he went on.

"And it won't be too much longer before there's another fish kill."

"Time for one, ain't it Paw?" Bean said.

"It is. It is." Jesse looked at Aunt May and thought about how much she hated Paw selling rotten fish.

"Listen, Jesse," Bean said, "how about seining today?"

"Sure."

"Where you goin?" Paw asked.

"Down in the Mock Orange Slough."

"That thing pretty full?"

"Sho is. And them fish are fightin each other for the air."

"Hell," Paw said, "let's go. Let's *all* go." He got up and went toward his trailer for the seine. Bean grabbed Jesse's arm. "Listen," he said, "we can't sell any more deer, and I'm scared to tell him."

"Why not?" Jesse asked. But Paw was already back, grinning with the net around his shoulders.

They waded in the muddy cool water up to their waists, quiet, tall Robert Elmer holding his corner of the net up and watching the surface nervously, Bean following on the bank with the long-handled dip net to separate quickly any snakes from the mass of trapped fish. Jesse and Paw waded with the other corner of the seine.

On their first pass they got a bucketful of bluegills and small catfish. They wiped the mud and sticks from the net to try again.

"Every time the river floods," Paw said, "it brings us all these here treasures."

"Sho does," Bean said.

"I think it's fine," Paw went on. "I think it's right nice of the old river."

A big fish swirled on the brown surface and they raised the seine quickly. It was a five pound bass and they were all grinning as they lifted him onto the weedy bank and watched him jump and flop and wave his gills.

"Aunt May'll like that!" Jesse said.

"What a fish!" Bean added.

"We not doin bad," Paw said. "No we not."

They all smiled in silence as they secured the bass with a bootlace through his lower lip and tied him down in the bucket with the smaller fish. If he was loose he might jump out and roll down the slope into the water again. It had happened to them once and they never forgot Paw's rage.

"Let's hit it!" Paw said.

They straightened out the seine and waded slowly into deeper water.

This time when they eased the corners up they felt a great weight in the center, and at first they thought they had a floating log. Then it was moving toward Robert Elmer and he was backing away and Paw yelled, "Don't you let go! Whatever you do, don't let go this sonofabitch!"

Robert Elmer's face was hard angles already but the bones stuck out through dark skin and he got his tight straight mouth like he always wore into fights. Just the mouth of the creature was showing and the jaws slammed chop-chop so loud that Robert Elmer's knuckles turned white. The rough back of the thing showed now and they all thought it was an alligator.

"I need to let go, Paw," Robert Elmer said. He never begged, and it was a strange voice in which he managed to ask.

"Not yet, boy! Not yet!"

He was backing toward the bank but the ragged back and the chopping big jaws were coming at him faster than he was walking.

"We got to see this thing!" Paw said, grinning.

"No, Paw! Now this is enough! Say I can let go!"

"You chicken, son?"

The question seemed to stop the creature itself, and they all waited motionlessly for an instant, Jesse trying to figure whether Paw was kidding or really testing Robert Elmer. Then it was swimming again and Robert Elmer yelled, "Paw!" but he never took his eyes from the moving water.

"Let go Robert Elmer!" Jesse yelled. "Let go! Let go!"

Robert Elmer looked at Paw once and saw his father unsmiling and daring him to do it.

Then the monster surfaced two feet from Robert Elmer's tight trembling hand and they all saw it was a huge alligator snapping turtle. It was over three feet long and its head was as big as a child's, floating square and malevolent on the surface. Its shell was covered with ragged ridges.

"Lift!" Paw cried, and they heaved their arms high, turning the turtle, and they hurried through the bottom mud to the near bank, and hauled the creature tangled and upside down and hissing and chopping into the weeds.

"I don't believe that!" Bean cried.

"Biggest one I ever seen," Paw said.

He held his own upside down palm near the turtle's foot and they were the same size, with the claws an inch long and the thing opening and closing like the hand of a witch.

Robert Elmer stood towering over the turtle, dripping and muddy up to his chest, not saying a word.

Paw was looking at him and laughing quietly, then louder.

"You sho held your ground, boy! I never seen the like of that! Didn't he?" He turned to Bean and Jesse. "Didn't he hold his ground?"

"He flat did," Bean said, chuckling.

Even Jesse began to smile.

"But *you,*" Paw said to Jesse angrily, "you hollered at him to quit! I heard you, too! Told him to disobey his Paw."

"Aw, Paw," Bean said.

"No, no! A time like this, we find out what everybody's made out of. Them damn people in town, most of them never find out. But once in a while, when you don't expect it, you get a look."

Robert Elmer broke the tension.

"What you want to do with him, Paw?"

They all looked at the great snapper, writhing in the net on his back.

"We could sell him to the fish store, couldn't we?" Robert Elmer said. "Make a lot of steaks."

"We'd have to be mighty careful," Paw said. "You boys may not get out of these woods enough to know about it, but them things are now *highly* protected by the law."

"Really?" Bean asked. "I was thinking Aunt May could flat cook us some stews from that sucker."

"She could, couldn't she?" Paw said.

"Let's let him go," Jesse said. "We'll get some little ones for the pot."

"Let him go?" Robert Elmer said. "Let him go and us have to wade in there again?"

"He could take off your foot, couldn't he?" Bean laughed.

"More than that," Paw said.

The turtle kept struggling, waving his head in circles in a slower and slower rhythm.

"Aw," Paw said, "we might let him go."

"No, Paw!" Robert Elmer said, "I say no!"

"Look out now, son. You doin good so far today. Don't push it."

"I want to eat him," Bean said.

"I'll tell you what I'd like to do," Paw said. "I wish we could get him to town just to show them folks. If some of them saw him, they'd come closer to stayin out of our swamp, wouldn't they?"

"They sure would," Bean said. "But how could we get him there? He must weigh two hundred pounds."

"I bet he does," Paw said. "He's the dadgumdest thing I ever saw. I think I want to let him go."

"Paw!"

"Hush, Robert Elmer. You don't have to kill every damn thing in the woods."

"But—"

"Hush! Sit down and rest a minute, let's think it over."

Jesse waited, hoping and afraid to say any more.

"Paw," Bean said, "I got some bad news to tell you, and I reckon I'll get it over with."

"Oh?"

"Yes, sir. I hate to tell this."

"Spit it out."

"Well, when I took the whiskey to the fish store yesterday, that feller said to tell you some people in Birmingham got caught servin deermeat in a cafe."

"And?"

"And, to save himself from going to jail, he told em it was *us* that sold it to him. Riggins ain't heard about it yet, but he will soon."

They were all silent, and the only sound was the turtle, moving its head in slow circles in the mud.

Jesse stared at the giant alligator snapper. He understood Bean's wanting to eat it, and Robert Elmer's wanting to sell it. That was all they knew about animals, all Paw had taught them. Aunt May had told Jesse about the massive rare turtles, how they live deep in a few rivers, and almost never appear in hill swamps. They live a long long time, she had said, and it's only right to let them go on living. There are plenty of common turtles around for soup.

They waited until Paw said, "And?"

"And that will shut the deermeat business down tight. Won't be a dollar in it before November."

Paw looked out over the slough a long time.

Jesse saw the cords in the back of his neck swell up and flex in and out.

"So we can't sell whiskey," he finally said, "and we can't sell deermeat."

Nobody answered him.

"What are we supposed to do now?" he said angrily.

The birds whistled softly to each other high above, where sunlight played on the tops of the tall thick trees.

Paw suddenly stared at the moving turtle, focusing on it as tensely as a cat on a mole.

He came to his feet and walked quickly to it, drawing his skinning knife from its sheath, and before Jesse realized what he was going to do he cut off the creature's head.

They had been gone for an hour.

Paw had carried off the bucket of fish and the torn seine to camp.

Robert Elmer and Bean had followed him with each side of the heavy turtle, dark blood marking the way behind them.

Jesse sat without tears beside the head which still moved its jaws slowly now and then, as if trying to taste something for the last time. So Aunt May would be cooking him after all.

He wondered how long it took to make the old turtle. And he wondered simply what difference it made after all when a thing died. It happened so matter-of-factly, like falling leaves or even more like the casual moving of a branch in the wind.

He wondered how life could be so tense and full of struggles and death be so natural as to seem almost innocent.

Still he couldn't convince himself of any natural order or sense to it, and he was left after the wide circle of his thoughts with a blind anger toward Paw that was greater than anything he'd felt before.

Bean had warned him long ago, that the only way to get their father's respect was to fight him, or at least offer to . . .

"But you can't fake it," Bean said. "When you threaten Paw you got to mean it."

"Is that what you did?"

"Me, and before me Robert Elmer. When we got big enough, and fed up enough."

"You actually fought *him?"*

"Robert Elmer traded a few licks. You know how big he is. But the thing is this, and remember it: I didn't care anymore whether I

was big enough or not. It didn't even matter to me if I killed him or he killed me. Do you understand?"

"I don't think so."

"You got to reach that point. You got to not care. If you care, he'll know it and he'll whip you or scare you to death."

"How can you not care?" Jesse asked.

"You have to answer that for yourself. I didn't understand it until he slapped me the last time and I just had to stand up."

"Does he know all this?"

"You mean is he just testing us?"

"Yeah."

"I don't know. Hell, don't ask me . . ."

Jesse had figured he was a coward, and Bean was not. But how could he face Paw yet, until he got bigger?

He dug a deep hole in the mud with his knife and buried the alligator snapper's head.

The body might be carried away to be food for Watersmith mammals, but the spirit of the old turtle, if there was a spirit, would remain here by the muddy slough.

There was something in the snapper's death that helped Jesse, gave him strength, and he reached inside himself to find it, drag it out into the sunlight. He felt guilty at first for the feeling, but he pulled at the thing and when he saw it he smiled a hard smile: his father was that cold, that sudden; it cut a great distance between him and Jesse.

As long as Jesse cared, Paw's coldness and meanness mattered too much. Jesse wanted, so much, to be close to his father, kept trying again and again.

But Jesse felt older and tougher today.

He looked at the grave of the turtle's soul and felt the tight lines of his own face, not the frightened boy worried sick over his secret bobcat, but more the face of his own brothers and even of Twaint.

He got to his feet and set off in the swamp, unafraid of snakes and squinting his eyes in newfound recklessness and bitterness. He felt like a Watersmith for the first time.

A Memory

EUDORA WELTY

ONE SUMMER MORNING when I was a child I lay on the sand after swimming in the small lake in the park. The sun beat down—it was almost noon. The water shone like steel, motionless except for the feathery curl behind a distant swimmer. From my position I was looking at a rectangle brightly lit, actually glaring at me, with sun, sand, water, a little pavilion, a few solitary people in fixed attitudes, and around it all a border of dark rounded oak trees, like the engraved thunderclouds surrounding illustrations in the Bible. Ever since I had begun taking painting lessons, I had made small frames with my fingers, to look out at everything.

Since this was a weekday morning, the only persons who were at liberty to be in the park were either children, who had nothing to occupy them, or those older people whose lives are obscure, irregular, and consciously of no worth to anything: this I put down as my observation at that time. I was at an age when I formed a judgment upon every person and every event which came under my eye, although I was easily frightened. When a person, or a happening, seemed to me not in keeping with my opinion, or even my hope or expectation, I was terrified by a vision of abandonment and wildness which tore my heart with a kind of sorrow. My father and mother, who believed that I saw nothing in the world which was not strictly coaxed into place like a vine on our garden trellis to be presented to my eyes, would have been badly concerned if they had guessed how frequently the weak and inferior and strangely turned examples of what was to come showed themselves to me.

I do not know even now what it was that I was waiting to see; but in those days I was convinced that I almost saw it at every turn. To watch everything about me I regarded grimly and possessively as a *need.* All through this summer I had lain on the sand beside the small lake, with my hands squared over my eyes, finger tips touching, looking out by this device to see everything: which appeared as a kind of projection. It did not matter to me what I looked at; from any observation I would conclude that a secret of life had been nearly revealed to me—for I was obsessed with notions about concealment, and from the smallest gesture of a stranger I would wrest what was to me a communication or a presentiment.

This state of exaltation was heightened, or even brought about, by the fact that I was in love then for the first time: I had identified love at once. The truth is that never since has any passion I have felt remained so hopelessly unexpressed within me or appeared so grotesquely altered in the outward world. It is strange that sometimes, even now, I remember unadulteratedly a certain morning when I touched my friend's wrist (as if by accident, and he pretended not to notice) as we passed on the stairs in school. I must add, and this is not so strange, that the child was not actually my friend. We had never exchanged a word or even a nod of recognition; but it was possible during that entire year for me to think endlessly on this minute and brief encounter which we endured on the stairs, until it would swell with a sudden and overwhelming beauty, like a rose forced into premature bloom for a great occasion.

My love had somehow made me doubly austere in my observations of what went on about me. Through some intensity I had come almost into a dual life, as observer and dreamer. I felt a necessity for absolute conformity to my ideas in any happening I witnessed. As a result, all day long in school I sat perpetually alert, fearing for the untoward to happen. The dreariness and regularity of the school day were a protection for me, but I remember with exact clarity the day in Latin class when the boy I loved (whom I watched constantly) bent suddenly over and brought his handkerchief to his face. I saw red—vermilion—blood flow over the handkerchief and his square-shaped hand; his nose had begun to bleed. I remember the very moment: several of the older girls laughed at the confusion and distraction; the boy rushed from the room; the teacher spoke sharply in warning. But this small happening which had closed in upon my friend was a tremendous shock to me; it was unforeseen, but at the same time dreaded; I recognized it, and suddenly I leaned heavily on my arm and fainted. Does this explain why, ever since that day, I have been unable to bear the sight of blood?

I never knew where this boy lived, or who his parents were. This occasioned during the year of my love a constant uneasiness in me. It was unbearable to think that his house might be slovenly and unpainted, hidden by tall trees, that his mother and father might be shabby—dishonest—crippled—dead. I speculated endlessly on the dangers of his home. Sometimes I imagined that his house might catch on fire in the night and that he might die. When he would walk into the schoolroom the next morning, a look of unconcern and even stupidity on his face would dissipate my dream; but my fears were increased through his unconsciousness of them, for I felt a mystery deeper than danger which hung about him. I watched everything he did, trying to learn and translate and verify. I could reproduce for you now the clumsy weave, the exact shade of faded blue in his sweater. I remember how he used to swing his foot as he sat at his desk—softly, barely not touching the floor. Even now it does not seem trivial.

As I lay on the beach that sunny morning, I was thinking of my friend and remembering in a retarded, dilated, timeless fashion the incident of my hand brushing his wrist. It made a very long story. But like a needle going in and out among my thoughts were the children running on the sand, the upthrust oak trees growing over the clean pointed roof of the white pavilion, and the slowly changing attitudes of the grown-up people who had avoided the city and were lying prone and laughing on the water's edge. I still would not care to say which was more real—the dream I could make blossom at will, or the sight of the bathers. I am presenting them, you see, only as simultaneous.

I did not notice how the bathers got there, so close to me. Perhaps I actually fell asleep, and they came out then. Sprawled close to where I was lying, at any rate, appeared a group of loud, squirming, ill-assorted people who seemed thrown together only by the most confused accident, and who seemed driven by foolish intent to insult each other, all of which they enjoyed with a hilarity which astonished my heart. There were a man, two women, two young boys. They were brown and roughened, but not foreigners; when I was a child such people were called "common." They wore old and faded bathing suits which did not hide either the energy or the fatigue of their bodies, but showed it exactly.

The boys must have been brothers, because they both had very white straight hair, which shone like thistles in the red sunlight. The older boy was greatly overgrown—he protruded from his costume at every turn. His cheeks were ballooned outward and hid his eyes, but it was easy for me to follow his darting, sly glances as he ran clumsily around the others, inflicting pinches, kicks, and idiotic sounds upon them. The smaller boy was thin and defiant; his white bangs were plastered down where he had thrown himself time after time headfirst into the lake when the older child chased him to persecute him.

Lying in leglike confusion together were the rest of the group, the man and the two women. The man seemed completely given over to the heat and glare of the sun; his relaxed eyes sometimes squinted with faint amusement over the brilliant water and the hot sand. His arms were flabby and at rest. He lay turned on his side, now and then scooping sand in a loose pile about the legs of the older woman.

She herself stared fixedly at his slow, undeliberate movements, and held her body perfectly still. She was unnaturally white and fatly aware, in a bathing suit which had no relation to the shape of her body. Fat hung upon her upper arms like an arrested earthslide on a hill. With the first motion she might make, I was afraid that she would slide down upon herself into a terrifying heap. Her breasts hung heavy and widening like pears into her bathing suit. Her legs lay prone one on the other like shadowed bulwarks, uneven and deserted, upon which, from the man's hand, the sand piled higher like the teasing threat of oblivion. A slow, repetitious sound I had been hearing for a long time unconsciously, I identified as a continuous laugh which came through the motionless open pouched mouth of the woman.

The younger girl, who was lying at the man's feet, was curled tensely upon herself. She wore a bright green bathing suit like a bottle from which she might, I felt, burst in a rage of churning smoke. I could feel the genie-like rage in her narrowed figure as she seemed both to crawl and to lie still, watching the man heap the sand in his careless way about the larger legs of the older woman. The two little boys were running in wobbly ellipses about the others, pinching them indiscriminately and pitching sand into the man's roughened hair as though they were not afraid of him. The woman continued to laugh, almost as she would hum an annoying song. I saw that they were all resigned to each other's daring and ugliness.

There had been no words spoken among these people, but I began to comprehend a progression, a circle of answers, which they were flinging toward one another in their own way, in the confusion of vulgarity and hatred which twined among them all like a wreath of steam rising from the wet sand. I saw the man lift his hand filled with crumbling sand, shaking it as the woman laughed, and pour it down inside her bathing suit between her bulbous descending breasts. There it hung, brown and shapeless, making them all laugh. Even the angry girl laughed, with an insistent hilarity which flung her to her feet and tossed her about the beach, her stiff, cramped legs jumping and tottering. The little boys pointed and howled. The man smiled, the way panting dogs seem to be smiling, and gazed about carelessly at them all and out over the water. He even looked at me, and included me. Looking back, stunned, I wished that they all were dead.

But at that moment the girl in the green bathing suit suddenly whirled all the way around. She reached rigid arms toward the screaming children and joined them in a senseless chase. The small boy dashed headfirst into the water, and the larger boy churned his overgrown body through the blue air onto a little bench, which I had not even known was there! Jeeringly he called to the others, who laughed as he jumped, heavy and ridiculous, over the back of the bench and tumbled exaggeratedly in the sand below. The fat woman leaned over the man to smirk, and the child pointed at her, screaming. The girl in green then came running toward the bench as though she would destroy it, and with a fierceness which took my breath away, she dragged herself through the air and jumped over the bench. But no one seemed to notice, except the smaller boy, who flew out of the water to dig his fingers into her side, in mixed congratulation and derision; she pushed him angrily down into the sand.

I closed my eyes upon them and their struggles but I could see them still, large and almost metallic, with painted smiles, in the sun. I lay there with my eyes pressed shut, listening to their moans and their frantic squeals. It seemed to me that I could hear also the thud and the fat impact of all their ugly bodies upon one another. I tried to withdraw to my most inner dream, that of touching the wrist of the boy I loved on the stair; I felt the shudder of my wish shaking the darkness like leaves where I had closed my eyes; I felt the heavy weight of sweetness which always accompanied this memory; but the memory itself did not come to me.

I lay there, opening and closing my eyes. The brilliance and then the blackness were like some alternate experiences of night and day. The sweetness of my love seemed to bring the dark and to swing me gently in its suspended wind; I sank into familiarity; but the story of my love, the long narrative of the incident on the stairs, had vanished. I did not know, any longer, the meaning of my happiness; it held me unexplained.

Once when I looked up, the fat woman was standing opposite the smiling man. She bent over and in a condescending way pulled down the front of her bathing suit, turning it outward, so that the lumps of mashed and folded sand came emptying out. I felt a peak of horror, as though her breasts themselves had turned to sand, as though they were of no importance at all and she did not care.

When finally I emerged again from the protection of my dream, the undefined austerity of my love, I opened my eyes onto the blur of an empty beach. The group of strangers had gone. Still I lay there, feeling victimized by the sight of the unfinished bulwark where they had piled and shaped the wet sand around their bodies, which changed the appearance of the beach like the ravages of a storm. I looked away, and for the object which met my eye, the small worn white pavilion, I felt pity suddenly overtake me, and I burst into tears.

That was my last morning on the beach. I remember continuing to lie there, squaring my vision with my hands, trying to think ahead to the time of my return to school in winter. I could imagine the boy I loved walking into a classroom, where I would watch him with this hour on the beach accompanying my recovered dream and added to my love. I could even foresee the way he would stare back, speechless and innocent, a medium-sized boy with blond hair, his unconscious eyes looking beyond me and out the window, solitary and unprotected.

First Love

EUDORA WELTY

WHATEVER HAPPENED, it happened in extraordinary times, in a season of dreams, and in Natchez it was the bitterest winter of them all. The north wind struck one January night in 1807 with an insistent penetration, as if it followed the settlers down by their own course, screaming down the river bends to drive them further still. Afterwards there was the strange drugged fall of snow. When the sun rose the air broke into a thousand prisms as close as the flash-and-turn of gulls' wings. For a long time afterwards it was so clear that in the evening the little companion-star to Sirius could be seen plainly in the heavens by travelers who took their way by night, and Venus shone in the daytime in all its course through the new transparency of the sky.

The Mississippi shuddered and lifted from its bed, reaching like a somnambulist driven to go in new places; the ice stretched far out over the waves. Flatboats and rafts continued to float downstream, but with unsignalling passengers submissive and huddled, mere bundles of sticks; bets were laid on shore as to whether they were alive or dead, but it was impossible to prove it either way.

The coated moss hung in blue and shining garlands over the trees along the changed streets in the morning. The town of little galleries was all laden roofs and silence. In the fastness of Natchez it began to seem then that the whole world, like itself, must be in a transfiguration. The only clamor came from the animals that suffered in their stalls, or from the wildcats that howled in closer rings each night from the frozen cane. The Indians could be heard from greater distances and in greater numbers than had been guessed, sending up placating but proud messages to the sun in continual ceremonies of dancing. The red percussion of their fires could be seen night and day by those waiting in the dark trance of the frozen town. Men were caught by the cold, they dropped in its snare-like silence. Bands of travelers moved closer together, with intenser caution, through the glassy tunnels of the Trace, for all proportion went away, and they followed one another like insects going at dawn through the heavy grass. Natchez people turned silently to look when a solitary man that no one had ever seen before was found and carried in through the streets, frozen the way he had crouched in a hollow tree, gray and huddled like a squirrel, with a little bundle of goods clasped to him.

Joel Mayes, a deaf boy twelve years old, saw the man brought in and knew it was a dead man, but his eyes were for something else, something wonderful. He saw the breaths coming out of people's mouths, and his dark face, losing just now a little of its softness, showed its secret desire. It was marvelous to him when the infinite designs of speech became visible in formations on the air, and he watched with awe that changed to tenderness whenever people met and passed in the road with an exchange of words. He walked alone, slowly through the silence, with the sturdy and yet dream-like walk of the orphan, and let his own breath out through his lips, pushed it into the air, and whatever word it was it took the shape of a tower. He was as pleased as if he had had a little conversation with someone. At the end of the street, where he turned into the Inn, he always bent his head and walked faster, as if all frivolity were done, for he was boot-boy there.

He had come to Natchez some time in the summer. That was through great worlds of leaves, and the whole journey from Virginia had been to him a kind of childhood wandering in oblivion. He had remained to himself: always to himself at first, and afterwards too—with the company of Old Man McCaleb, who took him along when his parents vanished in the forest, were cut off from him, and in spite of his last backward look, dropped behind. Arms bent on destination dragged him forward through the sharp bushes, and leaves came toward his face which he finally put his hands out to stop. Now that he was a boot-boy, he had thought little, frugally, almost stonily, of that long time . . . until lately Old Man McCaleb had reappeared at the Inn, bound for no telling where, his tangled beard like the beards of old men in dreams; and in the act of cleaning his boots, which were uncommonly heavy and burdensome with mud, Joel came upon a little part of the old adventure, for there it was, dark and crusted . . . came back to it, and went over it again. . . .

He rubbed, and remembered the day after his parents had left him, the day when it was necessary to hide from the Indians. Old

Man McCaleb, his stern face lighting in the most unexpected way, had herded them, the whole party alike, into the dense cane brake, deep down off the Trace—the densest part, where it grew as thick and locked as some kind of wild teeth. There they crouched, and each one of them, man, woman, and child, had looked at all the others from a hiding place that seemed the least safe of all, watching in an eager wild instinct for any movement or betrayal. Crouched by his bush, Joel had cried; all his understanding would desert him suddenly and because he could not hear he could not see or touch or find a familiar thing in the world. He wept, and Old Man McCaleb first felled the excited dog with the blunt end of his axe, and then he turned a fierce face toward him and lifted the blade in the air, in a kind of ecstasy of protecting the silence they were keeping. Joel had made a sound. . . . He gasped and put his mouth quicker than thought against the earth. He took the leaves in his mouth. . . . In that long time of lying motionless with the men and women in the cane brake he had learned what silence meant to other people. Through the danger he had felt acutely, even with horror, the nearness of his companions, a speechless embrace of which he had had no warning, a powerful, crushing unity. The Indians had then gone by, followed by an old woman—in solemn, single file, careless of the inflaming arrows they carried in their quivers, dangling in their hands a few strings of catfish. They passed in the length of the old woman's yawn. Then one by one McCaleb's charges had to rise up and come out of the hiding place. There was little talking together, but a kind of shame and shuffling. As soon as the party reached Natchez, their little cluster dissolved completely. The old man had given each of them one long, rather forlorn look for a farewell, and had gone away, no less preoccupied than he had ever been. To the man who had saved his life Joel lifted the gentle, almost indifferent face of the child who has asked for nothing. Now he remembered the white gulls flying across the sky behind the old man's head.

Joel had been deposited at the Inn, and there was nowhere else for him to go, for it stood there and marked the foot of the long Trace, with the river back of it. So he remained. It was a noncommittal arrangement: he never paid them anything for his keep, and they never paid him anything for his work. Yet time passed, and he became a little part of the place where it passed over him. A small private room became his own; it was on the ground floor behind the saloon, a dark little room paved with stones with its ceiling rafters curved not higher than a man's head. There was a fireplace and one window, which opened on the courtyard filled always with the tremor of horses. He curled up every night on a highbacked bench, when the weather turned cold he was given a collection of old coats to sleep under, and the room was almost excessively his own, as it would have been a stray kitten's that came to the same spot every night. He began to keep his candlestick carefully polished, he set it in the center of the puncheon table, and at night when it was lighted all the messages of love carved into it with a knife in Spanish words, with a deep Spanish gouging, came out in black relief, for anyone to read who came knowing the language.

Late at night, nearer morning, after the travelers had all certainly pulled off their boots to fall into bed, he waked by habit and passed with the candle shielded up the stairs and through the halls and rooms, and gathered up the boots. When he had brought them all down to his table he would sit and take his own time cleaning them, while the firelight would come gently across the paving stones. It seemed then that his whole life was safely alighted, in the sleep of everyone else, like a bird on a bough, and he was alone in the way he liked to be. He did not despise boots at all—he had learned boots; under his hand they stood up and took a good shape. This was not a slave's work, or a child's either. It had dignity: it was dangerous to walk about among sleeping men. More than once he had been seized and the life half shaken out of him by a man waking up in a sweat of suspicion or nightmare, but he dealt nimbly as an animal with the violence and quick frenzy of dreamers. It might seem to him that the whole world was sleeping in the lightest of trances, which the least movement would surely wake; but he only walked softly, stepping around and over, and got back to his room. Once a rattlesnake had shoved its head from a boot as he stretched out his hand; but that was not likely to happen again in a thousand years.

It was in his own room, on the night of the first snowfall, that a new adventure began for him. Very late in the night, toward morning, Joel sat bolt upright in bed and opened his eyes to see the whole room shining brightly, like a brimming lake in the sun. Boots went completely out of his head, and he was left motionless. The candle was lighted in its stick, the fire was high in the grate, and from the window a wild tossing illumination came, which he did not even identify at first as the falling of snow. Joel was left in the shadow of the room, and there before him, in the center of the strange multiplied light, were two men in black capes sitting at his table. They sat in profile to him, tall under the little arch of the rafters, facing each other across the good table he used for everything, and talking together. They were not of Natchez, and their names were not in the book. Each of them had a white glitter upon his boots—it was the snow; their capes were drawn together in front, and in the blackness of the folds, snowflakes were just beginning to melt.

Joel had never been able to hear the knocking at a door, and still he knew what that would be; and he surmised that these men had never knocked even lightly to enter his room. When he found that at some moment outside his knowledge or consent two men had seemingly fallen from the clouds onto the two stools at his table and had taken everything over for themselves, he did not keep the calm heart with which he had stood and regarded all men up to Old Man McCaleb, who snored upstairs.

He did not at once betray the violation that he felt. Instead, he simply sat, still bolt upright, and looked with the feasting the eyes do in secret—at their faces, the one eye of each that he could see, the cheeks, the half-hidden mouths—the faces each firelit, and strange with a common reminiscence or speculation. . . . Perhaps he was saved from giving a cry by knowing it could be heard. Then the gesture one of the men made in the air transfixed him where he waited.

One of the two men lifted his right arm—a tense, yet gentle and easy motion—and made the dark wet cloak fall back. To Joel it was like the first movement he had ever seen, as if the world had been up to that night inanimate. It was like the signal to open some heavy gate or paddock, and it did open to his complete astonishment upon a panorama in his own head, about which he knew first of all that he would never be able to speak—it was nothing but brightness, as full as the brightness on which he had opened his eyes. Inside his room was still another interior, this meeting upon which all the light was turned, and within that was one more mystery, all that was being said. The men's heads were inclined together against the blaze, their hair seemed light and floating. Their elbows rested on the boards, stirring the crumbs where Joel had eaten his biscuit. He had no idea of how long they had stayed when they got up and stretched their arms and walked out through the door, after blowing the candle out.

When Joel woke up again at daylight, his first thought was of Indians, his next of ghosts, and then the vision of what had happened came back into his head. He took a light beating for forgetting to clean the boots, but then he forgot the beating. He wondered for how long a time the men had been meeting in his room while he was asleep, and whether they had ever seen him, and what they might be going to do to him, whether they would take him each by the arm and drag him on further, through the leaves. He tried to remember everything of the night before, and he could, and then of the day before, and he rubbed belatedly at a boot in a long and deepening dream. His memory could work like the slinging of a noose to catch a wild pony. It reached back and hung trembling over the very moment of terror in which he had become separated from his parents, and then it turned and started in the opposite direction, and it would have discerned some shape, but he would not let it, of the future. In the meanwhile, all day long, everything in the passing moment and each little deed assumed the gravest importance. He divined every change in the house, in the angle of the doors, in the height of the fires, and whether the logs had been stirred by a boot or had only fallen in an empty room. He was seized and possessed by mystery. He waited for night. In his own room the candlestick now stood on the table covered with the wonder of having been touched by unknown hands in his absence and seen in his sleep.

It was while he was cleaning boots again that the identity of the men came to him all at once. Like part of his meditations, the names came into his mind. He ran out into the street with this knowledge rocking in his head, remembering then the tremor of a great arrival which had shaken Natchez, caught fast in the grip of the cold, and shaken it through the lethargy of the snow, and it was clear now why the floors swayed with running feet and unsteady hands shoved him aside at the bar. There was no one to inform him that the men were Aaron Burr and Harman Blennerhassett, but he knew. No one had pointed out to him any way that he might know which was which, but he knew that: it was Burr who had made the gesture.

They came to his room every night, and indeed Joel had not expected that the one visit would be the end. It never occurred to him that the first meeting did not mark a beginning. It took a little time always for the snow to melt from their capes—for it continued all this time to snow. Joel sat up with his eyes wide open in the shadows and looked out like the lone watcher of a conflagration. The room grew warm, burning with the heat from the little grate, but there was something of fire in all that happened. It was from Aaron Burr that the flame was springing, and it seemed to pass across the table with certain words and through the sudden nobleness of the gesture, and touch Blennerhassett. Yet the breath of their speech was no simple thing like the candle's gleam between them. Joel saw them still only in profile, but he could see that the secret was endlessly complex, for in two nights it was apparent that it could never be all told. All that they said never finished their conversation. They would always have to meet again. The ring Burr wore caught the firelight repeatedly and started it up again in the intricate whirlpool of a signet. Quicker and fuller still was his eye, darting its look about, but never at Joel. Their eyes had never really seen his room . . . the fine polish he had given the candlestick, the clean boards from which he had scraped the crumbs, the wooden bench where he was himself, from which he put outward—just a little, carelessly—his hand. . . . Everything in the room was conquest, all was a dream of delights and powers beyond its walls. . . . The light-filled hair fell over Burr's sharp forehead, his cheek grew taut, his smile was sudden, his lips drove the breath through. The other man's face, with its quiet mouth, for he was the listener, changed from ardor to gloom and back to ardor. . . . Joel sat still and looked from one man to the other.

At first he believed that he had not been discovered. Then he knew that they had learned somehow of his presence, and that it had not stopped them. Somehow that appalled him. . . . They were aware that if it were only before him, they could talk forever in his room. Then he put it that they accepted him. One night, in his first realization of this, his defect seemed to him a kind of hospitality. A joy came over him, he was moved to gaiety, he felt wit stirring in his mind, and he came out of his hiding place and took a few steps toward them. Finally, it was too much: he broke in upon the circle of their talk, and set food and drink from the kitchen on the table between them. His hands were shaking, and they looked at him as if from great distances, but they were not surprised, and he could smell the familiar black wetness of travelers' clothes steaming up from them in the firelight. Afterwards he sat on the floor perfectly still, with Burr's cloak hanging just beside his own shoulder. At such moments he felt a dizziness as if the cape swung him about in a great arc of wonder, but Aaron Burr turned his full face and looked down at him only with gravity, the high margin of his brows lifted above tireless eyes.

There was a kind of dominion promised in his gentlest glance. When he first would come and throw himself down to talk and the fire would flame up and the reflections of the snowy world grew bright, even the clumsy table seemed to change its substance and to become a part of a ceremony. He might have talked in another language, in which there was nothing but evocation. When he was seen so plainly, all his movements and his looks seemed part of a devotion that was curiously patient and had the illusion of wisdom all about it. Lights shone in his eyes like travelers' fires seen far out on the river. Always he talked, his talking was his appearance, as if there were no eyes, nose, or mouth to remember; in his face there was every subtlety and eloquence, and no features, no kindness, for there was no awareness whatever of the present. Looking up from the floor at his speaking face, Joel knew all at once some secret of temptation and an anguish that would reach out after it like a closing hand. He would allow Burr to take him with him wherever it was that he meant to go.

Sometimes in the nights Joel would feel himself surely under their eyes, and think they must have come; but that would be a dream, and when he sat up on his bench he often saw nothing more than the dormant firelight stretched on the empty floor, and he would have a strange feeling of having been deserted and lost, not quite like anything he had ever felt in his life. It was likely to be early dawn before they came.

When they were there, he sat restored, though they paid no more attention to him than they paid the presence of the firelight. He brought all the food he could manage to give them; he saved a little out of his own suppers, and one night he stole a turkey pie. He might have been their safety, for the way he sat up so still and looked at them at moments like a father at his playing children. He never for an instant wished for them to leave, though he would so long for sleep that he would stare at them finally in bewilderment and without a single flicker of the eyelid. Often they would talk all night. Blennerhassett's wide vague face would grow out of devotion into exhaustion. But Burr's hand would always reach across and take him by the shoulder as if to rouse him from a dull sleep, and the radiance of his own face would heighten always with the passing of time. Joel sat quietly, waiting for the full revelation of the meetings. All his love went out to the talkers. He would not have known how to hold it back.

In the idle mornings, in some morning need to go looking at the world, he wandered down to the Esplanade and stood under the trees which bent heavily over his head. He frowned out across the ice-covered racetrack and out upon the river. There was one hour when the river was the color of smoke, as if it were more a thing of the woods than an element and a power in itself. It seemed to belong to the woods, to be gentle and watched over, a tethered and grazing pet of the forest, and then when the light spread higher and color stained the world, the river would leap suddenly out of the shining ice around, into its full-grown torrent of life, and its strength and its churning passage held Joel watching over it like the spell unfolding by night in his room. If he could not speak to the river, and he could not, still he would try to read in the river's blue and violet skeins a working of the momentous event. It was hard to understand. Was any scheme a man had, however secret and intact, always broken upon by the very current of its working? One day, in anguish, he saw a raft torn apart in midstream and the men scattered from it. Then all that he felt move in his heart at the sight of the inscrutable river went out in hope for the two men and their genius that he sheltered.

It was when he returned to the Inn that he was given a notice to paste on the saloon mirror saying that the trial of Aaron Burr for treason would be held at the end of the month at Washington, capital of Mississippi Territory, on the campus of Jefferson College, where the crowds might be amply accommodated. In the meanwhile, the arrival of the full, armed flotilla was being awaited, and the price of whisky would not be advanced in this tavern, but there would be a slight increase in the tariff on a bed upstairs, depending on how many slept in it.

The month wore on, and now it was full moonlight. Late at night the whole sky was lunar, like the surface of the moon brought as close as a cheek. The luminous ranges of all the clouds stretched one beyond the other in heavenly order. They seemed to be the streets where Joel was walking through the town. People now lighted their houses in entertainments as if they copied after the sky, with Burr in the center of them always, dancing with the women, talking with the men. They followed and formed cotillion figures about the one who threatened or lured them, and their minuets skimmed across the nights like a pebble expertly skipped across water. Joel would watch them take sides, and watch the arguments, all the frilled motions and the toasts, and he thought they were to decide whether Burr was good or evil. But all the time, Joel believed, when he saw Burr go dancing by, that did not touch him at all. Joel knew his eyes saw nothing there and went always beyond the room, although usually the most beautiful woman there was somehow in his arms when the set was over. Sometimes they drove him in their carriages down to the Esplanade and pointed out the moon to him, to end the evening. There they sat showing everything to Aaron Burr, nodding with a magnificence that approached fatigue toward the reaches of the ice that stretched over the river like an impossible bridge, some extension to the west of the Natchez Trace; and a radiance as soft and near as rain fell on their hands and faces, and on the plumes of the breaths from the horses' nostrils, and they were as gracious and as grand as Burr.

Each day that drew the trial closer, men talked more hotly on the corners and the saloon at the Inn shook with debate; every night Burr was invited to a finer and later ball; and Joel waited. He knew that Burr was being allotted, by an almost specific consent, this free and unmolested time till dawn, to meet in conspiracy, for the sake of continuing and perfecting the secret. This knowledge Joel gathered to himself by being, himself, everywhere; it decreed his own suffering and made it secret and filled with private omens.

One day he was driven to know everything. It was the morning he was given a little fur cap, and he set it on his head and started out. He walked through the dark trodden snow all the way up the Trace to the Bayou Pierre. The great trees began to break that day. The pounding of their explosions filled the subdued air; to Joel it was as if a great foot had stamped on the ground. And at first he thought he saw the fulfillment of all the rumor and promise—the flotilla coming around the bend, and he did not know whether he felt terror or pride. But then he saw that what covered the river over was a chain of great perfect trees floating down, lying on their sides in postures like slain giants and heroes of battle, black cedars and stone-white sycamores, magnolias with their heavy leaves shining as if they were in bloom, a long procession. Then it was terror that he felt.

He went on. He was not the only one who had made the pilgrimage to see what the original flotilla was like, that had been taken from Burr. There were many others: there was Old Man McCaleb, at a little distance. . . . In care not to show any excitement of expectation, Joel made his way through successive little groups that seemed to meditate there above the encampment of militia on the snowy bluff, and looked down at the water.

There was no galley there. There were nine small flatboats tied to the shore. They seemed so small and delicate that he was shocked and distressed, and looked around at the faces of the others, who looked coolly back at him. There was no sign of a weapon about the boats or anywhere, except in the hands of the men on guard. There were barrels of molasses and whisky, rolling and knocking each other like drowned men, and stowed to one side of one of the boats, in a dark place, a strange little collection of blankets, a silver bridle with bells, a book swollen with water, and a little flute with a narrow ridge of snow along it. Where Joel stood looking down upon them, the boats floated in clusters of three, as small as water-lilies on a still bayou. A canoe filled with crazily wrapped-up Indians passed at a little distance, and with severe open mouths the Indians all laughed.

But the soldiers were sullen with cold, and very grave or angry, and Old Man McCaleb was there with his beard flying and his finger pointing prophetically in the direction of upstream. Some of the soldiers and all the women nodded their heads, as though they were the easiest believers, and one woman drew her child tightly to her. Joel shivered. Two of the young men hanging over the edge of the bluff flung their arms in sudden exhilaration about each other's shoulders, and a look of wildness came over their faces.

Back in the streets of Natchez, Joel met part of the militia marching and stood with his heart racing, back out of the way of the line coming with bright guns tilted up in the sharp air. Behind them, two of the soldiers dragged along a young dandy whose eyes glared at everything. There where they held him he was trying over and over again to make Aaron Burr's gesture, and he never convinced anybody.

Joel went, in all, three times to the militia's encampment on the Bayou Pierre, the last time on the day before the trial was to begin. Then out beyond a willow point a rowboat with one soldier in it kept laconic watch upon the north.

Joel returned on the frozen path to the Inn, and stumbled into his room, and waited for Burr and Blennerhassett to come and talk together. His head ached. . . . All his walking about was no use. Where did people learn things? Where did they go to find them? How far?

Burr and Blennerhassett talked across the table, and it was growing late on the last night. Then there in the doorway with a fiddle in her hand stood Blennerhassett's wife, wearing breeches, come to fetch him home. The fiddle she had simply picked up in the Inn parlor as she came through, and Joel did not think she bothered now to speak at all. But she waited there before the fire, still a child and so clearly related to her husband that their sudden movements at the encounter were alike and made at the same time. They stood looking at each other there in the firelight like creatures balancing together on a raft, and then she lifted the bow and began to play.

Joel gazed at the girl, not much older than himself. She leaned her cheek against the fiddle. He had never examined a fiddle at all, and when she began to play it she frightened and dismayed him by her almost insect-like motions, the pensive antennae of her arms, her mask of a countenance. When she played she never blinked an eye. Her legs, fantastic in breeches, were separated slightly, and from her bent knees she swayed back and forth as if she were weaving the tunes with her body. The sharp odor of whisky moved with her. The slits of her eyes were milky. The songs she played seemed to him to have no beginnings and no endings, but to be about many hills and valleys, and chains of lakes. She, like the men, knew of a place. . . . All of them spoke of a country.

And quite clearly, and altogether to his surprise, Joel saw a sight that he had nearly forgotten. Instead of the fire on the hearth, there was a mimosa tree in flower. It was in the little back field at his home in Virginia and his mother was leading him by the hand. Fragile, delicate, cloud-like it rose on its pale trunk and spread its long level arms. His mother pointed to it. Among the trembling leaves the feathery puffs of sweet bloom filled the tree like thousands of paradisical birds all alighted at an instant. He had known then the story of the Princess Labam, for his mother had told it to him, how she was so radiant that she sat on the roof-top at night and lighted the city. It seemed to be the mimosa tree that lighted the garden, for its brightness and fragrance overlaid all the rest. Out of its graciousness this tree suffered their presence and shed its splendor upon him and his mother. His mother pointed again, and its scent swayed like the Asiatic princess moving up and down the pink steps of its branches. Then the vision was gone. Aaron Burr sat in front of the fire, Blennerhassett faced him, and Blennerhassett's wife played on the violin.

There was no compassion in what this woman was doing, he knew that—there was only a frightening thing, a stern allurement. Try as he might, he could not comprehend it, though it was so calculated. He had instead a sensation of pain, the ends of his fingers were stinging. At first he did not realize that he had heard the sounds of her song, the only thing he had ever heard. Then all at once as she held the lifted bow still for a moment he gasped for breath at the interruption, and he did not care to learn her purpose or to wonder any longer, but bent his head and listened for the note that she would fling down upon them. And it was so gentle then, it touched him with surprise; it made him think of animals sleeping on their cushioned paws.

For a moment his love went like sound into a myriad life and was divided among all the people in his room. While they listened, Burr's radiance was somehow quenched, or theirs was raised to equal it, and they were all alike. There was one thing that shone in all their faces, and that was how far they were from home, how far from everywhere that they knew. Joel put his hand to his own face, and hid his pity from them while they listened to the endless tunes.

But she ended them. Sleep all at once seemed to overcome her whole body. She put down the fiddle and took Blennerhassett by both hands. He seemed tired too, more tired than talking could ever make him. He went out when she led him. They went wrapped under one cloak, his arm about her.

Burr did not go away immediately. First he walked up and down before the fire. He turned each time with diminishing violence, and light and shadow seemed to stream more softly with his turning cloak. Then he stood still. The firelight threw its changes over his face. He had no one to talk to. His boots smelled of the fire's closeness. Of course he had forgotten Joel, he seemed quite alone. At last, with a strange naturalness, almost with a limp, he went to the table and stretched himself full length upon it.

He lay on his back. Joel was astonished. That was the way they laid out the men killed in duels in the Inn yard; and that was the table they laid them on.

Burr fell asleep instantly, so quickly that Joel felt he should never be left alone. He looked at the sleeping face of Burr, and the time and the place left him, and all that Burr had said that he had tried to guess left him too—he knew nothing in the world except the sleeping face. It was quiet. The eyes were almost closed, only dark slits lay beneath the lids. There was a small scar on the cheek. The lips were parted. Joel thought, I could speak if I would, or I could hear. Once I did each thing. . . . Still he listened . . . and it seemed that all that would speak, in this world, was listening. Burr was silent; he demanded nothing, nothing. . . . A boy or a man could be so alone in his heart that he could not even ask a question. In such silence as falls over a lonely man there is child-like supplication, and all arms might wish to open to him, but there is no speech. This was Burr's last night: Joel knew that. This was the moment before he would ride away. Why would the heart break so at absence? Joel knew that it was because nothing had been told. The heart is secret even when the moment it dreamed of has come, a moment when there might have been a revelation. . . . Joel stood motionless; he lifted his gaze from Burr's face and stared at nothing. . . . If love does a secret thing always, it is to reach backward, to a time that could not be known—for it makes a history of the sorrow and the dream it has contemplated in some instant of recognition. What Joel saw before him he had a terrible wish to speak out loud, but he would have had to find names for the places of the heart and the times for its shadowy and tragic events, and they seemed of great magnitude, heroic and terrible and splendid, like the legends of the mind. But for lack of a way to tell how much was known, the boundaries would lie between him and the others, all the others, until he died.

Presently Burr began to toss his head and to cry out. He talked, his face drew into a dreadful set of grimaces, which it followed over and over. He could never stop talking. Joel was afraid of these words, and afraid that eavesdroppers might listen to them. Whatever words they were, they were being taken by some force out of his dream. In horror, Joel put out his hand. He could never in his life have laid it across the mouth of Aaron Burr, but he thrust it into Burr's spread-out fingers. The fingers closed and did not yield; the clasp grew so fierce that it hurt his hand, but he saw that the words had stopped.

And if a silent love had shown him whatever new thing he would ever be able to learn, Joel had some wisdom in his fingers now which only this long month could have brought. He knew with what gentleness to hold the burning hand. With the gravity of his very soul he received the furious pressure of this man's dream. At last Burr drew his arm back beside his quiet head, and his hand hung like a child's in sleep, released in oblivion.

The next morning, Joel was given a notice to paste on the saloon mirror that conveyances might be rented at the Inn daily for the excursion to Washington for the trial of Mr. Burr, payment to be made in advance. Joel went out and stood on a corner, and joined with a group of young boys walking behind the militia.

It was warm—a "false spring" day. The little procession from Natchez, decorated and smiling in all they owned or whatever they borrowed or chartered or rented, moved grandly through the streets and on up the Trace. To Joel, somewhere in the line, the blue air that seemed to lie between the high banks held it all in a mist, softly colored, the fringe waving from a carriage top, a few flags waving, a sword shining when some gentleman made a flourish. High up on their horses a number of the men were wearing their Revolutionary War uniforms, as if to reiterate that Aaron Burr fought once at their sides as a hero.

Under the spreading live-oaks at Washington, the trial opened like a festival. There was a theatre of benches, and a promenade; stalls were set out under the trees, and glasses of whisky, and colored ribbons, were sold. Joel sat somewhere among the crowds. Breezes touched the yellow and violet of dresses and stirred them, horses pawed the ground, and the people pressed upon him and seemed more real than those in dreams, and yet their pantomime was like those choruses and companies whose movements are like the waves running together. A hammer was then pounded, there was sudden attention from all the spectators, and Joel felt the great solidifying of their silence.

He had dreaded the sight of Burr. He had thought there might be some mark or disfigurement that would come from his panic. But all his grace was back upon him, and he was smiling to greet the studious faces which regarded him. Before their bright façade others rose first, declaiming men in turn, and then Burr.

In a moment he was walking up and down with his shadow on the grass and the patches of snow. He was talking again, talking now in great courtesy to everybody. There was a flickering light of sun and shadow on his face.

Then Joel understood. Burr was explaining away, smoothing over all that he had held great enough to have dreaded once. He walked back and forth elegantly in the sun, turning his wrist ever so airily in its frill, making light of his dream that had terrified him. And it was the deed they had all come to see. All around Joel they gasped, smiled, pressed one another's arms, nodded their heads; there were tender smiles on the women's faces. They were at Aaron Burr's feet at last, learning their superiority. They loved him now, in their condescension. They leaned forward in delight at the parading spectacle he was making. And when it was over for the day, they shook each other's hands, and Old Man McCaleb could be seen spitting on the ground, in the anticipation of another day as good as this one.

Blennerhassett did not come that night.

Burr came very late. He walked in the door, looked down at Joel where he sat among his boots, and suddenly stooped and took the dirty cloth out of his hand. He put his face quickly into it and pressed and rubbed it against his skin. Joel saw that all his clothes were dirty and ragged. The last thing he did was to set a little cap of turkey feathers on his head. Then he went out.

Joel followed him along behind the dark houses and through a ravine. Burr turned toward the Halfway Hill. Joel turned too, and he saw Burr walk slowly up and open the great heavy gate.

He saw him stop beside a tall camellia bush as solid as a tower and pick up one of the frozen buds which were shed all around it on the ground. For a moment he held it in the palm of his hand, and then he went on. Joel, following behind, did the same. He held the bud, and studied the burned edges of its folds by the pale half-light of the East. The bud came apart in his hand, its layers like small velvet shells, still iridescent, the shriveled flower inside. He held it tenderly and yet timidly, in a kind of shame, as though all disaster lay pitifully disclosed now to the eyes.

He knew the girl Burr had often danced with under the rings of tapers when she came out in a cloak across the shadowy hill. Burr stood, quiet and graceful as he had always been as her partner at the balls. Joel felt a pain like a sting while she first merged with the dark figure and then drew back. The moon, late-risen and waning, came out of the clouds. Aaron Burr made the gesture there in the distance, toward the West, where the clouds hung still and red, and when Joel looked at him in the light he saw as she must have seen the absurdity he was dressed in, the feathers on his head. With a curious feeling of revenge upon her, he watched her turn, draw smaller within her own cape, and go away.

Burr came walking down the hill, and passed close to the camellia bush where Joel was standing. He walked stiffly in his mock Indian dress with the boot polish on his face. The youngest child in Natchez would have known that this was a remarkable and wonderful figure that had humiliated itself by disguise.

Pausing in an open space, Burr lifted his hand once more and a slave led out from the shadows a majestic horse with silver trappings shining in the light of the moon. Burr mounted from the slave's hand in all the clarity of his true elegance, and sat for a moment motionless in the saddle. Then he cut his whip through the air, and rode away.

Joel followed him on foot toward the Liberty Road. As he walked through the streets of Natchez he felt a strange mourning to know that Burr would never come again by that way. If he had left in disguise, the thirst that was in his face was the same as it had ever been. He had eluded judgment, that was all he had done, and Joel was glad while he still trembled. Joel would never know now the true course, or the true outcome of any dream: this was all he felt. But he walked on, in the frozen path into the wilderness, on and on. He did not see how he could ever go back and still be the bootboy at the Inn.

He did not know how far he had gone on the Liberty Road when the posse came riding up behind and passed him. He walked on. He saw that the bodies of the frozen birds had fallen out of the trees, and he fell down and wept for his father and mother, to whom he had not said good-bye.

Why I Live at the P.O.

Eudora Welty

I WAS GETTING ALONG fine with Mama, Papa-Daddy and Uncle Rondo until my sister Stella-Rondo just separated from her husband and came back home again. Mr. Whitaker! Of course I went with Mr. Whitaker first, when he first appeared here in China Grove, taking "Pose Yourself" photos, and Stella-Rondo broke us up. Told him I was one-sided. Bigger on one side than the other, which is a deliberate, calculated falsehood: I'm the same. Stella-Rondo is exactly twelve months to the day younger than I am and for that reason she's spoiled.

She's always had anything in the world she wanted and then she'd throw it away. Papa-Daddy gave her this gorgeous Add-a-Pearl necklace when she was eight years old and she threw it away playing baseball when she was nine, with only two pearls.

So as soon as she got married and moved away from home the first thing she did was separate! From Mr. Whitaker! This photographer with the popeyes she said she trusted. Came home from one of those towns up in Illinois and to our complete surprise brought this child of two.

Mama said she like to made her drop dead for a second. "Here you had this marvelous blonde child and never so much as wrote your mother a word about it," says Mama. "I'm thoroughly ashamed of you." But of course she wasn't.

Stella-Rondo just calmly takes off this *hat*, I wish you could see it. She says, "Why, Mama, Shirley-T.'s adopted, I can prove it."

"How?" says Mama, but all I says was, "H'm!" There I was over the hot stove, trying to stretch two chickens over five people and a completely unexpected child into the bargain, without one moment's notice.

"What do you mean—'H'm!'?" says Stella-Rondo, and Mama says, "I heard that, Sister."

I said that oh, I didn't mean a thing, only that whoever Shirley-T. was, she was the spit-image of Papa-Daddy if he'd cut off his beard, which of course he'd never do in the world. Papa-Daddy's Mama's papa and sulks.

Stella-Rondo got furious! She said, "Sister, I don't need to tell you you got a lot of nerve and always did have and I'll thank you to make no future reference to my adopted child whatsoever."

"Very well," I said. "Very well, very well. Of course I noticed at once she looks like Mr. Whitaker's side too. That frown. She looks like a cross between Mr. Whitaker and Papa-Daddy."

"Well, all I can say is she isn't."

"She looks exactly like Shirley Temple to me," says Mama, but Shirley-T. just ran away from her.

So the first thing Stella-Rondo did at the table was turn Papa-Daddy against me.

"Papa-Daddy," she says. He was trying to cut up his meat. "Papa-Daddy!" I was taken completely by surprise. Papa-Daddy is about a million years old and's got this long-long beard. "Papa-Daddy, Sister says she fails to understand why you don't cut off your beard."

So Papa-Daddy l-a-y-s down his knife and fork! He's real rich. Mama says he is, he says he isn't. So he says, "Have I heard correctly? You don't understand why I don't cut off my beard?"

"Why," I says, "Papa-Daddy, of course I understand, I did not say any such of a thing, the idea!"

He says, "Hussy!"

I says, "Papa-Daddy, you know I wouldn't any more want you to cut off your beard than the man in the moon. It was the farthest thing from my mind! Stella-Rondo sat there and made that up while she was eating breast of chicken."

But he says, "So the postmistress fails to understand why I don't cut off your beard than the man in the moon. It was the farthest the government. 'Bird's nest'—is that what you call it?"

Not that it isn't the next to smallest P.O. in the entire state of Mississippi.

I says, "Oh, Papa-Daddy," I says, "I didn't say any such of a thing, I never dreamed it was a bird's nest, I have always been grateful though this is the next to smallest P.O. in the state of Mississippi, and I do not enjoy being referred to as a hussy by my own grandfather."

But Stella-Rondo says, "Yes, you did say it too. Anybody in the world could of heard you, that had ears."

"Stop right there," says Mama, looking at *me.*

So I pulled my napkin straight back through the napkin ring and left the table.

As soon as I was out of the room Mama says, "Call her back, or she'll starve to death," but Papa-Daddy says, "This is the beard I started growing on the Coast when I was fifteen years old." He would of gone on till nightfall if Shirley-T. hadn't lost the Milky Way she ate in Cairo.

So Papa-Daddy says, "I am going out and lie in the hammock, and you can all sit here and remember my words: I'll never cut off my beard as long as I live, even one inch, and I don't appreciate it in you at all." Passed right by me in the hall and went straight out and got in the hammock.

It would be a holiday. It wasn't five minutes before Uncle Rondo suddenly appeared in the hall in one of Stella-Rondo's flesh-colored kimonos, all cut on the bias, like something Mr. Whitaker probably thought was gorgeous.

"Uncle Rondo!" I says. "I didn't know who that was! Where are you going?"

"Sister," he says, "get out of my way, I'm poisoned."

"If you're poisoned stay away from Papa-Daddy," I says. "Keep out of the hammock. Papa-Daddy will certainly beat you on the head if you come within forty miles of him. He thinks I deliberately said he ought to cut off his beard after he got me the P.O., and I've told him and told him and told him, and he acts like he just don't hear me. Papa-Daddy must of gone stone deaf."

"He picked a fine day to do it then," says Uncle Rondo, and before you could say "Jack Robinson" flew out in the yard.

What he'd really done, he'd drunk another bottle of that prescription. He does it every single Fourth of July as sure as shooting, and it's horribly expensive. Then he falls over in the hammock and snores. So he insisted on zigzagging right on out to the hammock, looking like a half-wit.

Papa-Daddy woke up with this horrible yell and right there without moving an inch he tried to turn Uncle Rondo against me. I heard every word he said. Oh, he told Uncle Rondo I didn't learn to read till I was eight years old and he didn't see how in the world I ever got the mail put up at the P.O., much less read it all, and he said if Uncle Rondo could only fathom the lengths he had gone to to get me that job! And he said on the other hand he thought Stella-Rondo had a brilliant mind and deserved credit for getting out of town. All the time he was just lying there swinging as pretty as you please and looping out his beard, and poor Uncle Rondo was *pleading* with him to slow down the hammock, it was making him as dizzy as a witch to watch it. But that's what Papa-Daddy likes about a hammock. So Uncle Rondo was too dizzy to get turned against me for the time being. He's Mama's only brother and is a good case of a one-track mind. Ask anybody. A certified pharmacist.

Just then I heard Stella-Rondo raising the upstairs window. While she was married she got this peculiar idea that it's cooler with the windows shut and locked. So she has to raise the window before she can make a soul hear her outdoors.

So she raises the window and says, "*Oh!*" You would have thought she was mortally wounded.

Uncle Rondo and Papa-Daddy didn't even look up, but kept right on with what they were doing. I had to laugh.

I flew up the stairs and threw the door open! I says, "What in the wide world's the matter, Stella-Rondo? You mortally wounded?"

"No," she says, "I am not mortally wounded but I wish you would do me the favor of looking out that window there and telling me what you see."

So I shade my eyes and look out the window.

"I see the front yard," I says.

"Don't you see any human beings?" she says.

"I see Uncle Rondo trying to run Papa-Daddy out of the hammock," I says. "Nothing more. Naturally, it's so suffocating-hot in the house, with all the windows shut and locked, everybody who cares to stay in their right mind will have to go out and get in the hammock before the Fourth of July is over."

"Don't you notice anything different about Uncle Rondo?" asks Stella-Rondo.

"Why, no, except he's got on some terrible-looking flesh-colored contraption I wouldn't be found dead in, is all I can see," I says.

"Never mind, you won't be found dead in it, because it happens to be part of my trousseau, and Mr. Whitaker took several dozen photographs of me in it," says Stella-Rondo. "What on earth could Uncle Rondo *mean* by wearing part of my trousseau out in the broad open daylight without saying so much as 'Kiss my foot,' *knowing* I only got home this morning after my separation and hung my negligee up on the bathroom door, just as nervous as I could be?"

"I'm sure I don't know, and what do you expect me to do about it?" I says. "Jump out the window?"

"No, I expect nothing of the kind. I simply declare that Uncle Rondo looks like a fool in it, that's all," she says. "It makes me sick to my stomach."

"Well, he looks as good as he can," I says. "As good as anybody in reason could." I stood up for Uncle Rondo, please remember. And I said to Stella-Rondo, "I think I would do well not to criticize so freely if I were you and came home with a two-year-old child I had never said a word about, and no explanation whatever about my separation."

"I asked you the instant I entered this house not to refer one more time to my adopted child, and you gave me your word of honor you would not," was all Stella-Rondo would say, and started pulling out every one of her eyebrows with some cheap Kress tweezers.

So I merely slammed the door behind me and went down and made some green-tomato pickle. Somebody had to do it. Of course Mama had turned both the Negroes loose; she always said no earthly power could hold one anyway on the Fourth of July, so she wouldn't even try. It turned out that Jaypan fell in the lake and came within a very narrow limit of drowning.

So Mama trots in. Lifts up the lid and says, "H'm! Not very good for your Uncle Rondo in his precarious condition, I must say. Or poor little adopted Shirley-T. Shame on you!"

That made me tired. I says, "Well, Stella-Rondo had better thank her lucky stars it was her instead of me came trotting in with that very peculiar-looking child. Now if it had been me that trotted in from Illinois and brought a peculiar-looking child of two, I shudder to think of the reception I'd of got, much less controlled the diet of an entire family."

"But you must remember, Sister, that you were never married to Mr. Whitaker in the first place and didn't go up to Illinois to live," says Mama, shaking a spoon in my face. "If you had I would of been just as overjoyed to see you and your little adopted girl as I was to see Stella-Rondo, when you wound up with your separation and came on back home."

"You would not," I says.

"Don't contradict me, I would," says Mama.

But I said she couldn't convince me though she talked till she was blue in the face. Then I said, "Besides, you know as well as I do that that child is not adopted."

"She most certainly is adopted," says Mama, stiff as a poker.

I says, "Why, Mama, Stella-Rondo had her just as sure as anything in this world, and just too stuck up to admit it."

"Why, Sister," said Mama. "Here I thought we were going to have a pleasant Fourth of July, and you start right out not believing a word your own baby sister tells you!"

"Just like Cousin Annie Flo. Went to her grave denying the facts of life," I remind Mama.

"I told you if you ever mentioned Annie Flo's name I'd slap your face," says Mama, and slaps my face.

"All right, you wait and see," I says.

"I," says Mama, "*I* prefer to take my children's word for anything when it's humanly possible." You ought to see Mama, she weighs two hundred pounds and has real tiny feet.

Just then something perfectly horrible occurred to me.

"Mama," I says, "can that child talk?" I simply had to whisper! "Mama, I wonder if that child can be—you know—in any way? Do you realize," I says, "that she hasn't spoken one single, solitary word to a human being up to this minute? This is the way she looks," I says, and I looked like this.

Well, Mama and I just stood there and stared at each other. It was horrible!

"I remember well that Joe Whitaker frequently drank like a fish," says Mama. "I believed to my soul he drank *chemicals.*" And without another word she marches to the foot of the stairs and calls Stella-Rondo.

"Stella-Rondo? O-o-o-o-o! Stella-Rondo!"

"What?" says Stella-Rondo from upstairs. Not even the grace to get up off the bed.

"Can that child of yours talk?" asks Mama.

Stella-Rondo says, "Can she what?"

"Talk! Talk!" says Mama. "Burdyburdyburdyburdy!"

So Stella-Rondo yells back, "Who says she can't talk?"

"Sister says so," says Mama.

"You didn't have to tell me, I know whose word of honor don't mean a thing in this house," says Stella-Rondo.

And in a minute the loudest Yankee voice I ever heard in my life yells out, "OE'm Pop-OE the Sailor-r-r-r Ma-a-an!" and then somebody jumps up and down the upstairs hall. In another second the house would of fallen down.

"Not only talks she can tap-dance!" calls Stella-Rondo. "Which is more than some people I won't name can do."

"Why, the little precious darling thing!" Mama says, so surprised. "Just as smart as she can be!" Starts talking baby talk right there. Then she turns on me. "Sister, you ought to be thoroughly ashamed! Run upstairs this instant and apologize to Stella-Rondo and Shirley-T."

"Apologize for what?" I says. "I merely wondered if the child was normal, that's all. Now that she's proved she is, why, I have nothing further to say."

But Mama just turned on her heel and flew out, furious. She ran right upstairs and hugged the baby. She believed it was adopted. Stella-Rondo hadn't done a thing but turn her against me from upstairs while I stood there helpless over the hot stove. So that made Mama, Papa-Daddy and the baby all on Stella-Rondo's side.

Next, Uncle Rondo.

I must say that Uncle Rondo has been marvelous to me at various times in the past and I was completely unprepared to be made to jump out of my skin, the way it turned out. Once Stella-Rondo did something perfectly horrible to him—broke a chain letter from Flanders Field—and he took the radio back he had given her and gave it to me. Stella-Rondo was furious! For six months we all had to call her Stella instead of Stella-Rondo, or she wouldn't answer. I always thought Uncle Rondo had all the brains of the entire family. Another time he sent me to Mammoth Cave, with all expenses paid.

But this would be the day he was drinking that prescription, the Fourth of July.

So at supper Stella-Rondo speaks up and says she thinks Uncle Rondo ought to try to eat a little something. So finally Uncle Rondo said he would try a little cold biscuits and ketchup, but that was all. So *she* brought it to him.

"Do you think it wise to disport with ketchup in Stella-Rondo's flesh-colored kimono?" I says. Trying to be considerate! If Stella-Rondo couldn't watch out for her trousseau, somebody had to.

"Any objections?" asks Uncle Rondo, just about to pour out all the ketchup.

"Don't mind what she says, Uncle Rondo," says Stella-Rondo.

"Sister has been devoting this solid afternoon to sneering out my bedroom window at the way you look."

"What's that?" says Uncle Rondo. Uncle Rondo has got the most terrible temper in the world. Anything is liable to make him tear the house down if it comes at the wrong time.

So Stella-Rondo says, "Sister says, 'Uncle Rondo certainly does look like a fool in that pink kimono!' "

Do you remember who it was really said that?

Uncle Rondo spills out all the ketchup and jumps out of his chair and tears off the kimono and throws it down on the dirty floor and puts his foot on it. It had to be sent all the way to Jackson to the cleaners and re-pleated.

"So that's your opinion of your Uncle Rondo, is it?" he says. "I look like a fool, do I? Well, that's the last straw. A whole day in this house with nothing to do, and then to hear you come out with a remark like that behind my back!"

"I didn't say any such of a thing, Uncle Rondo," I says, "and I'm not saying who did, either. Why, I think you look all right. Just try to take care of yourself and not talk and eat at the same time," I says. "I think you better go lie down."

"Lie down my foot," says Uncle Rondo. I ought to of known by that he was fixing to do something perfectly horrible.

So he didn't do anything that night in the precarious state he was in—just played Casino with Mama and Stella-Rondo and Shirley-T. and gave Shirley-T. a nickel with a head on both sides. It tickled her nearly to death, and she called him "Papa." But at 6:30 A.M. the next morning, he threw a whole five-cent package of some unsold one-inch firecrackers from the store as hard as he could into my bedroom and they every one went off. Not one bad one in the string. Anybody else, there'd be one that wouldn't go off.

Well, I'm just terribly susceptible to noise of any kind, the doctor has always told me I was the most sensitive person he had ever seen in his whole life, and I was simply prostrated. I couldn't eat! People tell me they heard it as far as the cemetery, and old Aunt Jep Patterson, that had been holding her own so good, thought it was Judgment Day and she was going to meet her whole family. It's usually so quiet here.

And I'll tell you it didn't take me any longer than a minute to make up my mind what to do. There I was with the whole entire house on Stella-Rondo's side and turned against me. If I have anything at all I have pride.

So I just decided I'd go straight down to the P.O. There's plenty of room there in the back, I says to myself.

Well! I made no bones about letting the family catch on to what I was up to. I didn't try to conceal it.

The first thing they knew, I marched in where they were all playing Old Maid and pulled the electric oscillating fan out by the plug, and everything got real hot. Next I snatched the pillow I'd done the needlepoint on right off the davenport from behind Papa-Daddy. He went "Ugh!" I beat Stella-Rondo up the stairs and finally found my charm bracelet in her bureau drawer under a picture of Nelson Eddy.

"So that's the way the land lies," says Uncle Rondo. There he was, piecing on the ham. "Well, Sister, I'll be glad to donate my army cot if you got any place to set it up, providing you'll leave right this minute and let me get some peace." Uncle Rondo was in France.

"Thank you kindly for the cot and 'peace' is hardly the word I would select if I had to resort to firecrackers at 6:30 A.M. in a young girl's bedroom," I says back to him. "And as to where I intend to go, you seem to forget my position as postmistress of China Grove, Mississippi," I says. "I've always got the P.O."

Well, that made them all sit up and take notice.

I went out front and started digging up some four-o'clocks to plant around the P.O.

"Ah-ah-ah!" says Mama, raising the window. "Those happen to be my four-o'clocks. Everything planted in that star is mine. I've never known you to make anything grow in your life."

"Very well," I says. "But I take the fern. Even you, Mama, can't stand there and deny that I'm the one watered that fern. And I happen to know where I can send in a box top and get a packet of one thousand mixed seeds, no two the same kind, free."

"Oh, where?" Mama wants to know.

But I says, "Too late. You 'tend to your house, and I'll 'tend to mine. You hear things like that all the time if you know how to listen to the radio. Perfectly marvelous offers. Get anything you want free."

So I hope to tell you I marched in and got that radio, and they could of all bit a nail in two, especially Stella-Rondo, that it used to belong to, and she well knew she couldn't get it back, I'd sue for it like a shot. And I very politely took the sewing-machine motor I helped pay the most on to give Mama for Christmas back in 1929, and a good big calendar, with the first-aid remedies on it. The thermometer and the Hawaiian ukulele certainly were rightfully mine, and I stood on the step-ladder and got all my watermelon-rind preserves and every fruit and vegetable I'd put up, every jar. Then I began to pull the tacks out of the bluebird wall vases on the archway to the dining room.

"Who told you you could have those, Miss Priss?" says Mama, fanning as hard as she could.

"I bought 'em and I'll keep track of 'em," I says. "I'll tack 'em up one on each side the post-office window, and you can see 'em when you come to ask me for your mail, if you're so dead to see 'em."

"Not I! I'll never darken the door to that post office again if I live to be a hundred," Mama says. "Ungrateful child! After all the money we spent on you at the Normal."

"Me either," says Stella-Rondo. "You can just let my mail lie there and *rot*, for all I care. I'll never come and relieve you of a single, solitary piece."

"I should worry," I says. "And who you think's going to sit down and write you all those big fat letters and postcards, by the way? Mr. Whitaker? Just because he was the only man ever dropped down in China Grove and you got him—unfairly—is he going to sit down and write you a lengthy correspondence after you come home giving no rhyme nor reason whatsoever for your separation and no explanation for the presence of that child? I may not have your brilliant mind, but I fail to see it."

So Mama says, "Sister, I've told you a thousand times that Stella-Rondo simply got homesick, and this child is far too big to be hers," and she says, "Now, why don't you all just sit down and play Casino?"

Then Shirley-T. sticks out her tongue at me in this perfectly horrible way. She has no more manners than the man in the moon. I told her she was going to cross her eyes like that some day and they'd stick.

"It's too late to stop me now," I says. "You should have tried that yesterday. I'm going to the P.O. and the only way you can possibly see me is to visit me there."

So Papa-Daddy says, "You'll never catch me setting foot in that post office, even if I should take a notion into my head to write a letter some place." He says, "I won't have you reachin' out of that little old window with a pair of shears and cuttin' off any beard of mine. I'm too smart for you!"

"We all are," says Stella-Rondo.

But I said, "If you're so smart, where's Mr. Whitaker?"

So then Uncle Rondo says, "I'll thank you from now on to stop reading all the orders I get on postcards and telling everybody in China Grove what you think is the matter with them," but I says, "I draw my own conclusions and will continue in the future to draw them." I says, "If people want to write their inmost secrets on penny postcards, there's nothing in the wide world you can do about it, Uncle Rondo."

"And if you think we'll ever *write* another postcard you're sadly mistaken," says Mama.

"Cutting off your nose to spite your face then," I says. "But if you're all determined to have no more to do with the U.S. mail, think of this: What will Stella-Rondo do now, if she wants to tell Mr. Whitaker to come after her?"

"Wah!" says Stella-Rondo. I knew she'd cry. She had a conniption fit right there in the kitchen.

"It will be interesting to see how long she holds out," I says. "And now—I am leaving."

"Good-bye," says Uncle Rondo.

"Oh, I declare," says Mama, "to think that a family of mine should quarrel on the Fourth of July, or the day after, over Stella-Rondo leaving old Mr. Whitaker and having the sweetest little adopted child! It looks like we'd all be glad!"

"Wah!" says Stella-Rondo, and has a fresh conniption fit.

"*He* left *her*—you mark my words," I says. "That's Mr. Whitaker. I know Mr. Whitaker. After all, I knew him first. I said from the beginning he'd up and leave her. I foretold every single thing that's happened."

"Where did he go?" asks Mama.

"Probably to the North Pole, if he knows what's good for him," I says.

But Stella-Rondo just bawled and wouldn't say another word. She flew to her room and slammed the door.

"Now look what you've gone and done, Sister," says Mama. "You go apologize."

"I haven't got time, I'm leaving," I says.

"Well, what are you waiting around for?" asks Uncle Rondo.

So I just picked up the kitchen clock and marched off, without saying "Kiss my foot" or anything, and never did tell Stella-Rondo good-bye.

There was a girl going along on a little wagon right in front.

"Girl," I says, "come help me haul these things down the hill, I'm going to live in the post office."

Took her nine trips in her express wagon. Uncle Rondo came out on the porch and threw her a nickel.

And that's the last I've laid eyes on any of my family or my family laid eyes on me for five solid days and nights. Stella-Rondo may be telling the most horrible tales in the world about Mr. Whitaker, but I haven't heard them. As I tell everybody, I draw my own conclusions.

But oh, I like it here. It's ideal, as I've been saying. You see, I've got everything cater-cornered, the way I like it. Hear the radio? All the war news. Radio, sewing machine, book ends, ironing board and that great big piano lamp—peace, that's what I like. Butter-bean vines planted all along the front where the strings are.

Of course, there's not much mail. My family are naturally the main people in China Grove, and if they prefer to vanish from the face of the earth, for all the mail they get or the mail they write, why, I'm not going to open my mouth. Some of the folks here in town are taking up for me and some turned against me. I know which is which. There are always people who will quit buying stamps just to get on the right side of Papa-Daddy.

But here I am, and here I'll stay. I want the world to know I'm happy.

And if Stella-Rondo should come to me this minute, on bended knees, and *attempt* to explain the incidents of her life with Mr. Whitaker, I'd simply put my fingers in both my ears and refuse to listen.

FROM
Joiner

JAMES WHITEHEAD

LUCY DIED BEFORE I ever saw Bryan at an age old enough to remember it well. Daddy went to work at Hercules, the dynamite company in Hattiesburg, for the duration of the war, which war he missed because he lacks his thumb and first finger on his left hand, the result of another accident.

His first year or so at the old Chalmers' Mill in Bryan he was fitting a link belt back on the cogs, when an old one-eyed nigger switched the damn thing on and slowly ground them off, took off that finger and thumb, and caused him to crash and break his front teeth an instant before he let go of a scream I'm told you could hear over the entire terrible noise of the Mill going full blast. But Daddy never blamed anybody. He never blamed that blind nigger for making his left hand look like the terrible paw of some obscure animal.

What I remember first in my life is a dogtrot house at Rawles Springs, out from Hattiesburg, and it was there that Lucy got hers.

My sister was a corposant . . . foxfire . . .

For I've got a memory that goes back to three—and this thing was at five, and it's pretty goddamned vivid, praise God—it's enough to keep that good child, Lucy Patricia Joiner, and all other good children fast in my heart forever, including my own son Aubrey, whom Royal's getting.

Lucy was gawky like Momma, an energetic pale child with huge feet and the largest toes I ever saw. She was always rushing around on weekends and evenings, helping tend to me and the washing. She hustled around with wide blue eyes and short lashes, and she could be trusted with the wringer-type Maytag on the screen porch at an early age—and what I remember first about her is how she moved along the clothesline like it was an event in a girls' track meet. She had a step she did there in the hardyard in the sunshine—she pushed the wicker basket with her left foot, crimping those long toes over the rim, shoving. She could pluck the wooden pins from her mouth at an amazing rate. Pushing and bending, securing our clothes, white underthings, prints, and jeans and khakis, on the blue wire of the line.

Lucy was a dancer and I knew that never in the world could I do anything so worthwhile and graceful if I lived to be a hundred years old.

I loved my sister very much, and when she was prettied up in a dotted swiss dress at twelve, I guess you'd have to say there was something carnal about my feelings for her. (Mary, I grant you that.) So now I'm ready to offer the tragic event, *tragic* or *awful* or *terrible,* and probably I can be such a bastard about it because Mary Ann demands making an issue of it. There have been three big fires in my life and Mary Ann believes they constitute a psychic trinity, but they don't. It wasn't merely fire that got me out here in this house with her in exile. People react to different things in different ways.

It was an accident when Lucy backed too near the space heater and blazed up and ran past us all and out the screen door almost before the yelling started, and then the screaming. I finally knew it was an accident because Daddy's favorite saying has to do with trying to change what is in your power to change—*change what you're free to change, and try to forget the rest:* or did he say *forgive?* Hell, she even set the field on fire.

I was standing off across the room by the cypress dining table Daddy'd made (a magnificent gray thing with no nails in it)—I was watching Momma fuss around Lucy's 4-H party dress. And I think I remember drinking wonderfully lumpy and yellow-flecked and cold buttermilk straight out of the pitcher from the icebox, and in my memory's present eye R.S. and Momma are like wax figures from Madame Tussaud's (a rear view), for when the first smoke curled up, they were stiff and unnatural across the back and shoulders—Momma's blades like they'd split clean through her gilliflower cotton print.

Lucy Patricia broke from around them like they were a basketball screen and she was a small guard moving in for a quick lay-up. Out the kitchen door into the breezeway she ran on fire, out the front door of the house and into the hardyard on fire, and all the wax figures were alive and yelling and running after. Lucy's hair had been combed out and brushed, a yellow ribbon pulled tight at her crown—and just before I joined in the running I was thinking it didn't make any sense for her to be so dressed up and then catch fire.

We all followed after as she ran a zigzag course through the fallow field to the west of the house, and when we finally got to where she'd fallen over a worndown ancient cornrow, she was out cold and badly burned, but at least that terrible single syllable she'd been crying had gone away. R.S. said, "She's burned bad, but she'll make it." Her new dress was almost entirely gone, with only little patches of scorched slip stuck to her skin. And in the moonlight her face looked flushed and her body was reddish, but she didn't look entirely ruined. And there *was* a little fire around her in the brush and dock. It was sputtering and lapping slightly the way it does when farmers have their burn-offs under control. Daddy kept saying, "She's hurt O.K. but she'll be all right," as he knelt to lift her up—ole bearlike R.S. lifted her easily and gently into his arms and then ran a strange stiff jog across the field to the truck, leaving Momma and me alone. The motor caught the second time, but only one headlight went on in that instant before he turned out onto the road toward the hospital in Hattiesburg.

Momma didn't say very much the whole time they were gone, and neither did I. What she did was go back to the house and wet down some gunnysacks to beat the fire out with. Correct. She wet down two at the pump behind the house, then we walked back to where Lucy'd been, and she beat out the little fires that were left. She was strong against the fires, but she never went crazy and acted like they were to blame. Momma never lost her mind over it.

We did those things and then went inside to sit at the table and drink coffee until we heard from Daddy. Momma said a couple of times that Lucy'd be O.K., but when Daddy got back home it was to say that Lucy was dead. It was a cold December night in a drought and Lucy Patricia died of shock that night as much as anything else.

So there. Now we have it—Eugene "Sonny" Joiner did see his sister running and dying and crying out, like ambulant foxfire, across a dockfield some time near the end of World War II. And he remembers how the hair around her narrow face was singed—but her inexpensive casket was never opened—and *my* mother never got up from *her* pew to try and climb in with the dead child the way

Billy Weatherford's mother did, after I'd killed him. And our good Methodist preacher didn't tell us she died to teach us all a great goddamned *im*portant lesson about the meaning of LAF, which is exactly what that foot-washing, ignorant sonofabitch did at Billy's.

Daddy said close it, at the hospital, for we wanted to remember her the way she was in the time of her life with us and not the way some mortician imagined her; and at the Rawles Springs Methodist Missionary Chapel there was a quiet and decent celebration of the life of that energetic and good-natured and helpful young lady, attended by friends and family, including the Boykins (later to die by fire themselves), and Henry Smith, April's father (also to be burned)—all of them old friends from Bryan.

The preacher said the Lord Himself probably didn't have anything to do with Lucy's death. He was a fellow of about forty with blotchy skin and a B.D. from Emory Seminary named Taggart, Stream's daddy, and I can see now that what he said was absolutely miraculous for that time and place. He told the assembled congregation that though God created the world and loves His creation, loving man most of all, He requires man to *complete* His creation. I sat like a flat rock in a dry bed and listened the way a small child does in Mississippi when God is the subject—and Reverend Taggart was nervous about what he'd said. He was afraid that he'd suggested that maybe it was the parents' fault. Maybe the bereaved were blaming themselves for letting the girl get too close to the heater. He rolled his eyes up to the exposed ceiling beams, with what I now know was a God-get-me-through-this-hour look—he trembled there in his place, fluttering his long fingers on the front edge of the pulpit, and then he went cautiously on to say that sometimes things happen in this life that are *not* God's will—sometimes things happen not because of God's will and not because of human mistakes either—sometimes we suffer accidents . . . sometimes the good . . . sometimes the bad, and when the bad, even the entirely terrible, happen on us, God Himself grieves.

The preacher had struck vision he didn't expect.

His eyes shone with a look akin to joy. He pulled himself to his full strict height and spread his arms wide. He said: "Dear friends, the Lord God in Heaven Himself . . . *grieves* this child's death. The Great High God is . . . *confused* to see her here, and us in all our misery today. How *could* we love a God who never suffered our confusions?"

And he got away with it.

Nobody in the house knew or at that moment gave a rip about theology, so he got away with it. Damn near the whole small church broke out crying when Preacher Taggart said that. They did exactly what they had to do. Man, it was the kind of scene that broke Big Jim Agee's heart, and if Walker Evans had been there later at the graveside with us, his camera would have wept from its one keen eye.

All those fine adult people stood there under the loblollies and around Lucy's gravesite—the goddamned lonesome pines—and the cheap vault being lowered—and sometimes it happens exactly that way—the resin all beaded out like jewels on the coarse bark, and the air with a terribly beautiful hungry taste when you breathe it in, and the only hymn we sang was "Farther Along." *Farther along we'll know more about it, farther along we'll understand why!*

How does *that* grab you, Mary, me dear, me dear? Kinda makes you harelip, don't it? Kinda goes against the grain of all your foolish de-fense mechanisms, don't it? Decency. Decency. Decency. Decency. Decency. It was a decent afternoon with a lot of fellow feeling in the air. Pine needles and gumbo clay, pine barrens, and sweet songs—it was the goddamned animal at his best, and almost everybody came to the house for supper, Mrs. Boykin having brought it over from Bryan—she brought us black-eyed peas and ham, like it was New Year's Day. Tiny Mrs. Boykin had herself some proper traditions and a good deal of imagination to boot.

It was, in fact, a strangely good day and the first time I met and played with Royal and Stream and April. Reverend Taggart lived in Petal and didn't preach for us but every third Sunday, and of course I hadn't seen the children of my people's old friends yet—or didn't remember if I had. It was the day of the funeral and the day I met my lifelong friends, and also it was moving day, which is curious in a way, and something I never entirely understood about my parents. I can understand them wanting out of the house we were in then, and I can even understand how, in a troubled time, they'd want to be in the town they knew best, which was Bryan, but why did they bury Lucy in Rawles Springs?

Years later I asked Daddy why, and he said it's only forty miles from Rawles to Bryan. And Momma thought I was accusing her of something evil when I asked her the same question. "We get over there plenty often an' keep Lucy's the best in the world . . . Eugene?" My question moved and spooked her. And the nearest I can come is to say they're superstitious. They believed their luck was down.

"Daddy, you moved to change your luck didn't you?"

"I moved because I had to move," he said. And then he walked away. He had the Big Wheel Yazoo mower to oil.

The day of Lucy's funeral we all played outside after the early supper, while the adults were talking, packing and talking, and loading all our things into the pickups. We fell in with each other very comfortably, and it wasn't long before I took them out into the field to where the patch of burned grass was, which wasn't really a ghoulish thing for a small boy to do. We gathered in the burned place and waited in solemn anticipation for something that never quite happened. I remember them clearly. Royal was fat and active, and even when he was trying to be still he bounced like a redrubber ball that peels—and he made a kind of rolling motion when he ran, like there wasn't really any flat ground anywhere in the world. He featured himself as Lash LaRue and had a twenty-cent McCrory's whip to prove it with. And Stream was Stream—named Coldstream Taggart because his momma loved the Coldstream Guards she's seen in a movie travelogue once—Stream's a turkey always jabbing with his head and pecking around—and when he plays anything he's a chicken with its head off, a thrasher and a flopper, not a roller or a strider. The nicest thing you can call him is *loose.*

The day of Lucy's funeral we ended up by playing soldiers and grenades with pine cones.

What the hell? And, yes, there she was, little April. I remember she had some kind of plaid wool coat on, and that she was entirely white-headed, what my momma called a "perfect blond." She was frisky and agile and played what we boys wanted her to. We stood there in the burned grass and she picked up a little piece of scorched net, and she asked me if I wanted it. Royal bobs and bounces silently, and Stream groans, "OOoooo," then runs off to the trees and the gloaming.

She asks, "Would you want this?"

I said I didn't, and she looked embarrassed. She dropped it back on top of the old cornrow.

And nothing happened, absolutely nothing happened until Royal clicked his little whip. He tossed his red head from side to side, like he was working a crick out of his short, thick neck. Then he made as if he were boarding his trusty horse. "Giddyup, hoss," says Royal. We agreed we all had horses—we agreed that we were cavalry in World War II—so April and Royal and I galloped away toward the woods where Stream had gone, toward the woods where, in fact, the sun was going down.

FROM

Captain Blackman

JOHN A. WILLIAMS

Cadences

Outside, Cincinnati was gray with rain winding down the sky, but there was enough light and luxury in the Great Hall to dispel the sense of gloom that hung outside the windows, vainly trying to attack the interior of the huge estate and its inhabitants.

Lunch was over. The baroque room muffled the sounds of bottles and glasses, of Negro servants picked for their lightness of color, who padded like cougars on carpeted floors whisking away dishes, bowls, silver, and dressing the tables with crackling white damask covers. It was time for "refreshment" and the talk. Large bowls of pungent, hot spiced rum were brought in. Bottles of Old Robertson's Canadian lent the air of Delmonico's, Riley's and Delatour's to the room. Mint juleps, heavily sprigged and thickly sweet, came last.

Their accents revealed the places the men in the room came from: New York, Boston, Charleston, New Orleans, San Francisco. Random conversations were scheduled for now; later they'd come together at the big table for more formal discussions and dinner. The two sponsors of the meeting sat down in a corner.

"Cockrill, this drift to war is as incredible as it is ridiculous. How can New York and New Orleans go to war? We need each other; we're like the fingers on a hand."

"Then, by God, Cabot, you must stop this opposition to a protective tariff; we won't continue to provide you with cotton; we'll go to Europe."

Cabot sighed heavily. He knew that the Southerners were already firmly into the European markets. "Let's not play games. You're there already. American products don't belong in Europe, not yet, not when you've an obligation still to the American people. You've got to stop pushing for slavery in the West—I know there's lots of land out there; you fellows got us into that war just to expand slavery with your cotton farming. The idea is to withdraw *as painlessly as possible from slavery; your entire economy rests upon it—"*

"—and yours, dear Cabot."

"But, Cockrill, I'm saying that with immigration wide open now, it's time to change habits. How in the world can these poor Irish and Germans compete with slave labor? It can't *be done."*

"On the contrary, sir. Were it not for our holding four million or so slaves in bondage in the southeastern United States, there'd be no jobs at all anywhere for the immigrants. It is only because they are so constrained that this European rabble has any chance at all to seek work in your mills. In any case," Cockrill said sourly, "it's too late. The blacks will always be a factor in the labor market, North and South. Indirectly now. But say they were free and joined forces with the immigrants—oh, God, Cabot, what a mess that would be. As it is, we've right now got five million poor whites who hate the blacks because they do the work for nothing that the whites could do for pay. That is good, don't you think?"

Grimly Cabot said, "Sooner or later you've got to give up slavery, you, me, and set our base somewhere else—"

"Yes, and see them come together, the blacks and the whites, and then, my friend, what will we have?"

"You've got to do it, Cockrill. This is serious. In the past, you paid as little attention to our public pronouncements about the evils of slavery as we did to your claims of the blacks' natural backwardness—you've got too many mulattoes and quadroons down there for us to have taken you seriously. Now, it's different.

"Furthermore, we're opposed to the way you've captured political office in Washington with your representation based so much upon the slaves, the very persons you don't even consider to be people until its time for one of you to run for office. God! Open the West and we'd be overwhelmed—"

Cockrill said, "Property is property, Cabot, and according to law, you've got to own property to run for office."

"What we're basically talking about here, Cockrill, and you know it, is sharing the wealth, sharing the power. We will have our share, goddamnit, or there will be war."

"Now, now, Cabot, you know we couldn't do without you Yan-

kees. You loan us money, let us use your ships, but you ought to know that if there is war, we'll have England and France on our side, because they want the cotton. You could only win if the Almighty stepped in on your side."

"We don't want a war, Cockrill! Think what it'd do to the country."

Soothingly Cockrill said, "We've worked out things before and we can work them out again. The election won't matter, whether Lincoln or Douglas wins. There're certain hard realities that go with the office, you know—"

"My dear friend Cockrill," Cabot said, and he felt tears coming to his eyes. "We talk all about the matter, but not to it. We have got to move the base of economic power in this nation from slavery, or slavery will move us in one way or another. Now, you mark my words. Mark them well."

Languidly the Southerner said, sniffing of his mint, "Slavery is only a name. There are others, perhaps less offensive, that can serve just as well and mean, pretty nearly, the same thing."

THE TRAINING WAS all over now, Blackman thought. All that marching in the square in those bright uniforms with the women looking on; that was all over and this, coming up was the real thing. He nudged Little David Harrison and together they looked up at the ramparts of Port Hudson. The flat, brown Mississippi gurgled its way past, cooling the air, and all about them they heard the jangle of packs and rifles, of drums preparing to dress them into the line of attack.

Blackman pursed his lips in a silent whistle. This was gonna be something. "Good luck," he said to Little David.

"Yeah."

On the way to his men Blackman passed Flag Sergeant Anselmas Plancianois. "Ready, Sergeant?" Plancianois asked with a grin, as he nervously shifted his feet.

"I'm ready. How about you?"

"Ready's I'll ever be, and I'll bring the colors back in honor or tell the good Lord the reason why."

"Let's hope you won't have to do that, Sergeant," Blackman said.

Yeah, he thought, continuing on his way. When those balls start to fly he'll be talking out the other side of his mouth, just like all the rest of these bad-talking soldiers. Blackman felt his stomach fluttering and the palms of his hands growing water as he fell in with his company, row upon row of black faces, men with French names and hard-to-understand accents.

The long roll sounded on the drums. Blackman stared upward at the fortifications again. It was ten in the morning, the day settling firmly in the sky. The insects jabbed and whined at his face. Behind the rows of black troops, he knew that the generals, Banks and Ullman, were there, anxious to see how black troops fought, eager to spread the word of the success or failure of the Emancipation on this one battle.

Now the drums sounded common time and the lines marched forward. Blackman barked at his men, the better to conceal his rising fear, and they, the better to conceal theirs, glared back at him and thought, The big black bastard. His heart pounding, thudding against his rib cage, Blackman moved on as if in a dream.

Quick-time in a series of rolls and flams rocked off the drums and the bugles took up the call. Blackman felt the ground flowing back under him. The clatter of metal hooks sounded in unison as the waves of black men moved on, panting although they'd not really begun to exert themselves. Then: *double-quick time!* Blackman rushed over the ground now; he seemed to be out of breath already, but knew it was from fear, nothing else. For a ludicrous moment there came the twitter of diving swallows. Behind them the barrage lifted, and ahead the Rebels began theirs.

Black powder bursts puffed sharply among them. Blackman cowered at the whine of hot metal seeking flesh. Turning, he saw the lines uneven, bent backwards, strung out, and he shouted into the roar for them to come on. Sharply the bugles sounded the charge and the men, as though stung, leaped forward again, straightening their lines, bending them forward this time, and they burst into a clearing where some of the Rebel cannon had been fixed, firing at the gunners as they tried to escape. They were almost under the walls now and down from them poured Rebel fire, grape and ball, all singing and humming wildly as they slashed through flesh and bone.

Blackman found himself running almost alone; the first line had been decimated. Captain Cailloux ran up beside Blackman and, turning his back to the fort, shouted at the men, "Steady, steady," in both French and English, his blue-black skin covered with sweat sparkling in the sun. Desperate soldiers rallied to him and he turned to face the fort, lunged forward and took a charge in the arm. Horrified, Blackman slowed to help. The Captain waved him on. "Follow me! Follow me!" He took a shell directly in the torso. Blackman quivered at the sound and wanted to scream when he saw blood, bone and skin unraveling even as Cailloux was moving. He watched helplessly as the half mass of pulverized flesh staggered to the lip of a ditch and collapsed.

Even as he hurtled toward it, Blackman's mind screamed, a ditch! They hadn't said anything about a ditch. You just run up to the walls, batter them in or climb them, or go in through breaches made by our artillery. He was going so fast he couldn't stop; he gathered himself and sprung up and out and came down short of the other side, powering into brown water which gave off a sudden series of silver bubbles as he went under. For a second or two he took shelter in the calm depths. The battle seemed far away, and then in panic, he began to kick and struggle to the surface, nearer the sound of rifle and cannon and shouts. The blacks were bunched up on the lip. Officers among them were urging them back to try again. Struggling up through thick mud, Blackman watched them go, and return, all bent black men, rifles held high. They seemed to be moving slowly as they approached the lip, and then in a wave they took to the air and he heard and saw them fall short, some of them dead, and hit the water behind him. He grabbed a rock with one hand and with the other pulled at as many hands as he could, towing them toward his side of the ditch. Those who could climbed out and cowered under the walls, their rifles useless because of wet powder.

Anxiously, they glanced back across the ditch as the men hurtled up once more and flung their weary black bodies out over the water, some to drown, others to struggle up to where Blackman was, to become victims of the Rebel sharpshooters now shooting directly down from the walls and into the heads of those who'd made it across.

Retreat sounded. Blackman slipped his pack and the others followed suit; they went again into the water, easing past the bodies filling it, and back to the other side.

Later, relieved at having found Little David alive, the two men compared notes.

"We were by ourselves for four hours," Little David said. "And the center and left side sections didn't start their attacks. We took it all."

Blackman sat stolidly. He'd learned that the blacks'd been only one twelfth of the Union forces but had lost one eighth of the total, one tenth of the wounded and three fourths of the missing.

"Pigeons," Little David said. "Or sittin ducks."

Little David Harrison was a small man with a boy's face, but there was something huge and terrible about him, Blackman knew. He was a vicious fighter, a man who killed with equal facility in the heat of battle or the coldness of revenge. "There's no satisfaction like killin white men," he'd said. "Yankee or Rebel, it's all the same to me." And glancing at Blackman in what for him could've been called a gentle manner, he said, "You got too much compassion, or whatever, Abraham. Maybe that goes with bein big. I dunno."

"I kill like you kill, Little David."

The events of the day, like those of other days, would stay with Little David. All that white treachery. And black folks not seeing it just because, back there in January, Lincoln freed the slaves. Freed them because he didn't have a choice, Little David thought. But out here, along this Mississippi and a thousand other places black men were eager to let themselves be slaughtered because they believed in the sudden goodness of those who'd oppressed them for over two centuries.

Perhaps he shouldn't have said what he said to Abraham. Compassion wasn't the right word, or maybe it was in a sense too large for Little David to bother to understand. He has killed like me. Little David shifted his position. "You right, Abe. I didn't mean you're soft."

"Maybe the difference, Little David, is that I kill because I have to—"

Little David smiled, the same kind of smile Blackman observed he smiled when he was ready to sing one of his favorite songs. And Little David could sing. "You mean," Little David said, "I kill because I like to."

Blackman stood up. "We're just runnin off at the mouth, little man. Tired and scared and don't half know what it is we're sayin. Besides, it's time to move on to other places and other killings."

Killings at Milliken's Bend, and in southeast Kansas, brutal, hateful killings that had little to do with war, but everything to do with color, and it was these constant murders of black soldiers that made other black soldiers better fighters, Blackman observed, with each succeeding campaign. For the Rebels there was no such thing as a black prisoner of war. Each battle became a fight not for land or victory, but for survival. Whenever black men and white men locked in fearful, angry embrace, the terror of ugly death struck at both sides; when the balls ran out, they charged with bayonets. Rebel yells and black curses rent the air. Kill close up! Kill with bare hands! Steel! Feel their blood so slick on your hands you couldn't hardly hold your rifle. As if in some wild and ancient euphoria, time after time black and white danced, steel glinting where it wasn't already crimsoned, blood jetting suddenly in the bright sun, all to cries of "No quarter to the niggers!" "No quarter to the crackers!"

Behind their line of march the traded atrocities became legend: prisoners shredded by bayonets; prisoners decapitated; prisoners castrated; prisoners pulled asunder by horses. Still they marched on across the southland, ever fearful that worse could happen, and as they came into sight of Fort Wagner, they exchanged the bitter news of the Draft Riots in New York and of black people hung from lamp posts, beaten in the streets, murdered in alleys, old and young alike, orphans and attached.

So it did not help when they were dressed into line for the attack, the blacks in front, exhausted with travel from Folly and Morris islands, hungry from lack of food. Wagner shimmered before their eyes, a mirage, but a reality, and Blackman saw that even now there were men who were proud to be leading the attack, proud to be white men's cannon fodder, and when the bugles and drums sounded, like spurred horses they charged to the attack as they'd done so many times before, and Blackman moved with them, Little David at his side now, again engaged in survival.

The Colonel, leading the charge, was hit, but he continued, shouting and waving his sword, and Blackman hated him, wished him dead, prayed through gasps of breath for the violent death of this man who'd asked that his troops lead the charge. How much more can we prove, Blackman thought angrily, running hard, all the sounds of his being bubbling up into an angry, frustrated scream which even he couldn't hear for the cadence of war all around him.

Through sand, marsh and water they plunged, sound sucking in air and then exploding it, and up to the walls like crazed dogs, eager to attack and kill the targets for their being there in the first place, and from inside those walls came the old cries: "It's niggers! Kill the black sonsabitches!"

They're afraid, too, Blackman thought, as he blew the head off a whiskered man who'd thrust himself forward on the walls; out of the corner of his eye he saw Little David ram his bayonet into the face of another Rebel, where it stuck, and saw the face disintegrate when Little David pulled the trigger.

Damn the Union. Damn the Confederacy. Kill niggers. Kill crackers.

And, beat down from the walls, Blackman led his men back, reformed them and charged again, this time over the body of the Colonel, only to be beaten down again and again and again, leaving inside some of his troops who'd made it over the walls; Blackman ran back, his chest on fire, hands stiff on the gun he held only by force of habit. He already felt, imagined that he felt, crackers bayoneting him, slowly sawing off his prick, and his flesh crawled. The fate of the missing who'd not been lucky enough to be blown apart by a shell.

The next day, with a solitary drummer, Blackman led out the burial detail under a flag of truce. He always marveled at the quiet that hovered over battlefields after the fighting. Above the vomitus birds twittered and sand flies stung; the stiff sea breeze curled the stink of the dead across the island. Huge flies, glistening bluely, buzzed over shattered skin, sucked drying blood, busied themselves laying eggs that in a few hours would turn into maggots.

The Colonel was already buried. They told Blackman of his naked body, stomped, spat on, and otherwise defiled, and how he'd been put into a pit with his dead nigger soldiers. For a moment, Blackman wanted to uncover the mound, throw aside the black dead just to see what the crackers had really done to the Colonel. Had they cut off his prick, too? His head? Punctured him with their bayonets? He looked to the walls of the fort, gray in this morning light, and saw and smelled a sickness there, defined behind its ugliness; a glob, like the jellyfish on the beach, amorphous, yet containing dimension and sharp pain—a smell of impending decay.

Later, winding through Georgia, a hard, murderous regiment, their cheap, blue uniforms falling in patches from their bodies, they heard of Fort Pillow where General Nathan Bedford Forrest ordered the slaughter of three hundred black troops after they'd surrendered; they said the Mississippi, which flows fast and deep past Memphis, ran red with blood for two days, and that the black civilians fished out heads, arms, legs and torsos, and only six days later, while probing toward Atlanta, they heard of Poison Springs.

There black soldiers were left like hunks of buffalo meat on an Arkansas landscape.

The day they heard of Poison Springs was the day they gave up trying to stay human. The change was imperceptible, but it was change nonetheless. Blackman and Little David joined them in the grove that night, away from the white officers. One by one under the moonless sky they spoke the words, each of them, clearly.

"I swear by my ancestors, and by the Mother whose name is Africa, to kill with a swift, sure arm, without hesitation, and in revenge for my brothers at Fort Pillow and Poison Springs and wherever else black soldiers are made to die less than the men they are."

When the oath-taking was finished the chant began like the rustle of leaves in a light wind:

No quarter to the Rebels,
No quarter when they call,
No quarter to the Rebels,
Damn them, kill them all!

Now, Blackman thought, they could drink hot cow's blood and shit, and he dreamed back to Africa's warriors, and forward to 200,000 black Union soldiers who would take the oath and chant the litany; to the white soldiers caught in the path of the black phalanx who would know that their deaths were no longer necessary, but imperative, and understanding that, would tremble when, from outside their walls they heard the chant spring up on the morning wind, the night wind, the noon wind, growing in intensity, in pledge:

No quarter to the Rebels,
No quarter when they call,
No quarter to the Rebels,
Damn them, kill them all!

The Field of Blue Children

TENNESSEE WILLIAMS

THAT FINAL SPRING at the State University a restlessness came over Myra which she could not understand. It was not merely the restlessness of superabundant youth. There was something a little neurotic about it. Nothing that she did seemed quite satisfying or complete. Even when she returned from a late formal dance, where she had swung from partner to partner the whole evening through, she did not feel quite ready to tumble exhausted into bed. She felt as though there must be something still further to give the night its perfect fullness. Sometimes she had the almost panicky sensation of having lost or forgotten something very important. She would stand quite still for a moment with tightened forehead, trying to remember just what it was that had slipped from her fingers—been left behind in the rumble seat of Kirk's roommate's roadster or on the sofa in the dimly-lighted fraternity lounge between dances.

"What's the matter?" Kirk or somebody else would ask and she would laugh rather sharply.

"Nothing. I just felt like I'd forgotten something!"

The feeling persisted even when every article was accounted for. She still felt as though something were missing. When she had returned to the sorority house she went from room to room, exchanging anecdotes of the evening, laughing at them far more than their humor warranted. And when finally everyone else had gone to bed, she stayed up alone in her room and sometimes she cried bitterly without knowing why, crushing the pillow against her mouth so that no one could hear—or else she sat in pajamas on the window seat and looked out across the small university town with all its buildings and trees and open fields a beautiful dusky blue in the spring night, the dome of the administration building like a snowy peak in the distance and the stars astonishingly large and close—she felt as though she would strangle with an emotion whose exact nature or meaning she could not understand.

When half-drunken groups of serenaders, also restless after late dances, paused beneath her house, she turned on the bed lamp and leaned above them, patting her hands together in a pantomime of delighted applause. When they left, she remained at the window, looking out with the light extinguished, and it was sad, unbearably sad, to hear their hoarse voices retreating down moon-splashed avenues of trees till they could not be heard any longer or else were drowned in the noise of a starting motor whose raucous gravel-kicking departure ebbed quickly to a soft, musical hum and was succeeded at length by the night's complete blue silence.

Still seated at the window, she waited with tight throat for the sobbing to commence. When it did, she felt better. When it did not, her vigil would sometimes continue till morning began and the restless aching had worn itself out.

That spring she took Kirk Abbott's fraternity pin. But this did not radically change her manner of living. She continued to accept dates with other men. She went out almost wherever she was asked with almost whoever asked her, and when Kirk protested she didn't try to explain the fever that made her behave in this way, she simply kissed him until he stopped talking and was in a mood to forgive her for almost anything that she might conceivably do.

From the beginning of adolescence, perhaps earlier, Myra had written a little verse. But this spring it became a regular practice. Whenever the rising well of unexplainable emotion became so full that its hurt was intolerable, she found that it helped her a little to scribble things down on paper. Single lines or couplets, sometimes whole stanzas, leapt into her mind with the instant completeness of slides flashed on the screen of a magic lantern. Their beauty startled her: sometimes it was like a moment of religious exaltation. She stood in a frozen attitude; her breath was released in a sigh. Each time she felt as though she were about to penetrate some new area of human thought. She had the sensation of standing upon the verge of a shadowy vastness which might momentarily flower into a marvelous crystal of light, like a ballroom that is dark one moment and is the next moment illuminated by the sunlike brilliance of a hundred glass chandeliers and reflecting mirrors and polished floors. At such times she would turn out the light in her bedroom and go quickly to the window. When she looked out across the purple-dark town and the snowy white dome above the quadrangle, or when she sat as in a spell, listening to the voices that floated down the quiet streets, singers of blues-songs or laughing couples in roadsters, the beauty of it no longer tormented her, she felt instead a mysterious quietness as though some disturbing question had been answered and life had accordingly become a much simpler and more pleasurable experience.

"Words are a net to catch beauty!"

She wrote this in the back of a notebook toward the close of a lecture on the taxing powers of Congress. It was late in April when she wrote this—and from then on it seemed that she understood what she wanted and the hurt bewilderment in her grew less acute.

In the Poetry Club to which Myra belonged there was a boy named Homer Stallcup who had been in love with her for a year or more. She could tell this by the way that he looked at her during the club sessions, which were the only occasions on which they met. Homer never looked directly at her, his eyes slid quickly across her face, but something about his expression, even about the tense pose of his body as he sat gripping his knees, made her feel his awareness of her. He avoided sitting next to her or even directly across from her—the chairs were usually arranged in a circle—and because of this she had at first thought that he must dislike her, but she had come gradually to understand that his shyness toward her had an exactly opposite meaning.

Homer was not a fraternity member. He waited on tables at a campus restaurant, fired furnaces and did chores for his room and board. Nobody in Myra's social *milieu* knew him or paid him any attention. He was rather short, stocky and dark. Myra thought him good-looking, but certainly not in any usual way. He had intense black eyes, a straight nose with flaring nostrils, full, mobile lips that sometimes jerked nervously at the corners. All of his movements were overcharged. When he rose from a chair he would nearly upset it. When he lighted a cigarette his face would twist into a terrible scowl and he would fling the burnt match away like a lighted firecracker.

He went around a great deal with a girl of his own intellectual type, a girl named Hertha something or other, who was rather widely known on the campus because of her odd behavior. In classes she would be carried away by enthusiasm upon some subject, either literary or political, and she would talk so rapidly that nobody could understand what she was saying and she would splutter and gasp and make awkward gestures—as though she were trying to pluck some invisible object out of the air—till the room was in an uproar of amusement and the instructor had to turn his face to the blackboard to conceal his own laughter.

Hertha and this boy, Homer, made a queer picture together, she nearly a foot taller, often rushing along a foot or more in advance of him, clutching him by the coat sleeve as though afraid that he might escape from her, and every minute or so one or both of them bursting into violent laughter that could be heard for a block.

Homer wrote poetry of a difficult sort. It was uneven. Parts of it were reminiscent of Hart Crane, parts were almost as naïvely lucid as Sara Teasdale's. But there were lines and phrases which stabbed at you with their poignant imagery, their fresh observation. When he had given a reading at a symposium, Hertha would always leap out of her chair as though animated by an electric charge, her blinking, near-sighted eyes tensely sweeping the circle of superciliously smiling faces, first demanding, then begging that they concur in the extravagant praise which her moist lips babbled. Only Myra would say anything when Hertha had finished. The rest were too baffled or too indifferent or even too hostile. And Homer's face, darkly flushed, would be turned to his lap throughout the rest of the meeting. His fingers would fold down corners of the neat pages as though the poetry had been erased from them or had never been written on them, as though these pages were simply blank pieces of paper for his fingers to play with.

Myra always wanted to say something more, but her critical vocabulary was slight.

"I think that was lovely," she would say. Or "I liked that very much." And Homer would not lift his eyes, his face would turn even darker, and she would bite her tongue as though in remose for an unkind speech. She wanted to put her hands over his fingers, to make them stop crumpling the neat pages, to make them be still.

It was not till the last meeting of the year, in early June, that Myra had the courage to approach him. After that meeting she saw him standing by the water fountain at the end of the corridor. She rushed impulsively up to him and told him, all in one breath, that his was the best unpublished verse she'd ever heard, that he should submit it to some of the good literary magazines, that she thought the other members of the club were absolute fools for not understanding.

Homer stood with his fists clenched in his pockets. He did not look at her face the whole time she was speaking. When she had stopped, his excitement burst through. He tore a sheaf of manuscripts from his brief case and thrust them into her hands.

"Please read them," he begged, "and let me know what you think."

They went downstairs together. On the bottom step he tripped or slid and she had to catch his arm to prevent him from falling. She was both touched and amused by this awkwardness and by his apparent delight in walking beside her. As they went out of the white stone building the late afternoon sun, yellow as lemon, met their faces in a beneficent flood. The air was filled with the ringing of five-thirty bells and the pliant voices of pigeons. A white feather from one of the stirring wings floated down and lighted upon Myra's hair. Homer lifted it off and thrust it in his hatband, and all the way home, after leaving him, Myra could feel that quick, light touch of his fingers. She wondered if he would keep the pigeon's feather; treasure it, possibly, for a long while afterward because it had once touched her person.

That night, when the sorority house was submerged in darkness, she took out the sheaf of poems and read them through without stopping. As she read she felt a rising excitement. She did not understand very much of what she was reading, but there was a cumulative effect, a growing intensity in the sequence. When she had finished she found herself trembling: trembling as when you step from warm water into chill air.

She dressed and went downstairs. She didn't know what she was planning to do. Her movements were without any conscious direction. And yet she had never moved with more certainty.

She opened the front door of the sorority house, ran down the brick-paved walk, turned to the left and continued swiftly through the moonlit streets till she had reached Homer's residence. It startled her to find herself there. There were cicadas burring in the large oaks—she had not heard them until this moment. And when she looked upward she saw a close group of stars above the western gable of the large frame house. The Seven Sisters. They were huddled together like virgin wanderers through a dark forest. She listened and there was not a voice anywhere, nothing except the chant of cicadas and the faint, faint rustling of her white skirt when she moved.

She went quickly around the side of the house to the door that she had seen Homer come out of in the mornings. She gave two short, distinct raps, then flattened herself against the brick wall. She was breathing rapidly. After waiting a while, she knocked again. Through the glass pane she could see down a flight of stairs into the basement. The door of a lamplit room was open. She saw first a moving shadow, then the boy himself, catching a heavy brown robe about his body and frowning up at the door as he mounted toward it.

As the door came open she gasped his name.

For a whole minute, it seemed, he said nothing. Then he caught her arm and pulled her inside the door.

"Myra, it's you!"

"Yes, it's me," she laughed. "I don't know what came over me. I've been reading your poetry and I just felt like I had to see you at once and tell you. . . ."

Her breath gave out. She leaned against the closed door. It was her eyes this time, and not his, that looked for concealment. She looked down at the bottom of his ugly brown bathrobe and she saw his bare feet beneath it, large and bony and white, and the sight of them frightened her. She remembered the intense, fleeting way of his eyes sliding over her face and body and the way he trembled that afternoon when she came up to him in the corridor, how those large feet had tripped on the bottom stair and she had been forced to catch him to keep him from falling.

"There was one thing in particular," she went on with a struggle. "There was something about a field of blue flowers. . . ."

"Oh, yes," he whispered. "The blue children, you mean!"

"Yes, that was it!" Now she lifted her eyes, eagerly.

"Come down to my room, Myra."

"I couldn't!"

"You couldn't?"

"No, of course not! If anyone caught me. . . ."

"They wouldn't!"

"I'd be expelled!"

There was a slight pause.

"Wait a minute!"

He ran down three steps and turned.

"Wait for me just one minute, Myra!"

She felt her head nodding. She heard him running down the rest of the steps and into the basement room where he lived. Through the door she saw his shadow moving about the floor and the walls. He was dressing. Once he stepped into the portion of the bedroom that she could see through the half-open door and he stood in her sight naked from the waist up, and she was startled and strangely moved by that brief glimpse of his full, powerful chest and arms, strikingly etched with shadows thrown by the lamp. In that moment he acquired in her mind a physical reality which he had never had before. A very great physical reality, greater than she had felt in Kirk Abbott or in any of the other young men that she had gone with on the campus.

A minute later he stepped out of the door and closed it and came quietly up the short flight of steps to where she was standing.

"I'm sorry I took so long."

"It wasn't long."

He took her arm and they went out of the door and around to the front of the house. The oak tree in the front lawn appeared gigantic. Everything was peculiarly sharpened or magnified; even the crunch of gravel under their two pairs of white shoes. She expected to see startled, balloon-like heads thrust out of all the upstairs windows, to hear voices calling a shrill alarm, her name shouted from rooftops, the rushing of crowds in pursuit. . . .

"Where are we going?" she asked as he led her south along the brick walk.

"I want to show you the field I described in the poem."

It wasn't far. The walk soon ended and under their feet was the plushy coolness of earth. The moon flowed aqueously through the multitude of pointed oak leaves: the dirt road was also like moving water with its variations of light and shade. They came to a low wooden fence. The boy jumped over it. Then held out his arms. She stepped to the top rail and he lifted her down from it. On the other side his arms did not release her but held her closer.

"This is it," he told her, "the field of blue children."

She looked beyond his dark shoulder. And it was true. The whole field was covered with dancing blue flowers. There was a wind scudding through them and they broke before it in pale blue waves, sending up a soft whispering sound like the infinitely diminished crying of small children at play.

She thought of the view from her window at night, those nights when she cried bitterly without knowing why, the dome of the administration building like a white peak and the restless waves of moonlit branches and the stillness and the singing voices, mournfully remote, blocks away, coming closer, the tender, foolish ballads, and the smell of the white spirea at night, and the stars clear as lamps in the cloud-fretted sky, and she remembered the choking emotion that she didn't understand and the dread of all this coming to its sudden, final conclusion in a few months or weeks more. And she tightened her arms about the boy's shoulders. He was almost a stranger. She knew that she had not even caught a first glimpse of him until this night, and yet he was inexpressibly close to her now, closer than she had ever felt any person before.

He led her out over the field where the flowers rose in pale blue waves to her knees and she felt their soft petals against her bare flesh and she lay down among them and stretched her arms through them and pressed her lips against them and felt them all about her, accepting her and embracing her, and a kind of drunkenness possessed her. The boy knelt beside her and touched her cheek with his fingers and then her lips and her hair. They were both kneeling in the blue flowers, facing each other. He was smiling. The wind blew her loose hair into his face. He raised both hands and brushed it back over her forehead and as he did so his hands slipped down behind the back of her head and fastened there and drew her head toward him until her mouth was pressed against his, tighter and tighter, until her teeth pressed painfully against her upper lip and she tasted the salt taste of blood. She gasped and let her mouth fall open and then she lay back among the whispering blue flowers.

Afterward she had sense enough to see that it was impossible. She sent the poems back to the boy with a short note. It was a curiously stilted and formal note, perhaps because she was dreadfully afraid of herself when she wrote it. She told him about the boy Kirk Abbott whom she was going to marry that summer and she explained to Homer how impossible it would have been for them to try and go on with the beautiful but unfortunate thing that had happened to them last night in the field.

She saw him only once after that. She saw him walking across the campus with his friend Hertha, the tall, weedy girl who wore thick-lensed glasses. Hertha was clinging to Homer's arm and shaking with outlandishly shrill laughter; laughter that could be heard for blocks and yet did not sound like real laughter.

Myra and Kirk were married in August of that year. Kirk got a job with a telephone company in Poplar Falls and they lived in an efficiency apartment and were reasonably happy together. Myra seldom felt restless any more. She did not write verse. Her life seemed to be perfectly full without it. She wondered sometimes if Homer had kept on with his writing but she never saw any of it in the literary magazines so she supposed it couldn't have amounted to very much after all.

One late spring evening a few years after their marriage Kirk Abbott came home tired from the office hungry for dinner and found a scribbled note under the sugar bowl on the drop-leaf table.

"Driven over to Carsville for just a few hours. Myra."

It was after dark: a soft, moony night.

Myra drove south from the town till she came to an open field. There she parked the car and climbed over the low wooden fence. The field was exactly as she had remembered it. She walked quickly out among the flowers; then suddenly fell to her knees among them, sobbing. She cried for a long time, for nearly an hour, and then she rose to her feet and carefully brushed off her skirt and stockings. Now she felt perfectly calm and in possession of herself once more. She went back to the car. She knew that she would never do such a ridiculous thing as this again, for now she had left the last of her troublesome youth behind her.

Portrait of a Girl in Glass

TENNESSEE WILLIAMS

WE LIVED IN A third floor apartment on Maple Street in Saint Louis, on a block which also contained the Ever-ready Garage, a Chinese laundry, and a bookie shop disguised as a cigar store.

Mine was an anomalous character, one that appeared to be slated for radical change or disaster, for I was a poet who had a job in a warehouse. As for my sister Laura, she could be classified even less readily than I. She made no positive motion toward the world but stood at the edge of the water, so to speak, with feet that anticipated too much cold to move. She'd never have budged an inch, I'm pretty sure, if my mother who was a relatively aggressive sort of woman had not shoved her roughly forward, when Laura was twenty years old, by enrolling her as a student in a nearby business college. Out of her "magazine money" (she sold subscriptions to women's magazines), Mother had paid my sister's tuition for a term of six months. It did not work out. Laura tried to memorize the typewriter keyboard, she had a chart at home, she used to sit silently in front of it for hours, staring at it while she cleaned and polished her infinite number of little glass ornaments. She did this every evening after dinner. Mother would caution me to be very quiet. "Sister is looking at her typewriter chart!" I felt somehow that it would do her no good, and I was right. She would seem to know the positions of the keys until the weekly speed-drill got under way, and then they would fly from her mind like a bunch of startled birds.

At last she couldn't bring herself to enter the school any more. She kept this failure a secret for a while. She left the house each morning as before and spent six hours walking around the park. This was in February, and all the walking out-doors regardless of weather brought on influenza. She was in bed for a couple of weeks with a curiously happy little smile on her face. Of course Mother phoned the business college to let them know she was ill. Whoever was talking on the other end of the line had some trouble, it seems, in remembering who Laura was, which annoyed my mother and she spoke up pretty sharply. "Laura has been attending that school of yours for two months, you certainly ought to recognize her name!" Then came the stunning disclosure. The person sharply retorted, after a moment or two, that now she *did* remember the Wingfield girl, and that she had not been at the business college *once* in about a month. Mother's voice became strident. Another person was brought to the phone to verify the statement of the first. Mother hung up and went to Laura's bedroom where she lay with a tense and frightened look in place of the faint little smile. Yes, admitted my sister, what they said was true. "I couldn't go any longer, it scared me too much, it made me sick at the stomach!"

After this fiasco, my sister stayed at home and kept in her bedroom mostly. This was a narrow room that had two windows on a dusky areaway between two wings of the building. We called this areaway Death Valley for a reason that seems worth telling. There were a great many alley-cats in the neighborhood and one particularly vicious dirty white Chow who stalked them continually. In the open or on the fire-escapes they could usually elude him but now and again he cleverly contrived to run some youngster among them into the cul-de-sac of this narrow areaway at the far end of which, directly beneath my sister's bedroom windows, they made the blinding discovery that what had appeared to be an avenue of escape was really a locked arena, a gloomy vault of concrete and brick with walls too high for any cat to spring, in which they must suddenly turn to spit at their death until it was hurled upon them. Hardly a week went by without a repetition of this violent drama. The areaway had grown to be hateful to Laura because she could not look out on it without recalling the screams and the snarls of killing. She kept the shades drawn down, and as Mother would not permit the use of electric current except when needed, her days were spent almost in perpetual twilight. There were three pieces of dingy ivory furniture in the room, a bed, a bureau, a chair. Over the bed was a remarkably bad religious painting, a very effeminate head of Christ with teardrops visible just below the eyes. The charm of the room was produced by my sister's collection of glass. She loved colored glass and had covered the walls with shelves of little glass articles, all of them light and delicate in color. These she washed and polished with endless care. When you entered the room there was always this soft, transparent radiance in it which came from the glass absorbing whatever faint light came through the shades on Death Valley. I have no idea how many articles there were of this delicate glass. There must have been hundreds of them. But Laura could tell you exactly. She loved each one.

She lived in a world of glass and also a world of music. The music came from a 1920 victrola and a bunch of records that dated from about the same period, pieces such as *Whispering* or *The Love Nest* or *Dardanella*. These records were souvenirs of our father, a man whom we barely remembered, whose name was spoken rarely. Before his sudden and unexplained disappearance from our lives, he had made this gift to the household, the phonograph and the records, whose music remained as a sort of apology for him. Once in a while, on pay-day at the warehouse, I would bring home a new record. But Laura seldom cared for these new records, maybe because they reminded her too much of the noisy tragedies in Death Valley or the speed-drills at the business college. The tunes she loved were the ones she had always heard. Often she sang to herself at night in her bedroom. Her voice was thin, it usually wandered off-key. Yet it had a curious childlike sweetness. At eight o'clock in the evening I sat down to write in my own mouse-trap of a room. Through the closed doors, through the walls, I would hear my sister singing to herself, a piece like *Whispering* or *I Love You* or *Sleepy Time Gal*, losing the tune now and then but always preserving the minor atmosphere of the music. I think that was why I always wrote such strange and sorrowful poems in those days. Because I had in my ears the wispy sound of my sister serenading her pieces of colored glass, washing them while she sang or merely looking down at them with her vague blue eyes until the points of gem-like radiance in them gently drew the aching particles of reality from her mind and finally produced a state of hypnotic calm in which she even stopped singing or washing the glass and merely sat without motion until my mother knocked at the door and warned her against the waste of electric current.

I don't believe that my sister was actually foolish. I think the petals of her mind had simply closed through fear, and it's no telling how much they had closed upon in the way of secret wisdom. She never talked very much, not even to me, but once in a while she did pop out with something that took you by surprise.

After work at the warehouse or after I'd finished my writing in the evening, I'd drop in her room for a little visit because she had a restful and soothing effect on nerves that were worn rather thin from trying to ride two horses simultaneously in two opposite directions.

I usually found her seated in the straight-back ivory chair with a piece of glass cupped tenderly in her palm.

"What are you doing? Talking to it?" I asked.

"No," she answered gravely, "I was just looking at it."

On the bureau were two pieces of fiction which she had received as Christmas or birthday presents. One was a novel called the *Rose-Garden Husband* by someone whose name escapes me. The other was *Freckles* by Gene Stratton Porter. I never saw her reading the *Rose-Garden Husband,* but the other book was one that she actually lived with. It had probably never occurred to Laura that a book was something you read straight through and then laid aside as finished. The character Freckles, a one-armed orphan youth who worked in a lumber-camp, was someone that she invited into her bedroom now and then for a friendly visit just as she did me. When I came in and found this novel open upon her lap, she would gravely remark that Freckles was having some trouble with the foreman of the lumber-camp or that he had just received an injury to his spine when a tree fell on him. She frowned with genuine sorrow when she reported these misadventures of her story-book hero, possibly not recalling how successfully he came through them all, that the injury to the spine fortuitously resulted in the discovery of rich parents and that the bad-tempered foreman had a heart of gold at the end of the book. Freckles became involved in romance with a girl he called The Angel, but my sister usually stopped reading when this girl became too prominent in the story. She closed the book or turned back to the lonelier periods in the orphan's story. I only remember her making one reference to this heroine of the novel. "The Angel is nice," she said, "but seems to be kind of conceited about her looks."

Then one time at Christmas, while she was trimming the artificial tree, she picked up the Star of Bethlehem that went on the topmost branch and held it gravely toward the chandelier.

"Do stars have five points really?" she enquired.

This was the sort of thing that you didn't believe and that made you stare at Laura with sorrow and confusion.

"No," I told her, seeing she really meant it, "they're round like the earth and most of them much bigger."

She was gently surprised by this new information. She went to the window to look up at the sky which was, as usual during Saint Louis winters, completely shrouded by smoke.

"It's hard to tell," she said, and returned to the tree.

So time passed on till my sister was twenty-three. Old enough to be married, but the fact of the matter was she had never even had a date with a boy. I don't believe this seemed as awful to her as it did to Mother.

At breakfast one morning Mother said to me, "Why don't you cultivate some nice young friends? How about down at the warehouse? Aren't there some young men down there you could ask to dinner?"

This suggestion surprised me because there was seldom quite enough food on her table to satisfy three people. My mother was a terribly stringent housekeeper, God knows we were poor enough in actuality, but my mother had an almost obsessive dread of becoming even poorer. A not unreasonable fear since the man of the house was a poet who worked in a warehouse, but one which I thought played too important a part in all her calculations.

Almost immediately Mother explained herself.

"I think it might be nice," she said, "for your sister."

I brought Jim home to dinner a few nights later. Jim was a big red-haired Irishman who had the scrubbed and polished look of well-kept chinaware. His big square hands seemed to have a direct and very innocent hunger for touching his friends. He was always clapping them on your arms or shoulders and they burned through the cloth of your shirt like plates taken out of an oven. He was the best-liked man in the warehouse and oddly enough he was the only one that I was on good terms with. He found me agreeably ridiculous I think. He knew of my secret practice of retiring to a cabinet in the lavatory and working on rhyme schemes when work was slack in the warehouse, and of sneaking up on the roof now and then to smoke my cigarette with a view across the river at the undulant open country of Illinois. No doubt I was classified as screwy in Jim's mind as much as in the others', but while their attitude was suspicious and hostile when they first knew me, Jim's was warmly tolerant from the beginning. He called me Slim, and gradually his cordial acceptance drew the others around, and while he remained the only one who actually had anything to do with me, the others had now begun to smile when they saw me as people smile at an oddly fashioned dog who crosses their path at some distance.

Nevertheless it took some courage for me to invite Jim to dinner. I thought about it all week and delayed the action till Friday noon, the last possible moment, as the dinner was set for that evening.

"What are you doing tonight?" I finally asked him.

"Not a God damn thing," said Jim. "I had a date but her Aunt took sick and she's hauled her freight to Centralia!"

"Well," I said, "why don't you come over for dinner?"

"Sure!" said Jim. He grinned with astonishing brightness.

I went outside to phone the news to Mother.

Her voice that was never tired responded with an energy that made the wires crackle.

"I suppose he's Catholic?" she said.

"Yes," I told her, remembering the tiny silver cross on his freckled chest.

"Good!" she said. "I'll bake a salmon loaf!"

And so we rode home together in his jalopy.

I had a curious feeling of guilt and apprehension as I led the lamb-like Irishman up three flights of cracked marble steps to the door of Apartment F, which was not thick enough to hold inside it the odor of baking salmon.

Never having a key, I pressed the bell.

"Laura!" came Mother's voice. "That's Tom and Mr. Delaney! Let them in!"

There was a long, long pause.

"Laura?" she called again. "I'm busy in the kitchen, you answer the door!"

Then at last I heard my sister's footsteps. They went right past the door at which we were standing and into the parlor. I heard the creaking noise of the phonograph crank. Music commenced. One of the oldest records, a march of Sousa's, put on to give her the courage to let in a stranger.

The door came timidly open and there she stood in a dress from Mother's wardrobe, a black chiffon ankle-length and high-heeled slippers on which she balanced uncertainly like a tipsy crane of melancholy plumage. Her eyes stared back at us with a glass brightness and her delicate wing-like shoulders were hunched with nervousness.

"Hello!" said Jim, before I could introduce him.

He stretched out his hand. My sister touched it only for a second.

"Excuse me!" she whispered, and turned with a breathless rustle back to her bedroom door, the sanctuary beyond it briefly revealing itself with the tinkling, muted radiance of glass before the door closed rapidly but gently on her wraithlike figure.

Jim seemed to be incapable of surprise.

"Your sister?" he asked.

"Yes, that was her," I admitted. "She's terribly shy with strangers."

"She looks like you," said Jim, "except she's pretty."

Laura did not reappear till called to dinner. Her place was next to Jim at the drop-leaf table and all through the meal her figure was slightly tilted away from his. Her face was feverishly bright and one eyelid, the one on the side toward Jim, had developed a nervous wink. Three times in the course of the dinner she dropped her fork on her plate with a terrible clatter and she was continually raising the water-glass to her lips for hasty little gulps. She went on doing this even after the water was gone from the glass. And her handling of the silver became more awkward and hurried all the time.

I thought of nothing to say.

To Mother belonged the conversational honors, such as they were. She asked the caller about his home and family. She was delighted to learn that his father had a business of his own, a retail shoe store somewhere in Wyoming. The news that he went to night-school to study accounting was still more edifying. What was his heart set on beside the warehouse? Radio-engineering? My, my, my! It was easy to see that here was a very up-and-coming young man who was certainly going to make his place in the world!

Then she started to talk about her children. Laura, she said, was not cut out for business. She was domestic, however, and making a home was really a girl's best bet.

Jim agreed with all this and seemed not to sense the ghost of an implication. I suffered through it dumbly, trying not to see Laura trembling more and more beneath the incredible unawareness of Mother.

And bad as it was, excruciating in fact, I thought with dread of the moment when dinner was going to be over, for then the diversion of food would be taken away, we would have to go into the little steam-heated parlor. I fancied the four of us having run out of talk, even Mother's seemingly endless store of questions about Jim's home and his job all used up finally—the four of us, then, just sitting there in the parlor, listening to the hiss of the radiator and nervously clearing our throats in the kind of self-consciousness that gets to be suffocating.

But when the blanc-mange was finished, a miracle happened.

Mother got up to clear the dishes away. Jim gave me a clap on the shoulders and said, "Hey, Slim, let's go have a look at those old records in there!"

He sauntered carelessly into the front room and flopped down on the floor beside the victrola. He began sorting through the collection of worn-out records and reading their titles aloud in a voice so hearty that it shot like beams of sunlight through the vapors of self-consciousness engulfing my sister and me.

He was sitting directly under the floor-lamp and all at once my sister jumped up and said to him, "Oh—you have freckles!"

Jim grinned. "Sure that's what my folks call me—Freckles!"

"Freckles?" Laura repeated. She looked toward me as if for the confirmation of some too wonderful hope. I looked away quickly, not knowing whether to feel relieved or alarmed at the turn that things were taking.

Jim had wound the victrola and put on *Dardanella.*

He grinned at Laura.

"How about you an' me cutting the rug a little?"

"What?" said Laura breathlessly, smiling and smiling.

"Dance!" he said, drawing her into his arms.

As far as I knew she had never danced in her life. But to my everlasting wonder she slipped quite naturally into those huge arms of Jim's, and they danced round and around the small steam-heated parlor, bumping against the sofa and chairs and laughing loudly and happily together. Something opened up in my sister's face. To say it was love is not too hasty a judgment, for after all he had freckles and that was what his folks called him. Yes, he had undoubtedly assumed the identity—for all practical purposes—of the one-armed orphan youth who lived in the Limberlost, that tall and misty region to which she retreated whenever the walls of Apartment F became too close to endure.

Mother came back in with some lemonade. She stopped short as she entered the portieres.

"Good heavens! Laura? Dancing?"

Her look was absurdly grateful as well as startled.

"But isn't she stepping all over you, Mr. Delaney?"

"What if she does?" said Jim, with bearish gallantry. "I'm not made of eggs!"

"Well, well, well!" said Mother, senselessly beaming.

"She's light as a feather!" said Jim. "With a little more practice she'd dance as good as Betty!"

There was a little pause of silence.

"Betty?" said Mother.

"The girl I go out with!" said Jim.

"Oh!" said Mother.

She set the pitcher of lemonade carefully down and with her back to the caller and her eyes on me, she asked him just how often he and the lucky young lady went out together.

"Steady!" said Jim.

Mother's look, remaining on my face, turned into a glare of fury.

"Tom didn't mention that you went out with a girl!"

"Nope," said Jim. "I didn't mean to let the cat out of the bag. The boys at the warehouse'll kid me to death when Slim gives the news away."

He laughed heartily but his laughter dropped heavily and awkwardly away as even his dull senses were gradually penetrated by the unpleasant sensation the news of Betty had made.

"Are you thinking of getting married?" said Mother.

"First of next month!" he told her.

It took her several moments to pull herself together. Then she said in a dismal tone, "How nice! If Tom had only told us we could have asked you *both!*"

Jim had picked up his coat.

"Must you be going?" said Mother.

"I hope it don't seem like I'm rushing off," said Jim, "but Betty's gonna get back on the eight o'clock train an' by the time I get my jalopy down to the Wabash depot—"

"Oh, then, we mustn't keep you."

Soon as he'd left, we all sat down, looking dazed.

Laura was the first to speak.

"Wasn't he nice?" she said. "And all those freckles!"

"Yes," said Mother. Then she turned on me.

"You didn't mention that he was engaged to be married!"

"Well, how did I know that he was engaged to be married?"

"I thought you called him your best friend down at the warehouse?"

"Yes, but I didn't know he was going to be married!"

"How peculiar!" said Mother. "How very peculiar!"

"No," said Laura gently, getting up from the sofa. "There's nothing peculiar about it."

She picked up one of the records and blew on its surface a little as if it were dusty, then set it softly back down.

"People in love," she said, "take everything for granted."

What did she mean by that? I never knew.

She slipped quietly back to her room and closed the door.

Not very long after that I lost my job at the warehouse. I was fired for writing a poem on the lid of a shoe-box. I left Saint Louis and took to moving around. The cities swept about me like dead leaves, leaves that were brightly colored but torn away from the branches. My nature changed. I grew to be firm and sufficient.

In five years' time I had nearly forgotten home. I had to forget it, I couldn't carry it with me. But once in a while, usually in a strange town before I have found companions, the shell of deliberate hardness is broken through. A door comes softly and irresistibly open. I hear the tired old music my unknown father left in the place he abandoned as faithlessly as I. I see the faint and sorrowful radiance of the glass, hundreds of little transparent pieces of it in very delicate colors. I hold my breath, for if my sister's face appears among them—the night is hers!

Paul's Eyes

AUSTIN WILSON

PAUL HAD MAMA'S EYES. Everybody used to notice that, first thing, how he favored her. I thought that was the reason she always sided with him over me, him having those same pale blue eyes she did, eyes that sometimes had a kind of faraway look in them as if they were seeing something in the distance you'd missed, maybe something behind you, over your shoulder that you couldn't see, or maybe deep inside you that you couldn't see yourself if you looked in a mirror. When I remember that winter, it is always his eyes I think of first: looking up at me, begging to be taken along.

He was looking over Mama's shoulder. She was stooped down, her back to me, tying his shoes, then fixing his hat, and finally wrapping his face with the scarf that was hers, the only thing he was wearing that hadn't once been mine. The scarf was a blue plaid and seemed to bring his eyes out, the way it covered most of the rest of his face. I thought I might be able to slip out while she had her attention on him, but he had noticed me. His eyes filled with tears and he started whimpering. Mama stood up and turned around, her hands on Paul's shoulders, moving him around in front of her, but facing me, putting him between us. Before I looked down I saw both their eyes, hers burning into me, not tearfully begging like his.

"Just where do you think you're going, young man?" she asked.

"Nowhere," I said. Paul seemed to brighten up. I thought I'd get even with him, spoiling everything the way he did.

"You know you're supposed to be looking after your brother."

"Ma-uh-ma," I said, stretching it out to three syllables.

Paul was just turned five that winter. I was seven and a half, almost eight. I didn't think we looked like brothers at all, even when he was wearing some of my clothes that I could still remember. I felt it was like he was mocking me to be wearing my favorite clothes.

"Do I have to?" I whined.

"Here," she said, and slipped me a quarter. "Don't you cross the fence."

The money mollified me some, because I knew what I wanted to spend it on, but I felt I would have no fun at all if I had to stay on our side of the fence.

As Mama shut the door after us, I couldn't keep from looking in that direction, towards the far field, where if you slipped under the fence you'd be off our land and on government property, the old air base. It had been shut down for a long while now, ever since the war that I couldn't remember, and the county was always trying to get some industry to set up out there in some of the old hangars. The only one that ever moved there was the mobile home factory where Daddy worked. No planes ever landed there anymore, except cropdusters and there weren't even those in wintertime. It was too cold to bicycle or skate on the runways like I sometimes did with my friends from school. The wind seemed to blow especially hard on the runways and it was a good place to fly kites, though sometimes the cropduster pilots yelled at us and chased us away. But that was something for the spring, not the middle of winter. In the summer I used to pick blackberries there and come home, my hands stained with the purple juice, with a big bucketful for Mama. She worried about snakes in snake season and fussed about going where there might be some. She always took the berries, though. Now, in February, the only thing to do was to check on the lead mine and try out an idea I had. I thought Paul at least would be useful and dig some.

When the air base had been in use, there had been a rifle range for the men stationed there, and the mound of earth that had stopped the bullets behind the target area held what seemed an endless supply of lead. I had an old mold that had been my father's when he was a boy and a heavy cast iron ladle in which I could melt lead over a fire. The mold made soldiers, perfect Confederate soldiers that didn't even need to be painted since the lead gave them the proper grey color. The mold made two types of soldier, one standing, one kneeling, both with their rifles at their shoulders in firing position. Mother didn't like me playing with fire, so I had to make them away from the house, and I had gradually taken a fairly large supply of her kitchen matches for that purpose.

I kept the matches, my equipment for making the soldiers, and my stock of soldiers in a hiding place near the old rifle range. I didn't want Mama to know how many I had made. That day I wanted to mine some lead for some new soldiers, but I also had an idea for a more realistic battle.

The store across the highway from our house had some fireworks left from New Year's and now I had some money. We weren't supposed to cross the highway by ourselves but I led Paul across the road, both of us looking back to see if Mama was watching us.

"Now don't you tattle, you hear?" I said.

I knew immediately where to go in the store. I had seen them when I went with Mama to get groceries.

"Look," I said to Paul, holding one up by the stiff fuse.

"A little apple," he said.

"Stupid, don't you know anything? They're cherries, cherry bombs."

They were three for a quarter and the man didn't charge me anything for the tax. We ran out of the store, forgetting to look both ways as we raced across the highway, Paul stumbling and holding me back. But there was no traffic on the road. We skirted our house and made for the hole in the fence.

I set up the soldiers in ranks and wouldn't let Paul help. He was too clumsy, always knocking them over.

"Go dig over there." I pointed to the mound.

I buried one of the firecrackers in the middle of a group of the soldiers that I had set up in positions of battle, lit the fuse with one of Mama's kitchen matches, and ran back far enough to be safe. The cherry bomb was much louder than I had thought and it did a satisfying amount of damage to my ranks of soldiers. Paul came running to see what had happened. He was very excited, not scared like I thought he would be; he was jumping around and clapping his hands, shouting, "Let me. Let me do it. Please. Please."

"No," I told him, "you get back and stay away. This is mine."

"I'm telling," he whined.

"You better not. If you know what's good for you."

I set up another group of soldiers and another firecracker, and it too was better than I'd imagined. I was impressed with the way the cherry bomb made my ears ring after its explosion. I wanted to use the last one in a spectacular way, one that would send up more debris than the first two had. I looked around for something to put the firecracker in, but I couldn't see anything.

"Help me find something," I yelled at Paul, and he eagerly started looking, though he didn't really have any idea what I had in mind.

Finally, I found an old beer bottle, half full of earth and mud, and I positioned it in the midst of my soldiers, partially burying it. I dropped the firecracker down the opening, and ran for a short distance. Paul was right by me then.

But something happened. The dampness inside the bottle must have put the fuse out, I thought. I started to approach it, very slowly, giving the bomb a chance, when Paul ran ahead of me, saying, "Let me, let me."

I ran then, racing him to it, getting to it just as he was pulling the bottle out of the place where I had buried it. I reached for it, and was pulling it away from him. It was like a hand—a grown-up's hand—had shoved me hard in the chest and pushed me backwards. My head was ringing and my eyes were like after someone had taken my picture with a flashbulb on the camera.

I stood back up and I felt my hand tingling and then beating like my heart. It felt sort of like someone had spanked it with a ruler and I was surprised there was blood on it and that part of it was gone.

I held it up for Paul to see. "Look," I said. He was sitting on the ground, his head down. He turned his face around and upwards. Bright blood was spreading all over it.

I looked around wildly, and started screaming. And then Paul began echoing me.

I somehow got to the hangar where my father worked, led him to where Paul was, and he took us into town to the hospital.

I don't think I was ever able to look at Mama's eyes again after that; I was afraid that somehow they wouldn't be the same as they once were. Sometimes I couldn't help looking at Paul's eyes. One of them—the glass one that didn't quite have the right shade of blue—stared straight at me, boring into me, from his scarred face; the other quickly darted away, even before my eyes could, even before I could drop my eyes to my ruined hands.

FROM

Big Boy Leaves Home

Richard Wright

III

They stopped when they got to the end of the woods. They could see the open road leading home, home to ma and pa. But they hung back, afraid. The thick shadows cast from the trees were friendly and sheltering. But the wide glare of sun stretching out over the fields was pitiless. They crouched behind an old log.

"We gotta git home," said Big Boy.

"Theys gonna lynch us," said Bobo, half-questioningly.

Big Boy did not answer.

"Theys gonna lynch us," said Bobo again.

Big Boy shuddered.

"Hush!" he said. He did not want to think of it. He could not think of it; there was but one thought, and he clung to that one blindly. He had to get home, home to ma and pa.

Their heads jerked up. Their ears had caught the rhythmic jingle of a wagon. They fell to the ground and clung flat to the side of a log. Over the crest of the hill came the top of a hat. A white face. Then shoulders in a blue shirt. A wagon drawn by two horses pulled into full view.

Big Boy and Bobo held their breath, waiting. Their eyes followed the wagon till it was lost in dust around a bend of the road.

"We gotta git home," said Big Boy.

"Ahm scared," said Bobo.

"C mon! Les keep t the fields."

They ran till they came to the cornfields. Then they went slower, for last year's corn stubbles bruised their feet.

They came in sight of a brickyard.

"Wait a minute," gasped Big Boy.

They stopped.

"Ahm goin on t mah home n yuh better go on t yos."

Bobo's eyes grew round.

"Ahm scared!"

"Yuh better go on!"

"Lemme go wid yuh; they'll ketch me . . ."

"Ef yuh kin git home mabbe yo folks kin hep yuh t git erway."

Big Boy started off. Bobo grabbed him.

"Lemme go wid yuh!"

Big Boy shook free.

"Ef yuh stay here theys gonna lynch yuh!" he yelled, running.

After he had gone about twenty-five yards he turned and looked; Bobo was flying through the woods like the wind.

Big Boy slowed when he came to the railroad. He wondered if he ought to go through the streets or down the track. He decided on the tracks. He could dodge a train better than a mob.

He trotted along the ties, looking ahead and back. His cheek itched, and he felt it. His hand came away smeared with blood. He wiped it nervously on his overalls.

When he came to his back fence he heaved himself over. He landed among a flock of startled chickens. A bantam rooster tried to spur him. He slipped and fell in front of the kitchen steps, grunting heavily. The ground was slick with greasy dishwater.

Panting, he stumbled through the doorway.

"Lawd, Big Boy, whuts wrong wid yuh?"

His mother stood gaping in the middle of the floor. Big Boy flopped wordlessly onto a stool, almost toppling over. Pots simmered on the stove. The kitchen smelled of food cooking.

"Whuts the matter, Big Boy?"

Mutely, he looked at her. Then he burst into tears. She came and felt the scratches on his face.

"Whut happened t yuh, Big Boy? Somebody been botherin yuh?"

"They after me, Ma! They after me . . ."

"Who!"

"Ah . . . Ah . . . We . . ."

"Big Boy, whuts wrong wid yuh?"

"He killed Lester n Buck," he muttered simply.

"Killed!"

"Yessum."

"Lester n Buck!"

"Yessum, Ma!"

"How killed?"

"He shot em, Ma!"

"Lawd Gawd in Heaven, have mercy on us all! This is mo trouble, mo trouble," she moaned, wringing her hands.

"N Ah killed im, Ma . . ."

She stared, trying to understand.

"Whut happened, Big Boy!"

"We tried t git our cloes from the tree . . ."

"Whut tree?"

"We wuz swimmin, Ma. N the white woman . . ."

"*White* woman? . . ."

"Yessum. She wuz at the swimmin hole . . ."

"Lawd have mercy! Ah knowed yuh boys wuz gonna keep on till yuh got into somethin like this!"

She ran into the hall.

"Lucy!"

"Mam?"

"C mere!"

Mam?"

"C mere, Ah say!"

"Whutcha wan, Ma? Ahm sewin."

"Chile, will yuh c mere like Ah ast yuh?"

Lucy came to the door holding an unfinished apron in her hands. When she saw Big Boy's face she looked wildly at her mother.

"Whuts the matter?"

"Wheres Pa?"

"He's out front, Ah reckon."

"Git im, quick!"

"Whuts the matter, Ma?"

"Go git yo Pa, Ah say!"

Lucy ran out. The mother sank into a chair, holding a dish rag. Suddenly, she sat up.

"Big Boy, Ah thought yuh wuz at school?"

Big Boy looked at the floor.

"How come yuh didnt go t school?"

"We went t the woods."

She sighed.

"Ah done done all Ah kin fer yuh, Big Boy. Only Gawd kin help yuh now."

"Ma, don let em git me; don let em git me . . ."

His father came into the doorway. He stared at Big Boy, then at his wife.

"Whuts Big Boy inter now?" he asked sternly.

"Saul, Big Boys done gone n got inter trouble wid the white folks."

The old man's mouth dropped, and he looked from one to the other.

"Saul, we gotta git im erway from here."

"Open yo mouth n talk! Whut yuh been doin?" The old man gripped Big Boy's shoulders and peered at the scratches on his face.

"Me n Lester n Buck n Bobo wuz out on ol man Harveys place swimmin . . ."

"Saul, its a *white* woman!"

Big Boy winced. The old man compressed his lips and stared at his wife. Lucy gaped at her brother as though she had never seen him before.

"Whut happened? Can't yuh-all talk?" the old man thundered, with a certain helplessness in his voice.

"We wuz swimmin," Big Boy began, "n then a white woman comes up t the hole. We got up right erway t git our cloes sos we could git erway, n she started screamin. Our cloes wuz right by the tree where she wuz standin, n when we started t git em she jus screamed. We told her we wanted our cloes . . . Yuh see, Pa, she wuz standin right *by* our cloes; n when we went t git em she jus screamed . . . Bobo got the cloes, n then he shot Lester . . ."

"*Who* shot Lester?"

"The white man."

"Whut white man?"

"Ah dunno, Pa. He wuz a soljer, n he had a rifle."

"A soljer?"

"Yessuh."

"A *soljer?*"

"Yessuh, Pa. A soljer.

The old man frowned.

"N then whut yuh-all do?"

"Waal, Buck said, 'Hes gotta gun!' N we started runnin. N then he shot Buck, n he fell in the swimmin hole. We didn't see im no mo . . . He wuz close on us then. He looked at the white woman n then he started t shoot Bobo. Ah grabbed the gun, n we started fightin. Bobo jumped on his back. He started beatin Bobo. Then Ah hit im wid the gun. Then he started at me n Ah shot im. Then we run . . ."

"Who seen?"

"Nobody."

"Wheres Bobo?"

"He went home."

"Anybody run after yuh-all?"

"Nawsuh."

"Yuh see anybody?"

"Nawsuh. Nobody but a white man. But he didnt see us."

"How long fo yuh-all lef the swimmin hole?"

"Little while ergo."

The old man nervously brushed his hand across his eyes and walked to the door. His lips moved, but no words came.

"Saul, whut we gonna do?"

"Lucy," began the old man, "go t Brother Sanders n tell im Ah said c mere; n go t Brother Jenkins n tell im Ah said c mere; n go t Elder Peters n tell im Ah said c mere. N don say nothin t nobody but whut Ah tol yuh. N when yuh git thu come straight back. Now go!"

Lucy dropped her apron across the back of a chair and ran down the steps. The mother bent over, crying and praying. The old man walked slowly over to Big Boy.

"Big Boy?"

Big Boy swallowed.

"Ahm talkin t yuh!"

"Yessuh."

"How come yuh didnt go t school this mawnin?"

"We went t the woods."

"Didnt yo ma send yuh t school?"

"Yessuh."

"How come yuh didn't go?"

"We went t the woods."

"Don yuh know thas wrong?"

"Yessuh."

"How come yuh go?"

Big Boy looked at his fingers, knotted them, and squirmed in his seat.

"AHM TALKIN T YUH!"

His wife straightened up and said reprovingly:

"Saul!"

The old man desisted, yanking nervously at the shoulder straps of his overalls.

"How long wuz the woman there?"

"Not long."
"Wuz she young?"
"Yessuh. Lika gal."
"Did yuh-all say anythin t her?"
"Nawsuh. We jus said we wanted our cloes."
"N what she say?"
"Nothin, Pa. She jus backed erway t the tree n screamed."
The old man stared, his lips trying to form a question.
"Big Boy, did yuh-all bother her?"
"Nawsuh, Pa. We didn't *touch* her."
"How long fo the white man come up?"
"Right erway."
"Whut he say?"
"Nothin. He jus cussed us."
Abruptly the old man left the kitchen.
"Ma, cant Ah go fo they ketches me?"
"Sauls doin whut he kin."
"Ma, Ma, Ah don wan em t ketch me . . ."
"Sauls doin whut he kin. Nobody but the good Lawd kin hep us now."

The old man came back with a shotgun and leaned it in a corner. Fascinatedly, Big Boy looked at it.

There was a knock at the front door.
"Liza, see whos there."
She went. They were silent, listening. They could hear her talking.

"Whos there?"
"Me."
"Who?"
"Me, Brother Sanders."
"C mon in. Sauls waitin fer yuh."
Sanders paused in the doorway, smiling.
"Yuh sent fer me, Brother Morrison?"
"Brother Sanders, wes in deep trouble here."
Sanders came all the way into the kitchen.
"Yeah?"
"Big Boy done gone n killed a white man."
Sanders stopped short, then came forward, his face thrust out, his mouth open. His lips moved several times before he could speak.

"A *white* man?"

"They gonna kill me; they gonna kill me!" Big Boy cried, running to the old man.

"Saul, cant we git im erway somewhere?"

"Here now, take it easy; take it easy," said Sanders, holding Big Boy's wrists.

"They gonna kill me; they gonna lynch me!"

Big Boy slipped to the floor. They lifted him to a stool. His mother held him closely, pressing his head to her bosom.

"Whut we gonna do?" asked Sanders.

"Ah done sent fer Brother Jenkins n Elder Peters."

Sanders leaned his shoulders against the wall. Then, as the full meaning of it all came to him, he exclaimed:

"Theys gonna git a mob! . . ." His voice broke off and his eyes fell on the shotgun.

Feet came pounding on the steps. They turned toward the door. Lucy ran in crying. Jenkins followed. The old man met him in the middle of the room, taking his hand.

"Wes in bad trouble here, Brother Jenkins. Big Boy's done gone n killed a white man. Yuh-alls gotta hep me . . ."

Jenkins looked hard at Big Boy.

"Elder Peters says hes comin," said Lucy:

"When all this happen?" asked Jenkins.

"Near bout a hour ergo, now," said the old man.

"Whut we gonna do?" asked Jenkins.

"Ah wanna wait till Elder Peters come," said the old man helplessly.

"But we gotta work fas ef we gonna do anythin," said Sanders. "Well git in trouble jus standin here like this."

Big Boy pulled away from his mother.

"Pa, lemme go now! Lemme go now!"

"Be still, Big Boy!"

"Where kin yuh go?"

"Ah could ketch a freight!"

"Thas *sho* death!" said Jenkins. "Theyll be watchin em all!"

"Kin yuh-all hep me wid some money?" the old man asked.

They shook their heads.

"Saul, whut kin we do? Big Boy cant stay here."

There was another knock at the door.

The old man backed stealthily to the shotgun.

"Lucy, go!"

Lucy looked at him, hesitating.

"Ah better go," said Jenkins.

It was Elder Peters. He came in hurriedly.

"Good evenin, everbody!"

"How yuh, Elder?"

"Good evenin."

"How yuh today?"

Peters looked around the crowded kitchen.

"Whuts the matter?"

"Elder, wes in deep trouble," began the old man. "Big Boy n some mo boys . . ."

". . . Lester n Buck n Bobo . . ."

". . . wuz over on ol man Harveys place swimmin . . ."

"N he don like us niggers *none,*" said Peters emphatically. He widened his legs and put his thumbs in the armholes of his vest.

". . . n some white woman . . ."

"Yeah?" said Peters, coming closer.

". . . comes erlong n the boys tries t git their cloes where they done lef em under a tree. Waal, she started screamin n all, see? Reckon she thought the boys wuz after her. Then a white man in a soljers suit shoots two of em . . ."

". . . Lester n Buck . . ."

"Huummm," said Peters. "Tha wuz ol man Harveys son."

"Harveys son?"

"Yuh mean the one tha wuz in the Army?"

"Yuh mean Jim?"

"Yeah," said Peters. "The papers said he wuz here fer a vacation from his regiment. N tha woman the boys saw wuz jus erbout his wife . . ."

They stared at Peters. Now that they knew what white person had been killed, their fears became definite.

"N whut else happened?"

"Big Boy shot the man . . ."

"Harveys *son?*"

"He had t, Elder. He wuz gonna shoot im ef he didnt . . ."

"Lawd!" said Peters. He looked around and put his hat back on.

"How long ergo wuz this?"

"Mighty near an hour, now, Ah reckon."

"Do the white folks know yit?"

"Don know, Elder."

"Yuh-all better git this boy outa here right now," said Peters. "Cause ef yuh don theres gonna be a lynchin . . ."

"Where kin Ah go, Elder?" Big Boy ran up to him.

They crowded around Peters. He stood with his legs wide apart, looking up at the ceiling.

"Mabbe we kin hide im in the church till he kin git erway," said Jenkins.

Peters' lips flexed.

"Naw, Brother, thall never do! Theyll git im there sho. N anyhow, ef they ketch im there itll ruin us all. We gotta git the boy outta town . . ."

Sanders went up to the old man.

"Lissen," he said in a whisper. "Mah son, Will, the one whut drives fer the Magnolia Express Comny, is taking a truck o goods t Chicawgo in the mawnin. If we kin hide Big Boy somewhere till then, we kin put im on the truck . . ."

"Pa, please, lemme go wid Will when he goes in the mawnin," Big Boy begged.

The old man stared at Sanders.

"Yuh reckon thas safe?"

"Its the only thing yuh *kin* do," said Peters.

"But where we gonna hide im till then?"

"Whut time yo boy leavin out in the mawnin?"

"At six."

They were quiet, thinking. The water kettle on the stove sang.

"Pa, Ah knows where Will passes erlong wid the truck out on Bullards Road. Ah kin hide in one of them ol kilns . . ."

"Where?"

"In one of them kilns we built . . ."

"But theyll git yuh there," wailed the mother.

"But there ain no place else fer im t go."

"Theres some holes big ernough fer me t git in n stay till Will comes erlong," said Big Boy. "Please, Pa, lemme go fo they ketches me . . ."

"Let im go!"

"Please, Pa . . ."

The old man breathed heavily.

"Lucy, git his things!"

"Saul, theyll git im out there!" wailed the mother, grabbing Big Boy.

Peters pulled her away.

"Sister Morrison, ef yuh don let im go n git erway from here hes gonna be caught shos theres a Gawd in Heaven!"

Lucy came running with Big Boy's shoes and pulled them on his feet. The old man thrust a battered hat on his head. The mother went to the stove and dumped the skillet of corn pone into her apron. She wrapped it, and unbuttoning Big Boy's overalls, pushed it into his bosom.

"Heres somethin fer yuh t eat; n pray, Big Boy, cause thas all anybody kin do now . . ."

Big Boy pulled to the door, his mother clinging to him.

"Let im go, Sister Morrison!"

"Run fas, Big Boy!"

Big Boy raced across the yard, scattering the chickens. He paused at the fence and hollered back:

"Tell Bobo where Ahm hidin n tell im t c mon!"

IV

He made for the railroad, running straight toward the sunset. He held his left hand tightly over his heart, holding the hot pone of corn bread there. At times he stumbled over the ties, for his shoes were tight and hurt his feet. His throat burned from thirst; he had had no water since noon.

He veered off the track and trotted over the crest of a hill, following Bullard's Road. His feet slipped and slid in the dust. He kept his eyes straight ahead, fearing every clump of shrubbery, every tree. He wished it were night. If he could only get to the kilns without meeting anyone. Suddenly a thought came to him like a blow. He recalled hearing the old folks tell tales of blood-houns, and fear made him run slower. None of them had thought of that. Spose blood-houns wuz put on his trail? Lawd! Spose a whole pack of em, foamin n howlin, tore im t pieces? He went limp and his feet dragged. Yeah, thas whut they wuz gonna send after im, blood-houns! N then thered be no way fer im t dodge! Why hadnt Pa let im take tha shotgun? He stopped. He oughta go back n git tha shotgun. And then when the mob came he would take some with him.

In the distance he heard the approach of a train. It jarred him back to a sharp sense of danger. He ran again, his big shoes sopping up and down in the dust. He was tired and his lungs were bursting from running. He wet his lips, wanting water. As he turned from the road across a plowed field he heard the train roaring at his heels. He ran faster, gripped in terror.

He was nearly there now. He could see the black clay on the sloping hillside. Once inside a kiln he would be safe. For a little while, at least. He thought of the shotgun again. If he only had something! Someone to talk to . . . Thas right! Bobo! Bobod be wid im. Hed almost fergot Bobo. Bobod bringa gun; he knowed he would. N tergether they could kill the whole mob. Then in the mawning theyd git inter Will's truck n go far erway, t Chicawgo . . .

He slowed to a walk, looking back and ahead. A light wind skipped over the grass. A beetle lit on his cheek and he brushed it off. Behind the dark pines hung a red sun. Two bats flapped against that sun. He shivered, for he was growing cold; the sweat on his body was drying.

He stopped at the foot of the hill, trying to choose between two patches of black kilns high above him. He went to the left, for there lay the ones he, Bobo, Lester, and Buck had dug only last week. He looked around again; the landscape was bare. He climbed the embankment and stood before a row of black pits sinking four and five feet deep into the earth. He went to the largest and peered in. He stiffened when his ears caught the sound of a whir. He ran back a few steps and poised on his toes. Six foot of snake slid out of the pit and went into coil. Big Boy looked around wildly for a stick. He ran down the slope, peering into the grass. He stumbled over a tree limb. He picked it up and tested it by striking it against the ground.

Warily, he crept back up the slope, his stick poised. When about seven feet from the snake he stopped and waved the stick. The coil grew tighter, the whir sounded louder, and a flat head reared to strike. He went to the right, and the flat head followed him, the blue-black tongue darting forth; he went to the left, and the flat head followed him there too.

He stopped, teeth clenched. He had to kill this snake. Jus had t kill im! This wuz the safest pit on the hillside. He waved the stick again, looking at the snake before, thinking of a mob behind. The flat head reared higher. With stick over shoulder, he jumped in, swinging. The stick sang through the air, catching the snake on the side of the head, sweeping him out of coil. There was a brown writhing mass. Then Big Boy was upon him, pounding blows home, one on top of the other. He fought viciously, his eyes red, his teeth bared in a snarl. He beat till the snake lay still; then he stomped it with his heel, grinding its head into the dirt.

He stopped, limp, wet. The corners of his lips were white with spittle. He spat and shuddered.

Cautiously, he went to the hole and peered. He longed for a match. He imagined whole nests of them in there waiting. He put the stick into the hole and waved it around. Stooping, he peered again. It mus be awright. He looked over the hillside, his eyes coming back to the dead snake. Then he got to his knees and backed slowly into the hole.

When inside he felt there must be snakes all about him, ready to strike. It seemed he could see and feel them there, waiting tensely in coil. In the dark he imagined long white fangs ready to sink into his neck, his side, his legs. He wanted to come out, but kept still. Shucks, he told himself, ef there wuz any snakes in here they sho woulda done bit me by now. Some of his fear left, and he relaxed.

With elbows on ground and chin on palms, he settled. The clay was cold to his knees and thighs, but his bosom was kept warm by the hot pone of corn bread. His thirst returned and he longed for a drink. He was hungry, too. But he did not want to eat the corn pone. Naw, not now. Mabbe after erwhile, after Bobo came. Then theyd both eat the corn pone.

The view from his hole was fringed by the long tufts of grass. He could see all the way to Bullard's Road, and even beyond. The wind was blowing, and in the east the first touch of dusk was rising. Every now and then a bird floated past, a spot of wheeling black printed against the sky. Big Boy sighed, shifted his weight, and chewed at a blade of grass. A wasp droned. He heard number nine, far away and mournful.

The train made him remember how they had dug these kilns on long hot summer days, how they had made boilers out of big tin cans, filled them with water, fixed stoppers for steam, cemented them in holes with wet clay, and built fires under them. He recalled how they had danced and yelled when a stopper blew out of a boiler, letting out a big spout of steam and a shrill whistle. There were times when they had the whole hillside blazing and smoking. Yeah, yuh see, Big Boy wuz Casey Jones n wuz speedin it down the gleamin rails of the Southern Pacific. Bobo had number two on the Santa Fe. Buck wuz on the Illinoy Central. Lester the Nickel Plate. Lawd, how they shelved the wood in! The boiling water would almost jar the cans loose from the clay. More and more pineknots and dry leaves would be piled under the cans. Flames would grow so tall they would have to shield their eyes. Sweat would pour off their faces. Then, suddenly, a peg would shoot high into the air, and

Pssseeeezzzzzzzzzzzzzzzzzzzz . . .

Big Boy sighed and stretched out his arm, quenching the flames and scattering the smoke. Why didn't Bobo c mon? He looked over the fields; there was nothing but dying sunlight. His mind drifted back to the kilns. He remembered the day when Buck, jealous of his winning, had tried to smash his kiln. Yeah, that ol sonofabitch! Naw, Lawd! He didnt go t say tha! Whut wu he thinkin erbout? Cussin the dead! Yeah, po ol Buck wuz dead now. N Lester too. Yeah, it wuz awright fer Buck t smash his kiln. Sho. N he wished he hadnt socked ol Buck so hard tha day. He wuz sorry fer Buck now. N he sho wished he hadnt cussed po ol Bucks ma, neither. Tha wuz sinful! Mabbe Gawd would git im fer tha? But he didnt go t do it! Po Buck! Po Lester! Hed never treat anybody like tha ergin, never . . .

Dusk was slowly deepening. Somewhere, he could not tell exactly where, a cricket took up a fitful song. The air was growing soft and heavy. He looked over the fields, longing for Bobo . . .

He shifted his body to ease the cold damp of the ground, and thought back over the day. Yeah, hed been dam right erbout not wantin t go swimmin. N ef hed followed his right min hed neverve gone n got inter all this trouble. At first hed said naw. But shucks, somehow hed just went on wid the res. Yeah, he shoulda went on t school tha mawnin, like Ma told im t do. But, hell, who wouldn't git tireda awways drivin a guy t school! Tha wuz the big trouble awways drivin a guy t school. He wouldn't be in all this trouble now ef it wuznt fer that Gawddam school! Impatiently, he took the grass out of his mouth and threw it away, demolishing the little red school house . . .

Yeah, ef they had all kept still n quiet when tha ol white woman showed-up, mabbe shedve went on off. But yuh never kin tell erbout these white folks. Mabbe she wouldntve went. Mabbe tha white man woulda killed all of em! All *fo* of em! Yeah, yuh never kin tell erbout white folks. Then, ergin, mabbe tha white woman woulda went on off n laffed. Yeah, mabbe tha white man woulda said: *Yuh nigger bastards git t hell outta here! Yuh know Gawd-*

damn well yuh don berlong here! N then they woulda grabbed their cloes n run like all hell . . . He blinked the white man away. Where wuz Bobo? Why didnt he hurry up n c mon?

He jerked another blade and chewed. Yeah, ef pa had only let im have tha shotgun! He could stan off a whole mob wid a shotgun. He looked at the ground as he turned a shotgun over in his hands. Then he leveled it at an advancing white man. *Boooom!* The man curled up. Another came. He reloaded quickly, and let him have what the other had got. He too curled up. Then another came. He got the same medicine. Then the whole mob swirled around him, and he blazed away, getting as many as he could. They closed in; but, by Gawd, he had done his part, hadnt he? N the newspapersd say: NIGGER KILLS DOZEN OF MOB BEFO LYNCHED! Er mabbe theyd say: TRAPPED NIGGER SLAYS TWENTY BEFO KILLED! He smiled a little. Tha wouldn't be so bad, would it? Blinking the newspaper away, he looked over the fields. Where wuz Bobo? Why didnt he hury up n c mon?

He shifted, trying to get a crick out of his legs. Shucks, he wuz gittin tireda this. N it wuz almos dark now. Yeah, there wuz a little bittie star way over yonder in the eas. Mabbe tha white man wuznt dead? Mabbe they wuznt even lookin fer im? Mabbe he could go back home now? Naw, better wait erwhile. Thad be bes. But, Lawd, ef he only had some water! He could hardly swallow, his throat was so dry. Gawddam them white folks! Thas all they wuz good fer, t run a nigger down lika rabbit! Yeah, they git yuh in a corner n then they let yuh have it. A thousan of em! He shivered, for the cold of the clay was chilling his bones. Lawd, spose they found im here in this hole? N wid nobody t hep im? . . . But ain no use in thinkin erbout tha; wait till trouble come fo yuh start fightin it. But ef tha mob came one by one hed wipe em all out. Clean up the whole bunch. He caught one by the neck and choked him long and hard, choked him till his tongue and eyes popped out. Then he jumped upon his chest and stomped him like he had stomped that snake. When he had finished with one, another came. He choked him too. Choked till he sank slowly to the ground, gasping . . .

"Hoalo!"

Big Boy snatched his fingers from the white man's neck and looked over the fields? He saw nobody. Had someone spied him? He was sure that somebody had hollered. His heart pounded. But, shucks, nobody couldnt see im here in this hole . . . But mabbe theyd seen im when he wuz comin n had laid low n wuz now closin in on im! Praps they wuz signalin fer the others? Yeah, they wuz creepin up on im! Mabbe he oughta git up n run . . . Oh! Mabbe tha wuz Bobo! Yeah, Bobo! He oughta clim out n see ef Bobo wuz lookin fer im . . . He stiffened.

"Hoalo!"

"Hoalo!"

"Wheres yuh?"

"Over here on Bullards Road!"

"C mon over!"

"Awright!"

He heard footsteps. Then voices came again, low and far away this time.

"Seen anybody?"

"Naw. Yuh?"

"Naw."

"Yuh reckon they got erway?"

"Ah dunno. Its hard t tell."

"Gawddam them sonofabitchin niggers!"

"We oughta kill ever black bastard in this country!"

"Waal, Jim got two of em, anyhow."

"But Bertha said there wuz *fo!*"

"Where in hell they hidin?"

"She said one of em wuz named Big Boy, or somethin like tha."

"We went t his shack lookin fer im."

"Yeah?"

"But we didnt fin im."

"These niggers stick tergether; they don never tell on each other."

"We looked all thu the shack n couldnt fin hide ner hair of im. Then we drove the ol woman n man out n set the shack on fire . . ."

"Jeesus! Ah wished Ah coulda been there!"

"Yuh shoulda heard the ol nigger woman howl . . ."

"Hoalo!"

"C mon over!"

Big Boy eased to the edge and peeped. He saw a white man with a gun slung over his shoulder running down the slope. Wuz they gonna search the hill? Lawd, there wuz no way fer im t git erway now; he wuz caught! He shoulda knowed theyd git im here. N he didnt hava thing, notta thing t fight wid. Yeah, soon as the blood-houns came theyd fin im. Lawd, have mercy! Theyd lynch im right here on the hill . . . Theyd git im n tie im t a stake n burn im erlive! Lawd! Nobody but the good Lawd could hep im now, nobody . . .

He heard more feet running. He nestled deeper. His chest ached. Nobody but the good Lawd could hep now. They wuz crowdin all round im n when they hada big crowd theyd close in on im. Then itd be over . . . The good Lawd would have t hep im, cause nobody could hep im now, nobody . . .

And then he went numb when he remembered Bobo. Spose Bobod come now? Hed be caught sho! Both of em would be caught! Theyd make Bobo tell where he wuz! Bobo oughta not try to come now. Somebody oughta tell im . . . But there wuz nobody; there wuz no way . . .

He eased slowly back to the opening. There was a large group of men. More were coming. Many had guns. Some had coils of rope slung over shoulders.

"Ah tell yuh they still here, somewhere . . ."

"But we looked all over!"

"What t hell! Wouldnt do t let em git erway!"

"Naw. Ef they git erway notta woman in this town would be safe."

"Say, whuts tha yuh got?"

"Er pillar."

"Fer whut?"

"Feathers, fool!"

"Chris! Thisll be hot ef we kin ketch them niggers!"

"Ol Anderson said he wuz gonna bringa barrela tar!"

"Ah got some gasoline in mah car ef yuh need it."

Big Boy had no feelings now. He was waiting. He did not wonder if they were coming after him. He just waited. He did not wonder about Bobo. He rested his cheek against the cold clay, waiting.

A dog barked. He stiffened. It barked again. He balled himself into a knot at the bottom of the hole, waiting. Then he heard the patter of dog feet.

"Look!"

"Whuts he got?"

"Its a snake!"

"Yeah, the dogs foun a snake!"

"Gee, its a big one!"

"Shucks, Ah wish he could fin one of them sonfabitchin niggers!"

The voices sank to low murmurs. Then he heard number twelve, its bell tolling and whistle crying as it slid along the rails. He flattened himself against the clay. Someone was singing:

We'll hang ever nigger t a sour apple tree . . .

When the song ended there was hard laughter. From the other side of the hill he heard the dog barking furiously. He listened. There was more than one dog now. There were many and they were barking their throats out.

"Hush, Ah hear them dogs!"

"When theys barkin like tha theys foun somethin!"

"Here they come over the hill!"

"WE GOT IM! WE GOT IM!"

There came a roar. Tha mus be Bobo; tha mus be Bobo . . . In spite of his fear, Big Boy looked. The road, and half of the hillside across the road, were covered with men. A few were at the top of the hill, stenciled against the sky. He could see dark forms moving up the slopes. They were yelling.

"By Gawd, we got im!"

"C mon!"

"Where is he?"

"Theyre bringin im over the hill!"

"Ah got a rope fer im!"

"Say, somebody go n git the others!"

"Where is he? Cant we see im, Mister?"

"They say Berthas comin, too."

"Jack! Jack! Don leave me! Ah wanna see im!"

"Theyre bringin im over the hill, sweetheart!"

"AH WANNA BE THE FIRS T PUT A ROPE ON THA BLACK BASTARDS NECK!"

"Les start the fire!"

"Heat the tar!"

"Ah got some chains t chain im."

"Bring im over this way!"

"Chris, Ah wished Ah hada drink . . ."

Big Boy saw men moving over the hill. Among them was a long dark spot. Tha mus be Bobo; tha mus be Bobo theys carryin . . . Theyll git im here. He oughta git up n run. He clamped his teeth and ran his hand across his forehead, bringing it away wet. He tried to swallow, but could not; his throat was dry.

They had started the song again:

We'll hang ever nigger t a sour apple tree . . .

There were women singing now. Their voices made the song round and full. Song waves rolled over the top of pine trees. The sky sagged low, heavy with clouds. Wind was rising. Sometimes cricket cries cut surprisingly across the mob song. A dog had gone to the utmost top of the hill. At each lull of the song his howl floated full into the night.

Big Boy shrank when he saw the first tall flame light the hillside. Would they see im here? Then he remembered you could not see into the dark if you were standing in the light. As flames leaped higher he saw two men rolling a barrel up the slope.

"Say, gimme a han here, will yuh?"

"Awright, heave!"

"C mon! Straight up! Git t the other end!"

"Ah got the feathers here in this pillar!"

"BRING SOME MO WOOD!"

"Big Boy could see the barrel surrounded by flames. The mob fell back, forming a dark circle. Theyd fin im here! He had a wild impulse to climb out and fly across the hills. But his legs would not move. He stared hard, trying to find Bobo. His eyes played over a long dark spot near the fire. Fanned by wind, flames leaped higher. He jumped. That dark spot had moved. Lawd, thas Bobo; thas Bobo . . .

He smelt the scent of tar, faint at first, then stronger. The wind brought it full into his face, then blew it away. His eyes burned and he rubbed them with his knuckles. He sneezed.

"LES GIT SOURVINEERS!"

He saw the mob close in around the fire. Their faces were hard and sharp in the light of the flames. More men and women were coming over the hill. The long dark spot was smudged out.

"Everybody git back!"

"Look! Hes gotta finger!"

"C MON! GIT THE GALS BACK FROM THE FIRE!"

"Hes got one of his ears, see?"

"Whuts the matter!"

"A woman fell out! Fainted, Ah reckon . . ."

The stench of tar permeated the hillside. The sky was black and the wind was blowing hard.

"HURRY UP N BURN THE NIGGER FO IT RAINS!"

Big Boy saw the mob fall back, leaving a small knot of men about the fire. Then, for the first time, he had a full glimpse of Bobo. A black body flashed in the light. Bobo was struggling, twisting; they were binding his arms and legs.

When he saw them tilt the barrel he stiffened. A scream quivered. He knew the tar was on Bobo. The mob fell back. He saw a tar-drenched body glistening and turning.

"THE BASTARDS GOT IT!"

There was a sudden quiet. Then he shrank violently as the wind carried, like a flurry of snow, a widening spiral of white feathers into the night. The flames leaped tall as the trees. The scream came again. Big Boy trembled and looked. The mob was running down the slopes, leaving the fire clear. Then he saw a writhing white mass cradled in yellow flame, and heard screams, one on top of the other, each shriller and shorter than the last. The mob was quiet now, standing still, looking up the slopes at the writhing white mass gradually growing black, growing black in a cradle of yellow flame.

"PO ON MO GAS!"

"Gimme a lif, will yuh!"

Two men were struggling, carrying between them a heavy can. They set it down, tilted it, leaving it so that the gas would trickle down to the hollowed earth around the fire.

Big Boy slid back into the hole, his face buried in clay. He had no feelings now, no fears. He was numb, empty, as though all blood had been drawn from him. Then his muscles flexed taut when he heard a faint patter. A tiny stream of cold water seeped to his knees, making him push back to a drier spot. He looked up; rain was beating in the grass.

"Its rainin!"

"C mon, les git t town!"

". . . don worry, when the fire git thu wid im hell be gone . . ."

"Wait, Charles! Don leave me; its slippery here . . ."

"Ahll take some of yuh ladies back in mah car . . ."

Big Boy heard the dogs barking again, this time closer. Running feet pounded past. Cold water chilled his ankles. He could hear raindrops steadily hissing.

Now a dog was barking at the mouth of the hole, barking furiously, sensing a presence there. He balled himself into a knot and clung to the bottom, his knees and shins buried in water. The bark came louder. He heard paws scraping and felt the hot scent of dog breath on his face. Green eyes glowed and drew nearer as the barking, muffled by the closeness of the hole, beat upon his eardrums. Backing till his shoulders pressed against the clay, he held his breath. He pushed out his hands, his fingers stiff. The dog yawped louder, advancing, his bark rising sharp and thin. Big Boy rose to his knees, his hands before him. Then he flattened out still more against the bottom, breathing lungsful of hot dog scent, breathing it slowly, hard, but evenly. The dog came closer, bringing hotter dog scent. Big Boy could go back no more. His knees were slipping and slopping in the water. He braced himself, ready. Then, he never exactly knew how—he never knew whether he had lunged or the dog had lunged—they were together, rolling in the water. The green eyes were beneath him, between his legs. Dognails bit into his arms. His knees slipped backward and he landed full on the dog; the dog's breath left in a heavy gasp. Instinctively, he fumbled for the throat as he felt the dog twisting between his knees. The dog snarled, long and low, as though gathering strength. Big Boy's hands traveled swiftly over the dog's back, groping for the throat. He felt dognails again and saw green eyes, but his fingers had found the throat. He choked, feeling his fingers sink; he choked, throwing back his head and stiffening his arms. He felt the dog's body heave, felt dognails digging into his loins. With strength flowing from fear, he closed his fingers, pushing his full weight on the dog's throat. The dog heaved again, and lay still . . . Big Boy heard the sound of his own breathing filling the hole, and heard shouts and footsteps above him going past.

For a long, long time he held the dog, held it long after the last footstep had died out, long after the rain had stopped.

V

Morning found him still on his knees in a puddle of rainwater, staring at the stiff body of a dog. As the air brightened he came to himself slowly. He held still for a long time, as though waking from a dream, as though trying to remember.

The chug of a truck came over the hill. He tried to crawl to the opening. His knees were stiff and a thousand needle-like pains shot from the bottom of his feet to the calves of his legs. Giddiness made his eyes blur. He pulled up and looked. Through brackish light he saw Will's truck standing some twenty-five yards away, the engine running. Will stood on the runningboard, looking over the slopes of the hill.

Big Boy scuffled out, falling weakly in the wet grass. He tried to call to Will, but his dry throat would make no sound. He tried again.

"Will!"

Will heard, answering:

"Big Boy, c mon!"

He tried to run, and fell. Will came, meeting him in the tall grass.

"C mon," Will said, catching his arm.

They struggled to the truck.

"Hurry up!" said Will, pushing him onto the runningboard.

Will pushed back a square trapdoor which swung above the back of the driver's seat. Big Boy pulled through, landing with a thud on the bottom. On hands and knees he looked around in the semi-darkness.

"Where's Bobo?"

Big Boy stared.

"Wheres Bobo?"

"They got im."

"When?"

"Las night."

"The mob?"

Big Boy pointed in the direction of a charred sapling on the slope of the opposite hill. Will looked. The trapdoor fell. The engine purred, the gears whined, and the truck lurched forward over the muddy road, sending Big Boy on his side.

For a while he lay as he had fallen, on his side, too weak to move. As he felt the truck swing around a curve he straightened up and rested his back against a stack of wooden boxes. Slowly, he began to make out objects in the darkness. Through two long cracks fell thin blades of daylight. The floor was of smooth steel, and cold to his thighs. Splinters and bits of sawdust danced with the rumble of the truck. Each time they swung around a curve he was pulled over the floor; he grabbed at corners of boxes to steady himself. Once he heard the crow of a rooster. It made him think of home, of ma and pa. He thought he remembered hearing somewhere that the house had burned, but could not remember where . . . It all seemed unreal now.

He was tired. He dozed, swaying with the lurch. Then he jumped awake. The truck was running smoothly, on gravel. Far away he heard two short blasts from the Buckeye Lumber Mill. Unconsciously, the thought sang through his mind: Its six er-clock . . .

The trapdoor swung in. Will spoke through a corner of his mouth.

"How yuh comin?"

"Awright."

How they git Bobo?"

"He wuz comin over the hill."

"Whut they do?"

"They burnt im . . . Will, Ah wan some water; mah throats like fire . . ."

"Well git some when we pas a fillin station."

Big Boy leaned back and dozed. He jerked awake when the truck stopped. He heard Will get out. He wanted to peep through the trapdoor, but was afraid. For a moment, the wild fear he had known in the hole came back. Spose theyd search n fin im? He quieted when he heard Will's footstep on the runningboard. The trapdoor pushed in. Will's hat came through, dripping.

"Take it, quick!"

Big Boy grabbed, spilling water into his face. The truck lurched. He drank. Hard cold lumps of brick rolled into his hot stomach. A dull pain made him bend over. His intestines seemed to be drawing into a tight knot. After a bit it eased, and he sat up, breathing softly.

The truck swerved. He blinked his eyes. The blades of daylight had turned brightly golden. The sun had risen.

The truck sped over the asphalt miles, sped northward, jolting him, shaking out of his bosom the crumbs of corn bread, making them dance with the splinters and sawdust in the golden blades of sunshine.

He turned on his side and slept.

Almos' a Man

Richard Wright

Dave struck out across the fields, looking homeward through paling light. Whut's the usa talkin wid em niggers in the field? Anyhow, his mother was putting supper on the table. Them niggers can't understan nothing. One of these days he was going to get a gun and practice shooting, then they can't talk to him as though he were a little boy. He slowed, looking at the ground. Shucks, Ah ain scareda them even ef they are biggern me! Aw, Ah know whut Ahma do. . . . Ahm going by ol Joe's sto n git that Sears Roebuck catlog n look at them guns. Mabbe Ma will lemme buy one when she gits mah pay from ol man Hawkins. Ahma beg her t gimme some money. Ahm ol ernough to hava gun. Ahm seventeen. Almos a man. He strode, feeling his long, loose-jointed limbs. Shucks, a man oughta hava little gun aftah he done worked hard all day. . . .

He came in sight of Joe's store. A yellow lantern glowed on the front porch. He mounted steps and went through the screen door, hearing it bang behind him. There was a strong smell of coal oil and mackerel fish. He felt very confident until he saw fat Joe walk in through the rear door, then his courage began to ooze.

"Howdy, Dave! Whutcha want?"

"How yuh, Mistah Joe? Aw, Ah don wanna buy nothing. Ah jus wanted t see ef yuhd lemme look at tha ol catlog erwhile."

"Sure! You wanna see it here?"

"Nawsuh. Ah wans t take it home wid me. Ahll bring it back termorrow when Ah come in from the fiels."

"You plannin on buyin something?"

"Yessuh."

"Your ma letting you have your own money now?"

"Shucks. Mistah Joe, Ahm gittin t be a man like anybody else!"

Joe laughed and wiped his greasy white face with a red bandanna.

"Whut you plannin on buyin?"

Dave looked at the floor, scratched his head, scratched his thigh, and smiled. Then he looked up shyly.

"Ahll tell yuh, Mistah Joe, ef yuh promise yuh won't tell."

"I promise."

"Waal, Ahma buy a gun."

"A gun? Whut you want with a gun?"

"Ah wanna keep it."

"You ain't nothing but a boy. You don't need a gun."

"Aw, lemme have the catlog, Mistah Joe. Ahll bring it back."

Joe walked through the rear door. Dave was elated. He looked around at barrels of sugar and flour. He heard Joe coming back. He craned his neck to see if he were bringing the book. Yeah, he's got it! Gawddog, he's got it!

"Here, but be sure you bring it back. It's the only one I got."

"Sho, Mistah Joe."

"Say, if you wanna buy a gun, why don't you buy one from me? I gotta gun to sell."

"Will it shoot?"

"Sure it'll shoot."

"Whut kind is it?"

"Oh, it's kinda old. . . . A lefthand Wheeler. A pistol. A big one."

"Is it got bullets in it?"

"It's loaded."

"Kin Ah see it?"

"Where's your money?"

"Whut yuh wan fer it?"

"I'll let you have it for two dollars."

"Just two dollahs? Shucks, Ah could buy tha when Ah git mah pay."

"I'll have it here when you want it."

"Awright, suh. Ah be in fer it."

He went through the door, hearing it slam again behind him. Ahma git some money from Ma n buy me a gun! Only two dollahs! He tucked the thick catalogue under his arm and hurried.

"Where yuh been, boy?" His mother held a steaming dish of black-eyed peas.

"Aw, Ma, Ah jus stopped down the road t talk wid th boys."

"Yuh know bettah than t keep suppah waitin."

He sat down, resting the catalogue on the edge of the table.

"Yuh git up from there and git to the well n wash yosef! Ah ain feedin no hogs in mah house!"

She grabbed his shoulder and pushed him. He stumbled out of the room, then came back to get the catalogue.

"Whut this?"

"Aw, Ma, it's jusa catlog."

"Who yuh git it from?"

"From Joe, down at the sto."

"Waal, thas good. We kin use it around the house."

"Naw, Ma." He grabbed for it. "Gimme mah catlog, Ma." She held onto it and glared at him.

"Quit hollerin at me! Whut's wrong wid yuh? Yuh crazy?"

"But Ma, please. It ain mine! It's Joe's! He tol me t bring it back t im termorrow."

She gave up the book. He stumbled down the back steps, hugging the thick book under his arm. When he had splashed water on his face and hands, he groped back to the kitchen and fumbled in a corner for the towel. He bumped into a chair; it clattered to the floor. The catalogue sprawled at his feet. When he had dried his eyes, he snatched up the book and held it again under his arm. His mother stood watching him.

"Now, ef yuh gonna acka fool over that ol book, Ahll take it n burn it up."

"Naw, Ma, please."

"Waal, set down n be still!"

He sat down and drew the oil lamp close. He thumbed page after page, unaware of the food his mother set on the table. His father came in. Then his small brother.

"Whutcha got there, Dave?" his father asked.

"Jusa catlog," he answered, not looking up.

"Yawh, here they is!" His eyes glowed at blue and black revolvers. He glanced up, feeling sudden guilt. His father was watching him. He eased the book under the table and rested it on his knees. After the blessing was asked, he ate. He scooped up peas and swallowed fat meat without chewing. Buttermilk helped to wash it down. He did not want to mention money before his father. He would do much better by cornering his mother when she was alone. He looked at his father uneasily out of the edge of his eye.

"Boy, how come yuh don quit foolin wid tha book n eat yo suppah."

"Yessuh."

"How yuh n ol man Hawkins gittin erlong?"

"Shuh?"

"Can't yuh hear. Why don yuh listen? Ah ast yuh how wuz yuh n ol man Hawkins gittin erlong?"

"Oh, swell, Pa. Ah plows mo lan than anybody over there."

"Waal, yuh oughta keep yo min on whut yuh doin."

"Yessuh."

He poured his plate full of molasses and sopped at it slowly with a chunk of cornbread. When all but his mother had left the kitchen he still sat and looked again at the guns in the catalogue. Lawd, ef Ah only had the pretty one! He could almost feel the slickness of the weapon with his fingers. If he had a gun like that he would polish it and keep it shining so it would never rust. N Ahd keep it loaded, by Gawd!

"Ma?"

"Hunh?"

"Ol man Hawkins give yuh mah money yit?"

"Yeah, but ain no usa yuh thinin bout thowin nona it erway. Ahm keepin tha money sos yuh kin have cloes t go to school this winter."

He rose and went to her side with the open catalogue in his palms. She was washing dishes, her head bent low over a pan. Shyly he raised the open book. When he spoke his voice was husky, faint.

"Ma, Gawd knows Ah wans one of these."

"One of whut?" she asked, not raising her eyes.

"One of these," he said again, not daring even to point. She glanced up at the page, then at him with wide eyes.

"Nigger, is yuh gone plum crazy?"

"Aw, Ma—"

"Git outta here! Don't yuh talk t me bout no gun! Yuh a fool!"

"Ma, Ah kin buy one fer two dollahs."

"Not ef Ah knows it yuh ain!"

"But yuh promised me one—"

"Ah don care whut Ah promised! Yuh ain nothing but a boy yit!"

"Ma, ef yuh lemme buy one Ahll never ast yuh fer nothing no mo."

"Ah tol yuh t git outta here! Yuh ain gonna toucha penny of tha money fer no gun! Thas how come Ah has Mistah Hawkins pay yo wages t me, cause Ah knows yuh ain got no sense."

"But Ma, we needa gun. Pa ain got no gun. We needa gun in the house. Yuh kin never tell whut might happen."

"Now don yuh try to maka fool outta me, boy! Ef we did hava gun yuh wouldn't have it!"

He laid the catalogue down and slipped his arm around her

waist. "Aw, Ma, Ah done worked hard alls summer n ain ast yuh fer nothing, is Ah, now?"

"Thas whut yuh spose t do!"

"But Ma. Ah wants a gun. Yuh kin lemme have two dollah outa mah money. Please Ma. I kin give it to Pa. . . . Please, Ma! Ah loves yuh, Ma."

When she spoke her voice came soft and low.

"What yuh wan wida gun, Dave? Yuh don need no gun. Yuhll git in trouble. N ef yo Pa jus thought Ah letyuh have money t buy a gun he'd hava fit."

"Ahll hide it, Ma. It ain but two dollahs."

"Lawd, chil, whuts wrong wid yuh?"

"Ain nothing wrong, Ma. Ahm almos a man now. Ah wants a gun."

"Who gonna sell yuh a gun?"

"Ol Joe at the sto."

"N it don cos but two dollahs?"

"Thas all, Ma. Just two dollahs. Please, Ma."

She was stacking the plates away; her hands moved slowly, reflectively. Dave kept an anxious silence. Finally she turned to him.

"Ahll let yuh git the gun ef yuh promise me one thing."

"Whuts tha, Ma?"

"Yuh bring it straight back t me, yuh hear? It'll be fer Pa."

"Yessum! Lemme go now, Ma."

She stooped, turned slightly to one side, raised the hem of her dress, rolled down the top of her stocking, and came up with a slender wad of bills.

"Here," she said. "Lawd knows yuh don need no gun. But yer Pa does. Yuh bring it right back t me, yuh hear. Ahma put it up. Now ef yuh don, Ahma have yuh Pa lick yuh so hard yuh won ferget it."

"Yessum."

He took the money, ran down the steps, and across the yard.

"Dave! Yuuuuuh Daaaaaave!"

He heard, but he was not going to stop now. "Naw, Lawd!"

The first movement he made the following morning was to reach under his pillow for the gun. In the gray light of dawn he held it loosely, feeling a sense of power. Could killa man wida gun like this. Kill anybody, black or white. And if he were holding this gun in his hand nobody could run over him; they would have to respect him. It was a big gun, with a long barrel and a heavy handle. He raised and lowered it in his hand, marveling at its weight.

He had not come straight home with it as his mother had asked; instead he had stayed out in the fields, holding the weapon in his hand, aiming it now and then at some imaginary foe. But he had not fired it; he had been afraid that his father might hear. Also he was not sure he knew how to fire it.

To avoid surrendering the pistol he had not come into the house until he knew that all were asleep. When his mother had tiptoed to his bedside late that night and demanded the gun, he had first played 'possum; then he had told her that the gun was hidden outdoors, that he would bring it to her in the morning. Now he lay turning it slowly in his hands. He broke it, took out the cartridges, felt them, and then put them back.

He slid out of bed, got a long strip of old flannel from a trunk, wrapped the gun in it, and tied it to his naked thigh while it was still loaded. He did not go in to breakfast. Even though it was not yet daylight, he started for Jim Hawkins's plantation. Just as the sun was rising he reached the barns where the mules and plows were kept.

"Hey! That you, Dave?"

He turned. Jim Hawkins stood eyeing him suspiciously.

"What're yuh doing here so early?"

"Ah didn't know Ah wuz gittin up so early, Mistah Hawkins. Ah wuz fixin t hitch up ol Jenny n take her t the fiels."

"Good. Since you're here so early, how about plowing that stretch down by the woods?"

"Suits me, Mistah Hawkins."

"O.K. Go to it!"

He hitched Jenny to a plow and started across the fields. Hot dog! This was just what he wanted. If he could get down by the woods, he could shoot his gun and nobody would hear. He walked behind the plow, hearing the traces creaking, feeling the gun tied tight to his thigh.

When he reached the woods, he plowed two whole rows before he decided to take out the gun. Finally he stopped, looked in all directions, then untied the gun and held it in his hand. He turned to the mule and smiled.

"Know whut this is, Jenny? Naw, yuh wouldn't know! Yuhs jusa ol mule! Anyhow, this is a gun, n it kin shoot, by Gawd!"

He held the gun at arm's length. Whut t hell, Ahma shoot this thing! He looked at Jenny again.

"Lissen here, Jenny! When Ah pull this ol trigger Ah don wan yuh t run n acka fool now."

Jenny stood with head down, her short ears pricked straight. Dave walked off about twenty feet, held the gun far out from him, at arm's length, and turned his head. Hell, he told himself, Ah ain afraid. The gun felt loose in his fingers; he waved it wildly for a moment. Then he shut his eyes and tightened his forefinger. Bloom! The report half-deafened him and he thought his right hand was torn from his arm. He heard Jenny whinnying and galloping over the field, and he found himself on his knees squeezing his fingers hard between his legs. His hand was numb; he jammed it into his mouth, trying to warm it, trying to stop the pain. The gun lay at his feet. He did not quite know what had happened. He stood up and stared at the gun as though it were a living thing. He gritted his teeth and kicked the gun. Yuh almos broke mah arm! He turned to look for Jenny; she was far over the fields, tossing her head and kicking wildly.

"Hol on there, ol mule!"

When he caught up with her she stood trembling, walling her big white eyes at him. The plow was far away; the traces had broken. Then Dave stopped short, looking, not believing. Jenny was bleeding. Her left side was red and wet with blood. He went closer. Lawd, have mercy! Wondah did Ah shoot this mule? He grabbed for Jenny's mane. She flinched, snorted, whirled, tossing her head.

"Hol on now! Hol on."

Then he saw the hole in Jenny's side, right between the ribs. It was round, wet, red. A crimson stream streaked down the front leg, flowing fast. Good Gawd! Ah wuzn't shootin at tha mule. He felt panic. He knew he had to stop that blood, or Jenny would bleed to death. He had never seen so much blood in all his life. He chased the mule for half a mile, trying to catch her. Finally she stopped, breathing hard, stumpy tail half arched. He caught her mane and led her back to where the plow and gun lay. Then he stooped and grabbed handfuls of damp black earth and tried to plug the bullet hole. Jenny shuddered, whinnied, and broke from him.

"Hol on! Hol on now!"

He tried to plug it again, but blood came anyhow. His fingers were hot and sticky. He rubbed dirt into his palms, trying to dry them. Then again he attempted to plug the bullet hole, but Jenny shied away, kicking her heels high. He stood helpless. He had to do something. He ran at Jenny; she dodged him. He watched a red stream of blood flow down Jenny's leg and form a bright pool at her feet.

"Jenny . . . Jenny . . ." he called weakly.

His lips trembled! She's bleeding t death! He looked in the direction of home, wanting to go back, wanting to get help. But he saw the pistol lying in the damp black clay. He had a queer feeling that if he only did something, this would not be; Jenny would not be there bleeding to death.

When he went to her this time, she did not move. She stood with sleepy, dreamy eyes; and when he touched her she gave a low-pitched whinny and knelt to the ground, her front knees slopping in blood.

"Jenny . . . Jenny . . ." he whispered.

For a long time she held her neck erect; then her head sank, slowly. Her ribs swelled with a mighty heave and she went over.

Dave's stomach felt empty, very empty. He picked up the gun and held it gingerly between his thumb and forefinger. He buried it at the foot of a tree. He took a stick and tried to cover the pool of blood with dirt—but what was the use? There was Jenny lying with her mouth open and her eyes walled and glassy. He could not tell Jim Hawkins he had shot his mule. But he had to tell him something. Yeah, Ahll tell em Jenny started gittin wil n fell on the joint of the plow. . . . But that would hardly happen to a mule. He walked across the field slowly, head down.

It was sunset. Two of Jim Hawkins's men were over near the edge of the woods digging a hole in which to bury Jenny. Dave was surrounded by a knot of people; all of them were looking down at the dead mule.

"I don't see how in the world it happened," said Jim Hawkins for the tenth time.

The crowd parted and Dave's mother, father, and small brother pushed into the center.

"Where Dave?" his mother called.

"There he is," said Jim Hawkins.

His mother grabbed him.

"Whut happened, Dave? Whut yuh done?"

"Nothing."

"C'mon, boy, talk," his father said.

Dave took a deep breath and told the story he knew nobody believed.

"Waal," he drawled. "Ah brung ol Jenny down here sos Ah could do mah plowin. Ah plowed bout two rows, just like yuh see." He stopped and pointed at the long rows of upturned earth. "Then something musta been wrong wid ol Jenny. She wouldn't ack right a-tall. She started snortin n kickin her heels. Ah tried to hol her, but she pulled erway, rearin n goin on. Then when the point of the plow was stickin up in the air, she swung erroun n twisted herself back on it. . . . She stuck herself n started t bleed. N fo Ah could do anything, she wuz dead."

"Did you ever hear of anything like that in all your life?" asked Jim Hawkins.

There were white and black standing in the crowd. They murmured. Dave's mother came close to him and looked hard into his face.

"Tell the truth, Dave," she said.

"Looks like a bullet hole ter me," said one man.

"Dave, whut yuh do wid tha gun?" his mother asked.

The crowd surged in, looking at him. He jammed his hands into his pockets, shook his head slowly from left to right, and backed away. His eyes were wide and painful.

"Did he hava gun?" asked Jim Hawkins.

"By Gawd, Ah tol yuh tha wuz a gunwound," said a man, slapping his thigh.

His father caught his shoulders and shook him till his teeth rattled.

"Tell whut happened, yuh rascal! Tell whut . . ."

Dave looked at Jenny's stiff legs and began to cry.

"Whut yuh do wid tha gun?" his mother asked.

"Come on and tell the truth," said Hawkins. "Ain't nobody going to hurt you. . . ."

His mother crowded close to him.

"Did yuh shoot tha mule, Dave?"

Dave cried, seeing blurred white and black faces.

"Ahh ddinnt gggo tt sshoooot hher. . . . Ah ssswear ffo Gawd Ahh ddint. . . . Ah wuz a-tryin t sssee ef the ol gggun would sshoot—"

"Where yuh git the gun from?" his father asked.

"Ah got it from Joe, at the sto."

"Where yuh git the money?"

"Ma give it t me."

"He kept worryin me, Bob. . . . Ah had t. . . . Ah tol im t bring the gun right back t me. . . . It was fer yuh, the gun."

"But how yuh happen to shoot that mule?" asked Jim Hawkins.

"Ah wuznt shootin at the mule, Mistah Hawkins. The gun jumped when Ah pulled the trigger . . . N fo Ah knowed anything Jenny wuz there a-bleedin."

Somebody in the crowd laughed. Jim Hawkins walked close to Dave and looked into his face.

"Well, looks like you have bought you a mule, Dave."

"Ah swear fo Gawd, Ah didn't go t kill the mule, Mistah Hawkins!"

"But you killed her!"

All the crowd was laughing now. They stood on tiptoe and poked heads over one another's shoulders.

"Well, boy, looks like yuh done bought a dead mule! Hahaha!"

"Ain tha ershame."

"Hohohohoho."

Dave stood, head down, twisting his feet in the dirt.

"Well, you needn't worry about it, Bob," said Jim Hawkins to Dave's father. "Just let the boy keep on working and pay me two dollars a month."

"Whut yuh wan fer yo mule, Mistah Hawkins?"

Jim Hawkins screwed up his eyes.

"Fifty dollars."

"Whut yuh do wid tha gun?" Dave's father demanded.

Dave said nothing.

"Yuh wan me t take a tree lim n beat yuh till yuh talk!"

"Nawsuh!"

"Whut yuh do wid it?"

"Ah thowed it erway."

"Where?"

"Ah . . . Ah thowed it in the creek."

"Waal, c mon home. N firs thing in the mawnin git to tha creek n fin tha gun."

"Yessuh."

"Whut yuh pay fer it?"

"Two dollahs."

"Take tha gun n git yo money back n carry it t Mistah Hawkins, yuh hear? N don fergit Ahma lam you black bottom good fer this! Now march yosef on home, suh!"

Dave turned and walked slowly. He heard people laughing. Dave glared, his eyes welling with tears. Hot anger bubbled in him. Then he swallowed and stumbled on.

That night Dave did not sleep. He was glad that he had gotten out of killing the mule so easily, but he was hurt. Something hot seemed to turn over inside him each time he remembered how they had laughed. He tossed on his bed, feeling his hard pillow. N Pa says he's gonna beat me. . . . He remembered other beatings, and his back quivered. Naw, naw, Ah sho don wan im t beat me tha way no mo. . . . Dam em all! Nobody ever gave him anything. All he did was work. They treat me lika mule. . . . N then they beat me. . . . He gritted his teeth. N Ma had t tell on me.

Well, if he had to, he would take old man Hawkins that two dollars. But that meant selling the gun. And he wanted to keep that gun. Fifty dollahs fer a dead mule.

He turned over, thinking how he had fired the gun. He had an itch to fire it again. Ef other men kin shoota gun, by Gawd, Ah kin! He was still listening. Mebbe they all sleepin now. . . . The house was still. He heard the soft breathing of his brother. Yes, now! He would go down an get that gun and see if he could fire it! He eased out of bed and slipped into overalls.

The moon was bright. He ran almost all the way to the edge of the woods. He stumbled over the ground, looking for the spot where he had buried the gun. Yeah, here it is. Like a hungry dog scratching for a bone he pawed it up. He puffed his black cheeks and blew dirt from the trigger and barrel. He broke it and found four cartridges unshot. He looked around; the fields were filled with silence and moonlight. He clutched the gun stiff and hard in his fingers. But as soon as he wanted to pull the trigger, he shut his eyes and turned his head. Naw, Ah can't shoot wid mah eyes closed n mah head turned. With effort he held his eyes open; then he squeezed. Blooooom! He was stiff, not breathing. The gun was still in his hands. Dammit, he'd done it! He fired again. Bloooom! He smiled. Bloooom! Blooooom! Click, click. There! It was empty. If anybody could shoot a gun, he could. He put the gun into his hip pocket and started across the fields.

When he reached the top of a ridge he stood straight and proud in the moonlight, looking at Jim Hawkins's big white house, feeling the gun sagging in his pocket. Lawd, ef Ah had jus one mo bullet Ahd taka shot at tha house. Ahd like t scare ol man Hawkins jussa little. . . . Jussa enough t let im know Dave Sanders is a man.

To his left the road curved, running to the tracks of the Illinois Central. He jerked his head, listening. From far off came a faint hoooof-hoooof; hoooof-hoooof; hoooof-hoooof. . . . That's number eight. He took a swift look at Jim Hawkins's white house; he thought of Pa, of Ma, of his little brother, and the boys. He thought of the dead mule and heard hooof-hooof; hooof-hooof; hooof-hooof. . . . He stood rigid. Two dollahs a mont. Les see now . . . Tha means itll take bout two years. Shucks! Ahll be dam! He started down the road, toward the tracks. Yeah, here she comes! He stood beside the track and held himself stiffly. Here she comes, erroun the ben. . . . C mon, yuh slow poke! C mon! He had his hand on his gun; something quivered in his stomach. Then the train thundered past, the gray and brown boxcars rumbling and clinking. He gripped the gun tightly; then he jerked his hand out of his pocket. Ah betcha Bill wouldn't do it! Ah betcha. . . . The cars slid past, steel grinding upon steel. Ahm riding yuh ternight so hep me Gawd! He was hot all over. He hesitated just a moment; then he grabbed, pulled atop of a car, and lay flat. He felt his pocket; the gun was still there. Ahead the long rails were glinting in moonlight, stretching away, away to somewhere, somewhere where he could be a man. . . .

FROM

Snakes

AL YOUNG

FINALLY I KEEP TRYING to see myself emerging out of that shaky home scene, a home-grown nut, a peculiar lad who lived with his hard-working grandmother who spent all her extra money playing the numbers and playing them hard. She always wanted to hit lucky and ease out of the game, all the games.

When I was ten, Bo died and Claude took sick and didnt have the means or strength to look after me properly, so I was sent south to live with relatives. They were cousins but I called them Uncle Donald and Aunt Didi. They lived in a small town in Mississippi and were poor as church mice the first year I spent with them. We lived in a rickety old frame house out from Meridian and had neckbones, rice, or beans and rice for dinner a lot. Uncle Donald sold fruits and vegetables on the streets from an obsolescent truck and in summer was the original watermelon man.

Uncle Donald was also what they called a midnight rambler who drove Aunt Didi into fits. He liked to stay out late. The ruckus he kept up was continuous. He got into fights. Wherever he went there was commotion. But he had a talent for getting hold of a dollar and dollars were very scarce indeed.

He bought an old used humpback Ford and had the legend BLACKJACK TAXI CO. stenciled on the sides and drove around town picking up fares. Soon he had the good fortune to acquire three or four other cabs. Business was good, but there was only so much money to be made off black people who took taxis in a small southern town.

Uncle Donald started running whiskey for a black bootlegger who, allegedly, was being backed by a white man whom some people identified as being the governor himself. Within a year after I had come to live with them, quickly adjusting to the southern style of life and the funnytime public school system, Uncle Donald turned the house into a beer garden, a blind pig where people slipped to have a few drinks, gamble, dance, or just generally cut up and get their feet wet in the dry, dry state of Mississippi. The sheriff himself was often to be seen on the premises, a black gal on either arm, loaded to the jowls and red in the face, quivering when he put on his big white horse-laugh.

My second cousins and I, Aunt Didi's and Uncle Donald's children, were all around the same age. Their oldest boy, Jab, was exactly my age. We thought it was great that there was a party going on all the time. We were regularly called in after the sun went down and playtime was over, and hustled into a back bedroom from which we'd work our game of listening thru the walls, making numberless trips to the bathroom in order to get a peek at all the people and see what all the fuss was about that went on and on into the night.

Records would be playing, drinks poured; women and girls laughing and cackling in high black tones and registers. I used to sit with my cousin Jab by the wall next to the door and read comicbooks and dig all the sounds seeping thru. We'd split a pack of B-C Headache Powder, dump it into our palms and lap it up with a Coke or RC. We'd seen grown people down south doing that. We knew all the records by heart, all that blues and rhythm and blues, those jump numbers and jazz, even country and western sides, cracker music. "Wouldnt you like to be able to sing or play somethin when you grow up?" I asked Jab.

"Like what?"

"Like anything—just be able to make all that good sound come outta somethin and get paid a lotta money for it."

"How much money you think people that put out records get?"

"I dont know but I know it's a lot."

"A thousand dollars?"

"I dont know. A thousand maybe, five thousand, maybe even ten thousand. They get a lot all right."

"How you know?"

"Well, it's a lotta people buy they records, you know that."

"How many?"

"Look at how many records Uncle Donald and them buy—and that's just around here. Think about all over the state and all over the country and the world and everywhere."

"You think they get as much as a boxer?" Jab was hung up on becoming a prizefighter.

"Some of em do, I betcha that. I betcha it's a lotsa boxers dont make as much money as some of these people put out records."

"How much you wanna bet?"

"Bet a dime."

"Where you gon get a dime from?"

"I'll get it, dont worry bout that. You wanna bet or not?"

We worked up a routine for hustling drunk people on their way into or out of the bathroom. We knew how to get them into conversations that ended up with them shelling out a nickel, a dime, or sometimes even quarters. Whenever we managed to con someone—usually a half-high older man in a jolly mood—we'd get back into the room and dance and brag about how slick we thought we were.

The music, I noticed, seemed to make people happy. At least it made things seem more relaxed and pleasant. It was the music that was knocking me out. I thought about songs and listened to everything. When we went to church—one of those churches with a band full of trombones, trumpets, saxophones, piano, organ, tambourines, the works—I yawned and dozed thru the draggy sermons and more proper singing, knowing that things would get better as the meeting warmed up. As soon as the spirit would begin to hit, the band would let itself go and blast away, ladies fainting, me sitting there, sometimes trembling with fright but loving every minute of it; other times so quiet and caught up in the excitement that Aunt Didi would have to look around to see if I was still there.

Uncle Donald worked some kind of deal that resulted in an old beat-up upright with a couple of missing notes being hauled into the front room for the pleasure of piano-playing customers who got the urge. It was a rough-looking instrument, battered, many of the keys yellowed or chipped, but it had been newly tuned and had a curious oldtime sound that I found attractive. It must have gotten several years' worth of wear the first few months it was with us. House guests played away at it evenings and midnights, and during the day we kids banged at it, hunt and peck, diligently fashioning right- or lefthand versions of whatever tunes suited our fancy.

I learned that I wasnt bad at it and, before long, could rattle off just about any melody that struck my ear and from any number of starting points on the keyboard. Aunt Didi wanted me to take piano lessons but I thought that was too sissified and told her I wasn't interested.

Eventually my chance to learn a few things came up anyway. A thin man with a limp came in one afternoon in the summertime to take care of some business with Uncle Donald. It was very hot outdoors so a few of us were lolling around the kitchen drinking Kool-Aid and enjoying the electric breeze from the fan Uncle Donald had bought hot. Business transacted, the thin man sat down at the upright in the front room and began to play. Right away I could tell that he was so much better than most of the other casual players who'd been on the set. He played for a long time. I heard something different in the way he played, something new; a kind of modern touch I hadnt heard before, a certain feeling that I liked and wanted to learn. I thought feeling could be learned.

His name was Tull and he had at one time worked with some small bands out of New Orleans and Mobile, small combos mostly. He was really a trombone player but working out on piano was something of a hobby. "This is the way I relaxes myself," he told me.

Tull got into the habit of coming by just as the sun was going down to play ballads and blues for his own enjoyment for a couple of hours. Uncle Donald and Aunt Didi seemed to go for it too. Uncle Donald would be moving thru the house, suspenders unhitched and shaving lather smeared all over his wide jaws, getting ready for another hard night. "Hey, do that one again, Tull," he'd call out from the bathroom if a number came up that he really liked. Tull would go into it again with that tough but gentle unheard-of touch of his.

I got into the habit of copping out of whatever game we kids happened to have going whenever he came over. There was a field next to the house where you could sit and still hear the music pouring from the livingroom window. I'd hide out there in the weeds and wig out.

Soon I overcame my shyness enough to ask Tull if I could watch him while he played. He was amused that a skinny brat like me should be interested in watching him play. I watched closely too, checking all his fingerings out, thinking he didn't know what I was up to. But he was on to me all along. "All right, son," he said one day, "tell you what. I'mo show you how this piece go and I'mo show it to you slow. Now, when I come back here tomorrow, I expect you to sit down and play it for me just like I taught it to you." He sucked at a can of beer and played me the chords and melody of a blues Ive never heard anywhere since. I sat down on the stool next to him and watched every move he made. "Think you got it now?"

"Nope, nossir, but I think I get the general idea."

"Lemme hear you play a little taste of it back before I cut out cause I'm goin out on a run outta town and it aint no tellin when I might be back."

I made a couple of awkward attempts on the keys and stopped.

"Go on," Tull said, "that dont sound bad at all. Youll get it if you keep at it. Listen, just take your time, one note at a time over here with your right hand. Just take your time, that's all it is to playin the piano or anything else. Take your time and work it on out."

I went to bed that night feeling as if I had the key to all the secrets in the world.

"What you laughin to yourself about?" Jab asked me.

"Nothin."

"You are too. You got some money hid away, I betcha, that dont nobody know about."

"No, I'm just feelin pretty good, that's all."

"You cant jive me, you up to somethin, MC."

Inside of a week I had Tull's blues down pat and was making a nuisance of myself playing it over and over again around the house. I was waiting for him to turn back up so that he could listen to me. I knew he'd be proud.

Weeks went by and Tull didnt show. I went to Uncle Donald and asked about him. "O you mean Tull that use to come in here and be playin all that old good music on the piano? They got him over here in Louisiana or someplace, picked him up for somethin or other."

"Picked him up, sir?"

"That's right, picked him up."

"I dont think I know what you mean, Uncle Donald."

"I mean he in jail."

"In jail, what for?"

"Dont ask me."

"You mean they just put him in jail and dont nobody know what for? Did he rob somebody or kill somebody or somethin?"

Uncle Donald shook his head and yawned. "Learn to stay outta grown folkses business, boy. Scuse me, I have to go downtown and see a man about a dog."

FROM

River House

Stark Young

When he looked at his father and saw that pale, proud face of this man he loved but knew so little about, John felt all of a sudden the things he wanted to tell pouring up in his mind. But he could not begin. He stood running his hand through his hair, trying to think of how to start. Evelyn had said that she could never talk to her father and no longer tried. If she said anything he would only swell out in his big words that meant nothing, until you were sick at the very sound of him. But John would never have allowed himself even to think like that of his father. They had been loyal to each other like gentleman always, never meaning to be disloyal even in their thoughts, much less in what they said. He himself did not know at this moment how much it hurt him that, with all he wanted to say, he could say only, in a friendly voice and half smiling,

"So Cousin Tom is still making us a little visit, father?"

"Well this trip Tom's been with us three years, I believe. Why, son?"

"And Mr. Bobo a month."

"He'll stay till New Year's, I suppose. I recollect, come to think of it, Bahram generally stays till New Year's. I'd have sold old Fancy if it hadn't been for Bahram. I used to ride, as you know, but not now."

"You were a fine rider, father, everybody knew that."

"Well, I don't ride now; the car's enough, and you'll have one too now, of course, you and Evelyn. She drives, I suppose?"

John nodded his head.

"But Bahram wants the horse. So Fancy's out there eating his head off. Bahram's a great one for horseflesh."

"You'd know that," John said, "by all those horse phrases of his. So at River House we have horses and prophecy——"

"Well, your Cousin Tom is half-way through the Book of Revelations," said his father, smiling a little. "He's found some sort of black angel for Abolition, I believe. Or spotted beast."

"Father, how can you stand it, so much company like this and the same damn stories forever?"

It was not the thing he meant to say, for it lost the tone they had struck in the conversation.

"But, son," the major said, quietly still but in a changed manner, "what would you have me do? They are gentlemen. We must be social, you know. Even you young people these days must have some sociability left."

"I suppose so," John said.

"And old friends as well. I'm sorry they trouble you."

"Oh, no, it's not that. It's not that."

"No," his father said gently. "It's because you are tired."

"I think I feel rather lit up than tired." He began to walk about the room slowly, looking around as if to study it. "It hardly seems the same," he said.

"What?"

"The place, father, and this room."

His father looked quickly at him.

"Nothing has been changed, sir."

"I know, I know," John said, shaking his head.

"You've been under a strain. Almost anybody would find it hard to bear the sight of suffering in someone—" —He changed what he was going to say—"near death like that."

"Father, I want to try and tell you."

His father turned away from him and went over to the table.

"Son," he said, "you are sure you wouldn't rather wait, not talk now?"

John shook his head impatiently. "No, father."

"All right, then, you'd better sit down."

They sat down on the davenport at the two ends, John nearest the windows. There was one thing he had to say at once.

"Father, I'd always thought my mother was not to be loved or remembered."

His father got up and stood by the window, with his back to John. His voice trembled as he said, sternly,

"Nothing has been said to make you think so, I remind you of that, John."

"No, Father, I don't in the least mean to reflect on you, you've never said anything to me against my mother. Not a word."

"Not a word."

"No." His voice was full of regret for having spoken, and the major said quickly,

"That's all right, that's all right. Pray proceed."

His father did not leave the window or turn to him. There was a silence, neither of them moved; and John could see that clear profile that he had always admired, the high, pale forehead, the aquiline nose, the close line of the lips, still red like a young man's.

The last few days—what had happened in them was flooding into John's mind. His hands were motionless at his sides, and he seemed to be alone as he sat there, then he seemed to be with his mother, then alone again but somehow with her too.

He saw again the journey on the train. He was out of New Orleans and nearing New Iberia, where he was to stop. It was a hot day at the end of June and the passengers looked like people listening to dull music, let down and at the same time abandoned and dissolute. It was not the worst part of the day, for noon and the sweltering hours around three were well past, and in the shadows of the woods along the track the cool of evening was already coming on. But from the summer heat and the long day, people were still in a sort of vague excitement and prostration. There was something like the African desert—a trance and dream; he felt it in himself.

He had bought a newspaper but had not read it; and the book that Professor Daniel's wife, Harriet, his old friend and a sort of cousin, had given him lay closed on the seat. The afternoon sun fell through the west windows straight across the coach. The book was *The Forsyte Saga*—the first Galsworthy he had read since he was a Junior at Princeton—and he had not gone on reading it now because in the story what seemed to him poignant and ready to break your heart the author had not felt at all. All that big canvas of family generations, changes, fashions, epochs, death, new life and old, was laid out with great skill by this celebrated English author but without any sensitivity. Who was to bear the brunt of it all, then, for God's sake, unless it be the author? He had put the book down with a strange contempt, thinking of his own family at home, of his aunts and his father and the old place, and feeling in his breast a catch at the thought of them, and what he meant to them, and what they meant to him.

He thought of his last year in the St. Louis bank, with Tom Kelcey's father, thanks to Princeton, where Tom had been his best friend. Then of the two years before that at Princeton. It was his grandfather's college and his father liked the idea of sending his son there; he himself had belonged to a generation too poor after the Civil War to go away to school; the major was still touchy about his lack of education.

The two years before Princeton John had been at Le Flore College, staying at home. His father had talked of sending him away to Sewanee, which at River House was thought to be the last stronghold of the old gentility in Southern education, and then afterward perhaps to Princeton. There had been a good deal of talk about this. But the old bishop, who used to stay with them and be coddled and fed by Miss Ellen and Miss Rosa when he came to preach at St. Mary's, died; and the business ended by John's spending the two years at home and going to college from there. Le Flore was a mild old college, founded long ago by pious deacons and of late years turned more than Puritanical, even for a church school. It lacked now the class of students it had had in the old days, and was served now by a faculty that every year became more self-made and envious-minded. There had always been at Le Flore College a lack of erudition and sheer information, but this had once rested on an inherited conception of a society; and, through that, the education offered there had been made gracious and useful. But by the time John's generation came along the wind had gone out of it; Le Flore was a provincial little college, confused in its policy and without any standards beyond popular movements and the cheap cant of the day.

It had done nothing for him but give him a sense that the world is easy and human, and leave him alone, which was something; and living at home had divided his life so that the campus and college meant less to him than Princeton and seemed much vaguer. Fraternities were not allowed at Le Flore, they were denounced as undemocratic and even as unchristian by the trustees, most of whom were Methodist preachers—no Jesuit college could be more priest-ridden than was Le Flore by such men as these, despite their railing at the Catholics. Without fraternities to choose them for him, John had made his friends here and there among the four hundred students. But all these friends had gone back to their towns, Natchez, Yazoo City, Kosciusko, Jackson and the rest of these Mississippi places, and married or at least settled down, and, though they were only short journeys away, he felt that they were far more distant than even the Princeton men he had known, who were scattered from ocean to ocean. That feeling came from the provincial state of mind.

This strong thing, woven into his bones, that bound him to his family and made it what it was to be apart from them—his Aunt Rosa always said it was the Scotch in them, she felt it so deeply that she wanted to explain it for herself. He remembered how hard it had been a year ago leaving home to go to live in St. Louis, and what a struggle there had been in his mind. He remembered how it had been when he went away to Princeton. It had always been so. At Christmas going back and every autumn, there had been this strange pain and this pulling at his heart, at the thought of leaving the old place and his people; he remembered the nostalgia for it all, and how the first days in the new place he had gone to seemed harsh and lonely and distracted, and how they wrote from home that they missed him—it was the Scotch in them all, Miss Rosa said; Harriet, his cousin, said it was the Dandridge.

Before his college days and on back as far as he could remember, John had been at home with his father and his aunts. And before that, when he was three, as they had told him, his mother had gone away and never returned. He had not said, as he sat there on the train, "I wonder what my mother will be like?" or "I'll tell her about myself"—nothing so definite as that. His mother had no reality for him, not as an image or figure. No one in his family had talked of her to him; what he had asked as a child had been easily put off, no doubt; and later, when he was a little older, he had known by some instinct not to ask. He had some ideas of his mother but they had been long since left at the back of his mind, vague and neglected. She was a Louisiana woman, and none of her family lived in Mississippi, so that he never heard her spoken of in a place from which she had been gone for a generation; he—her son—was twenty-five.

His thoughts that day on the train had been broken into by the voices of two men who had the seat in front of him. One of them was young and sat in his shirt sleeves, with his collar open at the throat and his black and yellow striped cravat hanging from the rack overhead; the other was a man of fifty or more, dressed in blue seersucker. John heard the older man speaking of Memphis. It was as if he spoke of Le Flore almost, for Memphis was hardly two hours from Le Flore, where every one read the Memphis papers.

"Fast!" the man was saying. "Memphis, oh, boy!"

"Well," said the young man, "the girls got to keep up, I guess. The South's sure coming on for prosperity. Say, those parties! Say, how about Little Rock?"

But the older man was impressed by Memphis.

"Say how! Say, there's nothin' in Arkansas now like Memphis. Some of those babies!"

"They tell me some of 'em 're hottern'n the hinges of hell."

"And being so pretty as they are."

"I get you."

"You oughter look in on Memphis."

"Say, I will. I know the burg, but I'm not so much acquainted there as I might be."

They began to talk of their own adventures, a series of stupid and vulgar egotisms mixed with bootleg stories; the younger man was telling of a trained nurse he knew in Kansas City. John could remember how he listened vaguely. Then he remembered how, as the train went on through the level green country, the man's dull voice, harping on one dirty adventure after another, droned into the rumble of the wheels. Suddenly his imagination grasped the idea that he was about to see his mother.

At the hotel, when he arrived, he hurried through his bath but dressed himself carefully, and at the very last changed to another necktie, the blue looked black, he chose one that was red and gray. The fact that some one is dying of whom we have no image or conception cannot mean the same poignancy to us as it does with those whom we have seen and known, so greatly is our life all images and sounds, and dear to us for that. He had forgotten for the moment that his mother was so ill and had thought only of the meeting with her. He had felt a sense of coquetry, almost, in the event. And yet at the same time he knew that, for a man such as he was, there is no such thing as a woman's being merely his mother. He may or may not love her, but he is too sensitive not to have been touched long ago by the very idea of a mother as a woman whose body has survived the pain, whose mind has suffered hope, and whose soul encountered a strange soul, because of the child born to her.

This thought had been in John's mind more than he knew. And there was also the feeling that went with it: this pain and dream involved himself. He had a share in it and was drawn to her through it, in something he could have with no other person. How could she go away and leave him, seeing they had this together? There was an old hurt and resentment in him against his mother for that. He had not realized it in any clear shape, but it was there.

As he went down the old streets to the house where his mother lived, he saw beyond the trees the moon. It was in the first quarter. He had watched the young moon these nights at home, since he had come South again; and had seen the feather of it coming down the sky; and there came into his mind now, as he walked along, that old fancy of his, strong almost as a superstition. Every month when he looked up and saw the new moon he felt that it would bring him some good fortune. Then he came to the house where his mother lived, and went around the veranda and up a stair. The nurse met him at the door, Miss Thompson, a fat young woman, with a rosy Scotch face. He had to wait a few minutes before he could see his mother; an injection she had had must take effect; and the nurse spoke of the attacks that had lately grown worse; the strain of the summer heat had been too much for her heart. The nurse knew his mother's affairs and about her family, and expected no explanations from him. She said how much John looked liked his mother, and left him to go to the sick woman. He caught a glimpse of his mother's room through the half-open door, the old-style walnut bed, the white curtains at the windows. Then the nurse called him in and he saw his mother.

In the middle of the room he stopped for a moment looking at her. She lay with her hands raised to him, he saw how white and transparent they were. He saw the dark hair and brown eyes, the fairness, the smile, and heard her voice saying, "John? You've come?" The light in her eyes was what he saw. He fell on his knees and buried his head in his mother's bosom, her hands on his hair.

She kept saying,

"This is my son, nurse, this is my son. He has come to see me."

He had not moved, but had felt a kind of divine quiet stealing through him, such as he had never felt before, and the sensation that he had had a moment before, of pain and sobbing, passed away into a gentle peace.

Presently when he raised his head to look at her, she said,

"And your father, is he well?"

"Yes." He was almost whispering to her.

"He doesn't have his headaches any more?"

"Not that I ever heard of, mother."

"I'm glad, I've wondered if he had. And you?"

"I'm fine."

He could say no more, for the nurse came to send him away. She was afraid of more for one visit. He was to come in the morning, not before nine.

"Good night, my darling," his mother said, "you get some rest."

"Good night, mother," he said and kissed her.

"Here, kiss me again," she said, and he leaned over again and kissed her.

That was all their meeting, nothing else said. Afterward he walked about the streets, filled with a strange new life. For all the brief visit in his mother's room the thoughts in his head were crowded and wandering as if after some long conversation. He knew that something had passed into him. He saw the moon again, drifting downward in the sky and his fancy about the new moon seemed now to be an old truth, as he stood looking out from his window at the hotel, excited and sleepy at the same time, like a child. The night before he had been awake until daylight, when the heat in the sleeping-car had cooled. The gentle stir of the trees outside in the night wind was like that coolness coming in at the windows of the train; he lay in his bed and heard it as he fell asleep.

When John went the next morning to see his mother, the nurse told him that she was dead. She had died in the night, shortly after midnight.

It was the heat, the nurse said, and added bluntly, partly the heat and partly the shock of seeing him.

Miss Thompson did not let him see his mother again. His mother had asked that he go home, with the memory of her as they had been together, not this other remembrance. He was not to remain for any arrangements or funeral services, they had all been provided for.

Miss Thompson knew his mother's affairs. During the years away from her husband his mother had taken nothing from him. There had been a small property of her own, some land near the town, which a cousin who managed her business for her had sold and put the money into an annuity that ended with her life. She had come back to New Iberia because of two or three cousins still living there, and they had been very kind. But there was no need for John to call on them, as he might feel he should do; and when Miss Thompson said that, he understood that his mother had wished to prevent his hearing any sad accounts of her life. She did not wish to burden him with memories that could do no good.

He sat for a little while talking with the nurse about his mother. Miss Thompson had been with her only a few months over a year and during that time his mother had been ill, but they used to talk, Miss Thompson sitting in the armchair by the bed. His mother had spoken often of River House and her son and her husband, always gently as if they were her dearest memories. Sometimes she spoke of walking in a pavilion by the river. She used to say a lot of things that Miss Thompson would never forget. Once she said, "Sometimes I hear the leaves rustling along the river," Miss Thompson remembered her saying that, though you couldn't see why anybody'd remember it especially. Once she said, "No, I know there could be something worse than losing those you love; it would be to stop loving them." Miss Thompson remembered the day his mother had said that, once when there had been a storm and from the trees branches had been scattered over the grass and wet leaves on the window-sill.

There was a photograph of John that had been sent to his mother by some one, only the picture without any letter. Miss Thompson brought it for him to see before she went to put it back under the pillow. He looked at the picture of himself and on the back of it, where there was written in Miss Rosa's cramped little hand:

John Dandridge
21 years.

When he offered to help with the expenses of the burial, Miss Thompson refused, they were not even to discuss it. The only thing for him to do, she said, was to carry out his mother's wishes and go away and remember everything of last night.

Miss Thompson put her hand on his shoulder.

"I'd do it if I were you, Mr. John," she said.

He nodded his head, promising that he would.

"It's not everybody would do it, I know that. They'd insist on doing the proper thing themselves. It's nice you aren't that way about it."

"All right," he said.

She shook hands to say good-bye, and turned abruptly to go into the room. For a moment he stood outside the door, not certain what he meant to do. He might sit there a while and think over things, knowing that for the last time he would be near all that kept his mother most nearly his, her body. Then he heard the girl sobbing aloud, and talking to the dead woman as if it were to a child. Hearing that he turned quickly away and down the stair. He came a second time into the street, and started to walk down one block after another under the trees.

He was one of those people, often highly sensitive, that cannot realize things at once. It was as if he got the physical experience first and then only gradually the other. For many people something that befalls them strikes them then and there with its full meaning; their senses and their reason take in what has happened in their lives. From this full realization they gradually lose the exact impression their senses received, sounds, smells and images grow dimmer in their memories, even if the meaning of the thing remains almost as strong as ever. For John it was different. A great piece of good fortune, something that he had dreamed of and longed for to give him happiness, or some great loss, from which afterward the pain would ache in him, growing fuller instead of being dulled with time, did not quite come home to him at the moment it happened. He felt the event at the moment, his senses were taking it in, and the exact image of it would survive in his memory to make the realization more poignant; but realization itself came later.

But now that a night had passed and his mother was dead, the sense not of her death but of what had come to him from seeing her, began to spread into a fuller meaning. He was not sorry that he and his mother had not talked longer, that he had not known more about her; he did not miss her physically—the comfort of her presence—as he would have missed some one he had been with all his life. An exaltation crept over him. Was it, far back in his mind the triumph of something that partook of the soul's last and dearest dream—the mastery of death? He was exalted with a sense of the soul's immortality; he knew that at that moment his mother was more alive to him than any one who was breathing in the flesh. He could see her eyes and her hands, and could hear her voice saying, "This is my son. He has come to see me."

At the sight of his mother one feeling had followed another, two waves of feeling that were like shocks. There came first the shock of seeing, then and in a moment, that life could be so beautiful in any one, so fine, that the human body could carry so the burden and the light of its soul, that the sight of a face could draw out his heart suddenly and fill it.

After this feeling, flowing back over it, had come the second shock, the realization of how he had misjudged her. The irony of it!

But if you have not known your mother—he stopped and leaned against a tree, putting his hands up against it, his face toward it, and biting his lips together—if you haven't known your mother—he turned and walked on along the street.

Nothing had ever been said against his mother at River House; his father, speaking of her only when he had to, and that was rarely, had always said, "Your mother, John," and if there was company "Mrs. Dandridge." His aunts had never talked of his mother to him; and since they never said anything evil of anybody, their very silence about her seemed to imply all the more against her. He had early been told that his mother had gone away. And so he had thought that some way or other she was a bad woman, he had put her down as that. And then he saw her——

As he walked along, a man and a girl, side by side, the man much older, the girl not eighteen and laughing as she went, though the look on her face was neither contented nor merry, passed him. After them two old men with shovels. He thought bitterly, accusing himself. "And we may be doing the same thing with everybody. What do I know of them? Misjudging them, like a fool!"

Does a man long always, even when he does not know it, to go back to the comfort of that protecting body, the shadow of those wings? he wondered. He could remember as a little boy lying sometimes on the floor, crying and kicking his heels into the carpet, some curious defeat and strangeness baffling him. His father would only go out of the room, without punishing him, without speaking to him. His aunts had done what they could to comfort him, stroking his hands, taking patiently his spite at them at such a moment and his roughness. He remembered all that now, and that sadness of spinster love; they had tried to give him what he lacked from his mother, and to find what they lacked from never having had a child. Had the little boy resented sometimes this devotion in them, by some instinct knowing that he had been denied what he should have had?

As he grew older he had tried not to think of his mother at all; sometimes he had sat very still, with his eyes on the floor, putting the dull pain out of his mind. How much force his father must have had that his sisters should have been so sure not to go contrary to his wishes in this matter, and that others in the family or friends had not asked questions and babbled what they learned from him! They must have known they would get short answers. What love his sisters had had for him! And yet they loved John himself also, how could they have let him grow up with this doubt and shame in his child's heart? And so, thinking of his mother like that, he had gone to see her. And then he saw her——

He stopped walking, his eyes suddenly full of tears.

Then all at once he realized that he was no longer crying. An incident long forgotten had come into his mind. They were in the sitting-room at River House, the three of them, he and his two aunts. He must have been seven then, almost eight perhaps. Miss Ellen was sitting by a window that looked into the formal garden. Miss Rosa was at the bookshelves taking out the volumes of some worn set and gently dusting the covers. Now and then she stopped to look at the engravings in the books.

"They are all frayed out these books," she said.

"No wonder, Sis Rosa," said her sister, "I suppose father bought them before you were born, child."

"No, Tellie, father never bought them, they were some that belonged to Sis Bedie, I remember very well."

"Oh," Miss Ellen said, in a low voice.

"Poor child," Miss Rosa said gently, "I reckon she was very unhappy."

"Yes, Rosa."

"Only God can read our hearts, I know, but I often wish things could have been different for Bro' Hugh and her."

"Yes."

He was a little boy then, and since then he had grown to be a man, but if he had known then at seven all that he had since learned from his education and experience, he could not have understood any more deeply than he did what his aunts felt and what it meant; in the light of everything and as a man now, he knew that. He had understood it completely, and had gone upstairs quietly and taken out his box of toys without making any more noise than he could help, and begun to play with them on the floor of his room.

His aunts never knew that he had heard them that day, but he remembered now as he walked along, his little aunt's sorrow for his mother. Then he understood something. What had most made his aunts do as his father willed, was pity. The thought of what their brother felt and what had fallen to him in life, made them do anything he wished.

Sitting there on the sofa at River House not moving, John felt his thoughts cover all this and then suddenly go back to that first day, on the train, and the picture of his father that quivered in his mind, this father that was now there in the room with him and waiting to hear what he had to say. On the train he had had in his mind his father. His mother was dying and his father had said that he should go and see her, though it was a hard thing to put on him. His father would know that it was a hard thing, and though he said nothing about it, would know what it would be like for John. But that would make no difference. In his mind's eye he saw that fine head, the flare of the nostrils and tightening of the lips at certain times. It was right that he should be sent to Louisiana to see his mother. His father's conduct in life was to do always what you will not regret or despise, whatever it cost him or cost others.

Then he raised his eyes and saw his father looking at him.

"Well, father—" he said.

"Yes, John."

He did not look his father in the eyes again but began to tell of his visit to his mother. When he stopped at last he did not know quite what he had said.

He saw that his father had gone to the long table behind him and sat there with his hands resting against the edge and his head bowed, his eyes looking down.

John got up and stood facing him.

"Look, father, I want to try and tell you," he began. "I want to tell you—" he left off, for his father had turned his head away.

"Did she have a good nurse?"

"Oh, yes, fine," John said.

"And she looked—pale, I reckon."

"Yes, pale; but her eyes were full of life, I can see her eyes now." John found himself now unable to look at his father and began to walk back and forth in the room.

"Yes, I know, son, you must excuse me," the major began, going back to John's remark of a moment ago, and as if that about his mother had not been said, "I know. I can see you're like a man that's seen a vision, that's all lifted out of himself, of course I see that, boy. Go on."

"Well, seeing my mother like that, and seeing what she was, I felt that she would keep me—" John began, but saw that for a second time his father did not hear anything he said. He felt himself go hot in the head.

"Well, I know I'm not a Southern gentleman, of course. I know these feelings are not to be mentioned." He began speaking scornfully and felt a hard antagonism against this man who was his father. He wanted to give him a cut and to hurt him. But suddenly, after a moment, he heard his own voice as if striking against an empty void, ugly and cruel, and almost as quickly he looked up and saw that his father's eyes were closed as if he minded nothing you might say, and felt now only his own grief.

"Father, I'm sorry, I just haven't got any sense," he burst out; but again as his father lifted his eyes and looked at him, he saw that nothing he had said had been heard. He said no more, and made no effort then to say anything more of what he had felt or of what his mother had given him; nothing of what had filled him and made him wonder—that strange new freedom, which had come from the force of that other soul working in him. He said nothing of how he had gone along the streets, to the hotel and to the train for home, feeling a kind of peace like a child's in doing her will, and listening to the sweetness of people's voices along the way.

After a while he looked up and saw his father's eyes resting steadily on him, hungry beneath their mask of cold light.

"Son, may I ask how all this will affect you, in the future I mean?" he said.

John did not answer for a moment. He was afraid of talking like a prig or sounding ecstatic. His father did not give him very long. Looking fixedly at his son, he said,

"To stay here with us?"

That was all it meant to him.

"Yes, father," John said, sadly.

"I know you'd like me to tell you what the trouble was, why your mother went away as she did. You certainly have a right to expect it now. After this."

"Well, naturally, sir. I've been wondering since I saw her. I don't know what to think. I've thought and thought."

"That's only natural." Major Dandridge looked at him almost defiantly. "I suppose now you blame me for most of it."

"No, no, father," John said, quickly, "I don't feel there's any use blaming anybody."

He was thinking humbly, "Things happen too deep down in us for that. In our own souls we must kneel down—" where had he read that? In some foreign novel—away back in college. In our own souls we must kneel down—But he said nothing more.

Major Dandridge waited a while before he spoke. He was controlling himself rigidly. Then he said,

"I'll tell you some time, son. Not now. If you'll excuse me. But as soon as I can. I mean I'd as lief wait."

"You tell me when you feel like it, father. I understand how it is."

"All right, I will then," the major said, knowing how bare, when the time came, would be the account he would give.

He had not, perhaps, encouraged John to talk of what he felt inside himself, after seeing his mother. Southern people of the major's generation did not speak of their innermost selves. You might spout or be poetical or even hysterical. But you did not analyze yourself to others—that was what he had a revulsion from, this subjectivity, dwelling on yourself. And out of *noblesse oblige* you did not whine. What was this whining about yourself that had come into modern life? You meet it everywhere, even in Le Flore. And yet—you could not say that John had done any whining. "It wouldn't be fair to say that," the major thought. Well, at any rate he resented any talking in a subjective way, and had not encouraged John to do it.

His thoughts turned suddenly to his own case.

He looked at his son.

"John, you think I was right to send you to see your mother, don't you?"

"Yes, sir, of course."

The major said nothing more, but he thought, "Yes, he thinks it was hard for him, however. Well, what about me?" Had he sent his son to see this dying woman from some *noblesse oblige?* Had his own grief been so great that he had sent his son, when he himself could not go? Had he been so grieved that he wanted to take this risk of losing his son to a rival? "It wasn't easy for me, by God," he thought, "sending my son off to someone who might take him away from me. Is he here now, taking her part against me?"

"What, father?" John asked, seeing his searching look.

"Nothing."

They could hear Miss Rosa come down the stair outside and knock at the door. Before either of them had answered she opened it.

At the sight of the two men she thought she was going to cry, but instead she came gaily toward them, with her clumsy little movement.

"My stars, Bro' Hugh," she said, "it's too funny, you ought to see the hubbub upstairs."

John rose to meet her, and her brother got up and placed a chair for her.

"What is it, Rosie? You've been having a lark, I can see by your eyes," he said.

"No, it's Tellie's having a lark. Thank you I can't sit down. She puts it up it's me but it's Tellie, honestly. You know how she is about these things."

"I know you girls have got your heads full of romance."

They were getting Evelyn settled, she said, and one of her trunks would not open; she wanted to try her brother's keys. He took his keyring from his pocket and gave it to her.

On the way out she stopped at the piano where John was standing and gave him a pat on the arm.

"Well, how are the young ladies?" he said.

"Oh, son, two old things! We're the lucky ones, to have our boy back again!"

"Your nice, lovely nephew, ain't dat so?"

"Son, you better not be talking like that, you'll get the habit like I do. You'd better be careful, dearest."

"Yes, mam."

"Well, now then, that's right." She must feed him up again, she thought, and have him quiet down, stop that twitching his hands. "Our nephew back again," she went on. "And all last year you were far away and the year before farther away in Princeton. We'll never let you out of our sight again." She added, gravely, "Son, you'll worry yourself into your grave. Try not to worry about what can't be helped, honey. What's the matter is we've all handed you down feelin's that can't do you any good, not in this world these days. That's about all we have given you, I'm afraid, just a lot of feelin's and things that can't do you any good."

"Write down Rosa Hartwell Dandridge for a big silly," he said, and put his arm around Miss Rosa's shoulder and kissed her brow. She looked up at him for a moment. She knew, somehow, that her nephew was a good man, and that goodness was life finding itself; wrong was what killed life. She could not have explained this but said her prayers every night for his safety and believed that her nephew's heart was pure.

"No, she's not silly, either," was all she said, and hurried out, looking down at the keys with a frown, as if opening a trunk was a very serious matter.

One of his aunts' coming in like that reminded John that, though they would not ask, they must be told something about his marriage. And first he must tell his father.

MISSISSIPPI WRITERS

WILLIAM ATTAWAY (1911) was born in Greenville, Mississippi. An outstanding interpreter of the Great Migration, Attaway was himself a member of a migrant professional family. His father, a physician, did not want his children to grow up in the South so, when Attaway was still quite young, packed up his family and moved to Chicago. While in high school, Attaway tried his hand at scriptwriting for his sister's amateur dramatic groups. His sister Ruth later became a successful actress.

Upon graduation from high school, he enrolled at the University of Illinois. "I had all the advantages," he later wrote, "that a self-made man imagines are good for an only son. But after my father's death I rebelled and spent my time hoboing." He worked as a laborer and a seaman and took a number of odd jobs before returning to the University of Illinois to complete his education. Back in Urbana, Illinois, he experimented with both one-act plays and short stories, publishing a few pieces in literary magazines and newspapers.

Out of college, he spent a year traveling around the country gathering materials for his first novel; he finally arrived in New York City to earn his living as a free-lance writer. There he was a part of the Harlem Renaissance and lived near artist Romare Bearden and writer Ralph Ellison. His first novel, *Let Me Breathe Thunder,* was published in 1939. In his second novel, *Blood on the Forge* (1941), he confronted directly many of the problems faced by blacks who migrated northward during the first decade of the twentieth century.

In the fifties he turned to writing for radio, films, and television. During the latter part of that decade, he wrote for such television programs as "Wide Wide World" and "The Colgate Hour." One of his most famous scripts in the sixties was an hour-long special on black humor, "A Hundred Years of Laughter." Shown on television in 1964, it was the first time comedians Redd Fox, Moms Mabley, Flip Wilson, and others had been seen on television. Attaway was the first black writer to write scripts for television and for films. A composer as well as a writer, he has arranged songs for Harry Belafonte and authored the *Calypso Song Book* (1957). He has composed over 500 songs, some 150 of which are calypsos. In 1967 he published *Hear America Singing,* a children's book with an introduction by Harry Belafonte. In this important work he tells the stories of about a hundred songs as sung by pioneers, soldiers, workers, and country and city dwellers. Attaway currently lives and writes in Los Angeles.

FREDERICK BARTHELME (1943) was born in Houston, Texas. He received degrees from Tulane University, the University of Houston, and Johns Hopkins University. Since 1978 Barthelme has been director of the Center for Writers at the University of Southern Mississippi. An editor of the *Mississippi Review*, he is also a frequent contributor to the *New Yorker*.

Moon Deluxe (1983), his first collection of short stories, was praised by Raymond Carver as being "superbly written, and very funny." One critic notes that "Barthelme's characters inhabit a world of Subarus and suburban swimming pools, of polo shirts and quick-food stands and neighborhood traffic jams. From these townscapes Barthelme has distilled with splendid economy of means and trenchant wit something of the strangeness of life, its surprising encounters and bizarre juxtapositions. While depicting the commonplace, his stories take on the atmosphere of quiet meditations, now amusing, now troubling, now unexpected, but invariably suffused with a quality of reticent but deep-felt affection." Barthelme captures the humor and dignity of our ordinary lives.

CHARLES G. BELL (1916) was born in Greenville, Mississippi. After graduating in 1936 from the University of Virginia with a degree in physics, Bell went to Oxford University as a Rhodes Scholar. Since then he has had a varied career as a novelist, poet, educator, scientist, and humanist. Bell has been at work since the late 1930s on a synthesis of history, thought, and the arts titled "Symbolic History: A Drama of the Western Arts." He now teaches at St. John's College in Santa Fe, New Mexico.

In a 1963 essay, "The Symbolic Landscape," published in the *Delta Review* Bell writes, "To write about Greenville and the Delta—what else have I been doing all these years? . . . Polarities are unavoidable. Unavoidable too is the mind's struggle to reconcile them. In my second book of poems, *Delta Return* (1956), and my first novel, *The Married Land* (1962), the Delta and its Queen City are always central, and the effort is to get them attuned to the world-field. All this about my writing would be inappropriate if I thought the problems only mine. But the Delta is what I call a symbolic landscape, and a symbolic landscape is shared." In addition to the two previously mentioned books, Bell has published another volume of poetry, *Songs for a New America* (1953), and a novel, *The Half Gods* (1968).

Of his childhood Bell says that his father was a "reforming idealist" who entered politics thinking he could clean up the state; his mother, from the hills, was "an idealist of a more mystical kind." His boyhood was spent, he says, "in trees and on the river, as far from books as I could manage. Then I got caught in the current, beginning with the more romantic things, astronomy and atomic physics."

LERONE BENNETT, JR., (1928) was born in Clarksdale, Mississippi, but moved with his family to Jackson, Mississippi, when young. After high school, he went to Atlanta to attend Morehouse College, from which he graduated in 1949. After further study at Atlanta University, Bennett became a journalist and worked for the *Atlanta Daily World* (1949–53), *Jet* magazine (1953), and *Ebony* magazine as an associate editor from 1954–57. In 1958 he became the senior editor of *Ebony*, a position he holds today. Bennett is a historian, critic, poet, essayist, and writer of short stories. His *Before the Mayflower; A History of the Negro in America, 1619–1966* is considered by many the "bible of black history."

In an interview with Felicia Lee of *USA Today* Bennett says, "Black history studies saved my life. It's made it possible for me to have some sense of why black people are where they are; why black people are what they are. It's given me a sense of optimism." His love for black history was ignited, as he was growing up in Jackson, by the "extraordinary" teachers in the public schools, and grew stronger as he sought understanding of Jackson. "I developed the mad idea that if I mastered the written word I could figure out why Mississippi existed, why black people lived as they did. I *had* to know," he said. "It was a matter of life and death. It had nothing to do with academics, it had nothing to do with books. I had friends who were whipped, attacked. I was threatened. It was rare for a black person to reach adulthood without having that kind of an experience."

There were good times for Bennett too, of course—having his first newspaper editorial published when he was eleven; playing clarinet and saxophone in a jazz band; being the editor of his high school yearbook and newspaper; and editing the newspaper at Morehouse College.

Concluding the interview he said, "We have to go back to the beginning and create a common American history—one that takes into account that America is not a creation of white people alone. In too many presentations we pop up suddenly as slaves, and Lincoln 'frees' us. We came here before the Mayflower, and . . . we were essentially involved in creating the economic settlement of this country. It is my view that it's impossible for white people to understand themselves and this country without understanding black history."

BESMILR BRIGHAM (1923), who is part Choctaw, was born Bess Miller Moore in Pace, Mississippi. She received a bachelor of journalism degree from Mary Hardin-Baylor University in Belton, Texas, and later studied at New School for Social Research in New York City. Her poems and short stories have been frequently anthologized from appearances in the *Southern Review*, the *Atlantic Monthly*, *Harper's Bazaar*, *North American Review*, *Open Places*, *Southwest Review*, and other literary journals. Brigham received a National Endowment for the Arts grant to complete her book of poetry, *Heaved from the Earth* (1971).

Concerning her development as a writer, brigham says, "i wanted to write when i was very young, and as a child i wrote poems, from what was about me, what i saw, felt, and loved. Three of my poems were printed in the *Commercial Appeal* (Memphis), and i received for each a small leather book that was a reprint of a classic. You write where you are, from what you touch, from what is a part of you. You write happily and you learn to write by the writing itself. You grow as you continue to learn, through dissatisfaction or whatever that makes you question and so learn."

Brigham and her husband Roy have lived in Oklahoma, Texas, France, Nicaragua, Alaska, Canada, and Mexico, and are now in Arkansas. She writes, "Reflections are often in my work, of Mississippi, the place of my roots."

JACK BUTLER (1944) was born in Alligator, Mississippi. He received a B.A. in English and a B.S. in mathematics from Central Missouri State and an M.F.A. in creative writing from the University of Arkansas. Butler spent his early years in a house on a Delta cotton field. The son of a Baptist preacher, he claims the King James Bible and science fiction as his two major literary influences. He describes himself as a generalist who is fascinated by "words, voices, trees, tones, stars, friends, work, rivers, calculus, games, jokes, prayers, time, food, gravity, flesh, love, learning, and the miracle of the image."

Butler has made his home in Arkansas for most of the last seventeen years. His books include *West of Hollywood* (1980), *Hawk Gumbo and Other Stories* (1982), and *The Kid Who Wanted to Be a Spaceman* (1984). All three were published by August House. He has also published frequently in the *New Yorker* and many respected literary journals including *Poetry, New Orleans Review,* and *Texas Quarterly.* His works have won considerable attention and many awards.

PRICE CALDWELL (1940) was born in Tutwiler, Mississippi. After attending high school in Hattiesburg, he then received an A.B. from Davidson College and an M.A. and Ph.D. from Tulane University. Now an English professor at Mississippi State University, Caldwell is completing work on a novel.

Of Mississippi's influence on his writing, Caldwell says, "Mississippi, for me, is more elemental than other more progressive and homogenized parts of the country. Especially the Delta, where I was born. It's so flat: if you stand on a levee or a railroad bed you're on a high spot, and the horizon is visible in every direction. Farms and family houses and communities stand as sharply etched against that wide sky as against history. Nothing is current, faddish or novel, and the lives of our ancestors are as easy to imagine as our own.

"Then, too, Mississippians grow up at cultural distance from the pressures of fad and fashion in the rest of the country, with the result that we can see even our own social hypocrisies more clearly and with more elemental humanity. It could be true that many Mississippi writers write to correct the lies they were taught when they were young. But that's not so bad: in most of the rest of the country, the lies continue unnoticed."

ROBERT CANZONERI (1925) was born in San Marcos, Texas, and grew up in Clinton, Mississippi, the son of a Baptist minister. In 1942 he joined the United States Navy and upon discharge, attended Mississippi College, receiving a B.A. in 1948. An M.A. from the University of Mississippi followed in 1951. After teaching at several universities and colleges, Canzoneri received a Ph.D. from Stanford University. Since 1965 he has been at Ohio State University where he directs the creative writing program. His books include *"I Do So Politely": A Voice from the South* (1965), *Watch Us Pass* (1968), *Men with Little Hammers* (1969), *Barbed Wire and Other Stories* (1970), and *A Highly Ramified Tree* (1976), which won the Ohioana award for the best book of the year in the field of autobiography.

Wallace Stegner wrote of *Barbed Wire and Other Stories* that "there is not a story here that doesn't show a perceptive eye, a human sympathy, and a way with words above the ordinary."

HUBERT CREEKMORE (1907–1966) was born in Water Valley, Mississippi. He began writing poetry in high school and continued writing at the University of Mississippi, where he graduated in 1927. At Yale University he studied playwriting under George Pierce Baker. In 1940 Creekmore received an M.A. from Columbia University and in that same year published his first volume of poetry, *Personal Sun.* His experience in the United States Navy during World War II furnished the material for his second volume of poems, *The Long Reprieve and Other Poems from New Caledonia* (1946). Between 1946 and 1953 Creekmore wrote four books—*The Fingers of Night* (1946), *Formula* (1947), *The Welcome* (1948), and *The Chain in the Heart* (1953). His last novel chronicles the injustices faced by a black family in Mississippi through three generations from Reconstruction days to the Great Depression.

Creekmore spent the last years of his life editing and translating. He died in New York City in 1966.

BORDEN DEAL (1922) was born in Pontotoc, Mississippi, and lived in the state until he graduated from high school. Although, he said, writing was all he had wanted to do from the time he was six years old, it was 1948 before he was first published and not until seven years later could he devote himself completely to a literary career. In 1946 he entered the University of Alabama and in 1949 received a B.A. with a major in English and a minor in creative writing. He was a student of Hudson Strode.

A prolific writer, Deal has gained many honors including Guggenheim and MacDowell Colony fellowships as well as award recognition by the American Library Association. Some of his books include *Dunbar's Cove* (1957), *Dragon's Wine* (1960), *The Loser* (1964), *A Long Way to Go* (1965), *The Least One* (1967), and *The Other Room* (1974). The last two are autobiographical novels about growing up in north Mississippi.

His story "Antaeus" is not autobiographical, in that his family did not go north to find work like the family in the short story. "It is, rather," says Deal, "a fictional reflection of the historical mass exodus from the South (by both white and black) that began during World War II and continued through the fifties and sixties, finally reversing itself during the seventies. 'Antaeus' is thus a prime example of the changes which have taken place in the South; changes that have been the central theme in my books and short stories. I write about the new South, not the old; about people living and working and dreaming of the future, not of the past."

"Antaeus" has a curious publishing history. Written in the early fifties, the story, was, during the next ten years, rejected by virtually every popular and literary magazine in the United States. It finally appeared in the *Southwest Review*, which had turned it down twice. "Antaeus" has since been published in hundreds of textbooks and anthologies and has been made into a film. It is also the most reprinted piece, fiction or nonfiction ever published by the *Southwest Review*.

LOUIS DOLLARHIDE (1918) was born in America, Oklahoma. Educated at Mississippi College, Harvard University, and the University of North Carolina, he was for twenty-one years, a reviewer and columnist for the *Clarion Ledger/Jackson Daily News* (Jackson, Mississippi). Now a professor of English at the University of Mississippi, he has written plays, poetry, short fiction, and articles for scholarly journals and magazines. He is also co-editor (with Ann J. Abadie) of *Eudora Welty: A Form of Thanks* (1979). *Of Art and Artists: Selected Reviews of the Arts in Mississippi, 1955–1976* was published by the University Press of Mississippi in 1981.

Dollarhide offers this advice to students interested in becoming writers: "Observe the state, its people, all of them; its peculiar flavor; its differences, some good, some less desirable, that make it a unique corner of the world. Weigh it all, all your observations, and come to your own conclusions."

ELLEN DOUGLAS (1921) is the pen name of Josephine Ayres Haxton. Born in Natchez, Mississippi, she graduated from the University of Mississippi in 1942. In her acceptance speech as the first recipient of the Mississippi Institute of Arts and Letters Literature Award in 1979, Douglas noted that "it came to me that the trees, the landscape—water and forest, fields, and pastures, river and Delta and the dissolving hills—are a gift, the gift of my state, not just to me, but to us all; the place that informs all my books, the place that we—all of us—hold in precarious trust and must jointly cherish and guard, threatened now more than ever before by a rootless and destructive world."

As a writer concerned with the human condition, Douglas has used the gift from her state well. She has repaid her debt admirably with *A Family's Affairs* (1962, winner of the Houghton Mifflin-Esquire Fellowship Award and named by the *New York Times* critic Orville Prescott as one of the five best novels of the year), *Black Cloud, White Cloud* (1963, her story, "On the Lake," which became a part of that book's novella, "Hold On," was first published in the *New Yorker* and won an O. Henry Prize Award), *Where the Dreams Cross* (1968), *Apostles of Light* (1973, nominated for the National Book Award), *The Rock Cried Out* (1979, a Book-of-the-Month Alternate Selection and the winner of the Mississippi Institute of Arts and Letters Literature Award), and *A Lifetime Burning* (1982, awarded the Mississippi Institute of Arts and Letters Literature Award).

Douglas has anchored her fiction in time and place. This firm rooting provides great strength against the universal stresses of human existence. "Place is the repository of history," Douglas says, "Place is the means by which you enter a story. I need the familiarity of my own surroundings to hear the voice."

In addition to her fiction, Douglas has written a short study of Walker Percy's novel, *The Last Gentleman.* She received a grant from the National Endowment for the Arts, and has participated in a number of literary festivals and writing workshops. She has been writer-in-residence at Northeast Louisiana University, the University of Virginia, and now teaches at the University of Mississippi.

CHARLES EAST (1924) was born in Shelby, Mississippi, and grew up in Cleveland, Mississippi, where his family moved when he was twelve. He received a B.A. from Louisiana State University in 1948. In 1949 he went to New York City to work for *Collier's Magazine* and then to Baton Rouge where he worked for the *Morning Advocate* and the *State-Times.* In 1962 he joined the staff of Louisiana State University Press and from 1970–75 served as director. East has published in numerous literary magazines, including the *Virginia Quarterly Review,* the *Southern Review,* and the *Yale Review.* His collection of short stories, *Where the Music Was,* was published in 1965. He now works as a free-lance writer and editor.

In a 1971 interview with Gordon Weaver, East stated, "I was born in Mississippi and grew up there, and my material has come largely out of that experience. . . . It [Mississippi] is the place I unconsciously or subconsciously turn to when I sit down to write. . . . I grew up in a small town. I don't think that I would have written the same sort of thing, possibly may not have written at all, if I had grown up in a larger place. . . . I feel that coming out of this kind of world was important to me as a writer."

WILLIAM FAULKNER (1897–1962) was born in New Albany, Mississippi. When he was five years old his family moved to Oxford, where he lived most of his life except for brief periods spent in Hollywood and Charlottesville, Virginia. Faulkner's education was sporadic. Dropping out of high school in his senior year, he attended the University of Mississippi as a special student for only one year (1919–20). He was a voracious reader and, through his friend and earliest critic, Phil Stone, was introduced to modern writers, including the French Symbolist poets. Their influence, along with the influence of Hardy and Yeats, can be seen in Faulkner's first book, *The Marble Faun.*

Influenced by Sherwood Anderson, Faulkner wrote his first novel, *Soldiers' Pay,* which appeared in 1926. Its publication began an extraordinarily prolific career. The next decade produced eight novels, including many of the finest he would write: *The Sound and the Fury* (1929), *As I Lay Dying* (1930), *Light in August* (1932), and *Absalom, Absalom!* (1936). However, his creative output was not matched by financial returns, so, in 1932, Faulkner went to Hollywood as a screen writer, a position he kept, under financial duress, until 1948, when the commercial success of *Intruder in the Dust* and its subsequent sale to the movies, enabled him to return to Mississippi. With the exception of tours for the State Department and time spent as a writer-in-residence at the University of Virginia, he remained in Oxford the rest of his life. Faulkner won numerous awards for his fiction, including the 1949 Nobel Prize and two Pulitzer Prizes, one for *A Fable* (1954) and another for *The Reivers* (1962). He is considered by many critics to be the finest writer America has produced and one of the finest writers in the English language.

Robert Penn Warren has said, "The study of Faulkner's writing is one of the most challenging tasks in our literature. It is also one of the most rewarding." Faulkner, who admitted that he had learned to write "from other writers," advised hopeful poets and novelists to "read all you can."

SHELBY FOOTE (1916) was born in Greenville, Mississippi, where he was educated in the public schools. He attended the University of North Carolina from 1935–37 and served in Europe as a captain of field artillery during World War II. According to Foote, his parents were not literary. He writes, "My principal connection with a literary home was through my friendship with the Percys (William Alexander Percy, author of *Lanterns on the Levee,* and his three nephews, among them Walker Percy). There were literally thousands of books in the Percy house. It's probable that if those Percy boys hadn't moved to Greenville, I might never have become interested in literary things.

"I wrote five novels in five years in Greenville," Foote said, "I wrote all of them on Washington Avenue. But, that was the beginning of my writing life and sort of the first chapter of it." Twenty years elapsed after his first five novels, but in 1974 publication of his massive three-volume history, *The Civil War: A Narrative,* was completed. According to Polk and Scafidel (*An Anthology of Mississippi Writers,* 1979, University Press of Mississippi), Foote "brought to the writing of his heavily researched history not just the historian's reservoir of facts and dates but also the novelist's eye for meaningful detail and the capacity for understanding and depicting character. In addition, his history reflects the novelist's natural way with story-telling and a superb, clear, prose style." It was a unique achievement and won him a nomination for the Pulitzer Prize.

His first five novels were *Tournament* (1949), *Follow Me Down* (1950), *Love in a Dry Season* (1951), *Shiloh* (1952), and *Jordan County* (1954).

Foote's sixth novel, *September, September,* was published in 1977. He now lives in Memphis, Tennessee, and is working on his seventh novel.

RICHARD FORD (1944) was born in Jackson, Mississippi, and lived in the state until he graduated from high school. He received a B.A. from Michigan State University and an M.F.A. from the University of California. Recently Ford bought a house in Coahoma, Mississippi, where he will live intermittently.

Ford has published widely in periodicals such as *Esquire* and the *Paris Review.* His essay "The Three Kings: Hemingway, Faulkner, and Fitzgerald" appeared in the 50th Anniversary Edition (December 1983) of *Esquire. A Piece of My Heart* (1976), Ford's first novel, was published to critical acclaim. *Newsweek* noted "the beginning of a career that could turn out to be extraordinary." For his second novel, *The Ultimate Good Luck* (1981), Ford won fellowships from the Guggenheim Foundation and from the National Endowment for the Arts. He is working on his third novel, *The Sportswriter.*

In discussing motivation Ford has said, "I don't have any advice for people who would try to be writers. Everyone I know seems to have come to that decision from very different compulsions and talents and instincts. To try, then, to generalize about it, as though any but particular cases can be drawn—particular writers, particular stories, particular successes and failures—threatens to make the whole engagement more difficult, more mysterious, and much less interesting and pleasing than it actually, occasionally is."

ELLEN GILCHRIST (1935) was born in Vicksburg, Mississippi. She received a B.A. in philosophy from Millsaps College and did graduate work at the University of Arkansas in creative writing. She has served as contributing editor of the *Courier* in New Orleans and was the recipient in 1979 of a Fellowship Grant in Fiction from the National Endowment for the Arts. Also in 1979 her book of poems, *The Land Surveyor's Daughter,* was published by Lost Roads Press.

Her first collection of short fiction, *In the Land of Dreamy Dreams,* received the 1981 Mississippi Institute of Arts and Letters Literature Award. Her first novel, *The Annunciation* (1983), and her second short story collection, *Victory Over Japan,* (1984) were published by Little, Brown and Company. She lives in Arkansas and is completing another novel and a third collection of short stories.

Of the process of writing, Gilchrist says, "I no longer believe that I understand the creative process except for two or three things. I believe that it is some form of trusting yourself to know the truth and to be able to tell the truth past all the things which pass for facts. Truth is a beautiful and complex and very funny song. When I am lucky and trust myself I am able to sing it long enough to make a poem.

"The other thing that I believe is that a writer must be terribly healthy and very patient. It is hard work to be a writer. You have to make up the job as you go along. You have to keep on trying and believing in yourself when nothing seems to be happening and when what you are doing seems to be the most absurd activity in the world. But it is exciting work."

Edwin Granberry (1897) was born in Meridian, Mississippi. When he was ten his family moved to Florida, where he has lived most of his life. Granberry spent two years at the University of Florida and enlisted in the United States Marine Corps in World War I. After the war he went to Columbia University and received an A.B. in 1920. From 1922–24 he attended Harvard University as a member of George Pierce Baker's 47 Workshop where his play *Hitch Your Wagon to a Star* was the Workshop's last production before it moved to Yale University to become the Yale School of Drama. Among his classmates in the 47 Workshop were Thomas Wolfe, John Mason Brown, and Henry Cabot Lodge.

Of his early memories Granberry writes, "My recollections of Indians, prairie fires, and tornadoes are vivid. No wolves, but lots of howling coyotes. I have not written down these recollections, nor anything of my boyhood in Mississippi. However, what I soaked up of the out-of-doors (woods, creeks, animals, weather signs) have colored all my writing. You will see it especially in *The Erl King* and *A Trip to Czardis* (the novel, as well as in the short story)."

Granberry is the author of four novels—*The Ancient Hunger* (1927), *Strangers and Lovers* (1928), *The Erl King* (1930), and *A Trip to Czardis* (1966)—and numerous short stories. "A Trip to Czardis" won an O. Henry Prize Award for one of the best short stories published in 1932. Set in the Florida backwoods, the title derives from Granberry's Mississippi boyhood. The story is a powerful telling of a young boy's coming of age. As a child Granberry knew of Sardis, Mississippi, and, when time came to give the story a title, he took the name and spelled it "Czardis."

Writer-in-residence at Rollins College until his retirement in 1971, for over thirty years Granberry wrote the comic strip *Buz Sawyer.* He has worked intermittently on a novel based on his play *The Falcon,* produced at Rollins College in 1951.

Loyle Hairston (1926) was born in Macon, Mississippi, and lived there for fourteen years, at which time his family moved to St. Louis. After graduating from high school, he enlisted in the United States Navy and served two years. Upon discharge, he moved to New York City and attended New York University for three semesters. He was one of the founders of the Harlem Writers Guild, a workshop that is still active today and is a major influence on the development of contemporary black writing. His first published short story was "The Winds of Change." Hairston is widely published and is a frequent contributor to *Freedomways.* He still lives in New York City.

Hairston writes, "I wanted to be a writer. This irrational idea came to me during my unstable boyhood when I became a voracious reader of black newsweeklies, *The Chicago Defender* and *The Pittsburgh Courier.*

But it was really Jack London's autobiographical novel, *Martin Eden,* that sealed my doom. After that book the idea of being a writer grew to an obsession. St. Louis became stifling—too many people tried to make me come to my senses. Moreover, I didn't know a single writer or anyone vaguely interested in literature. Obviously, I needed 'breathing' room.

"In New York I enrolled in school as a GI Bill student, eventually studying for a while at New York University. But more important, I joined a writers' workshop and began my apprenticeship among such people as Alice Childress, Eugene Gordon, Julian Mayfield, John Henrik Clarke, John Hudson Jones, John O. Killens, Rosa Guy, Douglas Turner Ward, Paule Marshall, Lonnie Elder III, and Sarah Wright. A few years later some of us broke away and founded a new writers group, the Harlem Writers Guild."

MARTHA LACY HALL (1923) was born in Magnolia, Mississippi, and attended Whitworth College and Millsaps College. In the mid-fifties she became a member of the editorial staff of Louisiana State University Press, for whom she edited over a hundred books, including the Pulitzer Prize-winning *A Confederacy of Dunces* by John Kennedy Toole. Hall's short stories have appeared in the *Southern Review, New Orleans Review,* and the *Sewanee Review. Call It Living,* her first collection of short stories, was published by the Press of the Nightowl in 1981. Her second collection, *Music Lesson,* was published by the University of Illinois Press in 1984. Of her writing Walker Percy has said that her stories are "quiet, well crafted, and deceptive—deceptive because under the calm surface, as peaceful as Main Street in Magnolia, Mississippi, on a Sunday afternoon, lurk the secret and sometimes terrible motions of the human heart."

Hall herself says, "I write about people. Watching and listening to individuals has obviously made lasting impressions on me. I keep notebooks of odds and ends of experiences, and when I begin to write about an event or string of events, I always have a large cast waiting in the wings. But sometimes a character incubates in my head for years, and sooner or later I feel compelled to bring him or her out and build a story. Because I am an editor, I am, for better or worse, a very careful writer. I think, in essence, this is good, but sometimes I probably overdo it."

BARRY HANNAH (1942) was born in Meridian, Mississippi. His early home was near Forest, Mississippi, in Scott County. When he was young his family moved to Pascagoula and then to Clinton, where he grew up. Hannah received a B.A. from Mississippi College and an M.F.A. from the University of Arkansas. He has been writer-in-residence at Clemson University, Middlebury College, the University of Alabama, the University of Iowa, the University of Montana, Memphis State University, and currently the University of Mississippi.

His first novel, *Geronimo Rex* (1972), won a William Faulkner Prize. A second novel, *Nightwatchmen* (1973), was followed by *Airships* (1978), a collection of short stories, which won the Arnold Gingrich Short Fiction Award. Of the collection James Dickey wrote, "One reads Barry Hannah and is amazed! *Airships* places him in the very first rank of American literary artists, and leaves us breathless with the force of its feeling." Hannah's most recent novels, *Ray* (1980) and *The Tennis Handsome* (1983), have achieved international acclaim. He has been honored by the American Academy of Arts and Letters and has received, among his many honors, a Guggenheim Fellowship.

Hannah lives in Oxford, Mississippi, and is completing his fifth novel, *Maximum Ned.* To students interested in creative writing, he says, "Write more, talk less. Pretty soon you may have an *opus major.*"

EVANS HARRINGTON (1925) was born in Birmingham, Alabama. When he was three his family moved to Clinton, where his father, a Baptist minister, attended Mississippi College. After serving twenty-eight months in the United States Naval Air Corps, Harrington attended Mississippi College where he received a B.A. degree. His M.A. and Ph.D. are from the University of Mississippi. The author of four novels and thirteen short stories, he has been widely published in magazines including the *Saturday Evening Post* and the *Southern Review.*

Harrington has lived most of his life in Mississippi, and he feels that connection when he begins to write: "Most of my fiction stems from my uncle Scott Harrington's farm in the southeastern corner of Simpson County, where I spent many day-dreaming boyhood summers. When I think of a character as coming from there, he comes alive for me and scenes, dialogue, and action flow from my pen spontaneously. The experience gives me a deep pleasure. Once I have identified the character with that area, I can move him anywhere I please and he remains alive for me. Johnny Graves in *The Prisoners* (1956) comes from this area, though I place him in the state penitentiary, which resembles Parchman, where my father was chaplain in the early 1950's."

As chairman of the English department at the University of Mississippi, Harrington lives and writes in Oxford, Mississippi.

ROBERT HERRING (1938) was born in Charleston, Mississippi, and attended Baylor University and the University of Tennessee. He has published in a number of periodicals and is the author of *Hub* (1981), a novel which was listed by the American Library Association as one of the best books for young adults. The son of a Baptist minister, Herring says he has poured concrete in Missouri, sold mattresses door-to-door in Mississippi, desk-clerked and done construction work in Arkansas, been a guide in the Black Mountains of North Carolina, played piano and trumpet in a jazz band, and taught at various colleges. Currently he teaches English at Middle Tennessee State University. Herring's second novel, *McCampbell's War,* will be published by Viking Press in 1985.

Of his novel Herring writes, "*Hub* was a way of both recapturing forever, and forever letting go, of one portion of my childhood. It is the writer's obligation to find the narrative form and voice of the human experience; always he looks back to find where he must then proceed. *Hub* is, consequently, my teacher and my alma mater."

REBECCA HILL (1944) was born in Memphis, Tennessee. In 1946 her family moved to Soso, Mississippi, and she lived in the state until 1953 when she moved to Palos Park, Illinois. Hill graduated Phi Beta Kappa from Grinnell College. She studied at Manchester University in England before receiving an M.A. from Harvard University. As an editorial consultant and education writer, she spent several years researching and writing material on the parenting of infants. These studies, together with her work as a consultant on institutional sexism in education, had a strong influence on many of the ideas in her novel *Blue Rise* (1983), which won the Mississippi Institute of Arts and Letters Literature Award. Set in Mississippi, *Blue Rise* has won national attention and acclaim.

Hill writes: "Though we lived in Illinois for nearly twenty years, my family could never have been called expatriate Southerners; we were exiles. Always there was the sense of having taken a rear exit from the Garden of Eden. For twenty years the talk was about going home to Mississippi—a question of when, not if.

"I left Soso School after losing the election for Queen of the Third Grade to my best friend Jeannette. After baton practice one of those last afternoons in April, she promised she'd never stoop to playing with my rival, a wisp of a girl who was just one half of a pair of twins. A year later Jeannette's letter solemnly confessed she now played with Cecilia, hoped I didn't mind.

"Like the rest of my family, I minded such things for years. Now I was among people who, charged with the information that Soso School got out in April, said the South couldn't afford to heat its schools. How to reply to such ignorance? Heat a Mississippi school in April?

"The world holds a great assortment of Yankees, by which name any non-Southerner is correctly labeled; we all know how point of view determines who looks silly. For thirty years I lived in places where the South as I knew it was completely opaque. Thus to portray a sequence of events, the narrative thread had to be balanced with interpretation. Common values may not be assumed. Place is a variable; so is time, religion, sex, culture, and most everything else. Such variables have meaning for the interior process of individuals—which is what I hoped to show in the voice and characterization of Jeannine Hinton in *Blue Rise*."

KENNETH HOLDITCH (1933) was born in Ecru, Mississippi. He received a B.A. from Southwestern College at Memphis (now Rhodes College) and an M.A. and a Ph.D. in English from the University of Mississippi. Holditch is a professor of English at the University of New Orleans. He conducts literary tours of New Orleans; his book *In Old New Orleans* was published by the University Press of Mississippi in 1983.

Holditch says of his Mississippi heritage: "I would simply say that most of the inspiration I have received to write fiction or poetry has come from my background, and that background is, of course, inextricably linked with Mississippi. It has been said so often that one does not need to say again that more writers have come from our state than from any other—more good writers. There is a reason for that. I don't know what that reason is. Part of it certainly involves the agrarian atmosphere which was so much a part of the state when I was growing up. I think of what Berry Morgan once said to me in describing the state from which both of us came and from which both of us have drawn great strength: Mississippi is 'a schizophrenic piece of heaven.' That says it better than I could say it in any other words."

JAMES HUGHES (1957) was born in Gulfport, Mississippi. After receiving a B.A. from Goddard College, he did graduate work at the University of Arkansas. "An Open House," which appeared in the *New Yorker,* was his first submission. Of its publication in 1980 Hughes wrote: "As a twenty-two year old who's only been writing seriously for about a year and a half, I doubt there's much I could offer anyone in the way of writing tips. But about 'An Open House,' I should mention that what sparked the writing of this story were my own fears having to do with violence and physical injury, and my memories of the rather unusual family life I had growing up in Clinton, Mississippi."

DON LEE KEITH (1940) was born in Wheeler, Mississippi, in Prentiss County. He attended the University of Mississippi before moving to New Orleans to join the staff of the *Times-Picayune,* where he worked in the capacity of reporter, editorial writer, and senior feature writer. He has twice been nominated for the Pulitzer Prize, and in 1974 he received a grant from the National Endowment for the Arts. In 1976 he became associate editor of the *Courier* in New Orleans and later served as editor-in-chief of the *New Orleans Magazine.*

During the past two decades, Keith has been the recipient of more journalism awards from the Press Club of New Orleans than any other person in the organization's history. He was twice presented with the Alex Waller Memorial Award, the club's highest distinction for writing. Other honors have come in recognition of articles ranging in topic from politics to stripteasing.

Of his relationship with Mississippi, Keith writes: "While I moved from the state of Mississippi at age twenty-one, with trips back there afterwards limited to family visits or relatively brief assignments as a journalist, almost all my values were shaped by my early life in rural Mississippi and, consequently, are probably inescapably evident in most things I write, with the exception of reportage, of course. That may be a rather immoderately roundabout way of saying what has been said by others, both with kindly and unkindly intents, that there's a little bit of Prentiss County in everything I write."

JOHN LITTLE (1939) was born in Brandon, Mississippi, and grew up in Raleigh, Mississippi, in Smith County. Little received a pharmacy degree from the University of Mississippi and an M.F.A. in creative writing from the University of Arkansas. He currently teaches English at the University of North Dakota, where he chairs an annual writers' conference. In 1979 Little's collection of short stories, *Whistling Dixie,* was published.

Little writes: "Most of my stories come from experiences in Mississippi. Certainly my incentive to write comes from listening to Mississippians talk. They tell stories with energy, humor, and language that strikes a cord or rather that makes me want to record it. 'Wild Rabbits' is such a story. Byron's father was a customer in my family's drugstore in Raleigh. He was a con man who dealt with poverty by means of his wit, his tongue, his audacity. All of which make for good fiction. Mississippi is blessed with an abundance of such people. Growing up in Mississippi for a fiction writer is like growing up in heaven."

P. H. LOWREY (1923–1965) was born in Verona, Mississippi. He received a B.A. in 1947 from the University of the South, Sewanee, Tennessee, and an M.A. and a Ph.D. from the University of Chicago. Before joining the faculty of the University of Chicago in 1950, he taught at San Jose State College (1949–50) and served in the United States Navy (1943–46). After teaching at Vassar College for five years (1952–57), he returned to Chicago where he remained until his death in 1965. His stories appeared in many magazines, and his writings, many of which had been previously published, were collected in *The Great Speckled Bird and Other Stories* (1964). One of his stories, "Too Young to Have a Gun," won an O. Henry Prize Award. Some of the stories were written at Blue Mountain College, Blue Mountain, Mississippi, during 1954–55 under a fellowship from the Ford Foundation. While there he also worked on a novel.

Janet Lowrey writes: "My husband turned to the north Mississippi hills and bottomland (Tippah County) where his family had lived for more than a century for the source of most of his fiction. He felt a strong attraction to, and identification with, William Faulkner and his work. His thesis was on Faulkner criticism, and he wrote an important article, 'The Use of Time in William Faulkner's Work,' which was published in the English Institute Essays."

BEVERLY LOWRY (1938) was born in Memphis, Tennessee, but grew up in Greenville, Mississippi. She spent two years at the University of Mississippi and graduated from Memphis State University. Of her first novel, *Come Back, Lolly Ray* (1977), a critic wrote in the *New York Times Book Review* that "what Lowry shares with that great southern tradition of fiction is an aptitude for the dramatic, a gift for metaphor and elaboration, a vision of the past abiding in and sometimes overwhelming the present." *Emma Blue,* her second novel, was published in 1978. Her third novel, *Daddy's Girl,* won the Jesse Jones Award for the best work of fiction written in 1981.

Lowry has taught creative writing at the University of Houston, and her short stories and articles have appeared in the *Black Warrior Review,*

Vanity Fair, Viva, Houston Review, Texas Monthly, and *Mississippi Review* among others. Winner of a National Endowment for the Arts Fellowship in 1979 and a Guggenheim Fellowship in 1983, Lowry lives in San Marcos, Texas, and is at work on her fourth novel. She is the past president of the Texas Institute of Letters.

Lowry writes: "Growing up in Greenville meant growing up in a town the patron saint of which was a poet/scholar as well as a soldier. William Alexander Percy was our greatest hero. From the time I was in elementary school I always knew it was not only respectable to be a writer but honorable; desirable. The literary tradition in Greenville is strong. Who our next writer would be was always pondered. Teachers were on the lookout. The effect of this is invaluable. I always pay homage, whenever I am asked."

TOM MCHANEY (1936) was born in Paragould, Arkansas. He was educated at Mississippi State University and received his Ph.D. from the University of South Carolina. Before becoming a professor of English at Georgia State University, he taught at the University of Mississippi.

McHaney is the author of *William Faulkner's "The Wild Palms": A Study* (1975) and *William Faulkner: A Reference Guide* (1976). He has also published articles on Faulkner and other figures in American literature and has lectured widely in the United States and abroad. His short stories have appeared in the *Georgia Review, Prairie Schooner, Cimarron Review, Atlanta Magazine,* and *Transatlantic Review.*

McHaney has said he grew up simultaneously from the age of two between his mother in Arkansas and his father in Tupelo, Mississippi. "Memphis," he writes, "was a kind of mythical state capital to my mythical mid-South state, and I find even now that it takes two events to make a story in my mind, sometimes events which occurred each in a different state. I suppose the tension between my two lives helps make fiction happen. For me, fiction comes from trying to make two lives, or two different times or places fit together."

BIRTHALENE MILLER was born in Choctaw County, Mississippi, and has spent all her life in the state. Her stories have appeared in *Southern Exposure, Laurel Review, Moving Out,* and the *Black Warrior Review.* "The Lonesomes Ain't No Spring Picnic" was her first published short story.

About her experiences in Mississippi, she writes: "Time never runs in a straight line, but like the twisting path of a rampant river, it twines around and into itself. Yesterday becomes today and today becomes tomorrow and yet they are all the same. Whatever affects us when we are young determines the person we are today and the person we will be tomorrow. It is this yesterday self still living in us that exerts the strongest force upon our writing. When I was a child, it infuriated me to hear people say a woman shouldn't speak in church. When I sat down to write 'The Lonesomes Ain't No Spring Picnic,' I only knew I was going to write about a little girl and her grandmother. The story and the characters evolved out of my yesterday self. The characters wrote their own story."

Miller admits to "a lifelong rapacious appetite for written words." For her "the South of today is fast changing from the one it was when I was growing up in a sharecropper's shack. In many ways, though, it's still the same. Many of the same contradictions and the same conflicts remain largely unchanged. The sense of place is balanced by the sense of displacement."

"The Lonesomes Ain't No Spring Picnic" was also anthologized in *Speaking for Ourselves: Women of the South* (1984) edited by Maxine Alexander and published by Pantheon Books.

WILLIAM MILLS (1935) was born in Hattiesburg, Mississippi, and received a Ph.D. in literature from Louisiana State University. He is the author of two poetry collections, *Watch for the Fox* (1974) and *Stained Glass* (1979). A third book of poetry will be published by Louisiana State University Press in 1985. Among Mills's other books are *The Stillness in Moving Things: The World of Howard Nemerov* (1975) and *I Know a Place* (1976), a collection of short stories published by the Press of the Nightowl. Currently he travels and writes articles on nature and the environment.

When asked about his story, "To Pass Him Out," Mills responded: "The kind of experience I wrote about was little discussed in the country where I lived, and trying to verify such a fugitive affair was almost as difficult as it was for the boy in the story, who is confused and mystified by the old woman's several married names and the words he hears. In country communities there would often be a woman who nursed people and when a family considered its 'loved one' to be beyond hope, the nurse would be apprised of this, often indirectly, and she would do the mercy killing (a pillow over the face during the night for the weak ones). The family was very grateful, of course. Over time this old woman's 'mercy' has gone slightly awry. What has happened I intended to be at first mysterious to the reader, as to the boy, and then hoped the reader would work his way via the better known expression 'to pass on.'"

BERRY MORGAN (1919) was born and grew up in Port Gibson, Mississippi. She attended Loyola University (1947) and Tulane University (1948–49) and has been writing ever since she can remember. In addition to writing, Morgan has worked as an executive secretary, as a real estate specialist, and as a free-lance editor. She has run a plantation in Mississippi, a cattle farm in West Virginia, and has taught creative writing at Northeast Louisiana University.

Pursuit, her first novel, was published in 1966, and for it she received a Houghton Mifflin Literary Fellowship Award, given to new authors considered by the publishers to possess great potential. In the same year, her short stories began to appear in the *New Yorker*. *The Mystic Adventures of Roxie Stoner*, a collection of sixteen stories, all concerning the title character, was published by Houghton Mifflin in 1974. Most of her fiction has been set in and around her mythical King County, Mississippi.

Of her title character, Morgan has said: "I would like to be Roxie Stoner. She's my ideal. . . . Just certain calculating devices have been left out of her mind—whether they were trained out or whether it's a birth defect, I don't know. This lack makes her very strong."

WILLIE MORRIS (1934) was born in Jackson, Mississippi, but moved with his family in 1935 to Yazoo City, Mississippi. He attended the University of Texas where he received a degree in English and became editor of the *Daily Texan.* After graduation in 1956, he received a Rhodes Scholarship to Oxford University and studied modern history at New College until 1959. For three years (1960–63) he was editor of the *Texas Observer,* a political and literary journal based in Austin. In 1963 he was employed by *Harper's Magazine* in New York. In 1967, when he was thirty-two, he became editor-in-chief of *Harper's,* substantially attracting first-rate fiction and essays, but resigned in 1971 in an editorial dispute. He has, since then, worked as a free-lance writer and lecturer, and has produced numerous articles and essays. Since his return to Mississippi, Morris has lived in Oxford and is the journalist-in-residence at the University of Mississippi.

His books include *North Toward Home* (1967), *Good Old Boy* (1971), *Yazoo: Integration in a Deep-Southern Town* (1971), *The Last of the Southern Girls* (1973), *James Jones: A Friendship* (1978), *Terrains of the Heart and Other Essays on Home* (1981), *The Courting of Marcus Dupree* (1983), and *Always Stand in Against the Curve* (1983). His classic *North Toward Home* received a Houghton Mifflin Literary Fellowship Award.

In "A Sense of Place and the Americanization of Mississippi," Morris writes: "It is no accident that Mississippi produced Faulkner, the greatest of all the American novelists, and perhaps the greatest of all novelists, and Eudora Welty, and Walker Percy, and Shelby Foote, and the distinguished others. I must add that I, as a younger writer, am proud to be part of this remarkable heritage. These impulses of the imagination that gave us our literature were an expression of many things: the act of speech . . . the language of music . . . the love of place . . . the ineluctable perception of a common past . . . and at the very base of all this was that rarest and most indispensable sustenance for literature: and that is memory.

"The young people of Mississippi must learn to remember who they are, and where they come from. They must be encouraged to remember; there is a message to be carried."

LEWIS NORDAN (1939) was born in Jackson, Mississippi, and attended school in Itta Bena, Mississippi. He received a B.A. from Millsaps College, an M.A. from Mississippi State University, and a Ph.D. from Auburn University. Widely published in such periodicals as *Harper's, Redbook,* and the *Greensboro Review,* he won the John Gould Fletcher award for fiction in 1977. Nordan is now assistant professor at the University of Pittsburgh, where he teaches creative writing. His collection of short stories, *Welcome to the Arrow-Catcher Fair,* was published by Louisiana State University Press in 1983.

Regarding the writer's relationship to his home state, he says, "A large body of Mississippi writers, white as well as black, do not live in Mississippi, and for their own reasons cannot. We are, in no romantic sense, expatriates. We will always be Mississippians—we will return to its swamps and cross its bridges and hear the stories, its rhythms will be our ritual, people will know us by them. And yet we could not write of our sweet home, or be proud of it, until we were gone from it and certain we would not return to live. We ache for Mississippi, but to its rich images and good people we are blinded by its light, we are smothered in its air. Still, we carry it in us, and it is a celebration so to do."

GLORIA NORRIS was born in Holcomb, Mississippi. She graduated magna cum laude from the University of Southern Mississippi and received an M.A. from Ohio State University. Norris is editor-in-chief of the Book-of-the-Month Club and lives in New York City. Her short stories have appeared in the *Sewanee Review,* and three of her stories—"When the Lord Calls," "Revive Us Again," and "Holding On"— have won O. Henry Prize Awards in 1983, 1984, and 1985 respectively. In 1985 her first novel will be published by Alfred A. Knopf. In addition to fiction, Norris (with Jo Ann Miller) wrote *The Working Mother's Complete Handbook* (1979). In 1983 the *Ladies Home Journal* named Norris, along with Mississippian Leontyne Price, as one of "America's 100 Most Important Women."

Norris feels that growing up in Mississippi presents a unique opportunity for young writers: "Unlike those in more urban areas, Mississippi young people have a rare chance growing up to know humans of all ages and all stations of life. The experience can give you a much richer appreciation of the variety of human experience and human character. Since Mississippians tend to stay in the same place over several generations, you also have a chance—increasingly rare in America—to observe the continuity of lives and families. How many times have you heard someone observe 'That's just like a Smith—they all have bad tempers.' Or 'He's the spitting image of his granddaddy.' Or 'You can see Jones written all over her.' Or 'That's your daddy's side of the family coming out in you!' The great advantage for your understanding of life is that you can learn something about not just your friends your own age, but about their parents and their grandparents and great-grandparents. You get a sense of how the choices made by one woman or man determine the fates—and future choices—of their children and grandchildren. Perhaps most of all, Mississippi exercises a hold on those who grow up here because the society has the warmth and inclusiveness of a close-knit clan. When one Mississippian meets a stranger also from Mississippi, neither one can rest until they find some tie in common—a person they both know, a hurricane they both remember, or a town they both lived near. It's as though they think it unfriendly and uncivilized not to be bound together by some thread. No matter how far away from Mississippi you go, you'll never feel you don't 'belong' there."

WALKER PERCY (1916) was born in Birmingham, Alabama. After the death of his parents, he and two brothers were adopted by their father's first cousin, William Alexander Percy, and raised in Greenville, Mississippi. He graduated from the University of North Carolina in 1937 with a B.A. in chemistry and upon graduation became a student at the College of Physicians and Surgeons, Columbia University. He received his M.D., with honors, in 1941. During his internship at Bellevue Hospital in New York, Percy contracted tuberculosis and was forced in 1942 to convalesce in the Adirondacks. In 1944 he returned to Columbia to teach, but suffered a relapse, after which he retired from medicine.

While convalescing Percy read the great Russian novelists, the modern French novelists, Kierkegaard, and many of the other existentialists. He began to write and in 1961 his first novel, *The Moviegoer,* was published; in 1962 it won the National Book Award. Since then he has published articles, essays, and novels. In addition to *The Moviegoer,* Percy's fiction and nonfiction books include *The Last Gentleman* (1966), *Love in the Ruins* (1971), *The Message in the Bottle* (1975), *Lancelot* (1977), *The Second Coming* (received the 1980 Mississippi Institute of Arts and Letters Literature Award), and *Lost in the Cosmos* (1983). With each publication Percy's writing receives more international attention and praise.

In "Cinematographic Souvenir of Greenville," Percy writes: "When I attended Greenville High School in the 1930's, which was the Golden Age of the movies, it was a great thing to go to the 'show' after school . . . then they had movies in the afternoon. You would walk all the way from the old high school to the Paramount, carrying a girl's books maybe, and afterwards walk home. High school students didn't have cars in the thirties. I also remember the old Grand on Main Street near the levee. It had been an old vaudeville house, but that was before my day. They showed westerns there and I seem to remember a piano player. The balcony had the biggest rats in Greenville. . . ."

To Percy, the writing of a novel is a process of discovery, but a process with ground rules: "If you're interested in writing, you'd better enjoy reading. If you don't enjoy reading, if you prefer TV, forget it."

THOMAS HAL PHILLIPS (1922) was born near Corinth, Mississippi. He attended Alcorn Agricultural High School in Kossuth and received a B.S. degree from Mississippi State University. Upon graduation, he entered the United States Navy and served in the amphibious forces in North Africa, Italy, and France. When the war ended, Phillips returned to the South and attended the University of Alabama, where he took creative writing courses and eventually received an M.A. degree. His first novel, *The Bitterweed Path,* was presented as his M.A. thesis. From 1948 to 1950 Phillips taught at Southern Methodist University and spent 1950 to 1951 in France on a Fulbright Fellowship. Afterward he returned to Mississippi.

His novels include *The Bitterweed Path* (1950), *The Golden Lie* (1951), *Search for a Hero* (1952), *Kangaroo Hollow* (1954), and *The Loved and the Unloved* (1955). Phillips has been involved in the production and writing of a number of films including *Tarzan's Fight for Life, Ode to Billy Joe, Walking Tall II, Barn Burning, Roll of Thunder, Hear My Cry,* and *Huckleberry Finn.* He worked on the Emmy award winning *Autobiography of Miss Jane Pittman,* and has been involved in a number of Robert Altman films, including *Thieves Like Us, California Split, Nashville,* and *Buffalo Bill.* Many awards have been given to Phillips, including a Julius Rosenwald Fellowship, a Saxton Memorial Award, two Guggenheim Fellowships, and an O. Henry Prize Award for "The Shadow of an Arm."

STERLING D. PLUMPP (1940) was born in Clinton, Mississippi. In 1955 his family moved to Jackson, Mississippi, where he completed school. After being selected for a scholarship, Plumpp studied for two years at St. Benedict's College and in 1968 received a B.A. in psychology from Roosevelt University. He is currently assistant professor in the Black Studies Program at the University of Illinois at Chicago.

Plumpp's writings include six books of poetry, prose, and essays. In 1972 Third World Press published *Black Rituals.* A book of black psychological essays, it is a probing analysis of the black man's way of coping in a technological, urbanized, and industrialized society. His books of poetry include *Portable Soul* (1969), *Half Black, Half Blacker* (1970), *Steps to Break the Circle* (1974), *Clinton* (1976), and *The Mojo Hands Call, I Must Go* (1982). The latter, published by Thunder's Mouth Press, won the 1983 Carl Sandburg Literary Award for Poetry. In 1982 Plumpp edited a collection titled *Somehow We Survive: An Anthology of South African Writing.*

Concerning his development as a writer, Plumpp says, "When I was thirty, I found my writing voice and the ability to master techniques to reflect my inner self. The more I wrote about the South, the more tranquil my voice was. By viewing my soul through Mississippi, I could maneuver into the reservoir of my being without first having to plod through attacks against whites; I could see the survival lines of my people concealed in the many ways they did things. Though there will be other places in my life none will be home, as close and as painfully or joyfully familiar as Mississippi."

JESSIE SCHELL (1941) was born in Greenville, Mississippi. She received a B.A. and an M.F.A. from the University of North Carolina at Greensboro. Her poetry and prose have been published in the *Greensboro Reader,* the *Greensboro Review, Vanderbilt Poetry Review,* the *Virginia Quarterly Review, New Orleans Review,* the *Georgia Review,* and *Atlantic.* Seven of her short stories have appeared in *McCalls,* and her stories "Alvira, Lettie, and Pip" and "Undeveloped Photographs" were selected for O. Henry

Prize Awards (1975 and 1978 respectively). Her novel *Sudina,* published in 1967 under her maiden name of Jessie Rosenberg, was reprinted in 1978 by Avon under her married name. It is the story of a young southern girl's search for identity.

Schell says, "My growing-up years in the Mississippi Delta gave me a sense of the world which has served me well ever since, and will always be an endless source of delight, for which I'm grateful: a sense of the music of language, of joy in the landscape, of family and regional ties. Mississippi people taught me the lasting delight of story-telling, and in their daily lives, practiced its art instinctively. I treasure the time I spent there and find that I use that time, that place, and all the people I knew there constantly in everything that I try to write today."

PATRICK D. SMITH (1927) was born in Mendenhall, Mississippi. He graduated from Hinds Junior College and holds a B.A. and an M.A. in English from the University of Mississippi. From 1959–62 he taught at Hinds Junior College, Raymond, Mississippi, and served as director of public relations. From 1962–66 he was director of public relations at the University of Mississippi; in 1966 he moved to Florida and has since served as director of public relations for Brevard Community College in Cocoa.

Smith is the author of six novels, two of which, *Forever Island* (1973) and *Angel City* (1978), have been nominated for the Pulitzer Prize. His first novel, *The River Is Home* (1953), won the Gold Medal of the International Mark Twain Society and the Canadian Fiction Award. *Forever Island* was included in a volume of Reader's Digest Condensed Books and has been published in nineteen foreign countries. *Angel City* has been made into a film.

Smith lives on Merritt Island in Florida and has served for six years on the professional staff of the annual Rollins College Writers' Conference in Winter Park. His latest novel, *A Land Remembered,* was published in 1984. In 1983 Smith traveled to the Soviet Union, and he is currently writing about his experiences in a book titled *In Search of the Russian Bear.*

ELIZABETH SPENCER (1921) was born in Carrollton, Mississippi, to a family that had lived in Carroll County since the 1830s. In 1942 she received a B.A. in English from Belhaven College, Jackson, Mississippi. Upon graduation, she attended Vanderbilt University where she received an M.A. degree. Afterwards Spencer taught at Northwest Mississippi Junior College, Senatobia, Mississippi, at Belmont College, Nashville, Tennessee, and at the University of Mississippi. It was at the University of Mississippi that Spencer wrote her first novel, *Fire in the Morning.* She has, since that time, been a full-time writer. Spencer has received many awards for her writing including a Guggenheim Fellowship (1953), the Rosenthal Foundation Award of the American Academy of Arts and Letters (1956), the *Kenyon Review* Fellowship in Fiction (1957), the

McGraw-Hill Fiction Award (1960), the Henry Bellamann Award for creative writing (1968), and, most recently, the Award of Merit Medal for the Short Story by the American Academy of Arts and Letters (1983).

Spencer's books include *Fire in the Morning* (1948), *This Crooked Way* (1952), *The Voice at the Back Door* (1956), *The Light in the Piazza* (1960), *Knights and Dragons* (1965), *No Place for an Angel* (1967), *Ship Island and Other Stories* (1968), *The Snare* (1972), *The Stories of Elizabeth Spencer* (1981), and *The Salt Line* (1984).

Of her native state Spencer writes: "Mississippi gave a wonderful cross-current to writing—when I was growing up the old had been set in its ways since the Civil War, but the new was making itself felt. Writers respond especially to this sort of tension. Then, too, there was such a wide variety of individuals, so many wildly different characters, everyone with his own story, all to be met with daily. The challenge was not where to find material but how best to use it in a modern fiction which would engage intelligence and feeling. All my early books came out of Mississippi and many still do . . . memory keeps so many things, and rather than lose them, it may even make them richer."

JAMES STREET (1903–1954) was born in Lumberton, Mississippi. His father, a lawyer, moved his family within the state to Poplarville, Hattiesburg, and Laurel as his practice developed. Street began working for the Laurel *Daily Leader* at age fourteen and at seventeen, after a brief period of hoboing in the West, became a reporter for the *Hattiesburg American.* In 1924, after attending a Baptist seminary, he became the youngest ordained Baptist minister in the United States. He left the ministry in 1926 and became a reporter, eventually working for the *Arkansas Gazette,* then for the Associated Press in Memphis, Nashville, Atlanta, and New York. In New York a feature article he had written attracted the attention of William Randolph Hearst, and Street was hired to write for the New York *American* in 1933.

In 1936 he published a book of short sketches about the South titled *Look Away! A Dixie Notebook.* His first novel, *Oh, Promised Land,* appeared in 1940. In that same year he resigned his position and moved to Natchez, Mississippi, where he wrote *In My Father's House* (1941). Returning to New York the following year, he lived there until 1945. During that time he wrote his popular novel, *The Gauntlet* (1945). In 1945 Street settled in Chapel Hill, North Carolina. He remained a successful professional writer for the rest of his life. Nearly all his novels were best sellers, and some sold over a million copies. Three of his books *The Biscuit Eater* (1941), *Tap Roots* (1942), and *Good-bye, My Lady* (1954) were made into films. "Weep No More, My Lady," is a good introduction to *Good-bye, My Lady.*

About his inspiration for "Weep No More, My Lady" Street writes, "The success of 'The Biscuit Eater' . . . urged me to do another boy-dog story, but I didn't have any plot. I happened to be in Natchez, Mississippi, writing a book *(In My Father's House)* and met a man who sold tobacco in a saloon. He loved dogs and had seen the movie of 'The Biscuit Eater' three times. He called it 'The Dog Biscuit.' He told me about the African basenji, the barkless dog. I didn't believe him. Then he got a magazine and showed me a picture and a story about an English lady who had the breed.

"The idea of a dog that couldn't bark just interested me. I wrote the magazine for information and learned that a Canadian dog fancier had the breed. From him, I got details about the dogs. Then I remembered a story that hadn't sold. It was called 'A Can of Peaches.' So I took the characters from 'A Can of Peaches' and wrote them into 'Weep No More, My Lady.' It was published in the *Saturday Evening Post.*"

CHESTER SULLIVAN (1939) was born in Hattiesburg, Mississippi. He attended schools in Mize and in Seminary, Mississippi, before moving to Texas where he received a Ph.D. from Texas Christian University. While he was teaching creative writing at Tarleton State College, his first novel, *Alligator Gar,* was published and received the Texas Institute of Letters Jesse Jones Award for the best work of fiction written in 1973. *Alligator Gar* is the tale of a young man's need to belong to the land he was born on in the Piney Woods of Tongs, Mississippi. Sullivan's second book, *Sullivan's Hollow* (1978), published by the University Press of Mississippi, presents a history of Sullivan's Hollow, Mississippi—a place purportedly synonymous with lawlessness.

Sullivan teaches at the University of Kansas and has published many short stories in journals and magazines. He is at work on a novel and a collection of short stories. He writes, "I spent my formative years in rural, Mississippi, in the Piney Woods. That experience has had a profound influence on all of my writing, and on my state of mind."

MILDRED D. TAYLOR was born in Jackson, Mississippi, and grew up in Toledo, Ohio, with yearly trips back to the South. After graduating from the University of Toledo, she spent two years in Ethiopia with the Peace Corps. Returning to the United States, she recruited for the Peace Corps before entering the School of Journalism at the University of Colorado. There, as a member of the Black Student Alliance, she worked with students and university officials in structuring a Black Studies program.

Song of the Trees (1975), Taylor's first book about the Logan family of Mississippi, won the Council on Interracial Books Award in the African American category. It was also a *New York Times* Outstanding Book of the Year in 1975. The *Times* called it "triumphant . . . a true story and truly told." Her second book, *Roll of Thunder, Hear My Cry* (1976), won many honors including the prestigious Newbery Award from the American Library Association. It was also made into a film. A sequel, *Let the Circle Be Unbroken,* was published in 1981.

In her 1977 acceptance speech for the Newbery Award, Taylor said: "I will continue the Logans' story with the same life guides that have always been mine, for it is my hope that these books, one of the first chronicles to mirror a black child's hopes and fears from childhood innocence to awareness to bitterness and disillusionment, will one day be instrumental in teaching children of all colors the tremendous influence that Cassie's generation—my father's generation—had in bringing about the great Civil Rights Movement of the fifties and sixties. Without understanding that generation and what it and the generations before it endured, children of today and of the future cannot understand or cherish the precious rights of equality which they now possess, both in the North and in the South. If they can identify with the Logans, who are representative not only of my family but of the many black families who faced adversity and survived, and understand the principles by which they lived, then perhaps they can better understand and respect themselves and others."

FRANK TRIPPETT (1926) was born in Columbus, Mississippi, and grew up in Aberdeen, Mississippi. He attended Mississippi College, Duke University, the University of Mississippi, Vandercook College of Music, and the University of the State of New York. Trippett's first job as a journalist was with the Meridian (Mississippi) *Star*. He worked for the Fredericksburg (Virginia) *Free Lance-Star* and the St. Petersburg (Florida) *Times* before joining the staff of *Newsweek* in 1961. Twice he was a joint winner of the National Headliner Award for Distinguished Journalism and recipient of an American Political Science Association citation for distinguished reporting. His *The States: United They Fell* (1967) provides an analysis and description of state legislatures. Among his writings are *The First Horsemen* (1974), a narrative history of the ancient Scythians, and *Child Ellen*, a novel published in 1975.

Trippett's articles have been published in the *New York Times Sunday Magazine, Saturday Review, People, Life, Reader's Digest, New Republic, Intellectual Digest, Psychology Today, Geo,* and many more. His most recent awards were the 1981 American Bar Association "Silver Gavel" for distinguished writing on the law and the 1982 National Space Club citation for distinguished writing on space.

Since 1977 Trippett has been a senior writer and essayist on the staff of *Time* magazine.

MARGARET WALKER (1915) was born in Birmingham, Alabama, the daughter of a music teacher and a minister of the Methodist Church; she grew up in Alabama, Louisiana, and Mississippi. Walker received a B.A. from Northwestern University in 1935 and an M.A. and a Ph.D. from the University of Iowa. In 1942, after working for the WPA on its Federal Writers Project, Walker began teaching at West Virginia State College in the English department. In the same year *For My People,* her first book, was published as a volume in the Yale Series of Younger Poets. In 1949 Walker joined the faculty at Jackson State University as a professor of English and later became director of the Institute for the Study of History, Life, and Culture of Black People. Her novel *Jubilee,* published in 1966, won a Houghton Mifflin Literary Fellowship Award and became an international best seller. Her other books include *Prophets for a New Day* (1970), *How I Wrote Jubilee* (1972), *October Journey* (1973), and *A Poetic Equation: Conversations Between Nikki Giovanni and Margaret Walker* (1974).

Her novel *Jubilee* is an inspiring story for all black Americans struggling for freedom and equality. In it Walker incorporated into the fictionalized life of her maternal great-grandmother actual historical events from slavery to Reconstruction.

Retired from teaching at Jackson State University, Walker is completing a biography of Richard Wright entitled *The Daemonic Genius of Richard Wright* to be published by Howard University Press. She is working on a new collection of poems titled *This Is My Century: Black Synthesis of Time.*

At the 1980 inauguration of Governor William F. Winter, Walker spoke of her link to Mississippi: "My family has been involved in education for black people in Mississippi for over one hundred years. In 1878 my great uncle, James A. Ware (the Jim of *Jubilee*), and my grandfather, the Reverend Edward Lane Dozier, a Baptist minister (who married Minna in my story) came to the Mississippi Delta and established a school for black children in the oldest black Baptist Church in Greenville. Uncle Jim died there in 1932. During the school year 1920–21 my mother and father taught school at old Haven Institute in Meridian and there I went to school for the first time. In the 1940s my sister came to Prentiss Institute for her first teaching experience and I have been in Mississippi since 1949 at Jackson State University where I retired in May."

LUKE WALLIN (1943) was born in Columbus, Mississippi. He received a B.A. in philosophy from Mississippi State University, an M.A. in philosophy from the University of Alabama, and an M.F.A. in creative writing from the University of Iowa. He taught philosophy for several years at the School of Visual Arts in New York City and has written for television. His own show for children, "The Enchanted Swamp," was broadcast on Alabama ETV in 1979. His first novel, *The Redneck Poacher's Son,* was a 1981 Best Book for Young Adults. *Blue Wings,* his second book, was published in 1982. Wallin's 1984 novel, *In the Shadow of the Wind,* takes place in 1835 during the Trail of Tears of the Creek Indians. Currently teaching writing at the University of Tennessee in Chattanooga, Wallin lives in Rising Fawn, Georgia.

To students he writes: "As a young person growing up in Mississippi, you will have noticed how different it seems to be from everywhere else. Even in the face of TV culture, we maintain strong traditions of our own. Some of these are corrupt, based on slavery, racism, and social injustice: but another part is quite wonderful. This is our folk culture, our closeness to the earth, animals, weather, and each other. . . . It is no accident that Mississippi has produced so many fine writers and musicians. These people felt the same pressures and confusions that you feel, and instead of joining the Klan or becoming bitter (violent toward themselves), they managed to make stories and songs from their lives. . . . Read your Mississippi authors and listen to the songs with a special ear: more than anyone else, all this was made for you."

EUDORA WELTY (1909) was born in Jackson, Mississippi. Educated in Jackson's public schools, she began writing and drawing very early, publishing poems and sketches in *St. Nicholas* magazine as early as 1920. After attending Mississippi State College for Women (now Mississippi University for Women) for two years, she transferred to the University of Wisconsin, graduating with a B.A. in 1929. In 1930 she attended Columbia University School of Business, but returned to Mississippi in 1931 when her father died. In Jackson, she worked in a variety of jobs before going to work for the WPA, traveling across the state taking photographs and writing copy for several small newspapers.

Two of her short stories "Death of a Traveling Salesman" and "Magic" were published in *Manuscript* magazine in 1936. Her first book, *A Curtain of Green,* appeared in 1941, and was a critical success. Her second volume, *The Robber Bridegroom,* appeared in 1942, and firmly established her reputation as a writer. Since the 1943 publication of *The Wide Net and Other Stories,* Welty has published *Delta Wedding* (1946), *The Golden Apples* (1949), *The Ponder Heart* (1954), *The Bride of the Innisfallen and Other Stories* (1955), *The Shoe Bird* (1964), *Losing Battles* (1970), *One Time, One Place* (1971), *The Optimist's Daughter* (1972), *The Eye of the Story* (1977), *The Collected Stories of Eudora Welty* (1980), and *One Writer's Beginnings* (1984) among others.

Welty has received great international attention and praise. Her many honors include the Pulitzer Prize, the American Book Award for fiction, the Gold Medal for the Novel by the National Institute of Arts and Letters, and the Howells Medal for Fiction by the American Academy of Arts and Letters. *One Writer's Beginnings,* a collection of 1983 lectures given at Harvard University, put her on the best-seller list. In 1984 the University Press of Mississippi published *Conversations with Eudora Welty,* interviews collected by Peggy Whitman Prenshaw.

In "Place in Fiction," she writes, "I think the sense of place is as essential to good and honest writing as a logical mind; surely they are somewhere related. It is by knowing where you stand that you grow able to judge where you are. Place absorbs our earliest notice and attention, it bestows on us our original awareness; and our critical powers spring up from the study of it and the growth of experience inside it. It perseveres in bringing us back to earth when we fly too high. It never really stops informing us, for it is forever astir, alive, changing, reflecting, like the mind of man itself. One place comprehended can make us understand other places better."

Novelist Reynolds Price says of Welty, "In all of American fiction, she stands for me with her only peers—Melville, James, Hemingway, and Faulkner—and among them, she is in some crucial respects the deepest, the most spacious, the most life-giving."

JAMES WHITEHEAD (1936) was born in St. Louis, Missouri, but grew up in Jackson, Mississippi. He earned a B.A. and an M.A. from Vanderbilt University and an M.F.A. in creative writing from the University of Iowa in 1965. He has taught at Millsaps College, at the University of Iowa, and is currently teaching in the creative writing program at the University of Arkansas. Whitehead was awarded the Robert Frost Fellowship of the Bread Loaf Writers' Conference in 1967 and a Guggenheim Fellowship in fiction in 1972. His poems have appeared in many reviews and journals including the *Southern Review, Mississippi Review, New Orleans Review, Poetry Now,* the *Vanderbilt Poetry Review,* and the *Greensboro Review.*

Domains, his first book of poems, was published in 1966. *Joiner* (1971), his first novel, was given critical acclaim. George Garrett wrote, "*Joiner* would be a fine book in any season. In ours it is more than that. James Whitehead has undertaken and achieved a rare and wonderful thing—an original work of art." His second book of poems, *Local Men,* was published in 1979.

Whitehead writes, "In spite of some tough times, I surely enjoyed my childhood and adolescence in Mississippi, and *Joiner* is often a celebration of such a growing up, though not exactly mine."

JOHN A. WILLIAMS (1925) was born in Hinds County near Jackson, Mississippi, but he grew up in Syracuse, New York, where his parents had met and married. However, following an old custom, they returned "down home" for the birth of their first child. When Williams was about one year old, his parents returned to Syracuse.

Before he finished high school, Williams joined the United States Navy (1943), serving as a hospital corpsman until his discharge in 1946. Returning to Syracuse, he completed high school, took a B.A. degree at Syracuse University, and did some graduate work. He has worked as European correspondent for *Ebony* and *Jet* magazines (1958–59) and as African correspondent for *Newsweek* (1964–65).

Williams books include *The Angry Ones* (1960), *Night Song* (1961), *Sissie* (1963), *Journey Out of Anger* (1965), *This Is My Country Too* (1965), *The Man Who Cried I Am* (1967), *Captain Blackman* (1972), *Flashbacks: A Twenty-Year Diary of Article Writing* (1973), and *!Click Song* (1982) among others.

In *Lives of Mississippi Authors 1817–1967*, Professor Jerry W. Ward, Jr., writes: "The fact that Williams was born in the 1920's, when great numbers of blacks migrated northward in search of economic, social, and political advantages, has had a lasting impact on his work, for he is keenly aware of what it means to be the product of transplanted roots. Mississippi can claim him as one of her native sons by virtue of birth, but the enduring attitudes that give shape and substance to his writing are those formed in a northern milieu."

Williams has co-produced, written, and narrated several programs for National Educational Television. He received a grant from the National Endowment for the Arts for *!Click Song* and currently is a professor of English at Rutgers University.

TENNESSEE WILLIAMS (1911–1983) was born in Columbus, Mississippi. After living his early years in various Mississippi towns, his family moved to St. Louis. This environment, and its effect on the young Williams, is described in his play *The Glass Menagerie* and his short story "Portrait of a Girl in Glass." Williams attended the University of Missouri from 1929 to 1931, when he was withdrawn by his father because of his failure to pass ROTC. He then worked for three years (1931–34) at the International Shoe Company in St. Louis and, as a way of escaping tedium, began to write more and more. Quitting his job, he attended Washington University before receiving a B.A. degree from the University of Iowa in 1938.

Williams revised an earlier script called "The Gentleman Caller" into *The Glass Menagerie.* It opened in Chicago on December 26, 1944 and was his first professional success. In 1945 it moved to Broadway. With this impressive start, Williams began his career as one of the world's most popular playwrights. He won two Pulitzer Prizes, one for *A Streetcar Named Desire* and another for *Cat on a Hot Tin Roof,* and four New York Drama Circle Critics Awards for these two plays, as well as for *The Glass Menagerie* and *The Night of the Iguana.* Many of Williams's plays have been made into films.

After changing his name to "Tennessee," the first work to bear his new name was "The Field of Blue Children," printed in *Story* in September 1939. About his name change Williams writes, "I was christened Thomas Lanier Williams. It is a nice enough name, perhaps a little too nice. It sounds like it might belong to the son of a writer who turns out sonnet sequences to Spring. As a matter of fact, my first literary award was $25.00 from a Woman's Club for doing exactly that, three sonnets dedicated to Spring. I hasten to add that I was still pretty young. Under that name I published a good deal of lyric poetry which was a bad imitation of Edna Millay. When I grew up I realized this poetry wasn't much good and I felt the name had been compromised so I changed it to Tennessee Williams, the justification being mainly that the Williamses had fought the Indians for Tennessee and I had already discovered that the life of a young writer was going to be something similar to the defense of a stockade against a band of savages."

AUSTIN WILSON (1943) was born in Waycross, Georgia. He received an A.B. from Valdosta State College, an M.A. from the University of Georgia, and a Ph.D. from the University of South Carolina. Since 1976 Wilson has taught in the English department at Millsaps College in Jackson, Mississippi. He has published in *Mississippi Review* and *The Apalachee Quarterly* among others. "Paul's Eyes" and a number of his other short stories were written in Mississippi.

RICHARD WRIGHT (1908–1960) was born near Natchez, Mississippi, the son of a country schoolteacher mother and an illiterate sharecropper father. Because of his mother's illness and his father's eventual abandonment, his childhood was one of poverty, frequent moves from relative to relative, and interrupted schooling. His story "The Voodoo of Hell's Half Acre" was, however, published in Jackson, Mississippi, in the local black newspaper when Wright was fifteen. In 1925 he graduated from the ninth grade at Smith-Robertson Public School in Jackson at the head of his class.

Wright was a voracious reader. While working in Memphis, Wright discovered the work of H. L. Mencken and began to read some of the works mentioned in Mencken's *Prefaces,* along with a wide variety of other works. In 1927 he moved to Chicago, where he would remain for ten years. In 1932 Wright joined the American Communist Party, believing that he had finally found a group interested in the plight of the American black. He had begun writing poetry and short stories earlier, and now, on behalf of the Party, his work began to appear in such publications as *New Masses, Left Front,* and *Partisan Review.*

In 1937 Wright moved to New York, where he was Harlem editor of the *Daily Worker.* His first book, *Uncle Tom's Children,* was published in 1938. This was followed by his two most famous works. *Native Son,* published in 1940, is the tragic tale of a Mississippi-born black in Chicago. Its success was phenomenal, and assured Wright a place in American literature. In 1945 *Black Boy,* an autobiographical work based on his traumatic childhood in Mississippi, was released.

By 1944 Wright had left the Communist Party and in 1946, unreconciled to the continuing racism in the United States, he moved his family to Paris, France. There he was to remain, with brief stays in England, until his death. During his stay there he was active in establishing such organizations as the Society of African Culture and worked with such African leaders as Leopold Senghor, later president of Senegal, and Aime Cesaire from Martinique. Among his nonfiction works of this time are *Black Power* (1954) and *Pagan Spain* (1957).

Wright's fiction includes *The Outsider* (1953) and *Savage Holiday* (1954). In addition, three works were published posthumously—*Eight Men* (1961), *Lawd Today* (1963), and *American Hunger* (1977).

AL YOUNG (1930) was born in Ocean Springs, Mississippi, and grew up in the South, the Midwest, and on the West Coast. Educated at the University of Michigan and the University of California at Berkeley as a Spanish teacher, he continues his life-long study of human speech and language. Along the way, he has been a professional musician, disk jockey, medical photographer, railroad man, warehouseman, laboratory aide, clerk-typist, job interviewer, janitor, editor, and screenwriter. Moreover, he has taught writing and literature at such institutions as Stanford, Foothill Community College, Colorado College, the University of Washington, and the University of California at both Santa Cruz and Berkeley.

How Is Angelina? (1975), *Sitting Pretty* (1976), and *Ask Me Now* (1980) are among his most recent novels. His books of poetry—*Dancing* (1969), *The Song Turning Back Into Itself* (1971), *Geography of the Near Past* (1976), and *The Blues Don't Change* (1982) have met with critical success.

Film assignments have included scripts for Dick Gregory, Sidney Poitier, Bill Cosby, and Richard Pryor. His work has been translated into Norwegian, Swedish, Italian, Japanese, Spanish, Polish, Russian, French, and Chinese.

Young is the recipient of the Joseph Henry Jackson Award, National Arts Council Awards for editing and poetry, a Wallace Stegner Fellowship, a National Endowment for the Arts Fellowship, the Pushcart Prize, and a Guggenheim Fellowship.

Bodies & Soul, his book of essays of musical memoirs, was published by Creative Arts Book Company in 1981. *Snakes* (reprinted in 1981 by Creative Arts Book Company), is a classic novel written about MC, a young black man with his head full of music. It is written with the rhythms and nuances of a musical score. *Rolling Stone* magazine said of it: "The reader glides through *Snakes* enjoying it, but not noticing how subtly beautiful it is until the very end . . . Al Young opts for art and attains it."

STARK YOUNG (1881–1963) was born in Como, Mississippi, and moved to Oxford, Mississippi, in 1895. He attended the University of Mississippi, from which he received a B.A. with honors in 1901. In 1902 he earned an M.A. in English from Columbia University. Returning to Mississippi, he taught at Water Valley, then at the University of Mississippi. From 1907 to 1915, he taught at the University of Texas and from 1915 to 1921 at Amherst College, Amherst, Massachusetts. In 1921 Young resigned from academic life and began writing and reviewing on a full-time basis in New York. He became drama critic for the *New Republic* and an editor of *Theatre Arts Magazine.*

In the next forty years, Young distinguished himself as a translator (his translations of Chekhov are still the most widely used), critic, poet, novelist, essayist, editor, painter, and playwright. He wrote thirty plays, many of which he directed. He is best remembered for his novel, *So Red the Rose* (1934), a story of the Civil War that preceeded *Gone with the Wind,* but never attained its popularity or commercial success. He died in New York on January 6, 1963.

Professor John Pilkington writes in *Lives of Mississippi Authors 1817–1967:* "In *River House* (1929), Young indicated his awareness of the erosion of Southern family life and the depressing effects of industrialization. Still, he defended the basic validity of the traditional Southern emphasis upon man's responsibility to his fellowmen in society and the need of every man to relate to a code or standard outside himself. At the end of this novel, the hero abandons the old Southern mansion for a job in St. Louis, but he takes with him the conviction that the Southern ideal of the 'life of the affections' and social responsibility will be valid guides to purposeful conduct wherever he lives."